S0-AEX-629

AMERICAN GOVERNMENT AND POLITICS TODAY

1991–92 EDITION

1991–92 EDITION

AMERICAN GOVERNMENT AND POLITICS TODAY

STEFFEN W. SCHMIDT
Iowa State University

MACK C. SHELLEY, II
Iowa State University

BARBARA A. BARDES
Loyola University of Chicago

WEST PUBLISHING COMPANY
Saint Paul   New York   Los Angeles   San Francisco

COPY EDITOR: Elaine Levin
COMPOSITION: Parkwood Composition Service
ILLUSTRATIONS: Brenda Booth, John & Jean Foster, Rolin Graphics, and Patrick Moloney
COVER: © Eric Meola, The Image Bank

Photo credits appear following index.

COPYRIGHT ©1985, 1987, 1989   **By WEST PUBLISHING COMPANY**
COPYRIGHT ©1991   **By WEST PUBLISHING COMPANY**
50 W. Kellogg Boulevard
P.O. Box 64526
St. Paul, MN 55164-0526

All rights reserved

Printed in the United States of America

98 97 96 95 94 93 92 91   8 7 6 5 4 3 2 1 0

Library of Congress Cataloging-in-Publication Data

Schmidt, Steffen W.
  American government and politics today.—1991–1992 ed. / Steffen
  W. Schmidt, Mack C. Shelley II, Barbara A. Bardes.
      p. cm.
  Rev. ed. of: American government and politiccs today / Barbara A.
Bardes, Mack C. Shelley II, Steffen W. Schmidt, 3rd ed. ©1990.
  Includes bibliographical references and index.
  ISBN 0-314-77461-0 (hard)
  1. United States—Politics and government. I. Shelley, Mack C.,
1950–   . II. Bardes, Barbara A. III. Title.
JK274.S428 1991
820,973—dc20   90-25199
                                    CIP

CONTENTS IN BRIEF

CONTENTS

CHAPTER 10
Campaigns, Candidates, and Elections   281

CHAPTER 11
The Media   325

CHAPTER 15
The Judiciary   469

■ PART FIVE   PUBLIC POLICY   497

■ PART SIX   STATE AND LOCAL POLITICS   593

CHAPTER 19
State and Local Government   595

The United States faces a very different world in the 1990s. Old barriers that seemed permanent, such as the Berlin Wall and the Iron Curtain, have disappeared. New relationships are developing in almost every part of the globe; the United States and the Soviet Union are negotiating further arms reductions in Europe, the two Germanies have become one, the once-powerful OPEC alliance has faltered, and Western Europe is about to become a single economic trading unit. All of these changes have made American citizens much more aware of our nation's position in the global community. Our economic strength depends on the strength of the global economy. At the same time, the environmental integrity of the planet Earth—depends on actions by other nations as well as those taken by our citizens.

Perhaps even more striking has been the enthusiastic embrace of democratic processes by the people of other nations. The newly free nations of Eastern Europe are experimenting with American-style political campaigns and elections. New political parties are being created overnight. Questions of domestic policy and how the government should regulate the economy are debated in foreign capitals with the strengths and weaknesses of the American experience clearly in mind.

Given the rapid changes in the world scene, it is even more important that American citizens understand their own political institutions and think critically about the choices the United States must make in the 1990s. Should the United States continue to play the role of global policeman in the coming decades, as it has done in Grenada, Panama, and the Middle East. To what extent can our military forces be reduced and resources diverted to other needs? What are the political priorities of the American people, and can they be met by our system of campaigns and elections? These and many other questions will occupy our student-readers in the future. It is the goal of the 1991–1992 edition of *American Government and Politics Today* to enable students to perceive and understand both the dynamics of political change and the institutions and processes that make it possible for the American political system to survive in this changing world. We want students to gain a comprehensive understanding of the system and its historical origins while at the same time to be stirred by the excitement of current events. We hope to develop the ability of students to think critically about political institutions, the political culture, and policies so that they may be better equipped to act as citizens of the United States and of the world.

■ A TOTAL LEARNING/TEACHING PACKAGE

This text, along with its numerous supplements, constitutes what we believe to be a total learning/teaching package. Specifically, the text itself contains numerous pedagogical aids and high-interest additions, such as:

1. *A Preview of Contents to Each Chapter.* To give the student an understanding of what is to come, each chapter starts out with a topical outline of its contents.

2. *What If . . .?* To stimulate student interest in the chapter topics, each chapter begins with a hypothetical situation that we call "What If . . .?" For example, in Chapter 10 we ask the hypothetical question, "What If . . . Voting Were Compulsory?"

3. *Marginal Definitions.* Because terminology is often a stumbling block to understanding, each important term is printed in boldface and a glossary definition appears in the margins adjacent to the boldfaced terms. Additionally, all of the marginal definitions are contained alphabetically in a glossary at the end of the text.

4. *Did You Know?* Throughout the text, in the margins, are various facts and figures that we call "Did You Know?" They add relevance, humor, and a certain amount of fun to the student's task of learning about American government and politics.

5. *Profiles and Highlights.* Every chapter is enlivened with profiles of key individuals who have made unique contributions to the American political system. Also included in every chapter are Highlight boxes, which take a closer look at some of the interesting aspects of topics discussed in the chapter.

6. *Getting Involved.* Because we believe that the best way for students to get a firmer understanding of the American political system is by direct participation, we offer suggestions on ways for them to get involved in the system. At the end of each chapter, there are suggestions of where to write, whom to call, and what to do.

7. *Point-by-Point Chapter Summary.* At the end of each chapter, the essential points in the chapter are presented in a point-by-point format for ease of review and understanding.

8. *Questions for Review and Discussion.* To elicit student interest and discussion in and out of class, there are two to five questions for review and discussion at the end of each chapter.

9. *Selected References.* Important and understandable references are given at the end of each chapter. Each reference is annotated to indicate its usefulness and the area that it covers.

10. *Tables, Charts, and Photos.* As you can readily see, the text uses tables and charts, as well as photos, to summarize and illustrate important institutional, historical, or economic facts.

■ CRITICAL PERSPECTIVES FOR ANALYSIS

The enthusiastic reception given to Critical Perspectives that appeared in previous editions induced us to include a Critical Perspective in every chapter of this edition. These are short essays in which we examine newer theories about what has happened in American political history, what is happening, or what might happen in the future. The student is asked to examine a particular theory more critically than he or she might normally do within the text itself. The Critical Perspectives that have been chosen for this edition are:

Chapter 2   Was the Constitution Designed to Benefit an Economic Elite?
Chapter 3   Is Federalism a Solution to the Problems of Nationalism?
Chapter 4   Procedural and Substantive Due Process, or Fairness of Means and Ends
Chapter 5   How Much Progress in Race Relations?
Chapter 6   What Is the Future of Social Security?
Chapter 7   Race and Bias in Public Opinion Polling
Chapter 8   The Logic of Collective Action
Chapter 9   The Rise and Fall of the Major Party
Chapter 10   Voting in the Noninformation Age
Chapter 11   What's in the News?
Chapter 12   At Home with House Members
Chapter 13   The Presidents' Personality
Chapter 14   Should There Be Reregulation?
Chapter 15   Will the Federal Judiciary Become More Conservative?
Chapter 16   Have We Solved Our Banking Crisis?
Chapter 17   Prohibition in Retrospect: Can We Learn Any Lessons?
Chapter 18   Bound to Lead? Hard versus Soft Power
Chapter 19   Did the Tax Revolt Really Happen?

■ EMPHASIS ON CRITICAL THINKING

To make certain that the student understands our emphasis on *Critical Thinking* within each Critical Perspective, we have added two or three exercises in *Critical Thinking*. Suggested approaches to using these exercises are given in the *Instructors Manual*. If the student uses our accompanying booklet, *Handbook on Critical Thinking and Writing in American Politics*, with the exercises in critical thinking, he or she will have a strong basis for analyzing not only American politics but all other college subjects as well.

■ THE ANNOTATED U.S. CONSTITUTION

So that this book can serve as a reference, we have included important documents for the student of American government to have close at hand. Of course, every college American government text includes the U.S. Constitution. We believe that this document—and students' understanding of it—is so important that we have made a major change in this edition. You and your students will find a fully annotated U.S. Constitution at the beginning of the Appendix section. Although no reading of a summary of the U.S. Constitution can be thought of as a substitute for word-for-word analysis, an overall view is sometimes helpful for the student in order to understand the finer points within each part of our Constitution.
   We also have the following appendices:

■ The Declaration of Independence
■ A list of presidents of the United States with pertinent biographical information
■ Federalist Papers #10 and #51

■ AN EXPANDED APPENDIX ON RESEARCH TECHNIQUES

Because many students are asked to do a research project, we have added a new appendix on how to do research in government and political science. Included in that appendix are a discussion of scientific approaches to politics, suggested reference sources, and suggested step-by-step procedures for choosing and analyzing a research topic.

■ 1990 ELECTION RESULTS TALLIED AND ANALYZED

Because we believe that students respond positively to up-to-date information, we have ensured high student interest by including the latest congressional and state election results from November 1990. These results are discussed in Chapter 7 on public opinion, Chapter 9 on political parties, Chapter 10 on campaigns and voting, Chapter 11 on the media and Chapter 12 on Congress. The analysis of the election in these chapters includes election results that show the strengths of incumbency in congressional elections and a preview of the impact of redistricting.

■ EXPANDED SUPPLEMENTS PACKAGE

We have developed, in conjunction with a number of our colleagues, supplementary teaching materials that, we believe, are among the best available today. For the 1991–1992 edition, we have greatly expanded the supplements package.

Study Guide

The student Study Guide was written by James McElyea of Tulsa Junior College, Oklahoma. Each chapter provides learning objectives, a topical outline, a list of terms and concepts, and a variety of self-study questions. The Study Guide contains an essay describing how students can develop and improve their study skills for the American government course. The Study Guide is available for student purchase. Also available is a new computerized study guide, MicroGuide. The questions from the written study guide are on disk allowing students to practice taking computerized tests. Test questions include multiple-choice, true/false, and fill-in-the-blank. You can also edit the existing questions or add your own test questions. MicroGuide runs on IBM PCs and compatables or the Apple Macintosh and is available free to adopters.

Instructor's Manual with Test Bank

The Instructor's Manual was written by Michael Dinneen of Tulsa Junior College and includes learning objectives and an annotated chapter outline with numerous teaching suggestions, examples, ideas for presentation, and supplemental lecture ideas. In the instructor's manual are suggested answers to Exercises in Critical Thinking found at the end of each Critical Perspective in the text. The test bank for the 1991–1992 edition has been thoroughly revised with many new items added. The test bank consists of multiple-choice, short-answer, and essay questions.

Computerized Instructor's Manual

The entire Instructor's Manual is now available on disk in ASCII format. It can be coded for practically any word-processing program that you are using. You can modify the Instructor's Manual to meet your own needs and specifications.

Computerized Testing

A computerized testing program, WESTEST, containing the test questions from the Instructor's Manual, is available with this text. WESTEST may be obtained for the IBM PC and compatibles or the Apple Macintosh family of microcomputers. WESTEST allows instructors to create new tests, modify existing tests, change the questions from West's original test bank, and print tests in a variety of formats. Instructors can add questions of their own to the test bank. Instructors should contact their West sales representative to inquire about acquiring WESTEST.

West's Computerized Study Guide—Microtest

A Computerized Study Guide is available with this edition. West's Computerized Study Guide allows students the opportunity to practice taking quizzes and tests on either IBM PC and compatibles or Apple Macintosh family of microcomputers and Macintosh computers. This new software contains a variety of self-testing formats, including multiple-choice, true/false, and essay. The instructor is able to add or edit the material. West's Computerized Study Guide is available free to adopters.

Videotapes

We are pleased to announce that Schmidt, Shelley, and Bardes, *American Government and Politics Today* was selected as the recommended text for the new Dallas County Community College District telecourse, "Government by Consent," which began in 1990. The telecourse is distributed through Dallas Telecourse and the PBS Adult Learning Service to educational institutions.

All qualified adopters of *American Government and Politics Today* are able to select three special half-hour videotapes from this exciting, new telecourse. The program is devoted to topics central to the study of American government and includes interviews with major contemporary decision makers.

An Introduction to Critical Thinking and Writing in American Politics

In keeping with the emphasis on critical thinking in this edition, we have written a handbook entitled *An Introduction to Critical Thinking and Writing in American Politics*. This handbook introduces students to a series of critical-thinking techniques that will allow them to make better use of the information they receive about the political sphere from campaign speeches, mass media, and privately sponsored publications. Although the examples used in the handbook relate specifically to American politics, the techniques in critical thinking presented can be of value to the students in all their college courses, as well as if their day-to-day activities. *An Introduction to Critical Thinking and Writing in American Politics* is available free, at the instructor's option, to all students who purchase a new copy of *American Politics and Government Today, 1991–1992.*

Enrichment Lectures

Each chapter has an Enrichment Lecture by the authors that includes full references plus one transparency. These provide additional lecture topics in outline form and are based on the ideas presented in the "What If . . .?" segments that open each chapter.

Transparency Acetates

A set of approximately fifty full-color transparency acetates of key graphs, tables and diagrams found in the text is available to adopters of this text.

■ ACKNOWLEDGMENTS

Since we started this project a number of years ago, a sizable cadre of individuals has helped us in various phases of the undertaking. The following academic reviewers offered numerous constructive criticisms, comments, and suggestions during the preparation of all previous editions.

Sharon Z. Alter
William Rainey Harper College

Kevin Bailey
North Harris Community College, Texas

Clyde W. Barrow
Texas A&M University

Ralph Bunch
Portland State University

Carol Cassell
University of Alabama

Robert E. Craig
University of New Hampshire

Doris Daniels
Nassau Community College, New York

Michael Dinneen
Tulsa Junior College

Gavan Duffy
University of Texas at Austin

George C. Edwards, III
Texas A&M University

Dale Grimnitz
Normandale Community College

Stefan D. Haag
Austin Community College, Texas

David N. Hartman
Rancho Santiago College

Robert M. Herman
Moorpark College, California

Michael Hoover
Seminole Community College

J. C. Horton
San Antonio College, Texas

Willoughby Jarrell
Kennesaw College, Georgia

Loch K. Johnson
University of Georgia

John D. Kay
Santa Barbara City College, California

Charles W. Kegley
University of South Carolina

Dale Krane
Mississippi State University

Samuel Krislov
University of Minnesota

Sue Lee
Center for Telecommunications
Dallas County Community
College District

Carl Lieberman
University of Akron, Ohio

Orma Linford
Kansas State University

James D. McElyea
Tulsa Junior College, Oklahoma

William P. McLauchlan
Purdue University

William W. Maddox
University of Florida

S. J. Makielski, Jr.
Loyola University, New Orleans

Jarol B. Manheim
George Washington University

J. David Martin
Midwestern State University, Texas

Bruce B. Mason
Arizona State University

Stanley Melnick
Valencia Community College

Robery Mittrick
Luzerne County Community College

Stephen Osofsky
Nassau Community College

John P. Pelissero
Loyola University of Chicago

Charles Prysby
University of North Carolina

Donald R. Ranish
Antelope Valley College, California

Curt Reichel
University of Wisconsin

Russell D. Renka
Southeast Missouri State University

Eleanor A. Schwab
South Dakota State University

Len Shipman
Mount San Antonio College,
California

Scott Shrewsbury
Mankato State University, Minnesota

Gerald S. Strom
University of Illinois at Chicago

John R. Todd
North Texas State University

B. Oliver Walter
University of Wyoming

Thomas L. Wells
Old Dominion University

Jean B. White
Weber State College

Allan Wiese
Mankato State University

Robert D. Wrinkle
Pan American University

The 1991–1992 edition of this text is the result of our working closely with a large set of reviewers who each offered us penetrating criticisms, comments, and suggestions for improving the text. While we haven't been able to take account of all requests, each of the reviewers listed below will see many of his or her suggestions taken to heart.

Lynn R. Brink, Ed.D
North Lake College
Irving, Texas

Marshall L. DeRosa, Ph.D.
Louisiana State University
Baton Rouge, Louisiana

Dr. Barbara L. Brown
Southern Illinois University at
Carbondale
Carbondale, Illinois

Dr. Charles T. Barber
University of Southern Indiana
Evansville, Indiana

Joel L. Franke
Blinn College
Brenham, Texas

Ray Leal, Ph.D.
Southwest Texas State University
San Marcos, Texas

Dr. Donald Gregory
Stephen F. Austin State University
Nacogdoches, Texas

Dr. Jean Wahl Harris
University of Scranton
Scranton, Pennsylvania

Frank J. Coppa
Union County College
Cranford, New Jersey

Paul Holder
McClennan Community College
Waco, Texas

Mark C. Ellickson
Southwestern Missouri State
University
Springfield, Missouri

Carol Stix
Pace University
Pleasantville, New York

Robert Mittrick
Luzerne County Community College
Nanticoke, Pennsylvania

Many individuals helped during the research and editorial stages of this project. For their help we wish to thank David Schier, Suzanne Jasin, and Eric Hollowell. Our longtime editor at West Publishing Company, Clyde Perlee, Jr., offered strong support and accurate guidance at every phase of this project. He remains the object of our sincere appreciation, as does the project editor, Bill Stryker. We also wish to thank Jan Lamar for her developmental guidance and her ability to get all of the teaching supplements out on time.

Any errors that remain are our own. We welcome any and all comments from instructors and students alike. Comments that we have received on the first three editions have helped us improve it. Nonetheless, we know that we need to continue to make changes as the needs of instructors and students change.

Steffen Schmidt   Mack Shelley   Barbara Bardes

A GLOBAL PERSPECTIVE
DEMOCRACY IS SWEEPING THE WORLD!

Addressing the students at Westminster College in 1946, Winston Churchill, prime minister of England, pronounced, "An iron curtain has descended across the continent." The iron curtain Churchill referred to was the domination of all of Eastern Europe by the Soviet Union. For more than forty years, the nations of Eastern Europe were governed by Marxist authoritarian regimes which recognized only one political party—the Communist party. All of the na-

tions belonged to the Warsaw Pact, a mutual defense alliance directed by the Soviet Union. The Soviet army invaded Hungary in 1956 and Czechoslovakia in 1968 to quash popular uprisings against the Communist governments in those countries. Each of the economies of the Eastern European nations was modeled after the Soviet system, with centralized planning, state ownership of most industries and farms, and very little private enterprise.

In November 1989, the world

watched in amazement as the Berlin Wall was breached by citizens of East and West Berlin while government troops stood by. Although there had already been a movement toward democracy in Poland and a flood of East Germans moving to the West, the tearing down of the Berlin Wall represented the end of the Iron Curtain to millions in the East and in the West.

As the televised pictures of the nonstop party atop the Berlin Wall flashed around the world, many asked, How would the So-

The Brandenberg Gate: symbol of German unity.

Students celebrate on the breached Berlin Wall.

Romanians queue to vote in free elections, 1990.

viet Union respond? When the days passed and the Soviet Union offered mild encouragement to talks between the two Germanies, it was clear that the political situation in Moscow had changed dramatically. Mikhail Gorbachev, the Soviet president, who was concentrating his efforts on economic and political reform at home, had decided to allow the Eastern European nations to pursue their own paths. This tolerance, however, was limited to the former Soviet satellites. When Lithuania, one of the Soviet Republics, declared independence, Gorbachev denied the legitimacy of the action and imposed an economic embargo on the formerly independent Baltic state.

Encouraged by the Polish reforms and the opening of the border between East and West Germany, the other nations of Eastern Europe moved toward democracy with astonishing speed. As indicated on the map, Hungary held elections on March 25, Poland elected a Solidarity-led government in April, and East Germany voted in a conservative government in early May 1990. The Romanians deposed their dictator, and after a period of violence, moved toward democratic elections. The Czechoslovakians installed a provisional government headed by playwright and former political prisoner Vaclav Havel, and in June 1990 Havel's democratic

Civic Forum triumphed in the elections.

Did these nations immediately opt for an American-style democracy? What aspects of our well-tried Constitution appealed to these new democratic governments?

Unlike the writers of our Constitution, who had several months to meditate on its features and then waged a lengthy campaign for its ratification, the new democracies of Eastern Europe moved first to organize elections. Previously, no organized political opposition was permitted. New political parties were formed overnight, often led by former dissidents and intellectuals with virtually no political experience. They turned to political consultants in the United States (both the Democrats and Republicans sent teams) to help organize political campaigns. West German political parties "invaded" East Germany to organize their elections. Even the chancellor of West Germany arrived to stump for his counterpart in the East.

Celebrating the centennial of the Statue of Liberty. For emerging democracies throughout the world, the American system serves as a model.

Questions of how parties were to be regulated, how regions and ethnic groups were to be represented, how new parliaments were to be organized, were left for later discussion. Democratic elections were the first priority. Citizens celebrated liberty at the ballot box.

Later the questions of establishing priorities and government institutions and building a political culture will demand answers.

Can these new governments agree on the type of economic system to be developed? Can ancient ethnic tensions be resolved? Will the people have enough faith in democracy to support the government through economic and political crises? Perhaps the United States will be able to contribute more than its techniques of political campaigning in the turbulent years to come in Eastern Europe.

THE AMERICAN SYSTEM

CHAPTER 1

AMERICAN DEMOCRACY AND POLITICAL CULTURE

WHAT IF . . . WE HAD NO GOVERNMENT?

Imagine that the citizens of the United States had voted to eliminate all governments—national, state, and local. Americans just decided that they could manage their own affairs and live peaceably without government-imposed policies, taxes to pay for those policies, laws, or courts to enforce them.

Living without government-imposed laws would mean that every individual would be responsible for his or her own behavior. There would be no speed limits and no age limit for buying alcohol or obtaining a driver's license. Individuals who wished to marry might be joined by a religious ceremony, but would not need to go to divorce court when the relationship ended.

For many Americans, the most appealing aspect of living without government would be the end of taxation. No sales tax would be paid to the city or state for any purchase. No property taxes would be due. There would be no income taxes deducted from your earnings each payday. Of course, without any form of revenue, there would be no government programs. There would be no Social Security monthly checks for the retired worker, no government-provided compensation or medical treatment for veterans, no welfare programs for the poor, no national parks (the land would probably be sold to private corporations), no

military establishment, and no *public* postal service.

How would these services, at least some of which seem to be vital to society as we know it, be provided? In some cases, society might resurrect the customs of earlier times. Local communities often tried to provide for the poor through charity or by offering work and shelter at a community "poor farm." Other services would be taken over by private corporations. Parks might become private concerns, like today's amusement parks, charging higher entrance fees. Postal services, which already have competition in the marketplace for package delivery, would also be furnished by private enterprise. One might expect that mail delivery in rural areas, on mountaintops, and in other remote places would be more expensive than in densely settled areas.

It may be that Americans could find ways to replace all of the services of the government, but who would guard the nation from potential invaders? One possibility would be a citizen militia

which would be open to all individuals who could train voluntarily and defend their community with weapons.

To some, life without government would appear to be a paradise. If you see human beings as basically peaceful and willing to respect one another's property and interests, then there would be limited need for government interference. If, however, human beings are, as Thomas Hobbes suggested, selfish, passionate, and aggressive, a society without government would soon deteriorate into bloodshed, greed, and chaos as individuals tried to take what they wanted from their neighbors and disputes were settled with weapons. With no government, of course, there would be no courts to decide any kind of conflict between citizens and no sheriff or police, or other authority to carry out the judgment of the court.

Many primitive societies flourished for generations without the formal governmental structures of the modern world. Individuals in those societies grew up,

had families, lived contented or not-so-contented lives, and died as respected elders of the community. Yet all of those societies had informal structures of power—the tribal chief or matriarch, the shaman or medicine man—who judged disputes and made some decisions for the community. The members of the society were not governed by laws but by cultural beliefs about what is right and what is wrong that were transmitted through the generations. Life today seems to have become too complex and the demands of the citizens too great to live without government.

---

1. *Which government services do you think are nonessential? Do you think these could be better provided in another way?*
2. *How could individuals settle conflicts without laws and courts?*
3. *Could private corporations provide services such as highway maintenance and postal services? How would they charge for such services?*

"This country, with all its institutions, belongs to the people who inhabit it. Whenever they shall grow weary of the existing government, they can exercise their constitutional right of amending it, or their revolutionary right to dismember or overthrow it."[1] With these words, Abraham Lincoln underscored the most fundamental concept of American government—that the people control the government, and not vice versa. Furthermore, the people have the right to change the government through established procedures or, if that fails, by more extreme measures.

Recently, we have witnessed the citizens of Eastern Europe claiming the right to control their own destinies and, in many cases, demanding new **institutions** of government that will better meet their needs. For the first time in more than forty years, the citizens of Poland, Hungary, (former) East Germany, Romania, Bulgaria, and Czechoslovakia formed competing political parties, organized election campaigns, and turned out to vote for new political leaders. For them, the fundamental questions of politics—who governs, who makes the decisions that will change people's lives, who enforces the laws and how—are immediate and exhilarating.

In contrast, in the United States, where the right to vote has been ensured for more than 200 years, voting turnout has been steadily declining. Barely one-half of the eligible voters usually participate in electing the president, and even fewer vote in state or local contests. For many Americans the institutions of government are remote and complicated; the problems of daily life outweigh interest in political issues.

As Lincoln well understood, politics will only involve Americans if they understand the institutions, the players in the political arena, and the stakes of the game. The goal of this textbook is to reveal the political processes by which people try to influence decisions and the institutions of government where decisions are made. To begin, we explore the nature of politics and how our political system deals with the universal question of who governs.

INSTITUTIONS
Long-standing, identifiable structures or associations that perform functions for society.

[1]*The Oxford Dictionary of Quotations,* 3rd ed. (Oxford, England: Oxford University Press, 1980), p. 314.

Hungarians cast their ballots in the first free elections since the second World War. Why are elections so fundamental to the establishment of a democratic regime?

■ WHAT IS POLITICS?

POLITICS
According to David Easton, the "authoritative allocation of values" for a society; according to Harold Lasswell, "who gets what, when, and how" in a society.

SOCIAL CONFLICT
Disagreements arising in society because of differing beliefs, values, and attitudes; conflicts over society's priorities and competition for scarce resources.

If there were no government, there would be no **politics** as we understand the concept. Although there are probably as many definitions of politics as there are political scientists, most definitions lead us to look at politics as a way of resolving **social conflict.**

All national societies require cohesion and a high level of cooperation among their members to survive and prosper. At the same time, each nation must deal with conflict among its citizens. To maintain a vital degree of unity and cooperation, ways must be found to channel and to resolve conflict in order to keep it from threatening the very existence of the society.

Conflicts arise in societies because their members are distinct individuals with their own unique needs, values, and perspectives. Individuals and groups compete with one another in at least three respects. First, because of their differing beliefs, rooted in religious or personal values, individuals may disagree over basic issues of right and wrong. The intensely bitter debate that has raged in recent years over abortion is an example of this kind of conflict. Second, because of their differing needs and values, individuals may disagree about society's priorities. In the 1990s, Americans will debate whether the government's main concern should be social justice and welfare or saving the environment. This is the latest version of the "guns or butter" dilemma that has faced nations for centuries. Third, individuals compete for scarce resources. Income is a good example. There is never enough of it to go around to satisfy everyone's demands. Thus many political debates can be analyzed in terms of

Conflict resolution in a congressional committee. Where else within government could you observe conflict?

the distribution of income. Underlying most debates about taxes, for example, is the question of which group will part with more of its income to pay for the nation's priorities.

Harold Lasswell, one of this century's most influential political scientists, fashioned a definition of politics that captures these conflicts: Politics is a process that determines "who gets what, when, and how" for a society. This definition implies that people (the "who") are in conflict over values (the "what"). Another implication is that a society needs to have a set of procedures to resolve the question of who gets what. Thus politics not only recognizes the reality of social conflict but the need for ways to solve these conflicts. It is important to note that conflict is seen as natural and inevitable in any social system. Differences of opinion or values are not inherently bad in a society. The process of resolving conflict can be an opportunity for clarifying values and making change possible.

Another leading political scientist, David Easton, has formulated one of the most widely used definitions of politics, one that is similar to Lasswell's. Easton defines politics as the "authoritative allocation of values" for a society. This means that politics encompasses all of the activities involved in the conflict over who receives benefits from the society. These benefits, or values, may include status, welfare payments, or a law dealing with prayer in the public schools. Easton further specifies that conflict resolution must be authoritative. Authoritative decisions are those that can be backed up by legitimate power. This concept of **authority** is very important for helping us understand politics and the role of government in society.

What Does Government Do?

If politics refers to conflict and conflict resolution, **government** refers to the structured arrangement through which the decisions resolving conflict are made. Some societies, such as families or tribes, may be small enough that they do not need permanent structures to make these decisions. The group may collectively and in very informal ways allocate values for the whole society. This would be a community that has politics but no government. But once a society reaches a certain level of complexity, there is likely to emerge a particular person or group of people who make decisions allocating values for the society. With the establishment of these decision makers, we have arrived at the concept of government.

Governments range in size from the chief of a primitive tribe to the massive **bureaucracy** of People's Republic of China. To carry out its function of making rules to resolve social conflict, governments often are comprised of multiple decision-making bodies and permanent organizations such as the bureaucracy. The government's activities range from simply outlining the rules or laws that regulate individual behavior to the implementation of **public policies** that are intended to fulfill specific national goals. As an example of the former, state governments set the age and qualifications necessary to obtain a driver's license. The national government, on the other hand, has adopted a policy to improve the quality of air by closely regulating the kinds of automobile engines that can be sold and the gasoline that they burn in order to reduce the level of some pollutants in the air of American cities.

The government's environmental policy requires that individuals use un-leaded gasoline, which costs more than leaded fuel, in all cars produced after

DID YOU KNOW?

That the word *politikos* (pertaining to citizen or civic affairs) was used by the Greeks thousands of years ago, and that the English word *politics* entered the language around 1529?

AUTHORITY
The features of a leader or an institution that compel others to grant it obedience, usually because of ascribed legitimacy. For most societies, government is the ultimate authority in the allocation of values.

GOVERNMENT
Individuals, institutions, and processes that make society's rules about conflict resolution and the allocation of resources and that possess the power to enforce them.

BUREAUCRACY
A large organization that is structured hierarchically to carry out particular functions.

PUBLIC POLICIES
What the government decides to do or not to do.

DID YOU KNOW?

That the phrase "In God We Trust" was made the national motto on July 30, 1956, but had appeared on U.S. coins as early as 1864?

COMPLIANCE
Accepting and carrying out authoritative decisions.

LEGITIMACY
A status conferred by the people on the government's officials, acts, and institutions through their belief that the government's actions are an appropriate use of power by a legally constituted governmental authority following correct decision-making policies; regarded as rightful and entitled to compliance and obedience on the part of citizens.

POWER
The ability to cause others to modify their behavior and to conform to what the power holder wants.

TOTALITARIAN
A form of government that controls all aspects of the political and social life of a nation. All power resides with the government. The citizens have no power to choose the leadership or policies of the country.

ANARCHY
The state of having no government and no laws. Each member of the society governs him- or herself.

DEMOCRACY
A system of government in which ultimate political authority is vested in the people. Derived from the Greek words *demos* ("the people") and *kratos* ("authority").

1975. Why do most citizens obey this law or, for that matter, the 65 mile-per-hour speed limit on most interstate highways? One reason that citizens obey the government is because people believe that it has the authority to make such laws. By authority, we mean the ultimate right to force **compliance** with its decisions. In general, Americans also believe that the laws should be obeyed because they possess the quality of **legitimacy,** that is, they are appropriate and rightful. The laws are an appropriate use of power by the legally constituted government following correct decision-making procedures. To say that authority is legitimate is to suggest strongly an obligation to comply with its decisions—even a moral obligation.

What Is Power?

Another and perhaps more fundamental answer to why we comply with onerous rules is because we understand that the government has the **power** to enforce these laws. Although we may obey the speed limit and acknowledge the legitimacy of pollution control laws, we also support the right of the government to use force to make other citizens obey the same laws.

Power is a particular kind of relationship between two actors. If Smith is able to make Brown do something that Brown would otherwise not do, we say that Smith has power over Brown. That power may be exercised through persuasion, command, or physical coercion, as well as myriad other ways. In the same way, we perceive an interest group such as the National Rifle Association as powerful if it is successful in having gun control regulations weakened. Often, we talk of the power of presidents to convince Congress to pass legislation that they have requested. In many respects, power is at the heart of "who gets what."

■ WHO GOVERNS?

One of the most fundamental questions of politics is who or what groups control the government. Who has the power to make laws and enforce obedience in the society? At one extreme are societies that are governed by a **totalitarian** regime. In this form of government, a small group of leaders or a single individual—a dictator—makes all political decisions for the society. Every aspect of political, social, and economic life is controlled by the government. The people have no power to influence the government or select its leadership.

In contrast to totalitarian government is **anarchy,** which is the state of no government. The situation presented in the *What If. . .* at the beginning of this chapter would be defined as anarchy. Every individual governs him- or herself in a society in which there are no laws and no government.

The United States is a **democracy.** Derived from the Greek, the word means "government by the people." The ultimate power to control the government, including changing its institutions and choosing the political decision makers, rests with the citizens. Democracy, however, can take many forms. The earliest and purest form was originated by the ancient Greeks.

The Athenian Model of Direct Democracy

The government of the ancient Greek city-state of Athens is often considered to be the historical model for a **direct democracy.** In fact, the system was not a pure system of direct democracy because the average Athenian was not a participant in every political decision. Nonetheless, all major issues, even if decided by the committees of the ruling Council, were put before the assembly of all citizens for a vote. Moreover, about one in six citizens held some political office in any given year. Since positions were usually held only for one year and were rotated from one citizen to another quite often, most citizens did, in fact, participate in governing. The most important feature of Athenian democracy was that the **legislature** was composed of all of the citizens. Women, foreigners, and slaves, not being citizens, were excluded.

Direct democracy in Athens is considered to have been an ideal form of democracy because it demanded a high level of participation from every citizen. All important decisions were put to a vote of the entire citizenry so that public debate over political issues was a constant feature of social life.

Direct democracy also has been practiced in some Swiss cantons, in New England town meetings, and in some midwestern township meetings in the United States. New England town meetings, which include all of the voters who live in the town, continue to make important decisions for the community—such as levying taxes, hiring city officials, and deciding local ordinances—by majority vote. Some states provide a modern adaptation of direct democracy for their citizens: In thirty-nine states, representative democracy is supplemented by the **initiative** or the **referendum**—a process by which the people may vote directly on laws or constitutional amendments. The **recall** process, which is available in thirteen states, allows the people to vote to remove an incumbent from state office.

DIRECT DEMOCRACY
A system of government in which political decisions are made by the people directly, rather than by their elected representatives; probably possible only in small political communities.

LEGISLATURE
A government body primarily responsible for the making of laws.

INITIATIVE
A procedure whereby voters can propose a law or a constitutional amendment.

REFERENDUM
An act of referring legislative (statutory) or constitutional measures to the voters for approval or disapproval.

RECALL
A procedure allowing the people to vote to dismiss an elected official from state office before his or her term has expired.

An example of direct democracy: A town meeting in Vermont. What are the impediments to using such a system on a larger scale?

DID YOU KNOW?

That parents are more successful in getting their children to agree with them on what party to support than in getting them to agree on policy issues such as school prayers or free speech?

CONSENT OF THE PEOPLE
The idea that governments and laws derive their legitimacy from the consent of the people living under them.

REPRESENTATIVE DEMOCRACY
A form of government in which representatives elected by the people make laws and policies.

UNIVERSAL SUFFRAGE
The right of all adults to vote for their representatives.

The Founders' Fear of Direct Democracy

Although they were aware of the Athenian model, the framers of the U.S. Constitution—for the most part—were opposed to such a system. For many centuries preceding this country's establishment, any form of democracy was considered to be dangerous and to lead to instability. But in the eighteenth and nineteenth centuries, the idea of government based on the **consent of the people** gained increasing popularity. Such a government was the main aspiration of the American and French revolutions, as well as of many subsequent ones. Few of the revolutions' advocates, however, were ready to embrace direct democracy on the Athenian model. Generally, the masses were considered to be too uneducated to govern themselves, too prone to the influence of demagogues, and too likely to abrogate minority rights.

In the *Federalist Papers,* James Madison defended the new scheme of republican government in the Constitution, while warning of the problems inherent in a "pure democracy":

> [A] pure democracy . . . can admit of no cure for the mischiefs of faction [groups pursuing some special interest]. A common passion or interest will, in almost every case, be felt by a majority of the whole . . . and there is nothing to check the inducements to sacrifice the weaker party or an obnoxious individual. Hence it is that such democracies have ever been spectacles of turbulence and contention, and have ever been found incompatible with personal security or the rights of property; and have in general been as short in their lives as they have been violent in their deaths.[2]

Like many other politicians of his time, Madison feared that pure, or direct, democracy would deteriorate into mob rule. What would keep the majority of the people, if given direct decision-making power, from abusing the rights of individuals?

Representative Democracy

The framers of the U.S. Constitution settled on a republican form of government, which is also known as a **representative democracy.** The people hold the ultimate power over the government through the election process, but policy decisions are all made by national officials. Even this distance between the people and the government was not sufficient; other provisions in the Constitution made sure that the Senate and the president would be selected by political elites rather than by the people. This moderate form of democratic government came to be widely accepted throughout the Western world as a compromise between the desire for democratic control and the needs of the modern state.

Principles of Democratic Government.   As practiced in the United States and many European countries, democratic government emphasizes certain values and procedures. All representative democracies rest on the rule of the people as expressed through the election of government officials. In the twentieth century, **universal suffrage** is the rule. In the 1790s, only free white males were able to vote and, in some states, they had to be property owners

---

[2]James Madison, in Alexander Hamilton, James Madison, and John Jay, *The Federalist Papers,* No. 10 (New York: Mentor Books, 1961), p.81.

PROFILE

Thomas Jefferson

"I have sworn upon the altar of God eternal hostility against every form of tyranny over the mind of man."

T here is perhaps no better representative of the spirit of the early American political climate and no clearer proponent of the modern American political culture than Thomas Jefferson. It was Jefferson's eloquence, for example, that crafted the strong statements in the Declaration of Independence that established the foundation for our views about the relationship between the people and their government:

We hold these Truths to be self-evident, that all Men are created equal, that they are endowed by their Creator with certain unalienable Rights, that among these are Life, Liberty, and the Pursuit of Happiness—That to secure these Rights, Governments are instituted among Men, deriving their just Powers from the Consent of the Governed, that whenever any Form of Government becomes destructive of these Ends, it is the Right of the People to alter or to abolish it, and to institute new Government, laying its Foundation on such Principles and organizing its Powers in such Form, as to them shall seem most likely to effect their Safety and Happiness.

Not all of Jefferson's views were written into the Declaration of Independence. For example, Jefferson's attacks on King George III of England for failing to abolish the slave trade (even though Jefferson was a slave owner) were stricken from the final version of the document.

Thomas Jefferson was born at Shadwell, Virginia, on April 13, 1743. He attended the College of William and Mary and subsequently studied law, science, and philosophy. After drafting the Declaration of Independence while a member of the Continental Congress, he was elected to the Virginia House of Delegates in 1776. Three years later, he became governor of Virginia. British occupation and political complexities led him to retire to his home at Monticello, Virginia. He became a member of the Continental Congress again in 1783, for which he drafted provisions for the subsequent Northwest Ordinance that forbade slavery north of the Ohio River and helped establish the decimal system.

Jefferson was appointed minister to France in 1785 and secretary of state in 1789. He resigned that cabinet post in 1793 because of continued differences with Secretary of the Treasury Alexander Hamilton over plans for a strong, centralized, executive-centered government bordering on monarchy. He ran as the Democratic-Republican nominee for president in 1796, lost to John Adams, and became Adam's vice president. Jefferson and Aaron Burr received equal numbers of electoral votes in the 1800 presidential contest, but Jefferson became president by a vote of the House of Representatives when Hamilton threw his Federalist support in the House to Jefferson. His first term was highlighted by the Louisiana Purchase (1803), which brought huge western territories into the union. Following reelection against Federalist Charles C. Pinckney in 1804, Jefferson pursued an unpopular embargo policy to try to keep the United States out of the Napoleonic Wars that ravaged Europe.

He retired to Monticello in 1809, later founded the University of Virginia, and developed his interests in education, science, architecture, and music. He died at Monticello on July 4, 1826, the same day that John Adams passed away.

It has been said that the greatest assemblage of intellectual talent that ever gathered in the White House occurred when Thomas Jefferson dined alone.

Citizens must register before casting their ballots. Do you think voter participation would increase if such registration were not required?

MAJORITY
More than 50 percent.

MAJORITY RULE
A basic principle of democracy asserting that the greatest number of citizens in any political unit should select officials and determine policies.

LIMITED GOVERNMENT
A form of government based on the principle that the powers of government should be clearly limited either through a written document or through wide public understanding; characterized by institutional checks to ensure that governments serve the public rather than private interests.

as well. Women did not receive the right to vote in national elections in the United States until 1920, while the right to vote of African Americans was not really secured until the 1960s.

Granting every person the right to participate in the election of officials recognizes the equal voting power of each citizen. This emphasis on the equality of every individual before the law is central to the American system. Since everyone's vote counts equally, the only way to make fair decisions is by some form of **majority** will. But to ensure that **majority rule** does not become oppressive, modern democracies also provide guarantees of minority rights. If certain democratic principles did not protect minorities, the majority might violate the fundamental rights of members of certain groups, especially groups that are unpopular or dissimilar to the majority population. In the past, the majority has imposed such limitations on African Americans, Native Americans, women, and Japanese Americans, to name only a few.

One way to guarantee the continued existence of a representative democracy is to hold free, competitive elections. Thus the minority always has the opportunity to win elective office. For such elections to be totally open, freedom of the press and speech must be preserved so that opposition candidates may present their criticisms of the government. Americans are not always prepared to tolerate the political opinions of parties or individuals that run counter to our political culture, and in times of crisis our tolerance tends to be even lower.

Constitutional Democracy.   Another key feature of Western representative democracy is that it is based on the principle of **limited government.** Not only is the government dependent on popular sovereignty but the powers of the government are also clearly limited, either through a written document or through widely shared beliefs. The U.S. Constitution sets down the fundamental structure of the government and the limits to its activities. Such limits are intended to prevent political decisions based on the whims or ambitions of individuals in government rather than on constitutional principles.

DID YOU KNOW?

That the Greek philosopher Aristotle favored enlightened despotism over democracy, which to him meant mob rule?

■ DO WE HAVE A DEMOCRACY?

The sheer size and complexity of American society make it unsuitable for direct democracy on a national scale. Some scholars suggest that representative democracy is also difficult to achieve in any modern state. They point to the low level of turnout for presidential elections and the even lower turnout for local ones. Research based on polling the public during election campaigns has shown that many Americans are neither particularly interested in politics nor well informed. Few are able to name the persons running for Congress in their district and even fewer can discuss the positions that candidates have espoused. Members of Congress claim to represent their constituents, but few constituents follow the issues, much less communicate their views to the representatives. For the average citizen, the national government is too remote, too powerful, and too bureaucratic to be influenced by one vote.

Democracy for the Few

If the ordinary citizens are not really making policy decisions with their votes, who is? One answer to this question is proposed by a group of theorists who suggest that **elites** really govern the United States. Proponents of **elite theory** see society much like Alexander Hamilton, who said,

> All communities divide themselves into the few and the many. The first are the rich and the wellborn, the other the mass of the people. . . . The people are turbulent

ELITES
The upper socioeconomic classes who control political and economic affairs.

ELITE THEORY
A perspective holding that society is ruled by the elite.

Donald Trump's yacht symbolizes the wealth of America's elite. Considering their wealth and resources, do members of this strata hold the same political values as the average American?

DID YOU KNOW?

That in 1990 there were 504,501 elected officials in the United States, which was more than all the bank tellers in the country?

and changing; they seldom judge or determine right. Give therefore to the first class a distinct, permanent share in the government. They will check the unsteadiness of the second, and as they cannot receive any advantage by a change, they therefore will ever maintain good government.

Elite theory describes an American mass population that is uninterested in politics and willing to let leaders make the decisions. Some versions of elite theory posit a small, cohesive elite class that makes almost all the important decisions regarding the nation,[3] whereas others, holding a more democratic view, suggest that voters choose among competing elites. New members of the elite are recruited through the educational system so that the brightest children of the masses allegedly have the opportunity to join the elite strata.

In such a political system, the primary goal of the government is stability, because elites do not want any change in their status. Major social and economic change only takes place if elites see their resources threatened. This selfish interest of the elites does not mean, however, that they are necessarily undemocratic. Political scientists Dye and Ziegler note that American elites are perceived as more devoted to democratic principles and rights than are most members of the mass public.[4]

Elite theory can neither be proved nor disproved, since it is not possible to identify with certainty the members of the ruling elite. Some governmental policies, such as tax loopholes for the wealthy, may be perceived as elitist in nature, whereas others benefit many members of the public. Elite theory does increase our awareness of the power of elected leaders, even in a democracy.

Democracy for Groups

A different school of thought looks at the characteristics of the American electorate and finds that our form of democracy is based on group interests. Even if the average citizen cannot keep up with political issues or cast a deciding vote in any election, the individual's interests will be protected by groups that represent him or her.

PLURALISM
A theory that views politics as conflict among interest groups. Political decision making is characterized by bargaining and compromise.

Theorists who subscribe to **pluralism** as a way of understanding American politics see all persons as naturally social and inclined to form associations. These groups of like-minded individuals will present their demands to government. In the pluralists' view, politics is the struggle among groups to gain benefits for their members. Given the structures of the American political system, group conflicts tend to be settled by compromise and accommodation so that each interest is satisfied to some extent.[5]

Pluralists see public policy as resulting from group interactions carried out within Congress and the executive branch. Because there are a multitude of interests, no one group can dominate the political process. Furthermore, since most individuals have more than one interest, conflict among groups does not divide the nation into hostile camps.

There are a number of flaws in some of the basic assumptions of this approach. Among these are the relatively low number of people who formally join interest groups, the real disadvantages of pluralism for the poorer citizens,

[3]Michael Parenti, *Democracy for the Few,* 4th ed. (New York: St. Martin's Press, 1983).
[4]Thomas Dye and Harmon Zielger, *The Irony of Democracy,* 8th ed. (Duxbury, Mass.: Wadsworth, 1990).
[5]David Truman, *The Governmental Process* (New York: Knopf, 1951); Robert Dahl, *Who Governs?* (New Haven, Conn.: Yale University Press, 1961).

and pluralism's belief that group decision making always reflects the best interests of the nation.

Both pluralism and elite theory attempt to explain the real workings of American democracy. Neither approach is complete, nor can either be proven. The elitist perspective reminds us that the Founders were not great defenders of the mass public and suggests that people need constant motivation to stay involved in the political system. In contrast, the pluralist view underscores both the advantages and the disadvantages of Americans' inclination to join, to organize, and to pursue benefits for themselves. It points out all of the places within the American system in which interest groups find it comfortable to work. With this knowledge, the system can be adjusted to keep interest groups within the limits of the public good.

■ IDEAS AND POLITICS: POLITICAL CULTURE

In spite of its flaws and weaknesses, most Americans are proud of their political system and support it with their obedience to the laws, their patriotism, or their votes. Given the diverse nature of American society and the wide range of ethnic groups, economic classes, and other interests, what gives Americans a common political heritage? One of the forces that unites Americans is the **political culture,** which can be defined as a patterned set of ideas, values, and ways of thinking about government and politics. For Americans, the political culture includes such symbolic elements as the flag, the Statue of Liberty, and the Lincoln Memorial; ideas such as the belief that one is innocent until proven guilty; and deeply held values, including equality, liberty, and the right to hold property.

The degree to which Americans subscribe to a single set of values is surprising if you consider that virtually all U.S. citizens are descended from immigrants. The process by which such beliefs and values are transmitted to individuals is known as **political socialization.** Historically, the political parties

POLITICAL CULTURE
The pattern of beliefs and attitudes toward government and the political process held by a community or nation.

POLITICAL SOCIALIZATION
The process through which individuals learn a set of political attitudes and form opinions about social issues. The family and the educational system are two of the most important forces in the political socialization process.

The Amish are one of many groups within the United States who do not share all of the values of the dominant culture, preferring to maintain their own customs and traditions. Is the existence of such groups a threat to majority values?

Americans differ over the right to free expression, especially with regard to the flag. Here, individuals protest the right of others to burn the flag.

LIBERTY
The greatest freedom of individuals that is consistent with the freedom of other individuals in the society.

EQUALITY
A concept that all people are of equal worth.

played an important role in teaching new residents how to participate in the system in return for their votes. Frequently, the parties also provided the first economic opportunity in the form of jobs to immigrants and their families.

Another major force for the socialization of Americans—past and present—has been the school system. The educational process continues to socialize the children of immigrants and native-born Americans by explicitly teaching such basic political values as equality and liberty. Perhaps the school system is even more successful in teaching loyalty to our political system. From introducing a benevolent police officer to first-graders to playing the national anthem at high school graduation, American schools emphasize patriotism and citizenship.

A Political Consensus

Usually, the more homogeneous a population, the easier it is to have a political culture that can be characterized by a political consensus. One of the reasons that Great Britain maintains a limited government without a written charter is that there exists considerable consensus within the population with respect to the political decision-making process of government. Even when a nation is heterogeneous in geography and ethnic background, such as the United States, it is possible for shared cultural ideas to develop. We have already discussed one of the most fundamental ideas in American political culture—democracy. There are other concepts related to the notion of democracy that are also so fundamental to American political culture that they are beyond debate, although individual Americans may interpret their meaning quite differently. Among these are liberty, equality, and property.

Liberty.   **Liberty** can be defined as the greatest freedom of individuals that is consistent with the freedom of other individuals in the society. In the United States, liberty includes religious freedom, both the right to practice whatever religion one chooses and freedom from any state-imposed religion. The basic guarantees of liberty are found not in the body of the U.S. Constitution but in the Bill of Rights, the first ten amendments to the Constitution. The process of ensuring liberty for all Americans did not end with the adoption of the Bill of Rights but has continued through the political struggles of groups such as African Americans, women, and those who hold unpopular opinions.

The concept of liberty has both personal and political dimensions. Most Americans feel that each individual has the right to free expression and to choose whatever path he or she might want to take, economically, socially, and politically. The idea of liberty also has a specific meaning in the political process. Freedom of speech, freedom of the press, and the freedom to organize groups for political action are essential to maintaining competition for office and for the free and open discussion of political issues.

Equality.   The Declaration of Independence states, "All men are created equal." Today, that statement has been amended by the political culture to include groups other than white males—women, African Americans, Native Americans, Asian Americans, and others. The definition of **equality,** however, still is unclear to most Americans. Does equality mean simply political equality—the right to register, to vote, and to run for political office? Does equality mean equal opportunity for individuals to develop their talents and skills? If the latter is the meaning of equality, what should the United States do to

HIGHLIGHT

Religion and American Political Culture

Given the strongly religious origins of the founders of the United States in the seventeenth and eighteenth centuries, it may not seem surprising that American culture is replete with religious symbols and practices. These practices spill over into the political arena on many occasions. Our coins and paper currency bear the motto, "In God We Trust," daily sessions of Congress begin with a prayer, and presidents are sworn into office with one hand on the Bible.

This cultural norm of religious expression in politics is traceable to patterns of belief shown in recent public opinion polls. A recent Gallup poll study showed the following attitudes toward religion: 57 percent of respondents agreed that "religion can answer all or most of today's problems," whereas just 23 percent felt that "religion is largely old-fashioned and out of date"; two-thirds reported that they were a member of a church or synagogue; almost 90 percent said they have prayed to God, and about one-third reported praying twice a day or more. Seventy-two percent believe the Bible to be the word of God, whereas only 23 percent held that it is not; 94 percent believed in "God or a universal spirit," 66 percent believed in a personal God who watches over and judges people like the God of biblical

revelation; 71 percent expressed a belief in life after death, with an identical 71 percent believing in a heaven and 53 percent in a hell. Thirty-three percent of adult Americans fit the definition of "evangelicals," meaning they describe themselves as "born-again Christians," have encouraged other people to believe in Jesus Christ, and believe in a literal interpretation of the Bible.

In some respects, these results suggest a very different social climate for the growth of a political system than exists in other countries in the world. Of sixteen countries in one study, Americans ranked behind only South Africans in the extent to which they believe that God is extremely important in their lives.

Belief in life after death also sets Americans apart from much of the rest of the world. For the same sixteen countries, only the Republic of Ireland and Northern Ireland have higher proportions of believers in an afterlife—76 percent and 71 percent, respectively. At the other end of the spectrum of belief is Denmark, where only 26 percent believe in life after death.

Some changes have taken place in the religious underpinnings of American society, as measured by public opinion surveys. Gallup reports, for example, a decline from 81 percent to 61 percent in the last three decades in the percent-

age of Americans who believe that religion can answer all or most of today's problems; also, the percentage saying that religion is very important in their lives declined from 75 percent to 56 percent in that same period, whereas the proportion of adults who can be classified as "evangelicals" increased from 17 percent in 1981 to 22 percent.

Given results like these, it is possible to understand why Jimmy Carter was successful with his openly "born-again" posture as a presidential candidate in 1976, why Ronald Reagan and the Republican party have so ardently pursued the votes of evangelicals, why moral issues such as abortion or prayer in public schools can spark so much political activity, and why ministers such as Jesse Jackson, Martin Luther King, Jr., and Pat Robertson can have such an impact on American politics as candidates or as supporters of major pressure groups. Christian broadcaster and evangelist Pat Robertson even ran for president in 1988. In 1990, he returned to politics with the launching of a new religious coalition to train conservative Christians to shape government policy. The primary political goals of the Christian Coalition are to make abortion a crime, to make school prayer legal, and to protect the presence of religious symbols on government property.

---

ensure equal opportunities for those who are born poor, handicapped, or female? Most Americans believe strongly that all persons should have the opportunity to fulfill their potential, but many disagree about whether it is the government's responsibility to eliminate all economic and social differences.

Property.   Many Americans probably remember that the **inalienable rights** asserted in the Declaration of Independence are the rights to "life, liberty, and the pursuit of happiness." The inspiration for that phrase, however, came from the writings of an English philosopher, John Locke, who clearly stated that man's rights were to life, liberty, and **property.** In American political culture, the pursuit of happiness and property are considered to be closely related.

INALIENABLE RIGHTS
Rights held to be inherent in natural law and not dependent on government; as asserted in the Declaration of Independence, the rights to "life, liberty, and the pursuit of happiness."

PROPERTY
As conceived by the political philosopher John Locke, a natural right superior to human law (laws made by government).

Americans place tremendous value on owning land, on acquiring material possessions, and on the monetary value of jobs rather than on social status. Property can be seen as giving its owner political power and the liberty to do whatever he or she wants. At the same time, the ownership of property immediately creates inequality in society. But the desire to own property is so widespread among all classes of Americans that socialist movements, which advocate the redistribution of wealth and property, have had a difficult time securing a wide following here.

Democracy, liberty, equality, and property—these concepts lie at the core of American political culture. Other issues such as majority rule, **popular sovereignty,** and **fraternity** are closely related to them. For most Americans these fundamental principles are so deeply ingrained that they rarely think about what they might mean today.

Subcultures and Political Conflict

Not all Americans share equally in this dominant political culture. Native Americans and Hispanic citizens have tried to preserve their respective cultures and languages in the face of pressure to conform to the national standard. As larger numbers of Asian, Latin American, and East European immigrants join the society, the question of how to integrate these diverse cultures into the dominant American culture becomes more urgent. To what extent can we become a more multicultural society and yet sustain some level of consensus? Some groups in the nation have rejected the majority emphasis on individual economic achievement and material possessions and advocate instead communities based on the sharing of resources and true direct democracy.

In addition to alternative or minority subcultures, which reject part of all of the dominant culture, there exist multiple perspectives on how fundamental values relate to today's policy dilemmas. Indeed, political conflict over the application of these ideas, over choices among policies, and even over which problems are most in need of solving, is inevitable and unending. What the political culture does is to provide a common ground for the debate and a common set of rules within which debate, however intense, can be carried on.

■ IDEAS AND POLITICS: IDEOLOGY

An **ideology** is a closely linked set of beliefs about the goal of politics and the most desirable political order. True ideologies are well-organized theories that can guide virtually every decision that an individual or society can make. As discussed in the Highlight on page 20, the major ideologies of our time are usually represented as a continuum from far left to far right according to their view of the power of government. Few Americans, however, order their views on politics according to the more extreme ideologies. In fact, the American political spectrum has been dominated for decades by two relatively moderate ideological positions: **liberalism** and **conservatism.**

American liberals believe that government should take strong, positive action to solve the nation's economic and social problems. They believe it is the obligation of the government to enhance opportunities for economic and social

POPULAR SOVEREIGNTY
The natural rights' concept that ultimate political authority rests with the people.

FRATERNITY
From the Latin *fraternus* ("brother"), the term *fraternity* came to mean, in the political philosophy of the eighteenth century, the condition in which each individual considers the needs of all others; a brotherhood. In the French Revolution of 1789, the popular cry was "liberty, equality, and fraternity."

IDEOLOGY
A comprehensive and logically ordered set of beliefs about the nature of people and the institutions of government.

LIBERALISM
A set of beliefs that includes the advocacy of positive government action to improve the welfare of individuals, support for civil rights, and a tolerance for political and social change.

CONSERVATISM
A set of beliefs that includes a limited role for the national government in helping individuals, support for traditional values and life-styles, and a preference for the status quo.

Hispanic Americans show their support for Dukakis in the 1988 campaign. Do Hispanics represent a political subculture?

equality for all people. Following this view, liberals tend to support government programs to reduce poverty, to redistribute income from wealthier citizens to poorer ones, and to regulate the activities of business. In general, liberals are also more tolerant of social change and resist efforts to restrict the rights of individuals to choose alternative life-styles.

Conservatives give a higher priority to the value of property and preservation of the social order than do liberals. Conservatives believe that the individual is primarily responsible for his or her own well-being and achievements. They are less supportive of government policies that attempt to change the social or economic status of individuals. In general, conservatives believe that many activities of the government could be eliminated or could be better performed by the private sector. In recent years, the conservative movement has also espoused a return to traditional social values—strengthening the family, opposing abortion, and supporting prayer in the public schools. Conservatives believe that traditional values will help preserve order in the society, whereas liberals see the imposition of those values as restricting the liberty of individuals.

There are also smaller groups of Americans who consider themselves to be communists, socialists, or libertarians, but these ideologies play little part on the national political scene.

HIGHLIGHT

Ideologies: Competing Visions of Power

Political ideologies offer their adherents well-organized theories that propose goals for the society and the political means by which those goals can be achieved. At the core of every political ideology is a set of values that guides its theory of governmental power. If we compare political ideologies on the basis of how much power the government should have within a society, we can array them on a continuum from left to right as shown in the first box below.

For each of these ideological positions, the amount of power granted to the government is intended to achieve a certain set of goals within the society, and the perfect society would completely achieve these values. The values are arrayed in the second box below.

In the United States, there are adherents of each of these ideological positions. However, given the wide acceptance of shared cultural values, only two of these belief systems have consistently played a central part in American political debates: liberalism and conservatism.

How Much Power Should the Government Have?

Marxism-Leninism	Socialism	Liberalism	Conservatism	Libertarianism
Central control of economy and political system	Active government control of major economic sectors	Positive government action in economy and to achieve social goals	Positive government action to support capitalism; action to uphold certain values	Government action only for defense; no regulation of economy or individual behavior

What Values Should the Government Pursue?

Marxism-Leninism	Socialism	Liberalism	Conservatism	Libertarianism
Total equality and security; unity and solidarity	Economic equality; community	Political liberty; economic security; equal opportunity	Political liberty; economic liberty; order	Total political and economic liberty for individuals

■ THE UNITED STATES IN A TURBULENT WORLD

As the United States looks to the future, it faces many questions about the nation's position in the world and the ability of its political system to deal with massive international change. The changing political system of the Soviet Union demands the creation of a new relationship with a former adversary. Not only will there be a challenge to its economic power when the nations of Western Europe become a single economic entity after December 31, 1992, but also the Pacific Rim nations—Japan, Korea, Singapore, Taiwan—continue to grow as economic competitors to the United States.

The August, 1990 invasion of Kuwait by the armed forces of Iraq challenged the United States to define its world role in the post-Cold War era. Should the United States retreat from the center stage and allow the United Nations to resolve the situation or should it continue to play the role of world peacekeeper, using its military force to maintain stability? The Bush administration responded by sending more than 200,000 troops as well as air and sea power to defend Saudi Arabia from the Iraqi threat. Americans debated the purposes of the response: was the United States trying to force Iraqi dictator Saddam Hussein out of Kuwait because the invasion was morally wrong or was the United States simply trying to secure its energy supply and stabilize the world economy? The strength of Bush's response also alarmed Arab-Americans who feared discrimination by other Americans. Their fears reflected those of the many other immigrant groups who have made America a multicultural society.

In some ways, the United States is well positioned to meet the challenges of the next decade. The political system of the nation is stable and well established. The administration of George Bush is more moderate than that of his predecessor, Ronald Reagan, and, at least in its early actions, enjoyed wide popular support. The economy generally remained strong until 1991, increasing the number of jobs available for Americans.

Yet the very stability of our political system raises questions about whether the political structures, the political parties, and the voters themselves are adaptable enough to respond to the new world that we face. Are the structures of our government—the executive branch, the houses of Congress, the judiciary, the bureaucracy—responsive enough to chart a new role for the United States in world politics? Can the political parties rally themselves to debate that world role? Can the political system really become multicultural and grant political power to all of the old and new minority groups that will make up the nation in the future? Can the government propose new policies to keep American industry competitive with a unified Europe, the Pacific Rim, and the newly awakened Eastern-bloc nations?

All of these questions and many more will confront the United States in the years to come. The political system is in place. What we look at in the chapters to follow are the institutions and political processes that have been established to govern the nation. What we critically examine is whether that political system has the dynamism to meet the challenges of the future.

GETTING INVOLVED

Seeing Democracy in Action

One way to begin understanding the American political system is to observe a legislative body in action. There are thousands of elected legislatures in the United States at all levels of government. You might choose to visit the city council, a school board, the township board of trustees, the state legislature, or the U.S. Congress. Before attending a business session of the legislature, try to find out how the members are elected. Are they chosen by the "at-large" method of election so that each member represents the whole community, or are they chosen by specific geographical districts or wards? Some other questions you might want to ask are: Is there a chairperson or official leader of the body who controls the meetings and who may have more power than the other leaders? What are the responsibilities of this legislature? Are the members paid political officials or do they volunteer their services? Do the officials serve as full-time or part-time employees?

When you visit the legislature, keep in mind the theory of representative democracy. The legislators or council members are elected to represent their constituents. Observe how often the members refer to the voters or to their constituents or to the special needs of their community or electoral district. Listen carefully for the sources of conflict within a community. If there is a debate, for example, over a zoning decision that involves the issue of land use, try to figure out why some members oppose the decision. Perhaps the greatest sources of conflict in local government are questions of taxation and expenditure. It is important to remember that the council or board is also supposed to be working toward the good of the whole; listen for discussions of the community's priorities.

If you want to follow up on your visit and learn more about representative government in action, try to get a brief interview with one of the members of the council or board. In general, legislators are very willing to talk to students, particularly if they also are voters. Ask the member how he or she sees the job of representative. How can the wishes of the constituents be identified? How does the representative balance the needs of the ward or district with the good of the whole community? You also might ask the member how he or she keeps in touch with constituents and informs them of the activities of the council.

After your visit to the legislative body, think about the advantages and disadvantages of representative democracy. Do you think the average citizen would take the time to consider all of the issues that representatives must debate? Do you think that, on the whole, the elected representatives act responsibly for their constituents?

To find out when and where the local legislative bodies meet, look up the number of the city hall or county building in the telephone directory and call the clerk of council. For information on the structure of your local government, contact the local chapter of the League of Women Voters.

CHAPTER SUMMARY

1. Most definitions of politics are based on the idea of social conflict, which invariably arises because of differing beliefs and values and competition for scarce resources.

2. Harold Lasswell defined politics as a process that determines "who gets what" in a society. David Easton defined politics as the "authoritative allocation of values" within a society.

3. For most complex societies, government is the ultimate authority that allocates values and makes decisions about conflict resolution.

4. To say that a government is authoritative implies a reasonable expectation that there will be compliance with its value-allocating decisions. This authority is based on the power to enforce rules, legitimacy, and compliance.

5. The framers of the Constitution warned against the inherent problems of a pure direct democracy: the inability of uneducated masses to govern themselves, the potentially disruptive influence of demagogues, and the threat to minority rights.

6. The U.S. political system is a representative, rather than a direct, democracy. The people hold ultimate power over the government through the election process, but they empower representatives to make decisions on their behalf.

7. Since everyone has an equal vote in a democracy, decisions are made by majority rule. To prevent oppression by the majority, certain rights are protected for the minority.

8. Elite theory sees the power in society resting with a small group of leaders who come from the upper social and economic classes. The masses are viewed as apathetic and uninterested in politics.

9. Pluralism assumes that groups are the basis of all political activity. Public policy results from group conflict and from bargaining among groups within Congress and the other institutions of government.

10. Americans share a common set of beliefs about the government which is called the political culture.

11. Concepts that are fundamental to American political culture are learned through a process of political socialization. Among these core concepts are liberty, equality, and property. These principles, subscribed to by men such as Thomas Paine, Thomas Jefferson, and James Madison, sometimes conflict with each other when applied to current problems.

12. Although Americans share in the same political culture, there are two major viewpoints within the electorate, liberalism and conservatism, which take different positions on many issues. Each of these represents a different political ideology.

QUESTIONS FOR REVIEW AND DISCUSSION

1. What decisions does the national government make that affect your life and work? What direct power does the national government have over you?

2. Think about how political decisions are made in your city or community. Are there certain individuals or social groups that seem to predominate in decision making? How are such elite groups controlled by the voters?

3. Think about your own family and schooling. How did you learn about the concepts of liberty, equality, and opportunity? How did you find out the difference between Republicans and Democrats? Has your political socialization continued in your adult years? Through what agencies, or sources of information, has that socialization occurred?

SELECTED REFERENCES

Robert A. Dahl, *Modern Political Analysis,* 4th ed. (Englewood Cliffs, N.J.: Prentice-Hall, 1984). Definitions and explanations of politics and political analysis, political influence, political systems, and political socialization.

Robert A. Dahl, *A Preface to Economic Democracy* (Berkeley: University of California Press, 1985). Dahl argues that social and political equality in the United States can be achieved within a framework of liberty if "workplace democracy" would be realized. Liberty, justice, and efficiency, he proposes, could all be achieved with such a radical transformation of the American social vision.

Harold Lasswell, *Politics: Who Gets What, When and How* (New York: McGraw-Hill, 1936). A classic work defining the nature of politics.

Linda J. Medcalf and Kenneth M. Dolbeare, *Neopolitics: American Political Ideas in the 1980s* (New York: Random House, 1985). An incisive examination of labels such as liberalism, neoliberalism, democratic neopopulism, democratic socialism, neoconservatism, conservatism, and New Right populist conservatism in modern American political thought.

Jack C. Plano and Milton Greenberg, *The American Political Dictionary,* 6th ed. (New York: Holt, Rinehart and Winston, 1982). Nearly 1,200 terms, organizations, court cases, and important statutes are defined in this useful reference work.

Donald L. Robinson, *Government for the Third American Century* (Boulder, Co.: Westview Press, 1989). The author asks whether a system based on an eighteenth-century constitution can meet the challenges of the twenty-first century and then offers interesting ideas for numerous basic constitutional reforms.

Harold W. Stanley and Richard G. Niemi, *Vital Statistics on American Politics,* 2nd ed. (Washington, D.C.: Congressional Quarterly Press, 1990). This valuable reference contains over 200 tables and figures on a wide range of topics covering almost all aspects of American politics.

Alexis de Tocqueville, *Democracy in America,* edited by Phillips Bradley (New York: Vintage Books, 1945). An account of life in the United States by a French writer who traveled through the nation in the 1820s.

Kenneth D. Wald, *Religion and Politics in the United States* (New York: St. Martin's Press, 1987). This book emphasizes the profound influence of religion on American politics and government, and the diversity of conservative and liberal political values that can be traced to the role of religion in American society.

THE CONSTITUTION

WHAT IF . . . WE HAD A CONSTITUTIONAL CONVENTION IN 1994?

Consider some possible amendments to the Constitution that have been proposed over the last few years: mandatory prayer in the public schools, a balanced federal budget, a prohibition against abortion, an injunction against desecrating the American flag. Not surprisingly, opponents are against calling a national constitutional convention to consider such amendments. Others have a more serious worry—that the second constitutional convention would follow the pattern of the first one in Philadelphia, in which major changes to the basic document were made.

All agree that amending our Constitution through normal channels is difficult at best. Even though there have been more than 7,000 bills introduced into Congress proposing amendments to the Constitution, only 33 were approved by two-thirds of both the House and Senate and sent to the states for ratification.

The Constitution itself does not provide the guidelines for another constitutional convention. Undoubtedly, a convention would operate under rules laid down by Congress, but once it got under way, it could probably modify those rules or interpret them as desired

by the majority (over 50 percent, three-fifths, two-thirds, or whatever was decided on). Let's say that Congress called the convention for a very narrow purpose, such as balancing the federal budget. There is no practical way for Congress to tie the convention members' hands once the convention is underway. Who knows what additional proposals might be introduced?

You can think of some outrageous possibilities, such as repealing the Thirteenth Amendment and thereby allowing slavery; or tampering with the structure of the executive branch by calling for a plural presidency; or eliminating the office of vice president; or repealing the First Amendment's protection of freedom of speech. Such proposals are possible, but highly improbable. To some extent, the potential for drastic proposals would be a function of who were selected as representatives to the national constitutional convention. Depending on whatever statutory law or ad hoc provisions exist in a given state, each state might send delegations selected in very different ways. States with conservative legislatures or governors probably would send delegates who were strongly antiabortion, pro-balanced budget, and in favor of public school prayer. The opposite would occur in delegations from states with more liberal legislators and governors.

A lot of people over the years offered ideas for amending the Constitution that could surface at a new constitutional convention. In 1876, for example, a group of Pennsylvanians proposed to eliminate the Senate because it was an aristocratic body that favored the wealthy. In 1933, Washington State Representative Wesley Lloyd proposed an amendment limiting personal wealth to no more than $1 million. In 1873, President Grant requested an amendment to give the president a line-item veto, by which the president could veto just one part or parts of a bill. Many other presidents, including Reagan and Bush, have pushed for such an amendment.

When all is said and done, the comparison between the Philadelphia Convention in 1787 and a constitutional convention, in, say, 1994, should not be exaggerated. We don't have many Frank-

lins, Washingtons, Jeffersons, Madisons, and Hamiltons in our midst who are going to articulate and politically craft the outlines of an entirely new constitution. Moreover, it would be awfully hard to duplicate the secrecy with which the Philadelphia Convention met. The prying eyes and ears of the media would make it unlikely that major surprises would be sprung on an unsuspecting nation.

The openness of the convention might even prevent any proposals for truly radical changes in the constitutional status quo. Finally, the rest of the world would be watching—something that really wasn't happening in 1787.

But a limited convention still is a possibility, and, if it occurred, it could make important changes in our lives, such as requiring that the federal government raise taxes every time it wants to increase spending or that schoolchildren start every school day with a moment of silence or prayer. To some, such changes would be welcome; to others, they would be fraught with threats to the nation's future.

---

1. *Would a new U.S. Constitution be as short as the original, or would it include many more details?*
2. *Which groups would be most powerful at a 1994 Constitutional Convention?*

We the People of the United States, in Order to form a more perfect Union, establish Justice, insure domestic Tranquility, provide for the common defence, promote the general Welfare, and secure the Blessings of Liberty to ourselves and our Posterity, do ordain and establish this Constitution for the United States of America.

Every schoolchild in America has at one time or another been exposed to these famous words from the Preamble to the United States Constitution. The document itself is remarkable: As constitutions go, it is short; and since its ratification on June 21, 1788, relatively few amendments have been added to it. What is even more remarkable is the fact that it has remained largely intact for over two hundred years, making it the oldest written constitution in the world today.

How and why this Constitution was created is a story that has been told and retold. It is worth repeating because the historical and political context in which this country's governmental machinery was formed is essential to understanding American government and politics today. The Constitution was not the result of completely creative thinking, nor were its provisions ungrounded in political thought. The delegates to the Constitutional Convention in 1787 brought with them two important sets of influences: their political culture and their political experience. In the years between the first settlements in the New World and the end of the Confederation, Americans had developed a political philosophy about how people should be governed and had tried out numerous forms of government. These experiences provided the tools with which the Constitution was constructed.

> **DID YOU KNOW?**
>
> That the first English claim to territory in North America was made by John Cabot, on behalf of King Henry VII, on June 24, 1497?

■ THE STARVING TIME

The first British outpost in North America was set up by Sir Walter Raleigh in the 1580s for the purpose of harassing the Spanish treasure fleets. Located in Roanoke Island Colony, it stands as one of history's great mysteries: After

The starving time.

DID YOU KNOW?

That the first permanent European colony in North America was founded at St. Augustine, Florida, on September 8, 1565, by Pedro Menendez de Aviles?

REPRESENTATIVE ASSEMBLY
A legislature composed of individuals who represent the population.

a short absence to resupply the colony, Raleigh's captain, John White, returned in 1590 to find no trace—living or dead—of the small colony's inhabitants. Roanoke has ever after been referred to as the "lost colony."

In 1607, a group of farmers were sent over to establish a trading post, Jamestown, in what is now Virginia. The Virginia Company of London was the first to establish successfully a permanent British colony in the Americas. The king of England gave the backers of this colony a charter granting them "full power and authority" to make laws "for the good and welfare" of the settlement. The Jamestown colonists instituted a **representative assembly**, setting a precedent in government that was to be observed in later colonial adventures.

Unfortunately, Jamestown was not a commercial success. Of the 105 men who landed, 67 died within the first year. But 800 new arrivals in 1609 added to their numbers. By the spring of the next year, frontier hazards had cut their numbers to 60! Of the 6,000 people who left England for Virginia between 1607 and 1623, 4,000 of them perished. The distinguished historian Charles Andrews has called this the "starving time for Virginia."[1]

Pilgrims, the *Mayflower,* and the Compact

The first New England colony was established in 1620. A group of English Puritans, calling themselves pilgrims, came over on the ship *Mayflower* to the New World, landing at Plymouth (Massachusetts). Before going on shore, the adult males—women were not considered to have any political status—drew up the Mayflower Compact, which was signed by forty-one of the forty-four men aboard the ship on November 21, 1620. The reason for the compact was obvious: Being outside the jurisdiction of the Virginia Company of London, which had chartered their settlement in Virginia, not Massachusetts, and fearful of the consequences of having no political institutions, the pilgrim leadership wanted to form a government.

[1]Charles M. Andrews, *The Colonial Period of American History,* vol. 1 (New Haven: Yale University Press, 1934), p. 110.

The signing of the Compact aboard the *Mayflower.* What was the significance of this document?

Rather than being a constitution, the compact was a political agreement later linked the seventeenth and eighteenth-century ideas of a **social contract.** Developed by such philosophers as John Locke, Thomas Hobbes, and Jean-Jacques Rousseau, the social contract theory says that a government arises out of the *voluntary* act of free persons. The theory is that government exists only to serve the will of the people, who are its sole source of power and who are free to withhold that power. The Mayflower Compact's historical and political significance is that it served as a prototype for similar compacts (in American history) and that it depended on the consent of the individuals involved. The compact bound the signers to majority-rule government, pending receipt of a royal charter. According to Samuel Eliot Morison, the compact proved the determination of the English immigrants to live under the rule of law, based on the *consent of the people.*[2]

More Colonies, More Government

A second outpost in New England was set up by the Massachusetts Bay Colony in 1630. Then followed Rhode Island, Connecticut, New Hampshire, and others. By 1732, the last of the thirteen colonies, Georgia, was established. During the colonial period, Americans developed a concept of limited government, which followed from the establishment of the first colonies under Crown charters. Although theoretically London governed the colonies, in practice, partly owing to the colonies' distance from London, the colonists exercised a large measure of self-government. The colonists were able to make their own laws, as in the Fundamental Order of Connecticut in 1639. The Massachusetts Body of Liberties in 1641 supported the protection of individual rights and was made a part of colonial law. In 1682, the Pennsylvania Frame of Government was passed. It, along with the Pennsylvania Charter of Privileges of 1701, established the rationale for our modern Constitution and Bill of Rights. All of this legislation enabled the colonists to acquire crucial political experience. After independence in 1776, the states quickly set up their own constitutions.

■ BRITISH RESTRICTIONS AND COLONIAL GRIEVANCES

The Navigation Acts of 1651–1750 were the earliest general restrictions on colonial activity. These acts imposed the condition that only English ships (including ships of its colonies) could be used for trade within the British Empire. Starting in 1763, British restrictions were intensified. The Proclamation of 1763 declared that no colonial settlement could be established west of the Appalachians. In 1764, the Sugar Act was passed to pay for wars that the British had waged (to a significant degree, on behalf of the colonies). As with the previous Molasses Act of 1733, many colonists were unwilling to pay the required tax.

Further oppressive legislation was to come. In 1765, the British Parliament passed the Stamp Act, providing for internal taxation, or, as the colonists'

SOCIAL CONTRACT
An agreement between individuals to establish a government and to abide by its rules. Early theorists saw the social contract as an agreement between the ruler and the people.

MILESTONES IN EARLY U.S. POLITICAL HISTORY	
1585	British outpost set up in Roanoke
1607	Jamestown established, Plymouth Company lands settlers
1620	Mayflower Compact signed
1630	Massachusetts Bay Colony set up
1639	Fundamental Orders of Connecticut adopted
1641	Massachusetts Body of Liberties adopted
1682	Pennsylvania Frame of Government passed
1701	Pennsylvania Charter of Privileges written
1732	Last of thirteen colonies established
1756	French and Indian War declared
1765	Stamp Act, Stamp Act Congress meets
1770	Boston Massacre
1774	First Continental Congress
1775	Second Continental Congress, Revolutionary War begins
1776	Declaration of Independence signed
1777	Articles of Confederation drafted
1781	Last state signs Articles of Confederation
1783–1789	"Critical period" in U.S. history, weak national government
1786	Shays's Rebellion
1787	Constitutional Convention

[2]See Morison's "The Mayflower Compact" in *An American Primer,* ed. Daniel J. Boorstin (Chicago: University of Chicago Press, 1966), p. 18.

King George III (Great Britain, 1760–1820)

FIRST CONTINENTAL CONGRESS
The first gathering of delegates from the thirteen colonies, held in 1774.

SECOND CONTINENTAL CONGRESS
The 1775 Congress of the colonies that established the Continental Army.

COMMON SENSE
Thomas Paine's best-selling pamphlet that argued for a new government in the colonies.

Stamp Act Congress assembled in 1765 called it, "taxation without representation." The colonists boycotted the Stamp Act, and the success of the boycott (the Stamp Act was repealed a year later) generated a feeling of unity within the colonies. The British, however, continued to try to raise revenue in the colonies. When duties on glass, lead, paint, and other items were passed in 1767, the colonists boycotted the purchase of English commodities in return. Continual negotiations between the colonists and the British took place until 1773. Finally, the Coercive Acts ("Intolerable Acts") were passed in 1774, closing Boston Harbor and placing the government of Boston under direct British control. The colonists were outraged—and they responded.

■ THE COLONIAL RESPONSE: THE CONTINENTAL CONGRESSES

New York, Pennsylvania, and Rhode Island proposed the convening of a colonial congress. The Massachusetts House of Representatives requested that all colonies hold conventions to select delegates to be sent to Philadelphia for such a congress. The **First Continental Congress** was held at Carpenter's Hall on September 5, 1774. It was a gathering of delegates from twelve of the thirteen colonies (Georgia did not attend until 1775). At that meeting, there was little talk of independence. The Congress passed a resolution requesting that the colonies send a petition to King George III expressing their grievances. Resolutions were also passed requiring that the colonies raise their own troops and boycott British trade. The British government condemned the Congress's actions, treating them as open acts of rebellion.

What is important politically is that the First Continental Congress represented the nation's first formal act of cooperation among the colonies. The congressional delegates declared that in every county and city a committee was to be formed whose mission was to spy on the conduct of friends and neighbors and to report to the press any violators of the trade ban. In spite of the antilibertarian nature of these committees, their formation was another act of cooperation among the colonies, which represented a step toward the formation of a national government.

By the time the **Second Continental Congress** met in May 1775 (this time all the colonies were represented), fighting had already broken out between the British and the colonists. One of the main actions of the Second Congress was to establish an army. It did this by declaring the militia that had gathered around Boston an army and naming George Washington as commander in chief. The participants in that Congress still attempted to reach a peaceful settlement with the British Parliament. One declaration of the Congress stated explicitly that "we have not raised armies with ambitious designs of separating from Great Britain, and establishing independent states." But by the beginning of 1776, military encounters had become increasingly frequent.

Public debate was acrimonious. Then Thomas Paine's pamphlet *Common Sense* appeared in Philadelphia bookstores. It was a colonial bestseller.[3] Many agreed that Paine did make common sense when he argued:

> A government of our own is our natural right: and when a man seriously reflects on the precariousness of human affairs, he will become convinced, that it is infinitely

---

[3]To do relatively as well today, a book would have to sell between eight and ten million copies in its first year of publication.

wiser and safer, to form a constitution of our own in a cool and deliberate manner, while we have it in our power, than to trust such an interesting event to time and chance.[4]

Students of Paine's pamphlet point out that his arguments were not new—they were common in tavern debates throughout the land. Rather, it was the near poetry of his words—which were at the same time as plain as the alphabet—that struck his readers.

■ DECLARING INDEPENDENCE

The Resolution of Independence

On April 6, 1776, the Second Continental Congress voted for free trade at all American ports for all countries except Great Britain. This act could be intrepreted as an implicit declaration of independence. The next month, the Congress suggested that each of the colonies establish state governments unconnected to Britain. Finally, on July 2, the Resolution of Independence was adopted by the Second Continental Congress:

> RESOLVED, That these United Colonies are, and of right ought to be free and independent States, that they are absolved from allegiance to the British Crown, and that all political connection between them and the state of Great Britain is, and ought to be, totally dissolved.

The actual Resolution of Independence was not legally significant. On the one hand, it was not judicially enforceable, for it established no legal rights or duties. On the other hand, the colonies were already, in their own judgment, self-governing and independent of Britain. Rather, the Resolution of Independence and the subsequent Declaration of Independence were necessary to establish the legitimacy of the new nation in the eyes of foreign governments, as well as in the eyes of the colonists themselves. What the new nation needed most was supplies for its armies and a commitment of foreign military aid. Unless it projected an image as being separate and independent from Britain, no foreign government would enter into a contract with its leaders.

July 4, 1776—The Declaration of Independence

By June 1776, Thomas Jefferson was already writing drafts of the Declaration of Independence in the second-floor parlor of a bricklayer's house in Philadelphia. Upon adoption of the Resolution of Independence, Jefferson had argued that a declaration putting forth clearly the causes that compelled the colonies to separate from England was necessary. He did that in the task assigned to him, enumerating the major grievances. Some of his work was amended to gain unanimous acceptance; (for example, his condemnation of slavery was eliminated to satisfy Georgia and North Carolina), but the bulk of it was passed intact on July 4, 1776. On July 19, the modified draft became "the unanimous declaration of the thirteen United States of America." On August 2, it was signed by the members of the Continental Congress. The first printed version carried only the signatures of the congress's president, John Hancock, and secretary, Charles Thompson.

[4]*The Political Writings of Thomas Paine,* vol. 1. (Boston: J. P. Mendum Investigator Office, 1870), p. 46.

DID YOU KNOW?

That in the "Boston Massacre" of March 5, 1770, British troops killed five civilians who were allegedly rioting, including Crispus Attucks, a black man who was reportedly a leader of the group?

Copyright 1985 Sidney Harris.

DID YOU KNOW?

That the first legislative assembly in America, the Virginia House of Burgesses, which met on August 9, 1619, had all its acts reviewed by the Virginia Company in London?

NATURAL RIGHTS
Rights held to be inherent in natural law, not dependent on governments. John Locke stated that natural law, being superior to human law, specifies certain rights of "life, liberty, and property." These rights, slightly altered to become "life, liberty, and the pursuit of happiness," are asserted in the Declaration of Independence.

CONSENT OF THE GOVERNED
The government is based on the consent or will of the people and can be abolished by them.

UNICAMERAL LEGISLATURES
Legislatures with only one legislative body, as compared with bicameral (two-house) legislatures, such as the United States Congress. Nebraska is the only state in the Union with a unicameral legislature.

Perhaps the most revolutionary concept in the Declaration was the assumption, inspired by the ideas of John Locke, that people have **natural rights** ("unalienable Rights") including "life, liberty, and the pursuit of happiness." Governments are established to secure these rights, and governments derive their power "from the **consent of the governed**." The Declaration went even further and claimed that whenever any form of government "becomes destructive to these ends, it is the Right of the People to alter or to abolish it, and to institute a new government."

■ THE RISE OF REPUBLICANISM

Not everyone had agreed with the notion of independence. There were recalcitrant colonists in the middle and lower southern colonies who demanded as a condition of independence that it be preceded by the formation of a strong central government. But the anti-Royalists in New England and Virginia, who called themselves Republicans, were against a strong central government, opposing monarchy, executive authority, and virtually any form of restraint upon the power of local groups. These so-called Republicans were a major political force from 1776 to 1780. Indeed, they almost prevented victory over the British by their unwillingness to cooperate with any central authority.

During this time, all the states adopted written constitutions. Eleven of the constitutions were completely new, whereas two of them—those of Connecticut and Rhode Island—were old royal charters with minor modifications. Republican sentiment led to increased power for the legislatures. In Pennsylvania and Georgia, **unicameral** (one-body) **legislatures** were unchecked by executive or judicial authority. Basically, the Republicans attempted to maintain the politics of 1776. In almost all states, the executive branch was emasculated; the legislative branch was expanded.

The signing of the Declaration of Independence. What political principles were used as a basis of this document?

■ THE ARTICLES OF CONFEDERATION: PROMISE AND REALITY

The fear of a powerful central government led to the passage of the Articles of Confederation. The term **confederation** is important; it means a voluntary association of *independent* **states,** in which the member states agree to only limited restraints on their freedom of action. As a result, confederations seldom have an effective executive authority.

Even though Richard Henry Lee first proposed the establishment of the confederation on June 6, 1776, it wasn't until November 15, 1777, that the Second Continental Congress agreed to a draft for the Articles, and March 1, 1781, that the last state, Maryland, agreed to sign.

Under the Articles, the thirteen original colonies, now states, established a government of the states on March 1, 1781—the Congress of the Confederation. The Congress was a unicameral assembly of so-called ambassadors from each state, with each state possessing a single vote. Each year the Congress would choose one of its members as its president, but the Articles did not provide for a president of the United States. The Congress was authorized to appoint an executive committee of the states "to execute in the recess of Congress, such of the powers of Congress as the United States, in Congress assembled, by the consent of nine [of the thirteen] states, shall from time to time think expedient to vest with them. . . ." The Congress was also allowed to appoint other committees and civil officers necessary for managing the general affairs of the United States. The Articles did not establish a separate judicial institution, although Congress had certain judicial functions. In addition, the Congress could regulate foreign affairs and establish coinage and weights and measures, but it lacked an independent source of revenue and any executive machinery to enforce its desires on individual citizens throughout the land. Figure 2-1 illustrates the structure of the confederal government under the Articles of Confederation; Table 2-1 summarizes the powers—and the lack of powers—of Congress under that system.

The Articles guaranteed each state its sovereignty:

> Each state retains its sovereignty, freedom and independence, and every power, jurisdiction, and right, which is not by this Confederation expressly delegated to the United States in Congress assembled.

Accomplishments under the Articles

Although the Articles of Confederation had many defects, there were also some accomplishments during the eight years of their existence. Certain states' claims to western lands were settled. Maryland had objected to the claims of Massachusetts, New York, Connecticut, Virginia, the Carolinas, and Georgia. It was only after these states consented to give up their land claims to the United States as a whole that Maryland signed the Articles of Confederation. Another accomplishment under the Articles was the passage of the Northwest Ordinance of 1787, which established a basic pattern of government for new territories north of the Ohio River.

Finally, the Articles created a sort of "first draft" for the Constitution of the United States that was to follow. In a sense, it was an unplanned applied experiment to try out some of the principles of government set forth in the Declaration of Independence.

CONFEDERATION
A political system in which states or regional governments retain ultimate authority except for those powers they expressly delegate to a central government. A voluntary association of independent states, in which the member states agree to limited restraints on their freedom of action.

STATE
A group of people occupying a specific area and organized under one government; either a nation or a subunit of a nation.

FIGURE 2-1
The structure of the confederal government under the Articles of Confederation

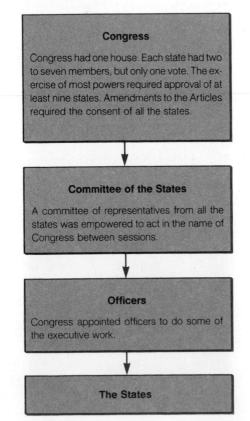

Congress
Congress had one house. Each state had two to seven members, but only one vote. The exercise of most powers required approval of at least nine states. Amendments to the Articles required the consent of all the states.

Committee of the States
A committee of representatives from all the states was empowered to act in the name of Congress between sessions.

Officers
Congress appointed officers to do some of the executive work.

The States

TABLE 2-1
Powers of the Congress of the Confederation

Congress Had Power to	Congress Lacked Power to
■ Declare war and make peace	■ Provide for effective treaty-making power and control foreign relations; it could not compel states to respect treaties
■ Enter into treaties and alliances	
■ Establish and control armed forces	
■ Requisition men and money from states	■ Compel states to meet military quotas; it could not draft soldiers
■ Regulate coinage	■ Regulate interstate and foreign commerce; it left each state free to set up its own tariff system
■ Borrow money and issue bills of credit	
■ Fix uniform standards of weight and measurement	■ Collect taxes directly from the people; it had to rely on states to collect and forward taxes
■ Create admiralty courts	
■ Create a postal system	■ Compel states to pay their share of government costs
■ Regulate Indian affairs	
■ Guarantee citizens of each state the rights and privileges of citizens in the several states when in another state	■ Provide and maintain a sound monetary system or issue paper money; this was left up to the states, and monies in circulation differed tremendously in value
■ Adjudicate disputes between states upon state petition	

Weaknesses of the Articles

Although Congress had the legal right to declare war and to conduct foreign policy, it did not have the right to demand revenues from the states. It could only *ask* for them. Also, the actions of Congress required the consent of nine states, and any amendments to the Articles required the unanimous consent of the Congress and confirmation by every state legislature. Further, the Articles did not create a national system of courts.

Basically, the functioning of the government under the Articles depended on the good will of the states. Article III of the Articles simply establishes a "league of friendship" among the states—no national government was intended.

Perhaps the most telling weakness of the Articles was their inability to give the Continental Congress the power to tax. When states refused to send money to support the government (not one state met the financial requests made by Congress under the Articles), Congress resorted to selling off western lands to speculators or issuing bonds that sold for less than their face value. Due to a lack of resources, the Continental Congress was forced to disband the army, even in the face of serious Spanish and British military threats. Although it was permitted to do so, Congress really did not have the power to raise and maintain an army.

Shays's Rebellion and the Need for Revision of the Articles

By 1786, in the city of Concord, Massachusetts, the scene of one of the first battles of the Revolution, there were three times as many people in prison for debts as there were for all other crimes combined. In Worcester County, the

Shays's Rebellion. What weaknesses in the Articles of Confederation caused this uprising?

ratio was even higher—twenty to one. Most of the prisoners were small farmers who couldn't pay their debts owing to the disorganized state of the economy. In August 1786, mobs of musket-bearing farmers led by former revolutionary captain Daniel Shays seized county courthouses and disrupted the trials of the debtors. Shays's men then launched an attack on the federal arsenal at Springfield, but they were repulsed.

Shays's Rebellion demonstrated the economic decline of the nation. Interstate trade conflicts, inflation, disruption of overseas trade, and the collapse of the U.S. bond market that occurred under the weak central government sowed fear and confusion among citizens and businesses. The Articles of Confederation could not provide the type of central government that would ensure the growth of the country.

> **DID YOU KNOW?**
>
> That on July 4, 1776, on the day the Founding Fathers signed the Declaration of Independence, King George III of England wrote in his diary, "Nothing of importance happened today."

■ DRAFTING THE CONSTITUTION

The Annapolis Convention

Shays's Rebellion was but one indication that America was in crisis by the winter of 1786–87. Finally, when the Continental Congress was unable to pass an amendment giving itself an independent source of revenue from import duties, its members became desperate. But as it was clearly impossible for the Congress to achieve unanimity on any important issue, there seemed little reason to call a constitutional convention.

As an alternative, the Virginia legislature called for a meeting of all the states, ostensibly to discuss commercial problems only. It was evident to those in attendance (including Alexander Hamilton and James Madison) that the national government had serious weaknesses which had to be addressed if it were to survive. Among the most important problems to be solved were the relationship between the states and the central government, the powers of the national legislature, the need for executive leadership, and the establishment of policies for economic stability. At this Annapolis meeting, a call was issued to all the states for a general convention to meet in Philadelphia in May of 1787 "to consider the exigencies of the union." When the members of the Second Continental Congress realized that the Philadelphia meeting would in fact take place, they approved the convention in February 1787, but they made it explicit that the convention was "for the sole and express purpose of revising the Articles of Confederation." Those in favor of a stronger national government—the Federalists, as they were to be called—had different ideas.

The Philadelphia Convention

The designated date for the opening of the convention was May 14, 1787. Since few of the delegates had actually arrived in Philadelphia by that time, however, it was not formally opened in the East Room of the Pennsylvania State House[5] until May 25. By this time, fifty-five of the seventy-four delegates chosen for the convention had arrived. (Of those fifty-five, only about forty played active roles at the convention.) Rhode Island was the only state that refused to send delegates.

---

[5]The State House was later named Independence Hall. This was the same room in which the Declaration of Independence had been signed eleven years earlier.

George Washington presiding at the
Constitutional Convention in 1787.

Not a Commoner Among Them

Who were the fifty-five delegates? They certainly did not represent a cross
section of eighteenth-century American society. Consider the following facts:

1. Thirty-three were members of the legal profession.
2. Three were physicians.
3. Almost 50 percent were college graduates.
4. Seven were former chief executives of their respective states.
5. Six were large plantation owners.
6. Eight were important businessmen.[6]

They were also relatively young by today's standards: James Madison was
thirty-six, Alexander Hamilton was only thirty-two, and Jonathan Dayton of
New Jersey was twenty-six. The venerable Benjamin Franklin (see Profile in
this chapter), however, was eighty-one and had to be carried in on a portable
chair borne by four prisoners from a local jail. Not counting Franklin, the
average age was just over forty-two.

Collectively, these men had extensive public experience. They had strong
personal, political, and moral views, taking active roles in religious and political
groups. Many had fought in the Revolution. More than half had been members
of the Continental Congress, the Congress under the Confederation, or both.
Eight had served in state constitutional conventions. Two were college presidents; three were professors.

Historian Charles Beard suggested in 1913 that the delegates represented
the economic elite and that they designed and drafted the Constitution to
benefit themselves rather than the majority, who were heavily indebted farmers
and property owners (see this chapter's Critical Perspective).[7] Beard's thesis

[6]Charles Warren, *The Making of the Constitution* (New York: Barnes & Noble, 1967), pp. 55–60.
[7]Charles Beard, *An Economic Interpretation of the Constitution* (New York: Macmillan, 1913).

PROFILE

Benjamin Franklin

"We must indeed all hang together, or, most assuredly, we shall all hang separately."

R emember that *time* is money. He that can earn ten shillings a day by his labour, and goes abroad, or sits idle, one half of that day, though he spends but sixpence during his diversion of idleness, ought not to reckon *that* his only expense; he has really spent, or rather thrown away, five shillings besides." Such were the words of Benjamin Franklin in his *Advice to a Young Tradesman,* published in 1748. A better example of the cost of time would be hard to find.

Franklin's aphorisms were undoubtedly colored by his strict Calvinist upbringing. The true Calvinist was a driven man, described by British economist R. H. Tawney as "tempered by self-examination, self-discipline, self-control . . . the practical ascetic, whose victories are won not in the cloister, but on the battlefield, in the counting house, and in the market." Calvin himself referred to God as the "great task maker" and looked around for tasks man should undertake. Ben Franklin claimed that he was a freethinker, but his father's continual exhortations—such as "Seest thou a man diligent in his business. He shall stand before kings"—must have had some effect.

Franklin was born in 1706 and raised in Boston. Family funds were insufficient for him to aim for Harvard, so he turned his hand to printing and

went to Philadelphia in 1723. Deciding that London was the place to perfect his printing knowledge, he spent two years there working and living the Bohemian life. Within a few years he began to prosper as a master printer. His simple writing style and great clarity of expression also started to bring in rewards. *Poor Richard's Almanac,* published annually between 1732 and 1757, was one of Franklin's most profitable enterprises, selling ten thousand copies a year. When he was twenty-three years old, Franklin wrote his first treatise on economics: *A Modest Inquiry into the Nature and Necessity of a Paper Currency* (1729). Coincidentally, Franklin was the first to start printing Pennsylvania paper currency.

Franklin was a crusader for learning and also a good businessman. He introduced printing and news publications to many communities throughout the colonies. He also helped start the present University of Pennsylvania in 1751. In 1753, he was named deputy postmaster general of the colonies.

Ben Franklin was also one of the first persons in America to use the techniques of advertising to increase business. When he started his *General Magazine,* he advertised his own "Pennsylvania Fire Place." The copy he wrote was persuasive: Franklin criticized ordinary fireplaces because they caused drafts that made "women . . . get cold in the head, rheums, and defluxions, which fall into their jaws and gums . . . [destroying] . . . early, many a fine set of teeth."

During the Revolution, Franklin helped draft the Declaration of Independence, which he also signed. Dispatched as envoy of the new government to France in 1776, proclaiming "our cause is the cause of all mankind," he began the successful diplomatic mission that enlisted foreign support for the Revolution. He signed the first U.S. treaty of alliance with France in 1778 and the treaty of peace with Great Britain in 1783. He died in 1790.

To practical men, especially the officers of savings banks ("a penny saved is a penny earned"), Ben Franklin seemed to be the epitome of good sense and morality. To others he appeared to be a materialistic opportunist. But, as John Adams once said, Franklin's "reputation was more universal than that of Leibniz, Newton, or Voltaire, and he was the first civilized American."

DID YOU KNOW?

That one state (Rhode Island) never sent a delegation to the Constitutional Convention?

has been disputed by other scholars who point out the diverse economic positions of the delegates. Interests other than wealth played a part in generating support for the Constitution. Some of the wealthiest delegates, such as Elbridge Gerry and George Mason, were opposed to the Constitution, whereas some who were less well-off and deeply in debt, such as Madison and Hamilton, were its strongest advocates.

The delegates may also be characterized as astute politicians who were attempting to develop a pragmatic plan to save the new nation.[8] With the exception of age, they were quite similar to the members of Congress today. In the One Hundred Second Congress (1991–1993), for example, over 180 representatives and over 60 senators are lawyers, whereas African Americans, Hispanics, Native Americans, and women are underrepresented.

The Working Environment

The conditions under which the Founding Fathers worked for 115 days were far from ideal and were made even worse by the necessity of maintaining total secrecy. The framers of the Constitution felt that if public debate were started on particular positions, delegates would have a more difficult time compromising or backing down to reach agreement. Consequently, the windows were usually shut in the East Room of the State House. Since the summer was quickly upon the delegates, the air became heavy, humid, and hot by noon of each day. Also, when the windows were open, flies swarmed into the room. The delegates did, however, have a nearby tavern and inn to which they retired each evening. The Indian Queen became the informal headquarters of the delegates.

Factions Among the Delegates

"You know, the idea of taxation with representation doesn't appeal to me very much either."

Drawing by Handelsman; © 1970 The New Yorker Magazine, Inc.

Fortunately, we know much about the proceedings at the convention because James Madison kept a daily, detailed personal journal. A majority of the delegates were strong nationalists—they wanted a central government with real power, unlike that of the central government under the Articles of Confederation. Washington and Franklin preferred limited national authority based on a separation of powers, but they were apparently willing to accept any type of national government, as long as the other delegates approved it. A few pronationalists, led by Gouverneur Morris of Pennsylvania and John Rutledge of South Carolina, distrusted the ability of the common people to engage in self-government.

Among the nationalists were several monarchists, including Alexander Hamilton, who was responsible for the Annapolis Convention's call for the Constitutional Convention. In a long speech on June 18, he presented his views: "I have no scruple in declaring . . . that the British government is the best in the world and that I doubt much whether anything short of it will do in America." Hamilton wanted the American president to hold office for life and to have absolute veto power over the legislature.

Another important group of nationalists were of a more democratic stripe. Led by James Madison of Virginia and James Wilson of Pennsylvania, these

[8]John Roche, "The Founding Fathers: A Reform Caucus in Action," *American Political Science Review,* 61 (December 1961), pp. 799–816.

CRITICAL PERSPECTIVE

Was the Constitution Designed to Benefit an Economic Elite?

One of the great debates surrounding American political history is whether the U.S. Constitution really was designed to protect all the people against the power of government and their own excesses, or whether it was written to serve the interests of the people and groups that wielded *economic* power in the United States after the Revolution. In other words, was the American Constitution a democratic constitution, or was it instead a means by which a dominant economic and social class maintained its power over a subordinate class of citizens?

Like most good arguments about American history and politics, this dispute does not have a clear answer. Nonetheless, the battle lines between competing points of view on this essential issue were drawn very sharply in a book that appeared in 1913, *An Economic Interpretation of the Constitution of the United States,* by Charles A. Beard. The book caused immediate controversy, and the ripples from that original storm continue to be felt today.

As summarized by historian Robert E. Brown in his 1956 book, *Charles Beard and the Constitution: A Critical Analysis of "An Economic Interpretation of the Constitution,"* Beard's thesis has two main points. First, the U.S. Constitution was produced by individuals representing money, public securities, manufacturing, and trade and shipping, whose concerns were to maintain their wealth and the political power that wealth could buy. These powerful economic groups, working through their politically active members, began the push for a new convention in Philadelphia to replace the Articles of Confederation and thereby replace a central government that was too weak to help them protect their economic advantages. Beard saw the entire Constitution as an economic document, very much like a contract, in which such groups laid out their philosophy that the claims of private property were superior to those of government and that private property could not be controlled by popular majorities. Furthermore, Beard argued, the same economic interests that controlled the Philadelphia Convention also controlled the state ratification conventions that adopted the Constitution. He pointed out that the debates in the state conventions often pitted small farmers and debtors, opposed to the Constitution, against the propertied interests who supported the Constitution because they saw it as economically beneficial.

The second essential point to Beard's thesis is that the Constitution was imposed by undemocratic methods to prevent democratic majorities from exercising real power. Beard noted, for example, that there was never any popular vote held on whether to have a constitutional convention in the first place. In addition, the masses who did not own enough property to be eligible to vote or to hold office were excluded from participation, so that about three-fourths of the adult men in the country did not vote on the Constitution (women could not vote), and the document was ratified by perhaps only one-sixth of the eligible adult males. Also, Beard cited evidence that in five states there was considerable doubt that majorities of the voters really had supported ratification.

In contrast to Beard's view, Robert E. Brown and other historians of American colonial politics argue that early America was not as undemocratic as Beard alleged. Brown found that most white males were able to vote during the colonial era and that Beard therefore was wrong to suggest that the Founding Fathers had pulled off a coup d'état of sorts at the Constitutional Convention. The arguments against Beard also hold that the fundamentally republican ideology of the American Revolution precluded the emergence of Beard's version of a domineering elite. Among the proponents of this alternative view are historians Bernard Bailyn, Gordon Wood, and J.G.A. Pocock.

In his Introduction to the 1935 edition of the book, Beard attempted to clarify his position. He said: "It was largely by recognizing the power of economic interests in the field of politics and making skillful use of them that the Fathers of the American Constitution placed themselves among the great practicing statesmen of all ages and gave instructions to succeeding generations in the art of government. . . . It is for us, recipients of their heritage, to inquire constantly and persistently, when theories of national power or states' rights are propounded: 'What interests are behind them and to whose advantage will changes or the maintenance of old forms accrue?' By refusing to do this we become victims of history—clay in the hands of its makers."

Exercise in Critical Thinking

1. What evidence is there that the Constitution works for the benefit of wealthier Americans?

2. Most of our congressional representatives are well-educated professionals. Can such members of the elite truly represent lower-income and minority citizens?

Elbridge Gerry

BICAMERAL LEGISLATURE
A legislature made up of two chambers, or parts. The United States Congress, composed of the House of Representatives and the Senate, is a bicameral legislature.

democratic nationalists wanted a central government founded on popular support.

Still another faction consisted of nationalists who would only support a central government if it were founded on very narrowly defined republican principles. This group was a relatively small number of individuals, including Edmund Randolph and George Mason of Virginia, Elbridge Gerry of Massachusetts, and Luther Martin and John Francis Mercer of Maryland.

Most of the other delegates of Maryland, New Hampshire, Connecticut, New Jersey, and Delaware were concerned about only one thing—claims to western lands. As long as those lands became the common property of all states, they were willing to support a central government.

Finally, there was a group of delegates who were totally against a national authority. Two of the three delegates from New York quit the convention when they saw the nationalist direction of its proceedings, leaving Alexander Hamilton alone.

Politicking and Compromises

The debates at the convention started on the first day. James Madison had spent months reviewing European political theory. When his Virginia delegation arrived ahead of most of the others, it got to work immediately. By the time Washington opened the convention, Governor Edmund Randolph of Virginia was immediately able to present fifteen resolutions. In retrospect this was a masterful stroke on the part of the Virginia delegation: It immediately set the agenda for the remainder of the convention. There was no talk about whether the convention should go beyond its initial mandate, even though the delegates had, in principle, been sent to Philadelphia for the sole purpose of amending the Articles of Confederation, not to write a new constitution.

The Virginia Plan.   Randolph's fifteen resolutions proposed an entirely new national government under a constitution. It was, however, a plan that not surprisingly favored the large states, including Virginia. Basically, it called for the following:

1. A **bicameral** (two-house) **legislature,** the lower house chosen by the people and the smaller upper house by the elected members of the lower house. The number of representatives would be proportional to population, thus favoring the large states. The legislature could void any state laws.
2. The creation of an unspecified national executive, elected by the legislature.
3. The creation of a national judiciary appointed by the legislature.

It did not take long for the smaller states to realize they would fare poorly under the Virginia plan, according to which Virginia, Massachusetts, and Pennsylvania would form a majority in the national legislature. The debate on the plan lasted about two weeks. It was time for the small states to come up with their own plan.

The New Jersey Plan.   On June 15, lawyer William Paterson of New Jersey offered an alternative plan. After all, argued Paterson, under the Articles of Confederation all states had equality; therefore, the convention had no power to change this arrangement. He proposed the following:

1. The fundamental principle of the Articles of Confederation—one state, one vote—would be retained.
2. Congress would be able to regulate trade and impose taxes.
3. All acts of Congress would be the supreme law of the land.
4. Several people would be elected by Congress to form an executive office.
5. The executive office would appoint a supreme court.

Basically, the New Jersey plan was simply an amendment of the Articles of Confederation. Its only notable feature was its reference to the **supremacy doctrine,** which was later included in the Constitution.

The "Great Compromise."   The delegates were at an impasse. Most wanted a strong national government and were unwilling even to consider the New Jersey plan. But when the Virginia plan was brought up again, the small states threatened to leave. It wasn't until July 16 that the **Great Compromise** was achieved. Roger Sherman of Connecticut proposed the following:

1. A bicameral legislature in which the House of Representatives would be apportioned according to the number of free inhabitants in each state, plus three-fifths of the slaves.
2. An upper house, the Senate, which would have two members from each state elected by the state legislatures.

This plan, often called the Connecticut Compromise because of the role of the Connecticut delegates in the proposal, broke the deadlock. The large-state versus small-state controversy had been resolved. So too had another major issue—how to deal with slaves in the representational scheme. Slavery was legal everywhere except in Massachusetts, but it was concentrated in the South. The South wanted slaves to be counted equally in determining representation in Congress (but equal representation meant equal taxation). The South wanted to avoid equal taxation. Sherman's three-fifths compromise solved the issue, satisfying those northerners who felt that slaves should not be counted at all and those southerners who wanted them to be counted as free whites. Actually, Sherman's Connecticut plan spoke of three-fifths of "all other persons" (and that is the language in the Constitution itself). It is not hard to figure out, though, who those other persons were.

Other Issues, Other Compromises.   The slavery issue was not completely eliminated by the three-fifths compromise. Many delegates were opposed to slavery and wanted it banned entirely in the United States. Charles Pinckney of South Carolina led strong southern opposition to this idea. Finally, the delegates agreed that Congress could limit the importation of slaves after 1808. The compromise meant that the issue of slavery itself was never addressed. The South won twenty years of unrestricted slave trade and a requirement that escaped slaves in free states be returned to their owners in slave states.

The agrarian South and the mercantile North were in conflict. The South was worried that the northern majority in Congress would pass legislation unfavorable to its economic interests. Since the South depended on exports of its agricultural products, it feared the imposition of export taxes. In return for acceding to the northern demand that Congress be given the power to regulate commerce among the states and with other nations, the South obtained a promise that export taxes would not be imposed. Even today, such

DID YOU KNOW?

That the delegates to the Constitutional Convention signed the document by geographic order, starting with New Hampshire—the northernmost state—and finishing with Georgia—the southernmost state?

SUPREMACY DOCTRINE
A doctrine that asserts the superiority of national law over state or regional laws. This principle is rooted in Article VI of the Constitution, which provides that the Constitution, the laws passed by the national government under its constitutional powers, and all treaties comprise the supreme law of the land.

GREAT COMPROMISE
The compromise between the New Jersey and the Virginia plans that created one chamber of the Congress based on population and one chamber that represented each state equally. Also called the Connecticut Compromise.

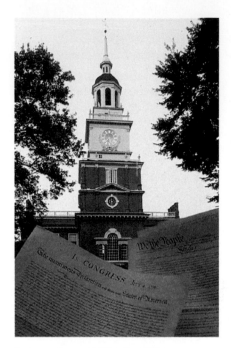

Independence Hall, where the constitution was drafted.

SEPARATION OF POWERS
The principle of dividing governmental powers among the executive, the legislative, and the judicial branches of government.

CHECKS AND BALANCES
A major principle of the American governmental system whereby each branch of the government exercises a check upon the actions of the others. Separation of powers, divided power, and checks and balances limit government's power by pitting power against power. For example, the president checks Congress by holding veto power, Congress has the purse strings, and Congress approves presidential appointments.

ELECTORAL COLLEGE
A group of persons called electors selected by the voters in each state; this group officially elects the president and vice president of the United States. The number of electors in each state is equal to the number of each state's representatives in both houses of Congress.

taxes are prohibited. The United States is one of the few countries that does not tax its exports.

There were other disagreements. The delegates could not decide whether to establish only a Supreme Court or to create lower courts as well. They deferred the issue by mandating a Supreme Court and allowing Congress to establish lower courts. They also disagreed over whether the president or the Senate would choose the Supreme Court justices. A compromise was reached, with the agreement that the president would nominate the justices and the Senate would confirm the nomination.

These compromises as well as others resulted from the recognition that if one group of states refused to ratify, the Constitution was doomed.

Working Toward the Final Document

The Connecticut Compromise was reached by mid-July. The makeup of the executive branch and the judiciary, however, was left unsettled. The remaining work of the convention was turned over to a five-man Committee of Detail, which presented a rough draft of the Constitution on August 6. It made the executive and judicial branches subordinate to the legislative branch.

The major issue of **separation of powers** had not yet been resolved. The delegates were concerned with structuring the government to prevent the imposition of tyranny—either by the majority or by a minority. It was Madison who devised a governmental scheme—sometimes called the Madisonian model—to achieve this: The executive, legislative, and judicial powers of government were to be separated so that no one branch had enough power to dominate the others. The separation of powers was by function, as well as by personnel, with Congress passing laws, the president enforcing and administering laws, and the courts interpreting laws in individual circumstances.

Each of the three branches of government would be independent of the others, but they would have to cooperate to govern. Figure 2-2 outlines these **checks and balances.** The president has veto power over congressional acts. Congress controls the budget and must approve presidential appointments. The Supreme Court consists of judges appointed by the president but with the advice and consent of the Senate.[9] Madison also wanted to prevent branches from abdicating their power to other branches. Note that our Constitution forces cooperation between at least two branches. But with checks and balances, we see simultaneous protection of the independence of each branch, yet forced dependence: Congress can pass a law; the executive branch must enforce and administer it.

Some delegates favored a plural executive made up of representatives from the various regions. This was abandoned in favor of a single chief executive. Others argued that Congress should choose the executive. However, to make the presidency completely independent of the proposed Congress, an **electoral college** was adopted, probably at Franklin's suggestion. To be sure, the electoral college (discussed in Chapter 10) made for a cumbersome presidential election process, but it further buttressed the notion of separation of powers (and mainly insulated the president from direct popular control). The seven-

---

[9]After *Marbury v. Madison* in 1803 (1 Cranch 137; see the Appendix at the end of this chapter which discusses legal citations), the Supreme Court became part of this checks and balances system through judicial review and the limited right to declare the policies of the other two branches of government unconstitutional. See Chapter 15.

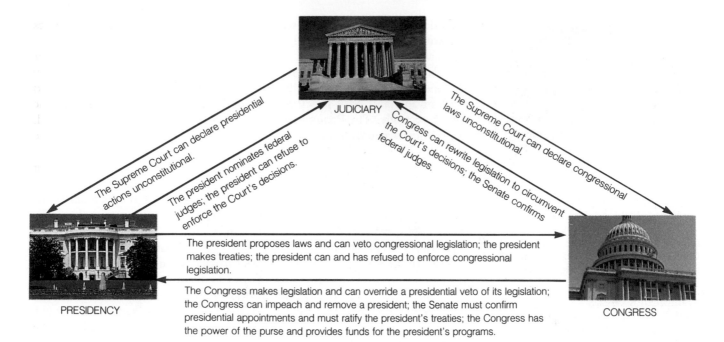

JUDICIARY

The Supreme Court can declare presidential actions unconstitutional.

The president nominates federal judges; the president can refuse to enforce the Court's decisions.

Congress can rewrite legislation to circumvent the Court's decisions; the Senate confirms federal judges.

The Supreme Court can declare congressional laws unconstitutional.

The president proposes laws and can veto congressional legislation; the president makes treaties; the president can and has refused to enforce congressional legislation.

The Congress makes legislation and can override a presidential veto of its legislation; the Congress can impeach and remove a president; the Senate must confirm presidential appointments and must ratify the president's treaties; the Congress has the power of the purse and provides funds for the president's programs.

PRESIDENCY

CONGRESS

year single term that some of the delegates had proposed was replaced by a four-year term and the possibility of reelection.

On September 17, 1787, the Constitution was approved by thirty-nine delegates. Of the fifty-five who had originally attended, only forty-two remained. Only three delegates refused to sign the Constitution. Others disapproved of at least parts of it but signed anyway to begin the ratification debate.

The Constitution that was to be ratified established the following fundamental principles:

1. Popular sovereignty, or control by the people
2. A republican government in which the people choose representatives to make decisions for them
3. Limited government with written laws, in contrast to the powerful monarchical English government the colonists had rebelled against
4. Separation of powers with checks and balances among branches to prevent any one branch from gaining too much power
5. A federal system that allowed for states' rights because the states feared too much centralized control
6. Respect and protection for individuals' rights

■ THE DIFFICULT ROAD TO RATIFICATION

The Founding Fathers knew that **ratification** of the Constitution was far from certain. Indeed, since it was almost guaranteed that many state legislatures would not ratify it, the delegates agreed that each state should hold a special convention at which elected delegates would discuss and vote on the Constitution. Further departing from the Articles of Confederation, the delegates

FIGURE 2-2
Checks and Balances
The major checks and balances among the three branches are illustrated here. Some of these checks are not mentioned in the Constitution, such as judicial review—the power of the courts to declare federal or state acts unconstitutional—or the president's ability to refuse to enforce judicial decisions or congressional legislation. Checks and balances can be thought of as a confrontation of powers or responsibilities. Each branch delays or checks the action of another; two branches in conflict have powers that can result in balances or stalemates, requiring one branch to give in or both to reach a compromise.

RATIFICATION
Formal approval.

DID YOU KNOW?

That of the fifty-five delegates who attended the Constitutional Convention, sixteen failed to sign and some of the thirty-nine signatories approved only with reservations?

FEDERALISTS
The name given to those who were in favor of the adoption of the United States Constitution and the creation of a federal union. They favored a strong central government.

ANTI-FEDERALISTS
Those individuals who opposed the ratification of the new Constitution in 1787.

John Jay

agreed that as soon as nine states (rather than all thirteen) approved the Constitution, it would take effect and the Congress could begin to organize the new government.

Delaware was the first to ratify on December 7, 1787, less than three months after the signing of the final document. The vote was unanimous. Pennsylvania and New Jersey ratified soon thereafter, on December 12 and 18, respectively. The Pennsylvania vote was 43 to 23, while the New Jersey convention was unanimous.

The Federalists Push for Ratification

The two opposing forces in the battle of ratification were the Federalists and Anti-Federalists. The **Federalists**—those in favor of a strong central government and the new Constitution—had an advantage over the **Anti-Federalists,** who wanted to prevent the Constitution (in its then-current form) from being ratified. In the first place, the Federalists had assumed a positive name, leaving their opposition the negative label of *Anti*-Federalist. More importantly, the Federalists had attended the Constitutional Convention and knew of all the deliberations that had taken place, whereas their opponents had no such knowledge since those deliberations were not open to the public. Thus the Anti-Federalists were at a disadvantage in terms of information about the document. The Federalists also had time, power, and money on their side. Communications were slow, and those who had access to the best communications were Federalists—mostly wealthy bankers, lawyers, plantation owners, and merchants living in urban areas where communication was better. The Federalist campaign was organized relatively quickly and effectively to elect Federalists as delegates to the state ratifying conventions. The Anti-Federalists, however, had at least one strong point in their favor: They stood for the status quo. In general, the greater burden is placed on those advocating change.

The Federalist Papers.   In New York opponents of the Constitution were quick to attack it. Alexander Hamilton answered their attacks in newspaper columns over the signature "Caesar." When the Caesar letters had little effect, Hamilton switched to the pseudonym Publius and brought on board two collaborators—John Jay and James Madison. In a very short period of time, those three political figures wrote a series of eighty-five essays in defense of the Constitution and of a republican form of government. These widely read essays appeared in New York newspapers from October 1787 to May 1788 and were reprinted in the newspapers of other states. Although we do not know for certain who wrote every one, it is apparent that Hamilton was responsible for about two-thirds of the essays, including the most important ones interpreting the Constitution, explaining the various powers of the three branches, and presenting a theory of judicial review. Madison's *Federalist Paper* No. 10 (see Appendix D), however, is considered a classic in political theory, dealing with the nature of groups—or factions, as he called them. In spite of the rapidity with which *The Federalist Papers* were written, they are considered by many to be perhaps the best example of political theorizing ever produced in the United States.[10]

---

[10]Some scholars believe that *The Federalist Papers* played only a minor role in securing ratification of the Constitution. Even if this is true, they still have lasting value as an authoritative explanation of the Constitution.

The Anti-Federalist Response. The Anti-Federalists used such pseudonyms as Montezuma and Philadelphiensis in their replies. Many of their attacks against the Constitution were also brilliant. They claimed that it was a document written by aristocrats and would lead to aristocratic tyranny. More importantly, the Anti-Federalists believed the Constitution would create an overbearing and overburdening central government inimical to personal liberty. (The Constitution said nothing about liberty of the press, freedom of religion, or any other individual liberties.) They wanted to include a list of guaranteed liberties, or a bill of rights. Finally, the Anti-Federalists decried the weakening of the power of the states.

The Anti-Federalists cannot be dismissed as a bunch of unpatriotic extremists. They included such patriots as Patrick Henry and Samuel Adams. They were arguing what had been the most prevalent view of the time, derived from the French political philosopher Montesquieu, who believed that liberty was only safe in relatively small societies governed by direct democracy or by a large legislature with small districts. The Madisonian view favoring a large republic, particularly expressed in *The Federalist Papers* Nos. 10 and 51 (which can be found in the Appendix D), was actually the more *un*popular view of the time. Madison was probably convincing because citizens were already persuaded that a strong national government was necessary to combat foreign enemies and to prevent domestic insurrections. Still, some researchers believe it was mainly the bitter experiences with the Articles of Confederation that created the setting for the ratification of the Constitution, rather than Madison's arguments.[11]

The March to the Finish. The struggle for ratification continued. After Delaware, Pennsylvania, and New Jersey, Georgia ratified unanimously on January 2, 1788, and, on January 9, Connecticut voted for ratification by a margin of 3 to 1. There was a bitter struggle in Massachusetts, but clever politicking by the Federalists brought a close but successful ratification vote on February 6, 1788, even though some historians believe the Anti-Federalists were a majority in the state at that time. In the spring of 1788, Maryland and South Carolina ratified by sizable majorities. On June 21, 1788, by a 57 to 46 margin, New Hampshire became the ninth state to ratify. The Constitution was now formally in effect, but that meant little without the large states of New York and Virginia. During that summer, New York and Virginia agreed to the new Constitution by slender majorities. It took another sixteen months for North Carolina to ratify. Rhode Island did not ratify until May 29, 1790, and then by a margin of only two votes. (See Table 2-2.)

Was the Constitution Truly Favored by the Majority?

Political scientists and historians still debate whether the Constitution was actually favored by the popular majority. The delegates at the various state ratifying conventions had been selected by only 150,000 of the approximately four million citizens of that time. That does not seem very democratic—at

---

[11]Of particular interest is a current view of the Anti-Federalist position contained in Herbert J. Storing, *What the Anti-Federalists Were For* (Chicago: University of Chicago Press, 1981). Storing also edited seven volumes of the Anti-Federalist writings, *The Complete Anti-Federalist* (Chicago: University of Chicago Press, 1981). See also Jackson Turner Main, *The Anti-Federalist* (Chapel Hill: University of North Carolina Press, 1961).

TABLE 2-2
Ratification of the Constitution

State	Date	Vote For–Against
Delaware	Dec. 7, 1787	30–0
Pennsylvania	Dec. 12, 1787	46–23
New Jersey	Dec. 19, 1787	38–0
Georgia	Jan. 2, 1787	26–0
Connecticut	Jan. 9, 1788	128–40
Massachusetts	Feb. 6, 1788	187–168
Maryland	Apr. 28, 1788	63–11
South Carolina	May 23, 1788	149–73
New Hampshire	June 21, 1788	57–46
Virginia	June 25, 1788	89–79
New York	July 26, 1788	30–27
North Carolina	Nov. 21, 1789*	184–77
Rhode Island	May 29, 1790	34–32

*Ratification was originally defeated on August 4, 1788 by a vote of 184–84

least not by today's standards. (On election day in 1988, for example, 91.6 million persons—of 182.6 million people of voting age—voted in the presidential election.) Even Federalist John Marshall believed that in some of the adopting states a majority of the people opposed the Constitution.[12] We have to realize, however, that the adoption of the Constitution was probably as open a process as was reasonable at that time. Transportation and communication were rudimentary and slow. It would have been difficult to discover the true popular opinion, even if the leaders of the new nation had been concerned to do so.

In any event, as soon as the Constitution was ratified, the movement to place limits on the power of the national government began.

James Madison

■ THE BILL OF RIGHTS

Bills of rights had been included in state constitutions at least as early as 1776 when George Mason of Virginia wrote the Virginia Declaration of Rights. That document was modeled on the traditional rights established in England and present in the British Bill of Rights of 1688.

Ratification in several important states could not have proceeded if the Federalists had not assured the states that amendments to the Constitution would be passed to protect individual liberties against incursions by the national government. Many of the recommendations of the state ratifying conventions included specific rights that were later considered by James Madison as he labored to draft what became the Bill of Rights.

[12]Beard, p. 299.

Ironically, Madison had a year earlier told Jefferson, "I have never thought the omission [of the Bill of Rights] a material defect" of the Constitution. But Jefferson's enthusiasm for a bill of rights apparently influenced Madison, as did his desire to gain popular support for his election to Congress. He promised in his campaign letter to voters that once elected he would force Congress to "prepare and recommend to the states for ratification, the most satisfactory provisions for all essential rights."

Madison had to cull through more than two hundred state recommendations. It was no small task, and in retrospect he chose remarkably well. (One of the rights appropriate for constitutional protection that he left out was equal protection under the laws—but that was not commonly regarded as a basic right at that time. It wasn't until 1868 that an amendment guaranteeing that no state shall deny equal protection to any person was ratified. The Supreme Court has applied this guarantee to actions of the federal government.)

The final number of amendments that Madison came up with was sixteen. Congress tightened the language somewhat and eliminated four of the amendments. Of the remaining twelve, two—dealing with the apportionment of representatives and the compensation of the members of Congress—were not ratified by the states. Eventually, Supreme Court decisions led to legislative reforms relating to apportionment.

> **DID YOU KNOW?**
>
> That the first ten amendments to the Constitution (the Bill of Rights) originally were twelve? (Two were never ratified.)

Drawing by Handelsman; © 1990 The New Yorker Magazine, Inc.

"Let me give you a lesson in American history: James Madison never intended the Bill of Rights to protect riffraff like you."

HIGHLIGHT

Are Americans Ignorant about the Constitution?

In connection with the celebration of the 200th anniversary of the U.S. Constitution, the Hearst Corporation conducted a nationwide survey to measure the public's understanding of the Constitution. Some of the results of this survey reveal a shockingly low level of knowledge about the fundamental document of the American political structure and about how that structure operates.

Among the findings from the Hearst survey were the following:

■ 64 percent of the respondents believed that the Constitution establishes English as the official language of the United States and requires its use in schools and by government.
■ 26 percent confused the Constitution with the Declaration of Independence, believing that it was drafted to declare American independence from England.
■ Only 41 percent could correctly identify the Bill of Rights as the first ten amendments to the Constitution.

■ 49 percent believed that the president can suspend the Constitution in time of war or national emergency, although 79 percent correctly knew that a president cannot alone conclude treaties with foreign nations.
■ 45 percent think that the fundamental tenet of Marxian socialism, "From each according to his ability, to each according to his need," is part of the Constitution.

On December 15, 1791, the national Bill of Rights was adopted when Virginia agreed to ratify the ten amendments. The basic structure of American government had already been established, and now the fundamental rights of individuals were protected, at least in theory, at the national level. Unfortunately, the proposed amendment that Madison characterized as "the most valuable amendment in the whole lot"—which would have prohibited the *states* from infringing on the freedoms of conscience, press, and jury trial— had been eliminated by the Senate. Thus the Bill of Rights as adopted did not limit state power, and the individual had to rely on the guarantees contained in the particular state constitution or state bill of rights. The country had to wait until the violence of the Civil War before significant limitations on state power became part of the national Constitution. (The Highlight above presents some startling statistics on Americans' ignorance of the Constitution.)

■ ALTERING THE CONSTITUTION

The Formal Amendment Process

The original U.S. Constitution is short (see Appendix B). It is only 7,000 words long, whereas the state constitutions of Alabama and New York are 174,000 words and 80,000 words, respectively. One of the reasons it is short is that the framers intended it to be only a framework for governing, to be interpreted by succeeding generations. One of the reasons it has remained short is because the formal amending procedure does not allow for changes to be made easily. Article V of the Constitution outlines the way in which amendments may be proposed and ratified (see Figure 2-3).

Two formal methods of proposing an amendment to the Constitution are available: (1) a two-third vote in each house of Congress or (2) a national convention called by Congress at the request of two-thirds of the state legislatures. There has yet to be a successful amendment proposal using the second

FIGURE 2-3
The Formal Constitutional Amending Procedure

There are two ways of proposing amendments to the U.S. Constitution and there are two ways of ratifying proposed amendments. Among the four possibilities, the usual route has been proposal by Congress and ratification by state legislatures. Only in the case of ratification of the Twenty-first Amendment in 1933 repealing the Eighteenth Amendment (Prohibition) was ratification by state conventions used. The Constitution has never been amended by two-thirds of the states requesting a national convention to be called by Congress and then having the proposed amendment ratified by the legislatures of three-fourths of the states or by state conventions.

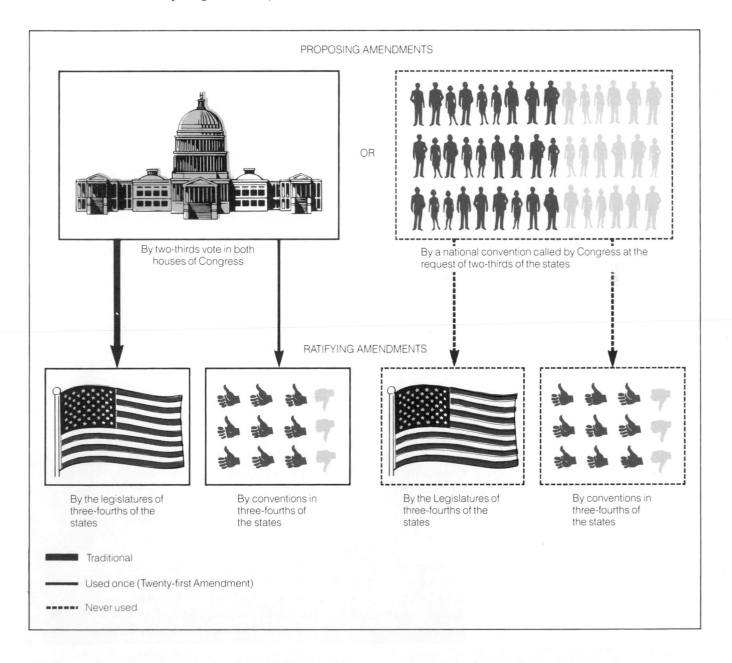

PROPOSING AMENDMENTS

OR

By two-thirds vote in both houses of Congress

By a national convention called by Congress at the request of two-thirds of the states

RATIFYING AMENDMENTS

By the legislatures of three-fourths of the states

By conventions in three-fourths of the states

By the Legislatures of three-fourths of the states

By conventions in three-fourths of the states

Traditional

Used once (Twenty-first Amendment)

Never used

DID YOU KNOW?

That the First Congress in 1789, considered 145 proposed amendments to the brand-new Constitution, of which 12 were submitted to the states and 10 were ratified?

method, although the balanced budget amendment—first proposed in 1975—has come close.

Ratification can occur by one of two methods: (1) by a positive vote in three-fourths of the legislatures of the various states or (2) by special conventions called in the states for the specific purpose of ratifying the proposed amendment, and a positive vote in three-fourths of them. The second method has been used only once, to repeal Prohibition. That situation was exceptional because it involved an amendment—the Twenty-first—to repeal an amendment—the Eighteenth, which had created Prohibition. State conventions were necessary for repeal because the "pro-dry" legislatures in the more conservative states would never have passed the repeal. (It should be noted that Congress determines the method of constitutional amendment ratification to be used by all states.)

Many Amendments Proposed, Few Accepted.   Congress has considered more than 7,000 amendments to the Constitution. Only 33 have been submitted to the states after having been passed by Congress, and only 26 have been ratified. (See Table 2-3) It should be clear that the process is much more difficult than a chart like Figure 2-3 can indicate. Because of competing social and economic interests, the requirement that two-thirds of both the House and Senate approve the amendments is difficult to achieve. Thirty-four senators, representing only seventeen sparsely populated states, could block any amendment. After approval by Congress, the process becomes even more arduous. Three-fourths of the state legislatures must approve the amendment, and it therefore must have wide popular support across parties and in all regions of the country.

The proposed Twenty-seventh Amendment—the Equal Rights Amendment (ERA)—failed to obtain ratification by the legislatures of three-fourths of the states within the time limits set by Congress, although it was reintroduced into Congress in 1985. The proposed Twenty-eighth Amendment, which would have guaranteed congressional representation to the District of Columbia, fell far short of the thirty-eight needed before its August 22, 1985, deadline.

Senators display the text of a proposed Constitutional amendment to ban the burning of the flag. Why does the process for adopting such amendments require extraordinary majorities both in the Congress and the states?

The 27th Amendment

"The Congress and the States shall have power to prohibit the physical desecration of the Flag of the United States."

A reading of Article V of the Constitution reveals that the framers of the Constitution specified no time limit on the ratification process. The courts nonetheless have held that amendments must be ratified within a "reasonable" time. Congress is to decide what is reasonable. Since 1919, most proposed amendments have included a requirement that ratification be obtained within seven years. This was the case in the proposed ERA. When three-fourths of the states had not ratified in time, Congress extended the limit for an additional three years and three months. That extension expired on June 30, 1982, without the amendment being ratified.

The National Convention Provision.   The Constitution provides for a national convention requested by the legislatures of two-thirds of the states to propose a constitutional amendment. This procedure has never been used, but

TABLE 2-3
Amendments to the Constitution

Amendments	Subject	Year Adopted	Time Required for Ratification
1st–10th	The Bill of Rights	1791	2 years, 2 months, 20 days
11th	Immunity of states from certain suits	1795	11 months, 3 days
12th	Changes in electoral college procedure	1804	6 months, 3 days
13th	Prohibition of slavery	1865	10 months, 3 days
14th	Citizenship, due process, and equal protection	1868	2 years, 26 days
15th	No denial of vote because of race, color, or previous condition of servitude	1870	11 months, 8 days
16th	Power of Congress to tax incomes	1913	3 years, 6 months, 22 days
17th	Direct election of U.S. senators	1913	10 months, 26 days
18th	National (liquor) prohibition	1919	1 year, 29 days
19th	Women's suffrage	1920	1 year, 2 months, 14 days
20th	Change of dates for congressional and presidential terms	1933	10 months, 21 days
21st	Repeal of the 18th Amendment	1933	9 months, 15 days
22nd	Limit on presidential tenure	1951	3 years, 11 months, 3 days
23rd	District of Columbia electoral vote	1961	9 months, 13 days
24th	Prohibition of tax payment as a qualification to vote in federal elections	1964	1 year, 4 months, 9 days
25th	Procedures for determining presidential disability, presidential succession, and filling a vice presidential vacancy	1967	1 year, 7 months, 4 days
26th	Minimum voting age cannot be set above 18 in any election	1971	3 months, 7 days

DID YOU KNOW?

That on February 7, 1989, Iowa became the twenty-sixth state to ratify a proposed amendment to the Constitution—sponsored by James Madison—that was submitted to the states on September 25, 1789 (the amendment would prohibit members of Congress from raising their salaries between elections)?

there is a possibility that two-thirds of the legislatures will in fact jump on the bandwagon of the proposed amendment to require a balanced federal budget. By 1991, thirty-two of the required thirty-four states had called for a constitutional convention to draft a balanced budget amendment. What if the required thirty-four states passed resolutions to have such a convention? The Constitution is silent about the procedures to be followed. There is no precedent. Can the convention be limited to one specific issue? Does Congress have the legal authority to set the ground rules? Scholars disagree on these questions, and Congress fears a convention in which unrestrained representatives could propose any amendment, even one calling for a new form of government. There is also another problem: The resolutions passed by the various states and sent to Congress are not identical; they seek at least ten different forms of a constitutional amendment to balance the budget. What would be the format for drafting a single amendment? Congress has proposed a "Constitutional Convention Procedures Act" to exert control over a constitutional convention if in fact it were to occur. The federal government lawmakers are clearly worried about a convention free-for-all adding, deleting, or changing numerous amendments to the Constitution. (See the *What If . . . ?* that begins this chapter.)

Informal Methods of Constitutional Change

Formal amendments are one way of changing our Constitution, and, as is obvious by their small number, they have not been resorted to very frequently. If we discount the first ten amendments (the Bill of Rights), which passed soon after the ratification of the Constitution, there have been only sixteen formal alterations of the Constitution in the more than two hundred years of its existence.

But looking at the sparse number of formal constitutional changes gives us an incomplete view. The brevity and ambiguity of the original document has permitted great changes in the Constitution by way of changing interpretations over the course of time. As the United States grew, both in population and territory, new social and political realities emerged, and Congress, presidents, and the courts found it necessary to interpret the Constitution's provisions in light of these new realities. The Constitution has proved to be a remarkably flexible document, adapting itself time and again to new events and concerns.

Judicial Review

JUDICIAL REVIEW
The power of the Supreme Court or any court to declare federal or state laws and other acts of government unconstitutional.

Another way of changing the Constitution—or of making it more flexible—is through the power of **judicial review.** In the case of *Marbury v. Madison*[13] in 1803, the Supreme Court ruled a provision of an act of Congress to be unconstitutional. Chief Justice Marshall declared that it is "the province and duty of the Judiciary department to say what the law is." Although the case was primarily concerned with the power of the Supreme Court in relation to the other two branches of the federal government, the principle of judicial review itself opened the way for Congress and the executive branch to test the elasticity of the Constitution—that is, it allowed them to see how far and in what ways it could be "stretched" without breaking.

[13]1803 (1 Cranch 137). See Highlight in Chapter 15.

Interpretation, Custom and Usage

The Constitution has also been changed through its interpretation by both Congress and the president. Originally, the president had a staff consisting of personal secretaries and a few others. Today, because Congress delegates specific tasks to the president and the chief executive assumes political leadership, the executive office staff alone has increased to several thousand persons. The executive provides legislative leadership far beyond the intentions of the Constitution.

Changes in the ways of doing political business have also changed the Constitution. The Constitution does not mention political parties, yet these informal, "extraconstitutional" organizations make the nominations for offices, run the campaigns, organize the members of Congress, and in fact change the election system from time to time. The political party system, for example, has changed the way of electing the president. The Constitution calls for the electoral college to choose the best candidate. Today the people vote for electors who are pledged to the candidate of their party, effectively choosing the president themselves. Perhaps most strikingly, the Constitution has been adapted from serving the needs of a small, rural republic with no international prestige to providing a framework of government for an industrial giant with vast geographic, natural, and human resources.

> **DID YOU KNOW?**
>
> That a constitutional amendment opposed by the thirteen smallest states with less than 4 percent of the nation's population will not become part of the Constitution even though it had been ratified by the other thirty-seven states which have 96 percent of the population?

■ THE RESULT: IT HAS LASTED

There are those who say the Constitution has lasted because it furnished only an outline for government. Much was left unsaid so that political circumstances could be accounted for. Others might give credit for the flexibility of the document to the sharing of power among the three branches and the compromises this sharing encourages. Still others suggest that the doctrine of federalism solved the problems of governing many diverse territories within one nation. Most important, the Constitution articulates certain principles of democratic government—such as representation, majority rule, and protection for minorities—that have become the core of American political culture and that are the accepted "rules of the game" from the smallest town council to the halls of Congress.

How Can You Affect the U.S. Constitution?

The Constitution is an enduring document that has survived more than two hundred years of turbulent history. However, it is also a changing document. Twenty-six amendments have been added to the original Constitution. How can you, as an individual, actively help to rewrite the Constitution?

One of the best ways is to work for (or against) a constitutional amendment. At the time of this writing, four major issues are the subject of efforts to enact constitutional amendments—equal rights for women, antiabortion laws, balancing the federal budget, and limiting the size of the federal government. These four proposed amendments are supported and opposed by national coalitions of interest groups. If you want an opportunity to change the Constitution—or to assure that it isn't changed—you could work for or with one of the alliances of groups interested in the fate of these amendments.

The following contacts should help you get started on efforts to affect the U.S. Constitution directly.

Government Reform

An organization whose goal is to "reduce the size and cost of federal government to those functions specified in the U.S. Constitution" is the Liberty Amendment Committee of the U.S.A., P.O. Box 20888, El Cajon, CA 92021. The ultimate goal of LACUSA is to see the so-called Liberty Amendment (now pending in Congress) ratified and then to abolish the income tax.

An even more general goal—namely, to encourage Congress to call a constitutional convention (the most openended way to change the Constitution)—is pursued by Conservatives for a Constitutional Convention, P.O. Box 582, Desert Hot Springs, CA 92240.

The Movement for Economic Justice, 1638 R St., NW, Washington, D.C. is an activist organization seeking grassroots involvement. Its goals are to encourage greater government responsiveness in such areas as revenue-sharing, inflation, and "fundamental economic reform." It conducts programs and training conferences and issues newsletters.

Equal Rights for Women

One group exclusively dedicated to the passage of the ERA has been Catholic Women for the ERA, 2706 Glenview Ave., Cincinnati, OH 45206. Its main activity is to contact and lobby state legislators to encourage them to vote for a national equal rights amendment.

Perhaps the most active organization working against the ERA has been Eagle Forum, Box 618, Alton, IL 62002 (618-462-5415). Its founder and president, Phyllis Schafly, has been a major opponent of the amendment.

Abortion

One of the organizations whose primary goal is to secure the passage of the Human Life Amendment is the American Life Lobby, Route 6, Box 162-F, Stafford, VA 22554 (703-659-4193). The Human Life Amendment would recognize in law the "personhood" of the unborn, secure human rights' protections for the fetus from the time of fertilization, and prohibit abortion under any circumstances.

The National Abortion Rights Action League, 1424 K St., NW, Washington, D.C. 20005 (202-347-7774) is a political action and information organization working on behalf of "prochoice" issues—that is, the right of women to have control over reproduction. The organization has roughly 150,000 members.

CHAPTER SUMMARY

1. In 1607, the Virginia Company of London established the first permanent British settlement in North America. Of the 6,000 persons who left England between 1607 and 1623, 4,000 perished.

2. The first New England colony was established by the Plymouth Company in 1620. Its settlers drew up the Mayflower Compact, which was based on the consent of the signers.

3. During the colonial period, Americans developed a concept of limited government.

4. Starting in 1763, British restrictions on colonial activity intensified. The colonies responded through the First Continental Congress, their first formal act of cooperation, in which resolutions were passed expressing their grievances.

5. By the time the Second Continental Congress met in 1775, fighting had begun. Thomas Paine's *Common Sense*—recommending separation from Great Britain—was well received.

6. The Resolution of Independence was adopted on July 2, 1776, by the Second Continental Congress and approved on July 4. It was necessary to establish the legitimacy of the new nation in the eyes of foreign governments and in the eyes of Americans.

7. The Declaration of Independence was signed on August 2, 1776. It was based on the consent of the governed and assumed people had natural and "inalienable" rights.

8. Some colonists demanded the formation of a strong central government. The first "Republicans" opposed a strong central government.

9. On March 1, 1781, the newly established states passed the Articles of Confederation. Although some accomplishments took place during the eight-year existence of the Articles, they did not provide the type of central government that would ensure the growth of the country.

10. It became evident that the national government had serious weaknesses under the Articles of Confederation. A call was issued to all states for a general convention to meet in Philadelphia in May of 1787 "to consider the exigencies of the union."

11. The fifty-five delegates, mostly educated, upper-class individuals, met in secrecy to frame a new constitution. Trying to balance a number of competing interests—small states versus large states, North versus South, slave states versus nonslave states—they finally agreed on several compromises including the "Great Compromise."

12. The Framers divided the central government into the executive, legislative, and judicial branches (separation of powers) operating within a system whereby no one branch could dominate the other two (checks and balances).

13. Once the Constitution was signed by the delegates in September of 1787, it had to be ratified by nine of the thirteen states. The Federalists, favoring a strong central government, fought for its ratification. The Anti-Federalists sought to prevent ratification. By July 1788, supporters had persuaded the necessary nine states to ratify.

14. The framers did not initially consider the Bill of Rights necessary to protect the rights of citizens. They were persuaded by Madison and Jefferson, however, and in 1791 the national Bill of Rights was adopted in the form of the first ten amendments to the Constitution.

15. Amendments to the Constitution can be proposed by (a) a two-thirds vote in each house of Congress or (b) a national convention called by Congress at the request of two-thirds of the state legislatures. Ratification can occur by (a) a positive vote of three-fourths of the legislatures of the various states or (b) special conventions called in the states for the specific purpose of ratifying the proposed amendment and a positive vote in three-fourths of them. Only twenty-six amendments to the Constitution have been ratified.

16. The Constitution has been adapted to meet the needs of a changing nation through the informal means of judicial review and by congressional and presidential interpretations.

QUESTIONS FOR REVIEW AND DISCUSSION

1. The writing of the Constitution can be seen as the first real working of group interest or pluralism in the United States. What kinds of bargains or compromises were struck in the writing of this document? How were the various interests in the thirteen colonies protected by the provisions of the Constitution?

2. Although the Constitution calls for separation of powers, a more accurate description of the system might be one of "separate branches sharing powers." What provisions of the Constitution require that the branches cooperate, or "share," power in order for the government to function?

3. List all the ways that the rights of the individual states are protected in the Constitution. Which provisions make it clear that the federal government has the ultimate power?

4. Why have so few amendments been added to the Constitution? How do the amendments that have been adopted reflect broad societal changes that have taken place since 1789?

SELECTED REFERENCES

Charles A. Beard, *An Economic Interpretation of the Constitution* (New York: Macmillan, 1913). A classic interpretation of the motives of the founders of the republic, which emphasizes their own economic interests in the success of the nation.

Richard Beeman, Stephen Botein, and Edward C. Carter II, eds., *Beyond Confederation: Origins of the Constitution and American National Identity* (Chapel Hill, NC: University of North Carolina Press, 1987). This collection of essays discusses the current debate over the intentions of the framers of the Constitution.

Richard B. Bernstein and Kym S. Rice, *Are We to Be a Nation? The Making of the Constitution* (Cambridge: Harvard University Press, 1987). The story of the revolution in political thought that led to the Constitution, presented in words and pictures.

Robert A. Bernstein, *Elections, Representation, and Congressional Behavior: The Myth of Constituency Control* (Englewood Cliffs, NJ: Prentice-Hall, 1989). This book addresses the issue of how citizens and constituents exercise control over the policy positions and decisions of members of Congress and then offers suggestions for changes in the electoral system to improve representation.

Edward S. Corwin, *The Constitution and What It Means Today,* 14th ed. rev. by Harold W. Chase and Craig R. Ducat (Princeton, N.J.: Princeton University Press, 1978). A detailed analysis of the meaning and interpretation of the Constitution through court cases.

Alexander Hamilton, James Madison, and John Jay, *The Federalist Papers* (Cambridge: Harvard University Press, 1961). The complete set of columns from the *New York Packet* defending the new Constitution.

Leonard W. Levy, Kenneth L. Karst, and Dennis J. Mahoney, eds., *Encyclopedia of the American Constitution* (Riverside, N.J.: Macmillan, 1986). This truly remarkable resource book contains roughly 2,000 articles by 262 leading constitutional scholars, covering every major aspect of the Constitution and including a discussion of all the current, hotly debated issues.

Clinton Rossiter, *1787: The Grand Convention* (New York: Macmillan, 1966). A readable and interesting account of the Constitutional Convention in Philadelphia.

Herbert J. Storing, *The Complete Anti-Federalist,* 7 vols. (Chicago: University of Chicago Press, 1981). An examination of those opposed to the Constitution.

James L. Sundquist, *Constitutional Reform and Effective Government* (Washington, D.C.: Brookings Institution, 1986). The author reviews the heated debate over constitutional reform, first analyzing the basic assumptions of the 1787 debates and then exploring the workable and desirable modifications that could strengthen and modernize American government.

APPENDIX TO CHAPTER TWO

How to Read Case Citations and Find Court Decisions

Many important court cases are discussed in references in footnotes throughout this book. Court decisions are recorded and published. When a court case is mentioned, the notation used to refer to, or to cite, it denotes where the published decision can be found.

State courts of appeal decisions are usually published in two places, the state reports of that particular state and the more widely used *National Reporter System* published by West Publishing Company. Some states no longer publish their own reports. The *National Reporter System* divides the states into the following geographic areas: Atlantic (A. or A.2d where 2d refers to second series), South Eastern (S.E. or S.E.2d), South Western (S.W. or S.W.2d), North Western (N.W. or N.W.2d), North Eastern (N.E. or N.E.2d), Southern (So. or So.2d), and Pacific (P. or P.2d).

Federal trial court decisions are published unofficially in West's *Federal Supplement* (F.Supp.), and opinions from the circuit courts of appeals are reported unofficially in West's *Federal Reporter* (F. or F.2d). Opinions from the United States Supreme Court are reported in the *United States Reports* (U.S.), the *Lawyer's Edition of the Supreme Court Reports* (L.Ed.), West's *Supreme Court Reporter* (S. Ct.), and other publications. The *United States Reports* is the official edition of the United States Supreme Court decisions published by the federal government. Many early decisions are missing from these volumes. An unofficial and more complete edition of Supreme Court decisions, the *Lawyer's Edition of the Supreme Court Reports,* is published by the Lawyers Cooperative Publishing Company of Rochester, New York. West's *Supreme Court Reporter* is an unofficial edition of decisions dating from October 1882. These volumes contain headnotes and brief editorial statements of the law involved in the case.

State courts of appeal decisions are cited by giving the name of the case; the volume, name, and page number of the state's official report (if the state publishes its own reports); the volume, unit, and page number of the *National Reporter;* and the volume, name, and page number of any other selected reporter. Federal court citations are also listed by giving the name of the case and the volume, name, and page number of the reports. In addition to the citation, this textbook lists the year of the decision in parentheses, for example, the case *United States v. Curtiss-Wright Export Co.*, 299 U.S. 304 (1936). The Supreme Court's decision of this case may be found in volume 299 of the *United States Reports* on page 304. The case was decided in 1936.

CHAPTER 3

FEDERALISM

CHAPTER CONTENTS

WHAT IF . . . THERE WERE NO CENSUS?

The U.S. Constitution requires a head count of Americans every ten years. The first census was organized by Secretary of State Thomas Jefferson and started on the first Monday of August 1790. It was supervised by 17 U.S. marshals, involved 650 assistants, took 18 months, cost about $45,000 (one penny per person) produced 54 pages, and found a little under 4 million people.

The 1990 census cost over $3.6 billion ($10.40) per capita), involved almost half a million temporary workers who used over 9 million pencils. The results yielded more than 6 billion facts, 420,000 pages of reports and found 250 million Americans.

What if there were no census?

Census results are used to draw congressional district maps and assign House seats to states based on population. Without a census it would be virtually impossible to determine equitable representation. Because of population shifts, the northern states are expected to lose approximately eighteen seats after the 1990 census, with New York and Pennsylvania hardest hit, each losing two or three seats. The South and West will gain, with California adding six or seven new House members and Florida and Texas each gaining three or four. If we had no census it would be impossible to provide one-person, one-vote representa-

tion in Congress since we would not know where persons are. Growth areas of the country would remain underrepresented and areas with declining numbers would have too many seats in Congress.

Inequitable political representation has produced grave consequences in other countries. In England, for example, "rotten boroughs" (areas that had lost people through migration) retained their power long after jobs and people had moved to new industrial areas, which couldn't effectively redirect government policy to meet their needs.

In Lebanon, where government was based on a complicated formula in which power was distributed according to the numbers of Moslems and Christians, growth of the Moslem population was much greater than that of Christians. The Christians who controlled the government simply re-

fused to hold a new census because they knew they would lose considerable influence. This produced such frustration that Moslems increasingly resorted to violence to gain proportional power. In part, the current violence and political crisis in Lebanon is the result of not having a census!

Many federal programs are based on demographic data provided by the census. The allocation of federal money for such programs as education, welfare, law enforcement, and women and infant care depend on accurate knowledge of where Americans reside. Without a census, the level of funding in different parts of the country of these programs would be seriously out of line with actual need.

The census is also used for state and local decision making, such as projecting needs

for schools, roads, hospitals, housing, law enforcement, economic development, and myriad other activities. Planning for these and producing effective government and realistic spending and taxation would be almost impossible without a census.

In the 1990 census, a special effort was made to count the homeless who cannot be reached by the mailed census forms which are based on residential addresses. Homelessness is a serious problem in the United States, and without the census the details necessary to enact programs to assist the homeless (many of whom are children) would remain a mystery.

Finally, undocumented (illegal) immigrants were also counted in 1990 because, although not citizens or legal residents of the United States, they have a great impact on state and local economies.

The census is and remains one of the most powerful tools of government. It is an essential instrument for keeping federalism dynamic and successful.

---

1. *It is predicted that the United States will reach zero population growth within thirty years. When it does, will the census still be important? Why?*

2. *Do the census results have any impact on the Senate? Why?*

3. *How does the census help local decision making?*

How many separate governments do you think exist in the United States? One national government and fifty state governments, plus local governments, create a grand total of more than 80,000 governments in all! The breakdown can be seen in Table 3-1. Those 80,000 governments contain about 500,000 elected officeholders. Visitors from France or the Soviet Union are often awestruck by the complexity of our system of government. Consider that a criminal action can be defined by state law, by national law, or by both. Thus the alleged criminal can be prosecuted in the state court system or in the national court system (or both). Often, economic regulation over exactly the same matter exists at the local level, the state level, and the national level—generating multiple forms to be completed, procedures to be followed, and laws to be obeyed. Numerous programs are funded by the national government but administered by state and local governments.

There are various ways of ordering relations between central governments and local units. Federalism is one of these ways. Understanding federalism and how it differs from other forms of government is important in understanding the current American political system.

■ THREE SYSTEMS OF GOVERNMENT

There are basically three ways of ordering relations between central governments and local units: (1) a unitary system, (2) a confederal system, and (3) a federal system. The most popular, both historically and today, is the unitary system.

TABLE 3-1
The Number of Governments in the United States Today
With more than 80,000 separate governmental units in the United States today, it is no wonder that intergovernmental relations in the United States are so complicated. Actually, the number of school districts has decreased over time, but the number of special districts created for single purposes, such as flood control, has increased from only about eight thousand during World War II to almost thirty thousand today.

Federal government		1
State governments		50
Local governments		83,153
Counties	3,042	
Municipalities	19,205	
(mainly cities or towns)		
Townships	16,691	
(less extensive powers)		
Special districts	29,485	
(water, sewer, etc.)		
School districts	14,730	
	83,153	
TOTAL		83,204

SOURCE: U.S. Department of Commerce, *Statistical Abstract of the United States* 1990 (Washington, D.C.: U.S. Government Printing Office, 1990).

UNITARY SYSTEM
A centralized governmental system in which local or subdivisional governments exercise only those powers given to them by the central government.

A Unitary System of Government

A **unitary system** of government is the easiest to define: Unitary systems allow ultimate governmental authority to rest in the hands of the national, or central, government. Consider a typical unitary system—France. There are departments in France and municipalities. Within the departments and the municipalities are separate government entities with elected and appointed officials. So far, the French system appears to be very similar to the United States system; but the similarity is only superficial. Under the unitary French system, the decisions of the governments of the departments and the municipalities can be overruled by the national government. Also, the national government can cut off the funding of many departmental and municipal government activities. Moreover, in a unitary system such as in France, all questions related to education, police, the use of land, and welfare are handled by the national government.[1] Britain, Sweden, Israel, Egypt, Ghana, and the Philippines also have unitary systems of government.

CONFEDERAL SYSTEM
A league of independent states, each having essentially sovereign powers, wherein the central government created by such a league has only limited powers over the states.

A Confederal System

You were introduced to the elements of a **confederal system** of government in Chapter 2, when we examined the Articles of Confederation. A confederation is the opposite of a unitary regime. It is a league of independent states, in which a central government or administration handles only those matters of common concern expressly delegated to it by the member states. The central governmental unit has no ability to make laws directly applicable to individuals unless the member states explicitly support such laws. The United States under the Articles of Confederation and the Confederate States during the American Civil War were confederations. There are no pure confederations in the world today (with the exception, perhaps, of the United Nations), although Switzerland officially is a confederation of 23 sovereign cantons.

FEDERAL SYSTEM
A system of government in which power is divided by a written constitution between a central government and regional, or subdivisional, governments. Each level must have some domain in which its policies are dominant and some genuine political or constitutional guarantee of its authority.

EXTRAORDINARY MAJORITY
A majority that is greater than 50 percent plus one. For example, ratification of amendments to the U.S. Constitution requires the approval of two-thirds of the House and the Senate and three-fourths of the states.

A Federal System

Between the unitary and confederal forms of government lies the **federal system.** In this system, authority is divided, usually by a written constitution, between a central government and regional, or subdivisional, governments (often called constituent governments). The central government and the constituent governments both act directly on the people through laws and through actions of elected and appointed governmental officials. Within each government's sphere of authority, each is supreme in theory. Contrast a federal system to a unitary one in which the central government is supreme and the constituent governments derive their authority from it. A key feature of all federal systems is that changes in their written constitution must be approved by **extraordinary majorities** of the legislature of both the national government and some of the subnational units (the states, in the United States). Australia, Canada, Mexico, India, Brazil, Germany, and Yugoslavia are examples of nations with federal systems. See Figure 3-1 for a comparison among the three systems.

---

[1] New legislation is altering somewhat the unitary character of the French political system, however. In March 1982, a major decentralization law was adopted by the socialist government of François Mitterand.

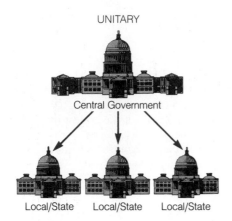
UNITARY
Central Government
Local/State   Local/State   Local/State

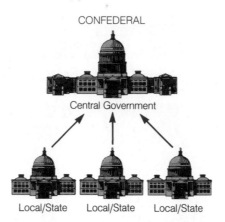
CONFEDERAL
Central Government
Local/State   Local/State   Local/State

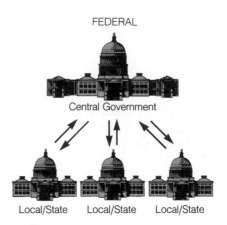
FEDERAL
Central Government
Local/State   Local/State   Local/State

Why a Federal System?

There are currently 170 countries in the world. None of them has a truly confederal system of government. Almost all have a unitary system. The United States is one of the few nations that has a truly federal system of government power.

The Historical Reasons for Federalism

There are historical, as well as practical, reasons why the United States developed in a federal direction. Some of these reasons are discussed below.

Common Problems. As you have seen in Chapter 2, the historical basis of the federal system was laid down in Philadelphia at the Constitutional Convention where strong national government advocates (see Profile of Alexander Hamilton in this chapter) opposed equally strong states' rights advocates. This dichotomy continued through to the ratifying conventions in the several states. The resulting federal system was a compromise. The appeal of federalism was that it retained state traditions and local power, while establishing a strong national government capable of handling common problems. Dealing with common problems was not the only reason that a federal system seemed to suit the United States well. A variety of characteristics—social and geographical—created the need for some type of federal system.

Size and Regional Isolation. At the time of the Philadelphia Convention, the thirteen colonies taken together were geographically larger than England or France. Slow travel and communication combined with geographical spread contributed to the isolation of many regions within the colonies. It could, for example, take up to several weeks for all of the colonies to be informed about one particular political decision. Even if the colonial leaders had agreed on the desirability of a unitary system, the problems of size and regional isolation would have made such a system operationally difficult.

Sectionalism and Political Subcultures. The American way of life has always been characterized by a number of political subcultures, dividing along the lines of race, wealth, education, religion, and, more recently, age and sexual

FIGURE 3-1
The Flow of Power in Three Systems
In a unitary system, the flow of power is from the central government uniquely to the local and state governments. In a confederal system, the flow of power is in the opposite direction—from the state and local governments to the central government. Finally, in a federal system the flow of power is, in principle, both ways.

PROFILE

Alexander Hamilton

"The more close the union of the states, and the more complete the authority of the whole, the less opportunity will be allowed the stronger states to injure the weaker."

The modern form of American federalism, consisting of a strong national government and subsidiary states, was endorsed both in theory and in practice by Alexander Hamilton. A New York lawyer educated at King's College (now Columbia University), Hamilton was a colleague of George Washington and a delegate to the Philadelphia Constitutional Convention. He later led the forces in favor of ratification of the Constitution at the New York State convention. Hamilton's successful politicking for ratification in that state was highlighted by a series of eighty-five public letters, which were printed in New York City newspapers from October 27, 1787 to August 16, 1788. The letters represented the joint work of Hamilton, James Madison, and John Jay and have come to be known as *The Federalist Papers*. About two-thirds of them are attributable to Hamilton.

Hamilton's admiration for a strong and energetic national government is evident in *The Federalist Papers*. He wrote that "the vigor of government is essential to the security of liberty" and that the fledgling nation confronted the alternatives of "adoption of the new Constitution or a dismemberment of the Union." History and common sense showed that "if these States should either be wholly disunited, or only united in partial confederacies, the subdivisions into which they might be thrown would have frequent and violent contests with each other." A divided nation of sovereign states would also be easy prey for the divide-and-

conquer tactics of other nations." A firm Union will be of the utmost moment to the peace and liberty of the States as a barrier against domestic faction and insurrection," whereas weak confederations would lead to "incurable disorder and imbecility in the government." The Constitution was not designed to abolish state governments, but to make them "constituent parts of the national sovereignty" by Senate representation and by their reserved powers.

A vigorous national government working for a common interest would also provide economic benefits from "an active commerce, an extensive navigation, [and] a flourishing marine," and the nation would be able to compete against European commercial power. "An unrestricted intercourse between the States themselves will advance the trade of each by an interchange of their respective productions, not only for the supply of reciprocal wants at home, but for exportation to foreign markets."

Hamilton, who became the nation's first secretary of the treasury in the cabinet of George Washington from 1789 to 1795, worked vigorously to implement these ideas. His views about strong national government have become dominant in U.S. history.

preferences. Subcultures associated with geography naturally developed because different groups of individuals became concentrated in different regions. For example, the Puritans who founded New England had, according to Daniel Elazar, a moralist subculture, viewing politics as the road to a good society.[2] The agricultural society of the South generated a traditionalist subculture, stressing not only tradition but also family and community. Finally, the Middle Atlantic states seemed to engender an individualist subculture, where politics was viewed as simply another business.

The existence of diverse political subcultures would appear to be at odds with a political authority concentrated solely in a central government. Had the United States developed into a unitary system, the various political sub-

[2]Daniel J. Elazar, *American Federalism: A View from the States* (New York: Crowell, 1966).

One of the advantages of federalism is that it allows states and local communities to preserve their own values through local policymaking. What might be some of the policy differences between rural communities and urban areas?

cultures certainly would have been less able to influence government behavior (relative to their own regions and interests) than they have done and continue to do in our federal system.

Other Arguments for Federalism

The arguments for federalism in the United States and elsewhere involve a complex set of factors, some of which we have already noted. First, for big countries, such as the United States, India, and Nigeria, federalism allows many functions to be "farmed out" by the central government to the states or provinces; the lower level of government, accepting these responsibilities, can thereby become the focus of political dissatisfaction rather than the national authorities. Second, even with modern transportation and communications systems, the sheer geographic or population size of some nations makes it impractical to locate all political authority in one place. Third, strong regional differences within a nation can be partly diffused by a federal arrangement of political power. Federalism is in part a means by which conflicting language groups (as in Canada), ethnic national groups (as in Yugoslavia), religious groups (as in India), tribal groups (as in Nigeria), or regional nationalist groups can find local outlets for their social and political interests and can therefore be better accommodated as a whole (see this chapter's Critical Perspective). Finally, federalism brings government closer to the people, allowing more direct access to and influence on government agencies and policies, rather than leaving the population restive and dissatisfied with a remote, faceless, all-powerful central authority.

In the United States, in particular, federalism historically has had special benefits as well as drawbacks. State government has long been a training ground for future national leaders. Recent presidents such as Jimmy Carter and Ronald Reagan first made their political mark as state governors, and many federal judges and members of Congress were initiated into politics and government on state courts or in state legislatures.

CRITICAL PERSPECTIVE

Is Federalism a Solution to the Problems of Nationalism?

In the Soviet Union, recent developments have opened up the possibility that the Baltic Republics—Latvia, Lithuania, and Estonia—as well as Soviet Georgia, Moldavia, the western Ukraine, and Muslim Azerbaijan, among other ethnically distinct and generally non-Great Russian portions of the Soviet Union, might all secede from the federal system of government that was established in the early 1920s under Lenin. In Canada, the Meech Lake accords, which were supposed to redesign the Canadian federal system so as to provide more equitable treatment to all provinces, were threatened by separatist sentiment in predominantly French Québec and by unwillingness on the part of much of English Canada to grant special status to *les Québeqois*. In the Middle East, complex ethnic patterns have led to separatist sentiment among Kurds living in Iran, Turkey, and Iraq who desire to form a nation of Kurdistan. Basques in Spain seek autonomy from the Spanish state, and members of that community have been engaged for years in often violent efforts to achieve that independence.

These are just a few examples of recent problems confronting modern nation–states. Virtually every large nation–state in the world today, in fact, could be said to be suffering from some degree of separatist sentiment among substantial segments of its population. These are groups that usually clash over matters of religion, race, income and social status, or ideology. After all, the United States as we know it today was reconstituted following an extremely violent interregional conflict between North and South from 1861 to 1865 which solidified the power of northern industry over the southern agrarian alternative, of union over separation, and of free labor over slave labor at a cost of hundreds of thousands of lives.

Are large, diverse nation–states inherently predisposed to these problems? Is federalism a solution to these difficulties around the world, or does it serve mainly to exacerbate tendencies that already exist for groups, especially those that identify themselves as unique in opposition to other groups with which they come into conflict, to use national political mechanisms to pursue their own agendas? One answer to these questions has been suggested by Leopold Kohr, author of *The Overdeveloped Nations: The Diseconomies of Scale* and *The Breakdown of Nations*.

Kohr's basic argument is that many of the worst economic problems of the modern era can be attributed to the excessive size of nations. He traces the problems of overdevelopment to "social overgrowth," which is expansion of the size of a society beyond its optimal limit, at which point it can grow further only at the cost of escalating difficulties. To Kohr, these problems will confront any overdeveloped political system, whether it is based on capitalist or socialist economic principles. This view leads him to argue for division instead of unification, and for a world of small competitive societies in which government and social complexity are reduced to a more human scale.

Kohr cites two leading examples of successful federal experiments—the United States and Switzerland. They are successful, he believes, because they have a central government that is weak except in times of crisis. It is wrong, Kohr argues, to attribute the relatively high political cohesiveness of these countries to the good will of their citizens and the presence of common cultural backgrounds within each country that might mitigate social and cultural conflicts. On the contrary, both countries are characterized by population with wide cultural differences. In the case of Switzerland, peoples of German, French, and Italian cultural ancestry live together, while the United States is typified by rather sharply distinctive regional cultures and by a strong propensity to maintain cultural distance from the country's predominantly English roots.

What makes federalism work well both in small Switzerland and in the very large United States is that neither country has a member unit that is strong enough to challenge the federal authority. Switzerland consists of twenty-three semi-autonomous cantons, whereas the United States is split up into fifty states that have some independent power base but no one of which could equal the authority exercised by the federal government. Both countries, in Kohr's assessment, have "incorporated into their structure the health-preserving principle of the small cell. And it is this, not wisdom, will, or culture, that accounts for their success." Larger political units that are strong enough to challenge other power centers for authority are, to Kohr, a guarantee of conflict that mirrors the larger European balance-of-power politics among nations, accentuated by nearly incessant warfare and diplomatic jockeying for advantage.

He finds other reasonably successful examples of federalism in Argentina, Brazil, Mexico, Venezuela, Australia, and, to a lesser extent, in Canada where English- and French-culture divisions threaten to break up a very decentralized federal system in which both predominantly English Ontario and predominantly French Québec are large enough to challenge the authority of the central authority in Ottawa. Unsuccessful cases of federal arrangements, to Kohr, include Germany before its unification under Bismarck, Indonesia, the League of Nations, the European Council, and the United Nations. Kohr attributes each case of federal failure to the presence of a single political component unit that was strong enough to unbalance the whole system by challenging the centralized authority.

CRITICAL PERSPECTIVE, CONTINUED

Does federalism have a future? Kohr argues that it does, but that a stable and long-lasting federal system will last only where small political units join together. He suggests, for example, that a federal system could be established throughout Europe, if it were based on relatively small ethnically distinct tribal, geographic, and political units, or on U.S.-style states that would break up the traditional European great powers into a large number of microstates.

Exercise in Critical Thinking

1. Within countries that currently have unitary systems, which groups would favor a change to a federal system and which groups would oppose such a change?
2. Look at the accompanying map. Which countries today would appear to be least in need of a federal system, and why?
3. Within the U.S. federal system, how does ethnic diversity manifest itself?

The European continent is home to a variety of ethnic cultures. As you can see, if each culture were a country, there would be many more nations in Europe.

SOURCE: Leopold Kohr, *The Breakdown of Nations* (New York: Rinehart & Company, 1957), p. 233.

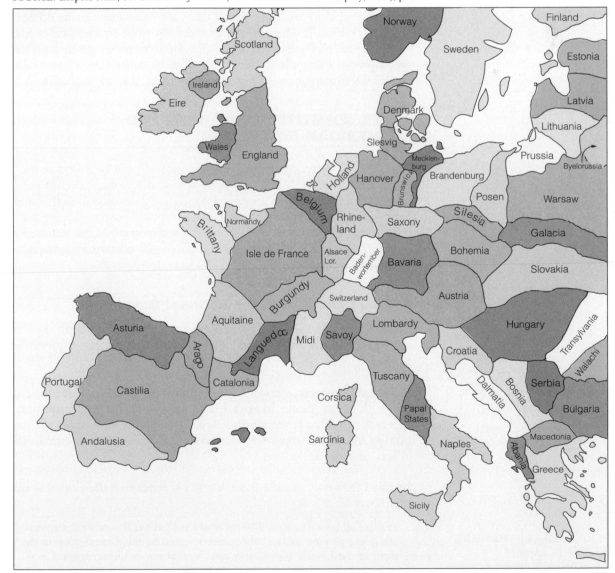

DID YOU KNOW?

That local governments, which can be created as well as abolished by their state, have no independent existence according to the Constitution, unlike the state and national governments?

Many people argue that the states have also been testing grounds for the introduction of bold new government initiatives. This was true, for example, with unemployment compensation, which began in Wisconsin; the enfranchisement of eighteen-year-old voters, where Georgia pioneered the way; state lotteries, which were spearheaded in their modern form in New Hampshire; and air pollution control, which was initiated in California. Of course, not everyone agrees that all of these developments were entirely beneficial, and other actions pioneered at the state level—such as Prohibition or Jim Crow laws—were either disastrous or morally bankrupt.

Arguments Against Federalism

Not everyone thinks federalism is such a good idea. Some see it as a way for powerful state and local interests to block progress and impede national plans. Political scientist William H. Riker condemns American federalism for perpetuating racism.[3] Smaller political units are more likely to be dominated by a single political group, and the dominant groups in some cities and states have resisted implementing equal rights for all minority groups. Others point out, however, that the dominant factions in other places have been more progressive in many areas, such as the environment, than the national government.

■ THE CONSTITUTIONAL BASIS FOR AMERICAN FEDERALISM

No mention of the designation "federal system" can be found in the United States Constitution. Nor is it possible to find a systematic division of governmental authority between the national and state governments in that document. Rather, the Constitution sets out different types of powers (Figure 3-2). These powers can be classified as (1) the delegated powers of the national government; (2) the reserved powers of the states; (3) concurrent powers; and (4) prohibited powers.

Powers Delegated to the National Government

The delegated powers of the national government include both expressed and implied powers, as well as resulting powers and the special category of inherent powers.

Expressed Powers.   Most of the powers expressly delegated to the national government are found in Article I, Section 8, of the Constitution. Some expressly delegated powers include setting standards for weights and measures, making uniform naturalization laws, admitting new states, establishing post offices, and declaring war.

Implied Powers.   Article I, Section 8:18, states that the Congress shall have the power

> to make all laws which shall be necessary and proper for carrying into execution the foregoing powers, and all other powers vested by this Constitution in the Government of the United States, or in any Department or Officer thereof.

ELASTIC CLAUSE, or NECESSARY AND PROPER CLAUSE
The clause in Article I, Section 8, which grants Congress the power to do whatever is necessary to execute its specific powers.

[3]William H. Riker, "Federalism," in Fred I. Greenstein and Nelson W. Polsby, eds., *Handbook of Political Science*, vol. 5 (Reading, Mass.: Addison-Wesley, 1975), p. 154.

This clause is sometimes called the **elastic clause,** or the **necessary and proper clause,** because it gives elasticity to our constitutional system. It gives Congress all those powers that can be reasonably inferred but are not expressly stated in the brief wording of the Constitution. It was first used in the Supreme Court decision of *McCulloch v. Maryland*[4] (discussed later in this chapter) to develop the concept of implied powers, through which the national government has succeeded in strengthening the scope of its authority to meet the numerous problems that the framers of the Constitution did not, and could not, anticipate.

[4] 4 Wheaton 316 (1819).

FIGURE 3-2
The American Federal System— Division of Powers between the National Government and the State Governments
We can separate the division of powers between national and state governments by looking at the powers granted by the Constitution to both the national governments and the state governments together. Then we look at the powers denied by the Constitution to each level of government.

POWERS GRANTED BY THE CONSTITUTION

National Government

IMPLIED
"To make all laws which shall be necessary and proper for carrying into execution the foregoing powers, and all other powers vested by this Constitution in the Government of the United States, or in any Department or Officer thereof."
(Article 1, Section 8.18)

EXPRESS
- To coin money
- To conduct foreign relations
- To regulate interstate commerce
- To levy and collect taxes
- To declare war
- To raise and support the military
- To establish post offices
- To establish courts inferior to the Supreme Court
- To admit new states

National and State Governments

CONCURRENT
- To levy and collect taxes
- To borrow money
- To make and enforce laws
- To establish courts
- To provide for the general welfare
- To charter banks and corporations

State Governments

RESERVED TO THE STATES
- To regulate intrastate commerce
- To conduct elections
- To provide for public health, safety, and morals
- To establish local governments
- To ratify amendments to the federal constitution
- To establish a state militia

POWERS DENIED BY THE CONSTITUTION

National Government

- To tax articles exported from any state
- To violate the Bill of Rights
- To change state boundaries

National and State Governments

- To grant titles of nobility
- To permit slavery
- To deny citizens the right to vote

State Governments

- To tax imports or exports
- To coin money
- To enter into treaties
- To impair obligations of contracts
- To abridge the privileges or immunities of citizens or deny due process and equal protection of the laws

The military might of the Federal government reminds us of the powers in foreign policy and warmaking that are reserved to the national government.

Resulting Powers.   Resulting powers are national powers that result when expressed powers are added together. For example, the central government's authority to make paper money legal tender for the payment of debts is the result of adding together the expressed powers to coin money, to borrow money, and to regulate interstate commerce.

Inherent Powers.   A special category of national powers that is not implied by the necessary and proper clause consists of what have been labeled the inherent powers of the national government. These powers derive from the fact that the United States is a sovereign power among nations, and, as such, its national government must be the only government that deals with other nations. Under international law, it is assumed that all nation-states, regardless of their size or power, have *inherent* in their existence as nations the right to ensure their own survival. To do this, each nation must have the ability to act in its own interest among and with the community of nations—by, for instance, making treaties, waging war, seeking trade, and acquiring territory.[5] The national government has these powers whether or not they have been enumerated in the Constitution. Some constitutional scholars categorize inherent powers as a third type of power, completely distinct from the delegated powers (both expressed and implied) of the national government.

Reserved Powers of the State Governments

The Tenth Amendment states that the powers not delegated to the United States by the Constitution, nor prohibited by it to the states, are reserved to the states respectively, or to the people. These are the reserved powers that the national government cannot usurp from, or deny to, the states. Such powers

[5]See especially *United States v. Curtiss-Wright Export Co.*, 299 U.S. 304 (1936), which upheld the validity of a joint resolution of Congress delegating the power to the president to prohibit arms shipments to foreign belligerents. See the appendix to Chapter 2 for more information about how court decisions are referenced.

Each state has its own laws regulating marriage. In what other areas do states have reserved and exclusive powers?

include each state's right to regulate commerce within its borders and to provide for a state militia. States also have the reserved power to make laws on all matters not prohibited to the states by the national or state constitutions and not expressly, or by implication, delegated to the national government. The states also have the **police power**—the authority to legislate for the protection of the health, morals, safety, and welfare of the people. On occasion, states have used their power to pass discriminatory legislation, such as anti-miscegenation laws prohibiting interracial marriages. These laws were passed on the assumption that since the Constitution did not grant such regulatory power to the national government, that power was reserved to the states acting through their legislatures. But when such laws were declared to be unconstitutional,[6] they immediately became unenforceable by the states.

Concurrent Powers

In certain areas, the Constitution gives national and state governments an equal right to pass legislation and to regulate certain activities. These are called concurrent powers. An example of a concurrent power is the power to tax. The types of taxation are divided between the levels of government. States may not levy a tariff (a set of taxes on imported goods); the federal government may not tax real estate; and neither may tax the facilities of the other. If the state governments did not have the power to tax, they would not be able to function other than on a ceremonial basis.

Other concurrent powers that are not specifically stated in the Constitution but only implied include the power to borrow money, to establish courts, and to charter banks and corporations. These powers are normally limited to the

POLICE POWER
The authority to legislate for the protection of the health, morals, safety, and welfare of the people. In the United States, police power is a reserved power of the states. The federal government is able to legislate for the welfare of its citizens through specific congressional powers such as control over interstate commerce.

[6]*Loving v. Virginia*, 388 U.S. 1 (1967).

DID YOU KNOW?

That the federal government of the United States was modeled, in part, on the sixteenth-century Iroquois confederacy of five Indian nations organized by the chiefs Dekanawide and Hiawatha?

geographical area of the state and to those functions not preempted by the Constitution or by the national government—such as the coinage of money and the negotiation of treaties.

The foregoing discussion of the constitutional basis for state power might give the impression that the power of the states today is derived solely from the Constitution. This would be a mistake, for the independence of the states rests, in large part, on the commitment of American citizens to the idea of local self-government. In addition, and perhaps more importantly, members of the national government—senators and representatives—are elected by their local constituencies. Except for the president, politicians in the national government have obtained their power by satisfying those local constituencies, rather than by satisfying some ill-defined, broad national constituency. Even the president must appeal to local constituencies to some degree, however, since the presidential candidate receiving the largest popular vote in a state wins all of that state's electoral votes. Furthermore, many of the programs paid for and undertaken by the national government are carried out by the state and local governmental units—for example, the interstate highway system, most of the welfare system, job creation programs, and environmental cleanup programs.

■ HORIZONTAL FEDERALISM

HORIZONTAL FEDERALISM
Activities, problems, and policies that require state governments to interact with each other.

So far we have examined only the relationship between central and state governmental units. But, of course, the states have numerous commercial, social, and other dealings among themselves. These interstate activities, problems, and policies make up what can be called **horizontal federalism.** The national Constitution imposes certain "rules of the road" on horizontal federalism, which have had the effect of preventing any one state from setting itself apart from the other states. The three most important clauses in the Constitution relating to horizontal federalism, all taken from the Articles of Confederation, require that:

1. Each state give full faith and credit to every other state's public acts, records, and judicial proceedings.
2. Each state extend to every other state's citizens the privileges and immunities of its own citizens.
3. Each state agree to render persons who are fleeing from justice in another state back to their home state when requested to do so.

The Full Faith and Credit Clause

FULL FAITH AND CREDIT CLAUSE
A section of the Constitution that requires states to recognize one another's laws and court decisions. It ensures that rights established under deeds, wills, contracts, and other civil matters in one state will be honored by other states.

Article IV, Section 1, of the Constitution provides that "full faith and credit shall be given in each state to the public acts, records, and judicial proceedings of every other state." This clause applies only to civil matters. It ensures that rights established under deeds, wills, contracts, and the like in one state will be honored by other states and that any judicial decision with respect to such property rights will be honored as well as enforced in all states. The **full faith and credit clause** was originally put in the Articles of Confederation to promote mutual friendship among the people of the different states. In fact, it has contributed to the unity of American citizens because it protects their legal rights as they move about from state to state. This is extremely important for the conduct of business in a country with a very mobile citizenry.

Privileges and Immunities

Privileges and immunities are defined as special rights and exemptions provided by law. Article IV, Section 2, indicates that "the citizens of each state shall be entitled to all privileges and immunities of citizens in the several states." This clause indicates that states are obligated to extend to citizens of other states protection of the laws, the right to work, access to courts, and other privileges they grant their own citizens. It means, quite simply, that a resident of Alabama cannot be treated as an alien when that person is in California or New York. He or she must have access to the courts of each state, to travel rights, and to property rights.[7]

PRIVILEGES AND IMMUNITIES
A section of the Constitution requiring states not to discriminate against one another's citizens. A resident of one state cannot be treated as an alien when in another state; he or she may not be denied such privileges and immunities as legal protection, access to courts, travel rights, or property rights.

Interstate Extradition

Article IV, Section 2, states that "a person charged in any state with treason, felony, or another crime who shall flee from justice and be found in another state, shall on demand of the executive authority of the state from which he fled, be delivered up, to be removed to the state having jurisdiction of the crime." The language here appears clear, yet governors of one state had not been legally required to **extradite** (render to another state) a fugitive from justice until 1987. (See Highlight on the case of Ron Calder.) The federal courts will not order such an action. It is rather the moral duty of a governor to do so, and, in fact, extradition is routinely followed in most cases. Governors who refuse to extradite are inviting retaliation from other states. In many cases, the question is moot because Congress has made it a federal crime to flee across state lines to avoid prosecution for certain felonies. Therefore, apprehension by federal agents puts the fugitive in national government hands, and that person is usually turned over to the state from which he or she fled.

EXTRADITE
To surrender an accused criminal to the authorities of the state from which he or she has fled; to return a fugitive criminal to the jurisdiction of the accusing state.

[7]Out-of-state residents have been denied lower tuition rates at state universities, voting rights, and immediate claim to welfare benefits. Actually, the courts have never established a precise meaning of the term *privileges and immunities*.

The Constitution requires freedom of travel between states. What might occur in the absence of such a requirement?

HIGHLIGHT

Changing Views on Extradition

In 1981, Ron Calder, an air traffic controller from Iowa, had a "fender bender" in a grocery shop parking lot in Aguadilla, Puerto Rico. The driver of the other car, Antonio de Jesus Gonzalez, allegedly became irate and began pounding on Calder's car with a metal pipe. Calder quickly backed out of the tight parking space, unaware that Mr. Gonzalez's pregnant wife was walking behind his car. She was run over and both she and the unborn infant died. Calder was arrested, charged with homicide, and released on bond.

Concerned about anti-American feel-ings and possible prejudicing of a jury by the extensive publicity generated by the case, Calder returned to Iowa. The governor of Puerto Rico asked the governor of Iowa to extradite him to the island so that Calder could stand trial. The Iowa governor refused, citing an 1861 ruling by the U.S. Supreme Court (the so-called Dennison rule) which upheld in that year the right of the governor of Ohio to refuse an extradition request by the governor of Kentucky of a "free man of color" on charges that he had helped a slave escape to freedom.

The Dennison rule had stood for 126 years. Then, in 1987, on appeal from Puerto Rico, the U.S. Supreme Court reversed itself and ordered the governor of Iowa to extradite Calder.

Justice Thurgood Marshall wrote in the majority opinion that the decision was based on the evolution of the American system away from a sharp separation between the states and the federal government. Marshall argued that the federal courts now have the authority to order a state to extradite a fugitive to another state.

The Peaceful Settlement of Differences between States

INTERSTATE COMPACTS
Agreements between two or more states. Agreements on minor matters are made without congressional consent, but any compact that tends to increase the power of the contracting states relative to other states or relative to the national government generally requires the consent of Congress. Such compacts serve as a means by which states can solve regional problems.

States are supposed to settle their differences peacefully. In so doing, they may enter into agreements called **interstate compacts**—if consented to by Congress. In reality, congressional consent is necessary only if such a compact increases the power of the contracting states relative to other states (or to the national government). Typical examples of interstate compacts are the establishment of the Port of New York Authority by the states of New York and New Jersey and the regulation of the production of crude oil and natural gas by the Interstate Oil and Gas Compact of 1935. The U.S. Supreme Court plays a major role in dealing with legal disputes between the states. Also, the Supreme Court plays a major role in dealing with disputes between the national government and the state governments. We consider the judicial system in more detail in Chapter 15.

■ THE SUPREMACY OF THE NATIONAL CONSTITUTION

SUPREMACY CLAUSE
The constitutional provision that makes the Constitution and federal laws superior to all state and local legislation.

The supremacy of the national constitution over subnational laws and actions can be found in the **supremacy clause** of the Constitution. The supremacy clause (Article VI, Paragraph 2) states:

This Constitution, and the laws of the United States which shall be made in pursuance thereof; and all Treaties made . . . under the Authority of the United States, shall be the supreme law of the Land; and the Judges in every State shall be bound thereby; any Thing in the Constitution or Laws of any State to the Contrary notwithstanding.

In other words, states cannot use their reserved or concurrent powers to thwart national policies. All national and state officers, as well as judges, must be bound by oath to support the Constitution. Hence any legitimate exercise of national governmental power supersedes any conflicting state action.[8] Of course, deciding whether a conflict actually exists is a judicial matter, as you will soon read about in the case of *McCulloch v. Maryland,* although such decisions may be politically charged.

Some political scientists believe that national supremacy is critical for the longevity and smooth functioning of a federal system. Nonetheless, the application of this principle has been a continuous source of conflict. Indeed, the most extreme result of this conflict was the Civil War, which we explore in more detail later.

DID YOU KNOW?

That under Article I, Section 10, of the Constitution, no state is allowed to enter into any treaty, alliance, or confederation?

■ MILESTONES IN NATIONAL GOVERNMENT SUPREMACY

Numerous court decisions and political events and even more numerous instances of bureaucratic decision making have given our national government a preponderance of significant political power. Such was not the case during the early days of the American republic. Historically, there are at least three milestones on the route to today's relatively more powerful national government. They are as follows:

1. The Supreme Court case of *McCulloch v. Maryland* (1819),[9] in which the doctrine of implied powers of the national government was clarified.
2. The Supreme Court case of *Gibbons v. Ogden* (1824),[10] in which the national government's power over commerce was defined for the first time in an expansive way.
3. The Civil War (1861–1865).

McCulloch v. Maryland (1819)

The U.S. Constitution says nothing about establishing a national bank. Article I, Section 8, gives Congress the power "to coin money, regulate the value thereof, and of foreign coin, and fix the standards of weights and measures. . . ." Nonetheless, at different times Congress chartered two banks—the First and Second Banks of the United States—and provided part of their initial capital; they were thus national banks.

Maryland was one of many states that opposed the existence of the Second Bank of the United States, claiming that it represented unfair competition against state banks and an overextention of centralized political power. Yielding to pressure from its state banks, the government of Maryland imposed a tax on the Second Bank's Baltimore branch. The branch's cashier, James William McCulloch, refused to pay the Maryland tax. Maryland took McCulloch to its state court. In that suit, the state of Maryland won. Since similar taxes were being levied in other states, the national government appealed the case to the Supreme Court, then headed by Chief Justice John Marshall.

---

[8]An excellent example of this is President Eisenhower's disciplining of Arkansas Governor Orval Faubus by calling up the National Guard to enforce the court-ordered desegregation of Little Rock High School. See R. Neustadt, *Presidential Power: The Politics of Leadership from FDR to Carter* (New York: Wiley, 1980).
[9]4 Wheaton 316 (1819).
[10]9 Wheaton 1 (1824).

HIGHLIGHT

The Seedier Side of *Gibbons* v. *Ogden*

What at first glance seems like a straightforward legal issue was actually a sensational battle between two men, a battle that physically and financially almost wrecked them. Gibbons was a belligerent southern planter. His sordid past included being campaign manager in an election in which there were more votes than voters. The loser in that election, James Jackson, attacked Gibbons in Congress, telling everyone who would listen about "this person . . . whose soul is faction and whose life has been a scene of political corruption. . . ." Gibbons obviously did not appreciate Jackson's remarks. He proposed a duel; shots were exchanged, though neither man was hit.

Gibbons's legal battle against Ogden (who was a former governor of New Jersey and a U.S. senator) became a personal vendetta. No expenditure was too large to make sure that Ogden lost. Daniel Webster was one of the prestigious attorneys that Gibbons hired. Gibbons even put a $40,000 contin-

Thomas Gibbons

Aaron Ogden

gency provision in his will to carry on the legal battle if he died before it was resolved.

During the lengthy litigation, Gibbons decided to visit Ogden's home. He challenged Ogden to a duel. Ogden

instead sued and won $5,000 against Gibbons for trespassing.

By the time the case ended, both Gibbons and Ogden had spent the greater part of their fortunes on legal fees.

years of the nation. This debate was sparked anew by the passage of the Tariff Acts of 1828 and 1830 by the national government, which the southern states believed were against their interests. The state of South Carolina attempted to nullify the tariffs, claiming that in cases of conflict between a state and the national government, the state should have the ultimate authority over its citizens.

NULLIFICATION
The act of nullifying or rendering void. John C. Calhoun asserted that a state had the right to declare a national law to be null and void and therefore not binding on its citizens, based on the assumption that ultimate sovereign authority rested with the several states.

Nullification and Secession.   Defending the concept of **nullification** was a well-educated and articulate senator from South Carolina, John C. Calhoun. Not a newcomer to politics, Calhoun had served the government in several capacities—as vice president under John Quincy Adams and Andrew Jackson, as secretary of state, and as secretary of war. Calhoun viewed the federal system as simply a compact (as in the Articles of Confederation) among sovereign states. The national government was not the final judge of its own power— the ultimate sovereign authority rested with the several states. It followed that the national government could not force a state and its citizens to accept a law against their will. In such cases, Calhoun argued, the state had the right to declare a national law to be *null and void* and therefore not binding on its

The Civil War was not fought just over the question of slavery. What else was at issue?

citizens. Within this theory of nullification is the concept of **interposition,** in which a state places itself between its citizens and the national government as a protector, shielding its citizens from any national legislation that may be harmful to them.[12]

Calhoun also espoused the political doctrine of the **concurrent majority,** in which he maintained that democratic decisions could be made only with the concurrence of all segments of society affected by the decision and that without that agreement a decision should not be binding on those whose interests it violates.

Calhoun's concurrent majority thesis was used by others later as a justification for the **secession** of the southern states from the Union. The ultimate defeat of the South, however, permanently lay to waste any idea that a state within the Union can successfully claim the right to secede. We live in "the indestructible union of indestructible states," as the Supreme Court has said. It is not without irony that the Civil War, brought about in large part because of the South's desire for increased states' rights, in fact resulted in the opposite—an increase in the political power of the national government. (See the Highlight on secession—Vermont style.)

War and Growth of the National Government.   Thousands of new employees were hired to run the Union war effort and to deal with the social and economic problems that had to be handled in the aftermath of war. A billion-dollar ($1.3 billion, which is about $10 billion in today's dollars) national government budget was passed for the first time in 1865 to cover the increased government expenditures. The first (temporary) income tax was imposed on citizens to help pay for the war. Civil liberties were curtailed in both the Union and in the Confederacy in the name of the wartime emergency. The distribution of pensions and widows' benefits also boosted the national government's social role. The North's victory set the nation on the path to a modern, industrial economy and society.

INTERPOSITION
The act in which a state places itself between its citizens and the national government as a protector, shielding its citizens from any national legislation that may be harmful to them. The doctrine of interposition has been rejected by the federal courts as contrary to the national supremacy clause of Article VI in the Constitution.

CONCURRENT MAJORITY
A principle advanced by John C. Calhoun whereby democratic decisions could be made only with the concurrence of all segments of society affected by the decision. Without their concurrence, a decision should not be binding on those whose interests it violates.

SECESSION
The act of formally withdrawing from membership in an alliance; withdrawal of a state from the federal union.

[12]Thomas Jefferson and James Madison also used the theory of interposition in the Kentucky and Virginia Resolutions of 1799, written to protest the Alien and Sedition Acts of 1798.

One result of the New Deal's WPA (Works Progress Administration), a wall mural in San Francisco. How did the WPA represent the shift to cooperative federalism?

COOPERATIVE FEDERALISM
The theory that the states and the national government should cooperate in solving problems.

that manufacturing could be regulated as interstate commerce by the national government.[16]

Some political scientists have labeled the era since 1937 as one of **cooperative federalism,** in which the states and the national government cooperate in solving complex common problems. Others see the 1937 decision as the beginning of an era of national supremacy, in which the power of the states has been consistently diminished. In particular, Congress can pass virtually any law that regulates almost any kind of economic activity, no matter where that activity is located. For all intents and purposes, the doctrine of dual federalism has been dead for quite some time, although, as we shall see, there were attempts at reviving it during the Reagan Administration.

The Growth of National-Level Powers

Even if the Great Depression had not occurred, we probably still would have witnessed a growth of national-level powers as the country became increasingly populated, industrial, and a world power. This meant that problems and situations that were once treated locally would begin to have a profound impact on Americans hundreds or even thousands of miles away.

For example, if one state is unable to maintain an adequate highway system, the economy of the entire region may suffer. If another state maintains a substandard educational system, the quality of the work force, the welfare rolls, and the criminal justice agencies in other states may be affected. So the death of dual federalism and the ascendancy of national supremacy had a very logical and very real set of causes. Our more mobile, industrial, and increasingly interdependent nation demanded more uniform and consistent sets of rules, regulations, and governmental programs. The shift toward a greater role for

[16]*NLRB v. Jones & Laughlin Steel Corporation,* 301 U.S. 1 (1937). For a different view of the historical significance of this decision, see Morton Grodzins, "Centralization and Decentralization in the American Federal System," in Robert A. Goldwin, ed., *A Nation of States: Essays on the American Federal System* (Chicago: Rand McNally, 1963).

the central government in the United States can nowhere better be seen than in the shift toward increased central government spending as a percentage of total government spending. Figure 3-3 shows that back in 1929, on the eve of the Great Depression, local governments accounted for 60 percent of all government outlays, whereas the federal government accounted for only 17 percent. After Roosevelt's New Deal had been in place for several years during the Great Depression, local governments gave up half their share of the government spending pie, dropping to 30 percent, and the federal government increased its share to 47 percent. Estimates are that in 1991, the federal government accounts for about 65 percent of all government spending.

The New Federalism

The third phase of federalism was labeled by President Richard Nixon as the **new federalism.** Its goal was to reduce the restrictions attached to federal grants—that is, to allow local officials to make the decisions about how the money is to be spent. The centerpiece of Nixon's new federalism was a **revenue-sharing program** that gave local and state officials considerable freedom in spending decisions.

President Ronald Reagan continued Nixon's emphasis on the new federalism. "It is my intention . . . [to restore] the powers granted to the federal government and those reserved to the states and to the people," said President Reagan in his first State of the Union address in 1982. Although President Reagan was referring to the boundaries between the powers of the national government and of the states, his new federalism, like Nixon's, was essentially a plan to give the states an increased ability to decide for themselves how government revenues should be spent.

During the Reagan administration, steps were also taken to privatize various federal programs, including housing, prisons, and hospitals. Reagan advocated relying more on private institutions and less on government to satisfy national goals. He reasoned that private firms guided by marketplace incentives would operate more efficiently than government. Thus, he maintained, costs could be cut and better services received if the federal bureaucracy were reduced.

President Bush's Views

During the first two years of Bush's presidency, his administration continued to implement the philosophy of the Reagan Administration. The goal contin-

NEW FEDERALISM
A plan to limit the national government's power to regulate and to restore power to state governments. Essentially, the new federalism was designed to give the states an increased ability to decide for themselves how government revenues should be spent.

REVENUE-SHARING PROGRAM
A program in which the federal government allocated funds to states and cities with virtually no strings attached. Recipient governments could use the funds in any way they saw fit.

FIGURE 3-3
The Shift Toward Central Government Spending
Before the Great Depression, local governments accounted for 60 percent of all government spending, with the federal government only accounting for 17 percent. By 1960, federal government spending was up to 64 percent, local governments accounted for only 19 percent, and the remainder was spent by state governments. The estimate for 1991 is that the federal government accounts for 65 percent and local governments for 16 percent.
SOURCE: *Government Finances,* U.S. Department of Commerce, Bureau of the Census, 1990.

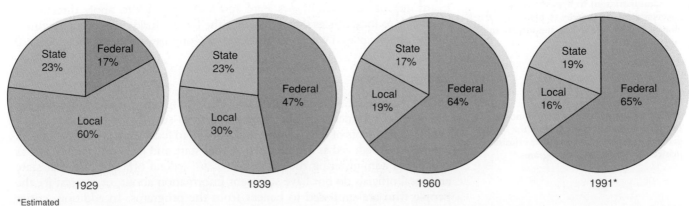

1929   1939   1960   1991*

*Estimated

DID YOU KNOW?

That forty counties in the north-west corner of Virginia split from that state after Virginia's secession from the Union and became the new pro-Union state of West Virginia?

ues to be to allow state and local governments to have increased freedom of action. No specific policy statements, however, with respect to the new federalism have been issued by the Bush Administration.

■ THE FISCAL SIDE OF FEDERALISM

Today, the national government collects over 60 percent of all tax dollars. As part of our system of cooperative federalism, the national government gives back to the states (and local governments) a significant amount—almost $125 billion projected in fiscal year 1991, although this amount represents a decline over earlier years. (The first decline in three decades occurred in fiscal year 1981–82.) There are basically three separate methods by which the national government returns nationally collected tax dollars to state and local governments: categorical grants-in-aid, block grants, and general grants-in-aid (general revenue sharing).

Categorical Grants-in-Aid

The modern concept of a federal government grant-in-aid was derived from a 1902 law providing that revenues from the sale of public lands were to be shared with certain states and territories for irrigation and land reclamation. Not until the administration of Franklin Roosevelt did restrictions and regulations accompany the **categorical grants.** These involved the establishment of agricultural extension programs, highway construction, vocational education, and maternal and child health. During Roosevelt's first two terms in office, categorical grants-in-aid increased from $200 million annually to $3 billion.

The number and scope of the categorical grants expanded further as part of the Great Society programs of President Lyndon Johnson (1963–69). Grants became available in the fields of education, pollution control, conservation, recreation, and highway construction and maintenance. For some of the categorical grant programs, the state and local governments must put up a share of the money, usually called **matching funds.** For other types of programs, the funds are awarded according to a formula that takes into account the relative wealth of the state, a process known as **equalization.**

In general, categorical grants have remained under fairly tight control by Congress. In a move to bypass the states, Congress established the **project grant** approach, which allows state and local agencies to apply directly for assistance to local offices that administer the federal funds. This way the funds can be directly placed where—in the eyes of Congress—they are most needed.

Block Grants

Block grants were introduced in 1966. These programs transfer funds to state and local governments in broadly defined areas such as health and criminal justice. Opponents of the block grant approach to federalism argue that overall federal aid is reduced as a consequence, that state and local officials are not as capable of administering the programs as are federal officials, and that state and local officials do not have sufficient information about, or interest in, the people who are supposed to benefit from the programs. In addition, critics

CATEGORICAL GRANTS
Federal grants-in-aid to states or local governments that are for very specific programs or projects.

MATCHING FUNDS
For many categorical grant programs, the state must "match" the federal funds. Some programs only require the state to raise 10 percent of the funds, whereas others approach an even share.

EQUALIZATION
A method for adjusting the amount of money that a state must put up to receive federal funds that takes into account the wealth of the state or its ability to tax its citizens.

PROJECT GRANT
An assistance grant that can be applied for directly by state and local agencies; established under a national program grant. Project grants allow Congress (and the administration) to bypass state governments and thereby to place the money directly where it is supposedly the most needed.

BLOCK GRANTS
Federal programs that provide funding to the state and local governments for general functional areas such as criminal justice or mental health programs.

say, a block grant approach to federalism contributes to increasing inequality among the states and is potentially harmful to the poor, because state legislatures are less likely to spend funds on social welfare programs than is the national government.

General Grants-in-Aid, or Revenue Sharing

In an effort to move away from national government involvement with categorical grants, the Nixon administration in 1972 asked Congress to remit to the states and local governments a certain percentage of tax income each year, on a more or less automatic basis, with few strings attached. Congress complied. One-third of the funds went to the states and two-thirds were sent directly to local governments. It is clear that the major impetus behind revenue sharing was President Nixon's desire to reduce the role of the national government while increasing that of the state and local governments. (Also, 1972 was an election year for Nixon.) The budget crisis confronting the federal government in the mid-1980s led Congress to abolish revenue sharing to local governments at the end of 1986.

■ FEDERALISM VERSUS REGIONALISM: THE SHIFT OF POWER FROM THE SNOWBELT TO THE SUNBELT

From 1950 to 1990, the **Snowbelt** states of the North increased 36.1 percent in population overall, where the **Sunbelt** states of the South and West increased 86.2 percent. Figure 3-4 shows projected regional job growth for the years 1987 to 2000. With the number of jobs increasing much faster in the Sunbelt than in the Snowbelt, the population shift should continue. This shifting population has meant an increasing amount of national government benefits

> **DID YOU KNOW?**
>
> That between 1980 and 1990, West Virginia (pop. 1.9 million) lost about 4 percent of its population while California gained 4.7 million people, growing by about 20 percent in the same period?

SNOWBELT
The northern states of the United States characterized by a harsh climate.

SUNBELT
The southern states of the United States characterized by mild and warm weather.

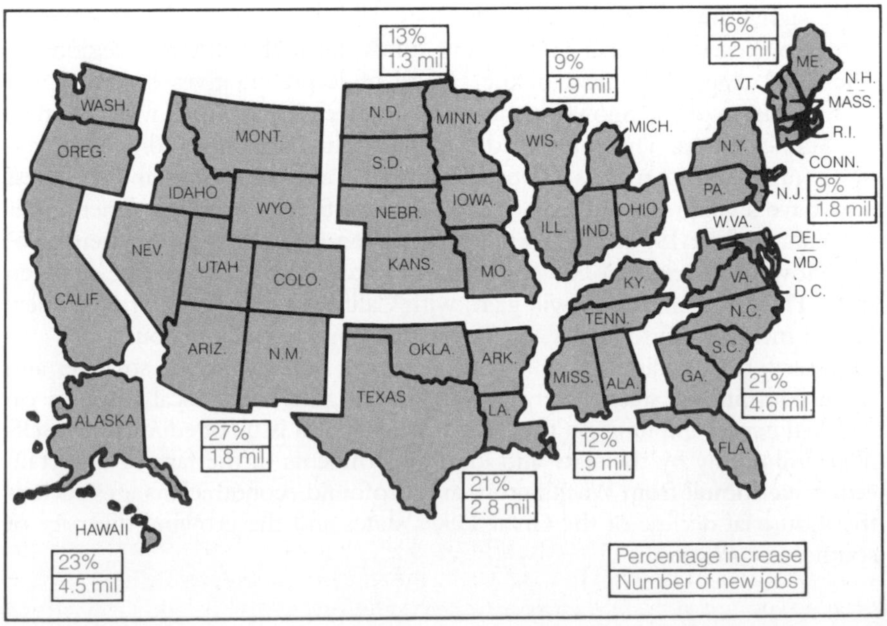

FIGURE 3-4
Regional Job Growth (1987–2000)
The number of jobs will grow much faster in the Sunbelt than in the Snowbelt, continuing the shift in population. How will this shift affect Congress's actions?
SOURCE: U.S. Department of Commerce, Bureau of the Census, 1990.

President Bush greets Arkansas governor Bill Clinton and Iowa governor Tery Branstad at the "education summit" called by the president. Which level of government—federal, state, or local—has the most responsibility for education?

obtained by the citizens of the Sunbelt states relative to those of the Snowbelt states. This has intensified regional conflict as the Snowbelt states have attempted to counter the changing power structure across the states. In part, this is a problem in horizontal federalism.

In the 1980s, shifting population combined with a reduction of the role of the federal government in domestic social programs to make regionalism a more significant force in national politics. We can expect to see increasing battles over how national government funds are to be allocated regionally. The 1982 reapportionment of the House of Representatives decreased the representation of the Snowbelt states by seventeen seats, which were given to the Sunbelt states. This intensified the Snowbelt coalition's efforts to obtain more funds, but its success has been limited because the South and the West now have a congressional majority for the first time. Reapportionment after the results of the 1990 census will further deteriorate the political strength of the Snowbelt states in Congress. Northern states are expected to lose eighteen seats. The South and West will gain, with California adding six or seven new House members and Florida and Texas each gaining three or four.

Other forces tending to regionalize American politics include stronger and more coordinated state governments, greater grass-roots local activism on national issues, emphasis on the fundamentally local issue of education, a self-help philosophy by the state and local governments in the face of uncertain economic stimuli from Washington, and profound economic changes such as the industrial decline of the Great Lakes states and the growing diversity of southern economies.

Expressing Your Views—Writing Letters to the Editor

Just about every day there is an issue concerning federalism that is discussed in the media. Advocates of decentralization—a shift of power from federal to state or local governments—argue that we must recognize the rights of states to design their own destiny and master their own fate. Advocates of centralization—more power to the national government—see the shift in power under decentralization as undermining the national purpose, common interests, and responsibilities that bind us together in pursuit of national goals. The big question is how much the national government should do for the people. Is it within the power of the national government to decide what the law should be on abortion? Before 1973, each state set its own laws without interference from the national government. Who should be responsible for the homeless? Should the national government subsidize state and local efforts to help them? Who is responsible for the nation's health care? Should the national government expand its role in this area?

You may have valid, important points to make on these or other issues. One of the best ways to make your point is by writing an effective letter to the editor of your local newspaper (or even to a national newspaper such as the *Wall Street Journal*). Here is what you should do to write an effective letter:

1. Use a typewriter and double-space the lines. If possible, use a word processor with a spelling checker and grammar checker.

2. Your lead topic sentence should be short, to the point, and powerful.

3. Keep your thoughts on target—choose only one topic to discuss in your letter. Make sure it is newsworthy and timely.

4. If you know that facts were misstated or left out in current news stories about your topic, supply them. The public wants to know.

5. Don't be afraid to express moral judgments. You can go a long way by appealing to readers' sense of justice.

6. Personalize the letter by bringing in your own experiences.

7. With appropriate changes, send it to the editors of more than one newspaper or magazine. Make sure, however, that the letters are not exactly the same.

8. Sign your letter and give your address and your phone number. If your letter is not published, try again. Eventually one will be.

CHAPTER SUMMARY

1. There are three basic models of ordering relations between central governments and local units: (a) a unitary system, (b) a confederal system, and (c) a federal system.

2. A unitary system, such as in France, is one in which the national government has ultimate authority. This system is most common.

3. A confederal system is a league of independent states, each having essentially sovereign powers. The central government handles only matters of common concern that have been expressly delegated to it by member states.

4. Somewhere between the unitary and the confederal forms of government lies the federal system. Here authority is divided between the central government and the regional, or subdivisional, governments.

5. Federalism is probably the best arrangement in large countries because of their size and consequent regional differences and political subcultures. Division of power between local and national governments brings government closer to the people and allows government to meet the local needs of its citizens. State governments in the United States have also served as testing grounds for future national leaders and bold new initiatives.

6. The Constitution expressly delegated certain powers to the national government in Article I, Section 8. The framers of the Constitution knew these powers would not be sufficient so they included the "elastic clause," giving Congress the right to pass laws "necessary and proper" to carrying out its enumerated powers.

7. Resulting powers are those held by the national government when several expressed powers are added together. Inherent powers are those held by the national government by virtue of its being a sovereign state with the right to preserve itself.

8. The Tenth Amendment to the Constitution states that powers not delegated to the United States by the Constitution, nor prohibited by it to the states, are reserved to the states respectively, or to the people.

9. In certain areas, the Constitution provides for concurrent powers, held by both national and state governments. The classic example of a concurrent power is the power to tax.

10. The three most important clauses in the Constitution relating to horizontal federalism require that (a) each state give full faith and credit to every other state's public acts, records, and judicial proceedings; (b) each state extend to every other state's citizens the privileges and immunities of its own citizens; and (c) each state agree to render persons who are fleeing from justice to another state back to their home state when requested to do so.

11. The supremacy clause of the Constitution states that the Constitution, congressional laws, and national treaties are the supreme law of the land. States cannot use their reserved or concurrent powers to override national politics.

12. *McCulloch v. Maryland* (1819) enhanced the implied power of the federal government through Chief Justice John Marshall's broad interpretation of the "necessary and proper" clause of Article I of the Constitution. The effects of the decision are part of a continuing debate about the boundaries between federal and state authority.

13. *Gibbons v. Ogden* (1824) enhanced and consolidated national power over commerce. Chief Justice Marshall interpreted the commerce clause of the Constitution broadly and held that the commerce power was complete in itself, with no limitations other than those found specifically in the Constitution. The regulation of commerce became one of the major issues in federal–state relations.

14. At the heart of the controversy that led to the Civil War was the issue of national government supremacy versus the rights of the separate states. The notion of nullification eventually led to the secession of the Confederate states from the Union. The South's desire for increased states' rights led rather to an increase in the political power of the national government.

15. In dual federalism, each of the states and the federal government remains supreme within its own sphere.

16. The era since the Depression has sometimes been labeled as one of cooperative federalism, in which states and the national government cooperate in solving complex common problems. Others view it as the beginning of an era of national supremacy.

17. The third phase of federalism was labeled new federalism by President Nixon and was revived by President Reagan. The goal of the new federalism was to decentralize federal programs, giving more responsibility to the states.

18. There are basically three separate methods by which the national government returns nationally collected tax dollars to state and local governments: (a) categorical grants-in-aid, (b) block grants, and (c) general grants-in-aid (revenue sharing). The grants differ in the restrictions and regulations attached to them by the federal government. Congress abolished revenue sharing in 1986 owing to large budget deficits.

19. Population shifts in the United States have created a change in the amount of benefits obtained by the citizens of the Sunbelt states relative to those of the Snowbelt states in the form of national revenues and programs. We can expect to see increasing battles over how national government funds are to be allocated regionally.

QUESTIONS FOR REVIEW AND DISCUSSION

1. The Constitution and federal law are supreme over state and local legislation. Can you think of several areas of law where local governments should have complete authority? Should the national government take full responsibility for protecting the environment?

2. Are the states unlikely to fund social welfare programs on their own if the federal government no longer sends grants for them? Why does the Congress prefer to keep control of such programs at the national level?

3. Should the federal government be responsible for distributing benefits and federal contracts equally among all the states? If population and industries shift from one region of the nation to another—for example, from the Snowbelt to the Sunbelt— is the federal government obligated to provide assistance for the states whose economies suffer?

4. By choosing a federal form for our government, the Founding Fathers assured the continued existence of regional differences. Choose four states from different sections of the country and list the ways in which their political interests differ from each other. On what kinds of national legislation will these differences surface? How do these differences affect the outcome of presidential elections?

SELECTED REFERENCES

Daniel J. Elazar, *American Federalism: A View from the States,* 3rd ed. (New York: Harper and Row, 1985). This is a classic book on the subject, with a focus on the politics of federalism—bargaining, negotiation, and cooperation. It also emphasizes the political subcultures of America and their impact on the states.

Morton Grodzins, *The American System* (Chicago: Rand McNally, 1974). A classic understanding of the modern federal system.

Alexander Hamilton, John Jay, James Madison, *The Federalist: A Collection of Essays Written in Favor of the New Constitution,* edited by George W. Carey and James McClellan. (Dubuque, Ia: Kendall/Hunt Publishing Co., 1990). This student-oriented edition makes these classic essays accessible to this generation and includes an introduction, analytical notes, a glossary, and an index.

Robert Higgs, *Crisis and Leviathan: Critical Episodes in the Growth of American Government* (New York: Oxford University Press, 1987). A study of the reasons for the growth in size and power of government in the United States.

David Osborne, *Laboratories of Democracy: A New Breed of Governor Creates Models for National Growth* (Boston: Harvard Business School Press, 1990). The author uses a series of six case studies of governors to describe and analyze the lessons of state-level innovation in areas such as economic development, technology, social policy, and welfare reform.

James C. Smith, *Emerging Conflicts in the Doctrine of Federalism: The Intergovernmental Predicament* (Lanham, Md.: University Press of America, 1984). Intergovernmental problems that interfere with the smooth operation and performance of government institutions, in particular the roles of different levels and jurisdictions, are concisely explored in this study.

Deil S. Wright, *Understanding Intergovernmental Relations,* 2nd ed. (Monterey, Calif.: Brooks/Cole 1982). National political authorities' relations with state and local officials, emphasizing the practice and problems of federalism.

A GLOBAL PERSPECTIVE
STRUGGLING FOR EQUALITY:
ETHNIC MINORITIES THROUGHOUT THE WORLD

All over the globe, people are expressing pride in their distinct ethnic and national identity. In perhaps most instances, such ethnic pride has led to increased tensions with other, majority groups. Like African Americans who began the civil rights movement in the United States in the 1960s, many ethnic and racial groups are demanding increased political and economic rights from their government or, in some cases, the right to establish a separate state. Perhaps the most well-known struggle for political equality has been in South Africa, where the black and colored, or mixed-race, citizens who comprise a majority are fighting against the white minority that controls the state. Nelson Mandela, the hero of the anti-apartheid movement and leader of the African National Congress, the primary opposition group, was released from prison in 1990 after serving more than twenty years for his political activities against the state. Mandela's persistence and courage is widely admired among peoples who feel that they are oppressed by their government.

Some of the ethnic tensions result from the desire of groups to establish a special identity within their own nation, such as the demand by French-speaking Canadians in Quebec for a constitutional provision recognizing their "distinct culture." Within the United States, as well as Canada, Native Americans have also demanded more cultural autonomy, especially when certain rights were provided for in early treaties. The Mohawk tribe of the

Nelson Mandela greets thousands after his release from prison.

Canadian–U.S. border region has disputed the right of the local Quebec government to build a golf course on Indian ancestral lands, while sport fishers in Wisconsin have opposed the Menominee tribe's treaty right to spearfish in local waters.

Long-standing conflicts in Southeast Asia continue to explode in violence. In the island nation of Sri Lanka, the civil war between the Tamil rebels, who embrace a different culture and religion from the majority, and the government, has taken many lives. In northwestern India, the dispute between India and Pakistan over the control of Kashmir, which shares a Muslim culture with Pakistan, has resulted in a number of violent incidents.

While the breakup of the Soviet bloc has done much to reduce conflict between the United States and the Soviet Union, it has exacerbated ethnic tensions within a number of the Eastern European states. Many of these nations were created after World War I with little regard for the ethnic nationalities who lived in them. As the accompanying map shows, many European peoples are ethnic minorities within another nation. In many cases,

Demonstrations for freedom in Azerbaidjan.

French speaking Canadians demonstrate in Quebec.

Ethnic conflict in the USSR: Kirghizia.

these minorities feel that they are oppressed by the national majority and hope to be reunited with their own cultural kin in a separate nation. In at least two of the Eastern European nations, Czechoslovakia and Yugoslavia, it is clear that the states are amalgams of several distinct entities. Recently, Czechoslovakia changed its name to include the two major nationalities, the Czechs and the Slovaks, excluding the Bohemians as a minority. It is now called the Czech and Slovak Federal Republic. Yugoslavia has never really tried to integrate its five peoples—the Croats, the Serbians, the Montenegrins, the Slovenes, and the Bosnians.

How such nations that are really conglomerations of several peoples resolve these conflicts and grant rights to their ethnic minorities may serve as a model for the future. It will be particularly important to the Soviet Union, a nation that is composed of dozens of nationalities, large numbers of Islamic citizens, and several major racial groups.

CIVIL RIGHTS AND LIBERTIES

CIVIL LIBERTIES

WHAT IF . . . THE MIRANDA RULES WERE ELIMINATED?

Since the mid-1960s, the criminal justice process in the United States has been governed largely by what have come to be known as the "Miranda rules." These rules, established by a 1966 Supreme Court decision, hold that criminal suspects must be treated in such a manner to decrease the probability that they will be convicted wrongly of crimes that they did not commit. For example, suspects have the right to remain silent. The rules exist to safeguard the accused against police officers who are overly zealous in their search for possible felons and against prosecutors who want to maintain or enhance their professional or political status by achieving high rates of convictions.

What might happen if the Miranda rules were eliminated? It is very difficult to know for certain, but some outcomes can be guessed at from the American experience with criminal justice procedures that were general before the introduction of the Miranda rules. It was once common, and might be again, for suspects to be subjected to the "third degree," which ranged from mild psychological pressure to violent physical and mental torture. The past record includes allegations, and proven instances, of beatings, threats of severe punishment, denial of access to legal counsel, incarceration without formal charges being filed, sleep deprivation, and suspects kept in handcuffs, sometimes

with their arms wrapped around radiators, among other violations of what we today would regard as the rights of criminal suspects. These actions and worse are common in other countries today that do not have Miranda-type protections for their citizens.

If you were arrested in a future America that did not have Miranda rules, what kind of treatment could you expect? The odds are that many, and even most, police officers and prosecutors would behave decently and with respect for whatever legal protections might remain. But there would without doubt be a strong incentive for law-enforcement officers to go out of their way to get a conviction. If you were ensnared in such a system, whether you were guilty or not, any of the following might happen. Depending on how serious the offense with which you were charged, you might be arrested in the middle of the night without being told why you were picked up by the police. Your arms might be handcuffed or tied very uncomfortably, and you would be compelled to accompany the arresting officers who could use whatever force would be needed to get your cooperation. You might demand to know why you were arrested, but the police would not be under any legal compulsion to tell you. Once in detention, you probably would not have the

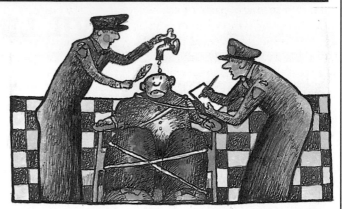

automatic right to make a telephone call to a lawyer who could give you legal advice or to contact your family to let them know what had happened to you.

Whether you are guilty of anything or not, it is often difficult to tell the truth if you are subjected to repeated threats, apparently helpful advice from some officers on how to avoid being verbally or even physically assaulted by the others (this is a version of the "good cop, bad cop" approach to gaining a suspect's cooperation), and the possible use of bright lights, sensory deprivation, truncheons, or beatings, which have been employed in the pre-Miranda past.

There are other reasons to expect that the excesses of the past might not be repeated if the *Miranda* rules were repealed. Educational levels among police officials are higher than before, and many are college-trained in the social sciences and related disciplines that encourage sensitivity to human rights. Furthermore, experi-

enced law-enforcement officers would have already become used to Miranda-governed procedures and trained in proper treatment of criminal suspects, and those habits would take some time to break. However, most public opinion polls indicate a hardening of popular attitudes toward crime and alleged criminals, including harsh treatment of drug dealers, rapists, child pornographers, and murderers. In that climate, police and the public tend not to make a clear distinction between those who actually are guilty of such offenses and those, like yourself, who may be merely suspected of committing crimes.

---

1. *Which groups would fare worse in the United States without Miranda rules and why?*
2. *What are the costs to society of retaining the Miranda rules?*
3. *"Only true criminals have to worry about the police." Comment on this statement.*

Most Americans believe they have more individual freedom than virtually any other people on earth. For the most part, this opinion is accurate. The freedoms that we take for granted—religion, speech, press, and assembly—are relatively unknown in many parts of the world. In many nations today, citizens have little chance of living without government harassment if they choose to criticize openly, through speech or print, the government or its actions. Indeed, if the United States suddenly had the same rules, laws, and procedures about verbal and printed expression that exist in many other countries, American jails would be filled overnight with transgressors.

■ CIVIL RIGHTS AND THE FEAR OF GOVERNMENT

Without government, people live in a state of anarchy. With unbridled government, men and women may end up living in a state of tyranny. The Founding Fathers wanted neither extreme. As we pointed out in Chapter 2, the Declaration of Independence was based on the idea of natural rights. These are rights discoverable in nature and history, according to such philosophers as John Locke and John Dickinson, who wrote that natural rights "are born with us; exist with us; and cannot be taken away from us by any human power."[1] Linked directly to the strong prerevolutionary sentiment for natural rights was the notion that a right was first and foremost a *limitation* on any government's ruling power. To obtain ratification of the Constitution by the necessary nine states, the Federalists had to deal with the colonists' fears of a too-powerful national government. The **Bill of Rights** was the result. When we speak of civil liberties in the United States, we are mostly referring to the specific limitations on government outlined in the first ten amendments to the U.S. Constitution, which were passed by Congress on September 25, 1789, and ratified by three-fourths of the states by December 15, 1791.[2]

BILL OF RIGHTS
The first ten amendments to the United States Constitution. They contain a listing of the rights a person enjoys and which cannot be infringed upon by the government, such as the freedoms of speech, press, and religion.

■ THE BILL OF RIGHTS

The First Amendment to the Constitution is for many the most significant part of the Bill of Rights, as well as the mainstay of the Declaration of Independence statement that all people should be able to enjoy life, liberty, and the pursuit of happiness. It is in this First Amendment that our basic freedoms of religion, speech, the press, assembly, and the right of petition are set forth. The first part of this chapter examines each of these freedoms in detail.

The Nationalization of the Bill of Rights

Most citizens do not realize that, as originally presented, the Bill of Rights limited only the power of the national government, not that of the states. In other words, a citizen in the state of Virginia in 1795 could not successfully sue in federal court against a law passed in Virginia that violated one of the amendments in the Bill of Rights. Each state had (and still has) its own

[1]Quoted in Bernard Bailyn, *The Ideological Origins of the American Revolution* (Cambridge, Mass.: Harvard University Press, 1967), p. 77.
[2]Note also that there is a distinction between the technical definitions of a civil *right* and a civil *liberty:* The former is government-granted, the latter is inherent.

constitution with its own bill of rights. Whereas the states' bills of rights were similar to the national one, there were some differences, and, perhaps more important, each state's judicial system interpreted the rights differently. A citizen in one state effectively had a different set of civil liberties from a citizen in another state. It was not until the Fourteenth Amendment was ratified in 1868 that our Constitution explicitly guaranteed to everyone due process of the law. Section 1 of that amendment provides that

> no State shall make or enforce any law which shall abridge the privileges or immunities of citizens of the United States; nor shall any State deprive any person of life, liberty, or property, without due process of law; nor deny to any person within its jurisdiction the equal protection of the laws.

Section 5 of the amendment explicitly gives Congress the power to enforce by appropriate legislation the provisions of the amendment. Note the use of the terms *citizens* and *person. Citizens* have political rights, such as voting and running for office, but no *person,* citizen or alien, can be denied civil rights (speech, press, and religion) nor have his or her property taken without equal recourse to the legal system.[3]

The Fourteenth Amendment itself was, as Kenneth Karst wrote, an act of **"positive law,"** that is, a law made to fit a particular circumstance. At the time of its passage, the sponsors of the Fourteenth Amendment had wished to extend to the South "a system of liberties and equality under the law that already existed elsewhere in the nation."[4]

The Incorporation Issue

The Fourteenth Amendment was passed as a standard that would guarantee both due process and equal protection under the laws for all persons. The courts did not agree. Many jurists still believed, as John Marshall stated in the *Barron v. Mayor of Baltimore* decision, that the states were "distinct governments framed by different persons and for different purposes."[5] Marshall's statement in the *Barron* decision was plain: The Bill of Rights limits only the national government and not the state governments. The *Barron* decision is still the general rule of law. We shall see, though, that it has been greatly modified in practice through later interpretations of the Fourteenth Amendment.

In 1873, in the *Slaughter-House Cases,*[6] the U.S. Supreme Court upheld the principle of **dual citizenship,** arguing that to deprive states of their authority and their identity would "fetter and degrade state governments." The Court refused to apply the guarantees of the Bill of Rights to the states under the Fourteenth Amendment's privileges and immunities clause. A Louisiana law prohibited livestock yards and slaughterhouses within New Orleans, except for the Crescent City Company's operation. Butchers and others adversely affected sought to have the law declared void, in part under the Fourteenth Amendment. The Supreme Court held that the Fourteenth Amendment creates two types of citizenship—federal and state—and that the privileges and immunities clause extends federal constitutional protection only to the privileges and immunities of national citizenship. The Court reasoned that the Louisiana

POSITIVE LAW
Laws made in and by legislatures to fit a particular circumstance.

DUAL CITIZENSHIP
The condition of being a citizen of two sovereign political units; being a citizen of both a state and the nation.

---

[3]Section 2 of the amendment contains the first use in the Constitution of *male.*
[4]Kenneth L. Karst, "Not One Law at Rome and Another at Athens: The Fourteenth Amendment in Nationwide Application," *Washington University Law Quarterly,* no. 3 (Summer 1972), p. 383.
[5]*Barron v. Mayor of Baltimore,* 7 Peters 243 (1833).
[6]83 U.S. (16 Wall) 36.

statute did not infringe on any of the privileges and immunities of national citizenship.

Only gradually, and never completely, did the Supreme Court accept the **incorporation theory**—that no state could act in violation of the U.S. Bill of Rights. By holding that those rights are protected against actions of the states, as well as of the national government, the Court has made their meanings uniform. In doing so, the Court has been deciding which rights are basic or essential to the American concept of ordered liberty. Table 4-1 shows the rights that the Court has incorporated into the Fourteenth Amendment and in which case it first applied these protections. The practical implementation of the Fourteenth Amendment has taken place relatively slowly through the doctrine of selective incorporation.

The last hundred years of Supreme Court decisions have bound the fifty states to accept most of the guarantees for their respective citizens that are contained in the U.S. Bill of Rights. The exceptions have usually involved the right to bear arms and to refuse to quarter soldiers and the right to a grand jury hearing. Thus, for all intents and purposes, the Bill of Rights provisions of the national Constitution must be uniformly applied by individual state governments to their laws and practices.

Just as judicial interpretation of the Fourteenth Amendment required more than a hundred years to "nationalize" the Bill of Rights, judicial interpretation has shaped the true nature of those rights as they apply to individuals in the United States. As we shall see in the following pages, there have been numerous

INCORPORATION THEORY
The view that most of the protections of the Bill of Rights are incorporated into the Fourteenth Amendment's protection against state governments.

TABLE 4-1
Incorporating the Bill of Rights into the Fourteenth Amendment

YEAR	ISSUE	AMENDMENT INVOLVED	COURT CASE
1925	Freedom of speech	I	*Gitlow v. New York*, 268 U.S. 652
1931	Freedom of the press	I	*Near v. Minnesota*, 283 U.S. 697
1932	Right to a lawyer in capital punishment cases	VI	*Powell v. Alabama*, 287 U.S. 45
1934	Freedom of religion	I	*Hamilton v. Regents of the University of California*, 293 U.S. 245
1937	Freedom of assembly and right to petition	I	*De Jonge v. Oregon*, 299 U.S. 353
1947	Separation of state and church	I	*Everson v. Board of Education*, 330 U.S. 1
1948	Right to a public trial	VI	In re *Oliver*, 333 U.S. 257
1961	No unreasonable searches and seizures	IV	*Mapp v. Ohio*, 367 U.S. 643
1962	No cruel and unusual punishment	VIII	*Robinson v. California*, 370 U.S. 660
1963	Right to a lawyer in all criminal felony cases	VI	*Gideon v. Wainwright*, 372 U.S. 335
1964	No compulsory self-incrimination	V	*Malloy v. Hogan*, 378 U.S. 1
1965	Right to privacy	I	*Griswold v. Connecticut*, 381 U.S. 479
1966	Right to an impartial jury	VI	*Parker v. Gladden*, 385 U.S. 363
1967	Right to a speedy trial	VI	*Klopfer v. North Carolina*, 386 U.S. 213
1973	No double jeopardy	V	*Colgrove v. Battin*, 413 U.S. 149

DID YOU KNOW?

That Samuel Argall, governor of Virginia from 1616 to 1618, punished those who failed to attend church with prison terms and forced labor and banned all forms of amusement on Sunday?

conflicts over the meaning of such simple phrases as freedom of press and freedom of religion. To understand what freedoms we actually have, we have to examine some of those conflicts.

■ FREEDOM OF RELIGION

In the United States freedom of religion consists of two principal precepts as they are presented in the First Amendment. The first has to do with separation of church and state, and the second guarantees free exercise of religion.

The Separation of Church and State

> Congress shall make no law respecting an establishment of religion, . . .

In the words of President Jefferson, the establishment clause was designed to create a "wall of separation of Church and State."[7] Perhaps Jefferson was thinking about the religious intolerance that characterized the first colonies. Although many of the American colonies were founded by groups in pursuit of religious freedom, they were nonetheless quite intolerant of religious nonconformity within their communities. He undoubtedly was also aware that state religions were the rule; among the original thirteen American colonies, nine of them had official religions.

The **establishment clause** in the First Amendment means at least the following:

> Neither a state nor the federal government can set up a church. Neither can pass laws which aid one religion, aid all religions, or prefer one religion over another. Neither can force nor influence a person to go to or to remain away from church against his will or force him to profess a belief or disbelief in any religion. No person can be punished for entertaining or professing religious beliefs or disbeliefs, for church attendance or nonattendance. No tax in any amount, large or small, can be

ESTABLISHMENT CLAUSE
The part of the First Amendment prohibiting the establishment of a church officially supported by the national government. It is applied to questions of state and local government aid to religious organizations and schools, of the legality of allowing or requiring school prayers, and of the teaching of evolution versus fundamentalist theories of creation.

[7]See Frank J. Sorauf, *Wall of Separation* (Princeton, N.J.: Princeton University Press, 1976).

Fundamentalists Vicki Frost and her husband challenged textbooks as being too secular and violating their freedom of religion. Can a public school teach about religion and still not violate the establishment clause?

levied to support any religious activities or institutions, whatever they may be called, or whatever form they may adopt to teach or practice religion. Neither a state nor the federal government can, openly or secretly, participate in the affairs of any religious organizations or groups and vice versa.[8]

The establishment clause covers all conflicts about such matters as state and local government aid to religious organizations and schools, the legality of allowing or requiring school prayers, and the teaching of evolution versus fundamentalist theories of creation.

The Issue of School Prayer.   Do the states have the right to promote religion in general, without making any attempt to establish a particular religion? That is the question in the issue of school prayer and was the precise question presented in 1962 in *Engel v. Vitale*,[9] the so-called Regents' Prayer Case in New York. The State Board of Regents of New York had suggested that a prayer be spoken aloud in the public schools at the beginning of each day. The recommended prayer was:

> Almighty God, we acknowledge our dependence upon Thee,
> And we beg Thy blessings upon us, our parents, our teachers, and our Country.

Such a prayer was implemented in many New York public schools.

A number of students' parents challenged the action of the regents, maintaining that it violated the establishment clause of the First Amendment. At trial the parents lost. However, the Supreme Court ruled that the regents' action was unconstitutional because "the constitutional prohibition against laws respecting an establishment of a religion must at least mean that in this country it is no part of the business of government to compose official prayers for any group of the American people to recite as part of a religious program carried on by any government."[10]

In 1963, the Supreme Court outlawed daily readings of the Bible and recitation of the Lord's Prayer in public schools.[11]

Children praying in school. Is this a violation of the First Amendment? If so, why?

Although the Supreme Court has repeatedly ruled against officially sponsored prayer and Bible-reading sessions in public schools, other means for bringing some form of religious expression into public education have been attempted. In 1983, the Tennessee legislature passed a bill requiring public school classes to begin each day with a minute of silence. This followed several years of efforts by the Tennessee legislature to bring "meditation, prayer, or silent reflection into school." Alabama also had a similar law. In 1985, the Supreme Court struck down as unconstitutional the Alabama law authorizing one minute of silence in all public schools for prayer or meditation. The majority of the court indicated that since the law specifically endorsed prayer, it appeared to support religion.[12]

Many school districts, particularly in the South, continue to operate in violation of the Court's prayer ban. A coalition of conservatives and southerners has proposed a constitutional amendment that would overturn the 1963 ruling.

Forbidding the Teaching of Evolution.   A rather short-lived effort by certain religious groups took place to forbid the teaching of evolution in public

[8]*Everson v. Board of Education,* 330 U.S. 1 (1947).
[9]370 U.S. 421.
[10]Ibid.
[11]*Abington School District v. Schempp,* 374 U.S. 203.
[12]*Wallace v. Jaffree,* 472 U.S. 38 (1985).

schools. One such law was passed in Arkansas, only to be struck down by the Supreme Court in the 1968 *Epperson v. Arkansas* case.[13] The Court held that the Arkansas legislation violated the separation of church and state, for it imposed religious beliefs on students. The Arkansas legislature then passed a law requiring the teaching of the biblical story of creation alongside with evolution. In the 1982 Supreme Court case *McLean v. Arkansas,* this law was declared unconstitutional.

Aid to Church-Related Schools.   Throughout the United States, all property owners except religious, educational, fraternal, literary, scientific, and similar nonprofit institutions must pay property taxes. A large part of the proceeds of such taxes goes to support public schools. But not all school-age children attend public schools. Fully 12 percent attend private schools, of which 85 percent have religious affiliations. Numerous cases have reached the Supreme Court in which the Court has tried to draw a fine line between permissible public aid to students in church-related schools and impermissible public aid to religion.

It is at the elementary and secondary level where these issues have arisen most often. In a series of cases, the Supreme Court has allowed states to use tax funds for lunches, textbooks, speech-and-hearing-problem diagnostic services, standardized tests, and transportation in church-operated elementary and secondary schools.[14] In a number of cases, however, the Supreme Court has held unconstitutional state programs helping church-related schools. In *Lemon v. Kurtzman,*[15] the Court judged that direct state aid might not be used to subsidize religious instruction. A Pennsylvania law had provided for state payments to private schools to cover costs of teachers' salaries in nonreligious courses. The Court held that this directly benefited parochial schools and the churches that sponsored them. The payments required close state supervision—too close. The Court in the *Lemon* case gave its most general statement on the constitutionality of governmental aid to religious schools, stating that the aid had to be secular in aim and that the government must avoid "an excessive entanglement with religion." In other cases, the Court has denied state reimbursements to religious schools for field trips and for developing achievement tests.

The Free Exercise of Religious Beliefs

FREE EXERCISE CLAUSE
The provision of the First Amendment guaranteeing the free exercise of religion.

The First Amendment constrains Congress from prohibiting the free exercise of religion. Does this **free exercise clause** mean that no type of religious practice can be prohibited or restricted by government? Certainly, a person can hold any religious belief that she or he wants; or a person can have no religious belief. When, however, religious *practices* work against public policy and the public welfare, the government can act. For example, regardless of a child's or parent's religious beliefs, the government can require certain types of vaccinations. Similarly, public school students can be required to study from textbooks chosen by school authorities. The sale and use of marijuana for religious purposes has been held illegal because a religion cannot make legal

[13]393 U.S. 97.
[14]See *Everson v. Board of Education,* 330 U.S. 1 (1947), *Meek v. Pittenger,* 421 U.S. 349 (1975), and *Committee for Public Education v. Regan,* 444 U.S. 646 (1980).
[15]403 U.S. 602 (1971).

HIGHLIGHT

Bible Clubs Get the Green Light

In 1984, Congress passed the federal Equal Access Act, which forbids discrimination against any student group on the basis of its religious, philosophical, or political viewpoint. Soon after, Bridget Murgans Mayhew, then a senior at Westside High School in Omaha, Nebraska, attempted to form a Christian bible club that was to meet after school on the school grounds. The public school district in Omaha said no. Mayhew sued. She won in the U.S. Court of Appeals for the Eighth Circuit in St. Louis. The Omaha school district appealed. On June 4, 1990, by a vote of eight to one, Ms. Mayhew prevailed. The Supreme Court rejected the argument that the 1984 Equal Access Act breached the constitutionally required separation between church and state. The federal law was not an unconstitutional "establishment of religion" by the government.*

Actually, the 1990 decision was simply an extension of the 1981 Supreme Court ruling in *Widmar v. Vincent*,** in which the Supreme Court held that public universities must permit student religious groups to meet on the same terms afforded other student organizations. Speaking for the Court, Justice Sandra Day O'Connor said, "We think the logic of *Widmar* applies with equal force to the Equal Access Act. We think that secondary school students are mature enough and are likely to understand that a school does not endorse or support student speech, that it merely permits [speech] on a nondiscriminatory basis."

*Board of Education of Westside Community Schools v. Mergens, __U.S. __ , 110 S.Ct. 2356.
**454 U.S. 263 (1981)

what would otherwise be illegal. Conducting religious rites that result in beheaded and gutted animals being left in public streets normally is not allowed.

The courts and lawmakers are constantly faced with a dilemma. On the one hand, no law may be made that requires someone to do something contrary to his or her religious beliefs or teachings because this would interfere with the free exercise of religion. On the other hand, if certain individuals, because of their religious beliefs, are exempted from specific laws, then such exemptions might tend to favor religion and be contrary to the establishment clause. The original view of the Court was that while religious beliefs are protected by the law, acting on those beliefs may not be. For instance, children of Jehovah's Witnesses are not required to say the Pledge of Allegiance at school,[16] but their parents cannot prevent them from accepting medical treatment (such as blood transfusions) if in fact their lives are in danger. The current view of the Court is that in all but a few situations a state is free to require everyone to comply with a law that is generally valid. A state can make exceptions for religious practices, but the Constitution does not require it to do so.[17]

■ FREEDOM OF EXPRESSION

Perhaps the most frequently invoked freedom that Americans have is the right to free speech and a free press without government interference. These rights guarantee each person a right of free expression by all means of communication and ensure all persons a full discussion of public affairs. Each of us has the right to have our say, and all of us have the right to hear what others say. For the most part, Americans can criticize public officials and their actions without fear of reprisal or imprisonment by any branch of the government.

[16]*West Virginia State Board of Education v. Barnette*, 319 U.S. 624 (1943).
[17]*Employment Division, Department of Human Resources of Oregon v. Smith*, __ U.S. __, 110 S.Ct. 1595 (1990).

DID YOU KNOW?

That noncitizens have as much right to the freedoms of speech, press, and religion as citizens do?

CLEAR AND PRESENT DANGER TEST
The test proposed by Justice Holmes for determining when government may restrict free speech. Restrictions are permissible, he argued, only when speech provokes a "clear and present danger" to the public order.

PREFERRED-POSITION TEST
A court test used in determining the limits of free expression guaranteed by the First Amendment, requiring that limitations only be applied on speech to avoid imminent, serious, and important evils.

SLIDING-SCALE TEST
Used as a criterion in cases in which a careful examination of the facts of each individual case must be undertaken.

BAD-TENDENCY RULE
Speech or other First Amendment freedoms may permissibly be curtailed if there is a possibility that such expression might lead to some "evil."

PRIOR RESTRAINT
Restraining an action before the activity has actually occurred. It involves censorship as opposed to subsequent punishment.

Permitted Restrictions

At various times, restrictions on expression have been permitted. A description of several such restrictions follows.

Clear and Present Danger.   When a person's remarks present a clear and present danger to the peace or public order, they can be constitutionally curtailed. Justice Holmes used this reasoning in 1919 when examining the case of a socialist who had been convicted for violating the Espionage Act. Holmes stated:

> The question in every case is whether the words are used in such circumstances and are of such a nature as to create a *clear and present danger* that they will bring about the substantive evils that Congress has a right to prevent. It is a question of proximity and degree. (Emphasis added)[18]

Thus, according to the **clear and present danger test,** expression may be restricted if evidence exists that such expression would cause a condition, actual or imminent, that Congress has the power to prevent. Commenting on this test, Justice Brandeis in 1920 said, "Correctly applied, it will reserve the right of free speech . . . from suppression by tyrannists, well-meaning majorities, and from abuse by irresponsible, fanatical minorities."[19] A related test includes the **preferred-position test.** This test comes almost as close to the position that freedom of expression may never be curtailed. Only if the government is able to show that limitations on speech are absolutely necessary to avoid imminent, serious, and important evils are such limitations allowed. Another test is called the **sliding-scale test.** Careful examination of the facts of each individual case must be undertaken.

The Bad-Tendency Rule.   According to the **bad-tendency rule,** speech or other First Amendment freedoms may permissibly be curtailed if there is a possibility that such expression might lead to some "evil." In *Gitlow v. New York,*[20] a member of a left-wing group was convicted of violating New York state's criminal anarchy statute when he published and distributed a pamphlet urging the violent overthrow of the United States government. In its majority opinion, the Court held that although the First Amendment afforded protection against state incursions on freedom of expression, Gitlow could be legally punished in this particular instance because his expression would tend to bring about evils that the state had a right to prevent.

No Prior Restraint.   **Prior restraint** is defined as restraining an activity before that activity has actually occurred. It involves censorship as opposed to subsequent punishment. Prior restraint of expression would require, for example, a permit before a speech could be made, a newspaper published, or a movie or TV show exhibited. Most, if not all, Supreme Court justices have been especially critical of any governmental action that imposes prior restraint on expression:

> A prior restraint on expression comes to this Court with a "heavy presumption" against its constitutionality. . . . The government thus carries a heavy burden of showing justification for the enforcement of such a restraint.[21]

The prior restraint case of the Pentagon Papers is discussed in the Highlight.

[18]*Schenck v. United States,* 249 U.S. 47 (1919).
[19]*Schaefer v. United States,* 251 U.S. 466 (1920).
[20]268 U.S. 652 (1925).
[21]*Nebraska Press Association v. Stuart,* 427 U.S. 539 (1976). See also *Near v. Minnesota,* 283 U.S. 697 (1931).

HIGHLIGHT

No Prior Restraint: The Case of the Pentagon Papers

On June 13, 1971, the *New York Times* carried the first article on a forty-seven volume classified U.S. government history of American policy in Vietnam from 1945 to 1967. The second article appeared the following day. A few days later, on June 18, the *Washington Post* also began a series on the secret study, based on documents it had secured. U.S. Attorney General John Mitchell obtained an injunction ordering the suspension of the publication of this material by both the *Times* and the *Post.* By June 24, both cases, *New York Times Co. v. United States* and *United States v. The Washington Post,* were before the Supreme Court.* The Justices

*403 U.S. 713.

were deeply divided on the constitutional issues raised by these cases.**

The key issue in the so-called Pentagon Papers was whether Americans had the right to know (and the press the right to inform them) of information that the government claimed might endanger national security. The First Amendment to the Constitution did not grant absolute rights to the press in publishing such material, and thus under certain circumstances prior restraint (government censorship) might be justified. Was this such a case? Would further publication immediately endanger

**According to Bob Woodward and Scott Armstrong, *The Brethren* (New York: Simon and Schuster, 1979).

national security or the lives and rights, for example, of hundreds of U.S. soldiers? Would publication jeopardize U.S. national security in the long run?

In an unusually speedy decision, reached after only four days in conference, the Court ruled six to three in favor of the newspapers' right to publish the information. The case affirmed the no prior restraint doctrine but left intact the government's right to prosecute after publication if the act of the publishers was claimed to be illegal.

The Protection of Symbolic Speech

Not all expression is in words or in writing. Gestures, movements, articles of clothing, and so on may under certain circumstances be considered **symbolic,** or nonverbal, **speech,** and such speech is given substantial protection today by our courts. During the Vietnam war (1964–1973), when students around the country began wearing black armbands in protest, a Des Moines, Iowa, school administrator issued a regulation prohibiting students in the Des Moines

SYMBOLIC SPEECH
Nonverbal expression of beliefs, which is given substantial protection by the courts.

Mary Beth Tinker and her brother John displaying the armbands that the Court ruled were "symbolic speech." How should the Court determine what constitutes such speech?

DID YOU KNOW?

That in 1990 the New York Federal Court of Appeals overturned a lower court's ruling that begging was a form of free speech protected by the First Amendment? The court also upheld the right of the state to ban loitering for the purpose of begging.

COMMERCIAL SPEECH
Advertising statements that have increasingly been given First Amendment protection.

School District from wearing them. The U.S. Supreme Court ruled that such a ban violated the free speech clause of the First Amendment. It reasoned that the school district was unable to show that the wearing of the black armbands had disrupted normal school activities. Furthermore, the school's ruling was discriminatory as it selected certain forms of symbolic speech for banning; lapel crosses and fraternity rings, for instance, symbolically speak of a person's affiliations, but these were not banned.[22] In 1989, in *Texas v. Johnson,* the Supreme Court ruled that state laws that prohibited the burning of the American flag as part of a peaceful protest also violated the freedom of expression protected by the First Amendment. Congress responded by passing the Flag Protection Act of 1989, which was ruled unconstitutional by the Supreme Court in June, 1990. Congress and President Bush immediately pledged to work for a constitutional amendment. See the Highlight on page 105 for a discussion of this controversy.

The Protection of Commercial Speech

Commercial speech is usually defined as advertising statements. Can advertisers use their First Amendment rights to prevent restrictions on the content of commercial advertising? Until the 1970s, the Supreme Court held that such speech was not protected by the First Amendment. By the mid-1970s, however, more and more commercial speech was brought under First Amendment protection. According to Justice Harry A. Blackmun, "Advertising, however tasteless and excessive it sometimes may seem, is nonetheless dissemination of information as to who is producing and selling what product for what reason and at what price."[23] If consumers are to make more intelligent marketplace decisions, they need to have the "free flow of commercial information," according to Blackmun and the Court.

Nonadvertising "speech" by businesses has also achieved First Amendment protection. In *First National Bank v. Belotti,*[24] the Supreme Court examined a Massachusetts statute prohibiting corporations from spending money to influence "the vote on any question submitted to the voters, other than one materially affecting any of the property, business, or assets of the corporation." That statute was struck down as unconstitutional because it unnecessarily prohibited "free speech." Some critics of the Court see in such decisions a strong bias toward property rights (the rights of corporations to use their property without regulation) and against the interests of consumers and the general citizenry. Similarly, the Court has held that a law forbidding a corporation from using bill inserts to express its views on controversial issues also violates the First Amendment.[25] On the other hand, laws limiting the amount that a corporation or an unincorporated association may contribute to a political candidate have been upheld.[26]

Unprotected Speech: Obscenity

Numerous state and federal statutes make it a crime to disseminate obscene materials. All such state and federal statutes prohibiting obscenity have been deemed constitutional if the definition of obscenity conforms with that of the

[22]*Tinker v. Des Moines School District,* 393 U.S. 503 (1969).
[23]*Virginia State Board of Pharmacy v. Virginia Citizens Consumer Council, Inc.,* 425 U.S. 748 (1976).
[24]435 U.S. 765 (1978).
[25]*Consolidated Edison Co. v. Public Service Comm'n,* 447 U.S. 550 (1980).
[26]*California Medical Ass'n v. Federal Election Comm'n.,* 453 U.S. 182 (1981).

HIGHLIGHT

Symbolic Speech and the American Flag

The flag is often displayed at political rallies and demonstrations to make a point, whether that point is to encourage feelings of patriotism or to provide a focus for protest. As a form of protest, during the Vietnam war, some Americans who opposed the role of the United States in that conflict burned American flags. In reaction, forty-eight states and the federal government outlawed burning or otherwise desecrating American flags. But the question remained whether burning the flag was symbolic speech protected under the Constitution.

During the 1984 Republican National Convention in Dallas, Texas, in a demonstration in front of city hall, Gregory Johnson doused an American flag with kerosene and set it on fire, as demonstrators chanted, "America, the red, white, and blue, we spit on you." Johnson was convicted of violating Texas's law against flag desecration. The Texas Court of Criminal Appeals overturned his conviction. The state appealed to the Supreme Court of the United States, arguing that the law was designed to preserve the flag as a "symbol of nationhood."

Two weeks before the fourth of July, 1989, the Supreme Court announced

its decision in the case—no law could prohibit political protesters from burning the American flag, as long as the protest was conducted peacefully. For the five to four majority, Justice Brennan wrote, "We do not consecrate the flag by punishing its desecration, for in

doing so we dilute the freedom that this cherished emblem represents."

Burning the flag was seen as a form of free expression. Brennan explained that "the Government may not prohibit the expression of an idea simply because society finds the idea itself offensive or disagreeable. . . . The way to preserve the flag's special role is not to punish those who feel differently about these matters. It is to persuade them that they are wrong."

The Court's decision evoked immediate reaction. Members of Congress introduced legislation effectively to overrule the decision. The Flag Protection Act of 1989 was passed, only to be declared unconstitutional by the Supreme Court in 1990. The controversy flared up again. A *New York Times*/CBS News poll taken in that summer found that 83 percent of Americans wanted flag burning to be against the law. Almost 60 percent favored a constitutional amendment. Supporters of such an amendment argue that the government has a legitimate right to preserve the flag's symbolic value even if doing so interferes with free speech.

---

then-current U.S. Supreme Court. Basically, the courts have not been willing to extend constitutional protections of free speech to what they consider obscene materials. For example, in *Roth v. United States*,[27] the Supreme Court stated, "Obscenity is not within the area of constitutionally protected speech or press."

But what is obscenity? As Justice Potter Stewart once said, even though he could not define it, "I know it when I see it."[28] The problem, of course, is that even if it were agreed on, the definition of obscenity changes with the times. Victorians deeply disapproved of the "loose" morals of the Elizabethan Age. The works of Mark Twain and Edgar Rice Burroughs have at times been considered obscene (after all, Tarzan and Jane were not legally wed).

The Supreme Court has grappled from time to time with the problem of specifying an operationally effective definition of obscenity. In the *Roth* case

[27]354 U.S. 476 (1957).
[28]*Jacobellis v. Ohio*, 378 U.S. 184 (1964).

Although pornography is not protected by the Constitution, it is difficult to define. Why do some communities ban movie theaters such as this while others do not?

in 1957, the Court coined the phrase "utterly without redeeming social importance." Since then Supreme Court justices have viewed numerous films to determine if they met this criterion. By the 1970s, the justices had recognized the failure of the *Roth* definition. In *Miller v. California,* Chief Justice Burger ultimately created a formal list of requirements, known as the Roth–Miller test of obscenity, that currently must be met for material to be legally obscene: (1) The average person finds that it violates contemporary community standards. (2) The work taken as a whole appeals to prurient interest in sex. (3) The work shows patently offensive sexual conduct. (4) The work lacks serious redeeming literary, artistic, political, or scientific merit.[29]

The problem, of course, is that one person's prurient interest is another person's artistic pleasure. The Court went on to state that the definition of prurient interest would be determined by the community's standards. The Court avoided presenting a definition of obscenity, leaving this determination to local and state authorities. Consequently, the *Miller* case has had widely inconsistent applications. Obscenity is still a constitutionally unsettled area, whether it deals with speech or printed or filmed materials. Feminists, often in alliance with religious fundamentalists, have begun a drive to enact new antipornography laws because of an increased amount of violence in pornography and more child pornography. In 1982, the Supreme Court upheld state laws making it illegal to sell material showing sexual performances by minors. Most recently, the Court has ruled that states can outlaw the possession of child pornography in the home. The Court reasoned that the ban on private possession is justified because owning the material perpetuates commercial demand for it and for exploitation of the children involved.[30]

Recently, governments and media groups have been confronted with the issue of regulating the lyrics and covers of record albums, the content of monologues by "shock" comedians, and other issues relating to obscenity in movies and television. In June, 1990 a federal judge in Florida ruled that a

[29]*Miller v. California,* 413 U.S. 5 (1973).
[30]*Osborne v. Ohio,* _____U.S. _____, 110 S.Ct. 1691 (1990).

The musicians of 2 Live Crew have been charged with obscenity in their performances although not convicted. To what extent should entertainment be censored to protect the community?

"rap" album by the group 2 Live Crew was obscene under the Supreme Court's 1973 criteria of contemporary community standards. Several days later, two members of the band were arrested in Broward County after a local live performance and at least one record-store owner was also arrested for continuing to sell the group's albums. The owner was convicted but not the singers.

Unprotected Speech: Slander

Can you say anything you want about someone else? Not really. Individuals are protected from **defamation of character,** which is defined as wrongfully hurting a person's good reputation. The law has imposed a general duty on all persons to refrain from making false, defamatory statements about others. Breaching this duty orally involves the wrongdoing called **slander.**[31]

Legally, slander is the public uttering of a statement that holds a person up for contempt, ridicule, or hatred. Slanderous public uttering means that the defamatory statements are made to, or within the hearing of, persons other than the defamed party. If one person calls another dishonest, manipulative, and incompetent when no one else is around, that does not constitute slander. The message is not communicated to a third party. If, however, a third party accidentally overhears defamatory statements, the courts have generally held that this constitutes public uttering and therefore slander, which is prohibited. Furthermore, any individual who repeats defamatory statements is legally responsible, even if that person reveals the source of such statements. Hence many radio stations have instituted seven-second delays for live broadcasts, such as talk shows, allowing them to "bleep" out possibly defamatory statements.

DEFAMATION OF CHARACTER
Wrongfully hurting a person's good reputation. The law has imposed a general duty on all persons to refrain from making false, defamatory statements about others.

SLANDER
The public uttering of a statement that holds a person up for contempt, ridicule, or hatred, when the defamatory statement is made to, or within the hearing of, persons other than the defamed party.

Fighting Words and Hecklers' Veto

The Supreme Court has created a limited class of speech "which by their very utterance inflict injury or intend to incite an immediate breach of peace that governments may constitutionally punish. . . ."[32] The reference here is to a prohibition on public speakers from using **fighting words.** These may include racial, religious, or ethnic slurs that are so inflammatory that they will provoke the "average" listener to fight. Under the Supreme Court leadership of Chief Justice Burger, fighting words were more and more narrowly construed. For example, a four-letter word used about the draft and emblazoned on a sweater is not considered a fighting word, unless it is directed at a specific person.

Members of a crowd listening to a speech are similarly prohibited from exercising a **hecklers' veto.** When hecklers do so, they are threatening disruption or violence and they are vetoing the essential rights of the speaker.

FIGHTING WORDS
Those words that when uttered by a public speaker are so inflammatory that they could provoke the average listener to violence; the words are usually of a racial, religious, or ethnic type.

HECKLERS' VETO
Boisterous and generally disruptive behavior by listeners of public speakers that, in effect, vetoes the public speakers' right to speak.

■ FREEDOM OF THE PRESS

Freedom of the press can be regarded as a special instance of freedom of speech. Of course, at the time of the framing of the Constitution, the press meant only newspapers, magazines, and perhaps pamphlets. As technology has modified the ways we disseminate information, so too have the laws touching on freedom of the press been modified. But what can and cannot

---

[31]Breaching it in writing involves the wrongdoing called *libel,* which is discussed in the next section.
[32]*Cohen v. California,* 403 U.S. 15 (1971).

be printed still occupies an important place in constitutional law (see Highlight on prior restraint and the Pentagon Papers in this chapter).

Defamation in Writing

LIBEL
Defamation of character in writing.

ACTIONABLE
Furnishing grounds for a lawsuit.

As slander is oral defamation, **libel** is defamation in writing. As with slander, the wrongdoing of libel is **actionable** only if the defamatory statements are observed by a third party. If one person writes another a private letter accusing him or her of embezzling funds, that does not constitute libel. It is interesting that the courts have generally held that dictating a letter to a secretary constitutes publication, and therefore, if defamation has occurred, the wrongdoing of libel is actionable.

Newspapers are often involved in libel suits. *New York Times Co. v. Sullivan* explored an important question about public officials and liability.[33] Sullivan, a commissioner of the city of Montgomery, Alabama, sued the *New York Times* for libel because it had printed an advertisement critical of the actions of Montgomery officials during the Civil Rights movement. Under Alabama law, the jury found that the statements were in fact libelous on their face, so that damages could be awarded to Mr. Sullivan without proof of the extent of any injury to him. The jury awarded him a half-million dollars and the Alabama Supreme Court upheld the judgment.

ACTUAL MALICE
Actual desire and intent to see another suffer by one's actions.

The U.S. Supreme Court, however, unanimously reversed the judgment. It found that Alabama's rule of liability as applied to public officials in performance of their duty deprived critics of their rights of free speech under the First and Fourteenth Amendments.[34] Speaking for the Court, Justice William J. Brennan, Jr., stated that libel laws such as those in Alabama would inhibit the unfettered discussion of public issues. The Court indicated that only when a statement was made with **actual malice** against a public official could damages be obtained.

A Free Press versus a Fair Trial: Gag Orders

Another major freedom of the press issue concerns newspaper reports of criminal trials. Amendment VI of the Bill of Rights guarantees a fair trial. In other words, the accused have rights. But the Bill of Rights also guarantees freedom of the press. What if the two appear to be in conflict? Which one prevails?

"GAG" ORDERS
Orders issued by judges restricting publication of news about a trial in progress or a pretrial hearing in order to protect the accused's right to a fair trial.

Jurors certainly may be influenced by reading news stories about the trial in which they are participating. In the 1970s, judges increasingly issued **"gag" orders** which restricted the publication of news about a trial in progress or even a pretrial hearing. A landmark case was decided by the Supreme Court in 1976,[35] based on the trial of E. C. Simants, who was charged with the murder of a neighboring family. Since the murder occurred in the course of a sexual assault, details of the crime were quite lurid. A local Nebraska judge issued an order prohibiting the press from reporting information gleaned in a pretrial hearing; since there were only 860 people in the town, the judge believed that such publicity would prejudice potential jurors.

[33]376 U.S. 254 (1964).
[34]Remember that the Fourteenth Amendment "nationalizes" most of the liberties listed in the Bill of Rights.
[35]*Nebraska Press Association v. Stuart*, 427 U.S. 539 (1976).

The Supreme Court unanimously ruled that the Nebraska judge's gag order had violated the First Amendment's freedom of the press clause. Chief Justice Burger indicated that even pervasive adverse pretrial publicity did not necessarily lead to an unfair trial, and that prior restraints on publication were not justified. Some justices even went so far as to indicate that gag orders are never justified.

In spite of the *Nebraska Press Association* ruling, the Court has upheld certain types of gag orders. In *Gannett Company v. De Pasquale,*[36] the highest court held that if a judge found a reasonable probability that news publicity would harm a defendant's right to a fair trial, the court could impose a gag rule: "Members of the public have no constitutional right under the Sixth and Fourteenth Amendments to *attend* criminal trials." The *Nebraska* and *Gannett* cases, however, involved pretrial hearings. Could a judge impose a gag order on an entire trial, including pretrial hearings? In *Richmond Newspapers, Inc. v. Virginia,*[37] the Court ruled that actual trials must be open to the public except under unusual circumstances.

Confidentiality and Reporters' Work Papers

By the 1980s, the courts had begun to rule in cases that involved the press's responsibility to law-enforcement agencies. In one, Myron Farber, a *New York Times* reporter who had possession of extensive notes related to a murder case, was jailed in 1978 in New Jersey for not turning this material over to law-enforcement officials. The Supreme Court refused to review the case.[38]

A widely publicized libel suit—*Carol Burnett v. The National Enquirer.*

Moreover, in several cases the police were permitted to search newspaper offices for documents related to cases under investigation. In general, the trend of the courts has moved in the direction of requiring the press to cooperate in criminal investigations to a much greater degree than it had before. These cases obviously raise a serious question about the confidentiality of working papers and background information that reporters obtain in the course of doing stories or investigative reporting. The question is not only who has the legitimate ownership and the right to privacy of those notes but also whether these decisions compromise the freedom of the press guaranteed by the Constitution.

One important case involved the *Stanford Daily.*[39] The campus newspaper of Stanford University had its offices searched by police officers with a search warrant who were looking for photographs that would identify demonstrators who may have been responsible for injuries to the police. In this particular case, the Court ruled that the protection of confidentiality, and therefore the protection of the First Amendment's guarantees of a free press, was less important under the specific circumstances than the needs of law-enforcement agencies to secure information necessary for prosecution. Congress responded to the *Stanford Daily* case by enacting the Privacy Protection Act.[40] This law applies to state as well as federal law-enforcement personnel. It limits their power to obtain evidence from the news media by search warrant and in many instances requires that they use a subpoena. Also, more than half the states have enacted so-called "shield laws." These laws protect reporters against having to reveal their sources and other confidential information.

[36]443 U.S. 368 (1979).
[37]448 U.S. 555 (1980).
[38]*New York Times Co. v. Jascalevich*, 439 U.S. 1317 (1978).
[39]*Zurcher v. Stanford Daily*, 436 U.S. 547 (1978).
[40]42 U.S.C. Sections 2000aa to 2000aa-12.

Other Information Channels: Motion Pictures, Radio, and TV

The Founding Fathers could not have imagined the ways in which information is disseminated today. Nonetheless, they fashioned the Constitution into a flexible instrument that could respond to social and technological changes. First Amendment freedoms have been applied differently to newer forms of information dissemination.

Motion Pictures: Some Prior Restraint.   The most onerous of all forms of government interference with expression is prior restraint. As we noted, the Supreme Court has not declared all forms of censorship unconstitutional but does require an exceptional justification for such restraint. Only in a few cases has the Supreme Court upheld prior restraint of published materials.

The Court's reluctance to accept prior restraint is less evident in the case of motion pictures. In the first half of the twentieth century, films were routinely submitted to local censorship boards. In 1968, the Supreme Court ruled that a film can only be banned under a law that provides for a prompt hearing at which the film is shown to be obscene. Today, few local censorship boards exist. Instead, audiences have come to rely on the film industry's rating system.

Radio and TV: Limited Protection.   Of all forms of communication, television is perhaps the most important and radio runs a close second. Radio and television broadcasting has the most limited First Amendment protection. In 1934, the national government established the Federal Communications Commission (FCC) to regulate electromagnetic wave frequencies. No one has a right to use the airwaves without a license granted by the FCC. The FCC grants licenses for limited periods and imposes numerous regulations on broadcasting. Although Congress has denied the FCC the authority to censor what is transmitted, the FCC can impose sanctions on those radio or TV stations broadcasting "filthy words," even if the words are not legally obscene.[41] Also, the FCC has occasionally refused to renew licenses of broadcasters who have presumably not "served the public interest." Perhaps one of the more controversial of the FCC's rulings was its **fairness doctrine,** imposing on owners of broadcast licenses an obligation to present "both" sides of significant public issues. In 1987, the FCC repealed the fairness doctrine because it determined that the doctrine was unconstitutional.

FAIRNESS DOCTRINE
An FCC regulation affecting broadcasting media, which required that "equal time" be made available to legitimate opposing political groups or individuals.

■ THE RIGHT TO ASSEMBLE AND TO PETITION THE GOVERNMENT

The First Amendment prohibits Congress from making any law that abridges "the right of the people peaceably to assemble and to petition the Government for a redress of grievances." Inherent in such a right is the ability of private citizens to communicate their ideas on public issues to government officials as well as to other individuals. The Supreme Court has often put this freedom on a par with the freedom of speech and of the press. Nonetheless, it has allowed municipalities to require permits for parades, sound trucks, and demonstrations,[42] so that public officials may control traffic or prevent demon-

---

[41]*Federal Communications Commission v. Pacifica Foundation,* 438 U.S. 726 (1978).
[42]*Davis v. Massachusetts,* 167 U.S. 43 (1897).

Members of the Ku Klux Klan march through Austin, Texas. What right are these people exercising?

strations from turning into riots. This became a major issue in 1977 when the American Nazi party wanted to march through the largely Jewish suburb of Skokie, Illinois. The American Civil Liberties Union (ACLU) defended the Nazis' right to march (in spite of its opposition to the Nazi philosophy). The Supreme Court let stand a lower court's ruling that the city of Skokie had violated the Nazis' First Amendment guarantees[43] by denying them a permit to do so.

The right to assemble has been broadly defined. For example, municipal and state governments do not have the right to require any organization to publish its membership list. This was decided in *NAACP v. Alabama*[44] when the state of Alabama required the National Association for the Advancement of Colored People to publish a list of its members. The Supreme Court held that the requirement was unconstitutional because it violated the NAACP's right of assembly, which the Court addressed in terms of freedom of association.

The courts have generally interpreted the right to parade and protest more narrowly than pure forms of speech or assembly. The Supreme Court has generally upheld the right of individuals to parade and protest in public places, but it has ruled against parades and protests when matters of public safety were at issue. In *Cox v. New Hampshire*[45] in 1941, the Court ruled that sixty-eight Jehovah's Witnesses had violated a statute prohibiting parading without a permit and upheld the right of a municipality to control its public streets.

[43]*Collin v. Smith,* 439 U.S. 916 (1978).
[44]357 U.S. 499 (1958).
[45]312 U.S. 569.

■ MORE LIBERTIES UNDER SCRUTINY: MATTERS OF PRIVACY

During the past several years, a number of civil liberties that relate to the right to privacy have become important social issues. Among the most important are the right to sexual freedom, the right to have an abortion, the many rights concerning new methods of reproduction, and the right to die.

The Right to Privacy

No explicit reference is made anywhere in the Constitution to a person's right to privacy. The courts did not take a very positive approach toward the right to privacy until relatively recently. For example, during Prohibition suspected bootleggers' telephones were routinely tapped and the information obtained was used as a legal basis for prosecution. In *Olmstead v. U.S.*,[46] the Supreme Court upheld such invasion of privacy. However, Justice Louis Brandeis, a champion of personal freedoms, strongly dissented when he argued that the framers of the Constitution gave every citizen the right to be left alone. He called such a right "the most comprehensive of rights and the right most valued by civilized men."

In the 1960s, the highest court began to modify its view. In *Griswold v. Connecticut*[47] in 1965, the Supreme Court overthrew a Connecticut law that effectively prohibited the distribution of contraceptives on the basis of the right to privacy. Justice William O. Douglas formulated a unique way of reading this right into the Bill of Rights. He claimed that the First, Third, Fourth, Fifth, and Ninth Amendments created "penumbras, formed by emanations from those guarantees that help give them life and substance," and went on to talk about zones for privacy that are guaranteed by these rights. When we read the Ninth Amendment, we can see the foundation for his reasoning: "The enumeration in the Constitution of certain rights, shall not be construed to deny or disparage others retained by the people." In other words, just because the Constitution, including its amendments, does not specifically talk about the right to privacy does not mean this right is denied to the people.

In a reversal to this trend, the Supreme Court ruled in 1986 that the right to privacy does not protect homosexual acts between consenting adults. It ruled that a Georgia law prohibiting sodomy—oral or anal sex—was constitutional.[48] About half the states have so-called sodomy laws, which are generally intended to restrict homosexual activities.

An important right to privacy issue, created in part by the new technology, is the amassing of information on individuals by government. The average American citizen has personal information filed away in dozens of agencies—such as the Social Security Administration and the Internal Revenue Service. Because of the threat of indiscriminate use of private information by nonauthorized individuals, Congress passed the Privacy Act in 1974. This was the first law regulating the use of federal government information about private individuals. Under the Privacy Act, every citizen has the right to obtain copies of personal records collected by federal agencies and to correct inaccuracies in such records. In addition, the act established a Privacy Protection Study Commission, which has found a wide range of abuses in this area.

[46]277 U.S. 438 (1928). This decision was reversed later in *Katz v. United States*, 389 U.S. 347 (1967).
[47]381 U.S. 479.
[48]*Bowers v. Hardwick*, 478 U.S. 186 (1986).

The use of lie detectors, or polygraphs, has been under scrutiny for many years. In 1988, Congress prohibited many uses of the polygraph by private employers for random employee examinations and for preemployment screenings. Such tests may still be used by federal, state, and local governments, by companies doing sensitive work for federal, military, or security agencies, or by companies dealing with controlled substances or those who provide private security services.

The Right to Abortion

Does a woman have the right to an abortion? The arguments for and against this extremely sensitive issue revolve around when who, if anyone, has the right to control reproduction. Before 1973, performance of an abortion was a criminal offense in most states. In 1973, however, the Supreme Court altered the law. In *Roe v. Wade*[49] the Court accepted the argument that the laws against abortion violated "Jane Roe's" right to privacy under the Constitution.[50] (See Profile on Justice Harry Blackmun, who wrote the majority opinion in this landmark case.) The Court refused to answer the question of when life begins. It simply said that "the right to privacy is broad enough to encompass a woman's decision whether or not to terminate her pregnancy." Note, though, that the Court did not say such a right was absolute. Rather, it asserted that any state could impose certain regulations that would safeguard the health of the mother and protect potential life.

Thus the Court balanced different issues when it decided that during the first trimester of pregnancy the state could not limit abortions except to require that they be performed by licensed physicians. Under the *Roe* decision, during the second trimester, the state was allowed to specify the conditions under which an abortion can be performed. During the final trimester, the state could regulate or even outlaw abortions to protect a "viable" fetus.

[49]410 U.S. 113 (1973).
[50]Jane Roe was not the real name of the woman involved in this case. It is a common legal pseudonym used to protect a person's privacy.

A major issue facing Americans continues to concern the right to have an abortion. What are the major differences in opinion about this issue?

PROFILE

Justice Harry Blackmun

"When those trained in the respective disciplines of medicine, philosophy, and theology are unable to arrive at any consensus, the judiciary, at this point in the development of man's knowledge, is not in a position to speculate as to the answer."

Justice Harry Blackmun had been on the Court for not much more than a year when he was given the assignment of writing the majority opinion in abortion cases that the Supreme Court had heard during its 1971 term. Although he was new on the Court, Justice Blackmun was not at all new to medical issues as they related to the law. Blackmun had been general counsel at the Mayo Clinic in Rochester, Minnesota, and had advised the staff there on the legality of abortions performed by the hospital.

In looking through available common law on the subject and examining the history of abortion in the United States and Great Britain, one of the things Blackmun discovered was that abortion had been a fairly accepted practice for many centuries, and it was only in the nineteenth century that it became a crime in the United States. Antiabortion laws were enacted largely to protect pregnant women because abortion was a very risky operation.

But the medical reality had changed. Abortion is now a relatively safe procedure with the use of modern drugs and surgical techniques, particularly in early pregnancy.

During the summer of 1972, Blackmun went back to Rochester and researched the question of abortion at the Mayo Clinic Medical Library. The basic issue that found its way into Blackmun's opinion on abortion was whether a woman had an absolute right to privacy or if and at what point a state government or the federal government had the right to step in to prevent the pregnant woman from doing with her body what she wished.

There was little guidance in the law about the point at which the state's interests should override the interests of the pregnant woman. Blackmun used the results of medical research and ac-

cepted medical practice as his guide: Pregnancy was divided into three trimesters of roughly equal stages of three months each. The basic conclusion in the medical world was that abortions were generally safe in the first trimester and with proper medical controls could be performed safely in the second trimester as well—that is, up until the time a woman is about six months pregnant. After the second trimester, though, the fetus becomes capable of surviving outside the womb.

Blackmun's conclusion was that at the end of the second trimester, some strong prohibitions would probably have to be included against a woman having an absolute right to an abortion. The sense of Blackmun's opinion was relatively liberal concerning abortion during the first two trimesters of pregnancy but rather conservative after the second trimester had ended and the third begun. On January 22, 1973, the U.S. Supreme Court handed down its ruling in *Roe v. Wade* and *Doe v. Bolton,* incorporating Harry Blackmun's opinion based on his medical background and legal expertise. Blackmun continued to support the right to an abortion in the 1989 *Webster* case. Dissenting from the majority, he said, "I fear for the future. I fear for the liberty and equality of the millions of women who have lived and come of age in the sixteen years since *Roe* was decided."

SOURCE: Bob Woodward and Scott Armstrong, *The Brethren* (New York: Simon & Schuster, 1979).

On July 3, 1989, the Supreme Court announced its decision in *Webster v. Reproductive Health Services,* a case which challenged very restrictive state laws on abortion. In a narrow five-to-four majority, the Court upheld the restrictions that Missouri placed on the performing of abortions, thus opening the way for many other states to enact similar or more restrictive laws. Specifically, the ruling allows states to pass laws that, like the Missouri statute, ban the use of public hospitals or other taxpayer supported facilities from performing abortions, bar public employees including doctors and nurses from assisting in abortions, and require the performance of viability tests on any fetus thought to be at least twenty weeks old. Although the *Webster* decision did not overturn the right to have an abortion, the Court's ruling was a major victory for antiabortion forces. Both pro- and antiabortion groups immediately announced plans to take the battle to the states. Antiabortion groups hope to pressure many states, particularly those with more conservative voters, to enact restrictive legislation. The prochoice forces began planning campaigns to defeat state legislators and other elected officials who support such legislation. The ultimate effect of the *Webster* decision is to make the right to obtain an abortion much more difficult in some states than in others. The five-to-four vote also signaled the emergence of a solid conservative majority on the Court.

The Right to Die

The question of whether the right to privacy includes the right to die is now a major point of controversy. Suicide and **euthanasia,** or mercy killing, are both illegal; but many extremely ill people do not want their lives prolonged through expensive artificial measures. These situations often end up in court because hospitals and doctors sympathetic to the patient's wishes do not want to be legally or morally responsible for giving the order to stop treatment.

EUTHANASIA
Killing incurably ill people for reasons of mercy.

The 1976 case of Karen Ann Quinlan was one of the first publicized right-to-die cases.[51] The parents of Quinlan, a young woman who had been in a coma since age twenty-one and kept alive by a respirator, wanted her respirator removed. The Supreme Court of New Jersey ruled that the right to privacy includes the right of a patient to refuse treatment and that patients unable to speak can exercise that right through a family or guardian. In its ruling on a 1985 case, the New Jersey Supreme Court set some clear guidelines for when care could be withheld for patients who cannot express their own wishes.[52] Care can be withheld if the patient would have definitely refused treatment, evidence suggests that treatment would have been refused, and the burdens of continuing care are greater than the benefits.

■ THE GREAT BALANCING ACT: THE RIGHTS OF THE ACCUSED VERSUS THE RIGHTS OF SOCIETY

The United States has one of the highest violent crime rates in the world. The statistics are quite shocking. Given so much crime in the United States, it is not surprising that many citizens have extremely strong opinions about the rights of those accused of criminal offenses. When an accused person, especially

[51]In re *Quinlan,* 70 N.J. 10, 355 A.2d 647.
[52]In re *Conroy,* 98 N.J. 321, 486 A.2d 1209.

CRITICAL PERSPECTIVE

Procedural and Substantive Due Process, or Fairness of Means and Ends

Due process of law is defined in Black's *Law Dictionary* (4th ed.) as

> . . . the right of the person affected thereby to be present before the tribunal which pronounces judgment upon the question of life, liberty, or property, in its most comprehensive sense; to be heard, by testimony or otherwise, and to have the right of controverting, by proof, every material fact which bears on the questions of right in the matter involved. If any question of fact or liability be conclusively presumed against him, this is not due process of law.

Due process, then, is concerned with certain fundamental rights recognized by the legal system. That system and its officers are responsible for ensuring that what are essentially rules of fair play are followed in making decisions, in ascertaining guilt or innocence, and in assessing who has been wronged. In short, "due process" means that the correct procedures have been followed and that everyone has been given an equal right to be heard. This focus on following the rules is often referred to as "procedural due process." The emphasis on doing things by the rules, almost without regard to whether the decision itself is fair, is the hallmark of procedural due process.

American law has, however, reflected both this procedural concern over means and a substantive concern over the ends to which the procedures lead. In other words, a decision to send someone to jail for fifty years for possession of one gram of marijuana may have been done with utmost procedural fairness, but the substance of the decision may lack fairness. This notion of "substantive due process" often takes the form of arguments over the equal protection clause of the Fourteenth Amendment to the Constitution. It lies at the heart of the use of the Fourteenth Amendment to selectively incorporate the provisions of the Bill of Rights into state law. This involves arguments over the "fundamental rights" that are not expressly laid out in the Bill of Rights but which ought to exist.

In the history of English (and, ultimately, American) law, the modern phrase "due process of law" is derived from the language of the English Magna Carta, which speaks of *per legem terrae,* or "by the law of the land." This was a guarantee to the barons of medieval Britain of the common-law rights of Englishmen, which were both procedural, such as the right to trial by one's peers, and substantive, including various liberties and the right to own and dispose of property. J. Roland Pennock, in the book *Due Process,* argues from this medieval origin of the concept that any distinction between procedural and substantive views of due process is "illusory."* Pennock

one who has confessed to some criminal act, is set free because of an apparent legal "technicality," many people may feel that the rights of the accused are being given more weight than the rights of society and of potential or actual victims. So why give criminal suspects rights? The answer is partly to avoid convicting innocent people, but mostly because all citizens have rights, and suspects are citizens.

The courts and the police must constantly engage in a balancing act of competing rights. At the basis of all discussions about the appropriate balance is, of course, the U.S. Bill of Rights. The Fourth, Fifth, Sixth, and Eighth Amendments specifically deal with the rights of criminal defendants.

Rights of the Accused

The basic rights of criminal defendants can be outlined as follows. Where appropriate, the specific amendment on which a right is based is given also.

CRITICAL PERSPECTIVE, CONTINUED

sees American history as characterized by using the concept of due process of law to limit the power of governments. In Pennock's view, the substantive emphasis on due process underlies the *Roe v. Wade* ruling that invalidated state legislation prohibiting abortions. The goal of substantive due process is to weigh contrasting claims of what is right, including an individual's claim against society's legislated attempts to protect people from themselves and from one another. For example, what is the correct decision on statutes that require motorcycle riders to wear crash helmets? The cyclist has a right to freedom, but that right has to be balanced against his or her safety and society's right not to be burdened with the death or injury that may result from a crash in which the cyclist was not protected by a helmet.

The issue of due process and the distinction between its procedural and substantive applications has become increasingly important with the growth of bureaucratic agencies that administer the affairs of government and that often make decisions of their own. How are people to be protected against arbitrary and unfair decisions by these nonelected government officials? How are your rights to privacy to be protected against intrusion by snoopy bureaucrats who have access to all sorts of information about you? This concern has been addressed by Jerry L. Mashaw in his book, *Due Process in the Administrative State*. Mashaw fears that the lack of protection against arbitrary bureaucratic actions may create a modern administrative state that acts as "an efficient machine for generating increasing numbers of inevitably arbitrary general rules, unconstrained by any operationally relevant constitutional limitation that might preserve the values of either democracy or

individualism."** Mashaw calls for a "dignitary perspective" on due process that emphasizes the rights of individuals to privacy, free expression, and religious freedom, among others, and that fuses administrative due process with the substantive due process found in the Supreme Court's incorporation doctrine and its development of nonenumerated constitutional rights in accordance with what he sees as the spirit of the Constitution. Of course, to those of opposite political views, this is the same as saying that the Supreme Court has a perfect right to "legislate," or to make law by judicial rulings that change society without resort to congressional or executive control.

*J. Roland Pennock and John W. Chapman, eds., *Due Process* (New York: New York University Press, 1977), p. xvi.
**Jerry L. Mashaw, *Due Process in the Administrative State* (New Haven, Conn.: Yale University Press, 1985), p. 41.

Exercise in Critical Thinking
1. Can you think of one or more government agencies that might follow procedural due process but violate individuals' substantive rights?
2. If Congress or a state legislature decides that driving without a license is punishable by two years in jail, isn't such a law legitimate and, by definition, fair?
3. Are the procedural rights of accused criminals too well safeguarded at the present time?

Limits on Conduct of Police and Prosecutors
- No unreasonable or unwarranted searches and seizures (Amend. IV)
- No arrest except on probable cause (Amend. IV)
- No coerced confessions or illegal interrogation (Amend. V)
- No entrapment
- Upon questioning, suspect must be informed of rights

Defendant's Pretrial Rights
- **Writ of habeas corpus** (Article I, Section 9)
- Prompt arraignment (Amend. VI)
- Legal counsel (Amend. VI)
- Reasonable bail (Amend. VIII)
- Defendant must be informed of charges (Amend. VI)
- Right to remain silent (Amend. V)

WRIT OF HABEAS CORPUS
Literally, "you should have the body." An order that requires jailers to bring a party before a court or judge and explain why the party is being held in prison.

DID YOU KNOW?

That in 1989, in a five-to-four decision, the U.S. Supreme Court ruled that the police do not need a search warrant to conduct low-altitude helicopter searches of private property?

Trial Rights
- Speedy and public trial before a jury (Amend. VI)
- Impartial jury selected from cross section of community (Amends. VI and VII)
- Trial atmosphere free of prejudice, fear, and outside interference
- No compulsory self-incrimination (Amend. V)
- Adequate counsel (Amend. VI)
- No cruel or unusual punishment (Amend. VIII)
- Appeal convictions
- No double jeopardy (Amend. V)

Extending the Rights of the Accused: *Miranda v. Arizona*

In 1963, near Phoenix, Arizona, a young woman was kidnapped and raped. A twenty-three-year-old mentally disturbed suspect, Ernesto Miranda, was arrested soon after the crime took place. After two hours of questioning, he confessed and was later convicted.

Miranda's counsel appealed his conviction. They argued that the police had never informed Miranda that he had the right to remain silent and the right to be represented by counsel. In 1966, a five-to-four majority of the U.S. Supreme Court ruled in Miranda's favor:

> Prior to any questioning, the person must be warned that he has a right to remain silent, that any statement he does make may be used against him, and that he has a right to the presence of an attorney, either retained or appointed.[53]

The majority voted to reverse the conviction on the basis of the Fifth and Sixth Amendments, but the minority complained that the majority was distorting the Constitution by placing the rights of criminal suspects above the rights of society as a whole—the balancing act was again in question. Police officials sided with the minority view, but many agreed with the majority that

[53]*Miranda v. Arizona*, 384 U.S. 436.

The war on drugs involves numerous "busts." What constitutional right is often at issue when such action is undertaken?

HIGHLIGHT

The Case of Clarence Earl Gideon

In 1962, Clarence Earl Gideon sent a petition to the Supreme Court to review his most recent conviction, for breaking into a pool hall and stealing some money in Panama City, Florida. That petition would not only change Gideon's life but would become a landmark case in constitutional law as well.

Clarence Gideon had been in trouble with the law during much of his life and in jail at least four times before for various minor crimes. Those who knew him, including his jailers, found him rather likeable and relatively harmless.

Gideon petitioned, claiming that his conviction and sentencing to a five-year term in prison violated the due process clause of the Fourteenth Amendment to the Constitution, which says that "no state shall . . . deprive any person of life, liberty, or property, without due process of the law." Gideon reported that at the time of his trial, when he asked for the assistance of a

lawyer, the court refused this aid. The heart of Gideon's petition lay in his notion that "to try a poor man for a felony without giving him a lawyer was to deprive him of due process of law."

The problem with Gideon's argument was that the Supreme Court had established a precedent twenty years

earlier in *Betts v. Brady,* * when it held that criminal defendants were not automatically guaranteed the right to have a lawyer present when they were tried in court except in capital cases.

Gideon was successful, with the help of his court-appointed lawyer, Abe Fortas, who later was named to the Supreme Court by President Johnson. In the case of *Gideon v. Wainwright* ** the Court decided in Gideon's favor, saying that persons who can demonstrate that they are unable to afford to have a lawyer present and are accused of felonies must be given a lawyer at the expense of the government. Gideon was retried, represented by an attorney appointed by the court, and found innocent of the charges.

*316 U.S. 455 (1942).
**372 U.S. 335 (1963).
SOURCE: Anthony Lewis, *Gideon's Trumpet* (New York: Vintage Books, 1964).

criminal law enforcement would be more reliable if it were based on independently secured evidence rather than on confessions obtained under adverse interrogation conditions in the absence of counsel.

Another extension of the rights of the accused was made by the Court in the case of Clarence Earl Gideon, described in the Highlight.

Recent Rulings and Their Impact on *Miranda*

The Supreme Court under Chief Justice Warren Burger did not expand the *Miranda* ruling but rather reduced its scope and effectiveness. Also, Congress in 1968 passed the Omnibus Crime Control and Safe Streets Act, which provided—among other things—that in federal cases a voluntary confession could be used in evidence, even if the accused was not warned of his or her rights.

Today, juries can even accept confessions without being convinced they were voluntary.[54] Even in cases that are not tried in federal court, confessions made by criminal suspects who have not been completely informed of their legal rights may be taken into consideration.[55] In 1984, the Court added

[54]See especially *Lego v. Twomey,* 404 U.S. 477 (1972).
[55]*Michigan v. Tucker,* 417 U.S. 433 (1974).

DID YOU KNOW?

That a study by sociologist Michael L. Radelet and philosopher Hugo Adam Bedau showed that between 1900 and 1985, 350 innocent persons were convicted of capital offenses, and that 23 of these convicts were executed, with 21 others winning last-minute reprieves?

EXCLUSIONARY RULE
A policy forbidding the admission of illegally seized evidence at trial.

another exception to the *Miranda* rule by allowing the introduction of evidence into the courtroom that was voluntarily given by the suspect before he had been informed of his rights. The Court held that when "public safety" required action (in this case, to find the loaded gun), police could interrogate the suspect before advising him of his right to remain silent.[56]

The Exclusionary Rule

At least since 1914, a judicial policy has existed forbidding the admission of illegally seized evidence at trial. This is the so-called **exclusionary rule.** Improperly obtained evidence, no matter how telling, until recently could not be used by prosecutors. The reasoning behind the exclusionary rule is that it forces police officers to gather evidence properly, in which case their due diligence will be rewarded by a conviction. There have always been critics of the exclusionary rule who argued that it permits guilty persons to be freed because of innocent errors.

This rule was first applied to state courts in the 1961 Supreme Court decision *Mapp v. Ohio.*[57] In this case, the Court overturned the conviction of Dollree Mapp for possession of obscene materials. Police found pornographic books in her apartment after searching it without a search warrant despite her refusal to let them in.

In a recent case in Massachusetts, the Court seemed to be loosening the severity of the exclusionary rule. A Boston police officer suspected a man of murder and wished to search his residence. He used a technically incorrect search warrant form. The Massachusetts Appeals Court threw out the conviction because of this technical defect. But the Supreme Court held that the officer acted in good faith and thereby created the "good faith exception."[58]

[56]*New York v. Quarles,* 467 U.S. 649 (1984).
[57]367 U.S. 643.
[58]*Massachusetts v. Sheppard,* 468 U.S. 981 (1984).

Dollree Mapp, a victim of an illegal search. What rule was violated by such a search?

Capital Punishment: Cruel and Unusual?

Amendment VIII prohibits cruel and unusual punishment. Until a Supreme Court decision in 1972,[59] the death penalty was not considered cruel and unusual punishment. Indeed, a number of states had imposed the death penalty for a variety of crimes and allowed juries to decide when the condemned could be sentenced to death.

But many believed, and in 1972 the Court agreed, that the imposition of the death penalty was random and arbitrary. For example, 53 percent of all persons executed from 1930 to 1965 were black, even though blacks constituted less than 10 percent of the population during that period. Changing attitudes toward the death penalty could be seen in the fact that the number of individuals who actually were executed dropped dramatically since the 1930s. In the decade 1930–1939, 1,666 persons were executed; from 1960 to 1969, fewer than 200 persons were executed.

The Supreme Court's 1972 decision stated that the death penalty as currently applied violated the Eighth and Fourteenth Amendments. It ruled that capital punishment is not necessarily cruel and unusual if the criminal has killed or attempted to kill someone. In its opinion, the Court invited the states to make more precise laws so that the death penalty would be applied more consistently. A majority of states have done so. In the 1990s, an increasing number of states are actually executing death-row inmates.

Issues surrounding the sanity of death-row inmates have come up in the last decade. In 1986, the Supreme Court ruled that the U.S. Constitution bars states from executing convicted killers who have become insane while waiting on death row (*Ford v. Wainwright*). In opposition, a 1989 ruling (*Penry v. Lynaugh*) the Supreme Court held that mentally retarded persons may be executed for murder. In the same year, the court found that defendants who were as young as sixteen could be executed if they committed a murder. Finally, in *Murray v. Giarrantano,* the court held that indigent death-row inmates have no constitutional right to a lawyer for a second round of state court appeals.

[59]*Furman v. Georgia,* 408 U.S. 238.

Since 1972 many states have executed death-row inmates. Some critics of capital punishment argue that execution violates what amendment?

DID YOU KNOW?

That the first public execution in the American colonies took place on September 30, 1630, when Pilgrim John Billington was hanged for murder?

When considering statistical evidence regarding one state's death-sentencing process, which the defendant claimed was racially discriminatory, the Supreme Court held that some disparities are an inevitable part of the criminal justice system and do not necessarily violate the Constitution.[60] In Georgia, in 1978, the defendant, a black man, was convicted of armed robbery and murder—shooting a white police officer in the face during the robbery of a store. The jury recommended the death penalty, and the trial court followed the recommendation. On appeal, the defendant presented a statistical study based on more than 2,000 murder cases that occurred in Georgia during the 1970s. The study purported to show that the death sentence was imposed more often on black defendants convicted of killing whites than on white defendants convicted of killing blacks. The Supreme Court decided that the statistics did not prove that race enters into capital sentencing decisions or that it was a factor in the defendant's case. The Court stated that the unpredictability of jury decisions does not justify their condemnation, since it is the jury's function to make difficult judgments. The Court explained that any method for determining guilt or punishment has its weaknesses and the potential for misuse. Despite such imperfections, the Court concluded, constitutional guarantees are met when the method has been made as fair as possible.

Capital punishment remains one of the most debated aspects of our criminal justice system. Those in favor of it maintain that it serves as a deterrent to serious crime and satisfies society's need for justice and fair play. Those opposed to the death penalty do not believe it has any deterrent value and hold that it constitutes a barbaric act in an otherwise civilized society. Recent public opinion polls have demonstrated that a large majority of Americans favor using the death penalty more frequently.

[60]*McCleskey v. Kemp,* 481 U.S. 279 (1987).

GETTING INVOLVED

Your Civil Liberties: Searches and Seizures

What happens if you are stopped by members of the police force? Your civil liberties protect you from having to provide any other information than your name and address. Indeed, you are not really required to produce evidence of identification, although it is a good idea to show this to the officers. Normally, even if you have not been placed under arrest, the officers have the right to frisk you for weapons and you must let them proceed. The officers cannot, however, check your person or your clothing further if, in their judgment, no weaponlike object is produced. Only if the officers have a search warrant or probable cause that they will likely find incriminating evidence if the search is conducted may they search you. Normally, it is unwise to resist physically the officers' attempt to search you if they do not have probable cause or a warrant; it is usually best simply to refuse orally to give permission for the search, preferably in the presence of a witness. Also, it is usually advisable to tell the officer as little as possible about yourself and the situation that is under investigation. Being polite and courteous, though firm, is better than acting out of anger or frustration and making the officers irritable. If you are told not to leave, that means you are under arrest. At that point, it is best to keep quiet until you can speak with a lawyer.

If you are in your car and are stopped by the police, the same fundamental rules apply. Always be ready to show your driver's license and car registration quickly. You may be asked to get out of the car. The officers may use a flashlight to peer into it if it is too dark to see otherwise. None of this constitutes a search. A true search requires either a warrant or probable cause. No officer has the legal right to search your car simply to find out if you may have committed a crime. Passengers in a car that has been stopped by the police are legally required only to give a name and address. Passengers are not even obligated to produce a piece of identification.

If you are in your residence and a police officer with a search warrant appears, you should examine the warrant before granting entry. A correctly made out warrant will state the exact place or persons to be searched, a description of the object sought, the date of the warrant (which should be no more than ten days old), and a signature of a judge or magistrate. If the search warrant is in order, you should not make any statement. If you believe it to be invalid, you should make it clear orally that you have not consented to the search, preferably in the presence of a witness. If the warrant is later proven to be invalid, normally any evidence obtained would be considered illegal. Officers who attempt to enter your home without a search warrant can do so only if they are pursuing a suspected felon into the house. Rarely is it advisable to give permission for a warrantless search. You must be the one to give permission for any evidence obtained to be legal. The landlord, manager, or head of a college dormitory cannot give legal permission. A roommate, however, can give permission for a search of his or her room, which may allow the police to search those areas in which you have personal belongings. If you find yourself a guest in a location for which there is a legal search, you may be legally searched also. But unless you have been placed under arrest, you cannot be compelled to go to the police station or into a squad car.

If you would like to find out more about your rights and obligations under the laws of searches and seizures, you might wish to contact:

The American Civil Liberties Union
22 East 40th Street
New York, NY 10016
(212) 725-1222

Legal Defense Fund
67 Winthrop Street
Cambridge, MA 02138
(617) 864-8680

CHAPTER SUMMARY

1. When we speak of civil liberties in the United States, for the most part we are referring to the specific limitations on government outlined in the first ten amendments to the U.S. Constitution. These include our basic freedoms of religion, speech, press, and assembly, and the right to petition.

2. As originally presented, the Bill of Rights limited only the power of the national government, not that of the states. It was not until the Fourteenth Amendment was ratified in 1868 that our Constitution explicitly guaranteed to everyone due process of the law.

3. For the most part, the last hundred years of Supreme Court interpretations of the Fourteenth Amendment have bound the fifty states to accept most of the guarantees for their respective citizens that are contained in the Bill of Rights.

4. The First Amendment freedom of religion implies both free exercise of religion and the separation of church and state.

5. The Supreme Court has ruled against officially sponsored prayer and Bible-reading sessions in public schools. A constitutional amendment to permit organized, recited prayers in public schools was rejected in the Senate on March 20, 1984. In cases regarding government financial aid to church-related schools, the Supreme Court has attempted to distinguish between permissible public aid to students as opposed to impermissible public aid to religion. As for the exercise of religion, when religious practices work against public policy and public welfare, the government can intervene.

6. The clear and present danger test is used in determining the limits of free expression. Other tests include the preferred-position test (more rigorous standards of review required because of importance), the sliding-scale test (careful examination of the facts of each individual case must be undertaken), and the bad-tendency test (speech having a tendency to bring "evil").

7. Prior restraint on expression and laws that are too vague or broad may be deemed unconstitutional.

8. The free speech clause normally protects symbolic speech, including the burning of the flag. Commercial speech and advertising statements have gradually been brought under the protection of the First Amendment.

9. Basically, the courts have not been willing to extend constitutional protections of free speech to what are considered obscene materials and to slander.

10. Abuses of free speech have included defamation of character in writing, or libel, and news reports of criminal trials when they interfere with a fair trial. The courts have moved in the direction of requiring the press to cooperate in criminal investigations if they have pertinent information.

11. The Supreme Court has not declared all forms of prior restraint or censorship to be unconstitutional but does require exceptional justification for such restraint.

12. The First Amendment protects the right to assemble peaceably and petition the government. The courts have generally upheld the right to parade and to protest in public places, but have ruled against such activities when public safety was threatened.

13. During the past several years, the right to privacy and the protections that it includes have become important social issues. They include the right to have an abortion and the right to die.

14. The police and the courts are constantly engaged in a balancing act between the rights of the accused versus the rights of society. The Fourth, Fifth, Sixth, and Eighth Amendments specifically deal with the rights of criminal defendants.

15. The exclusionary rule prohibits the use of illegally obtained evidence in a trial. The Supreme Court has recently relaxed this rule to allow improperly obtained evidence in certain cases.

16. In *Miranda v. Arizona* (1966), the Supreme Court ruled that criminal suspects must be immediately informed of their right to remain silent, that any statement they make can be used against them, and that they have the right to the presence of an attorney.

17. Amendment VIII prohibits cruel and unusual punishment. Capital punishment has been debated under this amendment.

QUESTIONS FOR REVIEW AND DISCUSSION

1. Although the Communist party was strictly outlawed in the United States for many years, today its candidates compete openly in presidential and other elections. What activities—speeches, printed publications, demonstrations—of the Communist party do you think could be considered illegal under the current laws?

2. Most conflicts concerning civil liberties involve the rights of the individual versus the rights of society as a whole. What religious practices might be considered a threat to society? On the other hand, what activities of certain missionary groups may be violating your right to be left alone?

3. The punishment of convicted criminals serves not only as retribution for the crime but also to satisfy the community's sense of justice. How should the courts balance the rights of the criminal against the rights of society—and the rights of the victim—to ensure fair treatment?

4. The criminal justice system in the United States is extremely overburdened. Many accused persons are either released owing to a failure in the system or agree to plea bargaining and forfeit a trial. What reforms might you suggest to make the judicial process both more efficient and more effective for the accused and for the courts?

5. The electronic era has created many legal situations that are not covered by the Constitution. To what extent should radio and television be covered by freedom of the press? Should videotape rentals be regulated to prevent the spread of pornography, especially to minors? Should computer communications be protected by the right to privacy?

SELECTED REFERENCES

John Brigham, *Civil Liberties and American Democracy* (Washington, D.C.: Congressional Quarterly Press, 1984). This book discusses fundamental civil liberties in the U.S. and the Supreme Court's role in guaranteeing those rights. Freedom of expression, press, speech, due process, and property rights are specifically treated.

Brookings Task Force on Civil Justice Reform, *Justice for All: Reducing Costs and Delay in Civil Litigation* (Washington, D.C.: Brookings Institute, 1990). This is a short but powerful report from a commission set up to look at ways of streamlining and reducing costs and delays in the American civil justice system.

William C. Culbertson, *Vigilantism: Political History of Private Power in America* (Westport, CT: Greenwood Press, 1990). This book examines the American people's history of taking the law into their own hands. The author asserts that private power has been instrumental in creating, distributing, and maintaining socially acceptable values and norms.

William A. Donohue, *The Politics of the American Civil Liberties Union* (New Brunswick, N.J.: Transaction Books, 1985). An interesting study of one of the most visible and active civil liberties groups in the United States, with specific emphasis given to the role of ideology and the political orientation of the ACLU.

Susan P. Fino, *The Role of State Supreme Courts in the New Judicial Federalism* (Westport, Conn.: Greenwood Press, 1987). An assessment of how state law is utilized to fashion rights not mandated by the Supreme Court's interpretation of the United States Constitution.

Nat Hentoff, *The First Freedom: The Tumultuous History of Free Speech in America* (New York: Delacorte, 1980). This is a lively account of the evolution of freedom of speech.

Anthony Lewis, *Gideon's Trumpet* (New York: Vintage, 1964). Absolutely essential reading for understanding how criminal rights cases reach the Supreme Court.

Robert J. Spitzer, *The Right to Life Movement and Third Party Politics* (Westport, Conn.: Greenwood Press, 1987). A study of the Right to Life political party in New York.

D. F. B. Tucker, *Law, Liberalism and Free Speech* (Totowa, N.J.: Rowman and Littlefield, 1986). Using the ideas of major contemporary philosophers, this book explores fundamental principles of freedom of speech and also provides specific applications to privacy, the public interest, the media, and authority.

WHAT IF . . . WE HAD UNRESTRICTED IMMIGRATION?

Until 1875, the United States was open to almost unlimited immigration. Only prostitutes and convicts were excluded. But government policy underwent many permutations since that time, so that by 1991 American immigration laws had become a complicated mix of quotas and special provisions—over thirty different categories. These include quotas by region of the world, country, skill, and economic condition (a special Hong Kong set-aside allowed in a large number of Hong Kong residents provided they would invest at least $1 million in the United States and hire at least ten Americans), relatives of U.S. citizens, refugees, those seeking temporary political asylum, and seasonal laborers (migrant workers). Under the most recent law, so-called "employer sanctions" impose fines and other penalties on persons (companies) knowingly hiring illegal aliens.

What if the United States were to return to an open immigration policy?

The world in the 1990s is characterized by easy transportation, mobility, and rapid, sometimes simultaneous, worldwide communications. People in every corner of the world can learn about life in the United States. For many in countries torn by strife and plagued by poverty and underdevelopment, the United States still seems a golden land of economic opportunity and political freedom. Moreover, the

(Nicaragua, El Salvador, Panama, or Guatemala) can make their way to the United States for relatively little cost by bus, train, hitchhiking, or even walking.

The arrival of these mil-"American way of life," including its popular culture of emblematic blue jeans, hamburgers, rock music, and other distinctive characteristics, has an enormous allure for people in Eastern Europe, the Soviet Union, and many other places.

Thus an open immigration policy, no questions asked, would clearly stimulate a huge number of persons to come to the United States or to send their children or other relatives.

Moreover, the United States has the longest open border between a developed country and a developing nation—Mexico. For Mexicans in poverty, crossing into the United States may be an opportunity to improve one's own and one's children's economic and social condition. Although not without hazard, crossing the border for many "illegals" can be done simply by walking through the shallow Rio Grande separating the two nations or by crawling through the holes in rickety fences separating Mexican and American towns in places such as Brownsville, El Paso, or San Diego. In addition, Central Americans and South Americans, whose countries are plagued by recession, runaway inflation, human rights abuses, or war

lions would have both negative and positive consequences.

On the negative side, U.S. institutions would be challenged by the surge of new persons requiring education, housing, health care, and other services. A relatively unmonitored immigration policy would no doubt allow in some criminals, human rights abusers, and drug dealers. The needs of sick persons seeking medical help, and the poor, unskilled, and unemployable among the newcomers would place severe strains on cities, counties, states, and the federal government. Racially, ethnically, and religiously diverse immigrant groups might clash with one another and increase the tension in U.S. neighborhoods, as has happened with Vietnamese and Koreans, on the one hand, and established African Americans, Hispanics, and European Americans, on the other, in New York City and other places.

There would, however, also be great advantages to open immigration. Entrepreneurs and others wishing to move away from places with an uncertain future (Hong Kong, for instance, which reverts to Chinese control in 1997) would bring their capital, skills, and energy which would stimulate business. The new wave of immigrants would bring with them their culture and, in the manner of traditional immigrant groups, greatly enrich American music, art,

dance, and a host of other cultural forms.

Finally, and most important, new immigrants would help ease the looming labor shortage, which (as a result of low U.S. birthrates and an aging population) threatens U.S. economic prosperity in the twenty-first century. In 1900, there were only 111 older Americans for every 1,000 working people. Now there are almost 300, and this figure is rising. This has resulted in a budget expenditure of over $350 billion in aid to the elderly. Immigrants are overwhelmingly working age (almost 50 percent are in the "early prime labor force age" of twenty to thirty-nine, compared with only 26 percent of current Americans). These new, young, working Americans would fill the jobs that now go begging and also create new jobs through entrepreneurship. They would pay local and state taxes and Social Security taxes, stimulate new housing and commercial construction, and inject vitality into the educational system, which in some places is shrinking because of a declining school-age population.

---

1. *When and where did* **your** *family come from?*
2. *Would they be able to emmigrate to the United States today?*
3. *What did they do for a living when they arrived?*

We hold these Truths to be self-evident, that all Men are created equal . . .

These are beautiful words, to be sure. But when they were written in 1776, the term *men* had a somewhat different meaning than it has today. It did not include slaves or women or Native Americans. So individuals in these groups were not considered equal. It has taken this nation over two hundred years to approach even a semblance of equality among all Americans.

The struggle for equality has not been easy. In this chapter, we show that it is continuing. It is a struggle perhaps best described as an effort to strengthen and to expand constitutional guarantees to *all* persons in our society. In this chapter and in the one that follows, we examine the rights of various minorities: African Americans, Mexican Americans and other Hispanics, Native Americans, Asian Americans, women, gays, the elderly, and juveniles.

Minority rights have often been called civil rights, and the quest for the expansion of minority rights has been called the civil rights movement. Since the civil rights movement started with the struggle for African-American equality, that story is told first. We begin by taking a look at the makeup of American society.

> **DID YOU KNOW?**
>
> That minorities will make up 35 percent of the U.S. population by the year 2010, and by the year 2025, minorities will account for 40 percent of young people 10 to 21 years of age?

■ THE DIVERSITY OF AMERICAN SOCIETY

A foreign visitor whose first stop in the United States is, say, a small town in the Midwest or a Los Angeles suburb might receive the impression that the population is entirely WASP (White Anglo-Saxon Protestants). But the facts are quite different. The United States is much more heterogeneous than it would seem at first glance and certainly more heterogeneous than any Western European country. The projection of population by race for 2000 shows that, although whites will still constitute a large majority of Americans, African Americans will make up 13.0 percent, Mexican Americans and other Hispanics 8.2 percent, and Asians 6.0 percent of the population of the United States.

Over the past two hundred years, more than 50 million persons emmigrated voluntarily to the United States. Of these, 37 million came from somewhere in Europe, over 5 million from Asia, 11 million from the Americas, 300,000 from Africa, and the rest from other places.

In terms of national origin, Table 5-1 shows that Anglo-Saxons are the largest group, but nearly as numerous are those claiming German or Irish

TABLE 5-1
The Six Largest Ethnic Groups in the United States in 1990

ANCESTRY	NUMBER (IN MILLIONS)	PERCENTAGE OF POPULATION
English	49.6	26.3
German	49.2	26.1
Irish	40.2	21.3
African	20.9	11.1
French	12.9	6.8
Italian	12.2	6.5

SOURCE: *Statistical Abstract of the United States.*

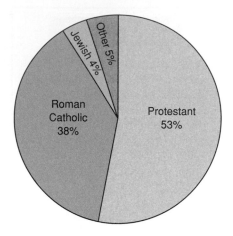

FIGURE 5-1
Religious Groups in the United States, 1990
SOURCE: Adapted from *Information Please Almanac.*

Dred Scott

descent. Also, the religious makeup of the American population certainly isn't homogeneous (Figure 5-1). Of those who express a religious affiliation in the United States, 53 percent are Protestant, 37 percent are Roman Catholic, 4 percent are Jewish, and 4 percent are of other religious persuasions. WASPs may constitute a large portion of our population, but this country is nonetheless made up of many diverse groups.

■ AFRICAN AMERICANS: THE CONSEQUENCES OF SLAVERY IN THE UNITED STATES

Article I, Section 2, of the Constitution stated that congressional representatives and direct taxes were to be apportioned among the states according to their respective numbers, obtained by adding to the total number of free persons "three-fifths of all other Persons." The "other persons" were, of course, slaves. A slave was thus equal to three-fifths of a white person.[1] As Lincoln stated sarcastically, "All men are created equal, except Negroes." Before 1863, the Constitution thus protected slavery and made equality impossible in the sense we use the word today. African-American leader Frederick Douglass pointed out that "Liberty and Slavery—opposite as Heaven and Hell—are both in the Constitution."

The constitutionality of slavery was confirmed just a few years before the outbreak of the Civil War in the famous *Dred Scott v. Sanford*[2] case of 1857. The Supreme Court held that slaves were not citizens of the United States, nor were they entitled to the rights and privileges of citizenship. The Court also ruled that the Missouri Compromise, which banned slavery in the territories, was unconstitutional. The *Dred Scott* decision had grave consequences. Most observers contend that the ruling contributed to making the Civil War inevitable. (In all fairness, it should be noted that the decision was not unanimous—the Court was divided six to three over the issue, and the nine justices filed eight separate opinions in the case.)

With the emancipation of the slaves by President Lincoln's Emancipation Proclamation in 1863 and the passage of the Thirteenth, Fourteenth, and Fifteenth Amendments following the Civil War, constitutional inequality was ended. The Thirteenth Amendment (1865) states that neither slavery nor involuntary servitude shall exist within the United States. The Fourteenth Amendment (ratified on July 9, 1868) tells us that *all* persons born or naturalized in the United States are citizens of the United States. Furthermore, "No State shall make or enforce any law which shall abridge the privileges or immunities of the citizens of the United States; nor shall any State deprive any person of life, liberty or property without due process of law; nor deny to any person within its jurisdiction the equal protection of the laws." The Fifteenth Amendment seems equally impressive: "The right of citizens of the United States to vote shall not be denied or abridged by the United States or by any State on account of race, color, or previous condition of servitude." (Pressure was brought to bear on Congress to include in the Fourteenth and Fifteenth Amendments a prohibition against discrimination based on sex, but with no success.) As we shall see, the words of these amendments had little immediate effect. Although slavery was legally and constitutionally ended,

[1]It may seem ironic that the median wage of blacks today is approximately three-fifths that of whites.
[2]19 Howard 393 (1857).

First reading of the Emancipation Proclamation, 1963.

politically and socially the idea of African-American inferiority has continued to the present time. In the following sections, we discuss several landmarks in the struggle of African Americans to overcome this inequality.

The Civil Rights Acts of 1865–1877

At the end of the Civil War, President Lincoln's Republican party controlled the national government and indeed most state governments, and the so-called Radical Republicans with their strong antislavery stance controlled the party. The Radical Republicans pushed through the Thirteenth, Fourteenth, and Fifteenth Amendments to the Constitution (the "Civil War amendments") and, from 1865 to 1877, succeeded in getting Congress to pass a series of civil rights acts that were aimed at enforcing these amendments. Even Republicans who were not necessarily sympathetic to a strong antislavery position wanted to undercut Democratic domination of the South. What better way to do so than to guarantee African-American suffrage? The civil rights acts that were passed from 1865 to 1877 were also supported by pro-industry legislators who believed that agrarian southern Democrats would impede industrialization.

The first Civil Rights Act under Reconstruction was passed in 1866 over the veto of President Andrew Johnson. That act extended citizenship to anyone born in the United States and gave African Americans full equality before the law. The act further authorized the president to enforce the law with national armed forces. Many considered the law to be unconstitutional, but such problems disappeared in 1868 with the adoption of the Fourteenth Amendment.

Among the six other civil rights acts in the nineteenth century, one of the more important was the Enforcement Act of May 31, 1870, which set out specific criminal sanctions for interfering with the right to vote as protected by the Fifteenth Amendment, or by the Civil Rights Act of 1866. Equally important was the Civil Rights Act of April 20, 1872, known as the Anti-Ku

DID YOU KNOW?

That by the time of the Revolution, African Americans made up nearly 25 percent of the American population of about three million?

Klux Klan Act. This act made it a federal crime for anyone to use law or custom to deprive an individual of his or her rights, privileges, and immunities secured by the Constitution or by any federal law. Section 2 of that act imposed detailed penalties or damages for violation of the act.

The last of these early civil rights acts, known as the Second Civil Rights Act, was passed on March 1, 1875. It declared that everyone is entitled to full and equal enjoyment of public accommodations, theaters, and other places of public amusement, and imposed penalties for violators. Unfortunately, the act was virtually nullified by the *Civil Rights Cases* of 1883 discussed below.

The civil rights acts of the 1870s are of special interest because they were an indication that congressional power or authority applied both to official, or government, action and to private action. The theory behind the acts was that if a state government failed to act, Congress could act in its absence. Thus Congress could directly legislate against private individuals who were violating constitutional rights of other individuals when state officials failed to protect those rights. At the time this was a novel theory and not truly accepted until the 1960s.

The Nullification of the Civil Rights Acts

The Reconstruction statutes, or civil rights acts, ultimately did little to secure equality for African Americans in their civil rights. Both the *Civil Rights Cases* and the case of *Plessy v. Ferguson* effectively nullified these acts.

The Civil Rights Cases. The Supreme Court invalidated the 1875 Civil Rights Act when it held in the *Civil Rights Cases*[3] of 1883 that the enforcement clause of the Fourteenth Amendment was limited to correcting actions by states in their official acts; thus the discriminatory acts of private citizens were not illegal. ("Individual invasion of individual rights is not the subject matter of the Amendment.") The 1883 Supreme Court decision met with widespread approval throughout most of the United States. Twenty years after the Civil War, the nation was all too willing to forget about the condition of African Americans in the prewar South. The other civil rights laws that the Court specifically did not invalidate became dead letters in the statute books, although they were never repealed by Congress.

Plessy v. Ferguson: **Separate but Equal.** A key decision during this period involved Homer Plessy, a Louisiana resident who was one-eighth African American. In 1892, he was riding in a train from New Orleans when the conductor made him leave the car, which was restricted to whites, and directed him to a car for nonwhites. At that time, Louisiana had a statute providing for separate railway cars for whites and African Americans.

Plessy went to court, claiming that such a statute was contrary to the Fourteenth Amendment's equal protection of the laws clause. In 1896, the U.S. Supreme Court rejected Plessy's contention, indicating that segregation alone did not violate the Constitution: "Laws permitting, and even requiring their separation in places where they are liable to be brought into contact do not necessarily imply the inferiority of either race to the other."[4] So was born the **separate but equal doctrine.**

SEPARATE BUT EQUAL DOCTRINE
The doctrine holding that segregation in schools and public accommodations does not imply the superiority of one race over another; rather, it implies that each race is entitled to separate but equal facilities.

[3]109 U.S. 3 (1883).
[4]*Plessy v. Ferguson*, 163 U.S. 537 (1896).

The only justice to vote against this decision was John Harlan, a former slaveowner. He stated in his dissent, "Our Constitution is color-blind, and neither knows nor tolerates classes among citizens." Justice Harlan also predicted that the separate but equal doctrine would "in time prove to be . . . as pernicious as the decision . . . in the Dred Scott Case."

For more than half a century, the separate but equal doctrine was accepted as consistent with the equal protection of the laws clause in the Fourteenth Amendment. In practical terms, the separate but equal doctrine effectively nullified this clause. *Plessy v. Ferguson* became the constitutional cornerstone of racial discrimination throughout the United States. Even though *Plessy* upheld segregated facilities in railway cars only, it was assumed that the Supreme Court was upholding segregation everywhere as long as the separate facilities were equal. The result was a system of racial segregation, particularly in the South, which required separate drinking fountains, separate seats in theaters, restaurants, and hotels, separate public toilets, and separate waiting rooms for the two races—collectively known as Jim Crow laws.

The End of the Separate but Equal Doctrine

A successful attack on the separate-but-equal doctrine began with a series of suits in the 1930s to admit African Americans to state professional schools. By 1950, the Supreme Court had ruled that African Americans who were admitted to a state university could not be assigned to separate sections of classrooms, libraries, and cafeterias. In 1951, Oliver Brown decided that his eight-year-old daughter, Linda Carol Brown, should not have to go to an all-nonwhite elementary school, twenty-one blocks from her home, when there was a white school only seven blocks away. The National Association for the Advancement of Colored People (NAACP), formed in 1909, decided to help Oliver Brown, and the results were monumental in their impact on American society. Actually, there was a series of cases, first argued in 1952, contesting state laws permitting or requiring the establishment of separate school facilities based on race. Following the death of Chief Justice Frederick M. Vinson and his replacement by Earl Warren, the Court asked for rearguments.

Brown v. Board of Education. The 1954 unanimous decision in *Brown v. Board of Education of Topeka*[5] established that public school segregation of races violates the equal protection clause of the Fourteenth Amendment. Chief Justice Warren stated that "to separate [African Americans] from others of similar age and qualifications solely because of their race generates a feeling of inferiority as to their status in the community that may affect their hearts and minds in a way unlikely ever to be undone." In other words, Warren said that separation implied inferiority, whereas the majority opinion in *Plessy v. Ferguson* had said the opposite. Legal pursuits still argue with the sociological rather than strictly legal criteria of the *Brown* decision.

"With All Deliberate Speed". The following year, in *Brown v. Board of Education*[6] (sometimes called the second *Brown* decision), the Court asked for rearguments concerning the way in which compliance with the 1954 decision should be undertaken. The Supreme Court declared that the lower courts must

[5]347 U.S. 483 (1954).
[6]349 U.S. 294 (1955).

DID YOU KNOW?

That the original Constitution failed to describe the status of a citizen or to describe how this status could be acquired?

Jim Crow laws resulted in the segregation of public facilities, such as this theater.

James Meredith

ensure that African Americans would be admitted to schools on a nondiscriminatory basis "with all deliberate speed." In other words, the high court told lower federal courts that they had to take an activist role in society. The district courts were to consider devices in their desegregation orders that might include "the school transportation system, personnel, [and] revision of school districts and attendance areas into compact units to achieve a system of determining admission to the public schools on a nonracial basis."

Reactions to School Integration

One unlooked-for effect of the "all deliberate speed" decision was that the term *deliberate* was used as a loophole by some jurists who were able to delay desegregation by showing that they were indeed acting with all deliberate speed but still were unable to desegregate. Another reaction to court-ordered desegregation was "white flight." In some school districts the public school population became 100 percent nonwhite when white parents sent their children to newly established private schools, sometimes known as "segregation academies."

The white South did not let the Supreme Court ruling go unchallenged. Arkansas's Governor Orval Faubus used the state's National Guard to block the integration of Central High School in Little Rock, Arkansas, in September 1957. The federal court demanded that the troops be withdrawn. Finally, President Eisenhower had to nationalize the Arkansas National Guard to quell the violence. Central High became integrated.

The universities in the South, however, remained segregated. When James Meredith, an African-American student, attempted to enroll at the University of Mississippi in Oxford in 1962, violence flared there as it had in Little Rock. Two men were killed and a number injured in campus rioting. President John Kennedy sent federal marshals and ordered federal troops to maintain peace and protect Meredith. One year later, George Wallace, governor of Alabama,

Little Rock Central High School, 1957

promised "to stand in the schoolhouse door" to prevent two African-American students from enrolling at the University of Alabama in Tuscaloosa. Wallace was forced to back down when Kennedy federalized the Alabama National Guard.

The Controversy Continues: Busing

In most parts of the United States, school integration is made difficult by housing segregation. Although it is true that a number of school boards in northern districts created segregated schools by the arbitrary drawing of school district lines, the concentration of African Americans and other minorities in well-defined geographical locations was the reason for the **de facto segregation** of northern public schools. Whether segregation was de facto or **de jure segregation,** the obvious solution seemed to be the transporting of some African-American schoolchildren to white schools and some white schoolchildren to nonwhite schools. Increasingly, the courts ordered school districts to engage in such **busing** across neighborhoods. Busing led to violence in some northern cities, as in south Boston where African-American students were bused into blue-collar Irish-Catholic neighborhoods.

Busing is unpopular with many groups. In the mid-1970s, almost 50 percent of the African Americans interviewed were opposed to busing and approximately three-fourths of the whites interviewed held the same opinion.[7] None-

[7]Dinae Ravitch, "Busing: The Solution That Has Failed to Solve," *New York Times,* December 21, 1975, Section 4, p. 3.

DID YOU KNOW?

That the Rhode Island colony enacted the first American law declaring slavery illegal, on May 18, 1652?

DE FACTO SEGREGATION
Racial segregation that occurs not as a result of deliberate intentions but because of past social and economic conditions and residential patterns.

DE JURE SEGREGATION
Racial segregation that occurs because of laws or administrative decisions by public agencies.

BUSING
The transportation of public school students from areas where they live to schools in other areas to eliminate school segregation based on residential patterns.

Busing in Boston. What legal process was used to require such an action?

DID YOU KNOW?

That during the 1964 Mississippi Summer Project, organized by students to register African-American voters, there were 1,000 arrests, 35 shooting incidents, 30 buildings bombed, 25 churches burned, 80 people beaten, and at least 6 murders?

theless, the Supreme Court upheld a number of busing plans. In 1971, the court upheld the right of judges to order school busing in the case of *Swann v. Charlotte-Mecklenburg Board of Education.*[8] In this case, the justices unanimously held that busing was permissible in school districts that had practiced deliberate segregation in the past. Two years later, in *Keyes v. School District No. 1,*[9] the Court ruled that the Denver school board had intentionally segregated a significant number of students. The Court determined that the Denver school board had to desegregate the school system completely. (The *Keyes* decision was reaffirmed in 1979 when the Court upheld crosstown busing plans in Dayton and Columbus, Ohio.[10]) In 1974, the Supreme Court, in a five to four vote, rejected a plan to bus children between Detroit and its suburbs. The Court determined in this case, *Milliken v. Bradley,*[11] that busing could not be ordered between the school districts unless there had been intentional action by the suburban district to segregate the city schools.

In an apparent reversal of previous decisions, the Supreme Court in June 1986 allowed the Norfolk, Virginia, public school system to end fifteen years of court-ordered busing of elementary schoolchildren.[12] Starting in the fall of 1986, the Norfolk schools were allowed to assign children to schools in their neighborhoods, even though ten of the city's thirty-five elementary schools would become 97 to 100 percent nonwhite. The Norfolk school board supported the decision. Its support was prompted by a drop from 32,500 whites attending public schools in 1970 when busing was ordered to fewer than 14,000 in 1985.

Lower federal courts have followed the Supreme Court's lead in allowing school districts to discontinue busing.[13] These and other cases hold that once a school district implements a plan to establish a racially neutral school system, the district is not responsible for any resegregation that results from changing demographics (such as "white flight"). Nevertheless, busing is still approved as a remedy for cases in which school districts are segregating students.[14]

■ THE CIVIL RIGHTS MOVEMENT

The *Brown* decision applied only to public schools. Not much else of the structure of existing segregation was affected. In December 1955, a forty-three-year-old African-American woman, Rosa Parks, boarded a public bus in Montgomery, Alabama (see Profile in this chapter). When it became crowded and several white people stepped aboard, she was asked to move to the rear of the bus, the "colored" section. She refused, was arrested, and was fined $10; but that was not the end of the matter. For an entire year, African Americans boycotted the Montgomery bus line. The protest was headed by a twenty-seven-year-old Baptist minister, Dr. Martin Luther King, Jr. During

[8]402 U.S. 1 (1971).
[9]413 U.S. 189 (1973).
[10]*Dayton Board of Education v. Brinkman,* 443 U.S. 526 (1979), and *Columbus Board of Education v. Penick,* 443 U.S. 449 (1979).
[11]*Milliken v. Bradley,* 418 U.S. 717 (1974).
[12]*Riddick v. School Board of City of Norfolk,* 627 F.Supp. 814 (1984), certiorari denied 107 S.Ct. 420 (1986).
[13]See, for example, *Flax v. Potts,* 864 F.2d 1157 (5th Cir. 1989) and *Price v. Austin Independent School District,* 729 F.Supp. 533 (W.D. Tex. 1990).
[14]*Keyes v. School District No. 1,* 895 F.2d 659 (10th Cir. 1990).

PROFILE

Rosa Parks

"My shoulder ached, I had had a bad day at work, I was tired from sewing all day, and all of a sudden everything was just too much."

She was an unlikely figure to be a rallying point for a major civil rights campaign in the heart of Alabama in the 1950s. On December 1, 1955, Rosa Parks, a forty-two-year-old seamstress, refused to give up her seat on a Montgomery, Alabama, bus to a white passenger. She was arrested for violating Alabama's segregation laws, spent the night in jail, and, by her act, spurred the African-American community to organize a total boycott of the Montgomery bus system. Rosa Parks's simple refusal to move to the back of the bus was the catalyst for the movement of African Americans to end segregation of buses, trains, lunch counters, and other public facilities in the South.

Rosa Parks was born on February 4, 1913, in Tuskegee, Alabama. Her father was a carpenter; her mother taught school. As a child she was soft spoken and mild mannered. Her early years were marked by fear of the Ku Klux Klan and their night raids on African-American families. After studying at Alabama State College, she worked briefly at clerical jobs, finally becoming a tailor's assistant at a Montgomery department store. Her husband, Raymond Parks, was a barber.

The only indicator of Rosa Parks's engagement in civil rights was her volunteer work for the NAACP, where she helped in the campaign to register African-American voters.

After working long days as a seamstress, Mrs. Parks often walked the mile home to her apartment because she found the bus system, with its segregated seating, a trial to endure. She claimed that if you did not passively follow the rules, "whites would accuse you of causing trouble when all you were doing was acting like a normal human being instead of cringing. You didn't have to wait for a lynching. You died a little each time you found yourself face to face with this kind of discrimination." On the day she finally rebelled, Mrs. Parks took the bus because

it was too hot to walk. Halfway through the trip, the bus filled up and the driver ordered the four African-American riders in Mrs. Parks's row to give up their seats to boarding white passengers. Mrs. Parks refused because, she recalls, "My shoulder ached, I had had a bad day at work, I was tired from sewing all day, and all of a sudden everything was just too much."

After Rosa Parks's arrest and harsh treatment in the Montgomery jail, the African-American community organized a boycott of the bus system that lasted for a year. Although the bus boycott was the beginning of civil rights activism in Alabama, Mrs. Parks suffered for her actions. She was fired from her job within two months, and her husband eventually lost his job as well. They were continually harassed by threatening telephone calls and racist intimidation. Rosa went to work for the group that coordinated the boycott and, within a short time, found herself speaking for civil rights throughout the country. Eventually, Rosa and her husband moved to Detroit where she became involved in community work and continued to work for civil rights.

Within ten years after Mrs. Parks's action, segregated facilities were outlawed by the Civil Rights Act of 1964, and Congress passed the Voting Rights Act of 1965 that provided real protection for African-American voters. Rosa Parks, the woman who wouldn't move to the back of the bus, was hailed by Martin Luther King as "the great fuse that led to the modern stride toward freedom."

the protest period, he went to jail,[15] and his house was bombed; but in the face of overwhelming odds, King won. In 1956, the federal district court issued an injunction prohibiting the segregation of buses in Montgomery. The era of civil rights protests had begun.

The following year, Martin Luther King formed the Southern Christian

[15]Read his "Letter from the Birmingham Jail" for a better understanding of this period.

DID YOU KNOW?

That by September 1961, more than 3,600 students had been arrested for participating in civil rights demonstrations and that 141 students and 58 faculty members had been expelled by colleges and universities for their part in civil rights protests?

Leadership Conference (SCLC). King's philosophy of nonviolent civil disobedience was influenced greatly by Mahatma Gandhi's life and teachings. Gandhi had led Indian resistance to the British colonial system from 1919 to 1947, using tactics such as demonstrations and marches as well as purposeful, public disobedience of unjust laws, while remaining nonviolent. King's followers successfully used these methods to widen public acceptance of their case. For the next decade, African Americans and sympathetic whites engaged in sit-ins, freedom rides, and freedom marches. In the beginning such demonstrations were often met with violence, but the contrasting image of nonviolent African Americans and violent, hostile whites created strong public support for the civil rights movement. When African Americans in Greensboro, North Carolina, were refused service at a Woolworth's lunch counter, they organized a sit-in that was aided day after day by sympathetic whites and African Americans. Enraged customers threw ketchup on the protestors. Some spat in their faces. But the sit-in movement continued to grow. Within six months of the first sit-in at the Greensboro Woolworth's, hundreds of lunch counters throughout the South were serving African Americans.

The sit-in technique was also successfully used to integrate interstate buses and their terminals, as well as railroads engaged in interstate transportation. Although buses and railroads that were engaged in interstate transportation were prohibited from segregating African Americans from whites,[16] they only stopped doing so after the sit-in protests.

The civil rights movement, with King at its head, gathered momentum in the 1960s. One of the most famous of the violence-plagued protests occurred in Birmingham, Alabama, in the spring of 1963, when Police Commissioner Eugene "Bull" Connor unleashed police dogs and used electric cattle prods against the protestors. People throughout the country viewed the event on national TV with indignation and horror, and such media coverage played a key role in the process of ending Jim Crow conditions in the United States. The ultimate result was that the most important civil rights act in the nation's history, passed in 1964.

In August 1963, Dr. Martin Luther King, Jr., organized a massive March on Washington for Jobs and Freedom. Before a quarter-million white and nonwhite Americans and millions watching on TV, Dr. King gave the world his dream (see Highlight). King's dream was not to be realized immediately. Eighteen days after his famous speech, four African-American girls attending Bible class in the basement room of the Sixteenth Street Baptist Church in Birmingham, Alabama, were killed by a bomb explosion.

Police dog attacks, cattle prods, high-pressure water hoses, beatings, bombings, and the March on Washington—all of these events led to an environment in which Congress felt compelled to act on behalf of African Americans. So came the second era of civil rights acts, the so-called Second Reconstruction period.

■ MODERN CIVIL RIGHTS LEGISLATION AND ITS IMPLEMENTATION

In the wake of the Montgomery bus boycott, public sentiment for stronger civil rights legislation put pressure on Congress and President Dwight David

---

[16]See *Morgan v. Commonwealth of Virginia*, 328 U.S. 373 (1946); and *Henderson v. United States*, 339 U.S. 819 (1950).

HIGHLIGHT

Martin Luther King, Jr.: "I Have a Dream"

On August 28, 1963, in the centennial year of the Emancipation Proclamation, a long-planned mass mobilization of civil rights supporters took place in the March on Washington for Jobs and Freedom. The march, attended by 250,000 African-American and white men and women, was a major event in the civil rights movement and in the leadership of Martin Luther King, Jr., head of the Southern Christian Leadership Conference. The March on Washington helped to generate political momentum that resulted in the landmark civil rights legislation of 1964 and 1968, and it also propelled Atlanta Baptist minister King to the forefront of the civil rights movement.

Local school bands provided early entertainment for the crowd gathered at the Washington Monument marshaling grounds. Joan Baez sang the anthem of the civil rights movement, "We Shall Overcome," and the mood was further enhanced by the songs of Peter, Paul, and Mary and the resounding voice of Odetta. Several minutes before the scheduled 11:30 A.M. starting time for the march to the Lincoln Memorial, the marchers set out behind the Kenilworth Knights, a local drum and bugle corps. The crowd moved too quickly for its leaders, who rushed to keep up with the marchers while marshals and news reporters tried to slow the human flow along Constitution and Independence Avenues.

At the Lincoln Memorial, more entertainers performed for the crowd massed around the reflecting pool and near the memorial steps. Performances of Bobby Darin, Josh White, Bob Dylan, Marian Anderson, Lena Horne, Mahalia Jackson, and others were interspersed with speeches by author James Baldwin, actors Paul Newman, Charlton Heston, Burt Lancaster, Sidney Poitier, Marlon Brando, Sammy Davis, Jr., and Harry Belafonte, Nobel Prize-

winner Dr. Ralph Bunche, and sports greats Jackie Robinson and Wilt Chamberlain.

The day's program included speeches by civil rights leaders John Lewis, Roy Wilkins, A. Philip Randolph, and Martin Luther King, Jr. The jobs, education, and antidiscrimination programs called for by earlier speakers were summarized in Dr. King's words:

> There will be neither rest nor tranquility in America until the Negro is granted his citizenship rights. The whirlwinds of revolt will continue to shake the foundations of our nation until the bright day of justice emerges. . . . I have a dream that my four little children will one day live in a nation where they will not be judged by the color of their skin but by the content of their character. . . . When we let freedom ring, when we let it ring from every village and every hamlet, from every state

and every city, we will be able to speed up that day when all God's children, black men and white men, Jews and Gentiles, Protestants and Catholics, will be able to join hands and sing in the words of that old Negro spiritual, "Free at last! Free at last! Thank God almighty, we are free at last!"

The contribution of Martin Luther King, Jr. to minority rights was officially recognized on October 20, 1983, when, after originally opposing the legislation, President Reagan signed into law an act establishing January 15, Martin Luther King, Jr.'s birthday, as a national holiday beginning in 1986.

Sources: David L.Lewis, *King: A Critical Bibliography* (New York: Praeger, 1970), pp. 210–232. Lenwood G. Davis, *I Have a Dream . . .: The Life and Times of Martin Luther King, Jr.* (Westport, Conn.: Negro Universities Press, 1969), pp. 132–140.

Civil rights laws have opened new opportunities to workers.

Eisenhower to act. The action taken was relatively symbolic. The Civil Rights Act of 1957 established a Civil Rights Commission and a new Civil Rights Division within the Justice Department. (President Reagan tried to abolish the Commission in 1983; Congress extended its life for another twenty years, after working out a compromise in which the president and congressional leaders would select its members.)

The growing number of demonstrations and sit-ins successfully created further pressure for more legislation through the classic democratic politics of mobilization of public opinion, coordinated with lobbying of political leaders. The Civil Rights Act of 1960 was passed to protect voting rights. Whenever a pattern or practice of discrimination was documented, the Justice Department, on behalf of the voter, could bring suit even against a state. The act also set penalties for obstructing a federal court order by threat of force and for illegally using and transporting explosives. But the 1960 Civil Rights Act, as well as that of 1957, had little substantive impact.

The same cannot be said about the Civil Rights Acts of 1964 and 1968, and the Voting Rights Act of 1965. Those acts marked the reassumption by Congress of a leading role in the enforcement of the constitutional notion of equality, for *all* Americans, as provided by the Fourteenth and Fifteenth Amendments.

The Civil Rights Act of 1964

As the civil rights movement mounted in intensity, equality before the law came to be "an idea whose time has come," in the words of conservative Senate Minority Leader Everett Dirksen. The 1964 legislation, the most far-reaching bill on civil rights in modern times, forbade discrimination on the basis of gender, race, color, religion, and national origin.

The major provisions of the act were as follows:

1. It outlawed arbitrary discrimination in voter registration.
2. It barred discrimination in public accommodations, such as hotels and restaurants, whose operations affect interstate commerce.

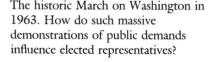

The historic March on Washington in 1963. How do such massive demonstrations of public demands influence elected representatives?

3. It authorized the federal government to sue to desegregate public schools and facilities.

4. It expanded the power of the Civil Rights Commission while extending its life.

5. It provided for the withholding of federal funds from programs administered in a discriminatory manner.

6. It established the right to equality of opportunity in employment.

Discrimination in housing was not covered by the 1964 act.

Several factors led to the passage of the 1964 act. As we noted, there had been a dramatic change in the climate of public opinion owing to violence perpetrated against protesting African Americans and whites in the South. Second, the assassination of President John F. Kennedy in 1963 had, according to some, a significant effect on the national conscience. Many believed the civil rights program to be the legislative tribute that Congress paid to the martyred Kennedy. Finally, the 1964 act could be seen partly as the result of President Lyndon B. Johnson's vigorous espousal of the legislation after his gradual conversion to the civil rights cause.

The act was passed in Congress only after the longest **filibuster** in the history of the Senate (eighty-three days) and only after **cloture** was imposed for the first time to cut off a civil rights filibuster.

The Civil Rights Act of 1968

Martin Luther King, Jr., was assassinated on April 4, 1968. Nine days after King's death, President Johnson signed the Civil Rights Act of 1968, which forbade discrimination in most housing and provided penalties for those attempting to interfere with individual civil rights, giving protection to civil rights workers, among others. Although the open-housing provision seemed important at the time, it was made obsolete by that summer when the Supreme Court prohibited discrimination in the sale and rental of all housing, using as a precedent the Civil Rights Act of April 9, 1866.[17] The Court held that Section 1 of the earlier act contains a broad prohibition against any racial discrimination in the sale or rental of property. It therefore forbids private development companies from refusing to rent to an individual simply because she or he is African American. The Court noted that racial discrimination "herds men into ghettos and makes their ability to buy property turn on the color of their skin."

Employment and Affirmative Action

Title VII of the Civil Rights Act of 1964 is the cornerstone of employment discrimination law, prohibiting discrimination in employment based on race, color, religion, sex, or national origin. Under Title VII, executive orders were issued that banned employment discrimination by firms that received any federal funding. The 1964 Civil Rights Act created a five-member commission, the **Equal Employment Opportunity Commission (EEOC),** to administer Title VII.

The EEOC can issue interpretive guidelines and regulations, but these do not have the force of law. Rather, they give notice of the commission's en-

[17]*Jones v. Mayer,* 329 U.S. 409 (1968).

DID YOU KNOW?

That in 1963 there were more than 10,000 demonstrations for racial equality?

FILIBUSTER
In the Senate, unlimited debate to halt action on a particular bill.

CLOTURE
A method invoked to close off debate and to bring the matter under consideration to a vote in the Senate.

EQUAL EMPLOYMENT OPPORTUNITY COMMISSION (EEOC)
A commission established by the 1964 Civil Rights Act to (1) end discrimination based on race, color, religion, sex, or national origin in conditions of employment and (2) promote voluntary action programs by employers, unions, and community organizations to foster equal job opportunities.

SUBPOENA
A legal writ requiring a person's appearance in court to give testimony.

AFFIRMATIVE ACTION
Policies issued in job hiring that give special consideration or compensatory treatment to traditionally disadvantaged groups in an effort to overcome present effects of past discrimination.

REVERSE DISCRIMINATION
The charge that affirmative action programs requiring preferential treatment or quotas discriminate against those who have no minority status.

Alan Bakke, admitted to medical school after a ruling by the U.S. Supreme Court against numeric minority quotas. Without some specific goals, how can institutions take affirmative action to provide access to minorities?

forcement policy. The EEOC also has investigatory powers: It has broad authority to require the production of documentary evidence, to hold hearings, and to **subpoena** and examine witnesses under oath.

To put teeth in the 1964 law, President Johnson applied the concept of **affirmative action** in 1965. Affirmative action can be defined as remedial steps taken to improve work opportunities for women, racial and ethnic minorities, and other persons considered to have been deprived of job opportunities in the past on the basis of other than work-related criteria.

Reverse Discrimination: Backlash

By the early 1970s, Labor Department regulations imposing numerical employment goals and timetables had been applied to every company that did more than $10,000 worth of business of any sort with the national government. Affirmative action plans were also required whenever an employer had been ordered to develop such a plan by a court or by the EEOC because of past discrimination. Finally, labor unions that had been found to discriminate against women or minorities were required to follow affirmative action plans.

Many people became convinced that affirmative action plans had a negative impact on whites, especially white males, and such plans began to be challenged in the courts. In *McDonald v. Santa Fe Trail Transportation Company*,[18] in 1976, the Supreme Court stated that "Title VII [of the 1964 Civil Rights Act] prohibits racial discrimination against the white petitioners upon the standards 'as would be applicable were they Negroes." Several employees had misappropriated the property of the Santa Fe Trail Transportation Company. Although the white employees were discharged, the black employees were reinstated. The issue of voluntary affirmative action programs was not, however, addressed in the *Santa Fe* case.

The Bakke Case.   Alan Bakke, a Vietnam war veteran and engineer who had been turned down for medical school at the Davis campus of the University of California, discovered that his academic record was better than some of the minority applicants who had been admitted to the program. He sued the University of California regents, alleging **reverse discrimination.** The Davis medical school had held sixteen places out of one hundred for educationally "disadvantaged students" each year, and the administrators at that campus admitted to using race as a criterion for admission for these particular minority slots. At trial in 1974, Bakke said that his exclusion from medical school violated his rights under the Fourteenth Amendment's provision for equal protection of the laws. The trial court agreed. On appeal, the California Supreme Court agreed also. Finally, the regents of the university appealed to the U.S. Supreme Court.

On June 28, 1978, the Supreme Court handed down its decision in *Regents of the University of California v. Bakke*.[19] The Court did not actually rule against affirmative action programs but did hold that Bakke must be admitted to the UC-Davis Medical School because its admission policy had used race as the *sole* criterion for the sixteen "minority" positions. But Justice Lewis Powell, speaking for the Court, indicated that race can be considered "as a factor" among others in admissions (and presumably hiring) decisions. In other words,

[18]427 U.S. 273 (1976).
[19]438 U.S. 265 (1978).

it is legal to give special consideration to "afflicted minority groups" in an effort to remedy past discrimination. Race can be one of many criteria for admission, but not the only one. So affirmative action programs were upheld as constitutional, but not if they were carried out as they had been at the UC-Davis Medical School.

The Weber Case.   In 1979, the issue of reverse discrimination in employment was addressed in *United Steelworkers of America v. Weber.*[20] The lower courts in that case had relied on the *Santa Fe* decision mentioned earlier and on Section 703(j) of the Civil Rights Act of 1964.

Using the language of *Santa Fe* and Section 703(j) as a basis for their decisions, the district court and the court of appeals held that the use of a racial quota to staff an apprenticeship program violated Title VII. What was at issue was Brian F. Weber's complaint that as a white employee in Kaiser Aluminum and Chemical Corporation's plant in Gramercy, Louisiana, he was denied his rightful place in a training program that would have raised his salary had he successfully completed it. Because of the affirmative action program in his union, he was passed over in favor of African Americans with less seniority.

Even though the lower courts held in his favor, in 1979 the Supreme Court reversed their decisions. The Court stated that the prohibition against racial discrimination in Title VII must be read against the background of the legislative history of Title VII calling for voluntary or local resolution of the discrimination problems and against the historical context from which the 1964 Civil Rights Act arose. In other words, the union apprenticeship program at Kaiser Aluminum violated the words of the Civil Rights Act of 1964, but not the spirit. Essentially, any form of reverse discrimination—even explicit quotas—is permissible provided that it is the result of a legislative, executive, or judicial finding of past discrimination.

The Court's More Recent Record on Reverse Bias

In 1984, in *Firefighters Local Union No. 1784 v. Stotts,*[21] the Court said that the layoffs of Memphis firefighters had to be done by seniority unless there were African-American employees who could prove they were victims of racial bias. But in 1986, in *Wygant v. Jackson Board of Education,*[22] the Court sent the signal that affirmative action could apply to hiring, but not to layoffs. This mixed message came from a case brought by a group of white teachers in Jackson, Michigan, challenging a labor contract that called for laying off three white teachers for every faculty member belonging to a minority group in order to preserve the school system's racial and ethnic ratios. In a five-to-four vote, the Court's majority said that the Jackson plan violated the Fourteenth Amendment's guarantee of equal protection of the laws. In a case involving Alabama state troopers, the use of temporary quotas to expand the access of blacks to the formerly all-white police force was upheld.

A more recent Supreme Court ruling dealt with whether whites could challenge employment decisions made on the basis of an earlier judgment that included goals for hiring African Americans as firefighters in the city of Bir-

[20]443 U.S. 1963 (1979).
[21]467 U.S. 561 (1984).
[22]476 U.S. 267 (1986).

Ku Klux Klan cross burning.

WHITE PRIMARY
State primary election that restricts voting only to whites; outlawed by the Supreme Court in 1944.

GRANDFATHER CLAUSE
A device used by southern states to exempt whites from state taxes and literacy laws originally intended to disenfranchise African-American voters. It allowed the voting franchise to anyone who could prove that his grandfather had voted before 1867.

mingham, Alabama. White firefighters who had not been parties in the earlier proceedings alleged that because of their race, they were being denied promotions in favor of less qualified African Americans. In a five to four decision, in June 1989, the Supreme court held that the white firefighters could challenge those employment decisions.[23]

The conservative shift of the Court has become evident in other recent cases. On affirmative action, the Court overturned a local government minority-preference program, signaling to dozens of cities and states that hundreds of affirmative action programs may also be invalid.[24] On racial discrimination, the Court has made it harder for minority workers to sue employers.[25] In another ruling, racial harassment was exempted from a widely used antibias law.[26]

■ THE VOTING RIGHTS ACT OF 1965

The Fourteenth Amendment provided for equal protection of the laws. The Fifteenth Amendment, ratified on February 3, 1870, stated that "the right of citizens of the United States to vote shall not be denied or abridged by the United States or by any State on account of race, color, or previous condition of servitude." Immediately after the adoption of those amendments, African Americans in the South began to participate in political life—but only because of the presence of federal government troops and northern Radical Republicans who controlled the state legislatures.

Historical Barriers to African-American Political Participation

This brief enfranchisement ended after 1877 when southern Democrats regained control of state governments. Social pressure, threats of violence, and the terrorist tactics of the Ku Klux Klan combined to dissuade African Americans from voting. Southern politicians, using everything except race as a formal criterion, passed laws that effectively deprived them of the right to vote.

This was the era of the **white primary** and the **"grandfather clause."** By using the ruse that political party primaries were private, southern whites were allowed to exclude African Americans. The Supreme Court in *Grovey v. Townsend*[27] upheld such exclusion. Indeed, it was not until 1944 in *Smith v. Allwright*[28] that the highest court finally found the white primary to be a violation of the Fifteenth Amendment. The Court reasoned that the political party was actually performing a state function in holding a primary election, not acting as a private group. By being denied a vote in the primary, African Americans had been prevented from participating in the selection of public officials from the end of Reconstruction until World War II. The grandfather clause allowed the voting franchise only to those who could prove that their grandfathers had voted before 1867. Most African Americans were automatically disenfranchised by this provision.

[23]*Martin v. Wilks*, 109 S.Ct. 2180 (1989).
[24]*Richmond v. J. A. Croson Co.*, 488 U.S. 469 (1989).
[25]*Wards Cove Packing Co. v. Atonio*, 109 S.Ct. 2115 (1989).
[26]*Patterson v. McLean Credit Union*, 109 S.Ct. 2363 (1989).
[27]295 U.S. 45 (1935).
[28]321 U.S. 649 (1944).

Another device to prevent African Americans from voting was the **poll tax,** requiring the payment of a fee to vote. This practice assured the exclusion of poor African Americans from the political process. It wasn't until the passage of the Twenty-fourth Amendment, ratified in 1964, that the poll tax as a precondition to voting was eliminated. That amendment, however, applied only to federal elections. In *Harper v. Virginia State Board of Elections,*[29] the Supreme Court declared that the payment of any poll tax as a condition for voting in any election is unconstitutional.

Actually, the poll tax had reduced the voting participation of both whites and nonwhites in five southern states, but it worked a greater hardship on African Americans because a higher proportion of them was poor. Also, the poll tax was unequally enforced among whites and nonwhites. The result was that poll tax states had turnouts in national elections equal to about 50 percent of those in states not having poll taxes.

By the 1960s, the distribution of seats in state legislatures among state voting districts had become another obstacle to African Americans' political participation. Frequent use of area instead of population as a basis for voting districts led to (white) rural representatives dominating state legislatures. In 1962, the Supreme Court decided that federal courts could hear cases involving state districting, and in 1964, the Court ruled that population is the only acceptable basis for the distribution of seats in a legislative body.[30]

As late as 1960, only 29.1 percent of African Americans of voting age were registered in the southern states, in stark contrast to 61.1 percent of whites. In 1965, Martin Luther King, Jr. took action to change all that. Selma, the seat of Dallas County, Alabama, was chosen as the site to dramatize the voting rights problem. In Dallas County, only 2 percent of eligible African Americans had registered to vote by the beginning of 1965. King organized a fifty-mile march from Selma to the state capital in Montgomery. He didn't get very far. Acting on orders of Governor George Wallace to disband the marchers, state troopers did so with a vengeance—with tear gas, night sticks, and whips.

[29]383 U.S. 663 (1966).
[30]*Baker v. Carr,* 369 U.S. 186 (1962); *Reynolds v. Sim,* 377 U.S. 533 (1964).

POLL TAX
A special tax that must be paid as a qualification for voting. The Twenty-Fourth Amendment to the Constitution outlawed the poll tax in national elections, and in 1966 the Supreme Court declared it unconstitutional in all elections.

African-American voter registration.

Once again the national government was required to intervene to force compliance with the law. President Johnson federalized the National Guard and the march continued. During the march, the president went on television to address a special joint session of Congress urging passage of new legislation to assure African Americans the right to vote. The events during the Selma march and Johnson's dramatic speech, wherein he invoked the slogan of the civil rights movement ("We shall overcome"), were credited for the swift passage of the Voting Rights Act of 1965.

Provisions of the Voting Rights Act of 1965

The act had two major provisions. The first one outlawed discriminatory voter registration tests. The second major section authorized federal registration of persons and federally administered voting procedures in any political subdivision or state that discriminated electorally against a particular group.[31] The act targeted counties, most in the South, where less than 50 percent of the eligible population was registered to vote. Federal voter registrars were sent to these areas to register African Americans who had been restricted by local registrars. Within one week after the act was passed, forty-five federal examiners were sent to the South. A massive voter registration drive covered the country.

In 1970, the Voting Rights Act was extended to August 1975. In 1975, Congress extended the act to August 1982, and it was again extended in 1983. The act originally brought federal supervision to areas of the country known for discriminating against African Americans in the voter registration process. But in 1970 and in 1975, the law was extended to other states and to other

---

[31]In addition, the act indicated that in Congress's opinion the state poll tax was unconstitutional.

Nelson Mandela addressing the Congress of the United States, after being freed from a South African prison. What does Mandela symbolize to people around the world?

CRITICAL PERSPECTIVE

How Much Progress in Race Relations?

One generation after the Civil Rights movement that began in the 1950s, the question of how much progress Americans have made toward eradicating racism is still unanswered. Although African Americans have been guaranteed legal equality for more than twenty-five years and have gained considerable political power, many scholars claim that the nation's commitment to equal opportunity has weakened in recent years.

On the positive side, African Americans register and vote in all states and, in many areas, elect black officials. By 1990, there were more than 7,000 black elected officials in the United States, including the mayors of New York, Detroit, Atlanta, Philadelphia, Los Angeles, and the District of Columbia. Thousands of African Americans hold jobs in the police, in fire protection, and other civil service positions. Perhaps more significant is the change in white attitudes. The proportion of white Americans who approve of integrated schooling has risen from 30 percent in 1942 to 91 percent in 1988; approval of equal hiring practices increased from 42 percent in 1944 to 96 percent, and those who feel that having a black neighbor is acceptable increased from 35 percent in 1942 to 86 percent in 1987.

The change in expressed attitudes toward equal opportunity does not, however, change the fact that African Americans still hold unequal status in American society. Although African-American median income was 62 percent of whites' in 1975, ten years later it dropped to 56 percent. The poverty rate among African-American families is three times the rate among whites, and the group that is poorest, the "underclass," has tripled in size since the 1970s. Although schools are integrated in most communities, housing is not. There have also been more incidents of racism in the 1980s and 1990s and increased numbers of complaints filed with the Equal Employment Opportunity Commission. One report summarized the nation as a "society which is less unequal but also less caring than it was in the 60s."

A Harris poll commissioned by the NAACP found that African Americans and whites are "worlds apart" on many race issues. For example 67 percent of whites felt that African Americans receive equal pay for equal work, while 66 percent of African Americans disagreed. Moreover, 61 percent of whites felt that African Americans are treated equally in the U.S.

criminal justice system, while 80 percent of African Americans disagreed.

Another phenomenon has begun to manifest itself in U.S. race relations—conflict *between* minorities. In Miami, Florida; Los Angeles, California; Dallas, Texas; and especially Chicago, Illinois, relations between African Americans and Hispanics (Latinos) have seriously deteriorated. In part, this is caused by the greater racial diversity in the Hispanic community which makes it easier for Hispanics to assimilate into white America (many Hispanics are fair skinned). Other factors contributing to this tension, according to researchers, are language differences, religion (Hispanics are largely Catholic), and the importance of the traditional two-parent and extended family in Hispanic culture (in contrast, in 1990 over 40 percent of all African-American families had no father present).

The most dramatic and tragic racial incidents have been the fights, beatings, and killings in New York: the Howard Beach and Bensonhurst (Brooklyn) incidents during which African-American youths died in confrontations with ethnic whites. Tension between African Americans and Korean grocers, whom the former accused of insulting treatment, resulted in a five-month boycott and demonstrations in front of Korean stores. The beatings of Vietnamese by African Americans, the killing of several Asian Americans by "skin heads," and a substantial overall rise in racially motivated violence and hate crimes across the country (even on college campuses) attest to the fact that the United States has a long way to go before finding racial harmony. In response to these incidents, the federal government and many states have enacted laws against hate crimes.

Exercise in Critical Thinking
1. Consider your own community: Has the status of African Americans and other minorities improved or declined in recent years?
2. How do you reconcile the more favorable views of whites toward integration with the increased segregation in schools in urban areas?
3. Why are white Americans so sure that equal opportunities exist for all?

groups, including Spanish-speaking Americans, Asian Americans, and Native Americans, including Alaskan natives. For example, the extended act requires that ballots be printed in both Spanish and English in areas where more than 5 percent of the population is Spanish speaking. As a result of this act and its extensions and of the large-scale voter registration drives in the South, the number of African Americans registered to vote climbed dramatically, until, by 1980, 55.8 percent of African Americans of voting age in the South were registered.

By 1986 the number of registered African-American voters nationally was more than 11 million. In that same year, there was a total of more than 5,000 black elected officials, including 18 at the national level, 336 at the state level, 2,977 at the local level, 563 in the judiciary, and 1,266 in various local school districts. Several of the largest cities in the United States have African-American mayors: New York, Los Angeles, Philadelphia, Detroit, and Seattle. In 1984, the Reverend Jesse Jackson became the first African-American candidate to compete seriously for the Democratic presidential nomination. In 1988, a renewed effort to register thousands more African Americans and other minority voters helped Jackson achieve an impressive total primary and caucus vote. During the early 1988 primaries, Jackson won more votes than any other democratic candidate. In 1989 Virginia became the first state to elect an African-American governor. (The Critical Perspective in this chapter discusses the state of race relations in the United States.)

■ HISPANICS IN AMERICAN SOCIETY

The second largest minority group in America can be classified loosely as Hispanics—or individuals of Spanish-speaking background. Even though this minority group represents over 8 percent of the American population, its diversity and geographical dispersion have hindered its ability to achieve political power, particularly at the national level. Mexican Americans constitute the majority of the Hispanic population. Of the over twenty million Hispanics in the United States, Mexican Americans are a majority. The next largest group is Puerto Ricans, then Cubans, and finally Hispanics from Central and South America.

Economically, Hispanics in the United States are less well off than non-Hispanic whites but a little better off than African Americans. About 27 percent of them live in poverty. Unlike the economic situation of African Americans, that of Hispanic Americans is worsening. The percentage of their population below the poverty level rose over three percentage points between 1982 and 1990. The unemployment rate for Hispanics decreased less than the rate for any other group, and Hispanics' real median income actually dropped during that period. Hispanic leaders have attributed these declines to language barriers and lack of training, which lead to low-paying jobs.

Politically, Hispanics are gaining power in some states. Table 5-2 shows how the number of Hispanics holding public office grew in certain states between 1973 and 1988.

Mexican Americans

Mexicans were not brought to the colonies by force. Some of them were in the southwestern territory of what eventually became the United States before the settlement of the eastern shores by the early English colonists. Indeed, Mexico formerly owned California as well as Arizona, New Mexico, Texas, Utah, Nevada, parts of Wyoming and Oklahoma, and most of Colorado during the early 1800s. By 1853, these territories had all been acquired by the United

TABLE 5-2
Hispanic Officeholders by Selected States, 1973 and 1986

STATE	1973	1986	% INCREASE
Arizona	95	232	144
California	231	450	95
Florida	13	45	246
New Mexico	366	588	61
New York	10	69	590
Texas	565	1,466	159

Source: "Latinos and State Government: Toward a Shared Agenda," by Rodolfo O. de la Garza et al., *Journal of State Government,* vol. 61, no. 2, March/April 1988, p. 78.

States (by purchase or by war) and were settled mainly by Anglos. It is interesting to note that the treaty ending the Mexican War in 1845 explicitly guaranteed all former citizens of Mexico then living in United States territory the same liberties, protections, and rights as any other American citizens. They did not receive this treatment, though. These Mexicans' rights were frequently violated as Anglos appropriated their land and harassed their persons.

Mexicans, though, have continued to settle in the United States, immigrating to this country primarily for economic reasons. The Mexican economy has greatly declined in recent years, and many Mexicans look to the United States for employment and a chance to better their lives. Most Mexican Americans still live in the southwestern United States, but many have moved to Indiana, Illinois, Pennsylvania, and Ohio.

Political Participation.   Mexican Americans have a very low level of political participation in national elections. In 1988, only 57 percent of Mexican Americans were registered to vote compared with 73 percent of Anglos. Mexican Americans have faced numerous barriers to voting, as have African Americans, not the least of which is the language barrier for those unable to read English. The Voting Rights Act extension of 1970 alleviated this problem somewhat by requiring ballots to be printed in both English and Spanish in districts where at least 5 percent of the registered voters are Spanish speaking.

Mexican Americans have also had little success in sending their own representatives to Congress. In 1976, the Hispanic caucus in the House of Representatives consisted of five people—a California Mexican American, two Texas Mexican Americans, the resident commissioner from Puerto Rico, and a Puerto Rican from New York City. In the One Hundred Second Congress, in 1991, the number of Hispanics had risen to 12. Mexican Americans have gained more political clout in local politics. For example, a Mexican American holds the office of mayor in Denver.

Political Organizations.   Mexican Americans have not, however, let the American political process pass them by. As far back as 1921, the Orden Hijos de America (Sons of America) was formed in San Antonio, Texas. Eight years later, in Corpus Christi, the League of United Latin American Citizens (LULAC) was established. Its goal, then and now, is to facilitate Hispanics' integration into American culture, using English as the primary language tool. Through numerous court battles, LULAC succeeded in removing discrimi-

DID YOU KNOW?

That the Hispanic population of the United States is approximately 21 million, a growth of 39 percent between 1980 and 1990? Hispanics make up 8.2 percent of the U.S. population and are expected to surpass African Americans as the largest minority in the next century.

natory barriers in public facilities, education, and employment in the Southwest for Hispanics.

In the 1960s, the Political Association of Spanish Speaking Organizations (PASO) in Texas, the Mexican American Political Association (MAPA) in California, and the American Coordinating Council on Political Education (ACCPE) entered numerous local political contests to elect Mexican Americans. They did not engage in economic or social struggles, however.

Mexican Americans have not been uniformly in favor of downplaying social and economic inequalities. One of those with different views is Cesar Chavez. In 1962, in California, Chavez began organizing farm workers into the United Farm Workers and started a five-year strike against central California grape growers to force them to recognize the union. The UFW organized a nationwide boycott of table grapes. Many responded out of sympathy with the strikers, who called their movement "La Causa." By 1975, Chavez and the UFW had convinced the California legislature to pass a bill that gave farm workers the same rights held by union members elsewhere.

Among the more controversial and well-publicized developments within the Mexican American, or Chicano, movement was the La Raza Unida Party (LRUP). La Raza Unida grew out of the first Chicano National Youth Movement meeting in Colorado in 1968. Chicanos, in forming La Raza Unida, hoped to show Anglo politicians that they were no longer dependent on them. They also desired to make the Chicano community aware of the possibilities of making change. The uniqueness of La Raza Unida lay in its being more than a political party. It was designed as "an ethnic institution that will break the cycle of Chicano repression by a variety of organizational efforts. La Raza Unida is not a vehicle for entering the mainstream of United States society, but is a safeguard for the Mexican American bilingual/bicultural uniqueness."[32] LRUP had some success in Colorado, Arizona, California, and New Mexico, as well as in Texas. Today it is not as active as it was in the 1970s.

[32]Matt S. Meyer and Feliciano Rivera, *The Chicanos* (New York: Hill and Wang, 1972), p. 277.

Spanish-language billboards in Miami, Florida.

Puerto Ricans

Because Puerto Rico is a U.S. Commonwealth, its inhabitants are American citizens. As such, they may freely move between Puerto Rico and the United States. Most of them who come to the continental United States reside in the New York–New Jersey area.

In Puerto Rico, Puerto Ricans use U.S. currency, U.S. mails, and U.S. courts. In Puerto Rico, they are also eligible for U.S. welfare benefits and food stamps, but they pay no federal taxes unless they move to the continental United States. By 1990, almost three-fourths of Puerto Ricans living in Puerto Rico were eligible for food stamps. Those who come to the mainland do not fare much better, owing to economic and language barriers and racial discrimination.

Puerto Ricans have had few political successes on the mainland. There are more than a million Puerto Ricans living in New York City, constituting at least 10 percent of the city's population. But only about 30 percent are registered to vote. Other dispiriting statistics show that currently there are only a few Puerto Rican city council members and only one Puerto Rican member of Congress. In New York City's massive bureaucracy, only a small percentage of the administrators are Puerto Rican.

Cuban Americans

Unlike their Hispanic brothers and sisters from Mexico and Puerto Rico, Cuban Americans chose to come to the United States for political, as well as economic, reasons. They left Cuba to escape the communist regime of Fidel Castro. Many of the emigrés came from the educated middle class, and, although they had to leave most of their financial assets behind, their education and training helped them to become established economically with relative ease. In Miami, for example, one can find numerous examples of former Cuban professionals who started out as taxi drivers and today own banks, retail stores, and law practices.

In 1980, President Carter allowed more than 150,000 Cubans to enter Florida through the so-called Mariel boatlift. This wave of Cuban immigrants was mostly lower class and unskilled. A thousand Mariel Cubans had been released from Cuban prisons and mental institutions. Their assimilation into even the heavily Latin-accented culture of Miami was noticeably less successful than that of their earlier compatriots.

Many Cubans who had been released from Cuban prisons to come to the United States in 1980 were detained in American prisons shortly after their arrival. In December 1987, after hearing rumors of an arrangement with the Castro government to send some prisoners back to Cuba, many of them panicked. Groups of Cuban detainees rioted and took hostages in Atlanta and Oakdale, Louisiana. After several days of tension, federal authorities agreed to review each of their cases individually.

A majority of Cuban Americans reside in southern Florida, although some live in New York City and elsewhere. Economically, they constitute a major force in the southern Florida region. Politically, they have been very successful in gaining power within city and county governments. Even Miami's mayor was born in Cuba. As a group, Cuban Americans are known for being staunchly anticommunist and strongly oppose any attempts of the American government to improve relations with communist Cuba. Militant Cuban-American orga-

> **DID YOU KNOW?**
>
> That Florida's 1.5 million Hispanics own 32,000 businesses that contribute almost $3 billion annually to the Florida economy?

nizations have actually denounced, threatened, or even bombed individuals and institutions in south Florida that they feel are pro-Castro or procommunist. Their political influence will certainly rise as their percentage of the population increases. In particular, in Dade County, it is estimated that (in the not-too-distant future) Hispanics, particularly Cubans, will constitute the majority of the county's population.

Bilingualism

All Hispanic groups are concerned about the preservation of their language and heritage. Bilingual education programs are supported by many Hispanic groups as a civil right. This claim was established by the Supreme court in 1974 when it required a school district in California to provide special programs for Chinese students with language difficulties if there were a substantial number of these children.[33] There is disagreement over the purpose of bilingual education. Some people feel such programs should be temporary, helping students only until they master English, whereas others want them to be permanent programs to help immigrant students preserve their cultural heritage.

Bilingualism extends beyond the education system. In many parts of the United States, signs, announcements, advertisements, and government documents are printed in languages other than English. Concern over the number of immigrants who do not speak English led California voters in 1986 to approve a law making English the state's official language. Similar measures were adopted by referendum in 1988 in Arizona, Colorado, and Florida. Members of Congress have even proposed an amendment to the U.S. Constitution making English our national language. Such laws affect government documents and official communication, not private use of language.

■ NATIVE AMERICANS

When America was "discovered," there were about ten million Native Americans, or "Indians," living in the New World. It is estimated that they inhabited areas from the north slope of Alaska to the southern tip of South America for at least thirty thousand years before Europeans arrived. (See Highlight on Native American democratic traditions.) By 1900, the number of Native Americans in the continental United States had declined to less than half a million owing to the effects of war and diseases brought to the continent by European immigrants. In the latest census, about 1.5 million individuals identified themselves as Indians. The five states with the largest Indian population are Oklahoma, Arizona, California, New Mexico, and Alaska.

Native Americans have not fared well economically, as is evident in Figure 5-2. From the point of view of health, Indians are even worse off than their economic status shows. Table 5-3 shows that the age-adjusted death rates per 100,000 of the population are two and sometimes three or more times the national average.

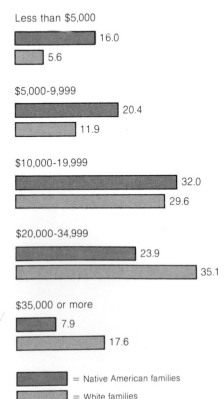

FIGURE 5-2
Native American and White Family Earnings Compared

Percentage of Native American and white families that earn --

Less than $5,000
16.0
5.6

$5,000-9,999
20.4
11.9

$10,000-19,999
32.0
29.6

$20,000-34,999
23.9
35.1

$35,000 or more
7.9
17.6

■ = Native American families
□ = White families

[33]*Lau v. Nichols,* 414 U.S. 563 (1974).

HIGHLIGHT

The Iroquois Confederacy and American Democratic Principles

A little-known fact about the development of American democratic principles is that Native-American political values greatly influenced them. It was out of a rich Native-American democratic tradition that many of the distinctive political beliefs of American life emerged. For example, long before Columbus reached American shores, Native-American tribes had universal suffrage for men as well as women, the patterns of states within a state that we call federalism, the habit of treating chiefs (their presidents) as servants of the people instead of as their masters (such as kings), and the insistence that the community must respect individual differences and aspirations.

Benjamin Franklin and other colonial leaders were impressed enough by the main features of the Iroquois Confederacy, consisting of five separate Native-American nations, that he presented a similar "Plan of Union" for the thirteen colonies in 1754.

At the Constitutional Convention in Philadelphia in 1787, John Rutledge read the following words from an Iroquois Treaty of 1520, "We, the people, to form a union, to establish peace, equity, and order . . ." The preamble to the United States Constitution was, indeed, based on the law of the land as it existed then.

In 1987, the United States Senate, with the House concurring, resolved

that "The Congress, on the occasion of the 200th anniversary of the signing of the United States Constitution, acknowledges the historical debt which this republic of the United States of America owes to the Iroquois Confederacy and other Indian nations for their demonstrations of enlightened, democratic principles of Government, and their example of a free association of independent Indian nations."

SOURCE: Dr. Jerry Stubben, Iowa State University

The Appropriation of Indian Lands

When the Continental Congress passed the Northwest Ordinance, it stated that "the utmost good faith shall always be observed towards the Indians; their lands and property shall never be taken from them without their consent; and their property rights, and liberty, they shall never be invaded or disturbed,

TABLE 5-3
Native Americans: Age-Adjusted Death Rates per 100,000 Population, 1989

	NATIVE AMERICANS (INCLUDING ALASKANS)	ALL RACES
Motor-vehicle accidents	44.1	17.1
All other accidents	37.4	16.7
Alcoholism	29.1	6.4
Diabetes	17.2	9.1
Homicide	17.1	8.9
Pneumonia, influenza	15.2	10.9
Suicide	14.8	10.8
Tuberculosis	3.5	0.4

Source: Indian Health Service, Center for Disease Control, 1990.

DID YOU KNOW?

That American Indians were not made citizens of the United States until an act of Congress on June 15, 1924?

unless in just and lawful wars authorized by Congress." In 1787, Congress designated the Indian tribes as foreign nations to enable the government to sign treaties with them about land and boundaries.

During the next hundred years, many agreements were made with the Indian tribes; however, many were broken by Congress, as well as by individuals who wanted Indian lands for settlement or exploration. In 1830, Congress instructed the Bureau of Indian Affairs to remove all Indian tribes to lands west of the Mississippi River to free land east of the Mississippi for white settlement. From that time on, Indians who refused to be "removed" to whatever lands were designated for them were forcibly moved. With the passage of the Dawes Act (General Allotment Act) of 1887, the goal of Congress became the "assimilation" of Indians into American society. Each family was allotted acreage within the reservation to farm, and the rest was sold to whites. The number of acres in reservation status was reduced from 140 million acres to about 47 million acres. Tribes that refused to cooperate with this plan lost their reservations altogether.

The U.S. Senate Subcommittee on Indian Education during the 1969 Congress issued its analysis of what had happened. The report declared:

> A careful review of the historical literature reveals that the dominant policy of the Federal Government toward the American Indian has been one of forced assimilation which has vacillated between the two extremes of coercion and persuasion. At the root of the assimilation policy has been a desire to divest the Indian of his land and resources.[34]

(Another kind of appropriation is discussed in a chapter Highlight, Skeletons in the Smithsonian's Closet.)

Native-American Political Response

Native Americans have been relatively unsuccessful in garnering political power. This is partly because the tribes themselves have no official representation in government and because the tribes are small and scattered. In the 1960s, the National Indian Youth Council (NIYC) was the first group to become iden-

[34]U.S. Senate, Subcommittee on Indian Education, *Indian Education: A National Tragedy—A National Challenge,* 91st Cong., 1st Sess. (1969), p. 9.

Navajo Council in Window Rock, Arizona.

HIGHLIGHT

Skeletons in the Smithsonian's Closet

The Smithsonian Museum of Natural History in our nation's capital has large collections of just about everything relating to America's past. Among its collection are fourteen thousand American Indian skeletons. In 1986, an Indian rights organization called the American Indians against Desecration (AIAD) argued that the skeletons are the sacred remains of Indians' ancestors. After all, most of the five hundred or more recognized American Indian tribes believe that the burial place of deceased Indians is indeed a sacred site. The removal, display, and even study of Indian remains, they maintained, violates their religious beliefs and traditions—their civil liberties. AIAD and other groups have asked the Smithsonian to return the skeletons for proper burial. "They do not do this with any other race of people but the red man," said AIAD head Jan Hammill. "Can you imagine if they had dug up white Americans—Catholics, Jews, Protestants—and put them on display in the

name of science? It would not be tolerated."*

The issue of Indian skeletons and Indian rights reflects the delicate balance among conflicting interests, beliefs, and

*"The Skeletons in the Smithsonian's Closet," *The Washington Post,* National Weekly Edition, March 17, 1986, p. 33.

rights. Responding to the demands and desires of American Indians, the Oklahoma State Museum recently returned all thirty-six Indian remains in its collections. These were buried at the famous Wounded Knee Cemetery in South Dakota. Other museums are considering similar actions.

tified with Indian militancy. At the end of the 1960s, a small group of persons identifying themselves as Indians occupied Alcatraz Island, claiming that the island was part of their ancestral lands. In 1972, several hundred Native Americans marched to Washington and occupied the Bureau of Indian Affairs (BIA, founded in 1824 as part of the War Department). They arrived in a caravan labeled "The Trail of Broken Treaties." In 1973, supporters of the American Indian Movement (AIM) took over Wounded Knee, South Dakota, which had been the site of the massacre of at least 150 Sioux Indians by the U.S. Army in 1890.[35] The goal of these demonstrations was to protest federal policy toward Native Americans.

The siege at Wounded Knee focused the anger of Native Americans on the BIA and the way their affairs were being administered by the agency. The American Indian Policy Review Commission, established by Congress, agreed in its 1977 report that the BIA mishandled Indian money, did not protect Indian property rights, and neglected Indian safety. The commission recommended that the BIA be replaced by a separate Department of Indian Affairs

[35]This famous incident was the subject of Dee Brown's best-selling book, *Bury My Heart at Wounded Knee* (New York: Holt, Rinehart, and Winston), published two years before the siege.

that would be divorced from the Department of the Interior. The commission's recommendation was not implemented.

Native Americans today face the continuing problem of dealing with a divided BIA. Some BIA bureaucrats want to maintain the dependency of the Native Americans on the reservation system run by the agency. Recently, however, the BIA has let more and more tribes control the police, job training, educational, and social programs that the BIA used to manage. Nonetheless, there are still numerous conflicts between Indian tribes and the BIA, as well as between them and state governments. Native Americans face the additional problem of being a fragmented political group now that a large number of their population do not live on reservations.

As more Americans have become aware of the concerns of Native Americans, Congress has started to compensate for past injustices. Courts, too, have shown a greater willingness to recognize Indian treaty rights. For example, cases dealing with the right of present-day Native Americans to a share of the annual salmon harvest in Washington involved, in part, enforcement of nineteenth-century treaty provisions.[36] In a decision that may open the way for other longstanding Native American claims, the Supreme Court ruled that three tribes of Oneida Indians could claim damages for the use of tribal land that had been unlawfully conveyed in 1795.[37] Lower court cases decided since this ruling may limit recovery on other similar claims, however.[38]

Asian Americans

Because Asian Americans have a relatively high median income, they are typically not thought of as being discriminated against. This certainly was not always the case. The Japanese Exclusion Act of 1882 prevented the Japanese from coming to the United States to prospect for gold or to work on the railroads or in factories in the West. Japanese-American students were segregated into special schools after the 1906 San Francisco earthquake so that white children could use their buildings. The 1941 Japanese bombing of Pearl Harbor intensified fear and hatred of the Japanese. Executive Order 9066, signed by President Franklin D. Roosevelt on February 19, 1942, set up "relocation" camps for virtually every Japanese American living in the United States. The Japanese were required to dispose of their property, usually at below-market prices. It wasn't until 1944 and 1945 that the relocation camps were closed and the prisoners freed after a December 18, 1944, Supreme Court ruling deemed such activity illegal.[39] Three Japanese Americans who had been jailed for resisting relocation during World War II successfully sued the United States in 1983. They won damages and their 1942 convictions were overturned because of their claim that the army lied about the possibility of security threats. In 1988, Congress provided funds to compensate former camp inhabitants or their survivors.

Both the Japanese and the Chinese have overcome initial prejudice to lead America's ethnic groups in median income and median education. Recently,

This American street scene contrasts a typical highrise apartment complex with an Asian shopping district. As Asian Americans increase in numbers, will their cultures be assimilated into the mainstream or will they be regarded as a threat to Anglo Americans?

[36]*United States v. Washington,* 384 F.Supp. 312 (W.D. Wash. 1974), aff'd 520 F.2d 676 (9th Cir. 1975), substantially aff'd, *Washington v. Washington State Commercial Passenger Fishing Vessel Association,* 443 U.S. 658 (1979).

[37]*County of Oneida v. Oneida Indian Nation,* 470 U.S. 226 (1985).

[38]For example, *Yankton Sioux Tribe of Indians v. South Dakota,* 796 F.2d 241 (9th Cir. 1986).

[39]See Dylan S. Meyer, *Uprooted American: The Japanese-American and the War Relocation Authority During World War II* (Tucson: University of Arizona Press, 1971).

however, a new group of Asians have had to fight discrimination—those from Southeast Asia. More than a million Indo-Chinese war refugees, most from Vietnam, have come into the United States in the last 15 years. Like their predecessors, the newer immigrants have quickly increased their median income; only about one-third of all such households receive welfare of any sort. Most have come with families and have been sponsored by American families or organizations, so they have had good support systems to help them get started. As with the Chinese and the Japanese, however, once they become established, they are seen as economic threats.

■ THE MELTING POT

No one really knows when the term *melting pot* was first applied to American society, although the phrase is derived from a play of that name by Israel Zangwill. Perhaps the last lines of Emma Lazarus's sonnet, "The New Colossus," engraved on a tablet inside the base of the Statue of Liberty, best synthesize the melting-pot idea.

> Give me your tired, your poor,
> Your huddled masses yearning to breathe free,
> The wretched refuse of your teeming shore.
> Send these, the homeless, tempest-tossed to me,
> I lift my lamp beside the golden door!

The earlier ethnic groups that came to the United States in the great waves of immigration that began after the Civil War were first northern Europeans and later eastern and southern Europeans. Then, as now, they were lured by the American Dream—the promise of economic security and freedom. Assimilation was the way by which the American Dream could be achieved.

Until the late nineteenth century, the United States imposed few limitations on immigration. Immigration laws became increasingly restrictive, although one of the largest waves of immigration occurred between 1901 and 1910, and included almost nine million people. After 1965, the government began to ease the restrictions. Between 1981 and 1990, there were an estimated eight to twelve million immigrants, including three to seven million illegal aliens. To deal with illegal immigration, Congress passed the Immigration Reform and Control Act of 1986. The new law authorized more border guards and provided penalties for employers who were caught hiring illegal aliens. The act also granted amnesty to illegal aliens who could prove they had been in the United States since 1981.

Today the melting-pot idea is being revised. A new emphasis on ethnic and racial pride has come to the fore with increased Asian and Hispanic immigration and African-American self-consciousness. Since 1977, four out of five immigrants have come from Latin America or Asia. If current rates continue, Hispanics will overtake African Americans as the nation's largest minority by the year 2020. By the year 2030, African Americans and Hispanics together will comprise 30 percent of the population. Americans do not have the same feelings toward all ethnic groups. Table 5-4 shows how these attitudes differ.

Ben Wattenberg of the American Enterprise Institute in Washington, D.C., says the United States is becoming the world's first "universal nation." We have always claimed to be one, but this really was not true until relatively recently. The "old guard" Anglo-Saxon Protestants will no longer dominate

TABLE 5-4
Public Attitudes Toward American Ethnic Groups

GROUP	HAS BEEN GOOD FOR COUNTRY	HAS BEEN BAD FOR COUNTRY	MIXED FEELINGS	DON'T KNOW
English	66%	6%	21%	8%
Irish	62	7	22	9
Jews	59	9	24	8
Germans	57	11	23	8
Italians	56	10	25	9
Poles	53	12	25	11
Japanese	47	18	26	9
Blacks	46	16	31	7
Chinese	44	19	27	10
Mexicans	25	34	32	10
Koreans	24	30	31	15
Vietnamese	21	38	31	11
Puerto Ricans	17	43	29	11
Haitians	10	39	26	26
Cubans	9	59	22	10

Source: "Asian Americans: A Growing Force," by Dinker I. Patel, *Journal of State Government*, vol. 61, no. 2, March/April 1988, p. 75.

American political life. We may see intense periods of conflict among African Americans and newly arrived Hispanics and Asians as they vie for jobs and political influence. On the other hand, if Hispanics and African Americans can form coalitions, perhaps with Asian Americans, their political strength can be increased dramatically, for they will have the numerical strength to make significant changes. African-American leader Jesse Jackson has attempted to form such a coalition. His 1984 and 1988 campaigns for the presidency were focused on and supported by a "Rainbow Coalition" of African Americans, Hispanics, Native Americans, women, and other minority groups.

America has been challenged and changed—and culturally enriched—time and again by immigrant peoples speaking other languages and observing different customs. The minority groups discussed here eventually will come to participate fully in the American system, and someday those thought of as "traditional Americans" may be of Hispanic or Asian origin, as well as Anglo-Saxon.

Citizenship and Immigrant Rights

A great debate has taken place in recent years over the issue of immigrant rights. The questions have included whether illegal immigrants can become citizens, whether employers are liable for hiring illegals, and whether the economy can absorb so many new workers. Legislation passed in 1986 created a new process by which illegal aliens who have resided in the United States since 1982 can apply to become legal residents, and, after five more years, citizens. Employers are required to certify the legal status of alien workers, or face fines. Although the law forbids discrimination against anyone on the basis of national origin, the new rules may, in fact, reinforce prejudices against minorities. Many organizations are concerned with the way the illegal immigrants are treated by federal and state police and immigration officials. Such groups want to maintain the nation's commitment to relatively free entry to people of all racial, ethnic, religious, political, and income backgrounds. Their goals are fair immigration rules, greater protection for resident illegal aliens, and a more pluralistic and tolerant culture.

You can become involved in this national controversy over immigration and citizenship policy in a number of ways. You can pay attention to the often contradictory policies that are proposed in Congress to deal with the problem. If you feel deeply enough about this issue, you might wish to join action organizations that lobby through influencing public opinion or by exerting direct pressure on Congress and the executive branch. Some of you may wish to help a sanctuary group that provides aid to illegal aliens. (Be aware, however, that such activity may be illegal and could lead to your being prosecuted by the government.) A safer means of taking similar action would be to lobby your local government to enact laws allowing aliens fleeing persecution to live in your community. The following organizations have been involved in the controversy over immigration and citizenship policies. Some groups are generally in favor of the right to immigrate:

Center for Immigrants' Rights
48 St. Marks Place
New York, NY 10003
(212) 505-6890

Citizens Committee for Immigration Reform
1120 Belleview
McLean, VA 22102
(703) 759-3326

National Center for Immigrants' Rights
1636 West Eighth St., Suite 215
Los Angeles, CA 90017
(213) 487-2531

National Immigration Project of the National Lawyers Guild
14 Beacon St., Suite 407
Boston, MA 02108

Other groups that usually support stricter enforcement of existing immigration laws or a more homogeneous culture include:

Federation for American Immigration Reform
1424 16th St., N.W., Room 701
Washington, D.C. 20036
(202) 328-7004

U.S. English
1424 16th St., N.W., Suite 714
Washington, D.C. 20036
(202) 232-5200

CHAPTER SUMMARY

1. Minority rights have often been called civil rights, and the quest for the expansion of minority rights has been called the civil rights movement. It has taken this nation two hundred years to reach a semblance of equality among its citizens, and the effort to expand constitutional guarantees to all individuals continues.

2. Before the Civil War, the Constitution protected slavery. It was confirmed in the *Dred Scott v. Sanford* case in 1857, which held that slaves could not become U.S. citizens, nor were they entitled to the rights and privileges of citizenship. With the emancipation of the slaves in 1863 and the passage of the Thirteenth, Fourteenth, and Fifteenth Amendments to the Constitution, this inequality was legally and constitutionally ended. Politically and socially, however, the badge of inferiority continued.

3. The first civil rights acts, passed from 1865 to 1877, were designed to enforce the civil rights amendments nationally. They ultimately did little to secure equality for African Americans.

4. In *Plessy v. Ferguson* (1896), the Supreme Court upheld a "separate but equal" doctrine, which became the constitutional cornerstone of racial discrimination throughout the United States.

5. In *Brown v. Board of Education* (1954), the Supreme Court finally reversed the 1896 decision and declared that enforced racial segregation in public schools was unconstitutional. Southern states continued to resist integration, and segregation continued on a de facto basis. Courts increasingly ordered busing to achieve integration, which has created a major controversy. The controversy continues as the Supreme Court, in June 1986, allowed the Norfolk, Virginia, public school system to end fifteen years of court-ordered busing of elementary school children.

6. By the 1960s, the quest for civil rights had led to a mass political movement with Martin Luther King, Jr. at its head.

7. Congress passed the Civil Rights Act of 1964, which banned discrimination against minorities in public accommodations and employment. The Civil Rights Act of 1968 forbade discrimination in housing.

8. The Equal Employment Opportunity Commission was created by the 1964 act to administer a program of affirmative action designed to increase the hiring of minority workers. Affirmative action was eventually seen to have a negative impact on whites, especially white males. This question of reverse discrimination reached the Supreme Court in the *Bakke* and *Weber* cases.

9. Historically, African Americans were effectively excluded from the election process through such methods as the poll tax, the grandfather clause, and literacy tests. The Voting Rights Act of 1965 outlawed discriminatory voter registration tests and authorized federal registration and federally administered voting procedures in any state or political subdivision evidencing electoral discrimination or unduly low registration rates.

10. The second largest minority group in America, Hispanics, or Spanish-speaking individuals, constitutes over 8 percent of the American population. Their diversity and geographical dispersion have hindered their ability to achieve political power, particularly at the national level, although a number of Hispanic groups have succeeded in removing some discriminatory barriers.

11. Of the nearly fifteen million Hispanics in the United States, Mexican Americans number about nine million. The next largest group is the Puerto Ricans, followed by the Cubans, then those from Central and South America.

12. Before the arrival of Europeans in the New World, Native Americans numbered about ten million. War and disease drastically reduced their numbers, and today there are approximately 1.5 million Native Americans in the United States. Statistically, they remain the least educated, most economically disadvantaged, and unhealthiest group in America. They have been relatively unsuccessful in garnering political power and face the continuing problem of dealing with a divided Bureau of Indian Affairs.

13. Among Asian Americans, Japanese and Chinese have overcome prejudice to lead America's ethnic groups in median income and median education. Southeast Asian immigrants—approximately a million in the last ten years—have quickly increased their median income; only about one-third of all such households receive welfare of any sort.

14. Since 1977, four out of five immigrants have come from Latin America or Asia. As the ethnic and racial makeup of this country changes, the "old guard" Anglo-Saxon Protestants will no longer dominate American political life. Minority groups will come to participate more fully in the American political system.

QUESTIONS FOR REVIEW AND DISCUSSION

1. According to the Supreme Court in *Brown v. Board of Education*, "separate but equal" is "inherently unequal." Why did the Court reject the idea of separate but equal in 1954? Why didn't segregation really provide equal opportunities for African Americans in the United States?

2. Even though the North fought the Civil War in part to liberate the slaves, the southern states were able to reestablish white domination within a generation after the war. Why did the North allow the disenfranchisement of African Americans in the South, even though it violated the Constitution? How did the Supreme Court's views of the proper powers of government work to support segregation in the South and industrialization in the North?

3. To what extent can the "American" culture absorb other, non-Anglo-Saxon cultures such as those of the American Indians, the Hispanics, or the Asians? How would "American culture" be changed if we came to have a multilingual, multiethnic society?

4. What is the purpose of affirmative action programs? Is it possible to institute such programs without practicing reverse discrimination?

SELECTED REFERENCES

Dee Brown, *Bury My Heart at Wounded Knee* (New York: Holt, Rinehart & Winston, 1971). An important examination of the treatment of Native Americans as the frontier pushed westward.

Stokely Carmichael and Charles V. Hamilton, *Black Power: The Politics of Liberation in America* (New York: Vintage Books, 1967). Classic expression of the politics of racism in the United States and of the struggle to overcome white domination.

Elizabeth O. Colton, *The Jackson Phenomenon: The Man, The Power, The Message* (New York: Doubleday, 1989). This book is a very interesting and personal perspective on Jesse Jackson's 1988 presidential campaign from the vantage point of an insider who was his campaign press secretary.

Stephen Cornell, *The Return of The Native: American Indian Political Resurgence* (New York: Oxford University Press, 1988). Considered to be the best study of Native Americans as an important and increasingly politicized ethnic minority.

Norman Dorsen, *Discrimination and Civil Rights* (Boston: Little, Brown, 1969). This is a classic book of constitutional cases in civil rights and is regularly updated.

Richard Kluger, *Simple Justice* (New York: Alfred A. Knopf, 1975). The history of the 1954 Supreme Court ruling on *Brown v. Board of Education* and African Americans' struggle for equality.

Aldon D. Morris, *The Origins of the Civil Rights Movement* (New York: The Free Press, 1985). This interesting book traces the alliances among African-American groups and the tactics they used in accelerating the civil rights movement in the United States.

Guadalupe San Miguel Jr., *"Let All of Them Take Heed": Mexican Americans and the Campaign for Educational Equality in Texas, 1910–1981* (Austin: University of Texas Press, 1987). A historical study of discrimination against Mexican Americans and their lack of educational opportunities in Texas.

Sidney Verba and Gary R. Orren, *Equality in America: The View from the Top* (Cambridge, Mass.: Harvard University Press, 1985). This fascinating book used an elite survey of 2,762 American leaders from a wide range of groups (business, labor, feminists, and so on) to determine the meanings and implications of equality and attitudes about equality in America.

C. Vann Woodward, *The Strange Career of Jim Crow* (New York: Oxford University Press, 1957). The classic study of segregation in the southern United States.

CHAPTER 6

STRIVING FOR EQUALITY

CHAPTER CONTENTS

WHAT IF . . . CONGRESS HAD A QUOTA SYSTEM FOR MEMBERSHIP?

We are used to thinking of the United States Congress as a representative institution of government—that is, the members of Congress are there to see to it that laws are enacted that make good sense and that are desired by the public. But in one sense of the word *representation,* Congress is far from the ideal of representing the public. If by *representation* we mean that the members of Congress are just like "us," in terms of age, race, ethnicity, sex, and the like, then by most assessments Congress is an extremely unrepresentative institution. For example, just 31 out of 535 members of the House and Senate in the 102nd Congress (1991–92) were female when that Congress was elected in 1990. That works out to only about 6 percent. If we look at the population of the entire United States at the beginning of the 1990s, the percentage of women is about 51.4 percent. In other words, the number of women in Congress would have to be about ten times what it currently is for women to be represented according to their numbers in the population.

Look at how African Americans are represented in Congress. In the 102nd Congress, there were 26 African American elected members. That is just a little over 4.8 percent of the total membership. This compares with 12.4 percent of the entire population that is African American. So African-American representation would have to increase by about three times to be consistent with the demographics of race.

What about Hispanics? The 102nd Congress has 12 members who are Hispanic, but just 10 of them are voting representatives of states (the other two serve as nonvoting delegates from Puerto Rico and the Virgin Islands). Barely 2 percent of the voting members of Congress, then, is Hispanic. Of the entire U.S. population, about 8.2 percent is of Hispanic origin.

What if Congress adopted a quota system for determining its membership, by an amendment to the Constitution? We know for certain that there would be far more people in the House and Senate who would be female, African American, Hispanic, or some combination of these. It is easy to imagine that a very different set of laws would be passed. Civil rights legislation should have easier passage, and so should bills or proposed constitutional amendments (such as the equal rights amendment) mandating gender equality.

Of course, these predictions are reasonable only if you believe that all women in Congress have about the same views, that all African Americans tend to think pretty much alike, and that Hispanics generally agree with one another on matters of public policy. We know this is not true for a whole range of issues, but it is still likely that the kinds of policy decisions made by Congress would change considerably if Congress were to apportion its membership by a quota system. It is guaranteed, at least, that the predominantly white, male, Anglo composition of Congress would change forever, and with that change would almost certainly come a major change in public policy decisions.

---

1. What would you propose about apportioning quotas in Congress among German, Italian, and Greek Americans?
2. Should there be apportioning quotas based on education? Age?

The paramount destiny and mission of women are to fulfill the noble and benign offices of wife and mother. This is the law of the Creator.

Words of centuries ago? Not quite. These words were part of a Supreme Court opinion rendered in the first case tried under the Fourteenth Amendment in 1873. The Court at that time upheld the denial of the right of women to practice law.[1] The sentiment that it is somehow more "natural" for women (than for men) to tend the household and the children is still very much alive. Old ways of thinking die hard, and those who favor complete equality among men and women—socially, politically, and economically—must still struggle with this age-old cultural tradition regarding the proper status of women in society.

■ WOMEN'S POSITION IN SOCIETY: HISTORICAL BACKGROUND

In some ancient civilizations, women were granted a number of rights and privileges. If we look at the Code of Hammurabi, which dates back to the eighteenth century B.C., we see that married women were granted a great deal of personal and financial freedom. Women could get a divorce on the grounds of adultery or cruelty (although a husband could divorce his wife at will), and women were allowed to trade on their own account. Many women were judges, scribes, and elders. In ancient Egypt, the status of women was still higher. There they owned property and mixed freely with men.

In those cultures that formed the basis of Western civilization, however, this was not the case. In the Hebraic culture of the Middle East—which became a part of the Christian heritage in the West—women were regarded as little more than vehicles for the pleasure and/or paternal ambitions of men. They were an order apart from male society and had virtually no political or economic rights. For example, if a woman became widowed, she was left to find her way back to her father's house or to beg for a living—or, in some cases, to starve. In the cultural traditions of Greece and Rome, the situation was not much different. The Greeks and Romans likewise regarded women as social ornaments and childbearing slaves.

In the Christian world of the late Middle Ages, women were usually excluded from all public affairs as well as from religious affairs. The church acted on St. Paul's injunction:

The women should keep silence in the Churches. For they are not permitted to speak.[2]

With the growth of towns and the creation of a middle class, however, women began to improve their social and economic status. They were increasingly allowed to take part in trade and to become members of the medieval craft guilds. At the time of the American Revolution, some women practiced trades, but most accepted their roles as wives or mothers.

[1]*Bradwell v. Illinois*, 16 Wall. 130 (1873).
[2]1 Cor. 14:34.

The words of Susan B. Anthony (1820–1906) are still used today by those who work for women's political equality.

The Early Feminist Movement in the United States

Women were considered citizens in the early years of the nation, but they had no political rights. The first political cause in which women became actively engaged was the slavery abolition movement—although male abolitionists felt that women should not take an active role on the subject in public. Separate female and male antislavery societies were founded in many states. When the World Antislavery Convention was held in London in 1840, women delegates were barred from active participation. Responding partly to this rebuff, two American delegates, Lucretia Mott and Elizabeth Cady Stanton, returned from that meeting with plans to work for women's rights in the United States.

In 1848, Mott and Stanton organized the first women's rights convention in Seneca Falls, New York. The three hundred persons who attended approved a declaration of sentiments: "We hold these truths to be self-evident: that all men *and women* are created equal. . . ." In the following twelve years, groups of feminists held seven conventions in different cities in the Midwest and in the East. With the outbreak of the Civil War, however, advocates of women's rights were urged to put their support behind the war effort, and most agreed.

SUFFRAGE
Right to vote; the franchise.

Elizabeth Cady Stanton (1815–1902)

The Suffrage Issue and the Fifteenth Amendment

"The right of citizens of the United States to vote shall not be denied or abridged by the United States or by any State on account of race, color, or previous condition of servitude." So reads Section 1 of Amendment XV to the Constitution, ratified on March 30, 1870. The campaign for passage of this amendment split the women's **suffrage** movement. Militant feminists wanted to add "sex" to "race, color, or previous condition of servitude." Other feminists, along with many men, opposed this view; they wanted to separate African-American suffrage and women's suffrage to ensure the passage of the amendment. So, although the African American press supported the women's suffrage movement, it became separate from the racial equality movement.

Still, some women attempted to vote in the years following the Civil War. One, Virginia Louisa Minor, was arrested and convicted in 1872. She appealed to the Supreme Court, but the Court upheld her conviction.[3]

Susan B. Anthony and Elizabeth Cady Stanton formed the National Suffrage Association in 1869. According to their view, women's suffrage was a means to achieve major improvements in the economic and social situation of women in the United States. In other words, the vote was to be used to obtain a larger end. Lucy Stone, however, felt that the vote was the only major issue. Members of the American Women's Suffrage Association, founded by Stone and others, traveled to each state, addressed state legislatures, wrote, published, and argued their convictions. They achieved only limited success. In 1890, the two organizations quit battling and joined forces. The National American Women's Suffrage Association had only one goal—the enfranchisement of women—but it made little progress.

By the early 1900s, small radical splinter groups were formed, such as the Congressional Union headed by Alice Paul. This organization worked solely for the passage of an amendment to the national Constitution. Willing to use "unorthodox" means to achieve its goal, this group and others took to the streets. There were parades, hunger strikes, arrests, and jailings. Finally, in 1920, seventy-two years after the Seneca Falls convention, the Nineteenth Amendment was passed: "The rights of citizens of the United States to vote shall not be denied or abridged by the United States or by any State on account of sex." Women were thus enfranchised.

Although today it may seem that the United States was slow to give women the vote, it was really not too far behind the rest of the world. The first countries to grant women electoral equality with men were New Zealand in 1893, Finland in 1906, Norway in 1913, and Denmark and Iceland in 1915. Toward the end of World War I, or soon after, many more Western nations granted women the right to vote.

Susan B. Anthony (1820–1906)

The Continued Struggle for Equal Status

Obviously, the right to vote does not guarantee political power. It has been more than half a century since women obtained the right to vote in most countries of the Western world, yet the number of women who have held high political positions can be counted on one's fingers. Women have become elected heads of state in India, Ceylon, Israel, Bolivia, Argentina, Barbados, the Phillipines, Pakistan, and England. There have been a few women ministers in a number of countries, but normally these ministries are concerned primarily with so-called "women's interests," such as family affairs or social welfare. In the United States, no woman has yet been nominated for president by a major political party—although the predictions are that we will see one elected in the next half-century. In Congress, the men's club atmosphere prevails. A few women senators have been elected. As of 1991, there were 29 women members of the House of Representatives—only 7 percent of the total. Of the more than 10,000 members of the House of Representatives who have served, only 1 percent have been women. No woman has yet held one of the major leadership positions in the House or in the Senate.

Women have also been meagerly represented in federal political appointments, although this situation is changing. Franklin Roosevelt appointed the

[3]*Minor v. Happersett*, 88 U.S. (21 Wall) 162 (1874).

DID YOU KNOW?

That in 1916, Jeannette Rankin became the first woman to be elected to the U.S. House of Representatives, four years before the Nineteenth Amendment gave women the right to vote?

first woman to a cabinet post—Frances Perkins, who was secretary of labor from 1933 to 1945. In 1969, President Nixon declared that "a woman can and should be able to do any political job that a man can do." But by the time of his resignation in 1974, he had not appointed a woman to either the cabinet or the Supreme Court. His successor, Gerald Ford, appointed a woman as secretary of housing and urban development. President Carter had three women in his cabinet. Ronald Reagan appointed women to two major cabinet posts and to head the U.S. delegation to the United Nations. He is also credited with an historical first in his appointment of Sandra Day O'Connor to the Supreme Court in 1981. President Bush has appointed one woman to a cabinet post and a woman served as his international trade negotiator.

Women have had more success at attaining elective office in state legislatures and local governments. Several women have been elected to governorships. Over 20 percent of the legislators in nine states are women, and the same is true of city council members in large and medium-size cities. Chicago, Houston, and San Francisco have had women mayors, as have 10 percent of U.S. cities with populations of more than thirty thousand.

The representation of women in political office does not reflect their participation as voters. As Table 6-1 indicates, the absolute turnout of women voters nationally is higher than that of male voters.

The National Organization for Women (NOW)

There was a hiatus between the nineteenth-century women's movement in the United States and the current feminist movement that began in the late 1950s. The women's movement of today is referred to by its members as the "second wave." Pioneering this second wave was Betty Friedan, whose book, *The Feminine Mystique,* was a spirited exploration of "sexism," or "the disease which has no name," in the suburbia of the 1950s.[4]

Although often identified as middle-class, the modern women's movement seeks to define sexism and to eradicate it from all spheres of life for all women. Perhaps the most prominent of the organizations associated with the women's movement is the National Organization for Women (NOW). NOW was formed in 1966 by Friedan and others who were dissatisfied with the lack of anti-sex-discrimination activity by the then-largest women's organizations—the National Federation of Business and Professional Women's Clubs and the League of Women Voters. The specific issue around which NOW coalesced was the

[4]Betty Friedan, *The Feminine Mystique* (New York: W. W. Norton, 1963).

TABLE 6-1
Voting and Registration, 1988

Voting participation by females has recently been equal to or greater than voting participation by males. Here we can see that in absolute terms, more females than males voted and registered in 1988.

	PERSONS OF VOTING AGE (MILLIONS)	PERSONS REPORTING THEY REGISTERED (MILLIONS)	PERSONS REPORTING THEY VOTED (MILLIONS)	PERSONS REGISTERED (PERCENT)
Male	82.4	63.4	37.7	76.9
Female	91.5	65.0	42.2	71.0

SOURCE: *Statistical Abstract of the United States, 1990,* p. 249.

failure of the Equal Employment Opportunity Commission (EEOC) to enjoin newspapers from running separate want ads for men and women. In June 1966, at the third annual Conference of State Commissions on the Status of Women, the attendees demanded a resolution condemning such sex discrimination in employment. They were told that the conference "was not allowed to pass such a resolution" or take any action for that matter. NOW was formed and immediately sent telegrams to the EEOC. After a series of tough battles, in 1968 NOW won its war against sex-segregated want ads.

NOW elected Betty Friedan as its first president and adopted a blanket resolution designed "to bring women into full participation in the mainstream of American society *now*, exercising all the privileges and responsibilities thereof in truly equal partnership with men." NOW grew from its original 300 members to over 300,000 members in 1991. It has continued to be one of the leading pressure groups in the struggle for women's rights. (See this chapter's Profile for information on one of NOW's current leaders.)

The Supreme Court and Sex Discrimination

Laws that include different provisions for men and women are not always struck down by the Supreme Court. The Court has established standards for determining whether gender classifications are acceptable. Unlike laws with racial classifications, which are always "suspect" and are invalidated unless the government can prove that the classifications are rational, laws that classify by sex are permissible as long as they are "reasonable." To be struck down they must be proven otherwise. This standard of "reasonableness" was established by the Court in 1971 in *Reed v. Reed*,[5] a case involving an Idaho law that gave men preference over women in administering estates of dead relatives. In 1973, the Supreme Court struck down a federal law providing that servicemen's wives automatically receive certain benefits but servicewomen's husbands receive these benefits only if they demonstrate a certain degree of need.[6] In this case, some of the justices unsuccessfully tried to change the standard applied to gender cases to the "suspect" standard applied to race cases.

NOW and the Equal Rights Amendment

Perhaps more than any other women's group, NOW has championed the passage of the Equal Rights Amendment (ERA)—the proposed Twenty-seventh Amendment to the U.S. Constitution—which states:

Equality of rights under the law shall not be denied or abridged by the United States or by any state on account of sex.

ERA was first introduced in Congress in 1923 by leaders of the National Women's Party who felt that getting the vote would not be enough to change women's status. After years during which the amendment was not even given a hearing in Congress, it was finally approved by both chambers in 1972.

As we noted in Chapter 2, any constitutional amendment must be ratified by the legislatures (or conventions) in three-fourths of the states before it can become law. Since the early 1900s, most proposed amendments have required that ratification occur within seven years of passage of the amendment by

DID YOU KNOW?

That according to the Population Crisis Committee, Sweden leads the world in the status accorded women, followed by Finland and then the United States? (Women in Bangladesh suffer the greatest discrimination.)

---

[5]404 U.S. 71 (1971).
[6]*Frontiero v. Richardson*, 411 U.S. 677 (1973).

PROFILE

Patricia Ireland

"In the last twenty years, our greatest achievement has been to change public opinion. In the next twenty years, our task is to translate that change in public opinion into a change in public policy."

Changing perceptions of the role and rights of women in American society have led to corresponding changes in our laws, particularly in the areas of family law and employment law. Many feminists argue that this is just the first step toward the achievement of true equality for women under the law. One such person is Patricia Ireland, a senior officer in the National Organization for Women (NOW), the most active feminist organization in America. Ireland is a committed feminist and an attorney who has used her considerable legal skills and talents in the effective promotion of women's rights.

Born in Oak Park, Illinois, in 1945, she was, as she describes it, "raised in a very traditional family with a full-time homemaking mother and a father who worked outside the home." She received a bachelor's degree from the University of Tennessee and went to graduate school with the idea of pursuing a teaching career in German and Spanish.

A turning point in her life occurred in 1971 when Ireland for the first time met a woman lawyer and realized that she, too, could go to law school. She began legal studies in 1972 at Florida State University in Tallahassee and graduated with honors from the University of Miami School of Law in 1975. While attending the University of Miami, she served on the editorial staffs of the *University of Miami Law Review* and the university's inter-American law journal, *Lawyer of the Americas*. Following graduation, Ireland joined a law firm specializing in corporate and commercial litigation and handled cases having to do with inter-American business transactions.

During her twelve-year tenure with the law firm, Ireland was also pursuing another, increasingly important, inter-

est. Almost immediately, she began to represent, *pro bono* (that is, for free), Dade County NOW—the local chapter of the National Organization for Women, and at the same time that she was advancing in her law firm, she became more and more committed to NOW's goals. She describes this change as an almost unconscious shift from thinking in terms of "my client/*they*" to "my client/*we*." She also was deeply involved in the campaign to ratify the Equal Rights Amendment. Ireland served on NOW's national board as the Southeast regional director, and in 1987, decided to devote her fulltime efforts to NOW. She ran for, and was elected, vice president. She has been a senior officer ever since.

Ireland finds her legal knowledge a great advantage in working for women's rights. She admits to what she calls a rather creative use of antitrust and racketeering laws to halt Operation Rescue's attempts to put abortion-performing clinics out of business through illegal means.

As a leader of NOW, Ireland has continued her efforts to promote the rights of women on a national and global level. Her aim has been to move women into positions of policy-making power, not only in law and government, but also in media, education, business, labor, and religion.

Congress. Supporters of ERA initially had until March 22, 1979, to obtain ratification by thirty-eight states.

ERA had tremendous popular support, especially among those who saw it as a way to invalidate numerous existing state laws that continue to maintain the inferior status of women by discriminating against them. By March 22, 1973, ERA had been ratified by thirty states—eight less than were needed. At the same time opposing forces were becoming organized and militant.

Opposition to ERA: The Conservative Reaction

Much of the responsibility for the defeat of ERA rests with the efforts of Phyllis Schlafly. Emphasizing the positive and unique qualities of the traditional role of women in society, Schlafly mobilized the sentiments of many women and men against ERA through the Stop-ERA and the Eagle Forum organizations. Schlafly claimed that pro-ERA groups were hostile to all the values women had traditionally held and to the general welfare of women. She felt the most "cruel and damaging sexual harassment taking place today" was not that which men inflicted on women but rather that which was directed "by feminists and their federal government allies against the role of motherhood and the role of the dependent wife."[7]

Phyllis Schlafly.

The necessary thirty-eight states failed to ratify the amendment within the seven-year period, in spite of the support given to ERA in numerous national party platforms and by six presidents and both houses of Congress. NOW boycotted nonratifying states. Nonetheless, the anti-ERA campaign was successful: As the deadline neared, five approvals were still lacking. Three states rescinded their ratification.[8] Congress decided to extend the deadline to June 30, 1982, but ERA again failed to receive the required number of ratifications.

Schlafly greeted the defeat of ERA with the statement that the amendment's failure to pass was "the greatest victory for women's rights since the women's suffrage amendment of 1920."[9] The National Organization for Women and related groups, however, have renewed the struggle. The Equal Rights Amendment has been reintroduced in Congress, and many years of renewed conflict over this issue can be expected.

■ FEDERAL RESPONSES TO SEX DISCRIMINATION IN JOBS

Although ERA did not pass, several efforts have been made by the federal government to eliminate sex discrimination in the labor market both before and after the introduction of the amendment.

Sex Discrimination and Title VII

Sex was included as a prohibited basis for discrimination in the job market under Title VII of the Civil Rights Act of 1964, although Title VII does not cover discrimination based on sexual preferences. Since its enactment, Title VII has been used to strike down so-called protective legislation, which prevents women from undertaking jobs deemed "too dangerous or strenuous by the state." In practice, such protective legislation often "protected" women from higher-paying jobs. Under the Equal Employment Opportunity Commission guidelines, such state statutes may not be used as a defense to a charge of illegal **sex discrimination.**

SEX DISCRIMINATION
Overt behavior in which people are given differential or unfavorable treatment on the basis of sex. Any practice, policy, or procedure that denies equality of treatment to an individual or to a group because of gender.

[7]Phyllis Schlafly's statement before a Senate labor subcommittee in 1981, quoted in the *Los Angeles Herald Examiner,* April 22, 1981, p. 2.
[8]But such rescinding (or taking back one's vote) may not be constitutional. Samuel S. Friedman argued this point in *ERA: May a State Change Its Vote?* (Detroit: Wayne State University Press, 1979).
[9]Marjorie P. K. Weiser and Jean S. Arbeiter, *Womanlist* (New York: Atheneum, 1981); and Carol Felsentha, "Phyllis Schlafly: The Sweetheart of the Silent Majority," in Peter Woll, ed., *Behind the Scenes in American Government* (Boston: Little, Brown, 1983), pp. 85–96.

DID YOU KNOW?

That the median weekly earnings for women working full time are about 70 percent of men's median weekly full-time earnings?

SEXUAL HARASSMENT
Harassment on the basis of sex, in violation of Title VII. This includes unwanted physical or verbal conduct or abuse of a sexual nature that interferes with a recipient's job performance or carries with it an implicit or explicit threat of adverse employment consequences.

Sexual harassment has also been outlawed by Title VII. In April 1980, the EEOC issued its first guidelines on the subject. Under the guidelines, all unwelcome sexual advances, requests, or other physical or verbal conduct of a sexual nature are illegal sexual harassment if submission is a condition of employment or a basis of pay, of promotion, or of other employment decisions. Also, if such unwanted conduct interferes with an employee's job performance or creates an intimidating, hostile, or offensive environment, it is illegal. The courts have gone so far as to hold the employer liable for illegal sexual harassment by supervisors, and EEOC guidelines go one step further—they hold an employer liable for a supervisor's conduct regardless of the employer's knowledge of such conduct or even when the employer has a policy forbidding such conduct.

The right of women to be free from sexual harassment on the job has been increasingly upheld by the Supreme Court in the last few years. In 1986, the court indicated that creating a hostile environment by sexual harassment, even if job status is not affected, violates Title VII.[10] According to Emily Spitzer, an attorney with the NOW Legal Defense and Education Fund, the 1986 Supreme Court decision "alerts employers and workers that treating women in a sexually harassing manner in the workplace isn't going to be condoned."[11]

In 1978, in a Title VII-based decision, the Supreme Court ruled that an employer (the City of Los Angeles) could not require female employees to make higher pension-fund contributions than male employees earning the same salary.[12] This and similar cases involving differential life insurance premiums for males and females (prohibited by a 1983 ruling) represent another set of issues on which Americans have been slowly redefining gender-based discrimination.[13]

The 1978 Pregnancy Discrimination Act amended Title VII to include job-related discrimination based on pregnancy, childbirth, or related medical con-

[10]*Meritor Savings Bank, FSB v. Vinson,* 477 U.S. 57 (1986).
[11]*Wall Street Journal,* June 20, 1986, p. 2.
[12]*Los Angeles v. Manhart,* 435 U.S. 702 at 710 (1978).
[13]*Congressional Quarterly, Guide to the U.S. Supreme Court* (Washington, D.C., 1979).

Women work alongside men in the United States army although they are barred from combat roles. In modern warfare, is it likely that such a prohibition will keep women soldiers out of conflict?

ditions. According to this amendment, health and disability insurance plans must cover pregnancy, childbirth, or related medical conditions in the same way as any other temporary disability. An employer must provide leaves of absence for pregnant women on the same terms and conditions as those given to any other worker for any other temporary disability. Also, simply because a woman is pregnant does not mean that she can be forced to take a maternity leave for any *specified* period of time. As long as she is capable of performing her duties, she must be allowed to work. The 1978 act applies both to married and unmarried women and to any aspect of employment.

DID YOU KNOW?

That in 1922, at age eighty-seven, Rebecca Latimer Felton was the first and oldest woman to serve in the U.S. Senate—although she was appointed as a token gesture and allowed to serve only one day?

The Equal Pay Act of 1963

The Equal Pay Act was enacted as an amendment to the Fair Labor Standards Act of 1938 and since 1979 has been administered by the Equal Employment Opportunity Commission. Basically, the act prohibits sex-based discrimination in the wages paid for equal work on jobs when their performance requires skills, effort, and responsibility under similar conditions. It is job content rather than job description that controls in all cases. For the equal pay requirements to apply, the act requires that male and female employees must work at the same establishment.

With equal-pay questions, the issue focuses more on the jobs performed by two employees and whether they are substantially equal than on the equivalence of employees' skills and training. But small differences in job content do not justify higher pay for one sex. The courts look to the primary duties of the two jobs. The jobs of a barber and a beautician are considered essentially "equal." So, too, are those of a tailor and a seamstress.

An example of pervasive sex discrimination in the workplace involved the Minnesota Mining and Manufacturing Company (3M). In August 1982, 3M decided to settle a number of sex-bias suits charging that 3M had discriminated against women in job assignments, wages, promotions, transfers, and other job-related areas. In this case, one thousand women had been forced to take

Day-care center for the children of hospital employees. Who should be responsible for paying for such services—parents or local, state, or the federal government?

T
ye
cc
isl

CO
The
con
wo
fact
suc
not
in
to
is
wo
pa

DID YOU KNOW?

That the most rapidly growing segment of the U.S. population is Americans aged eighty-five or older, who are estimated to amount to twenty-four million people, or eight percent of the total population, by the year 2040?

age seventy. Many states had already passed similar statutes. In 1986, mandatory retirement rules were finally outlawed, except for a few selected occupations, and the act's protection was extended to individuals over age seventy to whom it had not previously been available.

The Elderly and Politics

As voters, legislators, and activists, the elderly contribute significantly to American political life.

The Elderly as Voters.   If we use voter participation as a measure of political involvement, it is clear that the elderly are very active. Table 6-2 shows that of the six age categories listed, the over-sixty-five age group ranks first in voter registration and in actual turnout on election day. Whereas approximately 46 percent of all persons of voting age claim to have voted, in the over-sixty-five category the voting rate is 60.9 percent.

The Elderly as Legislators.   Whereas all other minority groups are very poorly represented in the Senate and in the House, such is the not the case for the elderly. In 1990, for example, the Senate had 29 members over the age of sixty and the House had 101. Table 6-3 shows the age categories of members of Congress for selected years.

The Elderly as Activists.   Today the elderly work for their interests through a number of large and effective political associations. The National Association of Retired Federal Employees, formed in 1921, currently has 450,000 members. In 1947, the National Retired Teachers' Association was established, and today it has more than half a million members. The largest of these groups is the American Association of Retired Persons, for those aged fifty and older, founded in 1958, with a current membership of more than thirty million. The latter two groups have united in a powerful joint effort to ensure beneficial

TABLE 6-2
Voter Participation by Age Groups, 1988

Voter participation seems to be positively correlated with age, as we can see in this table. The lowest participation is by 18–20-year-olds and the highest is by those 65 and over.			
AGE GROUP	**PERSONS OF VOTING AGE (MILLIONS)**	**PERCENT REPORTING THEY REGISTERED**	**PERCENT REPORTING THEY VOTED**
18–20	10.7	35.4%	18.6%
21–24	15.7	46.6%	24.7%
25–34	41.9	55.8%	35.1%
35–44	33.0	67.9%	49.3%
45–64	44.8	74.8%	58.7%
65 and over	27.7	76.9%	60.9%

SOURCE: *Statistical Abstract of the United States*, 1990, p. 262.

Americans over 65 are becoming an increasingly important political force.

TABLE 6-3
Ages of Members of Congress for Selected Years

Congressional Chamber and Year	AGE					
	Under 40	40–49	50–59	60–69	70–79	80 and Over
Representatives						
1973	45	132	154	80	20	2
1975	69	138	137	75	14	2
1977	81	121	147	71	15	—
1979	86	125	145	63	14	—
1981	94	142	132	54	12	1
1983	86	145	132	57	13	1
1985	71	154	131	59	17	1
1987	63	153	137	56	24	2
1989	38	165	131	79	20	2
Senators						
1973	3	25	37	23	11	1
1975	5	21	35	24	15	—
1977	6	26	35	21	10	2
1979	10	31	33	17	8	1
1981	9	35	36	14	6	—
1983	7	28	39	20	3	3
1985	4	27	38	25	4	2
1987	5	30	36	22	5	2
1989	0	29	41	22	6	2

SOURCE: *Harold W. Stanley and Richard G. Niemi,* **Vital Statistics on America's Politics,** *2nd ed., Washington D.C., Congressional Quarterly, Inc., 1990, p. 183.*

Senior citizens marching to save medical services.

treatment for the elderly by lobbying for legislation at the federal and state levels. They use the same staff in Washington and provide almost the same services to their members, including low-priced group insurance and travel programs.

In 1971, the Gray Panthers was formed to fight ageism, taking as its motto "Age and Youth in Action." It has about a hundred local groups in a number of cities and a small staff at its Philadelphia headquarters.

The National Council of Senior Citizens, established in 1960, is a politically oriented group of 3,300 local clubs. It keeps a close watch on congressional legislation affecting the elderly, informs members about important pending votes, and instructs them on how to lobby effectively for or against particular pieces of legislation.

■ THE RIGHTS OF THE HANDICAPPED

By the 1970s, the handicapped were becoming a political force. Congress passed the Rehabilitation Act in 1973 that prohibited discrimination against the handicapped in programs receiving federal aid. The Department of Health, Education, and Welfare (now Health and Human Services, or HHS), however, was slow to issue regulations needed to implement this act. When these regulations had still not been issued by April 1977, members of the American Coalition of Citizens with Disabilities staged a "wheel-in" by occupying several Washington HEW offices. A few weeks after this event, HEW passed the necessary regulations. There was still disagreement about what constituted discrimination. The handicapped wanted the right to physical access to be able to compete more effectively in the marketplace. This meant modifying physical structures so the handicapped could avoid the curbs, stairways, and other obstacles that make mobility difficult for them. A 1978 amendment to the Rehabilitation Act of 1973 established the Architectural and Transportation Barriers Compliance Board. Regulations for ramps, elevators, and the like in all federal buildings were implemented. Cost, however, created somewhat of an impediment. Estimates from as low as $4 billion to more than $7 billion were given as the cost of compliance over the next several decades. Faced with such estimates, the Reagan administration took some steps to rescind previous advances in this area.

Congress passed the Education for All Handicapped Children Act in 1975. Unofficially, this act has been referred to as the Bill of Rights for handicapped youth. It guarantees that all handicapped children will receive an "appropriate" education.

In 1990, Congress passed new legislation to provide expanded access to public facilities, including transportation. The Americans with Disabilities Act of 1990 (the "handicapped bill of rights") prohibits job discrimination against the 43.6 million Americans with physical and mental disabilities, including those with AIDS, and requires access to public buildings and public services. Physical access such as ramps, hand rails, and wheelchair accessible restrooms, counters, drinking fountains, telephones, doorways will need to be made wider, mass transit made more accessible. In addition many other steps must be taken to comply: car-rental companies will have to provide cars with hand controls for disabled drivers, and telephone companies will be required to have operators who pass on messages from the speech-impaired who use telephones with keyboards.

President Bush signs the civil rights for the handicapped bill. The new law requires corporations and public institutions to become much more accessible to disabled Americans. How will these new requirements be paid for?

What we will continue to observe in the future are the economic tradeoffs that have to be made when resources are allocated to benefit specially selected groups in society. It is not enough to state simply that the handicapped (or the elderly or any other disadvantaged group) should be given better treatment in America. How much better the treatment will become is both an economic and a political question.

■ THE RIGHTS AND STATUS OF JUVENILES

There are sixty-three million children who are American citizens. The definition of *children* ranges from under age sixteen to under age twenty-one, but, however defined, children form a large group of individuals in the United States and have the fewest rights and protections. The reason for this lack is the common presumption of society and its lawmakers that children are basically protected by their parents. This is not to say that children are the exclusive property of the parents, but rather that an overwhelming case in favor of *not* allowing parents to control the actions of their children must be presented before the state will intervene.

Voting, Marriage, and the Young

The Twenty-sixth Amendment to the Constitution, ratified on July 1, 1971, reads as follows:

> The right of citizens of the United States, who are eighteen years of age or older, to vote shall not be denied or abridged by the United States or by any State on account of age.

Why age eighteen? Why not seventeen or sixteen? Why did it take until 1971 to allow those between the ages of eighteen and twenty-one to vote?

DID YOU KNOW?

That in 1990 there were more than two million reported cases of child abuse, more than double the number reported fifteen years earlier?

CIVIL LAW
The law regulating conduct between private persons over noncriminal matters. Under civil law, the government provides the forum for the settlement of disputes between private parties in such matters as contracts, domestic relations, and business relations.

CRIMINAL LAW
The law that defines crimes and provides punishment for violations. In criminal cases, the government is the prosecutor since crimes are against the public order.

MAJORITY
Full age; the age at which a person is entitled by law to the management of his or her own affairs and to the enjoyment of civil rights.

NECESSARIES
In contracts, necessaries include whatever is reasonably necessary for suitable subsistence as measured by age, state, condition in life, and so on.

There are no easy answers to such questions. One cannot argue simply that those under twenty-one, or those under eighteen, are "incompetent." Incompetent at what? Certainly, one could find a significant number of seventeen-year-olds who can understand the political issues presented to them as well as can many eligible adults. One of the arguments used for granting suffrage to eighteen-year-olds was that because they could be drafted to fight in the country's wars, they had a stake in public policy. At the time, the example of the Vietnam war was paramount.

Have eighteen- to twenty-one-year-olds used their right to vote? Yes and no. Immediately after the passage of the Twenty-sixth Amendment, the percentage of eighteen- to twenty-year-olds registering to vote was 58 percent (in 1972), and 48.3 percent reported that they had voted. By the 1988 election, however, only 44.9 percent of this age group had registered and only 33.2 percent had voted.

The Rights of Children in Civil and Criminal Proceedings

Children today have limited rights in civil and criminal proceedings in our judicial system. Different procedural rules and judicial safeguards apply in civil and criminal laws. **Civil law** relates in part to contracts among private individuals or companies. **Criminal law** relates to crimes against society that are defined by society acting through its legislatures.

Private Contract Rights.   Children are defined exclusively by state law with respect to private contract negotiations, rights, and remedies. The legal definition of **majority** varies from eighteen to twenty-one years of age, depending on the state. If an individual is legally a minor, she or he usually cannot normally be held responsible for contracts entered into. In most states, only contracts entered into for so-called **necessaries** (things necessary for subsistence, as determined by the courts) can be enforced against minors. Also, when minors engage in negligent behavior, typically their parents are liable. If, for example, a minor destroys a neighbor's fence, the neighbor may bring suit against the child's parents, but not against the child.

Juvenile being arrested. Should juveniles be accorded all of the same rights that adults enjoy?

Criminal Rights.   One of the main requirements for an act to be criminal is intent. The law has given children certain defenses against criminal prosecution because of their presumed inability to have criminal intent.

Under **common law,** children up to seven years of age were considered incapable of committing a crime because they did not have the moral sense to understand that they were doing wrong. Children between the ages of seven and fourteen were also presumed to be incapable of committing a crime, but this presumption could be rebutted by showing that the child understood the wrongful nature of the act. Today, states vary in their approaches, but most states retain the common-law approach, although age limits vary from state to state. Other states have rejected the rebuttable presumption and simply set a minimum age for criminal responsibility.

All states have juvenile court systems that handle children below the age of criminal responsibility who commit delinquent acts. Their aim is allegedly to reform rather than to punish. In states that retain the rebuttable presumption approach, children who are beyond the minimum age but are still juveniles can be turned over to the criminal courts if the juvenile court determines that they should be treated as adults.

Procedural Rights in Criminal Trials.   Previously, if a child was picked up for illegal activities, that child could have been sentenced in juvenile court without a lawyer, without the child's parents being allowed to see the complaint against him or her, and without having counsel being able to cross-examine whoever made the complaint. In addition, in most states the child would have been unable to appeal his or her punishment to a higher court. Basically, the Bill of Rights did not apply to the young.

In 1967, all that changed. In a watershed case, the father of a child who had been sentenced in juvenile court to six years in an industrial school for one obscene phone call took his case all the way to the Supreme Court. The father argued that the Bill of Rights protects children, and noted that his child didn't have a lawyer, the parents couldn't see the complaint against the child, and no one could cross-examine the person who complained that the child had made the obscene phone call. Amazingly, if the child had been an adult (over eighteen), the maximum sentence in the state in which the presumed phone call was made would have been three months in jail or a fine of from $5 to $50.

The Supreme court, in *In re Gault*,[21] held that

> the Due Process Clause of the Fourteenth Amendment requires that in respect to proceedings to determine [juvenile] delinquency which may result in commitment to an institution in which the juvenile's freedom is curtailed, the child and his parent must be notified of the child's right to be represented by counsel retained by them, or if they are unable to afford counsel, that counsel will be appointed to represent the child.

In its majority opinion the Court, after reviewing reports on juvenile court proceedings, concluded that "juvenile court history has again demonstrated that unbridled discretion, however benevolently motivated, is frequently a poor substitute for principle and procedure." Finally, the Court stated that "under our Constitution, the condition of being a boy does not justify a **kangaroo court.**"

[21]387 U.S. 1 (1967).

Ronald Zamora, age fifteen, being tried for murder.

COMMON LAW
Judge-made law that originated in England from decisions shaped according to prevailing customs. Decisions were applied to similar situations and thus gradually became common to the nation. Common law forms the basis of legal procedures in the United States.

KANGAROO COURT
A mock hearing in which norms of justice and judicial procedure are ignored.

DID YOU KNOW?

That a recent Gallup poll found that 45 percent of adults would "vote against a public official regardless of other factors" if the candidate were a homosexual?

In spite of *In re Gault,* children still do not have the right to trial by jury or to bail. Also, parents can still commit their minor children to state mental institutions without allowing the child a hearing.

The Other Side of the Coin.   Although minors still do not normally have the full rights of adults in criminal proceedings, they have certain advantages. In felony, manslaughter, murder, armed robbery, and assault cases, juveniles are usually not tried as adults. They may be sentenced to probation or "reform" school for a relatively few years regardless of the seriousness of their crimes. However, most states allow juveniles to be tried as adults (often at the discretion of the judge) for certain crimes such as murder. When they are tried as adults, they are treated to due process of law and tried for the crime, rather than being given the paternalistic treatment reserved for the juvenile delinquent.

■ THE RIGHTS AND STATUS OF GAYS

Studies by Alfred Kinsey and his associates in the late 1940s, and early 1950s, coupled with more recent research, indicate there are perhaps twenty-five million Americans with varying degrees of homosexual orientation.[22] Gays, as they are most commonly called, therefore represent one of the most important minorities in the United States. Nonetheless, the rights of gays have only recently surfaced as a major issue on the American political and legal scene.

The Law and Public Attitudes

The status of gays came to national attention in 1977 when Anita Bryant, of Florida orange juice and television commercial fame, organized a "Save Our Children" campaign, whose purpose was to rescind the law protecting gays' legal rights in Dade County, Florida. The Dade County law protected homosexuals from discrimination in public accommodations, housing, and employment. Bryant's campaign against the gay community's effort to keep the law on the books was successful. In June 1977, Miami citizens voted two to one to repeal the law protecting gays. Similar laws were repealed in Eugene, Oregon; Wichita, Kansas; and St. Paul, Minnesota. In the 1990 primary, Broward County, Florida voters defeated a proposal designed to give gay people greater protection against discrimination (the so-called "human rights referendum") by a margin of 3-to-2. (See chapter Highlight on AIDS and gay politics.)

Until recently, homosexuality was illegal in virtually every state in the Union. Today twenty-nine states still have antihomosexual laws on the books. Recent Gallup polls show that 47 percent of Americans believe that private homosexual relations between consenting adults should not be considered illegal. Nonetheless, in the summer of 1986, the Supreme Court upheld an antigay law in the State of Georgia that made homosexual conduct between two adults a crime. Justice Byron White, in a written opinion, said that "we are quite unwilling" to "announce . . . a fundamental right to engage in homosexual sodomy."[23]

[22]Rhonda Rivera, "Homosexuality and the Law," in William Paul, James D. Weinrich, John C. Gonsirock, and Mary E. Hoxtedt, eds., *Homosexuality: Social, Psychological, and Biological Issues* (Beverly Hills, Calif.: Sage, 1982), pp. 25–26.
[23]*Bowers v. Hardwick,* 478 U.S. 186 (1986).

The Impact of AIDS on Gay Politics

One of the most adverse developments for the U.S. gay community has been the increasing problem of AIDS, or acquired immune deficiency syndrome. It is always fatal and in the United States has affected primarily homosexual males, intravenous drug users, and recipients of blood transfusions. When the potential impact of AIDS beyond the gay community became clearer, the politics of AIDS expanded. Children with AIDS were banned from schools by parent groups fearing transmission to their own children. Gays began to experience more job discrimination. Persons who tested positively for the virus were fired from their jobs.

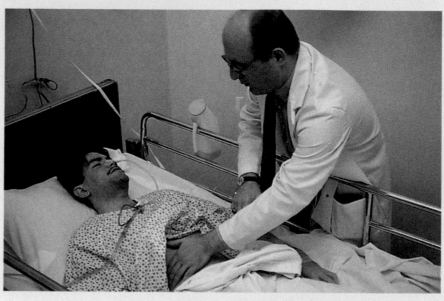

Rumors spread that AIDS could be contracted through touch and by saliva. In at least one case, a man was charged with attempted murder when he told police officers that he had AIDS and then spit at them. Anti-gay groups, especially religious conservatives, stated that AIDS was God's punishment for homosexual acts.

The rights of AIDS victims have become a concern. Gay groups have protested the lack of government effort to help find the cause and a cure. Public opinion on the whole has become more hostile to gay life-styles. The biggest reversal for gays came when the Office of Legal Counsel of the U.S. Department of Justice issued an opinion in June 1986 that said employers could dismiss gays who are determined to be carriers of the virus, when such firing can be justified as a prudent action to protect other employees.

Nevertheless, so far, no court has followed the Justice Department memorandum. Since it has been shown that AIDS is not transmitted by casual contact, courts have ruled that employment of persons with AIDS presents no public health risk in the workplace.* In fact, a recent survey revealed that many states have declared that their statutes prohibit such discrimination. In other recent cases, courts have ordered that in the absence of evidence that children with AIDS pose a real and valid threat to their classmates or teachers, they are otherwise qualified to attend regular classes.**

Recent polls have revealed that the public favors AIDS testing for immi-grants, prison inmates, members of the armed forces, couples applying for marriage licenses, and visitors from foreign countries. About half of those polled favored testing everyone. But the polls also showed increased compassion for AIDS victims and objection to terminating the employment of people with AIDS. A majority of those polled agreed that the government has done too little to combat the disease.

*Chalk v. United States Dist. Court Cent. Dist. of Cal., 840 F.2d 701 (9th Cir. 1988).
**Robertson v. Granite City Community Unit School Dist. No. 9, 684 F.Supp. 1002 (S.D. Ill.1988); Ray v. School Dist. of Desoto County, 666 F.Supp. 1524 (M.D. Fla.1987); Thomas v. Atascadero Unified School Dist., 662 F.Supp. 376 (C.D. Cal.1987).

A demonstration for more medical research for AIDS. To what extent is AIDS seen as a problem only for the gay community?

Almost one hundred cities throughout the United States currently have laws prohibiting discrimination against homosexuals in the areas of housing, education, banking, labor union employment, and public accommodations. Since 1982, Wisconsin has had on its books a general law prohibiting all discrimination against homosexuals. In 1989, Massachusetts passed a law specifically stating that the state does not endorse homosexuality nor recognize homosexual partnerships, but that no discrimination against homosexuals shall exist. In a number of states and localities, laws against "hate crimes" include actions taken against gays, even though the genesis of those laws was crimes against African Americans and Hispanics.

Gays and Politics

The number of gay organizations grew from fifty in 1969 to more than a thousand by the end of the 1970s. These groups have been active in exerting pressure on legislatures, the media, schools, and churches. In 1973, gay organizations succeeded in having the American Psychiatric Association remove homosexuality from its list of disorders. During the 1970s and 1980s, more than half the states repealed sodomy laws. The Civil Service Commission eliminated its ban on the employment of gays. In 1980, the Democratic party platform included a gay rights plank.

Politicians have not overlooked the potential significance of homosexual issues in American politics. Conservative politicians have been generally critical of gays. Liberals, however, have by and large begun to speak out for gay rights. Walter Mondale, former vice president of the United States and the winning contender for the Democratic party nomination for president in 1984, addressed a gay convention and openly bid for gays' political support.

In cities such as San Francisco, which is considered to be the gay capital of the United States, and Washington, D.C., the homosexual vote is considered to be a critical factor in politics. In 1979, gay political activist David Scott forced San Francisco Mayor Dianne Feinstein into a runoff primary election. In that same year, active gay voters in Washington, D.C., helped to elect Mayor Marion Barry. The gay community also supported Jesse Jackson's 1988 bid for the presidency and his "Rainbow Coalition." Gays have been elected to public offices, and gays in increasing numbers and from all walks of life declare themselves publicly. However, Americans do not appear to have accepted homosexuality as a normal and legitimate way of life. The controversy over the role of gays in American society will continue to occupy a great deal of public debate.

GETTING INVOLVED

What To Do About Discrimination

When you apply for a job, you may be subjected to a variety of possibly discriminatory practices—based on your race, gender, religion, and the like. You may also be subjected to a battery of tests, some of which you may feel are discriminatory. At both state and federal levels, the government has continued to examine the fairness and validity of criteria used in job-applicant screening. If you believe that you have been discriminated against by a potential employer, you may wish to consider the following steps:

1. Evaluate your own capabilities and determine if you are truly qualified for the position.
2. Analyze the reasons that you were turned down (or dismissed); do you feel that others would agree with you, or would they uphold your employer's claim?
3. If you still believe that you have been unfairly treated, you have recourse to several agencies and services.

You should first speak to the personnel director of the company and politely explain that you feel you have not been adequately evaluated. If asked, give the specifics of your concerns. If necessary, go into explicit detail and indicate that you feel that you may have been discriminated against. If a second evaluation is not forthcoming, contact the local branch of your state employment agency. If you still do not obtain adequate help, contact one or more of the following agencies, usually found by looking in your telephone directory under "state government" listings:

1. If a government entity is involved, a state ombudsman or citizen aide who will mediate may be available.
2. You may wish to contact the state civil rights commission, which will at least give you advice if it does not wish to take up your case.
3. The state attorney general's office will normally have a division dealing with discrimination and civil rights.
4. There may be a special commission or department specifically set up to help you, such as a women's status commission or a commission on Hispanic or Asian Americans. If you are a member of such a minority or a woman, contact the staff people of these commissions.
5. Finally, at the national level, you can contact the American Civil Liberties Union and you can also contact the most appropriate federal agency: Equal Employment Opportunity Commission, 2401 E St., NW, Washington, D.C. 20506.

CHAPTER SUMMARY

1. The earliest feminist movement in the United States was entwined with the struggle to abolish slavery. Later, the women's rights movement separated itself from the racial equality movement.
2. About 1870, women's organizations formed with the aim of achieving suffrage for women. In 1920, the Nineteenth Amendment was passed, granting women the right to vote.
3. The current feminist movement began in the late 1950s. The movement seeks to define sexism and to eradicate it from all spheres of life for all women. One of the leading pressure groups for women's rights today is the National Organization for Women (NOW).
4. The Supreme Court has stated that laws that classify by sex are permissible as long as they are "reasonable."
5. The proposed Twenty-seventh Amendment to the Constitution (the Equal Rights Amendment, or ERA) states, "Equality of rights under the law shall not be denied or abridged by the United States or by any State on account of sex." Anti-ERA groups, headed by Phyllis Schlafly, were successful in preventing ratification by the necessary number of states.

6. Under Title VII of the Civil Rights Act of 1964, sex discrimination in employment is prohibited. The Supreme Court has indicated in a recent case that creating a hostile environment by sexual harassment even if job status isn't affected also violated Title VII. As amended in 1978 by the Pregnancy Discrimination Act, sex discrimination based on pregnancy, childbirth, or related medical condition is also prohibited.
7. The Equal Pay Act of 1963 prohibits discrimination in the wages paid for equal work when its performance requires equal skills, effort, and responsibility under similar conditions. The issue of comparable worth is that women should receive equal pay, not just for equal work, but also for work of comparable skill, effort, and responsibility.
8. Of the American population, over 12 percent are sixty-five or older. Many are poor, burdened by medical costs, and unable to find work because of age discrimination in employment. The problems of aging and retirement will become increasingly important as the population continues to age.
9. The Age Discrimination in Employment Act of 1967 prohibits discrimination against individuals on the basis of age unless age is shown to be a bona fide occupational qualification reasonably necessary to the normal operation of a particular business. It

has been amended to cover state and local governments and to prohibit mandatory requirement of most employees under the age of seventy.

10. The elderly are involved politically through high voter turnout, representation in Congress, and very active political associations.

11. The rights of the handicapped became a political and economic issue in the 1970s and continues to be a controversial issue today.

12. Children form a large group of individuals in the United States but have the fewest rights and privileges. The Twenty-sixth Amendment extended the right to vote in national elections to all persons age eighteen and over.

13. Children have limited rights in civil and criminal proceedings in our judicial system. They are defined exclusively by state law with respect to private contract negotiations, rights, and remedies. States set minimum age requirements for criminal responsibility. The 1967 *In re Gault* decision extended the due process clause to juveniles.

14. The rights of gays, who comprise an estimated 10 percent of the U.S. adult population, have recently surfaced as a major issue on the American political and legal scene. In certain cities, gays have become politically active, and the homosexual vote is considered a critical factor in local politics. Gay political organizations have considerable power. However, Americans have not yet fully accepted homosexuality as a legitimate way of life.

QUESTIONS FOR REVIEW AND DISCUSSION

1. What beliefs about the nature of women made granting them the right to vote so difficult? To what extent do some of the same attitudes exist today?

2. Think about the concept of equal pay for comparable work. What kinds of jobs traditionally performed by men would be comparable in effort, skill, and worth, say, to an executive secretary or switchboard operator? How would the economy be affected if the wages for many "women's jobs" were greatly increased?

3. What changes in our patterns of family life and in societal values have led to the political activism of senior citizens? How has the establishment of the Social Security program changed our views of the relationship between government and the elderly?

SELECTED REFERENCES

Gary Burtless, ed., *Work, Health, and Income Among the Elderly* (Washington, D.C.: The Brookings Institution, 1987). A collection of papers examining economic implications of changing patterns among the elderly.

Sylvia Ann Hewlett, *A Lesser Life: The Myth of Women's Liberation in America* (New York: Morrow, 1986). One of the most controversial books on the women's struggle, it unfavorably compares the record of the United States with other countries, especially in Europe, in the area of women's social support and social legislation (maternity leave and day care, for example).

William W. Lammers, *Public Policy and the Aging* (Washington, D.C.: Congressional Quarterly Press, 1983). The author describes how the rapidly growing older population will affect the development of programs for the elderly. Specific public policies are explored in detail.

Keith T. Poole and Harmon Zeigler, *Women, Public Opinion, and Politics: The Changing Political Attitudes of American Women* (New York: Longman, 1985). A very important book which analyzes in detail the lack of cohesiveness of women and projects a growing liberal tendency among women, which the authors feel may shift American politics to the left in coming decades.

Gilbert Y. Steiner, *Constitutional Inequality: The Political Fortunes of the Equal Rights Amendment* (Washington, D.C.: Brookings Institution, 1985). A case study of the Equal Rights Amendment, this study dissects the difficulties in accomplishing fundamental policy changes through constitutional amendments.

Patricia A. Vardin and Ilene N. Brody, eds., *Children's Rights: Contemporary Perspectives* (New York: Teachers College Press, 1979). A valuable collection of essays on the rights of children in American politics.

A GLOBAL PERSPECTIVE
TECHNOLOGY CREATES THE GLOBAL VILLAGE

T he relationship of a people to its government has long been thought to be a purely internal matter. Each nation is a self-contained entity with its own governmental structures, its own political practices, its own set of rules for how the people exert influence on the structures of authority. Even though the United States and the Soviet Union, the leading world powers since 1947, adhered in principle to this notion of national self-determination, each has tried to influence the regimes of weaker states through subversion, economic sanctions, or, in some cases, through the use of force. Often, however, these efforts either were not acknowledged as governmental policies or their purpose was cloaked in camouflaging rhetoric.

Today, technological change has put the politics of one nation on the television screens of every nation. Rallies and repressions are visible to billions of people as they occur. Think about how the transmission of news has changed within this century. At

French and British journalists interview Americans in Operation Desert Shield.

the beginning of the twentieth century, news was printed and accompanied by photographs or drawings. It took months for reports of events in Africa to reach Europe or America. Later, the telephone made possible the reporting of events by on-the-scene journalists to their newsrooms if the lines were not cut. Events were transmitted to other nations by radio if broadcasts were not jammed. For the forty years following the establishment of the Iron Curtain after World War II, the United States supported radio broadcasting of news and music into the Eastern European nations via Radio Free Europe and the Voice of America. Listening to these broadcasts was illegal in many nations.

Although television brought pictures of worldwide events into the home, it is the development of satellite broadcasting, cable television, and the hand-held video camera that have really broken down national boundaries. The satellite broadcasting system makes possible the instantaneous transmission of pictures from anywhere in the world. Who can forget the sight of students tearing down the Berlin Wall in November 1989? Cable television, particularly the Cable News Network (CNN), is now available in most nations of the world, if only in hotel rooms and government offices. Prime ministers and members of the Soviet Politburo get their news from CNN. The hand-held video camera captures events that nations would prefer to censor—the student who faced down a tank in Tienanmen Square in Beijing in

Lenin's statute falls in Romania.

Chinese students create the "Goddess of Democracy" in Tiananmen Square.

the spring of 1989, people lined up patiently to vote in their first election in forty years in Czechoslovakia in June 1990, and the people of Lithuania linking hands across their nation for independence in the summer of that year. The Videotape, smuggled out, provides evidence for the world.

Because of the power of television, domestic politics become international. Our politics become theirs and their politics become ours. The events in Tienanmen Square make the Bush administration's relations with China an issue in presidential politics. The administration's lukewarm support of the Baltic republics' claims of independence are incorporated into constituency politics for some congresspersons.

The question of foreign priorities becomes part of the American budget debate: Do we spend some of the "peace dividend," if there is one, on aid to Central American democracies or on developing stable democratic regimes in Eastern Europe?

Daniel Ortega campaigns for election in Nicaragua.

Through the global network, we export our political techniques and our political culture. We also put our decision-making process on the world television network. American-style political campaigning, with its emphasis on style and image, is spreading throughout Europe. Daniel Ortega used glitzy television ads in his unsuccessful campaign for reelection in Nicaragua. Our cultural symbols—the Statue of Liberty, free elections, the open debate of our legislative bodies—are taken up by nations that have cultures far different from ours. We have, in fact, become part of one global village, and it seems very unlikely that the old boundaries of sight and sound can ever be erected again.

PEOPLE AND POLITICS

PUBLIC OPINION

WHAT IF . . . EXIT POLLS AND EARLY CALLS WERE BANNED?

In the early 1980s, the state of Washington passed a law that prohibited exit polling within 300 feet in any direction from a polling place. Because the success of exit polling depends on the interviewers' ability to convince people to participate in the poll immediately after they vote, the Washington law greatly restricted the ability of the pollsters to work. Although 300 feet does not sound like much, that distance would permit voters to get into their cars and drive away before being approached by interviewers. Since interviewers could not get a good sample of the voters, the exit polls would be flawed.

The Washington state law was passed by a legislature that was indignant over the exit polling and announcement at 6:00 P.M. Eastern time (3:00 P.M. Pacific time) that Jimmy Carter had been defeated by Ronald Reagan in 1980. West Coast politicians were infuriated by the networks' race to announce the Reagan landslide. Several local officials were defeated by close margins and they felt that the early call of the election may have discouraged their supporters from going to the polls.

Would it be possible to regulate exit polling and to prevent the announcement of election-day polling results throughout the United States? How would such a limit affect the political system?

If the media were able to carry out the polls but could not announce the results until, say, the next day or after the official vote count, there would be little reason for spending the money for such an exercise. The competition among the networks to have the earliest results would end and the ratings of the election-night broadcasts would undoubtedly decline. Without the early announcement of results, more voters might be motivated to go to the polls. In fact, if preelection polls showed that it would be a close election, party workers would have a strong incentive to get out the vote up to the very last moment. An increase in voter turnout would make a difference in some local elections as well.

Since the media could get some information about voting turnout and could, of course, poll up to the day before the election, the networks could still make some predictions about the results, but they could not make projections based on actual interviews. If the various

polling organizations decided not to continue exit polling, there would be little loss to society, since the main purpose of the polls is competition among the news organizations.

Limiting the ability of the media to broadcast the results of exit polls presents some disadvantages as well. Such regulation of the news media is certainly a restric-

tion on the freedom of speech and press. Even if the early calls were prohibited, there is little evidence that voter turnout would increase. Some studies of voting in the western states show that the early calls had no or very little effect on an individual's decision to vote. Limiting freedom of the press on the basis of skimpy evidence seems unwise.

Furthermore, early calls can only be said to have an effect in landslide elections because even the exit polls are not able to predict winners in close elections. So if a few individuals were discouraged from voting in a landslide election, it would have no effect on the results. Perhaps more necessary than regulating exit polls and early calls of elections is using the media to increase voter turnout in all types of elections.

---

1. *What situation could you imagine that would cause the Congress to try to eliminate exit polling?*
2. *Is the potential danger of early election projections great enough to restrict the freedom of the press?*
3. *If the media's election projections were restricted, do you think that interest in the election would increase or decrease?*

In an era of widespread public opinion polling, what role does public opinion play in the American political system? If the United States is a representative democracy, how powerful is the voice of the public, as it is expressed through polls, and how powerful should it be? Since our representatives in Washington and in the statehouse must make decisions on policies and issues that affect the people throughout the year, it would seem that the views of the public, as measured by polls, would help politicians in voting on the laws. Public opinion as expressed by polls, however, may be limited in its usefulness by its very character. After all, the pollster wrote the question, called the voters, and perhaps forwarded the results to the politicians. Public opinion, as gathered by commercial or academic polls, is not equivalent to constituents' writing to their representatives, nor does answering a poll require the effort of going out to vote. In fact, public opinion polls normally include the views of many individuals who do not vote.

DID YOU KNOW?

That 49 percent of the voters in 1988 didn't know that Lloyd Bentsen was the Democratic candidate for vice president?

■ HOW POWERFUL IS PUBLIC OPINION?

At various times in the recent history of the United States, public opinion has played a powerful role in presidential politics. Beginning in 1965, as public opinion became more divided over the war in Vietnam, numerous public expressions of opposition to the war took place, as measured by the polls and demonstrations in many cities. By 1968, when Lyndon Johnson was preparing to run for another term, public opinion against the war was expressed through a surge of support for antiwar candidate Senator Eugene McCarthy in the New Hampshire primary. Faced with public disapproval, Johnson dropped out of the race.

As the Watergate scandal of 1972 unfolded, revealing the role of President Nixon through congressional hearings and through tape recordings from his office, a similar groundswell of opinion against the president occurred. In this case, the disastrous fall in the president's approval ratings to less than 25 percent coincided with the decision by the House committee to vote articles of impeachment against the president. Nixon, facing an impeachment trial, resigned his office.

Both of these cases illustrate the power of public opinion when there is great public dissatisfaction with the government or with an official. On the positive side, high approval ratings for a president, such as George Bush maintained until late 1990, can be used to persuade Congress to support the president's program. Rarely, however, is public opinion so strongly expressed over a long period of time.

In most situations, public opinion is used by legislators, politicians, and presidents to shore up their own arguments. It provides a kind of evidence for their own point of view. If the results of polls do not support their position, they can either commission their own poll or ignore the polls. Regardless of the fact that 58 percent of Americans opposed giving aid to the *contras* in Nicaragua, President Reagan continued to press Congress for such assistance, asserting that the president should be the one to assess such risks. Similarly, public opinion favored passage of the Equal Rights Amendment but the necessary total of thirty-eight state legislatures could not be persuaded to ratify it. In neither of these cases, however, was public opinion overwhelmingly on one side or the other, highly emotional, or expressed in a crisis atmosphere.

Thus elected officials, although aware of the polls, could carry on their politics with little fear of reprisal from the voters. Public opinion, then, is neither all-powerful nor powerless.

■ DEFINING AND MEASURING PUBLIC OPINION

PUBLIC OPINION
The aggregate of individual attitudes or beliefs shared by some portion of adults. There is no one public opinion because there are many different "publics."

There is no one public opinion because there are many different "publics." In a nation of more than 250 million people, there may be innumerable gradations of opinion on an issue. What we do is describe the distribution of opinions among the public about a particular question. Thus we define **public opinion** as follows:

Public opinion is the aggregate of individual attitudes or beliefs shared by some portion of adults.

Although it might be said, for example, that public opinion favored the passage of the Equal Rights Amendment (ERA), a more accurate description of public opinion on that issue would be that 60 percent of the public supported the amendment, whereas 40 percent opposed it or had no opinion.

How is public opinion known in a democracy? In the case of the Vietnam war, it was made known by numerous antiwar protests, countless articles in magazines and newspapers, and continuing electronic media coverage of antiwar demonstrations. Normally, however, public opinion becomes known in a democracy through elections and, in some states, initiatives or referenda (see Chapter 19). Other ways are through lobbying and interest group activities, which are also used to influence public opinion.

Public opinion can be defined most clearly by its effect. As political scientist V. O. Key, Jr. said, public opinion is what governments "find it prudent to heed."[1] This means that for public opinion to be effective, enough people have

[1]*Public Opinion and American Democracy* (New York: Alfred A. Knopf, 1961), p. 10.

Union members protest cut in benefits. A strike can be seen as an expression of public opinion, but if the union does not get support from others, politicians will feel no effect.

to hold a particular view with such strong conviction that a government feels its actions should be influenced by it.

An interesting question arises as to when *private* opinion becomes *public* opinion. Everyone probably has a private opinion about the competence of the president, as well as private opinions about more personal concerns, such as the state of a neighbor's lawn. We say that private opinion becomes public opinion when the opinion is publicly expressed and if the opinion concerns public issues. When someone's private opinion becomes so strong that the individual is willing to go to the polls to vote for or against a candidate or an issue—or to participate in a demonstration, to discuss the issue at work, to be willing to speak out on local television, or to participate in the political process in any one of a dozen other ways—then that opinion becomes public opinion.

> **DID YOU KNOW?**
>
> That James Madison and others argued in the *Federalist Papers* that public opinion was potentially dangerous and should be diffused through a large republic with separation of government powers?

■ THE QUALITIES OF PUBLIC OPINION

At the beginning of the Vietnam war in the 1960s, public opinion about its conduct was not very clear, like a camera that is not focused. As the war progressed and U.S. involvement deepened and there was still no successful outcome and no end in sight, public opinion became increasingly clarified. Public opinion has identifiable qualities that change over time. Political scientists have identified at least five specific qualities relating to public opinion: (1) intensity, (2) fluidity, (3) stability, (4) quiescence, and (5) relevance. In addition, political knowledge affects opinion, and the distribution of opinion on an issue indicates the possibilities for conflict or compromise.

Intensity

How strongly people are willing to express their private opinions determines the **intensity** of public opinion. Consider an example that seems to be periodically in the news—gun control. Most Americans who have opinions about gun control do not have very strong opinions. A small percentage has extremely intense convictions pro or con. But the average intensity is still quite mild. In contrast, public opinion about the Iranian hostages in 1979 and 1980 was quite intense, on average. Most Americans were in favor of taking drastic measures to free the hostages. Of those who did have an opinion, only a few were just mildly interested in saving the hostages.

Intensity of public opinion is often critical in generating public *action*. Intense minorities can win on an issue of public policy over less intense majorities. There is often a relationship between intensity of opinion and its perceived relevance on the part of public policy makers.

INTENSITY
The strengths of a pro or con position concerning public policy or an issue. Intensity is often critical in generating public action; an intense minority can often win on an issue of public policy over a less intense majority.

Fluidity

Public opinion can change drastically in a very short period of time. When this occurs, we say that public opinion is fluid.

At the end of the Second World War, the American people were about evenly divided in their opinions of the United States's wartime ally, the Soviet Union. A 1945 Roper poll showed that about 39 percent of Americans saw the Soviets as peace loving, while 38 percent felt they were aggressive. During

The Gorbachevs meet Minnesotans during their trip to the United States. How did the Soviet president manage to gain such positive support in American opinion?

the years of the Cold War (1947 to, roughly, 1985), American opinion about the aims of the Soviet Union was very consistent, between 13 and 17 percent of the American people believing that the Soviet Union was peace loving and more than 60 percent seeing it as aggressive. Mikhail Gorbachev's leadership of the Soviet Union and his policy of openness toward the West created an extremely fluid state of opinion among Americans. As Americans watched his attempts at internal reform and his willingness to allow the Eastern European nations to pull away from the Communist orbit, American opinion about the Soviet Union changed quickly. Over a four-year period, between 1985 and the beginning of 1990, the number of Americans who saw the Soviet Union as peace loving increased from 17 to 36 percent. In an even quicker turnaround, during the same period, the proportion of the American public that held an unfavorable opinion about the Soviet Union dropped from 41 to 13 percent. The **fluidity** of American opinion was a response to the rapidly changing conditions in the Soviet Union and world politics.[2] Such fluidity in public opinion reflects public awareness of government policy and in turn influences government decision making.

Stability

Many individual opinions remain constant over a lifetime. Taken together, individual opinions that constitute public opinion may also be extremely stable, persisting for many years. Consider the effect of the Civil War on political attitudes in the South. It was the Republicans under Abraham Lincoln who, in the eyes of southerners, were responsible for the Civil War and the ensuing humiliations experienced by a defeated South. Consequently, the South became strongly Democratic. Until recently, it was called the **Solid South** because Democratic candidates always won. We can say that public opinion in the South in favor of Democrats and against Republicans had great **stability.**

FLUIDITY
The extent to which public opinion changes over time.

SOLID SOUTH
A term describing the disposition of the post-Civil War southern states to vote for the Democratic party. (Voting patterns in the South have changed.)

STABILITY
The extent to which public opinion remains constant over a period of time.

[2]*New York Times,* December 3, 1989.

Quiescence

Not all political opinions are expressed by the holders of opinions. There may be potential political opinions—those not yet realized. Political scientists call these **latent,** or quiescent, **public opinions.** Some say, for example, that Hitler exploited the latent public opinion of post-World War I Germany by forming the National Socialist party. The public was ripe for a leader who would militarize Germany and enforce discipline to put Germany back on its feet. Latent public opinion offers golden opportunities for political leaders astute enough to perceive and act politically on it.

When average citizens are asked to respond to highly complex issues about which they have imperfect knowledge, their opinions may remain latent. This was true, for example, of the antiballistic missile (ABM) program debated by the Senate in 1969. A Gallup poll in July of that year indicated that 59 percent of Americans were undecided about the value of the ABM program even though they knew about it. What the views of those citizens would have been if they had been better informed is unknown. Abstract poll questions dealing with a respondent's ideology also produce high proportions of responses indicating that the question deals with something that many people rarely think about.

LATENT PUBLIC OPINION
Unexpressed political opinions that have the potential to become manifest attitudes or beliefs.

Relevance

Relevant public opinion for most people is simply public opinion that deals with issues concerning them. If a person has a sick parent who is having trouble meeting medical bills, then the relevant public opinion for that person will be an opinion that is focused on the issues of Medicare and Medicaid. If another person likes to go hunting with his or her children, gun control becomes a relevant political issue. Of course, **relevance** changes according to events. Public concern about inflation, for example, was at an all-time low during the 1950s and early 1960s. Why? The United States had little inflation during that period. Public opinion about the issue of unemployment was certainly relevant during the Great Depression, but not during the 1960s when the nation experienced 102 months of almost uninterrupted economic growth from 1961 to 1969.

Certain popular books can make a particular issue relevant. The publication of *The Population Bomb*[3] by Paul Ehrlich in 1968 heralded nationwide concern with uncontrolled population growth. The population issue, although still far from resolved, is less in the public mind today. Indeed, public opinion polls rarely sample attitudes about it.

RELEVANCE
The extent to which an issue is of concern at a particular time. Issues become relevant when the public views them as pressing or of direct concern to them.

Political Knowledge

People are more likely to base their opinions on knowledge about an issue if they have strong feelings about the topic. Just as relevance and intensity are closely related to having an opinion, individuals who are strongly interested in a question will probably take the time to read about it.

Looking at the population as a whole, the level of political information is quite low. Survey research tells us that slightly less than 46 percent of adult Americans can give the name of their congressperson, and just 39 percent can

[3]New York: Ballantine Books, 1968.

"Are you uninformed or apathetic?"
"I don't know and I don't care."

"Why Are Your Papers in Order?" © 1984 by Peter C. Vey.

name both U.S. senators from their state. Only 30 percent know that the term of their congressional representative is two years, although almost 70 percent know the majority party in Congress. What these data tell us is that Americans do not expend much effort remembering political facts that may not be important to their daily lives.

Americans are also likely to forget political information quite quickly. Facts that were of vital interest to citizens at one time lose their meaning after the crisis has passed. In the 1985 *New York Times*/CBS News Survey on Vietnam, marking the tenth anniversary of the end of that conflict, 63 percent of those questioned knew that the United States sided with the South Vietnamese in that conflict. Only 27 percent remembered, however, which side in that conflict launched the Tet offensive, which was a major political defeat for American and South Vietnamese forces.[4]

If political information is perceived to be of no use for an individual or is painful to recall, it is not surprising that facts are forgotten. What is more disturbing is the inability of many citizens to give basic information about current issues. Members of Congress, who represent their constituents on complex and controversial issues, hope their constituents have informed opinions. Recent polls on the U.S. military involvement in Europe found that only 60 percent of the public knew that United States was a member of the North Atlantic Treaty Organization (NATO), which it has been since 1949 and 21 percent thought that the Soviet Union was also a member (NATO was founded to provide a unified defense against the Soviet Union).[5] Such a lack of information about an important defense structure indicates that many people have not cared to learn much about U.S. military commitments.

Consensus and Division

There are very few issues on which most Americans agree. The more normal situation is for opinion to be distributed among several different positions. Looking at the distribution of opinion can tell us how divided the public is on a question and give us some indication of whether compromise is possible. The distribution of opinion can also tell us how many individuals have not thought about an issue enough to hold an opinion.

CONSENSUS
General agreement among the citizenry on an issue.

DIVISIVE
Public opinion is polarized between two quite different positions.

When a large proportion of the American public appears to express the same view on an issue, we say that a **consensus** exists, at least at the moment the poll was taken. Figure 7-1 shows the pattern of opinion that might be called consensual. Issues on which the public is divided into widely differing attitudes are clearly **divisive** (Figure 7-2). If there is no possible middle position on such issues, we expect that the division will continue to generate political conflict.

Figure 7-3 shows a distribution of opinion indicating that most Americans either have no information about the issue or are not interested enough to formulate a position. This figure illustrates latent, or quiescent, opinion. Politicians may feel that the lack of knowledge gives them more room to maneuver or they may be wary of taking any action for fear that the opinion will crystallize after a crisis. It is possible that this pattern would be the most likely to occur if survey respondents were totally honest. Research has shown that some individuals will express nonexistent opinions to an interviewer on certain topics rather than admit their ignorance.

[4]*New York Times* Survey, February 23–27, 1985.
[5]*New York Times*/CBS News poll May 5–11, 1989.

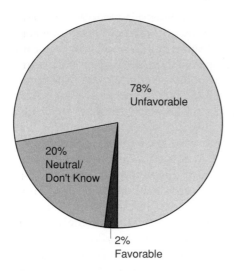

FIGURE 7-1
Consensus Opinion
After the Iranians held Americans hostage for more than a year, unfavorable feelings about Iran approached consensus. What conditions might change this view?
SOURCE: *New York Times*/CBS News Poll, September 21–22, 1987.

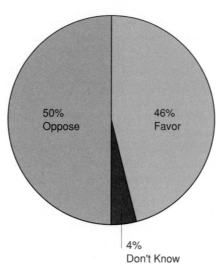

FIGURE 7-2
Divisive Opinion
Americans are almost evenly divided on using U.S. troops in a foreign nation to fight drug traffickers. Since the Vietnam war, Americans have strong differences over the use of troops abroad.
SOURCE: *Gallup Report,* October 1989.

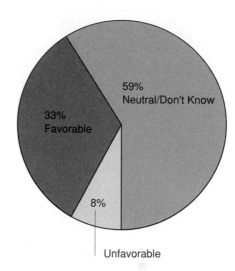

FIGURE 7-3
Latent Opinion
Few Americans have strong feelings about the Philippines in either direction, probably because they have little knowledge about the nation. What types of events might cause Americans to change their views?
SOURCE: *New York Times*/CBS News Poll, September 21–22, 1987.

■ MEASURING PUBLIC OPINION: POLLING TECHNIQUES

The History of Opinion Polls

Although some idea of public opinion can be discovered by asking persons we know for their opinions or by reading the "Letters to the Editor" sections in newspapers, most descriptions of the distribution of opinions are based on **opinion polls.** During the 1800s, certain American newspapers and magazines spiced up their political coverage by doing face-to-face straw polls or mail surveys of their readers' opinions. In this century, the magazine *Literary Digest* further developed the technique of opinion polls by mailing large numbers of questionnaires to individuals, many of whom were its own subscribers. From 1916 to 1936, more than 70 percent of the magazine's election predictions were accurate.

Literary Digest, however, suffered a major setback in its polling activities when it predicted that Alfred Landon would win over Franklin Delano Roosevelt in 1936, based on more than two million returned questionnaires. Landon won in only two states. A major problem with the *Digest's* polling technique was its continuing use of nonrepresentative respondents. In 1936, at the bottom of the Great Depression, those people who were the magazine's subscribers were, for one thing, considerably more affluent than the average American.

OPINION POLL
A method of systematically questioning a small, selected sample of individuals who are deemed representative of the total population. Widely used by government, business, university scholars, political candidates, and voluntary groups to provide reasonably accurate data on public attitudes, beliefs, expectations, and behavior.

DID YOU KNOW?

That for the 1984 presidential election between Ronald Reagan and Walter Mondale, the last pre-election Gallup poll missed the actual percentage of Reagan's popular vote support by only 0.2 percentage points?

Several newcomers to the public opinion poll industry accurately predicted Roosevelt's landslide victory. The organizations of these newcomers are still active in the poll-taking industry today: the Gallup poll of George Gallup, and Roper and Associates founded by Elmo Roper. Gallup and Roper, along with Archibald Crossley, developed the modern polling techniques of market research. Using personal interviews with small samples of selected voters (a few thousand) they showed they could predict with accuracy the behavior of the total voting population. We shall see how this is possible.

Government officials during World War II were keenly interested in public opinion about the war effort and about the increasing number of restrictions put on civilian activities. Improved methods of sampling were used, and by the 1950s a whole new science of survey research developed and spread to Western Europe, Israel, and other countries. Survey research centers sprang up throughout the United States, particularly at universities. Some of these survey groups are the American Institute of Public Opinion at Princeton, New Jersey, the National Opinion Research Center at the University of Chicago, and the Survey Research Center at the University of Michigan.

Sampling Techniques

How can interviewing several thousand voters tell us what tens of millions of voters will do? Clearly, it is necessary that the sample of several thousand individuals be representative of all voters in the population. Consider an analogy. Let us say we have a large jar containing pennies of various dates and we want to know how many pennies were minted within certain decades—1940–1949, 1950–1960, and so on. There are 10,000 pennies in the jar. One way to estimate the distribution of the dates on the pennies—without examining all 10,000—is to take a representative sample. This sample would be obtained by mixing the pennies up well and then removing a handful of them—perhaps 100 pennies. The distribution of dates might be as follows:

- 1940–1949: 5 percent
- 1950–1959: 5 percent
- 1960–1969: 20 percent
- 1970–1979: 30 percent
- 1980–present 40 percent

If the pennies are very well mixed within the jar and if you take a larger sample, the resulting distribution would probably approach the actual distribution of the dates of all 10,000 coins.

The most important principle in sampling, or poll taking, is randomness. Every penny or every person should have an *equal chance* of being sampled. If this happens, then a small sample should be representative of the whole group both in demographic characteristics (age, religion, race, living area, and the like) and in opinions. The most ideal way to sample the voting population of the United States would be to put all voter names into a jar—or a computer—and randomly sample, say, 2,000 of them. Because this is too costly and inefficient, pollsters have developed other ways to obtain good samples. One of the most interesting techniques is simply to choose a random selection of telephone numbers and interview the respective households. This technique produces an accurate sample at a low cost.

Telephone survey interviewers. Do you think that individuals respond honestly to telephone surveys? What might influence respondents to mislead the interviewer?

To ensure that the random samples include all living areas—rural, urban, Northeast, South, and so on—most survey organizations randomly choose, say, urban areas that they will consider as representative of all urban areas. Then they randomly select their respondents within that area. A generally less accurate technique is known as *quota sampling*. For this type of poll, survey researchers decide how many persons of certain types they need in the survey—such as minorities, women, or farmers—and then send out interviewers to find the necessary number of these types. This method is not only less accurate but it also may be biased if, say, the interviewer refuses to go into certain neighborhoods or will not interview after dark. Generally, the national survey organizations take great care to select their samples randomly because their reputations rest on the accuracy of their results. Usually, the Gallup or Roper polls interview about 1,500 individuals, and their results have a very high probability of being correct—within a margin of 3 percent. The accuracy with which the Gallup poll has predicted national election results is reflected in Table 7-1.

Similar sampling techniques are used in many other, nonpolitical situations. For the Nielsen ratings of TV programs, for example, representative households are selected by the A. C. Nielsen Company and a machine is attached to each household's TV set. The machine monitors viewing choices twenty-four hours a day and transmits this information to the company's central offices. A one-point drop in a Nielsen rating can mean a loss of revenue of millions of dollars to a TV network because a one-point drop indicates about 800,000 fewer viewers are watching a particular show. This means advertisers are unwilling to pay as much for viewing time. Indeed, advertising rates are based in many cases solely on Nielsen ratings. When you consider that only about 3,000 families have that little machine attached to their TV sets, it is apparent that the science of selecting representative samples has come a long way—at least far enough to convince major advertisers to accept advertising fees based on the results of those samples.

CRITICAL PERSPECTIVE, CONTINUED

into a sealed box, thus avoiding any personal interaction with the pollster.

Even in New York, where sealed ballot boxes were used for the exit polls, the results were not as close to the final outcome as usual. One factor accounting for this inaccuracy was the refusal of many urban voters to take part in exit polling. While only 10 percent of the voters in Iowa refuse to be interviewed after voting, nearly 40 percent of New Yorkers turn away from the pollsters. This high refusal rate means that the exit poll is not reaching an adequate sample of the voters, reducing its accuracy. Furthermore, many exit polls stop interviewing voters about an hour before polls close so the data can be analyzed for the evening news broadcast. If a candidate has a surge of late voters, their preferences will not be included in the exit poll results.

Exercise in Critical Thinking
1. Think about the actual purposes served by preelection and exit polls. If the main purpose is to provide news for the evening broadcast or the morning newspaper, should citizens cooperate with pollsters?
2. Could polls be improved and regain voter confidence if they were conducted according to certain standards of quality?
3. Does the emphasis on polling tend to make voters more cynical and less likely to vote?

Problems with Opinion Polls

One of the major problems with opinion polls of voter preferences is that they cannot be responsive to rapid shifts in public opinion, unless the polls are taken frequently and up until the last minute. A classic example of opinion polls falling short occurred during the 1980 presidential election when Ronald Reagan overtook President Carter at the last moment. Another problem may be racial bias, the subject of this chapter's Critical Perspective.

In addition, because opinion polls can be biased, they must always be interpreted with care. Only when the questions are phrased in a manner that precludes inadvertent bias can we have much faith in the results. Also, when we can see that polls taken at different time periods show a trend, we can increase our faith in them.

Any opinion poll contains *sampling error,* which is simply the difference between what the sample results show and what the true result would be if everybody had been interviewed. Basically, the greater the number of people who are interviewed and the closer the entire adult population is to being unanimous in their opinion, the smaller the sampling error becomes. (See chapter Highlight about three famous cases of national polling failure.)

The Polls and the 1988 Presidential Election

Public opinion polls that seek to identify the voters' preferences in the presidential election begin long before the primary elections. Usually, polls begin matching potential candidates against each other in the fall before the presidential contest.

In the fall of 1987, polls showed George Bush to be the most likely choice for the Republican nomination and Gary Hart the choice for most Democrats. In May 1988, Hart's withdrawal from the race opened the field for other Democratic contenders. Following a confusing and drawn-out period of vol-

HIGHLIGHT

When Polls Are Wrong

Between 1920 and 1932, the *Literary Digest* accurately projected the winners of each presidential election. The poll consisted of approximately ten million voters who received a mailing and returned their responses on presidential preference. In 1936, the results were tallied and reported on October 31: for Landon 57 percent, with 1,293,699 votes; for Franklin D. Roosevelt 43 percent and 972,897 ballots. When American voters actually went to their polling places in November, the results were quite different: Roosevelt got 62.5 percent of the vote and carried every state except Maine and Vermont.

What went wrong? First, the sample was selected from telephone directories and lists of automobile owners, creating a biased sample. Second, of the ten million questionnaires mailed, only about 20 percent were returned; thus, there was a strong self-selection among those who chose to answer. Third, the time lag between the early September mailing of the questionnaire and the election could not anticipate any changes in voter perception, campaign events, or even world or national events that by November would cause a shift in voter preferences. Finally, the poll neglected to take into account the fact that in 1936 the United States was still in the throes of a major national crisis. People were shifting allegiances. The New Deal coalition that Roosevelt was constructing recombined different and new groups of people; the working class and the less affluent were rallying behind FDR. The poll underrepresented this constituency and therefore had a disproportionate number of persons who would vote for Landon.

Polling techniques greatly improved in subsequent years. George Gallup, Jr.'s quota sampling technique used census data to identify the necessary percentages of relevant groups in the

population (by religion, gender, race, and so on) to make a poll more accurate. Nonetheless, a second and perhaps the most famous erroneous poll occurred in 1948 when Gallup projected that Thomas Dewey would defeat Harry Truman: The poll indicated that Truman would get 44.5 percent of the vote; he obtained 49.5 percent and won. The *Chicago Daily Tribune,* predicted the winner the night before the election with a banner headline that read "DEWEY DEFEATS TRUMAN."

Studies have demonstrated that quota sampling tends to underrepresent certain groups, in particular the poor, minorities, and the less educated, because in filling the assigned quotas, pollsters tend to avoid dangerous neighborhoods and other difficult polling obstacles. An entire quota may be filled from a single, relatively easy location (such as a "nice" apartment building where all of, say, the African-American quota can be completed). Moreover, in 1948, Gallup did his last poll two weeks before the election, thereby missing a last-minute shift to-

ward Truman. Subsequent polls have tried to correct these flaws by polling up to election day and providing more accurate samples of the electorate.

In spite of great refinements, a third major national polling failure occurred in 1980. Most polls showed the race between Reagan and Carter to be "too close to call." When Reagan beat Carter 51 percent to 41 percent, pollsters and the public were amazed at the magnitude of Reagan's victory. What went wrong? In essense, it was the major enemy of pollsters, last-minute surges. Almost up to election day, relatively large numbers of voters were undecided (some polls showed as many as 13 percent). In hindsight, it appears that almost all of the "undecided" went to Reagan. Polls done closest to election day revealed this trend. In fact, Carter's pollster, Patrick Caddell, looked at his figures the day before the election and told Carter aboard Air Force One that he would not win the election.

DID YOU KNOW?

That public opinion pollsters typically measure national sentiment among the more than 175 million adult Americans by interviewing only about 1,500 people?

atility among these candidates, Michael Dukakis emerged as the favorite. Among Republicans, despite some early caucus and primary defeats, Bush emerged as the consensus choice.

During the actual contest for the presidency, polls commissioned by the media tracked the voters' changing views. As shown in Figure 7-4, Dukakis held a strong lead over Bush at the end of the primary season. After the Democratic convention at the end of July, his lead was roughly seventeen percentage points. He let the lead slip away, however, and immediately after the Republican convention in late August, he trailed by about five points. Aided by his pollster Bob Teeter, whose Profile appears on p. 211, Bush's lead reached double digits. In early November, in a last-minute Democratic surge, Bush's lead fell only slightly.

Both campaigns relied heavily on private polling to plan strategy and to fine-tune their campaigns. Most commentators felt that the Bush campaign used polling more effectively to maximize support.

■ HOW PUBLIC OPINION IS FORMED

Most Americans are willing to express opinions on political issues when asked. How do individuals acquire these opinions and attitudes? Most views that are expressed as political opinions are acquired through a process known as **po-**

FIGURE 7-4
Tracking the 1988 Election:
Gallup Poll Results

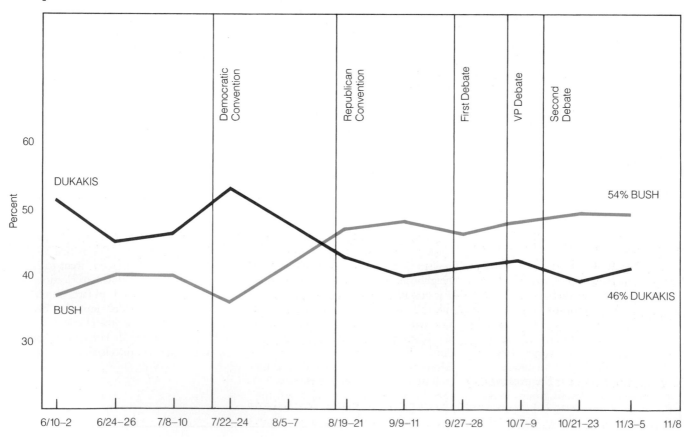

PROFILE

Robert Teeter

"To get results, you apply solutions to conditions as they exist."

The career of Bob Teeter, the professional pollster for George Bush's White House, is an illustration of the importance of public opinion to the conduct of the presidency. Teeter, a quiet, middle-aged native of Ann Arbor, Michigan, does more than periodically sample national opinion on issues such as the war on drugs and foreign policy; he is called on to use his expert knowledge to help President Bush formulate political strategy and national policy.

Teeter began his career sampling public opinion as a member of the polling firm Market Opinion Research, an organization that specializes in working for moderate Republican candidates. As one of the leaders of that firm, Teeter sampled public opinion for presidents Nixon and Ford as well as for many Republican senators and governors. A close friend of George Bush, he left his firm to become Bush's full-time adviser during the 1988 political campaign. After the election, there was speculation that Teeter would become

the resident pollster at the White House, following the example of Dick Wirthlin in the Reagan administration and Pat Caddell in the Carter years. Instead, Teeter opted for a consulting role outside the White House to give himself more time for long-range planning for Bush's future. Furthermore, Teeter has strong differences with White House Chief of Staff John Sununu, who has less confidence in polling data than does the president.

Unlike previous White House experts on public opinion, Teeter believes that

the president should move cautiously in making national policy. In this respect, he differs from Pat Caddell, the pollster for President Carter, who encouraged his boss to take innovative public positions. Teeter has argued that the president only needs to address a few major issues—such as drugs, crime, and the environment—to maintain his popularity. Only when George Bush's approval ratings slipped below 60 percent during 1988 did Teeter counsel Bush to make a bold initiative in Soviet-American relations to improve his leadership image.

One measure of the importance of Teeter's work is his income. In addition to the fees that he charges private clients, he receives a total of $15,600 monthly from the Republican National Committee and the Republican Senatorial Campaign Committee. He is also retained as an analyst for NBC news and the *Wall Street Journal*.

Given Teeter's old and trusted relationship with George Bush, it seems likely that he spends a great deal of his time planning for Bush's reelection campaign in 1992, as well as giving advice on issues ranging from managing a summit with Soviet leader Gorbachev to handling the economy.

---

litical socialization. By this we mean that individuals acquire their political attitudes, often including their party identification, through their relationships with their families, friends, and coworkers. The most important influences in that process are the following: (1) the family, (2) the educational environment and achievement of the individual, (3) the influence of peers, (4) the influence of religion, (5) economic status, (6) political events, (7) opinion leaders, (8) the media, and (9) race and other demographic traits. In addition to these influences, we also discuss the fairly recent phenomenon of the gender gap.

The Importance of the Family

The family is the most important force in political socialization. Not only do our parents' political attitudes and actions affect our adult opinions but also

POLITICAL SOCIALIZATION
The process by which individuals acquire political beliefs and attitudes.

"Glad you brought that up, Jim. The latest research on polls has turned up some interesting variables. It turns out, for example, that people will tell you any old thing that pops into their heads."

Drawing by Saxon: © 1984 The New Yorker Magazine, Inc.

the family links us to other socialization forces. We receive our ethnic identity, our notion of social class, our educational opportunities, and our early religious beliefs in the family. Each of these factors can also influence our political attitudes.

The clearest legacy of the family is partisan identification. If both parents identify with one party, there is a strong likelihood that the children will begin political life with the same party preference. Children do not "learn" such attitudes in the same way as they learn how to ride a bike. Rather, they learn by absorbing their parents' casual comments about political parties, their actions and conversation during election campaigns, and other intended clues.

In their study of political attitudes among adolescents, M. Kent Jennings and Richard G. Niemi[6] probed the partisan attachments of high school seniors and their parents during the mid-1960s. That parents successfully transmit their party identification to their children is evident from Table 7-2. Democratic parents tend to produce Democratic children about two-thirds of the time, and Independent and Republican parents both transmit their beliefs about parties only slightly less well. However, there is still a sizable amount of cross-generational slippage here. In all, Jennings and Niemi found that 59 percent of the children agreed with their parents' party ties.

In a 1973 reinterview of the same children and their parents,[7] Jennings and Niemi found that the younger people had become notably more independent of partisan ties, whereas their parents went through very little change. By 1973 a majority of the children deviated from their parents' partisanship.

[6]*The Political Character of Adolescence: The Influence of Families and Schools* (Princeton, N.J.: Princeton University Press, 1974).
[7]*Generations and Politics* (Princeton, N.J.: Princeton University Press, 1981).

These researchers also noted wide variance between the attitudes of the parents and children about specific political issues. They investigated parent-student attitudes on four issues: school integration, school prayers, allowing communists to hold elective office, and allowing speeches against churches and religion. There was only a moderate relationship between the generations' views on the first two issues and virtually no relationship at all on the last two issues.

Educational Influence on Political Opinion

Education is a powerful influence on an individual's political attitudes and on political behavior. Generally, the more education a person receives, the more liberal his or her opinions become. Students who go on to graduate training continue to become more liberal in their opinions. By *liberal,* we mean that the student is more likely to be tolerant of social change, to support social welfare programs, and to think that the United States should be active in international affairs. Individuals who have limited educational backgrounds are more likely to be isolationist in their foreign policy positions, more conservative in their social opinions, and less likely to support civil rights and civil liberties.

Peers and Peer Group Influence

Once a child enters school, the child's friends become an important influence on behavior and attitudes. As young children, and later as adults, friendships and associations in **peer groups** are influential on political attitudes. We must, however, separate the effects of peer group pressure on opinions and attitudes in general from peer group pressure on political opinions. For the most part, associations among peers are nonpolitical. It may be overgeneralizing to say that political attitudes are shaped by peer groups. This is more likely to occur when the peer group is actively involved in political activities.

Individuals who join interest groups based on ethnic identity may find, for example, a common political bond through working for the group's civil liberties and rights. Members of a labor union may feel strong political pressure to support certain prolabor candidates. African-American activist groups may consist of individuals who will exert mutual pressure to support government programs that will aid the African-American population.

> **DID YOU KNOW?**
>
> That a radio station in Iowa conducts "The Cess Poll" to assess voters' primary election preferences for president by measuring the drop in water pressure when people express their support for a candidate by flushing their toilets when the candidate's name is read over the air?

PEER GROUPS
Groups consisting of members sharing common relevant social characteristics. They play an important part in the socialization process, helping to shape attitudes and beliefs.

Patriotism is instilled in children through the process of political socialization. The children in this picture know that their parents approve of this display of support for the flag, thus enhancing their patriotic feelings.

TABLE 7-2
Student Party Identification by Parent Party Identification (in percent)

HIGH SCHOOL STUDENTS	PARENTS		
	Democratic	Independent	Republican
Democratic	66	29	13
Independent	27	55	36
Republican	7	17	51

SOURCE: Jennings and Niemi, p. 41.

DID YOU KNOW?

That young children first think of politics in terms of a benevolent president and a helpful police officer?

Religious Influence

Religious associations tend to create definite political attitudes, although why this occurs is not clearly understood. Surveys show that Roman Catholic respondents tend to be more liberal on economic issues than Protestants. Apparently, Jewish respondents are more liberal on all fronts than either Catholics or Protestants.[8] In terms of voting behavior, it has been observed that northern white Protestants are more likely to vote Republican, whereas northern white Roman Catholics more often vote Democratic; and everywhere in the United States, Jews mostly vote Democratic. These associations between religious background and political attitudes are partly derived from the ethnic background of certain religious groups and the conditions at the time their forebears immigrated to the United States. Germans who immigrated before the Civil War tend to be Republican regardless of their religious background, whereas Eastern European Catholics, who arrived in the late-nineteenth century, adopted the Democratic identity of the cities where they made their homes. The relationship between religion and voting in the 1988 presidential election is shown in Table 7-3

Sometimes a candidate's religion enters the political picture, as it did in the 1960 presidential election contest between Democrat John Kennedy and Republican Richard Nixon. The fact that Kennedy was a Catholic—the second nominated by a major party—polarized many voters. Among northern whites, Kennedy was supported by 83 percent of voting Catholics and by 93 percent of Jewish voters but by only 28 percent of the Protestants who voted.

The Influence of Economic Status and Occupation

How wealthy you are and the kind of job you hold are also associated with your political views. Social-class differences emerge on a wide range of issues. Poorer people are more inclined to favor government social welfare programs but are likely to be conservative on social issues such as abortion. The upper middle class is more likely to hold conservative economic views but to be tolerant of social change. People in lower economic strata also tend to be more isolationist on foreign policy issues and are more likely to identify with, and vote for, the Democratic party. Support for civil liberties and tolerance of different points of view tend to be greater among those with higher social

[8]See Robert S. Erikson, Norman R. Luttbeg, and Kent L. Tedin, *American Public Opinion: Its Origins, Content, and Impact,* 2nd ed. (New York: John Wiley, 1980).

TABLE 7-3
Religion and Voting

RELIGION	BUSH	DUKAKIS
White Protestant	66	32
Catholic	52	47
Jewish	35	64
White fundamentalist	81	18

SOURCE: *The New York Times,* July 17, 1988

status and lower among those with lower status. Probably, it is educational differences more than the patterns of life at home or work that account for this.

The Influence of Political Events

People's political attitudes may be shaped by political events and the nation's reactions to them. In the 1960s and 1970s, the war in Vietnam—including revelations about the secret bombing in Cambodia—and the Watergate break-in and subsequent cover-up fostered widespread cynicism toward government. In one study of the impact of Watergate, Christopher Arterton[9] found that school children changed their image of the president from a "benevolent" to a "malevolent" leader as the scandal unfolded. Negative views also increased about other aspects of politics and politicians.

When the events of an era produce a long-lasting political impact, **generational effects** result. Voters who grew up during the Great Depression were likely to form life-long attachments to the Democratic party, the party of Franklin D. Roosevelt. Similarily, there is some evidence that the years of economic prosperity under Ronald Reagan may have influenced young adults to identify with the Republican party. A poll taken in 1990 showed that 52 percent of 13–17-year-olds thought of themselves as Republicans compared with 32 percent as Democrats.[10]

GENERATIONAL EFFECTS
Events of a particular time period have a long-lasting effect on the political opinions or preferences of those individuals who came of political age at that time.

Opinion Leaders' Influence

We are all influenced by those with whom we are closely associated or whom we hold in great respect—friends at school, family members and other relatives, teachers, and so on. In a sense, these people are **opinion leaders,** but on an informal level; that is, their influence over us is not necessarily intentional or deliberate. Formal opinion leaders, such as a president, a lobbyist, a congress-person, or a news commentator, have as part of their job the task of swaying people's views. Their interest lies in defining the political agenda in such a way that discussions about policy options will take place on their terms.

OPINION LEADERS
Individuals able to influence the opinions of others because of position, expertise, or personality. Such leaders help to shape public opinion either formally or informally.

Media Influence

Newspapers, television, and other **media** act as sources of information, commentary, and images. Newspapers and news magazines (such as *Time* or *Newsweek*) are especially rich sources of knowledge about political issues. Some argue that newspaper editorials normally have a heavily pro-Republican and conservative slant, especially for presidential endorsements, and that columnists are often selected to reflect such biases. Journalists are perceived as having a counteracting Democratic and liberal bias. Television, the media source relied on by most Americans, conveys only limited political information about issues or candidates' qualifications. There seems to be no strongly partisan or ideological bias in television coverage, although the visual and mental images conveyed by TV clearly have a powerful impact.

MEDIA
The technical means of communication with mass audiences. The media have become extremely important in American political life as a means of informing and influencing millions of citizens.

---

[9]"The Impact of Watergate on Children's Attitudes toward Authority," *Political Science Quarterly*, vol. 89 (June 1984), pp. 269–288.
[10]*The Public Perspective*, May/June 1990, p. 105.

DID YOU KNOW?

That the results of 124 presidential preference polls were made public between September 1st and election day in 1988, compared to 44 such polls in 1984?

The Influence of Demographic Traits

African Americans show a much stronger commitment than whites to steady or more rapid racial desegregation. African Americans tend to be more liberal than whites on social welfare issues, civil liberties, and even foreign policy. Party preferences and voting among African Americans since the 1930s have very heavily supported the Democrats, and, as the Highlight, Competing Influences: Race and Wealth, indicates, wealth has little impact on African-American attitudes.

It is somewhat surprising that a person's chronological age has comparatively little impact on political preferences. Still, young adults are somewhat more liberal than older people on most issues and are considerably more progressive on such issues as marijuana legalization, pornography, civil disobedience, and racial and sexual equality.

The generally greater conservatism of older Americans may be explained in one or more ways: (1) Simply becoming older makes people more conservative. (2) People carry with them the values they learned when they first became politically aware, which are now considered relatively conservative. (3) People's attitudes are shaped by the events that unfold as they grow up. The most important of these explanations seems to be the third; that is, a person's views are mainly determined by when he or she happened to be born. If an individual grew up in an era of Democratic party dominance, then that person will be more likely to remain a Democrat throughout his or her life.[11]

Finally, attitudes vary from region to region, although such patterns probably are accounted for mostly by social class and other differences. Regional differences are relatively unimportant today. There is still a tendency for the East and West to be more liberal than most of the Midwest and the South, and for the South and East to be more Democratic than the West and the Midwest. More important than region is a person's residence—urban, suburban, or rural. Big cities tend to be more liberal and Democratic because of their greater concentration of minorities and newer ethnic groups, and smaller communities are more conservative and, outside the South, more Republican.

The Gender Gap

GENDER GAP
Most widely used to describe the difference between the percentage of votes a candidate receives from women voters and the percentage the candidate receives from men. The term was widely used after the 1980 presidential election.

Until the 1980s, there was little evidence that men's and women's political attitudes were very different. The election of Ronald Reagan, however, soon came to be associated with a **gender gap.** In a May 1983 Gallup poll, 43 percent of the women polled approved of Reagan's performance in office and 44 percent disapproved, versus 49 percent of men who approved and 41 percent who disapproved.[12]

In the 1988 election, the gender gap reappeared but in a modified form. Although the Democrats hoped that women's votes would add significantly to their totals, a deep split between men and women did not occur. The final polls showed that men voted 54 percent for Bush, as did 50 percent of the women. There is some evidence that women's votes did make a difference in congressional races.

Women also appear to hold different attitudes from their male counterparts on a range of issues other than presidential preferences. They are much more

[11]Robert Erikson, Norman Luttbeg, and Kent Tedin, *American Public Opinion,* 2nd ed., pp. 170–175.
[12]*The Gallup Report,* May, 1983.

HIGHLIGHT

Competing Influences: Race and Wealth

Two of the influences that seem to shape the opinions of Americans are race and income. As noted in the text, African Americans are more likely to be liberal on welfare and government spending issues than are whites, on the average, whereas individuals who earn higher incomes tend to be conservative on welfare and government spending issues. Presumably, high-income individuals perceive that it is in their best interest to have the government spend less on these programs because the wealthier classes pay more taxes and receive few of the benefits. Poorer Americans, whether African Americans or white, tend to approve of government spending on welfare programs because they are the principal beneficiaries of such expenditures.

One question that has interested social scientists and politicians is what happens to the political opinions of individuals who achieve a high income. Does becoming wealthy change the individual's political opinions? Do Americans who rise to the upper middle class become more Republican and conservative or do they remain loyal to the in-

terests of other African Americans who have not done as well?

Recent research shows that over the last fifteen years, African Americans as a group have maintained their liberal views. African-American respondents are almost twice as likely as whites to support government efforts to improve the standard of living for the poor. When the African-American respondents are divided into income groups, it becomes clear that wealthy African Americans do not become more conservative than those who have lower incomes. As the accompanying figure indicates, support for spending more on welfare does decline slightly among African Americans as their income increases, but the overall level of support for such government spending is twice as high as it is for whites of the same economic class. Not only do African Americans of the upper-income groups keep their liberal views but they also stay within the Democratic party. In 1984, surveys showed that 8 percent of the lowest-income African Americans were Republicans as compared with 11 percent of the upper-income African

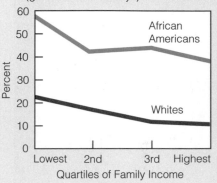

Support for Spending More on Welfare (general social surveys)

Americans. Keeter and Banks summarize their research by saying that "African Americans evidently continue to view political issues more in terms of their collective group situation than in terms of their personal economic circumstances."

Source: Scott Keeter and Elliott Banks, "An Examination of the Growth of Conservatism among Black Americans," paper presented at the annual meeting of the American Association for Public Opinion Research, Toronto, Canada, May 1988.

---

likely to oppose the use of force on domestic issues, such as capital punishment, and on foreign policy issues. A 1982 poll sponsored by the Chicago Council on Foreign Relations showed that only 34 percent of American women favored the government selling military equipment to other nations, whereas 50 percent of men supported this strategy. Other studies have shown that women are more concerned about risks to the environment, particularly from nuclear power, and are more supportive of social welfare than are men.[13] These differences of opinion appear to be growing and may become an important factor in future elections at national and local levels.

■ THE POLITICAL CULTURE OF AMERICANS

Americans are divided into a multitude of ethnic, religious, regional, and political subgroups. In many cases, members of these groups hold a particular

[13]Katherine Frankovic, "Sex and Politics—New Alignments, Old Issues," *PS*, 1982, pp. 439–448.

Reenacting the March on Washington.

POLITICAL CULTURE
That set of beliefs and values regarding the political system which are widely shared by citizens of a nation.

POLITICAL TRUST
The degree to which individuals express trust in the government and political institutions. This concept is usually measured through a specific series of survey questions.

set of opinions about government politics, about the goals of the society, and about the rights of their group and the rights of others. Given the diversity of American society and the wide range of opinions contained within it, how is it that the political process continues to function without being stalemated by conflict and dissension?

One explanation is rooted in the concept of the **political culture,** which can be described as a set of attitudes and ideas about the nation and the government. Our political culture is widely shared by Americans of many different backgrounds. To some extent, it consists of symbols, such as the American flag, the Liberty Bell, and the Statue of Liberty. One of the reasons that the renovation of the statue so strongly engaged the imagination of the citizens is because is symbolizes two major aspects of American political culture: the pursuit of liberty and the fact that most Americans are descended from immigrants who sought liberty and equality.

The elements of our political culture also include certain shared beliefs about the most important values in the American political system. Research by Donald Devine[14] suggests that there is a set of key values that is central to the political culture. Among the most important are three of the values from the revolutionary period: (1) liberty, equality, and property, (2) support for religion, and (3) a high value on community service and personal achievement. The structure of the government, particularly federalism, the political parties, the strength of Congress, and popular rule, were also found to be important values.

The political culture provides a general environment of support for the political system. If the people share certain beliefs about the system and a reservoir of good feeling exists toward the institutions of government, the nation will be better able to weather periods of crisis such as Watergate. This foundation of good will may combat cynicism and increase the level of participation in elections as well. During the 1960s and 1970s, survey research showed that the overall level of **political trust** declined steeply. A considerable proportion of Americans seemed to feel that they could not trust government officials and that they could not count on officials to care about the ordinary person. This index of political trust reached an all-time low in 1980, but since that year has begun to rebound (Table 7-4).

[14]Donald Devine, *Political Culture of the United States* (Boston, Little, Brown, 1972).

TABLE 7-4
Trends in Political Trust

How much of the time do you think you can trust the government in Washington to do what is right—just about always, most of the time, or only some of the time?											
	1964	1968	1972	1974	1976	1978	1980	1982	1984*	1986*	1988*
Percent saying:											
Always/ Most of the time	76	61	53	36	33	29	25	32	46	42	44
Some of the time/Never	22	36	45	61	63	67	73	64	51	55	54

SOURCE: The University of Michigan Survey Research Center, National Election Studies.
*The New York Times/CBS News surveys.

One way to test whether Americans really believe in the values that are central to the political culture is to examine the degree of **political tolerance** they are willing to show toward those who hold views differing strongly from their own. Researchers asked Americans if they would be willing to permit demonstrations by a number of groups who espouse particular opinions.[15] More than 80 percent of those asked were willing to permit demonstrations opposing crime in the community and pollution. About 60 percent felt that it would be acceptable to permit African-American militants or radical students to demonstrate, whereas only 40 percent would support efforts to march for the legalization of marijuana. Although we do not find that all Americans are willing to extend political tolerance to groups indiscriminately, it appears that the political culture is strong enough to provide freedom for many points of view.

POLITICAL TOLERANCE
The degree to which individuals are able to grant civil liberties to groups that have opinions differing strongly from their own.

■ PUBLIC OPINION ABOUT GOVERNMENT

A vital component of public opinion in the United States, as it reflects the nation's political culture and the patterns of political socialization in the country, is the considerable ambivalence with which the public regards many major national institutions. Table 7-5 shows trends from 1973 to 1989 in Gallup public opinion polls asking respondents to tell at regularly spaced intervals "how much confidence you, yourself, have" in the institutions listed. Over the years the military and religious organizations have ranked highest, but note the decline in confidence in churches following the numerous scandals concerning television evangelists of the last few years. The U.S. Supreme Court,

[15]David G. Lawrence, "Procedural Norms and Tolerance: A Reassessment," *American Political Science Review,* 70:88 (1976).

TABLE 7-5
Confidence in Institutions Trend

QUESTION: I am going to read a list of institutions in American society. Would you please tell me how much confidence you, yourself, have in each one—a great deal, quite a lot, some, or very little?

	PERCENT SAYING "GREAT DEAL" OR "QUITE A LOT"								
	1973	1975	1977	1979	1981	1983	1985	1987	1989
Church or organized religion	66%	68%	65%	65%	64%	62%	66%	61%	52%
Military	NA	58	57	54	50	53	61	61	63
U.S. Supreme Court	44	49	46	45	46	42	56	52	46
Banks & banking	NA	NA	NA	60	46	51	51	51	42
Public schools	58	NA	54	53	42	39	48	50	43
Congress	42	40	40	34	29	28	39	NA	32
Newspapers	39	NA	NA	51	35	38	35	31	NA
Big business	26	34	33	32	20	28	31	NA	NA
Television	37	NA	NA	38	25	25	29	28	NA
Organized labor	30	38	39	36	28	26	28	26	NA

NA = Not asked.
SOURCE: The Gallup Report, September, 1989.

which many people do not see as a particularly political institution although it is clearly involved in decisions with vitally important consequences for the nation, also scores well, as do banks and banking. Congress, however, ranks considerably below these other, more highly regarded institutions. Even less confidence is expressed in newspapers, big business, television, and organized labor, all of which are certainly involved directly or indirectly in the political process.

Although people may not have much confidence in government institutions, they nonetheless turn to government to solve what they perceive to be the major problems facing the country. Table 7-6, which is based on Gallup polls conducted over the years 1970 to 1990, shows that the leading problems have clearly changed over time. The public tends to emphasize problems that are real, timely, and important. It is not at all unusual to see fairly sudden and even apparently contradictory shifts in public perceptions of what government should do. Note the years 1975–1977 and 1980–1983, when both "high cost of living" and "unemployment" were at the top of the public's action agenda. These two problems are quite possibly contradictory; that is, reducing unemployment, everything else constant, is likely to produce inflationary pressures, and attempts to reduce inflation may have to be accompanied by more people unemployed so as to reduce inflationary pressures. In some instances, government cannot respond well to these contradictory demands from the public. Jimmy Carter, for example, was largely unable to resolve this dilemma. On the other hand, Ronald Reagan was much more successful in confronting much the same set of demands from public opinion, although Reagan benefited from very fortunate declines in energy prices and a climate of opinion that would tolerate very high rates of unemployment for a couple of years (1981–1982).

This gives rise to a critically important question: Is government really responsive to public opinion? One study by political scientists Benjamin I. Page and Robert Y. Shapiro[16] suggests that in fact the national government is very responsive to the public's demands for action. In looking at changes in public opinion poll results over time, Page and Shapiro show that when there is a noticeable change in what the public wants to see government do, government policy changes 43 percent of the time in a direction congruent with the change in public opinion, changes in the direction opposite to the change in opinion 22 percent of the time, and 33 percent of the time does not change even when public opinion demands that a change be made. So, overall, the national government could be said to respond to changes in public opinion about two-thirds of the time, and when government policy does change, it is usually (about two-thirds of the time) consistent with the change in public opinion. Page and Shapiro also show, as should be no surprise, that when public opinion changes more dramatically, say, by 20 percentage points rather than by just 6 or 7 percentage points, government policy is much more likely to be consistent with the changing public attitudes.

■ POLITICAL IDEOLOGY

Political candidates and officeholders in the United States are frequently identified as liberals or conservatives. In recent years, variations on these labels

TABLE 7-6
Most Important Problem Trend 1970–1990

Year	Problem
1990	War in Middle East
1989	War on drugs
1988	Economy, budget deficit
1987	Unemployment, economy
1986	Unemployment, budget deficit
1985	Fear of war, unemployment
1984	Unemployment, fear of war
1983	Unemployment, high cost of living
1982	Unemployment, high cost of living
1981	High cost of living, unemployment
1980	High cost of living, unemployment
1979	High cost of living, energy problems
1978	High cost of living, energy problems
1977	High cost of living, unemployment
1976	High cost of living, unemployment
1975	High cost of living, unemployment
1974	High cost of living, Watergate, energy crisis
1973	High cost of living, Watergate
1972	Vietnam
1971	Vietnam, high cost of living
1970	Vietnam

SOURCE: *The Gallup Report*, 1990.

[16]"Effects of Public Opinion on Policy," *American Political Science Review*, 77:175–190 (1985).

include post-Cold War liberals and neoconservatives. These terms refer loosely to a spectrum of political beliefs that are commonly arrayed on a single dimension from left to right. Each of the terms has changed its meaning from its origins and continues to change as the issues of political debate change. In the United States, however, the terms most frequently refer to sets of political positions that date from the Great Depression.

Liberals are most commonly understood to embrace national government solutions to public problems, to believe that the national government should intervene in the economy to ensure its health, to support social welfare programs to assist the disadvantaged, and to be tolerant of social change. Today, liberals are often identified with pro-women's rights positions, pro-civil rights policies, and opposition to increased defense spending. New York Governor Mario Cuomo and Massachusetts Senator Edward Kennedy are usually tagged as liberals.

In contrast, conservatives usually feel that the national government has grown too large, that the private sector needs less interference from the government, that social welfare programs should be limited, that state and local governments should be able to make their own decisions, and that the nation's defense should be strengthened. Some conservatives express grave concerns about the decline of family life and traditional values in this country; they would not be tolerant of gay rights laws, for example. Arizona Senator Barry Goldwater represented conservatism in the 1960s, whereas Senators Jesse Helms and Strom Thurmond are examples of today's variety.

When asked, Americans are usually willing to identify themselves on the liberal-conservative spectrum. More individuals are likely to consider themselves moderates than either liberal or conservative. As Table 7-7 shows, the number of conservatives increased and the number of liberals declined in the early Reagan years but, by 1986, the proportions were about the same as ten years earlier.

New York Governor Mario Cuomo, leading Democratic liberal (top); Senator Jesse Helms, Republican conservative (bottom).

TABLE 7-7
Ideological Self-Identification, 1976–1990
There has been relatively little change in the distribution of liberals and conservatives even after the election of self-described liberal or conservative presidents.

Year	Liberal	Moderate	Conservative	No Opinion
1976	21%	41%	26%	12%
1977	21	38	29	12
1978	21	35	27	17
1979	21	42	26	12
1980	19	40	31	11
1981	18	43	30	9
1982	17	40	33	11
1984	17	41	31	11
1986	20	45	28	7
1988	18	45	33	4
1990	20	48	28	6

SOURCE: *Gallup Reports,* New York Times/CBS News polls.

IDEOLOGUE
A term applied to an individual whose political opinions are tightly constrained, that is, who has opinions that are consistent with one another. Ideologues are often described as having a comprehensive world view.

Most Americans, however, do not fit into the categories as nicely as do Edward Kennedy or Jesse Helms. Such political leaders, who are quite conscious of their philosophical views and who hold a carefully thought out and consistent set of political beliefs, can be described as **ideologues.** Partly because most citizens are not highly interested in all political issues and partly because Americans have different stakes in politics, most people have mixed sets of opinions that do not fit into one ideological framework. Election research in the 1950s suggested that only a small percentage of all Americans, perhaps less than 10 percent, could be identified as ideologues. The rest of the public conceived of politics more in terms of the parties or of economic well-being.

Some critics of the American political system have felt that elections would be more meaningful and that the nation could face important policy problems more effectively if Americans were more ideological in their thinking. Public opinion research suggests that for most Americans, political issues are not as important as their daily lives most of the time. There is no evidence to suggest that forces are in place to turn Americans into highly motivated ideological voters.

■ PUBLIC OPINION AND THE POLITICAL PROCESS

Surveys of public opinion, no matter what fascinating questions they ask or how quickly they get the answers, are not equivalent to elections in the United States. Because not all Americans are equally interested in politics or equally informed, public opinion polls can suggest only the general distribution of opinion on issues. Many times, only a few citizens have formulated a preference, and these preferences will be changed by events.

Politicians, whether in office or in the midst of a campaign, see public opinion as important to their careers. The president, as well as governors, mayors, and other elected officials, realize that strong support by the public as expressed in polls is a source of power in dealing with other politicians. It is far more difficult for a senator to say no to the president if he is immensely popular and if polls show approval of his policies. Public opinion also helps political candidates identify the most important concerns among the public and may help them shape their campaigns successfully.

Public opinion is sometimes perceived as acting as a boundary for public officials. Although it cannot give exact guidance on what the government should do in a specific instance, the opinions measured in polls do set an informal limit on government action. Look at the highly controversial matter of abortion. Most Americans are moderates on this issue; they do not approve of abortion as a means of birth control but they do feel that it should be available under certain circumstances. But sizable groups of individuals express very intense feelings both pro- and antiabortion. Given this distribution of opinion, most elected officials would rather not try to change policy to favor either of the extreme positions. To do so would clearly violate the opinion of the majority of Americans. In this case, like many others, public opinion does not make public policy; rather, it restrains officials from taking truly unpopular actions. If officials do act in the face of public opposition, the consequences of such actions will be determined at the ballot box.

How to Read a Public Opinion Poll

We are inundated virtually every day with information from public opinion polls. The polls, often reported to us through television news, the newspaper, *Time* or *Newsweek* magazines, or radio, purport to tell us a variety of things: whether the president's popularity is up or down, whether the public is more willing than before to trust the Soviets on arms control agreements, whether gun control is more popular now than previously, or who is leading the pack for the next presidential nomination.

What must be kept in mind during this blizzard of information is that not all the poll results are equally good or equally believable. As a citizen, you need to be aware of what makes one set of public opinion poll results valid and other results useless or even dangerously misleading. You should be able to evaluate the results that are being forced on you by the media or by political groups or candidates.

The first question has to do with how the sample of people who were interviewed were selected. Pay attention only to opinion polls that are based on scientific, or random, samples, in which a known probability was used to select every person who was interviewed. These *probability samples,* as they are also called, can take a number of different forms. The simplest to understand is known as a *simple random sample*, in which everybody had an equal chance of being chosen to be interviewed. Other satisfactory ways of selecting samples are *systematic samples*, in which every tenth person, for example, might be selected from an alphabetized list of names; *stratified sampling*, in which the pollster has purposely selected a particular proportion or number of poll respondents who are, say, black, Jewish, or farmers and who otherwise might not get sufficient representation in the sample; or *cluster sampling,* in which people have been interviewed in randomly chosen geographical areas. As a rule, do not give credence to the results of opinion polls which use person-in-the-shopping-mall interviews on local television news segments. The problems with this kind of opinion taking, which is a special version of a so-called *accidental sample*, are that not everyone had a known or equal chance of being in the mall when the interview took place, and that it is almost certain that the people in the mall are not a reasonable cross-section of a community's entire population (shopping malls would tend to attract people who are disproportionately younger, female, mobile, and middle class). In general, if a pollster can't be specific about the odds of the results of the poll being correct, it means that some nonrandom, or nonprobability, sample has been taken and that the results are probably not very useful.

The reason why probability samples are useful whereas nonprobability samples are not is that when you know the odds that the particular sample would have been chosen randomly from a larger population, you can calculate the "sampling error," or the range within which the real results for the whole population would fall if everybody had been interviewed. Well-designed probability samples will allow the pollster to say, for example, that he or she is 95 percent sure that 61 percent of the public, plus or minus 4 percentage points, supports the development of the "Star Wars" strategic defense initiative. The range around the sample result becomes smaller, meaning that the guess about the actual proportion of Star Wars supporters is more precise, as the size of the sample gets bigger. It turns out that if you want to become twice as precise about a poll result, you would need to collect a sample four times as large. This tends to make accurate polls quite expensive and difficult to collect. Typically, national public opinion polls by, for example, the Gallup organization seldom interview more than about 1,500 respondents. With a sample of that size, Gallup is able to be correct to within about 3 percentage points of the probably true figures.

There are other important points to keep in mind when you are confronted with opinion poll results. How were people contacted for the poll—by mail, by telephone, in person in their homes, or in some other way? By and large, because of its lower cost compared with interviewing people in person, polling firms have recently turned more and more to telephone interviewing. This method can usually produce highly accurate results, but telephone interviews typically need to be short and deal with questions that are fairly easy to answer. Interviews in person are better for getting useful information about why a particular response was given to a question, but they take much longer to complete and are not as useful if results must be generated quickly. Results from mail questionnaires should be taken with a grain of salt, because usually only a small percentage of people complete them and send them back, and the kinds of people who fill them out are typically better educated, with higher incomes and more prestigious jobs, and are therefore not representative of the general population or its likely attitudes.

When you see the results from public opinion polls in this book, they are usually from probability samples, with the results having been gathered in personal interviews or over the telephone. The next time you see an opinion poll anywhere else, ask yourself how the results were collected and whether you should to believe what the poll seems to lead you to conclude.

CHAPTER SUMMARY

1. Public opinion is the aggregate of individual attitudes or beliefs shared by some portion of adults. It becomes known in a democracy through elections, initiatives, referenda, lobbying, and interest group activities.

2. Public opinion has at least five special qualities: (1) intensity—the strength of an opinion; (b) fluidity—the extent to which an opinion changes; (c) stability—the extent to which an opinion remains constant; (d) quiescence—latent opinions; and (e) relevance—the extent to which an issue is of concern at a particular time.

3. Most individuals remember relatively few political facts. They are most likely to remember political information about issues that are of great interest to them.

4. Consensus issues are those on which there is nearly total agreement within the public. Divisive issues are those on which large segments of the public hold fundamentally opposing views.

5. Most descriptions of the distribution of opinions are based on opinion polls. George Gallup, Elmo Roper, and Archibald Crossley developed modern polling techniques by using personal interviews with carefully drawn samples.

6. The most important principle in sampling techniques, or poll taking, is randomness. This nearly ensures that the sample is representative of the whole population.

7. One problem with opinion polls is that they cannot be responsive to rapid changes in public opinion. They may also be biased, and therefore should be interpreted with care.

8. Many people identify with their parents' political parties. An increasing number of young people have entered the electorate as independents, however.

9. The more education a person has, the more liberal and tolerant she or he is likely to be on most social issues, but not on economic issues.

10. Associations in peer groups, particularly when the peer group is politically active, help to determine political attitudes.

11. Other important determinants of political attitudes are religious affiliation, economic status, political events and the nation's reactions to them, opinion leaders, and the media.

12. In general, political attitudes vary with race, age, sex, and region.

13. Although Americans may be divided on specific issues or candidates, most subscribe to a similar set of beliefs about the nation and the government. This set of shared attitudes and values is called the political culture.

14. Most Americans are willing to identify themselves as liberals, moderates, or conservatives, although few individuals really hold the kind of organized beliefs about politics and government that can be called an ideology.

15. Public opinion can play an important part in the political process in election campaigns, in providing support for the president or others, or in limiting the acceptable actions of government officials.

QUESTIONS FOR REVIEW AND DISCUSSION

1. How does public opinion influence the formation of national policies? Is public opinion more powerful as a positive force for change or as a negative force opposing change?

2. Think about a current political problem—for example, U.S. policy towards Eastern Europe or oil politics in the Middle East. How have the opinions of your parents, your friends, or your teachers affected your own attitudes? To what extent are your views colored by your own political party identification?

3. Do you consider yourself to be a liberal, a conservative, or a moderate on political issues? Try to list all of the beliefs that you hold that create such an identity. To what extent do you feel close to politicians or elected officials who identify themselves in the same way?

SELECTED REFERENCES

Herbert Asher, *Polling and the Public, What Every Citizen Should Know* (Washington, D.C.: Congressional Quarterly Press, 1988). A basic guide to reading, analyzing, and learning from public opinion polls.

Irving Crespi, *Public Opinion, Polls and Democracy* (Boulder, Colorado: Westview Press, 1989). Crespi explores the reciprocal influences of polling, politics, and the media. He offers solutions to the often inappropriate uses of polls, and suggests reforms in media reporting methods.

Charles D. Elder and Roger W. Cobb, *The Political Uses of Symbols* (New York: Longman, 1983). How we react to political symbols with our emotions and intellect and how these symbols structure our political opinions.

Harry Holloway and John George, *Public Opinion: Coalitions, Elites, and Masses,* 2nd ed. (New York: St. Martin's, 1986). Public opinion and the 1984 election, shifting forms of conservatism and liberalism, attitudes of elites and the masses, and political socialization as the origin of opinions. Includes discussions of parties, interest groups, and the media, as well as ethnic groups and social class.

Michael Margolis and Gary A. Mauser, eds., *Manipulating Public Opinion: Essays on Public Opinion as a Dependent Variable* (Pacific Grove, Cal.: Brooks/Cole, 1989). This collection of empirical studies examines the ability of political elites to manage public opinion in election campaigns, in the development of public policy, and in the process of political socialization.

Keith T. Poole and L. Harmon Zeigler, *Women, Public Opinion, and Politics: The Changing Political Attitudes of American Women* (New York: Longman, 1985). Focuses on the relationship between attitudes for equality of women and attitudes about other issues, such as regulating the environment or defense spending. Women's political participation, ideological constraint on issues, and candidate preferences are addressed.

Jerry L. Yeric and John R. Todd, *Public Opinion: The Visible Politics,* 2nd ed. (Itasca, Ill.: F. E. Peacock, 1989). The relationship of public opinion to polling, public policy, and demographic factors is exlained in this text.

CHAPTER 8

INTEREST GROUPS

CHAPTER CONTENTS

What If Interest Groups' Campaign Spending Were Limited to
$1 per Member?

The Role of Interest Groups

Major Interest Groups

Interest Group Strategies

Regulating Lobbyists

Why Interest Groups Have So Much Power

WHAT IF . . . INTEREST GROUPS' CAMPAIGN SPENDING WERE LIMITED TO $1 PER MEMBER?

We now appear to be in a period of American political history when money is truly the mother's milk of politics. The 1988 congressional and presidential campaigns cost more than half a billion dollars. The rise of Political Action Committees (PACs) has opened the floodgates for money flowing into campaigns. In 1990, on the average, 40 percent of a House candidate's campaign funds came from PACs. Concern over the impact of money on politics, especially the argument that those politicians receiving the money return the favor, has led to a search for solutions.

What if groups were limited to spending only $1 for each member of the organization on political campaign contributions? Would the role of money in American politics change in dramatic ways? What would be some of the consequences of such a policy?

To begin with, lobby groups would probably begin an aggressive campaign to increase their membership. They would hire even more specialists in membership and fund raising. Today, even though Americans readily join organizations, it is safe to say that most of us simply rely on groups to which we do not belong but with whose objectives we agree to represent us. We may send a few dollars when asked, but we do not necessarily join formally.

Second, as a result of formal membership in special interest organizations, we would be bombarded with newsletters, telephone polls, and invitations to rallies and demonstrations. Thus Americans would likely be encouraged to become more militant and active in single-issue groups.

Third, the strengths of interest groups traditionally are evaluated by the nature of the group. Mass membership groups have their large numbers as a resource. They can write millions of letters, threaten to vote for the opposition candidate, march in protest, and in other ways make themselves felt in numbers. Other groups that do not have large numbers can use superior organization and money to press for their interests. A strict $1 per member limit on contributions to political campaigns would obviously shift the balance in favor of those organizations with mass memberships.

In the area of economic affairs, the AFL-CIO would be permitted to spend $13 million on politics, but the National Association of Manufacturers would be limited to $14,000.

On the very politicized issue of right to life versus freedom of choice, the National Right to Life organization could spend $12 million, while the National Abortion Rights Action League would be confined to $115,000.

In the area of gun control, the National Rifle Association would spend roughly $3 million, whereas the combined gun control lobby groups, National Coalition to Ban Handguns and Handgun Control, Inc., could only spend $300,000.

We can imagine that some groups and individuals would be tempted to inflate the numbers in their ranks. If the history of voting fraud and the growth of PACs are any lesson, monitoring, compliance, and enforcement of the dollar rule would quickly become a nightmare. The Federal Election Commission (FEC), charged with monitoring election finances, would not only have to check campaign contributions of interest groups against their stated membership numbers but would also have to spot-check membership rosters to verify the existence of persons claimed on the lists.

We would expect a massive proliferation of new interest groups, some legitimate, but many of them simply cloned from existing organizations and consisting of almost the identical members.

Thus the $1 member campaign finance reform effort would, in all probability, not significantly reduce the role of money in American politics.

---

1. *Is it more democratic for larger groups to spend more money, or does that unfairly punish small groups?*
2. *Why do so few Americans become active in interest groups?*

■ THE ROLE OF INTEREST GROUPS

DID YOU KNOW?

That the first labor organization in the United States was created by shoemakers' and coopers' guilds in Boston, Mass., in 1648?

Contrary to the expectations of most political analysts, Congress passed a massive tax reform bill in 1986, an election year. Like other tax bills which have gone before, this piece of legislation was a major source of concern for interest groups representing many sectors of American life. Lobbyists and staff members for interest groups spent long hours waiting outside the committee rooms for a chance to talk to the legislators as they left the meetings. Among the groups that were vitally interested in the legislation were bankers, stock-brokers, oil and timber interests, professionals, farmers, real estate investors, and state and local government officials.

By early summer, it was clear that the bill would emerge from committee with strong bipartisan support. There had been few opportunities for interest groups to influence committee decisions. The groups would have to decide a strategy for lobbying on the floor of Congress. Observers who watch such activities said that the size and complexity of the proposed reforms made the usual coalitions among interest groups hard to form. Some groups, such as the American Bankers Association, decided to support the Senate bill unchanged.

About 150 other groups formed an alliance, calling its organization the 15/27/33 Coalition. This label stood for the proposed new income-tax rate structure. This huge alliance included such diverse groups as Aetna Life Insurance, small businesses, and numerous women's groups. All agreed that the proposed measure was a "fair" bill and that the balance of tax rates should not be altered.

Among the groups that lobbied intensively for changes in the bill were representatives of the securities industry, the real estate industry, and elected officials of states and cities. The most successful lobbying group during the summer of 1986 had to be the state and local government officials. The original bill proposed that the deduction of state and local property and sales taxes be abolished. State officials protested strongly that this would be an unfair burden on taxpayers whose states had high property or sales taxes. The final bill kept the deduction for property taxes but eliminated it for sales taxes.

Although the tax reform bill escaped without major changes to benefit special interests, many industries or corporations were aided by the "transition" rules. These 682 rules, which were written into the law to ease the transition from the old law to the new, were buried in the bill. Among the forty-seven corporations which received rules with a net value of $20 million or more were United Telecom of Kansas City ($234 million savings in taxes), John Deere ($212 million), and Chrysler Corporation ($78 million). These rules, however, provided one-time benefits for specific corporations, not permanent loopholes for entire groups.[1]

What Is an Interest Group?

We have already used the term **interest group,** also called pressure group and sometimes lobby, but have not yet explicitly defined it. We may define this kind of group as follows:

> An interest group is any organized group whose members share common objectives. An interest group actively attempts to influence government policy makers through direct and indirect methods, including the marshalling of public opinion, lobbying

INTEREST GROUP
An organized group of individuals sharing common objectives who actively attempt to influence government policy makers through direct and indirect methods, including the marshalling of public opinion, lobbying, and electioneering.

[1]*Congressional Quarterly Weekly Report,* September 27, 1986, p. 2256.

Alexis de Tocqueville (1805–1859), the French social historian and traveler who first commented on Americans' predilection for group action.

members of Congress, and electioneering. Interest groups work to persuade decision makers in all three branches of government and at all levels of government.

How Widespread Are Interest Groups?

Alexis de Tocqueville observed in 1834 that "in no country of the world has the principle of association been more successfully used or applied to a greater multitude of objectives than in America."[2] But de Tocqueville probably could not have conceived of the more than 100,000 associations existing in the United States in the 1990s. It is estimated that about two-thirds of the U.S. population is formally associated with some type of group. Of course, the majority of these 100,000 groups do not strictly fit our definition of an interest group because they are not actively seeking to change or influence government policy. But we can be sure that the purpose of the roughly 1,200 organizations whose names begin with the word *National* listed in the Washington, D.C., telephone directory is to do just this. To this list, we can add many of the 600 organizations listed in the D.C. telephone directory whose first word is *American* or *Americans*. According to Norman J. Ornstein and Shirley Elder,[3] well over 10,000 separate groups exist for the purpose of influencing government policies. (Interest groups and lobbying are also international phenomena; see Highlight.)

■ MAJOR INTEREST GROUPS

Three of the most influential types of interest groups in the United States are business, agriculture, and labor. In terms of the amount of campaign funds provided by interest groups, we must add another category—the professional group, particularly the American Medical Association. Also to this list we must add public interest groups and public employee groups. There are also ethnic groups, conservation groups, and organizations to support almost any other cause, as Table 8-1 indicates.

Business Interest Groups

There are thousands of trade organizations, but most of them are quite ineffective in influencing legislation and administrative regulations. Three big business pressure groups are consistently effective: (1) the National Association of Manufacturers, (2) the United States Chamber of Commerce, and (3) the Business Roundtable.

The National Association of Manufacturers (NAM).   The annual budget of the NAM is more than $8 million, which it collects in dues from about 14,000 relatively large corporations. Organized in Cincinnati in 1895 as a predominantly small business association, the NAM became during the Depression of the 1930s primarily a proponent of the interests of large corporations. Of particular interest to the NAM is legislation that affects labor laws, minimum wage rates, corporate taxes, and trade regulations. The NAM's

[2]*Democracy in America*, vol. 1, ed. Phillips Bradley (New York: Alfred A. Knopf, 1980), p. 191.
[3]*Interest Groups, Lobbying and Policymaking* (Washington, D.C.: Congressional Quarterly Press, 1978), p. 23.

TABLE 8-1
Selected Lobby Registrations
The following groups, corporations, and individuals were among those registering with the Office of Records and Registration of the House of Representatives during one month in 1989.

LOBBY	TYPE	INTEREST
American Jewish Congress	Interest Group	Civil rights Pro-Israel
Anheuser-Busch Co., Inc.	U.S. corporation	Agriculture
B & E Tool Manufacturing	U.S. corporation	Tools
Center for Auto Safety	Nader public interest group	Auto safety
Chief Auto Parts	U.S. corporation	Auto parts
Colebrand, Ltd.	Foreign corporation	Engineering equipment
CSX Corporation	U.S. corporation	Railroads
Geo-Centers, Inc.	U.S. corporation	Defense industry
Industrias Trele	Foreign corporation	Unknown
LTV Corporation	U.S. corporation	Pensions
Mobil Oil Corporation	U.S. corporation	Oil spills
National Wildlife Federation	Interest group	Conservation
Nissan R & D	Subsidiary foreign corporation	Auto emissions
Organic Food Alliance	Interest group	Organic food
Public Broadcasting Corporation	Independent government corporation	Public TV
Villa Banfi	U.S. corporation	Wine

Washington national headquarters staff numbers about one hundred, of whom a dozen are full-time lobbyists.

The U.S. Chamber of Commerce. Sometimes called the National Chamber, this special interest organization represents more than 100,000 businesses. Dues from its members, which include upward of 3,500 local chambers of commerce, approach $30 million a year. In 1977, the National Chamber started the National Chamber Litigation Center—a public interest law firm, having the express purpose of countering what it regarded as antibusiness public interest law firms, one of which was started by Ralph Nader, champion of consumer interests. The National Chamber also organized Citizens' Choice in 1976. The latter is an interest group specifically designed to influence public opinion against high taxes and "increasing government interference" with individual lives. Citizens' Choice also lobbies in the halls of Congress.

Business Roundtable. Two hundred of the largest corporations in the United States send their chief executive officers to the Business Roundtable. This organization is based in New York, but it does its lobbying in Washington,

---

HIGHLIGHT

Lobbying—An International Phenomenon

The United States is not the only country in which special interests try to influence government to their advantage. In Japan, the farmers lobby the government through a powerful organization called the Central Union of Agricultural Cooperatives. The union, which favors tough restrictions on imported food and high prices for Japanese agricultural products, has threatened to unseat legislators if they allow the importing of foreign rice. The union is opposed by a consumer group that is attempting to lift the ban and thus lower prices for consumers.

In Great Britain, professional workers have long been organized into powerful associations. The British Medical Association has been waging a battle against the government to improve their salaries and working conditions in the government-run health-care system. Some of the association's methods are ingenious: Instead of general interest magazines in the doctors' waiting rooms, patients are likely to find political pamphlets from the association. Recently, a government minister had to undergo a twenty-minute lecture from his own doctor before treatment began.

Interest groups have even sprung up in the Soviet Union. Currently, there are few politically active business or agricultural groups. But ecologically oriented groups, which demonstrate in favor of stricter pollution controls, have organized at the grass-roots level. The largest of these is the Social-Ecological Union, with two hundred branches, mostly in European Russia. These Soviet interest groups agitate for democratic rights at the same time as they promote ecological politics: To secure their special interest, they must also struggle for the general interest they share in free expression.

D.C. Established in 1972, the Roundtable was designed to promote a more aggressive view of business interests in general, cutting across specific industries. Dues paid by the member corporations are determined by the companies' wealth. Roundtable members include American Telephone and Telegraph, General Motors, USX Corporation, and International Business Machines. The Roundtable opposed common-site picketing legislation, the proposed Consumer Protection Agency, automobile emissions standards, and industrial pollution control.

The Rainbow Warrior, flagship of the Greenpeace organization, represents this action-oriented interest group. Are the actions of Greenpeace against whaling ships justified by their cause?

Other Business-Oriented Interest Groups. The National Federation of Independent Business represents close to three-quarters of a million small business owners. By taking regular polls of its members, it is able to report their opinion to members of Congress. Also active in lobbying for policy changes that will benefit small business is the National Small Business Association, representing about 45,000 members.

Agricultural Interest Groups

American farmers and their workers represent less than 3 percent of the United States' population. In spite of this, farmers' influence on legislation beneficial to their interests has been enormous. In 1990, American farmers received more than $39 billion in direct and indirect subsidies from the federal government. Farm programs designed to keep farm incomes high involve price supports, target prices, soil conservation, and myriad other policies. Farmers have succeeded in their aims through very strong interest groups. The American Farm Bureau Federation, established in 1919, has three million members. It was instrumental in getting government guarantees of "fair" prices during the Depression in the 1930s.[4] In principle, the Federation, controlled by wealthier farmers, is no longer in favor of government price supports. These farmers, who are engaged in large-scale farming, do not need government price supports to compete effectively.

Another important agricultural special interest organization is the National Farmers' Union. The NFU was founded in 1902 and claims a membership of more than a quarter of a million today. The oldest farm lobby organization is the National Grange, founded in 1867. With a membership of more than half a million, it finds its support among New England, Middle Atlantic, and, to a lesser extent, Pacific dairy farmers. It champions basically the same causes as the National Farmers' Union, such as higher agricultural support prices.

[4]The Agricultural Adjustment Act of 1933 (declared unconstitutional) was replaced by the 1937 Agricultural Adjustment Act and later changed and amended several times.

> **DID YOU KNOW?**
>
> That the NRA (National Rifle Association) has a full-time Washington, D.C. staff of over 300 persons?

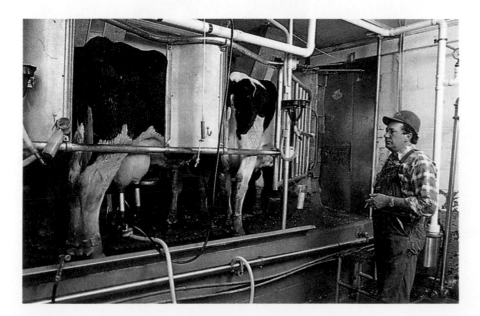

Dairy farmers are one of the best organized agricultural groups. How can such a small group wield so much political power?

Labor Interest Groups

LABOR MOVEMENT
In general, the term refers to the full range of economic and political expression of working-class interests; politically, it describes the organization of working-class interests.

POLITICAL ACTION COMMITTEES (PACs)
Committees set up by and representing corporations, labor unions, or special interest groups; PACs raise and give campaign donations on behalf of the organizations or groups they represent.

Interest groups representing the **labor movement** date back to at least 1886 with the formation of the American Federation of Labor (AFL). In 1955, the AFL joined forces with the Congress of Industrial Organizations (CIO), and today the combined AFL-CIO is an enormous union with a membership exceeding thirteen million workers. In a sense, the AFL-CIO is a union of unions. Its political arm is the Committee on Political Education (COPE), which cooperates with the CIO **Political Action Committee (PAC)** and the AFL League for Political Education. COPE's activities are funded by voluntary contributions from union members.

COPE has been active in state and national campaigns since 1956. In principle, it is used to educate workers and the general public on issues and candidates of interest to labor. Some critics of COPE allege that union members are pressured into making contributions to the organization. Other critics claim that its "education" is simply partisan political propaganda favorable to the Democratic party. The AFL-CIO through COPE has established policies on issues such as Social Security, housing, health insurance, and foreign trade.

Other unions are also active politically. One of the most widely known of these is the International Brotherhood of Teamsters, which was led by Jimmy Hoffa until his expulsion in 1967 because of alleged ties with organized crime. The Teamsters Union was established initially in 1903 and today has a membership of three million and an annual budget of $73 million.

Strikers outside the Hormel plant in Austin, Minnesota in 1989. Have unions lost some of their effectiveness?

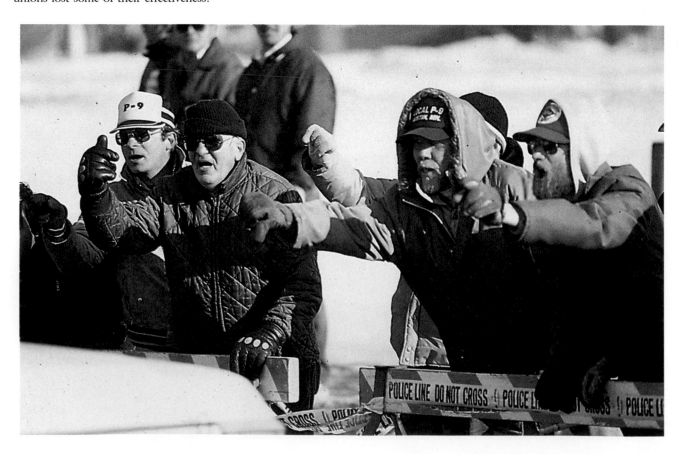

Another independent union is the United Auto Workers, founded in 1935. It now has a membership of 1.5 million with an annual budget of $230 million. Also very active in labor lobbying is the United Mine Workers (UMW) union, representing about 200,000 members.

Labor group pressure on Congress has been only partly successful. Although unions successfully allied themselves with civil rights groups in the 1960s, they lost on such issues as the Taft-Hartley Act of 1948, which put some limits on the right to strike and the right to organize workers. They were also frustrated in their efforts in 1975 and in 1977 to enact a bill designed to facilitate the picketing of construction sites.

The role of unions in American society has weakened in recent years, as is witnessed by a decline in union membership from 1945 to the present (Figure 8-1). The strength of union membership traditionally lay with blue-collar workers. But in the age of automation and with the rise of the **service sector,** blue-collar workers in basic industries (autos, steel, and the like) represent a smaller and smaller percentage of the total working population. Because of this decline in the industrial sector of the economy, national unions are looking to nontraditional areas for their membership, including migrant farm workers, service workers, and most recently public employees—such as police and fire-fighting personnel and teachers, including college professors.

SERVICE SECTOR
That sector of the economy that provides services—such as food services, insurance, and education—in contrast to that sector of the economy that produces goods.

Public Employee Interest Groups

The degree of unionization in the private sector has declined since 1965, but there has been growth in the unionization of public employees.

Membership in the three largest unions of government employees rose dramatically from 1960 to 1990. Table 8-2 shows the number of members in the three largest public employee unions, which grew more than 500 percent from 1960 to 1990.

Both the American Federation of State, County, and Municipal Employees and the American Federation of Teachers are members of the AFL-CIO's Public Employee Department. Originally, the public employee unions started

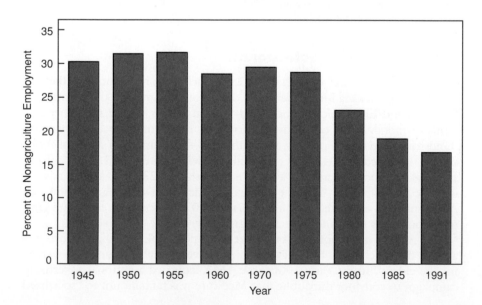

FIGURE 8-1
Decline in Union Membership as a Percentage of Nonagricultural Employment from 1945 to 1991

SOURCE: Leo Troy and Neil Sheflin, *U.S. Union Sourcebook* (West Orange, NJ: Industrial Relations Data and Information Services, 1985, and Bureau of Labor Statistics.

TABLE 8-2
The Growth in Public Employee Unionism
Should all public employee unions have the right to strike? If not, are the workers in an unfair position?

Union Name	1960	1979	1990
American Federation of State, County, and Municipal Employees	185,000	889,000	1,097,000
American Federation of Government Employees	70,000	236,000	163,000
American Federation of Teachers	56,000	423,000	484,000
Total	311,000	1,548,000	1,744,000

SOURCE: Bureau of Labor Statistics, 1990.

LATENT INTERESTS
Interests that are dormant or unexpressed. The group that holds these interests has never organized nor articulated them.

out as social and professional organizations. Over the years, they have become quite militant and are often involved in strikes. Many of these strikes are illegal because certain public employees do not have the right to strike and essentially sign a contract so stating. In August 1981, the Professional Air Traffic Controllers Organization (PATCO), in defiance of a court order, went on strike. The issues included wage levels, long hours, excess stress, insensitive Federal Aviation Administration (FAA) management, and other problems. President Reagan, convinced that public opinion was on his side, fired the strikers. Supervisors, nonstrikers, military personnel, and new trainees were rounded up to handle the jobs vacated by the terminated 16,000 air traffic controllers. On July 27, 1982, the union folded as a trustee padlocked the PATCO headquarters office. (A major irony is that PATCO was one of only a few unions to endorse Ronald Reagan's candidacy in 1980.)

Perhaps the most powerful of the interest groups lobbying on behalf of public employees is the National Education Association (NEA), a nationwide organization of about 1.8 million administrators, teachers, and others connected with education. The NEA is intensively involved in lobbying for increased public funding of education. The NEA sponsors regional and national conventions each year and has an extensive program of electronic media broadcasts, surveys, and the like.

Interest Groups of Professionals

Numerous professional organizations exist, including the American Bar Association, the Association of General Contractors of America, the Institute of Electrical and Electronic Engineers, the Screen Actors Guild, and others. In terms of money spent on lobbying, however, one professional organization stands out head and shoulders above the rest—the American Medical Association. Founded in 1947, it is now affiliated with more than 2,000 local and state medical societies and has a total membership of 237,000 and an administrative staff of 1,000. Together with the American Dental Association, the AMA spent an estimated $3.2 million in 1990 congressional campaign contributions in its efforts to influence legislation.

The AMA's most notable, but largely unsuccessful, lobbying effort was against the enactment of Medicare, which provides health insurance coverage for the elderly. In the early 1960s, the AMA launched a national advertising campaign to convince the public that Medicare was tantamount to "socialized

CRITICAL PERSPECTIVE

The Logic of Collective Action

One puzzle that has fascinated political scientists is the question of why some individuals join interest groups, whereas a great many more Americans do not. Everyone has some interest that could benefit from government action. For many groups, however, those remain unorganized, or **latent, interests.** Consider the women's movement. Until the 1960s, the interests of women in equal employment or equal educational opportunities had no representation. Even today, the membership of women's groups such as NOW or Women Employed is but a fraction of the women who share their goals.

It may be, according to the theory of Mancur Olson, that it simply is not rational for individuals to join most groups. His theory of collective action, first published in 1965, is controversial, but it offers an intriguing explanation for interest group membership and strength.

Olson introduces the idea of the "collective good." This concept refers to any public benefit that, if available to any member of the community, cannot be denied to any other member, whether or not he or she participated in the effort to gain the good. For example, women who regard themselves an antifeminists, or at least who would never join such an organization as NOW, still may avail themselves of equal employment opportunities although they never participated in the effort to change the laws. So equal employment is seen as a collective good.

Although collective benefits are usually thought of as coming from such public goods as clean air or the national defense, benefits are also bestowed by the government on subsets of the public. The price subsidies to dairy farmers or loans to college students are examples. Olson uses economic theory to propose that it is not rational for interested individuals to join groups that work for group benefits. In fact, it is often more rational for the individual to wait for others to procure the benefits and then share them.

Using agriculture as an example, Olson suggests that the solution to overproduction is for all farmers to cut production. The rational farmer, however, seeing that his small cutback will not really change the overall output, would be smarter to grow as much as possible so that if others cut production, prices would rise and he would profit from their actions. In the same fashion, individuals who would like government benefits will probably find it more rational to let others invest in the political effort from which they similarly will profit.

If so little incentive exists for individuals to join together, why are there thousands of interest groups lobbying in Washington? Olson's theory holds that if the contribution of an individual *will* make a difference to the effort, then it is worth it to join. Thus smaller groups, which seek benefits only for a small proportion of the population, are more likely to enroll members who will give time and money to the cause. Larger groups, which represent general public interests, like the women's movement or Common Cause, will have a difficult time getting individuals to join.

Olson's theory seems to have considerable validity. Certainly, the smaller, more cohesive groups have a larger presence in Washington than their size would warrant. Furthermore, these groups seem to have highly motivated members who will pressure their representatives to achieve their goals. If this aspect of Olson's theory is true, then smaller interests will always be overrepresented compared with the public interest.

Some larger interest groups, however, such as the National Education Association or the AFL-CIO, are also successful. Olson says that groups can increase their members by offering incentives to them. The NEA, for example, provides information, publications, insurance plans, and educational assistance to teachers. Furthermore, many organizations offer such benefits as free travel services (AAA), free admissions (to zoos, by the Audubon Society), or conventions (the American Legion). It is also true that if the cost of membership is low and the group provides other benefits, such as social opportunities, individuals may join, regardless of rational calculations. For the poorer members of the community, however, any cost of group membership is probably too high. Thus groups tend to be middle- and upper-class organizations.

Olson's theory presents complications for a democratic society. If groups that are smallest are likely to be most cohesive and determined to get benefits, the public interest may be injured. Similarly, if individuals who need the most assistance from the government—the least advantaged—are least likely to organize, policies that extend benefits to them are less likely to be promoted. For further reading on this complex and interesting theory, see Mancur Olson, *The Logic of Collective Action* (Cambridge, Mass.: Harvard University Press, 1965).

Exercise in Critical Thinking

1. What benefits have you gained from groups that you have joined?
2. Why have farmers remained such a potent political group?

medicine" and that private plans would offer better protection. This indirect lobbying, combined with direct pressure on members of Congress, delayed passage of the legislation until 1965 and ensured that the bill's language would protect and enhance doctors' incomes. More recently, the AMA has lobbied against present fees for services and stringent medical cost containment.

Public Interest Groups

PUBLIC INTEREST
The best interests of the collective, overall community; the national good, rather than the narrow interests of a self-serving group.

Public interest is a difficult term to define because, as we noted earlier, there are many publics in our nation of more than 250 million. It is nearly impossible for one particular public policy to benefit everybody, which makes it practically impossible to define the public interest. Nonetheless, over the past few decades, a variety of law and lobbying organizations have been formed "in the public interest." The most well known and perhaps the most effective are those public interest groups organized under the leadership of consumer activist Ralph Nader.

The story of Ralph Nader's rise to the top began in the mid-1960s after the publication of his book *Unsafe at Any Speed,* a lambasting critique of General Motors' purported attempt to keep from the public detrimental information about GM's rear-engine Corvair. Partly as a result of Nader's book, Congress began to consider testimony in favor of an automobile safety bill. GM made a clumsy attempt to discredit Nader's background. Nader sued, the media exploited the story, and, when GM settled out of court for several hundred thousand dollars, Nader became the recognized champion of consumer interests. Since then, Nader has turned over much of his income to the various public interest groups he has formed or sponsored. In all, there are more than fifteen national "Naderite" organizations promoting consumer interests.

Partly in response to the Nader organizations, numerous conservative public interest law firms have sprung up that are often pitted against the consumer groups in court. Some of these are the Mountain States Legal Defense Foundation, the Pacific Legal Foundation, the National Right-to-Work Legal Defense Foundation, the Washington Legal Foundation, and the Mid-Atlantic Legal Foundation.

One of the largest public interest pressure groups is Common Cause, founded in 1968, whose goal is to reorder national priorities toward "the public" and to make governmental institutions more responsive to the needs of the public. Anyone willing to pay dues of $15 a year can become a member. Members are polled regularly to obtain information about local and national issues requiring reassessment. Some of the activities of Common Cause have been (1) helping to assure passage of the Twenty-sixth Amendment (giving eighteen-year-olds the right to vote), (2) achieving greater voter registration in all states, (3) supporting the complete withdrawal of all U.S. forces from South Vietnam in the 1970s, and (4) promoting legislation that would limit campaign spending.

Other public interest pressure groups are active on a wide range of issues. The goal of the League of Women Voters, founded in 1920, is to educate the public on political matters; although generally nonpartisan, it has lobbied for the Equal Rights Amendment and for government reform. The Consumer Federation of America is an alliance of about two hundred local and national

Ralph Nader.

organizations interested in consumer protection. The American Civil Liberties Union dates back to World War I when, under a different name, it defended draft resisters. It generally enters into legal disputes related to Bill of Rights issues.

Single-Interest Groups

In recent years, a number of interest groups have formed that are focused on one issue. Environmental groups such as the Sierra Club and Friends of the Earth are especially active today. (See Profile on David Brower.) The abortion debate has created various antiabortion groups such as Right To Life and prochoice groups such as the National Abortion Rights Action League. Narrowly focused groups such as these may be able to call more attention to their respective causes because they have simple and straightforward goals and because their members tend to care intensely about the issue. Thus they can easily motivate their members to contact legislators or to organize demonstrations in support of their policy goals.

Foreign Governments

Home-grown interests are not the only players in the game. Washington, D.C., is also the center for lobbying by foreign governments as well as private foreign interests. Large research and lobbying staffs are maintained by governments of the largest U.S. trading partners, such as Japan, Korea, the Philippines, and the European Community (EC) countries. Even smaller nations such as those in the Caribbean engage lobbyists when vital legislation affecting their trade interests is considered. Frequently, these foreign interests hire ex-representatives or ex-senators to promote their positions on Capitol Hill.

Lobbyists wait outside a committee room to talk to congresspersons about the details of a bill. Should all such contacts be recorded and regulated?

■ INTEREST GROUP STRATEGIES

Interest groups employ a wide range of techniques and strategies to promote their policy goals. Although a few groups are successful at persuading the Congress and the president to endorse their programs completely, many are able to prevent legislation injurious to their members from being considered or to weaken such legislation. The key to success for interest groups is the ability to have access to government officials. To achieve this, interest groups and their representatives try to cultivate long-term relationships with legislators and government officials. The best of such relationships are based on mutual respect and cooperation. The interest group provides the official with excellent sources of information and assistance, and the official in turn gives the group opportunities to express its views.

The techniques used by interest groups may be divided into those that are direct and indirect. **Direct techniques** include all those ways in which the interest group and its lobbyists approach the officials personally to press their case. **Indirect techniques,** on the other hand, include strategies that use the general public or individuals to influence the government for the interest group.

DIRECT TECHNIQUES
Interest group activities that involve interaction with government officials to further the group's goals.

INDIRECT TECHNIQUES
Strategies employed by interest groups that use a third party, the general public, or other individuals to influence government officials.

PROFILE

David Brower

"The Earth's present brief tenants are indeed the last who will have the opportunity to know wildness as we have known it, unless we pass it on."

Called by some the number one conservationist in the United States, David Brower, 78 years old, has had a love affair with the wilderness since his childhood. Raised in Berkeley, California, the young Brower became a hiker and climber in the mountains of Yosemite. Whether he was frequently daydreaming about the wilderness or simply bored, Brower dropped out of college in his sophomore year and went to work in a factory on the assembly line. With his extensive experience in high mountain skiing and climbing, it is no surprise that he was recruited into the mountain troops in World War II, and spent much of his war service fighting in the Italian Alps.

At the end of the war, Brower came home to work as an editor at the University of California Press and to volunteer for the Sierra Club. He became the editor of the Sierra Club *Bulletin* and wrote *A Member's Handbook*. In 1952, Brower was named the first executive director of the Sierra Club as the organization moved into serious lobbying for protection of the wilderness. Brower took the lead in opposing the building of a series of dams on the Colorado River, which flows through the Grand Canyon, whose purpose was to provide enough water to satisfy the

needs of the Western states and provide water to Mexico as required by treaty. The Sierra Club fought the proposal but, at the last moment, agreed to drop its opposition to the Glen Canyon Dam if that were the only one built. As Brower puts it, "I saved Dinosaur [Canyon] but I killed Glen Canyon."

Under Brower's leadership, the Sierra Club grew in members and in political clout. It worked for the passage of the Wilderness Act in 1964 and against the building of the Alaska pipeline. Hundreds of thousands of acres of land were protected for the use of the public during the period of Brower's directorship. Brower broke with the Sierra Club over its support for building the Diablo Canyon nuclear plant in California, and was forced out of the club.

From running a club specializing in outdoor experiences and nature pub-

lishing, Brower turned to straight-out politics. Brower founded the Friends of the Earth to continue the nonprofit side of the work to save wilderness and the League of Conservation Voters as a lobbying organization to work the halls of Congress. Following the example of other well-known lobbies, the league quickly established a rating system which embarrassed the twelve legislators with the worst environmental records by naming them "The Dirty Dozen." The success of this tactic encouraged the league to expand its ratings to include each representative and send the ratings to his or her constituents.

David Brower has been fortunate enough to experience directly much of American wilderness—floating down the wild rivers, exploring the Arctic Wildlife Refuge, and climbing the highest peaks. Knowing that very few Americans could have those experiences, Brower has tried to educate Americans about the importance of the wilderness in sustaining life on earth through the Sierra Club books and calendars that have brought national parks and wilderness areas close to millions, through supporting research and educational efforts, and by hard lobbying against government agencies and corporations that oppose setting aside further lands for preservation. If Americans are more aware of their environment, more concerned about saving species and unique ecosystems, it is to the credit of David Brower and others like him who play hardball politics for what they see as the public interest.

Direct Techniques

Lobbying, publicizing ratings of legislative behavior, and providing campaign assistance, especially through political action committees, are the three main direct techniques used by interest groups.

Lobbying Techniques.   As might be guessed, the term **lobbying** comes from the original habit of private citizens regularly congregating in the lobbies of legislative chambers before a session. In the latter part of the nineteenth century, railroad and industrial interests openly bribed state legislators to pass legislation beneficial to their interests, giving lobbying a well-deserved bad name. Today, standard lobbying techniques still involve buttonholing senators and representatives in state capitols and in Washington, D.C., while they are moving from their offices to the voting chambers. Lobbyists, however, do more than that.

Lobbyists engage in an array of activities to influence legislation. These are, at a minimum, the following:

1. Engaging in private meetings with public officials to make known the lobbyist's clients' interests. Although acting on behalf of a client, often lobbyists provide needed information to senators and representatives (and government agency appointees) that they could not hope to obtain on their own. It is to the lobbyist's advantage to provide accurate information so that the policy maker will rely on this source in the future.
2. Testifying before congressional committees for or against proposed legislation.
3. Testifying before executive rule-making agencies, such as the Federal Trade Commission or the Consumer Product Safety Commission, for or against proposed rules.
4. Assisting the legislators or bureaucrats in drafting legislation or prospective regulations. Often, lobbyists can furnish legal advice on the specific details of legislation.
5. Inviting legislators to social occasions such as cocktail parties, boating expeditions, and other events. Most lobbyists feel that contacting legislators in a more relaxed social setting is effective. The extent to which legislators feel obligated to lobbyists for entertaining them is hard to gauge.
6. Providing political information to legislators and other government officials. Often the lobbyists will have better information than the party leadership about how other legislators are going to vote. In this case, the political information they furnish may be a key to legislative success.

The Ratings Game.   Many interest groups attempt to influence the overall behavior of legislators through their rating systems. Each year, the interest group selects those votes on legislation that it feels are most important to the organization's goals. Legislators are given a score based on the percentage of times that he or she voted with the interest group. The usual scheme ranges from 0 to 100 percent. If a legislator has a score of, for example, 90 percent on the Americans for Democratic Action rating, it means that she supported their positions to a high degree (Table 8-3). Such a high ADA score is usually interpreted as very liberal. The groups that use rating systems range from the Americans for Constitutional Action (considered to be conservative) to the League of Conservation Voters (environmental). One group identifies the

LOBBYING
The attempt by organizations or by individuals to influence the passage, defeat, or contents of legislation and of the administrative decisions of government. The derivation of the term may be traced back over a century ago to the habit of certain private citizens who regularly congregated in the lobby outside the legislative chambers before a session to petition legislators.

TABLE 8-3
ADA Ratings for 1989
The scores indicate the percentage of times the senator voted with the position taken by Americans for Democratic Action (ADA) in 1989.

Senator	Highest Rating
Leahy, D., Vt.	100%
Simon, D., Il.	100
Adams, D., Wash.	95
Harkins, D., Id.	95
Kerry, D., Mass.	95
Kohl, D., Wis.	95
Wirth, D., Col.	95
Biden, D., Del.	90
Bumper, D., Ark.	90
Mikulski, D., Md.	90

Senator	Lowest Rating
Burns, R., Mont.	0%
Cochran, R., Miss.	0
Gramm, R., Tex.	0
McCain, R., Ariz.	0
McClure, R., Id.	0
Murkowski, R., Alas.	0
Nickles, R., Ok.	0
Roth, R., Del.	0
Symms, R., Id.	0
Wallop, R., Wyo.	0

SOURCE: *Congressional Quarterly Weekly Report,* March 3, 1990, p. 705.

HIGHLIGHT

Delivering the Checks for the Letter Carriers

Although he may not be required to hand deliver the contributions from the National Association of Letter Carriers to the campaigns of their favorite senators and representatives, George B. Gould does keep in personal contact with all of the recipients of PAC money from the association. As the chief lobbyist for the Letter Carriers, Gould sits on the committee that decides which candidates receive PAC contributions and then meets with those individuals at receptions, dinners, and balls. It is not unusual for him to attend eight social events in one evening. His record is eighteen in one night.

Gould is considered a very prominent player in the PAC game because he represents one of the top ten PACs

in contributions to congressional candidates. In the 1987–88 election cycle, the Letter Carriers PAC gave $768,820 to 259 House and Senate candidates. Sixty-two of those candidates received at least $5,000 contributions each. Like most PACs, the Letter Carriers tend to give most to incumbents. As one lobbyist put it, "We know them, we've watched them, we've listened to them. It's so much easier to give to someone there."

With a huge campaign war chest, the Letter Carriers receive many requests for contributions. The association decides which candidates to support on the basis of the person's support of legislation important to the association, such as federal health and retirement

benefits. Candidates who receive support from the PAC are aware not only of the contribution but also of the fact that the association has close to 350,000 members, a sizable number of constituents.

Where does the Letter Carriers PAC get its funds? With its enormous roster of current and retired dues-paying members across the country, it raises money through voluntary contributions. Each year, about 46,000 members contribute. In Gould's view, this is simply a way for ordinary individuals to have an impact on the political process. As he notes, "It's more democratic to get it from PACs like ours, where the average donation is $26, then from $1,000 donors."

twelve legislators having what they see as the worst records on environmental issues and advertises that list as the "Dirty Dozen" (see Profile).[5] Needless to say, a senator or representative does not want to earn membership on this list.

Campaign Assistance.   Interest groups have additional strategies to use in their attempts to influence government policies. Groups recognize that the greatest concern of legislators is to be reelected, so they focus on their campaign needs. Associations with large memberships, such as labor unions or the National Education Association, are able to provide "manpower" for political campaigns, including precinct workers to get out the vote, volunteers to put up posters and pass out literature, and people to staff telephone banks for campaign headquarters.

In many states, where membership in certain interest groups is large, candidates vie for the group's endorsement in the campaign. Gaining that endorsement may be automatic or it may require that the candidate participate in a debate or interview with the interest group. Endorsements are important because the group usually publicizes its choices in its membership publication and because the candidate can use the endorsement in his or her campaign literature. Traditionally, labor unions such as the AFL-CIO and the UAW have endorsed Democratic party candidates. However, Republican candidates often try to persuade union locals to, at the minimum, refrain from any endorsement. Making no endorsement can then be perceived as disapproval of the Democratic party candidate.

[5]Bill Keller, "The Trail of the Dirty Dozen," *Congressional Quarterly Weekly Report,* March 21, 1981, p. 510.

PACs and Political Campaigns. Within the last ten years, the most important form of campaign help from interest groups has become the political contribution from a group's political action committee. The 1974 Federal Election Campaign Act and its 1976 amendments allow corporations, labor unions, and special interest groups to set up PACs to raise money for candidates (see Highlight on the National Association of Letter Carriers). For a PAC to be legitimate, the money must be raised from at least fifty volunteer donors and must be given to at least five candidates in the federal election. PACs can contribute up to $5,000 to each candidate in each election. Each corporation or each union is limited to one PAC. As you might imagine, corporate PACs obtain funds from executives in their firms and unions obtain PAC funds from their members.

The number of PACs has grown astronomically, as has the amount they spend on elections. There were about 600 political action committees in 1976; by 1991, there were more than 3,700. Corporate PACs are increasing at a rate greater than other varieties. The total amount of spending by PACs grew from $19 million in 1973 to $350 million in 1987–88. Of all of the campaign money spent by congressional candidates in 1984, about 41 percent came from PACs.[6] (Table 8-4 lists the PACs that spent the most in congressional races in 1980–1988.)

[6]Federal Election Commission Press Release, May 19, 1985, "PACs Support of Incumbents Increases in 1984 Elections," Washington, D.C.

DID YOU KNOW?

That in the 1988 congressional elections, political action committees gave almost $120 million to House and Senate races, over 80 percent of it to incumbents?

TABLE 8-4
Top PACs' Spending in Congressional Races, 1980–1988

Direct contributions to candidates.

Political Action Committee	1980	1984	1988
1. Realtors Political Action Committee (National Association of Realtors)	$1,536,573	$2,429,552	$3,040,969
2. American Medical Association Political Action Committee	1,348,985	1,839,464	2,316,496
3. BUILD-PAC (National Association of Home Builders)	379,391	1,625,539	1,448,560
4. National Education Association Political Action Committee	283,585	1,574,003	2,104,689
5. UAW V-CAP (United Auto Workers Volunteer Community Action Program)	1,422,731	1,405,107	1,953,099
6. Seafarers Political Activity Donation (Seafarers International Union)	685,248	1,322,410	n.a.
7. Machinists Non-Partisan Political League (International Association of Machinists and Aerospace Workers)	847,708	1,306,497	1,490,780
8. Active Ballot Club (United Food and Commercial Workers International Union)	569,775	1,271,974	1,152,110
9. Committee on Letter Carriers Political Education (National Association of Letter Carriers)	44,715	1,234,603	1,737,982
10. National Association of Retired Federal Employees Political Action Committee	8,200	1,099,243	1,979,850
11. Committee for Thorough Agricultural Political Education of Associated Milk Producers, Inc.	738,289	1,087,658	n.a.
12. Automobile and Truck Dealers Election Action Committee (National Automobile Dealers Association)	1,035,276	1,057,165	1,158,700
13. Public Employees Organized to Promote Legislative Equality (American Federation of State, County, and Municipal Employees)	338,035	905,806	1,663,386
14. National Association of Life Underwriters Political Action Committee	652,112	900,200	n.a.
15. BANKPAC (American Bankers Association)	592,960	882,850	1,151,050

NOTE: The data are based on a two-year election cycle and only include direct contributions to candidates for the House and Senate.
SOURCE: *Congressional Quarterly Weekly Report*, June 8, 1987, p. 1117, and various issues.

DID YOU KNOW?

That the leading Senate recipient of political action committee (PAC) money in the 1983–88 period (earning him the title of biggest "PAC-MAN") was Lloyd Bentsen, Democrat of Texas and the 1988 vice presidential candidate, who got over $2.6 million?

FIGURE 8-2
PAC Contributions to Congressional Candidates, 1972–1988

SOURCE: *Congressional Quarterly Weekly Report*, March 22, 1986, p. 657, *Federal Election Commission Report*, 1987, 1989.

Interest groups funnel PAC money to candidates whom they think can do the most good for them. Frequently, they make the maximum contribution of $5,000 per election to candidates who face little or no opposition. The summary of PAC contributions given in Figure 8-2 shows that the great bulk of campaign contributions goes to incumbent candidates rather than to challengers. Corporations are particularly likely to give money to Democrats in Congress as well as to Republicans, because many Democratic incumbents chair important committees or subcommittees. In the Senate, the Republicans held committee chairs from 1980 until 1986, so they reaped corresponding benefits in PAC money. Why, might you ask, would business leaders give to Democrats who may be more liberal than themselves? Interest groups see PAC contributions as a way to ensure access to powerful legislators, even if they may disagree with them some of the time. PAC contributions are, in a way, an investment in a relationship.

The campaign finance regulations clearly limit the amount that a PAC can give to any one candidate, but there is no limit on the amount that a PAC can spend on an independent campaign, either on behalf of a candidate or party or in opposition to one. One of the most prominent PACs in the United States is the National Conversative Political Action Committee, or NCPAC. This interest group espouses a conservative philosophy, opposing abortion, supporting prayer in school, and supporting a strong defense. In recent elections, NCPAC has targeted specific senators and representatives for defeat, spending large sums of money against them in primary and general elections. In general, NCPAC has not been successful in these efforts since 1980.

Indirect Techniques

By working through third parties, either constituents, the general public, or other groups, interest groups can try to influence government policy. Indirect

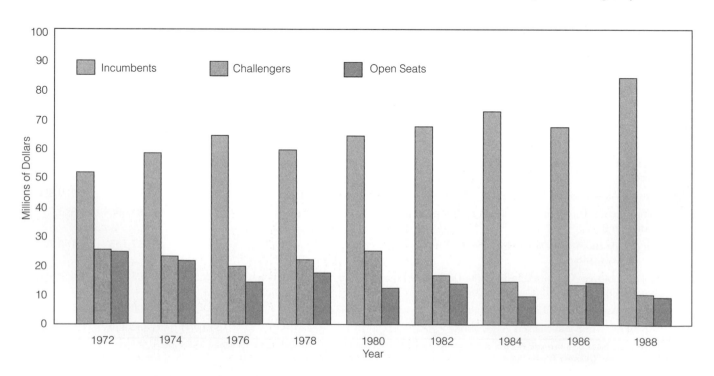

techniques mask the interest group's own activities and make the effort appear to be spontaneous. Furthermore, legislators and government officials are often more impressed by contacts from constituents than from the interest group's lobbyist.

Generating Public Pressure.   In some instances, interest groups try to produce a "groundswell" of public pressure to influence the government. Such efforts may include advertisements in national magazines and newspapers, mass mailings, television publicity, and demonstrations. Computers and satellite links make communication efforts even more effective. (See Highlight on High-Tech Lobbying.) Interest groups may commission polls to find out what the public sentiments are and then publicize the results. The intent of this activity is to convince policy makers that pubic opinion overwhelmingly supports the group's position.

Some corporations and interest groups also engage in a practice that might be called **climate control.** This strategy calls for public relations efforts, often not directly related to a specific political issue or legislation, aimed at improving the public image of the industry or group. Contributions by corporations and groups in support of public television programs, sponsorship of such events as Hands Across America, and commercials extolling the virtues of corporate research are examples of climate control. By building a reservoir of favorable public opinion, groups believe it less likely that their legislative goals will be met with opposition by the public.

CLIMATE CONTROL
Techniques to create favorable public opinion toward an interest group, industry, or corporation.

ACT UP, a group dedicated to increasing AIDS research, protests in Albany, New York. Why do groups stage such protests and seek to be arrested?

HIGHLIGHT

High-Tech Lobbying

Interest group activity has exploded in recent years. One particularly important aspect of lobbying in this new era is the use of modern technology to enhance the role of pressure groups. Such use is particularly striking in the case of the New Right groups on the conservative side of the political spectrum.

Lobbying organizations have for many years employed "grass-roots" tactics for influencing the outcomes of government decisions. These tactics have included soliciting citizens to send letters to members of Congress, mobilizing protest movements, and endorsing or attacking candidates during election campaigns. What is new, exciting, and potentially crucial in the struggle over who will have access to the levers of power in government is the availability of computer-based technology and expanded telecommunications facilities for communicating more effectively and more quickly to targeted segments of the population. Elected representatives may in fact not know which interest group was involved in the "write-your-congressperson" campaign and may even be unaware that any group was behind sophisticated letter-writing efforts in which every letter reads slightly differently and at least appears to have come from a different person with an equally intense interest in the issue at hand. Groups also generate massive telephone call-in efforts with instructions to each other to indicate a slightly different aspect of an issue that most concerns them. The goal of such campaigns, made possible by computer-controlled mass mailings to targeted citizens, is to produce at least the appearance that the interest group has a massive, unified, intense, and growing block of supporters.

The use of direct-mail methods to solicit small monetary contributions is among the most important reasons for the growth of conservative pressure groups in recent years. This has not only produced a considerable amount of money with which to finance conservative PACs, but also has produced very large lists of contributors and activists for future mobilization and has allowed the New Right to bombard average Americans with their views. These lists are readily tapped by the organizers of right-wing groups to generate pressure on Washington officials or on state and local political leaders. The critical thing to understand about the mailing lists, which are maintained by Richard Viguerie in Falls Church, Virginia, is that they allow the pressure groups to bypass the traditional media sources for communicating their views to the general public. As a consequence, individuals who are not in the network of these special interest groups may be caught unaware by major efforts by such groups to push for their views on major issues such as abortion, defense spending, or equal rights.

Not only computers but also advanced television technology has allowed New Right pressure groups to increase their role in American politics. The Rev. Jerry Falwell, leader of the Moral Majority, uses more than six hundred television and radio stations to carry his political messages during his weekly broadcasts of the "Old Time Gospel Hour." Other members of the "electronic church," such as Pat Robertson, have entered directly into electoral politics. Robertson was a candidate for the Republican nomination for president in 1988. Fundamentalist electronic ministers also rely on the use of direct-mail techniques. Such efforts resulted, for example, in a million letters and postcards sent to President Reagan supporting a constitutional amendment to allow prayer in public schools.

Business pressure groups have adopted the tactics that have been so successful for the New Right. Apart from the more traditional efforts of soliciting letters, telegrams, and phone calls to elected officials, the Chamber of Commerce has the computer capabilities to send targeted "action calls" in the form of bulletins distributed within particular congressional districts. The chamber has a major high-technology communications system available to send its interpretations of pending legislation and other matters to members; a monthly magazine (*Nation's Business*) with a circulation of 1.25 million; a weekly newsletter, *Washington Report,* sent to nearly a million members and friends of the chamber; a weekly televised syndicated program, "It's Your Business," carried on more than one hundred stations; a radio show, "What's the Issue?" discussing major national topics on more than four hundred stations; and Biznet, a highly ambitious closed-circuit tax-exempt television network, which in theory would allow the chamber to mobilize its members and supporters in only a matter of hours. Satellite television transmission by the U.S. Chamber of Commerce and computer real-time access are also planned. Future developments in high-tech lobbying will be limited only by the speed with which new technological innovations can be put in place.

Using Constituents as Lobbyists. One of the most effective interest group activities is the use of constituents to lobby for the group's goals. In the "shotgun" approach, the interest group tries to mobilize large numbers of constituents to write or phone their legislators or the president. Often, the group provides postcards or form letters for constituents to fill out and mail. These efforts are only effective on Capitol Hill when there is an extraordinary number of responses, since legislators know that the voters did not initiate the communication on their own.

A more influential variation of this technique uses only important constituents. Known as the "rifle" technique, or the "Utah plant manager's theory," the interest group contacts an influential constituent, for example, the manager of a local plant in Utah, to contact the senator from Utah.[7] Because the constituent is seen as responsible for many jobs or other resources, the legislator is more likely to listen carefully to his or her concerns about legislation than to a paid lobbyist.

Building Alliances. Another indirect technique used by interest groups is to join with other groups concerned about the same legislation in an alliance. Often, these groups will set up a paper organization with an innocuous name, such as the Coalition for American Rivers, to represent their joint concerns. In this case, the sponsoring groups, which included railroads, environmentalists, and others, who opposed the construction of the Alton Lock and Dam, contributed money to the "front" alliance, loaned lobbyists to it in Illinois, and paid the rent for its office.[8] The advantages of an alliance are that it looks as if larger public interests are at stake and it hides the specific interests of the individual groups involved. It is also an efficient device for keeping like-minded groups from duplicating one another's lobbying efforts.

■ REGULATING LOBBYISTS

In principle, lobbyists are regulated. In 1946, Congress made its first attempt to control lobbyists and lobbying activities through Title III of the Legislative Reorganization Act of 1946, otherwise known as the Federal Regulation of Lobbying Act. The act actually provided for publicity more than for regulation and neglected to specify which agency would enforce its provisions. Its specific provisions are as follows:

1. Any person or organization that receives money to be used principally to influence legislation before Congress must register.
2. Any individual lobbyist or a representative of a group who is registering must, under oath, give his or her name, address, place of employment, salary, amount and purpose of expenses, and duration of employment.
3. Every registered lobbyist must give quarterly reports on his or her activities; these reports are published in the *Congressional Record*.
4. Anyone failing to satisfy the specific provisions of the act can be fined up to $10,000 and receive a five-year prison term.

[7]Kay Lehman Schlozman and John T. Tierney, *Organized Interests and American Democracy* (New York: Harper and Row, 1986), p. 293.
[8]See T. R. Reid, *Congressional Odyssey* (San Francisco: W. H. Freeman, 1980) for the complete account of such lobbying activities.

DID YOU KNOW?

That there are over 10,000 lobbyists in Washington, D.C., the largest number (over 4,000) representing trade and professional associations and labor unions?

DID YOU KNOW?

That the overlapping membership in environmental interest groups that lobby Washington is over 2,000,000 people and growing fast?

In a famous case relating to the constitutionality of the lobbying act of 1946,[9] the Supreme Court emphasized that the intention of the act was simply to enable Congress to discover "who is being hired, who is putting up the money, and how much." The Court stated that the lobbying law does not violate due process, freedom of speech or press, or freedom of petition. But the Court narrowly construed the application of the act to only those lobbyists who *directly* seek to influence federal legislation. Any lobbyist indirectly seeking to influence legislation simply through public opinion does not fall within the scope of the activities regulated by the act.

Currently, about 6,500 lobbyists are registered under the act. The act has probably had no effect on the amount of money spent on lobbying and the types of activities engaged in by lobbyists. No enforcement agency has been created by Congress, and the public is almost totally ignorant of the publicity given in the quarterly reports. The problem facing Congress, of course, is that any stricter regulation of lobbying will run into constitutional problems because of the potential abridgement of First Amendment rights. Also, so long as the Supreme Court does not view indirect lobbying through attempts to change public opinion as falling under the purview of the act, lobbying will be difficult to control.

After the Watergate scandal in 1972, Congress attempted to pass a new bill that would make strict registration and reporting provisions a requirement. This 1976 bill, supported by Common Cause, failed under the combined attack of business, labor, and, interestingly enough, Ralph Nader. Obviously, public interest groups do not always see eye to eye. Whereas Common Cause is most concerned about good government—that is, better procedure—the Nader-type groups are more interested in substantive policy changes.

See the Highlight on Lobbying by Former Government Officials for an account of a prosecution under the 1978 Ethics in Government Act.

■ WHY INTEREST GROUPS HAVE SO MUCH POWER

It has been claimed that we are a nation of special interests. Organized interest groups have obtained special benefits for their members and blocked legislation that clearly seems to be supported by most citizens. The power of interest groups in the American political system probably results from a number of factors, some of which are inherent in the groups themselves and some of which are derived from the structure of our government.

Not all interest groups have an equal influence on government. Each has a different combination of resources to use in the policy-making process. Some groups are composed of members who have high social status and enormous economic resources, such as the National Association of Manufacturers. Other groups, such as labor unions, derive influence from their large membership. Still other groups, such as farmers or environmentalists, have causes that can claim strong public support even from those people who have no direct stake in the issue. Groups such as the National Rifle Association are well-organized and have highly motivated members. This enables them to channel a stream of mail toward Congress with a few days' effort.

Even the most powerful interest groups do not always succeed in their demands. Whereas the National Chamber of Commerce may be accepted as

[9]*United States v. Harris,* 347 U.S. 612 (1954).

HIGHLIGHT

Lobbying by Former Government Officials

In 1978, Congress passed the Ethics in Government Act as a reaction to the Watergate scandal during the Nixon administration. The main purpose of the act was to provide for independent investigations of present or former high-ranking government officials, unless the charges filed against an official are judged by the attorney general to be without merit. The act forbids former senior government employees to lobby their former agency on any matter for a year after leaving, to lobby any department for two years on an issue in which they had a direct responsibility, or to lobby for the rest of their lives on issues in which they participated "personally and substantially."

On May 29, 1986, Whitney North Seymour was appointed by a three-judge federal court to serve as a special prosecutor to investigate conflict-of-interest charges against former deputy White House Chief of Staff Michael K. Deaver. Deaver left the White House staff in May 1985 to become a highly paid lobbyist for foreign governments and business corporations. Deaver discussed with Robert McFarlane, the president's national security adviser at the time, some objections his client, the Commonwealth of Puerto Rico, had to a proposed revision in tax laws that would eliminate tax advantages for American businesses that invested in Puerto Rico and that could cause perhaps $600 million in economic losses. McFarlane was at the time directly in-

Michael Deaver, former member of the White House staff.

volved in looking into the possible revocation of this tax break. This occurred about two or three months after Deaver left office, in violation of the one-year prohibition on direct lobbying of his former White House colleagues.

In addition to these incidents, Deaver's work on behalf of the Daewoo Corporation, a large steel company in South Korea, and the U.S. defense contractor Rockwell International Corporation was also examined, following a series of allegations by Democrats on the Senate Judiciary Committee, by the General Accounting Office, and by the Office of Government Ethics. Finally, Deaver's work for the government of Canada in its dispute with the United

States over acid rain also allegedly violated the 1978 law.

For his efforts, Deaver was paid well by his clients: $105,000 by Canada, $250,000 by Rockwell International, $250,000 by Daewoo, and an undisclosed amount by Puerto Rico.

After a seven-week trial in late 1987, Deaver was found guilty and became the first person convicted under the Ethics in Government Act. In January 1988, a federal appeals court voted to strike down the provision of the law that authorizes judges to appoint special prosecutors to investigate high-level executive-branch crimes. But on June 29, 1988, the U.S. Supreme Court upheld the validity of the special prosecutor provisions.

The Deaver episode highlighted a continuing problem for the Reagan administration, whose high- and middle-level officials had frequently been investigated for improper or unethical conduct. Previous special prosecutors had examined charges against Reagan's former secretary of labor, Raymond Donovan, for taking payoffs and investigated allegations that Edwin Meese, formerly special counsel to Reagan and later attorney general, had committed eleven violations of government ethics. Both Donovan and Meese were cleared of those charges. Two previous investigations of Carter administration officials by special prosecutors also failed to produce convictions.

having a justified interest in the question of business taxes, many legislators might feel that the chamber should not engage in the debate over the size of the federal budget deficit. In other words, groups are seen as having a legitimate concern in the issues closest to their interests but not necessarily in broader issues. This may explain why some of the most successful groups are those that focus on very specific issues—tobacco farming, funding of abortions, handgun control—and do not get involved in larger conflicts. (See this chapter's Critical Perspective.)

DID YOU KNOW?

That the activities of interest groups at the state level has been growing much faster than in the nation's capital, with the number of registered lobbyists up over 40 percent in Sacramento, California, over 55 percent in Texas, and up at least 50 percent in Florida (from 2,000 to over 4,000)?

The structure of American government also invites the participation of interest groups. The governmental system has many points of access or places in the decision-making process where interest groups may focus an attack. If a bill opposed by a group passes the Senate, the lobbying efforts shift to the House of Representatives or to the president to seek a veto. If in spite of all efforts the legislation passes, the group may even lobby the executive agency or bureau that is supposed to implement the law and hope to influence the way in which the legislation is applied. In some cases, interest groups carry their efforts into the court system either by filing lawsuits or filing briefs as "friends of the court." The constitutional features of separation of powers and checks and balances encourage interest groups in their efforts.

The point is often made by lobbyists to members of Congress that interest groups are really constituents. If the group's needs are not met, the district may suffer economically, and the members of the group may vote against the legislator in the next election. When the argument is made to a member of Congress that voting against a new weapons system will result in the loss of jobs for constituents, the legislator can easily think of these constituents' votes in terms of the good of the district rather than of interest group pressure.

GETTING INVOLVED

The Gun Control Issue

I s the easy availability of handguns a major cause of crime? Do people have a right to firearms to defend home and hearth? These questions are part of a long-term and heated battle between organized profirearm and antifirearm camps. The disagreements run deeply and reflect strong sentiments on both sides. The fight is fueled by the one million gun incidents occurring in the United States each year—the murders, suicides, assaults, accidents, robberies, and injuries in which guns are involved. Proponents of gun control seek new restrictions on gun purchases—if not a ban on them entirely—while decreasing existing arsenals of privately owned weapons. Proponents of firearms are fighting back. They claim that firearms are a cherished tradition, a constitutional right, a vital defense need for individuals. They contend that the problem lies not in the sale and ownership of the weapons themselves but in the criminal use of firearms.

Michael Beard, director of the National Coalition to Ban Handguns, favors a total ban because "the only way to prevent the tragic loss of life—the thirty-two thousand lives a year we're losing to handguns—is to say: We no longer need handguns. They serve no valid purpose, except to kill people." Neal

James and Sarah Brady, leading the movement for handgun control after he was seriously wounded in the assassination attempt on President Reagan in 1981.

Know, director of the Institute for Legislative Action of the National Rifle Association of America, opposes a ban "because, among other reasons, it wouldn't work. It would not reduce the number of crimes committed. Are we going to assume that a person who will violate a law against rape, robbery, or murder will suddenly obey a gun law? I doubt it. There is no city, no state, no nation that has reduced its crime rate by the enactment of a gun law."*

The debate is intense and bitter. Gun control proponents accuse their adversaries of being "frightened little men living in a pseudomacho myth." Gun control opponents brand the other side as "new totalitarians" intent on curbing individual freedom.

The National Rifle Association, founded in 1871, is currently one of the most powerful single-issue groups on the American political scene. With some two million members and an annual budget of $30 million, the NRA is frequently successful in its efforts to block gun control legislation, elect officials sympathetic to its cause, and defeat candidates supportive of gun control. If you agree with the NRA's position and want to get involved in its efforts in opposition to gun control legislation, contact:

The National Rifle Association
1600 Rhode Island Ave., N.W.
Washington, D.C., 20036
202-828-6000

If, however, you are concerned with the increase in gun-related crimes and feel that stricter gun laws are necessary, you can get involved through these organizations:

Committee for the Study of Handgun Misuse
109 N. Dearborn St., Suite 704
Chicago, IL 60602
312-641-5593

The National Coalition to Ban Handguns
100 Maryland Avenue, N.E.
Washington, D.C. 20002
202-544-7190

Handgun Control, Inc.
810 18th St. N.W., Suite 705
Washington, D.C. 20006
202-638-4723

"Should Handguns Be Outlawed?" *U.S. News & World Report,* December 22, 1980, p. 23.

CHAPTER SUMMARY

1. An interest group is an organized group of individuals who share common objectives and who actively attempt to influence government policy.

2. Three of the most influential types of interest groups in the United States are business, agriculture, and labor.

3. Although there has been a decline in the percentage of nonagricultural workers who are union members, unions that represent public employees are increasing in strength.

4. Numerous professional organizations lobby to influence legislation; foremost among them in terms of money spent on lobbying is the American Medical Association (AMA).

5. Over the past decade, a variety of legal and lobbying organizations have been formed in the "public interest." The best known and perhaps most effective ones started under the leadership of Ralph Nader.

6. Lobbyists utilize a variety of direct techniques to influence legislation. These include testifying before congressional committees and rule-making agencies, providing information to legislators, making campaign contributions, and rating legislators' performance.

7. Most campaign contributions from interest groups are given through their Political Action Committees (PACs). New PACs are organized every year, with the corporate sector leading in growth. PACs give more money to incumbent legislators than to their challengers.

8. Interest groups can also use indirect techniques to influence policy making. Among these are campaigns to influence public opinion, campaigns to generate letters from the public, and using constituents to lobby for their cause.

9. The 1946 Legislative Reorganization Act was the first attempt to control lobbyists and lobbying activities through registration requirements. The Supreme Court narrowly construed it as applying only to lobbyists who directly seek to influence federal legislation.

10. The power of interest groups in the American political system derives partly from the structure of the government, which allows many points of access to the decision-making process, and partly from group characteristics, such as economic resources, social status, membership size, worthiness of the cause, and efficient organization.

QUESTIONS FOR REVIEW AND DISCUSSION

1. The American political system is sometimes described as one having "multiple cracks," or points of access for interest groups. If Congress is about to pass a law that adversely affects an interest group to which you belong, how can you lobby against it? How would you plan to lobby Congress, the executive branch, and the Supreme Court? How could you influence public opinion to support your point of view?

2. Think about your own interests—ethnic identity, religious affiliation, occupation, union, profession, hobby interests, and so on. How many interest groups might you belong to? Are you formally a member of any of these? If you are not a member, how are your interests represented? Which group represents the interests of the general public, say, for clean air or for lower taxes?

3. At the present time, PACs give disproportionate amounts of campaign contributions to incumbent legislators. How would the political process be changed if PACs were required to give equal amounts to challengers and incumbents, or if there were a limit on the percentage of campaign funds that could come from PACs? Where do PACs get their money?

SELECTED REFERENCES

Jeffrey M. Berry, *The Interest Group Society* (Glenview, Ill.: Scott, Foresman/Little, Brown, 1989). A comprehensive study of how interest groups are created, how they raise money, how they are staffed, and how they lobby. The role of interest groups in a democracy receives special attention.

David S. Broder, *Changing of the Guard: Power and Leadership in America* (New York: Simon and Schuster, 1980). The new generation of group leaders and its impact on the future of politics in the United States.

Alan J. Cigler and Burdette A. Loomis, eds., *Interest Group Politics*, 2nd ed. (Washington, D.C.: Congressional Quarterly Press, 1986). An in-depth discussion of what interest groups are, how they emerge and grow, and how they influence the legislative process.

A. Lee Fritschler and Bernard H. Ross, *How Washington Works: An Executive Guide to Government* (Cambridge, Mass.: Ballinger Publishing Co., 1987). This book provides a useful, practical perspective on how business executives can influence the federal government, how regulations are developed, how government supports business, and who the key government actors are.

David Rapp, *How the U.S. Got into Agriculture and Why It Can't Get Out* (Washington, D.C.: Congressional Quarterly Press, 1988). Explores how one pressure group became effective.

Kay Lehman Schlozman and John T. Tierney, *Organized Interests and American Democracy* (New York: Harper & Row, 1986). A systematic investigation of the activities and strategies of interest groups based on interviews with lobbyists and representatives of 175 groups.

CHAPTER 9

POLITICAL PARTIES

CHAPTER CONTENTS

WHAT IF . . . WE HAD A MULTIPARTY POLITICAL SYSTEM IN THE UNITED STATES?

The two-party system is an enduring feature of American government. In most elections, the contest is between two candidates, one from each of the major parties. In modern times, most members of Congress and state legislatures and all of the presidents have been either Democrats or Republicans.

Minor third parties have entered the arena, but historically it has been mostly a two-party affair. With few exceptions, the two major parties have accounted for about 90 percent of the total popular vote since the 1800s.

What if we had a multiparty system instead? Actually, such a system with competing political parties is much more common in Western democracies than the two-party system. As a modern, complex society with a wide variety of interests and opinions, it would seem the United States might be a likely candidate for a multiparty system.

Along with such a system, we would probably have

proportional representation. Legislative seats would be allocated to parties in proportion to the percentage of votes they won in the nation or a region. If a party or its candidates received 20 percent of the total vote, the party would have 20 percent of the seats in the legislature. It would be unlikely for one party to have exclusive government control.

Each party would be similar to a large interest group. Although still acting like a party, it would perform functions that in a two-party system only an interest group can perform. Parties representing interests would bargain with each other instead of interest groups bargaining with each other within a party. Each party would not have to win support from the large and heterogeneous groups they now need, but would achieve success by appealing to special groups.

It is difficult to say how many parties the United States would need to represent the diversity of American society. Would we need five or five hundred? We

would likely have parties representing many different groups: a farmer's party, an Hispanic party, a western party, a labor party, and so on. The various groups now working together in coalition within the Democratic and Republican parties might have less reason to seek consensus on issues of public policy.

Thinking about a multiparty system raises a number of questions about the existing American system.
1. *Why do we have only two parties, and how have they survived for more than one hundred years?*
2. *Why do American parties take such moderate positions, and how do they keep their electoral coalitions united?*
3. *What groups be better served by a multiparty system?*

■ WHAT IS A POLITICAL PARTY?

What are you? If that question were asked during a presidential election campaign, the answer would probably be "I'm a Republican" or "I'm a Democrat" or "I'm an Independent."[1] The answer would refer to a person's actual or perceived affiliation with a particular political party. In the United States, being a member of a political party does not require paying dues, passing an examination, or swearing an oath of allegiance. Well, if nothing is really required to be a member of a political party, what then is a **political party?**

A formal definition might be as follows:

> A political party is a group of individuals who organize to win elections, to operate the government, and to determine public policy.

With this definition, we can see the difference between an interest group and a political party. Interest groups do not want to operate government and they do not put forth political candidates—even though they support candidates who will promote their interests if elected or reelected. Another important distinction is that, whereas interest groups tend to sharpen issues, American political parties tend to blur their issue positions in order to attract voters.

A political party is not a **faction** (see Chapter 2). Factions, which historically preceded political parties, were simply groups of individuals who joined together to win a benefit for themselves, like the interest groups of today. They were limited to the period in our political history when there were relatively few elective offices and only a small percentage of the population could meet the requirements for voting. Today, we still use the term *faction,* but only for a particular group within a political party. For example, we speak of the conservative factions within the Republican and Democratic parties. A faction is founded on a particular philosophy, personality, or even geographical region. Sometimes a faction can be based on a political issue. The main feature differentiating a faction from a political party is that the faction generally does not have a permanently organized structure.

■ WHY DO PEOPLE JOIN POLITICAL PARTIES?

People join political parties for different reasons, according to political scientist James Q. Wilson.[2] These include solidary, material, and purposive (or ideological) incentives. Solidary incentives include enjoying the excitement of politics and using politics as a social outlet. Material incentives, such as those that created the support for big-city political machines, are operative when politics is seen as a means to employment or personal advancement. These jobs were often an important means of social mobility for aspirants to middle-class life. Finally, ideologically motivated people enter party activities to work for a clear-cut set of issue positions. Principle is more important than winning to those whose incentives are primarily ideological.

---

[1]In rare instances the answer might be "I'm a Libertarian" or "I'm a Socialist" or refer to some other less common political group.
[2]*Political Organizations* (New York: Basic Books, 1973).

DID YOU KNOW?

That in 1824 the voters were offered the choice between "John Quincy Adams who can write and Andy Jackson who can fight"?

POLITICAL PARTY
A group of individuals who organize to win elections, to operate the government, and to determine public policy.

FACTION
A group or bloc in a legislature or political party acting together in pursuit of some special interest or position.

DID YOU KNOW?

That Samuel J. Tilden, Democratic candidate for president in 1876, surveyed public attitudes by studying commencement addresses and Fourth of July orations?

■ POLITICAL PARTIES IN OTHER COUNTRIES

Although the individuals who claim to belong to the major American parties profess a similar political ideology, this is not a requirement for participation. Contrast this situation with membership in political parties in other countries. Members of the Communist party in the People's Republic of China, in Albania, and in Cuba must adhere to rigidly enforced (but often tactically shifting) party lines.

Countries vary widely in number of political parties and in the way political power is apportioned. Mexico has one dominant political party, but within it are relatively conservative and relatively liberal factions. This party is known as the *Partido Revolucionario Institucional* (Institutional Revolutionary Party), and its somewhat contradictory name conveys the nature of Mexican politics. The party grew out of popular revolutionary struggles in the late nineteenth and early twentieth centuries; however, today it must address the desires of modern Mexicans for stability.

In Italy, on the other hand, a variety of political parties vie for control and influence. Voters are splintered among the Christian Democrats, the former Communists, the Socialists, and a large number of minor parties, including the Social Movement party, the Social Democrats, the Radicals, the Republicans, the Liberals, and the Proletarian Unity party. Governments normally are formed by coalitions of the Christian Democrats and the Socialists along with some of the minor parties.

These different party structures grew out of historical events unique to each nation, as well as electoral laws that may favor either small parties (as in Italy) or only the biggest parties (as in the United States). What we are used to—that is, two relatively moderate political parties alternating in power peacefully—is not likely to exist in countries that have evolved differently from the United States.

A Jackson delegate at the 1988 Democratic convention.

■ FUNCTIONS OF POLITICAL PARTIES IN THE UNITED STATES

Political parties in the United States engage in a wide variety of activities. Many of those activities are discussed throughout this chapter. Political parties are expected to do the following, although no single party—state, local, or national—probably does them all.

1. Identify and publicize issues of a political and social nature.
2. Stimulate the public's interest in the political process.
3. Recruit party candidates and enter them in national, state, and local electoral campaigns.
4. Finance political party activity.
5. Accept responsibility for operating government while in power.
6. Provide an organized opposition to the political party operating the government.
7. Attempt to create a consensus that cuts across sectional or social class differences.
8. Provide an avenue for public service careers.

Students of political parties such as Leon D. Epstein[3] point out that the major functions of American political parties are carried out by a small, relatively loose-knit **cadre,** or nucleus, of party activists. This is quite a different arrangement from the more highly structured, mass-membership party organization typical of European working-class parties. American parties concentrate on winning elections rather than signing up large numbers of deeply committed, dues-paying members who believe passionately in the party's program.

CADRE
The nucleus of political party activists carrying out the major functions of American political parties.

■ A SHORT HISTORY OF POLITICAL PARTIES IN THE UNITED STATES

Political parties in the United States have a long tradition, dating back to the earliest years of this nation's history. The function and character of these political parties, as well as the emergence of the two-party system itself, have much to do with the unique historical forces operating from this country's beginning as an independent nation. It wasn't until the 1790s that political parties emerged in the United States (Figure 9-1). Generally, we can divide the evolution of our nation's political parties into six periods:

1. The creation of parties in the 1790s.
2. The era of onc-party rule, or personal politics, in the 1820s.
3. The period from Andrew Jackson's presidency to the Civil War, during which the Democrats and the Whigs were solidly established national parties.
4. The post-Civil War period, ending in 1896.
5. The progressive period, from 1896 to 1921.
6. The modern period, from Franklin Roosevelt's New Deal until today.

FEDERALISTS
The first American political party, led by Alexander Hamilton and John Adams. Many of its members had strongly supported the adoption of the new Constitution and the creation of the federal union.

ANTI-FEDERALISTS
The Anti-Federalists opposed the adoption of the Constitution because of its centralist tendencies and attacked the failure of the Constitution's framers to include a bill of rights.

The Formative Years: Federalists and Anti-Federalists

The first partisan political division in the United States occurred after the Constitutional Convention. The **Federalists** proposed adoption of the Constitution, while the **Anti-Federalists** were against ratification.

In September 1796, George Washington, who had served as president for almost two full terms, decided not to run again. In his farewell address, he made a somber assessment of the nation's future. Washington felt that the country might be destroyed by the "baneful effects of the spirit of party." He viewed parties as a threat to both national unity and the concept of popular government. Early in his career, Thomas Jefferson did not like political parties either. In 1789, he stated, "If I could not go to heaven but with a party, I would not go there at all."[4]

What Americans found out during the first decade or so after ratification of the Constitution was that even a patriot-king (as Washington has been called) could not keep everyone happy. There is no such thing as a neutral political figure who is so fair-minded that everyone agrees with him or her. During this period, it became obvious to many that something more permanent than a faction would be necessary to identify candidates for the growing

Thomas Jefferson.

[3]*Political Parties in Western Democracies* (New Brunswick, N.J.: Transaction, 1980).
[4]Letter to Francis Hopkinson written from Paris while Jefferson was minister to France. In John P. Foley, ed., *The Jeffersonian Cyclopedia* (New York: Russell & Russell, 1967), p. 677.

FIGURE 9-1
American Political Parties Since 1789

SOURCES: Congressional Quarterly, *Congressional Quarterly's Guide to U.S. Elections*, 2nd ed. (Washington, D.C.: Congressional Quarterly, 1985), p. 224; 1988: *Congressional Quarterly Weekly Report* (1988), p. 3184.

NOTE: The chart indicates the years parties either ran presidential candidates or held national conventions. The lifespan for many political parties can only be approximated because parties existed at the state or local level before they ran candidates in presidential elections, and parties continued to exist at local levels long after they ceased running presidential candidates. Not every party fielding a presidential candidate is represented in the chart. For instance, in 1988 at least nine other parties fielded such a candidate in at least one state.

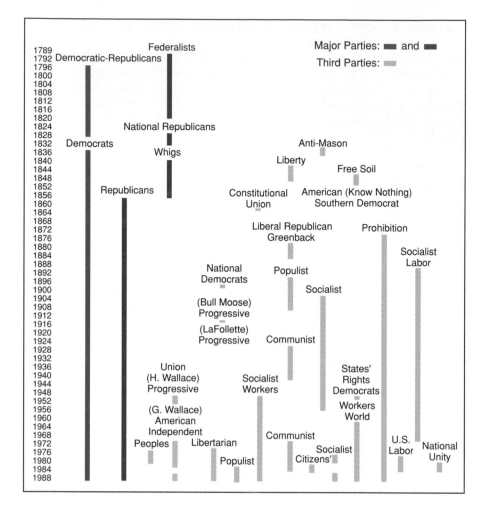

number of individuals who would be participating in elections. Thus, according to many historians, the world's first democratic political parties were established in this country. Also, in 1800 when the Federalists lost the presidential election to the Democratic Republicans (also known as Jeffersonians), one of the first peaceful transfers of power from one party to another was achieved.

The Era of Personal Politics

From 1816 to 1828, a majority of voters regularly elected Democratic Republicans to the presidency and to Congress. **Two-party competition** did not really exist. This was the so-called **era of personal politics,** when attention centered on the character of individual candidates rather than on party identification. Although opposing the Federalist belief in a stronger, more active central government during elections, the Democratic Republicans acquired the Louisiana Territory and Florida, established a national bank, enforced a higher tariff, and resisted European intrusion in the Western Hemisphere. Domestic tranquility was sufficiently in evidence that the administration of James Monroe came to be known as the **era of good feeling.**

TWO-PARTY COMPETITION
Two strong and solidly established political parties in competition for political control; both parties have a strong chance of winning an election.

ERA OF PERSONAL POLITICS
An era when attention centers on the character of individual candidates rather than on party identification.

ERA OF GOOD FEELING
The years from 1817 to 1825 when James Monroe was president and there was, in effect, no political opposition.

National Two-Party Rule: Democrats and Whigs

During the era of personal politics, one-party rule did not prevent Democratic Republican factions from competing against each other. Indeed, there was quite a bit of intraparty rivalry. Finally, in 1824 and 1828, Jeffersonian Republicans who belonged to the factions of Henry Clay and John Quincy Adams split with the rest of the party to oppose Andrew Jackson in those elections. Jackson's supporters and the Clay-Adams bloc formed separate parties as **Democrats** and **Whigs**, respectively. It was under Jackson's leadership that the Jeffersonians changed their name to the Democratic party. That same Democratic party is now the oldest continuing political party in the Western world.

The Whigs were those Jeffersonian Republicans who were often called the "National Republicans." At the national level, the Whigs were able to elect two presidents—William Henry Harrison in 1840 and Zachary Taylor in 1848. The Whigs, however, were unable to maintain a common ideological base when the party became increasingly divided over the issue of slavery in the late 1840s. During the 1850s the Whigs fell apart as a national party.

The Post-Civil War Period

The existing two-party system was disrupted by the election of 1860, in which there were four major candidates. Abraham Lincoln, the candidate of the newly formed **Republican party**, was the victor with a majority of the electoral vote, although with only 39.9 percent of the popular vote. This newly formed Republican party—not to be confused with the Jeffersonian Republicans—was created in the mid-1850s from the various groups that sought to fill the vacuum left by the disintegration of the Whigs. It took the label of Grand Old Party, or GOP. Its first national convention was held in 1856, but its presidential candidate, John C. Frémont, lost.

After the end of the Civil War, the South became heavily Democratic (the Solid South), and the North became heavily Republican. This era of Republican dominance was highlighted by the election of 1896 when the Republicans, emphasizing economic development and modernization under William McKinley, resoundingly defeated the Democratic and Populist candidate, William Jennings Bryan. The Republicans' control was solidified by winning over the urban working-class vote in northern cities. From the election of Abraham Lincoln until the election of Roosevelt in 1932, the Republicans won all but four presidential elections.

The Progressive Movement

In 1912, a major schism occurred in the Republican party when former Republican President Theodore Roosevelt ran for the presidency as a Progressive. Consequently, there was a significant three-way presidential contest. Woodrow Wilson was the Democratic candidate, William Howard Taft the regular Republican candidate, and Roosevelt the Progressive candidate. The Republican split allowed Wilson to be elected. The Wilson administration, although Democratic, ended up enacting much of the Progressive party's platform. Left without any reason for opposition, the Progressive party collapsed in 1921.

Republican Warren Harding's victory in 1920 asserted Republican domination of national politics until the Republicans' defeat by Franklin Roosevelt in 1932 in the depths of the Great Depression.

Andrew Jackson, founder of the modern Democratic Party.

DEMOCRATS
One of the two major American political parties evolving out of the Democratic Republican (Jeffersonian) group supporting Thomas Jefferson.

WHIGS
One of the foremost political organizations in the United States during the first half of the nineteenth century, formally established in 1836. The Whig party was dominated by the same anti-Jackson elements that organized the National Republican faction within the Jeffersonian Republicans and represented a variety of regional interests. It fell apart as a national party in the early 1850s.

REPUBLICAN PARTY
One of the two major American political parties, which emerged in the 1850s as an antislavery party. It was created to fill the vacuum caused by the disintegration of the Whig party. The Republican party traces its name—but not its ideology—to Jefferson's Democratic Republican party.

PROFILE

Ronald Brown

"We've got to reach out to the American people and give them a reason to vote for Democratic presidential candidates."

I t seemed to be a contradiction—a chairman of the Democratic National Committee who belonged to a prestigious Washington law firm and spared no effort to portray himself as a member of society's elite. Yet this was not the only surprise sprung by the national organization of "the party of the common people" in 1989: The aristocratic DNC chairman is, among other things, an African American.

Ronald Brown, whose father managed a hotel, grew up in the Harlem section of New York City. His family placed a high value on education, sending him to elite private schools where he was often the only African American.

Brown, after serving as an army officer in Europe, received a law degree from St. John's University in New York. He was quickly drawn into politics, becoming the National Urban League's chief lobbyist in 1967. In 1980, he became the director of Senator Ted Kennedy's Senate staff. After a short time in this position, he returned to the private practice of law. Politics seemed to pursue him, however, and in the spring of 1988, Jesse Jackson asked Ron Brown to be his manager at the Democratic National Convention in Atlanta. His election by party professionals to the national leadership was both a recognition of his political skill and a bold political gambit by the Democrats.

Ron Brown's assumption of the national leadership of the Democrats came at a time of crisis in the party's history. It had lost the last three presidential elections, and five of the last six; areas once solidly Democratic, such as the South, were experiencing steady inroads by the Republicans; middle-class, traditionally Democratic voters were leaving the party because they saw it as favoring higher taxes and unfair advantages for racial minorities. Indeed, some analysts foresaw the end of the Democratic party as a viable national force. The election of Ron Brown as chief national strategist, organizer, and fund raiser was a bold response to these problems. Because he is an African American, Democratic liberals and moderates hoped he would maintain the historic loyalty of the poor and racial minorities to the party. His organizational skills, talent for compromise, and establishment demeanor would, it was hoped, heal the rift between liberals and conservatives within the party, and bring middle-class voters back into the Democratic fold. The thinking that generated support for Brown as chairman was risky, however: Many southern Democrats opposed Brown because of his race, and some Democratic officials in that region actually changed their party affiliation to Republican after he assumed the chairmanship.

So far, the strategy that elevated Brown to the leadership of the party has been moderately successful: By persuading various Democratic candidates for state and local offices to work together, the party won important elections in Indiana, Virginia, and New York City in the spring of 1989. The national committee's willingness to invest time and money in these elections—a move that resulted from Brown's efforts—also helped bring victory for the party. The real test for Brown and the Democrats, however, will come in 1992 when they face their traditionally better-funded and better organized Republican rivals for national leadership.

The national chairperson, along with the national committee, attempts basically to maintain some sort of liaison among the different levels of the party organization. The fact is that the real strength and power of a national party is at the state level.

The State Organization

There are fifty states in the Union, plus the territories and the District of Columbia, and an equal number of party organizations for each major party. Therefore, there are more than a hundred state parties (and even more if we include local parties and minor parties). Since every state party is unique, it is impossible to describe what an "average" state political party is like. Nonetheless, state parties have several organizational features in common.

This commonality can be described in one sentence: Each state party has a chairperson, a committee, and a number of local organizations. In principle, the **state central committees**—the principal organized structure of each political party within each state—have similar roles in the various states. The committee, usually composed of those members who represent congressional districts, state legislative districts, or counties, has responsibility for carrying out the policy decisions of the party's state convention, and in some states the state central committee will direct the state chairperson with respect to policy making.

Also, like the national committee, the state central committee has control over the use of party campaign funds during political campaigns. Usually, the state central committee has little if any influence on party candidates once they are elected. In fact, state parties are fundamentally loose alliances of local interests and coalitions of often bitterly opposed factions.

State parties also loom importantly in national politics because of the **unit rule,** which awards electoral votes in presidential elections as an indivisible bloc (except in Maine). Presidential candidates concentrate their efforts in states in which voter preferences seem to be evenly divided or in which large numbers of electoral votes are at stake.

Local Party Machinery: The Grass Roots

The lowest layer of party machinery is the local organization, supported by district leaders, precinct or ward captains, and party workers. Much of the work is coordinated by county committees and their chairpersons. A local party organization is depicted in Figure 9-3. In the past, the institution of **patronage**—rewarding the party faithful with government jobs or contracts— held the local organization together. For immigrants and the poor, the political machine often furnished important services and protections. The big-city party machine was the archetypical example, and Tammany Hall, or the Tammany Society, which dominated New York government for nearly two centuries, was perhaps the highest refinement of this political form. (See Highlight, Tammany Hall: The Quintessential Local Political Machine.)

The last big-city local political machine to exercise a great deal of power was run by Chicago's Mayor Richard J. Daley, who was also an important figure in national Democratic politics. Daley, as mayor, ran the Chicago Democratic machine from 1955 until his death in 1976. The Daley organization,

---

DID YOU KNOW?

That the Democratic party in the United States is the oldest continuing political party in the Western world?

STATE CENTRAL COMMITTEE
The principal organized structure of each political party within each state. Responsible for carrying out policy decisions of the party's state convention.

UNIT RULE
All of a state's electoral votes are cast for the presidential candidate receiving a plurality of the popular vote.

Richard M. Daley, Mayor of Chicago. Son of the former mayor, Daley won office in a racially divisive election. Can such a mayor create a new coalition to govern such a racially mixed city?

DID YOU KNOW?

That in the history of this nation, parties identified as "conservative" and those identified as "liberal" have shared the presidency almost equally?

largely Irish in candidate origin and voter support, was split by the successful candidacy of African-American Democrat Harold Washington in the racially divisive 1983 mayoral election. He was reelected in 1987 but died within a year. A Washington supporter, Eugene Sawyer, became mayor after another bitter intraparty fight. In 1989, the son of Mayor Daley, Richard M. Daley, defeated Sawyer in the primary to become mayor. Although most African-American voters supported the African-American candidate, Daley garnered support from white, Hispanic, and Asian-American voters.

City machines are now dead, mostly because their function of providing social services (and reaping the reward of votes) has been taken over by state and national agencies. This trend began in the 1930s when the social legislation of the New Deal established Social Security and unemployment insurance. The local party machine has little if anything to do with deciding who is eligible to receive these benefits.

Local political organizations, whether located in cities, townships, or at the county level, still can contribute a great deal to local election campaigns. These organizations are able to provide the foot soldiers of politics, individuals who

FIGURE 9-3
The Structure of a Typical Local Party Organization

SOURCE: Based on the State of Iowa, as suggested by Dr. Lee Ann Osbun, Director, L.A.R.S. Consultants.

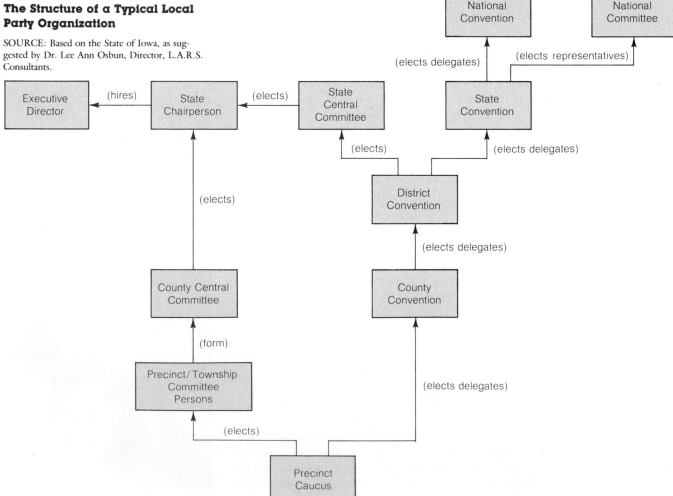

HIGHLIGHT

Tammany Hall: The Quintessential Local Political Machine

The Tammany Society dominated New York City politics for more than a century. Founded in 1786 with the express purpose of engaging in cultural, social, and patriotic activities, the society evolved into a major political force and became known as Tammany Hall. In the beginning, it organized and provided social services for the foreign born who made up the bulk of the Democratic party in New York City. One of its more notorious leaders was William Tweed, head of the so-called Tweed ring, whose scandals were unearthed by the *New York Times* in 1871. Readers were entertained and horrified by stories of millions of dollars in kickbacks through the letting of government contracts and the overlooking of civil and criminal violations, as well as phony leases and padded bills that were paid to members of the Tweed ring. As a result of the exposé, Tweed was imprisoned; but the other members of the ring managed to flee the country (as very wealthy men and women). Richard Crocker took over the leadership of Tammany Hall in 1886 and kept it until 1901.

Tammany Hall's influence declined when its slate of candidates was defeated in a reform movement in 1901. It wasn't until Franklin Roosevelt's victory in 1932 that Tammany lost its political clout almost completely—but only for a couple of decades. In the 1950s there was a short-lived resurgence in the influence of the Tammany Society. It has enjoyed no political influence in New York City politics since then.

TWEEDLEDEE AND SWEEDLEDUM.
(*A New Christmas Pantomime at the Tammany Hall.*)
Clown (to Pantaloon). "Let's Blind them with *this*, and then take *some more.*"

TWEED'S GIFT OF FIFTY THOUSAND DOLLARS TO THE POOR OF HIS NATIVE WARD.—"HARPER'S WEEKLY," JANUARY 14, 1871.

pass out literature and get out the vote on election day, which can be crucial in local elections. In many regions, local Democratic and Republican organizations still control some patronage, such as courthouse jobs, contracts for street repair, and other lucrative construction contracts. Local party organizations are also the most important vehicle for recruiting young adults into political work, since politics at the local level offers activists many opportunities to gain experience.

DID YOU KNOW?

That Millard Fillmore, former Whig president, ran for president in 1856 as the candidate of the Know-Nothing (or American) party?

■ WHY DO WE HAVE A TWO-PARTY SYSTEM?

It would be difficult to imagine a political system in the United States in which there were four, five, six, or seven major political parties. Of course, the United States has a two-party system, and that system has been around from about 1800 to the present. But considering the range of political ideology among voters and the variety of local and state party machines, the fact that we still have just two major political parties is somewhat unusual.

Strong competition between the parties at the national level has in general not filtered down to the state level. From 1900 to 1980, the Republicans won eleven presidential elections and the Democrats ten. In state and local elections, however, one-party dominance is the rule in many regions of the United States. The Solid South was almost totally Democratic at all levels of government from 1880 to 1944. The northeastern states and much of the Midwest were solidly Republican from approximately 1860 to 1930. As can be seen in Table 9-1, almost 60 percent of the states are dominated by either the Republican or Democratic party. In any event, we are still talking about either Democratic or Republican dominance—just two major parties.

There are several reasons why two major parties have dominated the political landscape in the United States for almost two centuries. These have to do

TABLE 9-1
Party Competition in the States, 1968–1988

AVERAGE PERCENTAGE OF REPUBLICAN WINS*				
0–20	21–40	41–60	61–80	81–100
Alabama	Alaska	Delaware	Arizona	Colorado
Arkansas	Illinois	Iowa	Kansas	Idaho
California	Montana	Maine	North Dakota	Indiana
Connecticut	Nebraska	New York	South Dakota	New Hampshire
Florida	Nevada	Ohio	Utah	Wyoming
Georgia	New Jersey	Pennsylvania	Vermont	
Hawaii	Oregon			
Kentucky	Washington			
Louisiana	Wisconsin			
Maryland				
Massachusetts				
Michigan				
Minnesota				
Mississippi				
Missouri				
New Mexico				
North Carolina				
Oklahoma				
Rhode Island				
South Carolina				
Tennessee				
Texas				
Virginia				
West Virginia				

*For this table, the percentage of wins is calculated by counting party control of the governorship and the upper and lower houses of the legislature. Thus if the Republicans won both houses of the Arizona legislature but not the governorship, their percentage would be 2 of 3 or 66.6 percent.
SOURCE: Harold W. Stanley and Richard G. Niemi, *Vital Statistics on American Politics* (Washington, D.C.: Congressional Quarterly Press, 1990).

with (1) the historical foundations of the system, (2) the self-perpetuation of the parties, (3) the commonality of views among Americans, (4) the winner-take-all electoral system, and (5) state and federal laws favoring the two-party system.

The Historical Foundation of the Two-Party System

As we have seen, the first two opposing groups in United States politics were the Federalists and the Anti-Federalists. The Federalists, who remained in power and solidified their identity as a political party, represented commercial interests—merchants, shipowners, and manufacturers. The Anti-Federalists, who gradually became known as the Democratic Republicans, represented artisans and farmers. These interests were also fairly well split along geographic lines, with the Federalists dominant in the North and the Democratic Republicans dominant in the South.

Two relatively distinct sets of interests continued to characterize the two different parties. During Andrew Jackson's time in power, eastern commercial interests were pitted against western and southern agricultural and frontier interests. Before the Civil War, the major split again became North versus South. The split was ideological—over the issue of slavery—as well as economic—the Northeast's industrial interests versus the agricultural interests of the South. After the Civil War and until the 1920s, the Republicans found most of their strength in the Northeast, the Democrats in the Solid South. The West and the Midwest held the balance of power at that time. This period until the 1920s has been called one of **sectional politics.**

Sectional politics gave way to **national politics** as the cities became more dominant and as industry flowed to the South and to the West. Some political scientists classify the period from 1920 to today as one of **class politics,** the Republicans generally finding support among groups of higher economic status and the Democrats appealing more to working-class constituencies.

Self-Perpetuation of the Two-Party System

As we saw in Chapter 7, most children identify with the political party of their parents. Children learn at quite a young age to think of themselves as either Democrats or Republicans. Relatively few are taught to think of themselves as Libertarians or Socialists or even independents. This generates a built-in mechanism to perpetuate a two-party system. According to most studies of the process of political socialization, psychological attachment to party identity intensifies during adulthood.[8]

Also, many politically oriented people who aspire to work for social change consider that the only realistic way to capture political power in this country is to be either a Republican or Democrat. Of course, the same argument holds for those who involve themselves in politics largely for personal gain. Thus, political parties provide avenues for the expression of the personal ambitions of politicians and supply government with men and women anxious to serve the public by satisfying their own goals.[9]

SECTIONAL POLITICS
The pursuit of interests that are of special concern to a region or section of the country.

NATIONAL POLITICS
The pursuit of interests that are of concern to the nation as a whole.

CLASS POLITICS
Political preferences based on income level and/or social status.

[8]See, for example, Lester W. Milbrath, *Political Participation: How and Why Do People Get Involved in Politics?* (Chicago, Ill.: Rand McNally, 1965), pp. 134–135.
[9]This is the view of, among others, Joseph Schlesinger. See his *Ambition and Politics: Political Careers in the United States* (Chicago, Ill.: Rand McNally, 1966).

DID YOU KNOW?

That New York sent two delegations to the 1848 Democratic convention—the Barnburners and the Hunkers?

ELECTORAL COLLEGE
A group of persons called electors who are selected by the voters in each state; this group officially elects the president and the vice president of the United States. The number of electors in each state is equal to the number of each state's representatives in both houses of Congress.

The Political Culture of the United States

Another determining factor in the perpetuation of our two-party system is the commonality of goals among Americans. Most Americans want continuing material prosperity. They also believe this goal should be achieved through individual rather than collective initiative. There has never been much support for establishing the government as the owner of the major means of production. Left-wing political movements wish to limit the ownership of private property. Most Americans take a dim view of such an attitude—private property is considered a basic American institution and the ability to acquire and use it the way one wishes is commonly regarded as a basic American right.

Another reason we have had a basic consensus about our political system and the two major parties is that we have largely managed to separate religion from politics. Religion was an issue in 1928 when Governor Alfred Smith of New York became the first Roman Catholic to be nominated for the presidency (he was defeated by Republican Herbert Hoover) and again in 1960 when John F. Kennedy was running for president. But religion has never been a dividing force triggering splinter parties. There has never been a major Catholic party or a Protestant party or a Jewish party or a Moslem party.

The major division in American politics has been economic. As we mentioned earlier, the Democrats have been known—at least since the 1930s—as the party of the working class, in favor of government intervention in the economy and more government redistribution of income. The Republican party has been known in modern times as the party of the middle and upper classes and commercial interests, in favor of a more uninhibited working of the market system and less redistribution of income.

Not only does the political culture support the two-party system but also the parties themselves are adept at making the necessary shifts in their platforms or electoral appeal to gain new members. Because the general ideological structure of the parties is so broad, it has been relatively easy for them to change their respective platforms or to borrow popular policies from minor parties to attract voting support. Both parties perceive themselves as broad enough to accommodate every group in society; the Republicans try to woo support from the African-American community, whereas the Democrats strive to make inroads in professional and business groups.

The Winner-Take-All Electoral System

At virtually every level of government in the United States, the outcome of elections is based on the plurality, winner-take-all principle. A plurality system is one in which the winner is the person who obtains the most votes, even if a majority is not obtained. Whoever gets the most votes gets everything. Since most legislative seats in the United States are elected from single-member districts in which only one person represents the constituency, the candidate who finishes second in such an election receives nothing for the effort.

The winner-take-all system also operates in the **electoral college** (see Chapter 10). Each state's electors are pledged to presidential candidates chosen by their respective national party conventions. During the popular vote in November, in each of the fifty states and in the District of Columbia, the voters choose one slate of electors from those on the state ballot. If the slate of electors wins a plurality in a state, *all* the electors so chosen—except in Maine, where electoral votes are apportioned among its U.S. Senate and House seats—then cast their ballots for the presidential and vice presidential candidates of the winning party. That means that if a particular candidate's slate of electors receives a plurality of 40 percent of the votes in a state, that candidate will receive all the state's electoral votes. Minor parties have a difficult time competing under such a system, even though they may influence the final outcome of the election. Because voters know that minor parties can't succeed, they often will not vote for minor party candidates, even if they are ideologically in tune with them.

Not all countries, or all states in the United States, use the plurality, winner-take-all electoral system. Some hold run-off elections until a candidate obtains at least one vote over 50 percent of the votes. Such a system may be used in countries with multiple parties. Small parties hope to be able to obtain a sufficient number of votes to at least get into a run-off election. Then the small-party candidate can form an alliance with one or more of those parties that did not make the run-off. Such alliances also occur in the United States, but with the plurality system these coalitions must normally be made before the first election since usually there is no run-off.

Now consider another alternative political system in which there is proportional representation with multimember districts. In Germany, each party submits its preferred list of candidates in order of preference. If, during the national election, party X obtains 12 percent of the vote, party Y 43 percent of the vote, and party Z the remaining 45 percent of the vote, then in parliament party X gets 12 percent of the seats, party Y gets 43 percent of the seats, and party Z gets 45 percent of the seats. Because even a minor party may still obtain at least a few seats in parliament, the smaller parties have a greater incentive to organize under such electoral systems than they do in the United States.

State and Federal Laws Favoring the Two Parties

Many state and federal election laws offer a clear advantage to the two major parties. In some states, the established major parties need gather only a few

DID YOU KNOW?

That the Democrats and Republicans each had exactly one woman delegate at their conventions in 1900?

Michael Dukakis, Lloyd Bentsen, Jesse Jackson, their families, and other Democratic party leaders at the close of the 1988 convention. What purpose do such displays of unity have for the party members and other viewers?

"Very Republican. I love it."

Drawing by B. Tobey © 1986 The New Yorker Magazine, Inc.

signatures to place their candidates on the ballot, whereas a minor party or an independent candidate must get many more signatures. The criterion for making such a distinction is often based on the total party vote in the last general election, penalizing the new political party that did not compete in the election.

At the national level, minor parties face different obstacles. All of the rules and procedures of both houses of Congress divide committee seats, staff members, and other privileges on the basis of party membership. A legislator who is elected on a minor party ticket, such as the Liberal party of New York, must choose to be counted with one of the major parties to get a committee assignment. The Federal Election Commission (FEC) rules for campaign financing also place restrictions on minor party candidates. Such candidates are not eligible for federal matching funds in either the primary or general election. In the 1980 election, John Anderson, running as an independent, sued the FEC for campaign funds, and the commission finally agreed to repay part of his campaign costs after the election in proportion to the votes he received.

How Do the Democratic and Republican Parties Differ?

The two major American political parties are often characterized as being too much like Tweedledee and Tweedledum, the twins in Lewis Carroll's *Through the Looking Glass*. When both parties nominate moderates for the presidency,

Republican delegates show their enthusiasm for the party. What personal benefits do these rank-and-file members gain from their activism for the party?

the similarities between the parties seem to outweigh their differences. Yet the political parties do generate strong conflict for political offices throughout the United States, and there are significant differences between the parties, both in the characteristics of their members and in their platforms.

Although Democrats and Republicans are not divided along religious or class lines to the extent of some European parties, certain social groups are more likely to identify with each. Since the New Deal of Franklin Roosevelt, the Democratic party has appealed to the more disadvantaged groups in society. African-American voters are far more likely to identify with the Democrats, as are members of union households, Jewish voters, and individuals who have less than a high school education. Republicans draw more of their support from college graduates, upper-income families, and professionals or business-persons. In recent years, more women have tended to identify themselves as Democrats than as Republicans.

The coalition of minorities, the working class, and various ethnic groups has been the core of Democratic party support since the presidency of Franklin Roosevelt. The social programs and increased government intervention in the economy that were the heart of Roosevelt's New Deal were intended to ease the strain of economic hard times on these groups. This goal remains important for many Democrats today. In general, Democratic identifiers are more likely to approve of social welfare spending, to support government regulation of business, to approve of measures to improve the situation of minorities, and to assist the elderly with their medical expenses. Republicans are more sup-portive of the private marketplace, and many feel that the federal government should be involved in fewer social programs. Table 9-2 shows that the general public shares this view of which groups are served by each party. It would seem that a larger proportion of the population falls into those groups that most people think are better served by the Democratic party than by the Republican party, yet the Republican party has captured the presidency in five of the last six elections. Turning from the interests of specific groups to the interest of the nation as a whole, Table 9-3 shows the percentages of the people

TABLE 9-2
Which Party Is Better?

In the view of the public, which party serves the interests of groups in society better?			
Better for	Republican	Democrat	Same/ Don't Know
Business and professional people	69%	16%	15%
White-collar workers	59	23	18
Skilled workers	41	39	20
Small business people	35	45	20
Farmers	31	45	24
Retired people	28	48	24
Unemployed people	26	52	22
Women	25	48	27
Labor union members	24	58	18
African Americans	19	60	21

SOURCE: *The Gallup Report*, January/February 1985.

who think that the Republican or Democratic party is better for preserving peace and promoting prosperity. Since 1984, a greater proportion of the public has felt that the Republican party was better able than the Democratic party to keep peace and to keep the country prosperous. If it is true, as some researchers suggest, that voters are more likely to consider the good of the whole nation rather than their individual interests in choosing a presidential candidate, the success of the Republican party is due to public perceptions of its effectiveness on the issues of peace and the economy.

These differences separating party identifiers are greatly magnified among the leadership of the Democrats and Republicans. Generally, a much greater percentage of Democratic leaders consider themselves to be liberals than do their followers, and Republican elites are far more likely to identify their philosophy as conservative than are their followers. Such differences are re-

TABLE 9-3
Public Perceptions of the Parties on Peace and Prosperity

WHICH PARTY IS BETTER FOR KEEPING PEACE?			WHICH PARTY IS BETTER FOR PROSPERITY?		
Year	Republican	Democrat	Year	Republican	Democrat
1980	25%	42%	1980	35%	36%
1982	29	38	1982	34	43
1984	38	38	1984	49	33
1986	34	29	1986	41	30
1988	43	33	1988	52	34
1989	45	31	1989	51	30

SOURCE: *The Gallup Report*, July 1989, p. 4.

flected in the party platforms that are adopted at each party's convention. Democratic platforms recently have stressed equality of opportunity, the government's responsibility to help citizens, and ending tax loopholes for business. Recent Republican platforms seek to ban abortions, oppose quotas to remedy discrimination, and increase defense spending. It is worth noting, however, that the strong differences between the attitudes of party elites and platforms tend to disappear during the election campaign as candidates try to win votes from partisans of all ideological persuasions and from independent voters as well.

> **DID YOU KNOW?**
>
> That it took 103 ballots for John W. Davis to be nominated at the Democratic national convention in 1924?

■ THE ROLE OF MINOR PARTIES IN U.S. POLITICAL HISTORY

Minor parties have a difficult if not impossible time competing within the two-party-dominated American system. Nonetheless, minor parties have had an important place in our political life. Frequently, dissatisfied groups have split from major parties and formed so-called **third parties,**[10] which have acted as barometers of changes in political mood. Such barometric indicators have forced the major parties to recognize new issues or trends in the thinking of Americans. Political scientists also believe that third parties have acted as a safety valve for dissident political groups, perhaps preventing major confrontations and political unrest.

THIRD PARTY
A political party other than the two major political parties (Republican and Democratic). Usually, third parties are composed of dissatisfied groups that have split from the major parties. They act as indicators of political trends and as safety valves for dissident groups.

Historically Important Minor Parties

Most minor parties that have endured have had a strong ideological foundation that is typically at odds with the majority mind-set. Ideology has at least two functions. First, the members of the minor party regard themselves as outsiders and look to one another for support; ideology provides tremendous psychological cohesiveness. Second, because the rewards of ideological commitment are partly psychological, these minor parties do not think in terms of immediate electoral success, and a poor showing at the polls does not dissuade either the leadership or the grass-roots participants from continuing their quest for change in American society. Some of the notable third parties that are still active include the following:

1. The Socialist Labor party, started in 1877.
2. The Socialist party, founded in 1901.
3. The Communist party, started in 1919 as the radical left wing that split from the Socialist party.
4. The Socialist Workers' party, a Trotskyite group, started in 1938.
5. The Libertarian party, formed in 1972 and still an important minor party.

As we can see from their labels, several of these minor parties have been Marxist oriented. The most successful was Eugene Debs's Socialist party, which captured 6 percent of the popular vote for president in 1912 and elected more than a thousand candidates at the local level. About eighty mayors were affiliated with the Socialist party at one time or another. It owed much of its success to the corruption of big-city machines and to antiwar sentiment. Debs's

Eugene V. Debs, founder of the Socialist party. Why have socialist parties had so little success in the United States?

[10]This term is erroneous because sometimes there have been third, fourth, fifth, and even sixth parties, but it has endured and we will use it here.

DID YOU KNOW?

That the political party with the most seats in the House of Representatives chooses the Speaker of the House, makes any new rules it wants, gets a majority of the seats on each important committee and chooses their chairs, and hires most of the congressional staff?

Socialist party was vociferously opposed to American entry into World War I, an opposition shared by many Americans. The other more militant parties of the left (the Socialist Labor, Socialist Workers', and Communist parties) have never enjoyed wide electoral success.

At the other end of the ideological spectrum, the Libertarian party supports a laissez-faire capitalist economic program combined with a hands-off policy on regulating matters of moral conduct.

In 1986, another minor party created a sensation by capturing the Democratic nominations for lieutenant governor and secretary of state in Illinois. Supporters of Lyndon LaRouche, an ultraconservative, self-sponsored candidate for president, had submitted petitions for the offices as Democrats and were elected over the candidates of the regular Democratic party in the primary. The LaRouche candidates had spent only a few hundred dollars on their campaigns, running on the platform that AIDS victims should be quarantined and drug dealers subjected to capital punishment. With almost no publicity and unidentified by the news media or the Democratic party, the LaRouche candidates capitalized on their ballot positions and the lack of voter information. Other LaRouche followers undertook a similar strategy. After a few LaRouche victories the Democratic and Republican parties worked aggressively to identify the LaRouche supporters for the voters and all were defeated.

Spin-off Minor Parties

The most successful minor parties have been spun off from major parties. The impetus for these **spin-off parties,** or factions, has usually been a situation in which a particular personality was at odds with the major party. The most famous spin-off was the Bull Moose Progressive party, which split from the Republican party in 1912 over the candidate chosen to run for president. Theodore Roosevelt rallied his forces and announced the formation of the Progressive party, leaving the regular Republicans to support William Howard Taft. Although the party was not successful in winning the election for Roosevelt, it did succeed in splitting the Republican vote so that Democrat Woodrow Wilson won.

Among the Democrats in recent years, there have been three splinter third parties: (1) the Dixiecrat (States Rights) party of 1948, (2) Henry Wallace's Progressive party of 1948, and (3) the American Independent party supporting George Wallace in 1968.

The strategy employed by Wallace in the 1968 election was to deny Nixon or Humphrey the necessary majority in the electoral college. Many political scientists (but not all) believe that Humphrey still would have lost to Nixon in 1968, even if Wallace hadn't run, since most Wallace voters would probably have given their votes to Nixon. The American Independent party mostly emphasized racial issues and to a lesser extent foreign policy. Wallace received 9.9 million popular votes and 46 electoral votes.

Other Minor Parties

There have been numerous minor parties that have coalesced around specific issues or aims. The goal of the Prohibition party, started in 1869, was to ban the sale of liquor. The Free Soil party, in evidence from 1848 to 1852, was dedicated to preventing the spread of slavery.

SPIN-OFF PARTY
A new party formed by a dissident faction within a major political party. Usually, spin-off parties have emerged when a particular personality was at odds with the major party.

Teddy Roosevelt, founder of the Bull Moose party.

Some minor parties have had specific economic interests as their reason for being. When those interests are either met or made irrelevant by changing economic conditions, these minor parties disappear. Such was the case with the Greenback party, which lasted from 1876 to 1884. It was one of the most prominent farmer-labor parties that favored government intervention in the economy. Similar to the Greenbacks but with broader support was the Populist party, which lasted from about 1892 to 1908. Farmers were the backbone of this party, and agrarian reform was its goal. In 1892, it ran a presidential candidate, James Weaver, who received one million popular votes and 22 electoral votes. The Populists for the most part joined with the Democrats in 1896 when both parties endorsed the Democratic presidential candidate, William Jennings Bryan.

The Impact of Minor Parties

Minor parties clearly have had an impact on American politics. What is more difficult to ascertain is how great that impact has been. Simply by showing that third-party issues were taken over some years later by a major party really doesn't prove that the third party instigated the major party's change. The

DID YOU KNOW?

That during the 1987–88 election cycle, the Republican party raised $263.3 million compared to the $127.9 million raised by the Democratic party?

case for the importance of minor parties may be strongest for the splinter parties. Splinter parties do indeed force a major party to reassess its ideology and organization. There is general agreement that Teddy Roosevelt's Progressive party and LaFollette's Progressive party caused the major parties to take up business regulation as one of their major issues.

Calling the United States a two-party system is an oversimplification. The nature and names of the major parties have changed over time, and smaller parties have almost always enjoyed a moderate degree of success. Whether they are splinters from the major parties or expressions of social and economic issues not addressed adequately by factions within the major parties, the minor parties attest to the vitality and fluid nature of American politics.

■ IS THE PARTY OVER?

PARTY IDENTIFICATION
Linking oneself to a particular political party.

Figure 9-4 shows **party identification** as measured by standard polling techniques from 1937 to 1989. What is quite evident is the rise of the independent voter combined with a more recent surge of support for the Republican party, so that the traditional Democratic advantage in party identification is relatively minor today.

In the 1940s, only about 20 percent of voters classified themselves as independents. By 1975, this percentage had increased to a third, and more recent

FIGURE 9-4
Party Identification from 1937 to 1989
SOURCE: *The Gallup Report*, May 1987, (January/February 1985); *The Gallup Opinion Index*, July 1979, October 1967; *The Gallup Report*, May 1990.

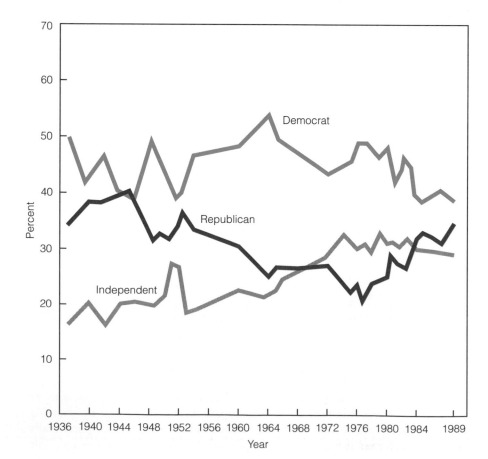

polls show it holding steady at about that level. The Democrats have at times captured the loyalty of about half the electorate, and the Republicans until 1960 had more than 30 percent support. By 1988, the Democrats could count on less than 40 percent and the Republicans more than a third of the electorate.

Not only have ties to the two major parties weakened in the last three decades, but also voters are less willing to vote a straight ticket, that is, to

TABLE 9-4
Political Party Identification, Cross Section, 1988

	Republican	Democrat	Independent
Sex			
Men	31%	37%	32%
Women	31	44	25
Age			
18–29	33	34	33
30–49	29	40	31
50 and over	31	46	23
Region			
East	29	45	26
Midwest	32	32	36
South	32	43	25
West	30	43	27
Race-ethnicity			
White	34	36	30
African American	10	74	16
Hispanic	21	57	22
Education			
Not high school graduate	21	51	28
High school graduate	31	41	28
College incomplete	31	39	30
College graduate	58	32	30
Occupation of chief wage earner			
Unskilled worker	25	46	29
Skilled worker	26	39	35
Manual worker	25	43	32
Clerical and sales	36	38	26
Professional and business	36	36	28
Household income			
Under $15,000	27	49	24
$15,000–$24,999	31	37	32
$25,000–$39,999	31	38	31
$40,000 and over	36	37	27
Religion			
Protestant	36	38	26
Catholic	24	46	30
Labor union			
Labor union family	23	49	28
Nonunion family	32	39	29
National	31	40	29

SOURCE: *The Gallup Poll,* 1988.

As party leader, President George Bush is expected to campaign for other Republican candidates. Here, he stumps for Clayton Williams, the unsuccessful candidate for governor in Texas. How important is Presidential assistance in state and local races?

TICKET SPLITTING
Voting for candidates of two or more parties for different offices. For example, a voter splits her ticket if she votes for a Republican presidential candidate and for a Democratic congressional candidate.

vote for all the candidates of one party. The percentage of voters who are *ticket splitters* has increased from 12 percent in 1952 to more than 28 percent in the presidential election of 1988. This trend, along with the increase in the number of voters who call themselves independents, suggests that parties have lost much of their hold on the loyalty of the voters. **Ticket splitting** and the rise of the independent voter have important policy effects. Since voters are quite likely to vote for a president of one party and a senator from another, it becomes less likely that one party will control both the executive and the legislature, thereby making conflict between the branches more frequent. Only in a situation like that of 1981, following the Reagan landslide, are members of Congress likely to follow the president's bidding eagerly.

There is considerable debate over the reasons for the upsurge in independent voters and split tickets. The increased importance of the media in American politics, the higher educational levels of Americans, and the mobility of American voters may all work to weaken party ties. What is clear is that the tendency to declare oneself an independent voter is more pronounced among some groups than others. Table 9-4 shows the breakdown of party identification in 1988 by demographic characteristics. As noted earlier, the youngest age groups, including those voters who are thirty or younger, are more likely to be Republican or independent than are older voters. Similarly, voters who have some college education are also more likely to be Republicans or independents than are those with a high school education or less.

GETTING INVOLVED

Electing Convention Delegates

The most exciting political party event, staged every four years, is the national convention. Surprising as it might seem, there are opportunities for the individual voter to become involved in nominating delegates to the national convention or in becoming such a delegate. For both the Republican and Democratic parties, most delegates must be elected at the local level—either the congressional district or the state legislative district. These elections take place at the party primary election or at a neighborhood or precinct caucus. If the delegates are elected in a primary, persons who want to run for these positions must file petitions with the board of elections in advance of the election. If you are interested in committing yourself to a particular presidential candidate and running for the delegate position, check with the local county committee or with the party's national committee about the rules you must follow.

It is even easier to get involved in the grass-roots politics of presidential caucuses. In some states, Iowa being the earliest and most famous one, delegates are first nominated at the local precinct caucus. According to the rules announced for the Iowa caucuses, anyone can participate in the caucus if he or she is eighteen years old, a resident of the precinct, and registered as a party member. These caucuses, as well as being the focus of national media attention in February, select delegates to the county convention who are pledged to specific presidential candidates. This is the first step toward going to the national convention.

At both the county caucus and convention level, both parties try to find younger members to fill some of the seats. Get in contact with the state or county political party to find out when the caucuses or primaries will be held. Then gather local supporters and friends and prepare to join in an occasion where political persuasion and debate are practiced at their best.

For further information about these opportunities (some states have caucuses and state conventions in every election year), contact the state party office or your local state legislator for specific dates and regulations or write to the national committees for their informational brochures on how to become a delegate.

Republican National Committee
Republican National Headquarters
310 1st Street, SE
Washington, D.C. 20003
202-484-6500

Democratic National Committee
Democratic National Headquarters
1625 Massachusetts Avenue, NW
Washington, D.C. 20036
202-797-5900

CHAPTER SUMMARY

1. A political party is a group of individuals who organize to win elections, to operate the government, and to determine public policy.

2. People join political parties for solidary, material, and purposive (or ideological) reasons.

3. Various party structures throughout the world grew out of historical events unique to each nation. Structures range from one major political party, as in Mexico, to a variety of political parties vying for control, as in Italy.

4. The evolution of our nation's political parties can be divided into six periods: (1) the creation and formation of political parties beginning in the 1790s; (2) the era of one-party rule, or personal politics, in the 1820s; (3) the period from Andrew Jackson's presidency to the Civil War, during which the Democrats and Whigs were the two solidly established national parties; (4) the post-Civil War period, ending in 1896 with solid control by the modern Republican party; (5) the progressive period,

from 1896 to 1921; and (6) the modern period, from Franklin Roosevelt's New Deal until today.

5. In theory, each of the American political parties has a standard, pyramid-shaped organization with a hierarchical command structure. In reality, the formal structure resembles a layer cake with autonomous strata more than it does pyramid.

6. The national party organization holds a national convention every four years to select presidential and vice presidential candidates, to write a party platform, to choose a national committee, and to conduct party business.

7. Each party chooses a national standing committee, elected by the individual state parties, to direct and coordinate party activities during the following four years. A national chairperson is chosen to manage the national election campaign.

8. Each state has a unique party organization, but each has a chairperson, a committee, and a number of local organizations.

9. The local party machinery is made up of district leaders, precinct or ward captains, and party workers. In the past, the local organization was held together by the institution or patronage—rewarding the party faithful with government jobs or contracts and immigrants and the poor with important social services.

10. Two major parties have dominated the political landscape in the United States for almost two centuries. The reasons for this include: (a) the historical foundations of the system, (b) the self-perpetuation of the parties, (c) the commonality of views among Americans, (d) the winner-take-all electoral system, and (e) state and federal laws favoring the two-party system.

11. Minor parties have emerged from time to time, often as dissatisfied splinter groups from within major parties that acted as barometers of changes in political moods.

12. Various enduring minor parties arose during this century with strong ideological foundations from both ends of the ideological spectrum.

13. Spin-off parties, or factions, usually have occurred when a particular personality was at odds with the major party, as Teddy Roosevelt's differences with the Republican party resulted in formation of the Bull Moose Progressive party. Numerous other minor parties have formed around single issues, such as the Prohibition party.

14. Minor parties have an impact on American politics by forcing major parties to reassess their ideologies and organizations or to take up particular issues.

15. From 1937 until recently, independent voters have formed an increasing proportion of the electorate, with a consequent decline of strongly Democratic or strongly Republican voters. The upsurge in independent voters has been seen most dramatically among new voters—the young and previously disenfranchised. In the 1980s, support increased for the Republican party.

QUESTIONS FOR REVIEW AND DISCUSSION

1. Some commentators have suggested that political parties are becoming obsolete in the United States. What functions of the parties are now being performed by the media? By the individual candidate or campaign organization? By the national government?

2. Although the political parties seem to have a formal organization and structure, the national offices are usually considered to be unimportant. Why is the power in American parties primarily at the county and state level? Why can't the national party control local parties?

3. What are the major differences on issues and in membership between the Democratic and Republican parties? What elements in the American political system tend to make them both move toward the political center?

SELECTED REFERENCES

Robert Kuttner, *The Life of the Party: Democratic Prospects in 1988 and Beyond* (New York: Penguin, 1987). The author argues that the Democratic Party has pursued a self-defeating strategy of moving away from progressive economic populism and towards becoming a technocratic, managerial party imitating the Republican party.

Seymour Martin Lipset, ed., *Party Coalitions in the 1980s* (San Francisco: Institute for Contemporary Studies, 1981). Describes parties as coalitions of voters and interests throughout American history. Special emphasis is placed on the 1980 election and the possible realignment of the electorate.

David R. Mayhew, *Placing Parties in American Politics* (Princeton, N.J.: Princeton University Press, 1986). Using sketches of each of the fifty states, this fascinating book analyzes the form, distribution, and effect of local political parties in the United States.

Steven J. Rosenstone, Roy L. Behr, and Edward H. Lazarus, *Third Parties in America: Citizen Response to Major Party Failure* (Princeton, N.J.: Princeton University Press, 1984). The authors' general theory of third-party voting is based on the factors of major party decline, attractive third-party candidates, and new voters with no loyalty to the two major parties.

James L. Sundquist, *Dynamics of the Party System: Alignment and Realignment of Political Parties in the United States* (Washington, D.C.: Brookings Institution, 1973). An analysis of three major realignments in party strength, why they happened, and what they meant.

CHAPTER 10

CAMPAIGNS, CANDIDATES, AND ELECTIONS

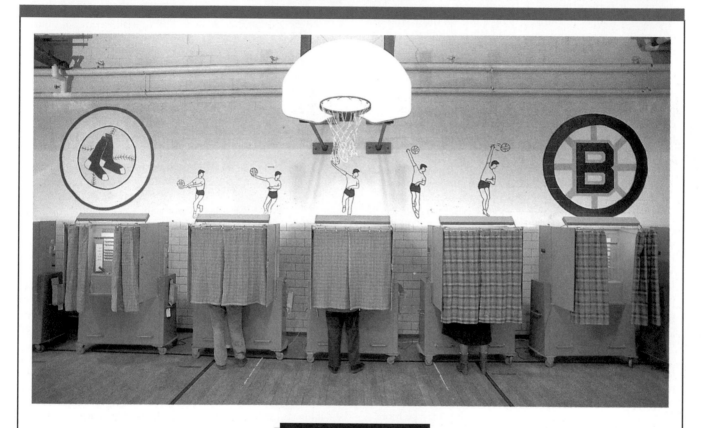

CHAPTER CONTENTS

WHAT IF . . . VOTING WERE COMPULSORY?

Casting a ballot is often seen as the prime symbol of a democracy. It is the way we choose our leaders, a source of legitimacy for our government, and a means by which citizens can influence public policy. For most Americans, voting is the only form of political participation they experience. Yet a large number of Americans do not vote. In 1990, only about one-third of those old enough to vote actually showed up at the polls to select their representatives and senators. In the 1988 presidential elections, only half of those eligible actually voted. Voter participation in the United States appears to be much lower than in other democracies, where 80 to 90 percent of the population go to the polls on voting day.

In the United States, our laws give Americans the right to vote, but they do not require us to vote. In some countries, voting is compulsory. What if we had

such a law making it compulsory for all eligible citizens to vote, perhaps by levying a fine on those who did not? What would the outcome be if *all* eligible U.S. citizens *had* to vote?

The immediate effects might not be that significant. Studies indicate that nonvoters' attitudes are similar to those of voters, so the results of elections would likely be very much the same. There would be about the same proportion of Democrats, about 4 percent fewer Republicans, and a similar proportion of independent voters.* Since nonvoters are usually less interested in politics and lack firm positions on issues, the new voters would probably not change issue preferences in the electorate. Nonvoters are not distinctly liberal or conservative.

The longer-term consequences are harder to calculate, but they may be more significant. Those who stay away from the polls tend to be the least educated, the poor, the young, the elderly,

minorities, southerners, and the unemployed. Parties and candidates do not have to make specific appeals to these groups because of their low voter turnout. But if these groups forming distinct constituencies were compelled by law to vote, their interests might be

given more attention. Perhaps the population would be better represented on the whole.

Some argue that the country would be worse off if its least-interested and least-informed citizens voted, that people who consider voting more trouble than it is worth are likely to make poor choices. Further, it would be unhealthy for a democracy to compel people to vote.

Others say that voting is not only a right but an obligation in a country that claims to have a representative government. Through elections, the people express approval or disapproval of the government's actions, and there would be a stronger sense of the government's legitimacy and of the worthiness of its elected officials if everyone voted. They would argue that where almost half the population avoids the polls, democracy functions badly.

*Raymond Wolfinger and Steven Rosenstone, *Who Votes?* (New Haven, Conn.: Yale University Press, 1980) ch. 6.

1. *How would compulsory voting change the outcomes of national elections?*
2. *Which groups might be better represented? Which interests might be poorly served by compulsory voting?*

■ THE PEOPLE WHO RUN FOR POLITICAL OFFICE

In the winter of 1988, thirteen men spent hundreds of hours tramping through the fields and farms of Iowa in search of voters who would support their bids for the presidency in the Iowa caucuses. Throughout the coldest winter of the last thirty-five years, seven Democrats and six Republicans did whatever they could to attract the attention of Iowa voters and the journalists who covered the campaign. By the day of the caucuses, February 8, virtually every candidate had posed with Iowa livestock, sat on a fence rail, and eaten a pork chop. Bruce Babbitt rode a bicycle in near-zero weather for almost twenty-three miles, while Michael Dukakis knocked on doors accompanied by the movie actor Richard Gere. The morning after the caucuses, the results were in: Bob Dole won the most Republican delegates and Richard Gephardt won the Democratic caucuses by a narrow margin over Paul Simon. Two months later, both men dropped out of the race after it became evident that George Bush and Michael Dukakis would be the nominees.

This discussion of the 1988 Iowa caucuses raises two important questions: Why would anyone want to undergo such an experience, and why does the American political system require such an endurance test? The answer to the first question lies in the forces that motivate individuals to run for office at all levels of government, and the answer to the second lies in the changing nature of the party system. There is no doubt that the prizes of the presidency—power, status, a place in history—make it the most sought-after office in the land. Furthermore, there is an excitement that seems to be intoxicating to the candidate and to the staff in the presidential race. Edmund Muskie described this feeling to journalist Elizabeth Drew:

> It's a very heady business, really, to suddenly find yourself near the top, and to breathe constantly the atmosphere of those who simply take it for granted that you're going to be the next President of the United States.[1]

Why They Run

People who choose to run for office can be divided into two groups—those who are "self-starters" and those who are recruited, or externally instigated. The volunteers, or self-starters, get involved in political activities to further their careers, to carry out specific political programs, or in response to certain issues or events. The campaign of Senator Eugene McCarthy in 1968 to deny Lyndon Johnson's renomination was rooted in McCarthy's opposition to the Vietnam war. His campaign became the model for many other peace activists in the years that followed.

Issues are important, but self-interest and personal goals—status, career objectives, prestige, and income—are central in motivating some candidates to enter political life. Political scientist Joseph Schlesinger suggests that personal ambition is a major force in politics, as political office is often seen as the stepping stone to achieving certain career goals. A lawyer or an insurance agent may run for office only once or twice and then return to private life with enhanced status. Other politicians may aspire to long-term political office—for example, county offices like commissioner or sheriff that sometimes offer attractive opportunities for power, status, and income and that are in

Diane Feinstein, the unsuccessful Democratic candidate for governor of California in 1990.

---

[1]"Running," *The New Yorker*, December 1, 1975, p. 61.

Dwight D. Eisenhower campaigning for president in 1952. Why would few presidential candidates take the time to ride in a parade today?

themselves career goals. Finally, we think of ambition as the desire for ever-more-important offices and higher status. Politicians who run for lower office and then set their sights on Congress or a governorship may be said to have "progressive" ambitions.[2]

Although we tend to pay far more attention to the flamboyant politician or to the personal characteristics of those with presidential ambitions than to their "lesser" colleagues, it is important to note that there are far more opportunities to run for office than there are citizens eager to take advantage of them. To fill the slate of candidates for election to such jobs as mosquito-abatement district commissioner, the political party must recruit individuals to run. The problem of finding candidates is compounded in states or cities where the majority party is so dominant that the minority candidates have virtually no chance of winning. In these situations, candidates are recruited by party leaders on the basis of loyalty to the organization and civic duty.

Who Runs?

There are few constitutional restrictions on who can become a candidate in the United States. As detailed in the Constitution, the requirements for a national office are as follows:

1. President: Must be a natural-born citizen and have attained the age of thirty-five years and be a resident of the country for fourteen years by the time of inauguration.

[2]Joseph Schlesinger, *Ambition in Politics: Political Careers in the United States* (Chicago: Rand-McNally, 1966), p. 6.

2. Vice President: Must be a natural-born citizen, have attained the age of thirty-five years, and not be a resident of the same state as the candidate for president.

3. Senator: Must be a citizen for at least nine years, have attained the age of thirty by the time he or she takes office, and be a resident of the state from which elected.

4. Representative: Must be a citizen for at least seven years, have attained the age of twenty-five by the time of taking office, and be a resident of the state from which elected.

The qualifications for state legislators are set by the state constitutions and likewise relate to age, place of residence, and citizenship. (Usually, the requirements for the upper house are somewhat higher than for the lower house.) The legal qualifications for running for governor or other state office are similar.

In spite of these minimal legal qualifications for office at both the national and state levels, a quick look at the slate of candidates in any election—or at the U.S. House of Representatives—will reveal that not all segments of the population take advantage of these opportunities. Holders of political office in the United States are overwhelmingly white and male. Until this century, politicians were also of northern European origin and predominantly Protestant. Laws enforcing segregation in the South and many border states, as well as laws that effectively denied voting rights to African Americans, made it impossible to elect African-American public officials in many areas where African Americans constituted a significant portion of the population. Since the passage of major civil rights legislation in 1964 and later, the number of African-American public officials has increased throughout the United States.

Until recently, women were generally considered to be suited only for lower-level offices, such as state legislator and school board member. The last ten years have seen a tremendous increase in the number of women who run for office, not only at the state level, but for the U.S. Congress as well. In 1990, 63 women ran for Congress and 31 were elected. Whereas African Americans were restricted from running for office by both law and custom, women were generally excluded by the agencies of recruitment—parties and interest groups—because they were thought to have no chance of winning or because they had not worked their way up through the party organization. They also had a more difficult time raising campaign funds. Today, it is clear that women are just as likely as men to participate in most political activities, and a majority of Americans say they would vote for a qualified woman or for an African American for president of the United States. The changing attitudes of voters toward women and African Americans holding high political office are illustrated in Figure 10-1.

Not only are candidates for office more likely to be male and white than female or African American, but they are also likely to be professionals, particularly lawyers, businesspeople, and teachers. Political campaigning and officeholding are simply easier for some occupational and economic groups than for others and can make a valuable contribution to certain careers. Lawyers, for example, have more flexible schedules than other professionals, can take time off for campaigning, and can leave their jobs to hold public office full time. Furthermore, holding political office is good publicity for their professional practice, and they usually have partners or associates to keep the

DID YOU KNOW?

That John Kennedy's margin of victory over Richard Nixon was less than two-tenths of one percent of the popular vote in the 1960 presidential election?

Geraldine Ferraro, the first woman to be nominated for vice president by a major party.

FIGURE 10-1
Changing Attitudes Toward an African American or Female Presidential Candidate
Do more people *say* they would vote for a woman or African American than actually would cast such a ballot?
SOURCE: *The Gallup Poll*, 1983, p. 114; *The Gallup Poll*, 1987, pp. 191–192.

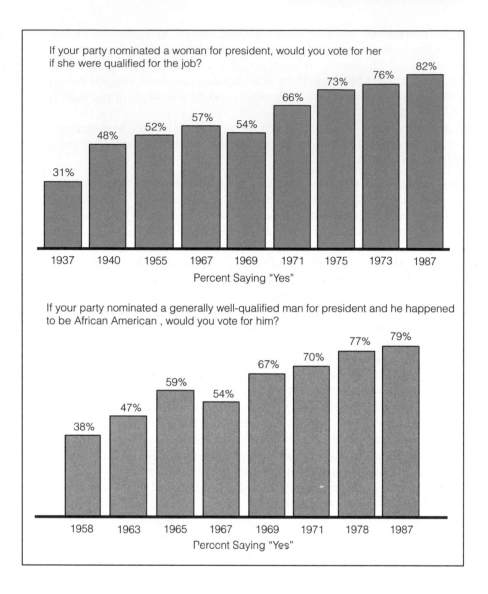

firm going while they are in office. Perhaps most importantly, many jobs that lawyers aspire to—federal or state judgeships, state attorney offices, or work in a federal agency—can be attained by political appointment. Such appointments most likely come to loyal partisans who have served their party by running for and holding office. Personal ambitions, then, are well served for certain groups by entering the political arena, whereas it could be a sacrifice for others whose careers demand full-time attention for many years.

■ THE MODERN CAMPAIGN MACHINE

American political campaigns are extravagant, year-long events that produce campaign buttons and posters for collectors, hours of film and sound to be relayed by the media, and eventually winning candidates who become the public officials of the nation. Campaigns are also enormously expensive; the total expenditures for 1990 were estimated at well over $1 billion for all congressional and local races in that year. Political campaigns exhaust candidates, their staff members, and the journalists covering the campaign—to say nothing of the public's patience.

The Changing Campaign

Campaigns seem to be getting longer and more excessive each year. The costs for candidates, primarily for media coverage, are rising; the candidates announce earlier; and the number of primaries, caucuses, and "beauty contests" increases with each presidential election. The goal of all this frantic activity is the same for all campaigns—to convince voters to choose a candidate or a slate of candidates for office. Part of the reason for the increased intensity of campaigns in the last decade is that they have changed from being party-centered to being candidate-centered in response to changes in the electoral system and to technological innovations such as computers (see Highlight, Politicians Discover the Computer Age).

To run a successful and persuasive campaign, the candidate's organization must be able to raise funds for the effort, to get coverage from the media, to produce and use paid political commercials and advertising, to schedule the candidate's time effectively with constituent groups and prospective supporters, to convey the candidate's position on the issues, to research the opposing candidate, and to get the voters to go to the polls. When party identification was stronger among voters and before the advent of television campaigning, a strong party organization on the local, state, or national level could furnish most of the services and expertise that the candidate needed. Political parties provided the funds for campaigning until the 1970s; parties used their precinct organizations to distribute literature, to register voters, and to get out the vote on election day. Less effort was spent on advertising for a single candidate's positions and character because the party label communicated that information to many of the voters.

One of the most important reasons that campaigns no longer depend on parties is that fewer people identify with them (see Chapter 9). Whereas in 1952, for example, about 47 percent of the voters declared themselves Democrats and 27 percent said they were Republicans, in 1988 only 40 percent claimed to be Democrats while 31 percent were Republicans. In 1952, only 22 percent of the voters were **independent voters;** in 1988 almost 29 percent classified themselves this way. Independent voters include not only those voters who are well educated and issue oriented but also many voters who are not very interested in politics or well-informed about candidates or issues. It is during the campaign that such voters can obtain the most information about the political stance of each candidate. There are two other important reasons for the relative weakness of political parties in campaigning. First is the inability of local and state parties to support campaigns financially owing to legal limits placed on campaign contributions and the related public financing of presidential campaigns. Second is the overwhelming importance of the media in campaigns—both for news coverage and for commercials. Media techniques are much more easily applied to individual candidates than to political parties, although the Republicans—in the first major advertising effort ever conducted by a political party—launched a series of theme commercials in 1980, urging viewers to "Vote Republican for a Change."

MAMIE START PACKING the KENNEDYS are COMING

INDEPENDENT VOTERS
Voters who disavow any party affiliation and cast their ballots based on their views of who is the best candidate.

A candidate's campaign staff using a computer to track the Iowa caucuses. Keeping track of individual voters makes possible personal appeals by candidates.

HIGHLIGHT

Politicians Discover the Computer Age

In a game in which handshaking and the personal touch are considered to be the most important way to gain votes, computers have finally come into their own as an important adjunct for the players. In the 1988 presidential campaign, desktop computers finally replaced typewriters. Campaign managers are increasingly aware of the wide range of tasks that computers can do for them. Experts estimate that some three hundred companies currently specialize in computer services and software for political campaigns.

Computers have taken on an amazing variety of jobs. Taking a cue from the business sector, Richard Gephardt used computers to dial voters in Michigan and give them a tape-recorded message. The Gephardt campaign also used computers to establish a network among all of the campaign offices with electronic mailboxes for the workers.

One of the things that computers do best is to sort voters into categories— male, female, upper income, African American, and so on. The biggest use for this talent is to create specialized mailing lists for fund raising. The Dukakis presidential campaign also used this sorting ability to create a bank of information about convention delegates. The Bush campaign's computer went a step further; it sent each newly elected Bush delegate a letter signed by the vice president, a questionnaire, and a certificate honoring his or her selection. The computer also kept information about each delegate's birthday, anniversaries, and other special information. Of course, the computer automatically prepared the correct letter or card and sent it to the delegate over the vice president's signature.

Other, more complicated uses for the computer include the Reagan-Bush computerized buying plan for political advertising. Special software was developed to keep track of rates, pricing, and scheduling data for the nation's television markets. The Dukakis campaign used the computer to store and categorize every news story about the presidential campaign. These stories were indexed so that any one could be recalled for reference in a speech or press release. It appears that, in addition to a media wizard and master fundraiser, campaigns from now on will also need a high-powered computer specialist.

The Professional Campaign

Whether the candidate is running for state legislator, for governor, for the U.S. Congress, or for the presidency, every campaign has some fundamental tasks to accomplish. What is most striking about today's campaigns is that many of these tasks are now put into the hands of paid professionals rather than volunteers or amateur politicians.

The most sought-after and possibly the most criticized expert is the **political consultant,** who for a large fee devises a campaign strategy, thinks up a campaign theme, and possibly chooses the campaign colors and candidate's portrait for all literature to be distributed. It is the paid consultant who suggests new campaign ideas to the candidate day by day and who decides what new advertising spots are needed. The consultants and the firms they represent are not politically neutral; most will work only for candidates from one party or only for candidates of a particular ideological persuasion. There are a couple of so-called "superfirms" that have reached the pinnacle of campaign management. These firms are so effective that they do not go to candidates; rather, the candidates must come to them. Two California firms, Spencer-Roberts, and Whitaker and Baker, handle Republican candidates only. It was one of them, Spencer-Roberts, to whom Ronald Reagan went in 1965 when he was thinking about running for governor in California. Reagan chose well. Spencer-Roberts helped him defeat Governor Edmund Brown. For the Democrats, nationally known consultants include Joseph Napolitan Associates, Peter Hart, and Patrick Caddell.

POLITICAL CONSULTANT
A paid professional hired to devise a campaign strategy and manage a campaign. Image building is the crucial task of the political consultant.

As more and more political campaigns are run exclusively by professional campaign managers, critics of the campaign system are becoming increasingly vociferous. Their worry is this: Professional campaign managers are concerned almost solely with personalities rather than with philosophies and issues. A professional campaign manager is a public relations person. He or she looks at an upcoming election as a contest of personalities rather than as a contest between two opposing parties or opposing principles. According to critics, professional campaign managers are willing to do anything to get their candidate to win, even if this means reshaping the public image of the candidate so that it bears little relation to reality.

Image building is seen to be the crucial task of campaign consultants, and is increasingly necessary to a successful campaign. Using public and private opinion polls as guidelines, consultants mold the candidate's image to meet the campaign's special needs. Image construction is a far cry from the "ear to the ground" technique used by party leaders in the past to select candidates and platforms. Yet the alternative to such image building is almost certain failure—regardless of the candidate's stand on significant issues. As Patrick Caddell, Jimmy Carter's pollster and consultant, once lamented; "Too many good people have been defeated because they tried to substitute substance for style."[3]

■ THE STRATEGY OF WINNING

The goal of every political campaign is the same: to win the election. In the United States, unlike some European countries, there are no rewards for a candidate who comes in second; the winner takes all. The campaign organization must plan a strategy to maximize the candidate's chances of winning. In making these strategic choices, a number of factors should be considered. One of the most important concerns is how well known the candidate is. If he or she is a highly visible incumbent, there may be little need for campaigning except to remind the voters of the officeholder's good deeds. If, however, the candidate is an unknown challenger or a largely unfamiliar character attacking a well-known public figure, the campaign must devise a strategy to get the candidate before the public.

In the case of the **independent candidate** or the candidate representing a minor party, the problem of name recognition is serious. There are usually a number of **third-party candidates** in each presidential election (see Table 10-1 for a list of those campaigning in the 1988 presidential race), and such candidates must present an overwhelming case for the voter to reject the major party candidate. Both the Democratic and the Republican candidates use the strategic ploy of labeling third-party candidates as "not serious" and therefore not worth the voter's time.

Because neither of the major parties can claim a majority of voters in its camp, the task that faces them is threefold. Each party and its presidential candidate must reinforce the party loyalty of its followers, motivate the undecideds or independents to vote for their candidate, and—the most difficult task—try to convince some followers of the other major party to cross party lines. The Republicans, having fewer adherents than the Democrats, spend

Precinct worker talking to a voter outside the polling place. What is the likely effect of giving voters a sample ballot?

IMAGE BUILDING
Using public and private opinion polls, the candidate's image is molded to meet the particular needs of the campaign. Image building is done primarily through the media.

INDEPENDENT CANDIDATE
A political candidate who is not affiliated with a political party.

THIRD-PARTY CANDIDATE
A political candidate running under the banner of a party other than the two major political parties.

[3]Quoted in Peter Woll, *Behind the Scenes in American Government: Personalities and Politics* (Boston: Little, Brown, 1983), p. 128.

DID YOU KNOW?

That it cost $40,000 a month plus expenses for Bob Dole to retain a political consultant for the 1988 presidential campaign?

more time and money trying to attract independents and Democrats, whereas the Democrats know they can win if they can secure all of the votes of their party plus a goodly share of the independents. To accomplish these tasks, the campaign organization, whether at the presidential level or otherwise, plans a mix of strategies using the media through campaign appearances, debates, and position papers to sway the voters.

The Value of Campaign Polls

Since the decision-making power for presidential nominations has shifted from the elites to the masses, one of the major sources of information for both the media and the candidates is polls. Poll taking is widespread during the primaries. Often presidential hopefuls will have private polls taken to make sure there is at least some chance they could be nominated and, if nominated, elected. Also, since the party nominees depend on polls to fine-tune their campaigns, during the presidential campaign itself continual polls are taken, not only by the regular pollsters—Roper, Harris, Gallup, and others—but also privately by each candidate's campaign organization.

In the 1980 presidential campaign, Jimmy Carter relied on constant rounds of polling conducted by his personal pollster, Patrick Caddell. Candidate Ronald Reagan used the skills of Richard Wirthlin and his staff to measure the pulse of the voters. Candidate George Bush used Bob Teeter. These private polls, as opposed to the independent public polls conducted by Gallup and

TABLE 10-1
Third Party Candidates in the 1988 Presidential Election Campaign
How many of these candidates received television news coverage?

Political Party	Candidate	Number of States Candidate was on the Ballot	Vote Totals
American	Delmar Dennis	2	3,475
American Independent	James C. Griffin	1	27,818
Consumer	Eugene J. McCarthy	4	30,905
Grassroots	Jack Herer	1	1,949
Independent	Louie G. Youngkeit	1	372
National Economic	Lyndon H. LaRouche, Jr.	12 plus D.C.	25,542
Libertarian	Ron E. Paul	46 plus D.C.	432,116
New Alliance	Lenora B. Fulani	50 plus D.C.	217,219
Peace and Freedom	Herbert Lewin	3	10,370
Populist	David E. Duke	12	47,047
Prohibition	Earl Dodge	4	8,002
Right to Life	William A. Marra	1	20,504
Socialist	Willa Kenoyer	6	3,882
Socialist Workers	James Warren	15 plus D.C.	15,604
Third World Assembly	John G. Martin	D.C.	236
Worker's League	Ed Winn	8 plus D.C.	18,662
Workers World	Larry Holmes	5	7,846

SOURCE: *Congressional Quarterly Weekly Report*, November 5, 1988, p. 3184.

PROFILE

Mario Cuomo

"If you can make compassion plausible to them and useful, then they are a compassionate people."

There are few politicians today who feel as comfortable about discussing philosophy as they do with shaking hands on the campaign trail. Mario Cuomo, the Democratic governor of New York, is one such official. Described by one political veteran as "a statesman ahead of his time," Cuomo mystified the press in 1988 by declaring that he was not a candidate for the Democratic presidential nomination—and then acting consistently with that pledge by neither seeking the nomination nor encouraging a draft. He is still seen as a possible candidate for that office in 1992, however.

Cuomo has generated much attention for reasons other than his intellectual bent and his ability to impress voters as more than a mere politician. His biography reads like a latter-day version of Abraham Lincoln's rise from log-cabin origins to high public office: The

son of penniless Italian immigrants, Cuomo raised himself from his humble origins by hard work and study, eventually earning a degree in law from St. Johns University in New York City. He did not run for public office until the age of forty-three, and then lost his first three elections. Eventually, Cuomo was elected lieutenant governor of New York state in 1978, then becoming governor in 1982 by a razor-thin electoral margin.

During his political career, Mario Cuomo's Italian heritage and his deeply ingrained Catholic religious beliefs have both helped and hurt him. Like John Kennedy before him, Cuomo has been at pains to emphasize that his religion in no way conflicts with his secular conception of public office. He took the controversial step of declaring that the government should not restrict a woman's ability to obtain an abortion—a position that may have helped dispel any image of him as a "Catholic politician," but that estranged him from both the church and his own political base in New York City.

During a period in which political liberals have been widely attacked for their ideals, Cuomo has unabashedly declared his belief that government should actively work to relieve the problems of minorities and the poor. At the same time, he has gained a reputation for political moderation. Cuomo supporters believe that the governor's brand of pragmatic liberalism might still be a political formula that will appeal both to the Democratic party and the nation as a whole during the next presidential campaign.

others, are for the exclusive and secret use of the candidate and his or her campaign organization.

By polling the potential voters in the state or nation, the candidate can find out his or her strengths and weaknesses and attempt to address problem areas through campaign advertising. As the election approaches, many candidates use **tracking polls,** which are polls taken almost every day, to find out how well they are competing for votes. Tracking polls, by indicating how well the campaign is going, enable consultants to fine-tune the advertising and the candidate's speeches in the last days of the campaign.

TRACKING POLLS
Polls taken for the candidate on a nearly daily basis as election day approaches.

■ WHERE DOES THE MONEY COME FROM?

In a book published in 1932 entitled *Money in Elections,* Louise Overacker had the following to say about campaign financing:

DID YOU KNOW?

That voter turnout in presidential elections as a proportion of eligible voters declined every year from 1960 to 1980?

The financing of elections in a democracy is a problem which is arousing increasing concern. Many are beginning to wonder if present-day methods of raising and spending campaign funds do not clog the wheels of our elaborately constructed mechanism of popular control, and if democracies do not inevitably become plutocracies.[4]

Although writing more than fifty years ago, Overacker touched on a sensitive issue in American political campaigns: the connection between money and elections. It is estimated that over $2 billion was spent at all levels of campaigning in 1988. At the federal level, a total of more than $248 million is estimated to have been spent in races for the House of Representatives, $180 million in senatorial races, and $220 million in the presidential campaign. Except for the presidential campaign in the general election, all of the other money had to be provided by the candidates and their families, borrowed, or raised by other means. For the general presidential campaign, most of the money comes from the federal government.

The road to election is long and takes, among other things, a lot of money (see Highlight, Some Big Spenders . . .). That money, as we have seen, is used for TV commercials, media consultants, campaign managers, and a host of other professional services. According to Mat Reese, president of Mat Reese and Associates, a campaign management firm, the single most important barrier in running for the House (and presumably the Senate) is the ability to pay for a modern campaign. Reese says he spends a lot of his time telling potential candidates that they can't afford to run:

> I've seen a lot of people with $50,000 in cash who can't raise another $250,000. I get almost rich men in here all the time, who say they've got $50,000 or $75,000 of their own money to run for Congress. And I have to be the one to tell them that that isn't enough.[5]

[4]Louise Overacker, *Money in Elections,* (New York: Macmillan, 1932), p. vii.
[5]Quoted in Walter Shapiro, "A House Full of Millionaires," *Harpers,* July 1982, p. 50.

How effective are signs like these?

HIGHLIGHT

Some Big Spenders in the History of Campaign Spending

Back in 1896, Boies Penrose spent more than half a million dollars (over $8.5 million in today's currency) to win a Senate seat from Pennsylvania. Most of that money went into bribes, because senators were not popularly elected but chosen by the state legislatures.

In 1980, Governor Jay Rockefeller of West Virginia spent more than $12 million on his reelection campaign. His opponent, Governor Arch Moore, used this fact to advantage in his slogan, "Make him spend it all, Arch."

By 1988, the amount of money spent for congressional campaigns had risen to unbelievable proportions. Can-

didates for the House of Representatives spent more than $243 million, and senatorial candidates spent $182 million, an average of $1.8 million per candidate. Spending enormous sums of money, however, does not guarantee victory, particularly when the money is spent to challenge a popular incumbent. In 1988, the most expensive race took place in California where Ed Zshau spent $11.7 million to challenge Alan Cranston. Cranston, the incumbent senator, spent $11 million to keep his seat.

The other big spenders in the 1988 senatorial campaign were:

- Pete Wilson, Rep., California (incumbent), $13 million;
- Connie Mack, Rep., Florida, $5.2 million;
- Frank Lautenberg, Dem., New Jersey, $7.3 million;
- Bob Graham, Dem., Florida (challenger), $6.1 million.

Campaigns in the House of Representatives are, on the average, much less expensive than in the Senate. However, spending more than a million dollars to win or retain a House seat is not unusual.

Although the total number of dollars being spent on financing campaigns is certainly not decreasing, the way in which campaigns are financed has changed rather dramatically in the last few years. In the wake of the scandals uncovered after the 1972 Watergate break-in, Congress and the Supreme Court reshaped the nature of campaign financing. It was discovered during the Watergate investigations that large amounts of money had been illegally funneled to Nixon's Campaign to Reelect the President (CREEP). Congress acted quickly to prevent such a situation occurring again. After all, those who make large campaign contributions presumably require something in return.[6]

There have been a variety of federal **corrupt practices acts** designed to regulate campaign financing. The first, passed in 1925, limited primary and general election expenses for congressional candidates. In addition, it required disclosure of election expenses and in principle put controls on contributions by corporations. However, numerous loopholes were found in the restrictions on contributions, and the acts proved to be ineffective.

In 1939, the **Hatch Act** (Political Activities Act of 1939) was passed in another attempt to control political influence buying. That act forbade a political committee to spend more than $3 million in any campaign and limited individual contributions to a committee to $5,000. Of course, such restrictions were easily circumvented by creating additional committees.

CORRUPT PRACTICES ACTS
A series of acts passed by Congress in an attempt to limit and regulate the size and sources of contributions and expenditures in political campaigns.

HATCH ACT
Passed in 1939, this act forbids a political committee to spend more than $3 million in any campaign and limits individual contributions to a committee to $5,000. The act was designed to control political influence buying.

The Federal Election Campaign Acts of 1972 and 1974

It wasn't until the 1970s that more effective regulation of campaign financing was undertaken. The **Federal Election Campaign Act of 1972** essentially replaced all past laws and instituted a major reform. The act placed no limit

FEDERAL ELECTION CAMPAIGN ACT OF 1972
An act to control the raising and spending of funds for political campaigns.

[6]See Chapter 8 for a discussion of the effective use of campaign contributions from the dairy lobby in obtaining a multimillion-dollar increase in federal dairy support prices.

on overall spending, but restricted the amount that could be spent on mass media advertising, including television. It limited the amount that candidates and their families could contribute to their own campaigns and required disclosure of all contributions and expenditures in excess of $100. In principle, the 1972 act limited the role of labor unions and corporations in political campaigns. It also provided for a voluntary $1 check-off on federal income tax returns for general campaign funds to be used by major party candidates (first applied in the 1976 campaign).

But the act still did not go far enough. In 1974, Congress passed another Federal Election Campaign Act. It did the following:

1. Created the **Federal Election Commission,** consisting of six nonpartisan administrators whose duties are to enforce compliance with the requirements of the act.

2. Provided public financing for presidential primaries and general elections. Any candidate running for president who is able to obtain sufficient contributions in at least twenty states can obtain a subsidy from the U.S. Treasury to help pay for primary campaigns. Each major party was given $9.2 million for the national convention in 1988. The major party candidates have federal support for almost all of their expenses, provided they are willing to accept campaign-spending limits.

3. Limited presidential campaign spending. Any candidate accepting federal support has to agree to limit campaign expenditures to the amount prescribed by federal law.

4. Limited contributions. Citizens can contribute up to $1,000 to each candidate in each federal election or primary; the total limit of all contributions from an individual is $25,000 per year. Groups can contribute up to a maximum of $5,000 to a candidate in any election.

5. Required disclosure. Periodic reports must be filed by each candidate with the Federal Election Commission, listing who contributed, how much was spent, and what the money was spent for.

The 1972 act limited the amount that each individual could spend on his or her own behalf. Senator Jim Buckley of New York challenged that aspect of the law, and the Supreme Court declared the provision unconstitutional in 1976.[7]

The Impact of the 1974 Act.   Who would benefit by severe limitations on the amount an individual could spend on her or his own campaign and the total amount that could be spent on a campaign altogether? Obviously, incumbents would benefit by such restrictions. Unfortunately for congressional incumbents, the 1976 Supreme Court decision eliminated restrictions on campaign spending for congressional seats. The Court ruled that the overall campaign-spending ceilings infringed First Amendment rights, and in a second opinion it held that it was unconstitutional to restrict in any way the amount congressional candidates or their immediate families could spend on their own behalf: "The candidate, no less than any other person, has a First Amendment right to engage in the discussion of public issues and vigorously and tirelessly to advocate his own election." The Court let stand the 1974 limits on individual contributions and on contributions by groups such as **political action com-**

FEDERAL ELECTION COMMISSION
Created by the 1972 Federal Election Campaign Act to enforce compliance with the requirements of the act; the commission consists of six nonpartisan administrators.

POLITICAL ACTION COMMITTEES (PACs)
Committees set up by and representing corporations, labor unions, or special interest groups; PACs raise and give campaign donations on behalf of the organizations or groups they represent.

[7]*Buckley v. Valeo,* 424 U.S. 1 (1976).

mittees (PACs). Candidates who do not want to have to depend on the kindness of strangers can do something else—take out loans.

The Growth in Political Action Committees (PACs). The 1974 act, as modified by certain amendments in 1976, allows corporations, labor unions, and special interest groups to set up political action committees (PACs) to raise money for candidates. For a PAC to be legitimate, the money must be raised from at least fifty volunteer donors and must be given to at least five candidates in the federal election. Each corporation or each union is limited to one PAC. As you might imagine, corporate PACs obtain funds from executives, employees, and stockholders in their firms, and unions obtain PAC funds from their members.

On March 27, 1990, in the case of *Austin* v. *Michigan State Chamber of Commerce,* No. 88-1569, the U.S. Supreme Court ruled 6–3 that the federal and state governments have the power to restrict the involvement of business corporations in political campaigns, by barring the expenditure of campaign funds on independent efforts on a candidate's behalf, such as newspaper advertisements. Corporations were left free to make political expenditures through their political action committees. At the time of the Court's action, both federal law and the laws of 21 states contained the limitation on corporate political spending.

> **DID YOU KNOW?**
> That, in 1962, Representative Clem Miller, a California Democrat, successfully defended his congressional seat against challenger Don Clausen despite the fact that Miller had died more than a month earlier in a plane crash?

■ RUNNING FOR PRESIDENT: THE LONGEST CAMPAIGN

The American presidential election is the culmination of two different campaigns linked by the parties' national conventions. The **presidential primary** campaign lasts officially from January until June of the election year, and the final presidential campaign heats up around Labor Day.

Primary elections were first mandated in 1903 in Wisconsin. The purpose of the primary was to open the nomination process to ordinary party members and to weaken the influence of party bosses in the nomination process. Until 1968, however, there were fewer than twenty primary elections for the presidency. They were generally "**beauty contests**" in which the contending candidates for the nomination competed for popular votes, but the results had little or no impact on the selection of delegates to the national convention. National conventions were meetings of the party elite—legislators, mayors, county chairpersons, and loyal party workers—who were mostly appointed to their delegations. These party faithful frequently voted as a bloc under the direction of their leaders. Chicago's Mayor Richard Daley was famous for the control he exercised over the Illinois delegation to the Democratic convention. National conventions saw numerous trades and bargains between competing candidates and the leaders of large blocs of delegate votes.

PRESIDENTIAL PRIMARY
A statewide primary election of delegates to a political party's national convention to help a political party determine its presidential nominee. Such delegates are either pledged to a particular candidate or unpledged.

BEAUTY CONTEST
A term used to describe a form of presidential primary in which contending candidates compete for popular votes but the results have little or no impact on the selection of delegates to the national convention.

Reforming the Primaries

In recent years, the character of the primary process and the makeup of the national convention have changed dramatically. The mass public, rather than party elites, now controls the nomination process owing to extraordinary changes in the party rules. After the massive riots outside the doors of the

DID YOU KNOW?

That only slightly more than one-third of eligible voters were esti-mated to have voted in the 1990 congressional elections?

1968 Democratic convention in Chicago, many party leaders pushed for se-rious reforms of the convention process. They saw the general dissatisfaction with the convention and the riots in particular as stemming from the inability of the average party member to influence the nomination system.

The Democratic National Committee appointed a special commission to study the problems of the primary system. Known as the McGovern-Fraser Commission, the group over the next several years formulated new rules for delegate selection that had to be followed by state Democratic parties. Al-though some of the state parties did not agree with the rules, the commission held the ultimate threat: If a state did not comply with the rules, its delegation would not be seated at the national convention. This penalty was carried out against Mayor Daley of Chicago in 1972.

The reforms instituted by the Democratic party, and imitated in most states by the Republicans, revolutionized the nomination process for the presidency. The most important changes require that convention delegates cannot be nominated by the elites in either party; they must be elected by the voters in primary elections, in caucuses held by local parties, or at state conventions. Delegates are mostly pledged to a particular candidate, although the pledge is not formally binding at the convention. The delegation from each state must also include a proportion of women, younger party members, and represen-tatives of the minority groups within the party. At first virtually no special privileges were given to elected party officials such as senators or governors, but in 1984, many of these officials returned to the Democratic convention as superdelegates.

Some political scientists believe these presidential primaries perform several useful functions. First, it is through primaries that a relatively unknown can-didate can get his or her "bandwagon" going. Primaries also provide an op-portunity for candidates to organize their campaigns and to try out different issue positions before the public. The long primary season stretching from February until mid-June can even be regarded as an endurance test, in which

Riots outside the 1968 Democratic convention in Chicago which influenced the party to reform its delegate selection rules.

Hubert Humphrey accepting the Democratic nomination for president in 1968. Why did the Humphrey nomination stir massive protests outside the convention hall in Chicago?

the voters can see how candidates stand up under stress. Finally, the primaries may put pressure on an incumbent to change his or her policy. Lyndon B. Johnson decided not to run for the presidency again after the 1968 New Hampshire primary showed he was losing party support.

Critics of the system argue that the primaries drag out the presidential election to such a length that by the time they are over, the public is tired of the whole business. The result is that people may take less interest in the general election.

The states that do not have presidential primaries use the **caucus** to choose convention delegates. The original definition of a caucus is a secret meeting of party leaders for the purpose of nominating the party's candidates. In the early years of this century, the caucus was frequently referred to as "the smoke-filled room." Caucuses are still in use by local parties in many states and counties

CAUCUS
A closed meeting of party leaders to select party candidates or to decide on policy. Also, a meeting of party members designed to select candidates and propose policies.

Party members caucus in the firehouse to choose delegates. It takes considerable confidence to speak up for less popular candidates in the caucus situation.

DID YOU KNOW?

That noncitizens were allowed to vote in some states until the early 1920s?

to determine which candidates will be endorsed by the party in primary elections. For the presidential nominating process, caucuses can be used to nominate the delegates to the national convention or to county and state conventions where the official delegates will be chosen. In the latter case, the caucus must be open to all members of the political party who live within the specified geographic area—precinct, legislative district, or county. These neighbors gather, discuss presidential candidates, decide who the delegates will be, and determine whether the delegates will be pledged to one or more presidential candidates. Some critics of the primary system feel that the caucus is a better way of finding out how loyal party workers feel about the candidates and that its more widespread use would lead to stronger political parties. (See Highlight for a discussion of some European alternatives to the American primary system.)

Types of Primaries

The two most common types of primaries are the closed primary and the open primary. In addition, there are the blanket primary and the run-off primary.

CLOSED PRIMARY
The most widely used primary, in which voters may participate only in the primary of the party with which they are registered.

Closed Primary. In a **closed primary,** the selection of a party's candidates in an election is limited to avowed or declared party members. In other words, voters must declare their party affiliation, either when they register or at the primary election. A closed-primary system makes sure that registered voters cannot cross over into the other party's primary in order to nominate the weakest candidate of the opposing party or to affect the ideological direction of that party. Regular party workers favor a closed primary because it promotes party loyalty and responsibility. Independent voters do not like closed primaries because they exclude such voters from participating in the nominating process.

OPEN PRIMARY
A direct primary in which voters may cast ballots in the primary of either party without having to declare their party registration. Once voters choose which party primary they will vote in, they must select among only the candidates of that party.

Open Primary. An **open primary** is a direct primary in which voters can vote in either party primary without disclosing their party affiliation. Basically, the voter makes the choice in the privacy of the voting booth. The voter must, however, choose one party's list from which to select candidates. Open primaries place no restrictions on independent voters. Few states use such a system.

BLANKET PRIMARY
A primary in which all candidates' names are printed on the same ballot, regardless of party affiliation. The voter may vote for candidates of more than one party.

Blanket Primary. A **blanket primary** is one in which the voter may vote for candidates of more than one party. Alaska, Louisiana, and Washington all have blanket primaries.

RUN-OFF PRIMARY
An election that is held to nominate candidates within the party if no candidate receives a majority of the votes in the first primary election.

Run-Off Primary. Some states have a two-primary system. If no candidate receives a majority of the votes in the first primary, the top two candidates must compete in another primary, called a **run-off primary.**

A National Presidential Primary?

There have been waves of popular demand for a single, nationwide presidential primary election. Its main advantage is that it would be more efficient and fairer than the existing expensive, long-drawn-out, state-by-state system of selecting candidates. If all of the voters could pick their party's nominee on the same day, they could choose from the whole field. In the current process,

HIGHLIGHT

No Primaries in Europe!

Most Americans have the chance to vote directly for their party's nominees for elective office in the primary election. This is the case in most elections for federal office and for a large proportion of state and local elections as well. When the presidency is at stake, primary elections in most states are held to select delegates, who go to the national conventions of the major parties to nominate a presidential candidate. Thus, for most important offices, Americans directly or indirectly pick the major party nominees.

This state of affairs, seemingly natural to Democrats and Republicans in the United States, is not followed exactly by any major European party. In Britain, the Labour and Conservative parties do rely on elections held by local party councils to determine who will be able to run for a seat in Parliament. Decisions of these local councils are reviewed by national committees of the parties, however, and in certain cases, the choice of the party rank and file can be overruled. The British system differs from the American even more markedly in the choice of the national party leader—the man or woman

who may become prime minister if the party wins a majority of seats in Parliament. The British Conservatives rely on a conference of sitting members of Parliament to select the party leader; the process by which this is accomplished can take no more than three ballots, and thus it is possible for a Conservative leader (and possibly prime minister) to be the third choice of the Conservative parliamentary delegation—although possibly not of ordinary Conservative voters. The Labour party has an even more complicated system of electing its leader: The local party organizations count for a small percentage of a weighted vote in the matter, along with a bloc of trade union votes and a third bloc of votes cast by sitting Labour members of Parliament. Under this arrangement, the individual party member has little say in selecting the party's nominee for prime minister.

The method of partial voter involvement in party nominations also exists in the Federal Republic of Germany. The Christian Democrats, for example, do allow local party members to select nominees for the Bundestag in district elections, but these selections are re-

viewed at the national level. The choice of party leader is reserved for sitting members of the Bundestag, much as with the British Conservatives; the parliamentary bloc in Germany, called the *Fraktion,* is under no obligation to pick a leader who is popular with rank-and-file Christian Democrats. In fact, Chancellor Helmut Kohl was a party functionary with no experience in the Bundestag before his selection.

The purest deviation from democratic or representative methods of party nomination can be found in the so-called Eurocommunist parties of France, Italy*, and Spain. In Italy, for example, nominations for parliamentary candidates and for party leader are more or less dictated by the party's central committee, and must normally be accepted by all the lower levels of party organization down to the factory party cell. These selections are made in accordance with several criteria; length of service in the party and political reliability may be more important than a candidate's potential popularity with the party faithful.

*The Italian communist party recently changed its name.

many candidates have dropped out of the race by the midpoint, and voters in the later primaries have fewer choices.

Arguments against a national presidential primary emphasize several factors. First, it might be very difficult for minor candidates to achieve any success when they have to compete everywhere at once with their limited resources. Second, since candidates would not be eliminated from the competition during the primary process, as at present, there would probably be a fragmented national delegate split, which might lead to convention outcomes being decided by the party leaders. (Some analysts feel that party leaders are well-qualified to judge the competing candidates, particularly as to their electability. Throwing the nomination into the convention might increase the influence of parties in the elections overall.) Third, an advantage of the current process is that details of the candidates' views or personality are revealed by having to be on display constantly and under widely varying conditions from state to

CREDENTIALS COMMITTEE
A committee used by political parties at their national convention to determine which delegates may participate. The committee inspects the claim of each prospective delegate to be seated as a legitimate representative of his or her state.

Citizens voting in the New Hampshire primary. Why does this presidential primary have such influence on the presidential campaign?

state. Finally, party organizations might be further weakened by even greater emphasis on candidates in the national media.[8]

On to the National Convention

Presidential candidates have been nominated by the convention method in every election since 1832. The delegates are sent from each state and are apportioned on the basis of state representation. There are delegate bonuses for states that had voting majorities for the party in the preceding elections. Parties also accredit delegates from the District of Columbia, the territories, and overseas groups.

At the convention, each political party uses a **credentials committee** to determine which delegates may participate. The credentials committee usually prepares a roll of all delegates entitled to be seated. Controversy arises when rival groups claim to be the official party organization for a county, district, or state. At that point, the credentials committee will make a recommendation, which is usually approved by the convention without debate or even a roll call. On occasion, conventions have rejected recommendations of the credentials committee, and in some cases the decision has been a decisive factor in the selection of the presidential nominee. At the Republican convention in 1952, two competing delegations supporting Eisenhower and Robert Taft arrived from five different southern states. It was because Eisenhower supporters succeeded in getting the credentials committee to approve their delegates that Eisenhower was nominated.

The Mississippi Democratic party split along racial lines in 1964 at the height of the civil rights movement in the Deep South. Separate all-white and mixed white and African-American sets of delegates were selected, and both factions showed up at the national convention. After much debate on party rules, the committee decided to seat the pro-civil rights forces and exclude those who opposed racial equality.

The goal of any presidential hopeful at the national convention is to obtain a majority of votes on the earliest ballot. Given that delegates generally arrive at the convention in various states of commitment to presidential candidates, a certain amount of politicking, logrolling, and promise making must take place in order to get delegate pledges. Much of this activity has been eliminated by convention reforms in both major parties that typically have required delegates to pledge themselves to a presidential candidate. Consequently, no convention since 1952 has required more than one ballot to choose a nominee. This surprising result is accomplished by a long-drawn-out single ballot during which delegations shift and realign so that the appearance, if not the actuality, of unity may be conveyed to the TV audience.

It is interesting to note that there is no federal regulation of conventions. Each party makes its own rules and policies itself as it sees fit. The typical convention lasts only a few days. The first day consists of speech making, usually against the opposing party. During the second day, there are committee reports, and during the third day, there is presidential balloting. On the fourth day, a vice presidential candidate is usually nominated, and the presidential nominee gives the acceptance speech.

---

[8]These and other arguments are presented in Nelson W. Polsby and Aaron Wildavsky, *Presidential Elections*, 6th ed. (New York: Charles Scribners' Sons, 1984), pp. 223–230.

■ THE ELECTORAL COLLEGE

Most voters who vote for the president and vice president think they are voting directly for a candidate. In actuality, they are voting for a slate of **electors** who will cast its ballots in the **electoral college.** Article II, Section 1, of the Constitution outlines in detail the number and choice of electors for president and vice president. The Founding Fathers wanted to avoid the selection of president and vice president by the excitable masses. Rather, they wished the choice to be made by a few supposedly dispassionate, reasonable men (but not women).

The Choice of Electors

Each state's electors are selected during each presidential election year. The selection is governed by state laws and by the applicable party apparatus (Table 10-2). After the national party convention, the electors are pledged to the candidates chosen. The total number of electors today is 538, equal to 100 senators, 435 members of the House, plus 3 electors for the District of Columbia, subsequent to the Twenty-third Amendment, ratified in 1961. Each state's number of electors equals that state's number of senators (two) plus its number of representatives.

The Electors' Commitment

If a plurality of voters in a state chooses one slate of electors, then those electors are pledged to cast their ballots later in December at the state capital for the presidential and vice presidential candidates for the winning party.[9] The Constitution does not, however, require the electors to cast their ballots for the candidate of their party.

The ballots are counted and certified before a joint session of Congress early in January. The candidates who receive a majority of the electoral votes (270) are certified as president-elect and vice president-elect. According to the Constitution, in cases in which no candidate receives a majority of the electoral vote, the election of the president is decided in the House from among the three highest candidates (decided by a plurality of each state delegation), each state having one vote. The selection of the vice president is determined by the Senate in a choice between the two highest candidates, each senator having one vote. Congress was required to choose the president and vice president in 1801 (Jefferson and Burr), and the House chose the president in 1825 (John Quincy Adams).

It is possible for a candidate to become president without obtaining a majority of the popular vote. There have been numerous minority presidents in our history, including Abraham Lincoln, Woodrow Wilson, Harry S Truman, John F. Kennedy, and Richard Nixon (in 1968). Such an event can always occur when there are third-party candidates.

Perhaps more distressing is the possibility of a candidate being elected when the candidate's major opposition receives a larger popular vote. This occurred on three occasions—in the elections of John Quincy Adams in 1824, Ruth-

DID YOU KNOW?

That from the end of the Civil War until the 1930s, African-American voters generally supported Republicans?

ELECTOR
The partisan slate of electors is selected early in the presidential election year by state laws and applicable political party apparatus, and the electors cast ballots for president and vice president. The number of electors in each state is equal to that state's number of representatives in both houses of Congress.

ELECTORAL COLLEGE
The constitutionally required method for the selection of the president and the vice president. To be elected president or vice president, the candidate must have a majority of the electoral votes (currently, 270 out of 538).

---

[9]An exception to this winner-take-all rule is Maine, where since 1969 two electors are chosen on the basis of the statewide vote and the other two according to which party carries each congressional district.

TABLE 10-2
Elector Selection Methods and Ballot Listing

State	Party Convention	Party Committee	Party Primary	Other	Electors' Names Not on Ballot	Electors' Names Appear on Ballot
Ala.		X[1]			X	
Alaska	X[2]					X
Ariz.	X		X			X
Ark.	X				X	
Cal.				X[3]	X	
Colo.	X[4]			X[4]	X	
Conn.	X[2]				X	
Del.	X[2]				X	
D.C.		X			X	
Fla.				X[5]	X	
Ga.	X[6]	X[6]			X	
Hawaii	X				X	
Idaho	X					X
Ill.	X				X	
Ind.	X				X	
Iowa	X				X	
Kan.	X					X
Ky.	X[2]				X	
La.		X[1]				X
Me.	X				X	
Md.	X[6]	X[6]			X	
Mass.		X			X	
Mich.	X				X	
Minn.	X				X	
Miss.			X			X
Mo.		X[6]			X	
Mont.	X[2]				X	
Neb.	X				X	
Nev.	X				X	
N.H.	X[7]				X	
N.J.		X			X	
N.M.	X				X	
N.Y.		X			X	
N.C.	X[2]				X	
N.D.	X					X
Ohio	X				X	
Okla.	X					X
Ore.	X[6]	X[6]			X	
Pa.	X[7]			X[8]	X	
R.I.	X[7]				X	
S.C.		X				X
S.D.	X					X
Tenn.		X[1]				X
Tex.	X[2]				X	
Utah	X				X	
Vt.	X[7]				X	
Va.	X[7]				X	
Wash.	X[2]				X	
W. Va.	X				X	
Wis.	X[7]				X	
Wyo.	X					X

[1] State law allows parties to choose means of selecting electors. Both parties chose to use party committees.

[2] State law allows parties to choose means of selecting electors. Both parties chose to use party conventions.

[3] California law contains separate provisions for the methods to be used by the Democratic and Republican parties in selecting electors. Each Democratic nominee for U.S. representative and the last two Democratic nominees for U.S. senator designate an elector. Certain Republican officials are designated as electors, and the Republican State Central Committee appoints the remaining electors.

[4] State law allows parties to choose means of selecting electors. The state Democratic Party chose to use the party convention method. The state Republican Party chose to have the party chairman select the electors based on recommendations of party officials.

[5] In Florida, the governor officially chooses the electors. However, he must choose only those electors selected by the parties' state executive committees.

[6] State law allows the parties to choose the method of selecting electors. The state Republican Party chose to use the party convention method, and the state Democratic Party chose to use the party committee method.

[7] Although termed a "convention," state law designates the party officials who meet to select electors.

[8] Pennsylvania law provides that the national Democratic and Republican parties' presidential nominees name their electors for Pennsylvania.

SOURCES: *Nomination and Election of the President and Vice President of the United States*, by Thomas M. Durbin and Michael V. Seitzinger (Washington, D.C.: U.S. Government Printing Office, 1980) and from secretaries of state, *Congressional Quarterly Weekly Report*, October 25, 1980, p. 3184.

erford B. Hayes in 1876, and Benjamin Harrison in 1888, all of whom won elections without obtaining a **plurality** of the vote.

Criticisms of the Electoral College

Beside the possibility of a candidate becoming president even though his or her major opponent obtains more popular votes, there are other complaints about the electoral college. The Founding Fathers' idea was to have electors use their own discretion to decide who would make the best president. But electors no longer perform the selecting function envisioned by the Founding Fathers, because they are committed to the candidate who has a plurality of votes in the general election.[10]

One can also argue that the current system, which gives all of the electoral votes to whomever has a statewide plurality, is unfair to other candidates and their supporters. The unit system of voting also means that presidential campaigning will be concentrated in those states that have the largest number of electoral votes and in those states where the outcome is likely to be close. All of the other states presumably get second-class treatment during the presidential campaign.

It can also be argued that there is something of a less-populous-state bias in the electoral college, because including Senate seats in the electoral vote total partly offsets the more-populous-states' edge in the House. A state such as Alaska (with two senators and one representative) gets an electoral vote for roughly each 71,000 people (based on the 1980 census), whereas Iowa gets one vote for each 365,000 people, and New York has a vote for every half-million inhabitants. (The 1990 census will change these numbers.)

Proposed Reforms

Many proposals for reform of the electoral college system have been advanced. The most obvious is to get rid of it completely and simply to have candidates elected on a popular-vote basis; in other words, a direct election, by the people, for president and vice president. This was proposed as a constitutional amendment by President Carter in 1977, but it failed to achieve the required two-thirds majority in the Senate in a 1979 vote. An earlier effort in 1969 passed the House, but a Senate vote was blocked by senators from less populous states and the South.

A less radical reform is a federal law that would require each elector to vote for the candidate who has a plurality in the state. Another system would eliminate the electors but retain the electoral vote, which would be given on a proportional basis rather than on a unit basis (winner take all). This method was endorsed by President Nixon in 1969.

The major parties are not in favor of eliminating the electoral college, fearing that it would give minor parties a more influential role. Also, less populous states are not in favor of direct election of the president because they feel they would be overwhelmed by the large urban vote.

[10]However, there have been revolts by a handful of **"faithless electors"**— in 1796, 1820, 1948, 1956, 1960, 1968, 1972, 1976, and 1988.

PLURALITY
The winning of an election by a candidate who receives more votes than any other candidate but not necessarily a majority. Most national, state, and local electoral laws provide for winning elections by a plurality vote.

"FAITHLESS" ELECTORS
Electors voting for candidates other than those within their parties. They are pledged, but not required by law, to vote for the candidate who has a plurality in the state.

■ HOW ARE ELECTIONS CONDUCTED?

AUSTRALIAN BALLOT
A secret ballot prepared, distributed, and tabulated by government officials at public expense. Since 1888, all states have used the secret Australian ballot rather than an open, public ballot.

The United States uses the **Australian ballot**—a secret ballot that is prepared, distributed, and counted by government officials at public expense. Since 1888, all states have used the Australian ballot, but before that many states used the alternatives of oral voting and differently colored ballots prepared by the parties. Obviously, knowing which way a person was voting made it easy to apply pressure to change his or her vote, and vote buying was common.

Office-Block and Party-Column Ballots

OFFICE-BLOCK BALLOT, OR MASSACHUSETTS BALLOT
A form of general election ballot in which candidates for elective office are grouped together under the title of each office. It emphasizes voting for the office and the individual rather than for the party.

PARTY-COLUMN BALLOT, OR INDIANA BALLOT
A form of general election ballot in which candidates for elective office are arranged in one column under their respective party labels and symbols. It emphasizes voting for the party rather than for the office or individual.

There are two types of ballots in use in the United States in general elections. The first, called an **office-block ballot** or sometimes a **Massachusetts ballot,** groups all the candidates for each elective office under the title of each office. Politicians dislike the office-block ballot because it places more emphasis on the office than on the party; it discourages straight-ticket voting and encourages split-ticket voting.

A **party-column ballot** is a form of general election ballot in which the candidates are arranged in one column under their respective party labels and symbols. It is also called the **Indiana ballot.** In some states, it allows voting for all of a party's candidates for local, state, and national offices by simply marking a single "X" or by pulling a single lever. Most states use this type of ballot. As it encourages straight-ticket voting, majority parties favor this form. When a party has an exceptionally strong presidential or gubernatorial can-

In the voting booth with the punch-card ballot. Are there any disadvantages of using such modern technology?

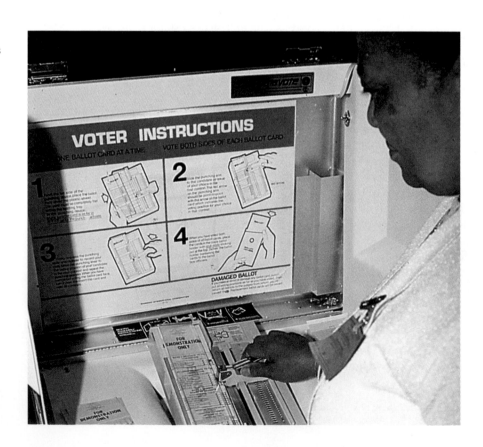

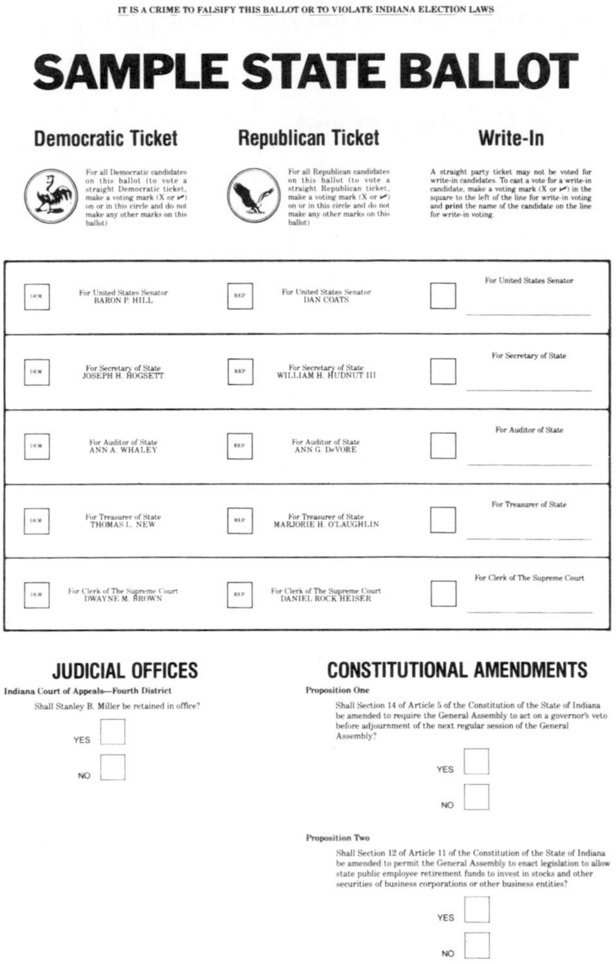

IT IS A CRIME TO FALSIFY THIS BALLOT OR TO VIOLATE INDIANA ELECTION LAWS

SAMPLE STATE BALLOT

Democratic Ticket

For all Democratic candidates on this ballot (to vote a straight Democratic ticket, make a voting mark (X or ✓) on or in this circle and do not make any other marks on this ballot)

Republican Ticket

For all Republican candidates on this ballot (to vote a straight Republican ticket, make a voting mark (X or ✓) on or in this circle and do not make any other marks on this ballot)

Write-In

A straight party ticket may not be voted for write-in candidates. To cast a vote for a write-in candidate, make a voting mark (X or ✓) in the square to the left of the line for write-in voting and **print** the name of the candidate on the line for write-in voting.

DEM	For United States Senator BARON P. HILL	REP	For United States Senator DAN COATS	For United States Senator
DEM	For Secretary of State JOSEPH H. HOGSETT	REP	For Secretary of State WILLIAM H. HUDNUT III	For Secretary of State
DEM	For Auditor of State ANN A. WHALEY	REP	For Auditor of State ANN G. DeVORE	For Auditor of State
DEM	For Treasurer of State THOMAS L. NEW	REP	For Treasurer of State MARJORIE H. O'LAUGHLIN	For Treasurer of State
DEM	For Clerk of The Supreme Court DWAYNE M. BROWN	REP	For Clerk of The Supreme Court DANIEL ROCK HEISER	For Clerk of The Supreme Court

JUDICIAL OFFICES

Indiana Court of Appeals—Fourth District

Shall Stanley B. Miller be retained in office?

YES ☐

NO ☐

CONSTITUTIONAL AMENDMENTS

Proposition One

Shall Section 14 of Article 5 of the Constitution of the State of Indiana be amended to require the General Assembly to act on a governor's veto before adjournment of the next regular session of the General Assembly?

YES ☐

NO ☐

Proposition Two

Shall Section 12 of Article 11 of the Constitution of the State of Indiana be amended to permit the General Assembly to enact legislation to allow state public employee retirement funds to invest in stocks and other securities of business corporations or other business entities?

YES ☐

NO ☐

Indiana ballot. How does this format encourage straight ticket voting?

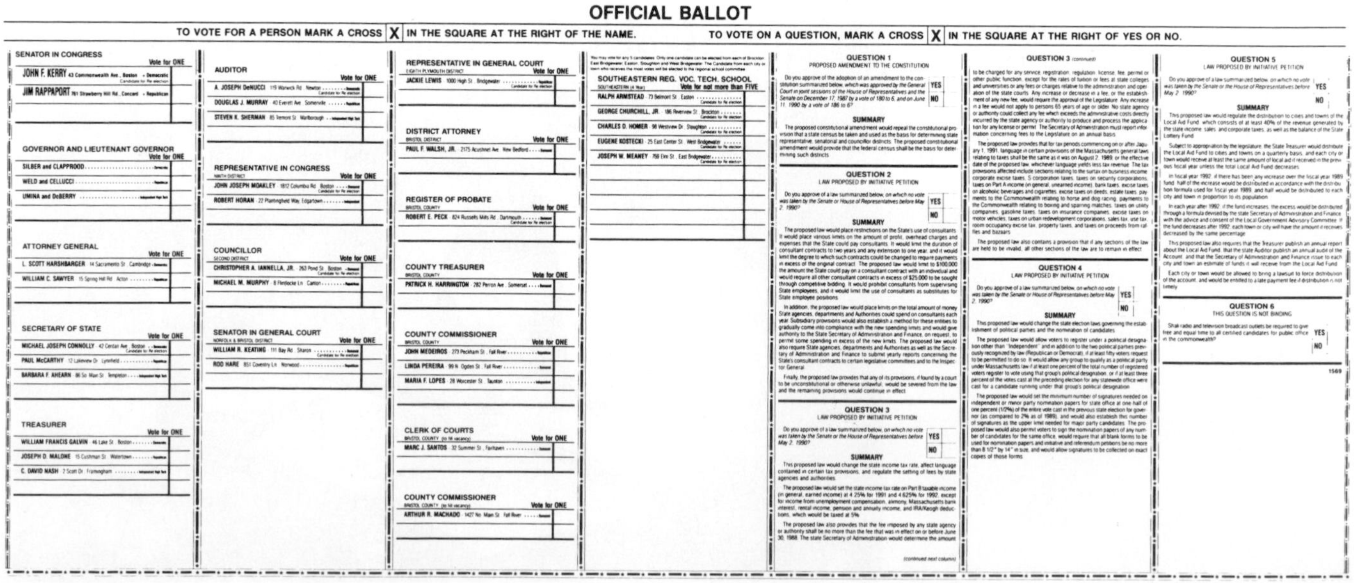

Massachusetts ballot. Grouping candidates by office encourages split-ticket voting.

OFFICIAL BALLOT

TO VOTE FOR A PERSON MARK A CROSS X IN THE SQUARE AT THE RIGHT OF THE NAME.   TO VOTE ON A QUESTION, MARK A CROSS X IN THE SQUARE AT THE RIGHT OF YES OR NO.

SENATOR IN CONGRESS — Vote for ONE
- JOHN F. KERRY 43 Commonwealth Ave., Boston — Democratic
- JIM RAPPAPORT 901 Strawberry Hill Rd., Concord — Republican

GOVERNOR AND LIEUTENANT GOVERNOR — Vote for ONE
- SILBER and CLAPPROOD
- WELD and CELLUCCI
- UMINA and DeBERRY

ATTORNEY GENERAL — Vote for ONE
- L. SCOTT HARSHBARGER 14 Sacramento St., Cambridge — Democratic
- WILLIAM C. SAWYER 15 Spring Hill Rd., Acton — Republican

SECRETARY OF STATE — Vote for ONE
- MICHAEL JOSEPH CONNOLLY 47 Gretan Ave., Boston — Democratic
- PAUL McCARTHY 12 Glenrose Dr., Lynnfield — Republican
- BARBARA F. AHEARN 98 So. Main St., Templeton — Independent

TREASURER — Vote for ONE
- WILLIAM FRANCIS GALVIN 46 Lake St., Boston — Democratic
- JOSEPH D. MALONE 16 Cushman St., Waterrown — Republican
- C. DAVID NASH 7 Scott Dr., Framingham — Independent

AUDITOR — Vote for ONE
- A. JOSEPH DeNUCCI 119 Warwick Rd., Newton — Democratic
- DOUGLAS J. MURRAY 40 Everett Ave., Somerville — Republican
- STEVEN K. SHERMAN 45 Tremont St., Marlborough — Independent

REPRESENTATIVE IN CONGRESS — Vote for ONE
- JOHN JOSEPH MOAKLEY 1012 Columbia Rd., Boston — Democratic
- ROBERT HORAN 22 Plantingfield Way, Edgartown — Republican

COUNCILLOR — Vote for ONE
- CHRISTOPHER A. IANNELLA, JR. 262 Pond St., Boston — Democratic
- MICHAEL M. MURPHY 8 Firebrook Ln., Canton — Republican

SENATOR IN GENERAL COURT — NORFOLK & BRISTOL DISTRICT — Vote for ONE
- WILLIAM R. KEATING 111 Bay Rd., Sharon — Democratic
- ROD HARE 851 Coventry Ln., Norwood — Republican

REPRESENTATIVE IN GENERAL COURT — EIGHTH PLYMOUTH DISTRICT
- JACKIE LEWIS 1000 High St., Bridgewater — Nonffilers — Candidate for Re-election

DISTRICT ATTORNEY — BRISTOL DISTRICT — Vote for ONE
- PAUL F. WALSH, JR. 2175 Acushnet Ave., New Bedford — Democratic — Candidate for Re-election

REGISTER OF PROBATE — BRISTOL COUNTY — Vote for ONE
- ROBERT E. PECK 624 Russells Mills Rd., Dartmouth — Democratic — Candidate for Re-election

COUNTY TREASURER — BRISTOL COUNTY — Vote for ONE
- PATRICK H. HARRINGTON 282 Pierce Ave., Somerset — Democratic — Candidate for Re-election

COUNTY COMMISSIONER — BRISTOL COUNTY — Vote for ONE
- JOHN MEDEIROS 379 Peckham St., Fall River — Democratic
- LINDA PERREIRA 98 N. Ogden St., Fall River — Democratic
- MARIA F. LOPES 28 Worcester St., Taunton — Democratic

CLERK OF COURTS — BRISTOL COUNTY — Vote for ONE
- MARC J. SANTOS 32 Somerset St., Fairhaven — Democratic

COUNTY COMMISSIONER — BRISTOL COUNTY (to fill vacancy)
- ARTHUR D. MACHADO 1427 No. Main St., Fall River — Democratic

REPRESENTATIVE IN GENERAL COURT — SOUTHEASTERN REG. VOC. TECH. SCHOOL — SOUTHEASTERN (4 Year) — Vote for not more than FIVE
- RALPH ARMSTEAD 73 Belmont St., Easton — Candidate for Re-election
- GEORGE CHURCHILL, JR. 186 Riverview Dr., Brockton — Candidate for Re-election
- CHARLES D. HOMER 98 Westview Dr., Stoughton — Candidate for Re-election
- EUGENE KOSTECKI 25 East Center St., West Bridgewater — Candidate for Re-election
- JOSEPH W. MEANEY 760 Elm St., East Bridgewater — Candidate for Re-election

QUESTION 1 — PROPOSED AMENDMENT TO THE CONSTITUTION

Do you approve of an amendment to the constitution summarized below, which was approved by the General Court in joint sessions of the House of Representatives and the Senate on December 17, 1987 by a vote of 180 to 6, and on June 11, 1990 by a vote of 186 to 6?

YES ☐   NO ☐

SUMMARY

The proposed constitutional amendment would repeal the constitutional provision that a state census be taken and used as the basis for determining state representative, senatorial and councillor districts. The proposed constitutional amendment would provide that the federal census shall be the basis for determining such districts.

QUESTION 2 — LAW PROPOSED BY INITIATIVE PETITION

Do you approve of a law summarized below, on which no vote was taken by the Senate or House of Representatives before May 2, 1990?

YES ☐   NO ☐

SUMMARY

The proposed law would place restrictions on the State's use of consultants. It would place various limits on the amount of profit, overhead charges and expenses that the State could pay consultants. It would limit the duration of consultant contracts to two years and any extension to one year, and it would limit the degree to which such contracts could be changed to require payments in excess of the original contract. The proposed law would limit to $100,000 the amount the State could pay on a consultant contract with an individual and would require all other consultant contracts in excess of $25,000 to be sought through competitive bidding. It would prohibit consultants from supervising State employees, and it would limit the use of consultants as substitutes for State employee positions.

In addition, the proposed law would place limits on the total amount of money State agencies, departments and Authorities could spend on consultants each year. Subsidiary processes would also establish a method for these entities to gradually come into compliance with the new spending limits and would give authority to the State Secretary of Administration and Finance, on request, to permit some spending in excess of the new limits. The proposed law would also require State agencies, departments and Authorities as well as the Secretary of Administration and Finance to submit yearly reports concerning the State's consultant contracts to certain legislative committees and to the Inspector General.

Finally, the proposed law provides that any of its provisions, if found by a court to be unconstitutional or otherwise unlawful, would be severed from the law and the remaining provisions would continue in effect.

QUESTION 3 — LAW PROPOSED BY INITIATIVE PETITION

Do you approve of a law summarized below, on which no vote was taken by the Senate or House of Representatives before May 2, 1990?

YES ☐   NO ☐

SUMMARY

This proposed law would change the state income tax rate, affect language contained in certain tax provisions, and regulate the setting of fees by state agencies and authorities.

The proposed law would set the state income tax (on personal, earned income) at 4.75% for 1991 and 4.625% for 1992, except for income from unemployment compensation, annuity, Massachusetts bank interest, rental income, pension and annuity income, and IRA/Keogh deductions, which would be taxed at 5%.

The proposed law also provides that the fee imposed by any state agency or authority shall be no more than the fee that was in effect on or before June 30, 1988. The State Secretary of Administration would then determine the amount

QUESTION 1 (continued)

to be charged for any service registration, regulation, license, fee, permit or other public function, except for the rates of tuition or fees at state colleges and universities or any fees or charges relative to the administration and operation of the state courts. Any increase or decrease in a fee, or the establishment of any new fee, would require the approval of the Legislature. Any increase in a fee would not apply to persons 65 years of age or older. No state agency or authority could collect any fee which exceeds the administrative costs directly incurred by the state agency or authority to produce and process the application for any license or permit. The Secretary of Administration must report information concerning fees to the Legislature on an annual basis.

The proposed law provides that for tax periods commencing on or after January 1, 1991, language in certain provisions of the Massachusetts general laws relating to taxes shall be the same as it was on August 7, 1989, or the effective date of the proposed law, whichever language yields less tax revenue. The tax provisions affected include sections relating to the surtax on business income, corporate excise taxes, corporation taxes, taxes on security corporations, taxes on Part A income on general, unearned income, bank taxes, excise taxes on alcoholic beverages and cigarettes, excise taxes on deeds, estate taxes, payments to the Commonwealth relating to horse and dog racing, payments to the Commonwealth relating to boxing and sparring matches, taxes on utility companies, gasoline taxes, taxes on insurance companies, excise taxes on motor vehicles, taxes on certain redevelopment corporations, sales tax, use tax, room occupancy excise tax, property taxes, and taxes on proceeds from oil and biotaxes.

The proposed law also contains a provision that if any sections of the law are held to be invalid, all other sections of the law are to remain in effect.

QUESTION 4 — LAW PROPOSED BY INITIATIVE PETITION

Do you approve of a law summarized below, on which no vote was taken by the Senate or House of Representatives before May 2, 1990?

YES ☐   NO ☐

SUMMARY

The proposed law would allow voters to register under a political designation other than 'Independent' and in addition to the two political parties previously recognized by law (Republican or Democratic). If at least fifty voters request to be permitted to do so, it would allow any group to qualify as a political party under Massachusetts law if at least one percent of the total number of registered voters register to vote using that group's political designation, or if at least three percent of the votes cast at the preceding election for any statewide office were cast for a candidate running under that group's political designation.

The proposed law would set the minimum number of signatures needed on independent or minor party nomination papers for state office at one half of one percent (1/2%) of the entire vote cast in the previous state election for governor (as compared to 2% as of 1989), and would also establish the number of signatures as the upper limit needed for major party candidates. The proposed law would also permit voters to sign the nomination papers of any number of candidates for the same office, would require that all blank forms to be used for nomination papers and initiative and referendum petitions be no more than 8½" by 14" in size, and would allow any signatures to be collected on exact copies of those forms.

QUESTION 5 — LAW PROPOSED BY INITIATIVE PETITION

Do you approve of a law summarized below, on which no vote was taken by the Senate or House of Representatives before May 2, 1990?

YES ☐   NO ☐

SUMMARY

This proposed law would regulate the distribution to cities and towns of the Local Aid Fund, which consists of at least 40% of the revenue generated by the state income, sales, and corporate taxes, as well as the balance of the State Lottery Fund.

Subject to appropriation by the Legislature, the State Treasurer would distribute the Local Aid Fund to cities and towns on a quarterly basis, and each city or town would receive at least the same amount of local aid it received in the previous fiscal year unless the total Local Aid Fund decreases.

In fiscal year 1992, if there has been any increase over the local year 1989 fund, half of the increase would be distributed in accordance with the distribution formula used for fiscal year 1989, and half would be distributed to each city and town in proportion to its population.

In each year after 1992, if the fund increases, the excess would be distributed through a formula devised by the State Secretary of Administration and Finance with the advice and consent of the Local Government Advisory Committee. If the fund decreases after 1992, each town or city will have the amount it receives decreased by the same percentage.

This proposed law also requires that the Treasurer publish an annual report about the Local Aid Fund, that the state Auditor publish an annual audit of the Account, and that the Secretary of Administration and Finance issue to each city and town an estimate of funds it will receive from the Local Aid Fund.

Each city or town would be allowed to bring a lawsuit to force distribution of the account, and would be entitled to a late payment fee if distribution is not timely.

QUESTION 6 — THIS QUESTION IS NOT BINDING

Shall radio and television broadcast outlets be required to give free and equal time to all certified candidates for public office in the commonwealth?

YES ☐   NO ☐

(continued next column)

COATTAIL EFFECT
The influence of a popular or unpopular candidate on the electoral success or failure of other candidates on the same party ticket. The effect is increased by the party-column ballot, which encourages straight-ticket voting.

CANVASSING BOARD
An official and normally bipartisan group on a county, city, or state level that receives vote counts from every precinct in the area. The state canvassing board obtains the voting results from all local boards, tabulates the figures, and certifies the winners.

POLL WATCHER
An individual appointed by a political party to scrutinize the voting process on election day. Usually, there are two poll watchers at every voting place, representing the Democratic and the Republican parties, both attempting to ensure the honesty of the election.

CHALLENGE
An allegation by a poll watcher that a potential voter is unqualified to vote or that a vote is invalid; designed to prevent fraud in elections.

didate to head the ticket, the **coattail effect** is increased by the party-column ballot.

Counting the Votes and Avoiding Fraud

State and local election officials tabulate the results of each election after the polls are closed. Although most votes are tallied electronically, there is still the possibility of voting fraud. To minimize this possibility, the use of canvassing boards is common. A **canvassing board** is an official body that is typically bipartisan. The canvassing boards tabulate and consolidate the returns and forward them to the state canvassing authority, which will usually certify the election of the winners within a few days. A state canvassing board often consists of ex officio members of the state government and is usually headed by the secretary of state. Typically, the extensive coverage of election returns by the mass media makes the results known to the public before certification by canvassing boards. It is only in very close elections that the final outcome turns on the official tabulation and certification.

To avoid fraud at the polling places themselves, each party may appoint **poll watchers** to monitor elections. In virtually all polling places throughout the country during partisan elections, major parties have their own poll watchers. Poll watching is particularly important when there is a challenge to an entrenched, local political machine. At any time, a poll watcher may make a **challenge,** which is an allegation that a potential voter is either unqualified or that his or her vote is invalid. Once a challenge is made, a bipartisan group of election judges in each precinct will decide on the merits of the challenge.

Vote fraud is something regularly suspected but seldom proved. Voting in the nineteenth century, when secret ballots were rare and people had a cavalier attitude toward the open buying of votes, was probably much more conducive to fraud than modern elections are. Nonetheless, stories persist in places such as Cook County, Illinois, about dead people miraculously voting, people voting more than once, or opponents' votes sinking into the Chicago River. Such allegations formed part of a continuing debate over the 1960 presidential

Election judges check the registration of each voter before giving out the ballot. Why do most local election boards require judges from both political parties at each precinct?

election, when John Kennedy officially defeated Richard Nixon by only 112,803 popular votes and by 303 to 219 electoral votes. Eleven states were decided by a margin of less than two percentage points. Allegations of fraud, paying off voters, and tampering with vote totals were rampant in Texas, Illinois, and New Jersey—states that were all carried narrowly by Kennedy. Most of the time for most elections, fraud is entirely absent.

■ VOTING IN NATIONAL, STATE, AND LOCAL ELECTIONS

In 1988, there were 183 million eligible voters. Of that number, 129 million, or 70 percent, actually registered to vote in the general presidential election. Of those who registered, 91.6 million actually went to the polls. The participation rate during the 1988 presidential election was only 71 percent of registered voters and 50.2 percent of eligible voters (see Table 10-3).

Figure 10-2 shows that the **voter turnout** in the United States compared with that of other countries places Americans in the bottom 20 percent. Figure 10-3 shows voter turnout for presidential and congressional elections from 1868 to 1988. The last "good" year of turnout for the presidential elections was 1960, when almost 65 percent of the eligible voters actually voted. We

> **DID YOU KNOW?**
>
> That among the members of the 1988 Electoral College who officially voted for George Bush for president were his son Neil, his brother, Prescott, and Penn State's football coach, Joe Paterno?

VOTER TURNOUT
The percentage of citizens taking part in the election process; the number of eligible voters that actually "turn out" on election day to cast their ballots.

TABLE 10-3
Elected by a Majority?
Most presidents have won a majority of the votes cast in the election. We generally judge the extent of their victory by whether they have won by more than 51 percent. Some presidential elections have been proclaimed *landslides,* meaning winning by an extraordinary majority of votes cast. However, as indicated below, no modern president has been elected by more than 38 percent of the total voting-age electorate.

YEAR—WINNER (PARTY)	PERCENTAGE OF TOTAL POPULAR VOTE	PERCENTAGE OF VOTING-AGE POPULATION
1932 —Roosevelt (D)	57.4	30.1
1936 —Roosevelt (D)	60.8	34.6
1940 —Roosevelt (D)	54.7	32.2
1944 —Roosevelt (D)	53.4	29.9
1948 —Truman (D)	49.6	25.3
1952 —Eisenhower (R)	55.1	34.0
1956 —Eisenhower (R)	57.4	34.1
1960 —Kennedy (D)	49.7	31.2
1964 —Johnson (D)	61.1	37.8
1968 —Nixon (R)	43.4	26.4
1972 —Nixon (R)	60.7	33.5
1976 —Carter (D)	50.1	26.8
1980 —Reagan (R)	50.7	26.7
1984 —Reagan (R)	58.8	31.2
1988 —Bush (R)	53.4	26.8

SOURCE: *Congressional Quarterly Weekly Report,* January 31, 1989, p. 137.

FIGURE 10-2
Voter Turnout in the United States Compared with Other Countries from Elections in 1981 through 1985.

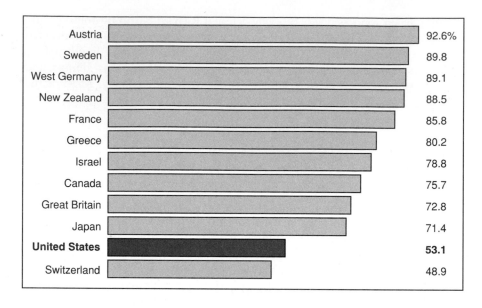

Austria	92.6%
Sweden	89.8
West Germany	89.1
New Zealand	88.5
France	85.8
Greece	80.2
Israel	78.8
Canada	75.7
Great Britain	72.8
Japan	71.4
United States	**53.1**
Switzerland	48.9

FIGURE 10-3
Voter Turnout for Presidential and Congressional Elections, 1868–1988

SOURCE: Historical Data Archive, Inter-university Consortium for Political and Social Research: U.S. Bureau of the Census, *Statistical Abstract of the United States: 1980,* 101st ed. (Washington, D.C.: U.S. Government Printing Office, 1980), p. 515; William H. Flanigan and Nancy H. Zingale, *Political Behavior of the American Electorate,* 5th ed. (Boston: Allyn and Bacon, 1983), p. 20; *Congressional Quarterly,* various issues.

can also see that voting for U.S. representatives is greatly influenced by whether there is a presidential election in the same year.

The same is true at the state level. When there is a race for governor, more participation occurs both in the general election for governor and in the election for state representatives. Voter participation rates in gubernatorial elections are also greater in presidential election years than when there is no president to choose. The average turnout in state elections is about 14 percentage points higher when a presidential election is held.

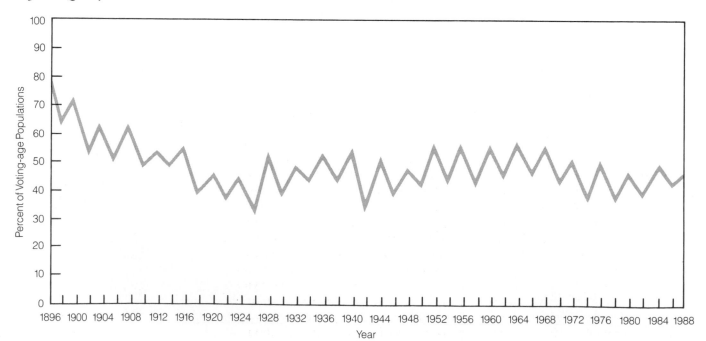

HIGHLIGHT

Voter Registration in Other Countries

The American system of preelection registration of voters has two features that tend to reduce citizen participation in elections: The first is a residency requirement which varies from locality to locality; the second, more important, feature is the requirement of registration weeks in advance of an election itself.

Most democracies have similar requirements regarding voter registration. Yet voter participation tends to be higher in these countries, even though voting is mandatory only in a few countries. The difference lies in the fact that governments in Europe and Oceania make a deliberate effort to ensure that all eligible voters are registered or make it easier to register ahead of an election than it is in the United States. In Europe, registration tends to be organized by the post office authorities, who have the duty to maintain the registration rolls. As they have the names and addresses of all residents in a given area, it is a simple matter to either solicit registration through the mail or to send a notice asking a potential voter to drop into the local post office to fill out a voter registration card.

In New Zealand, the convenience and efficiency of the system is reinforced by legal penalties for failing to register. The right—or perhaps it is better described as a duty—to register falls on all citizens of eighteen years of age or more who have a certain length of continuous residence within the country and within a district. Registration is run by the post office. The Kiwis have been done one better by their neighbors, the Australians, though, who have similar eligibility requirements, but who have made voting compulsory, in addition to registration.

Now consider local elections. In races for mayor, city council, county auditor, and the like, it is fairly common for only 25 percent or less of the electorate to vote. Is something amiss here? It seems obvious that people would be more likely to vote in elections that directly affect them. At the local level, each person's vote counts more (because there are fewer voters) and the issues—crime control, school bonds, sewer bonds, and so on—touch the immediate interests of the voters. The facts, however, do not fit the theory. Potential voters are most interested in national elections when a presidential choice is involved. Otherwise, voter participation in our representative government is very low (and, as we have seen, it is not overwhelmingly great even at the presidential level).

The Effect of Low Voter Turnout

There are two schools of thought concerning low voter turnout. Some view the decline in voter participation as a clear threat to our **representative democratic government.** Fewer and fewer individuals are deciding who wields political power in our society. Also, low voter participation presumably signals apathy about our political system in general. It also may signal that potential voters simply do not want to take the time to learn about the issues involved. When only a handful of people do take the time, it will be easier, say the alarmists, for an authoritarian figure to take over our government.

Others are less concerned about low voter participation. They believe that a decline in voter participation simply indicates there is more satisfaction with the status quo. Also, they believe that representative democracy is a reality even if a very small percentage of eligible voters vote. If everyone who does not vote believes the outcome of the election will accord with his or her own desires, then representative democracy is working. The nonvoters are obtaining the type of government—with the type of people running it—that they want to have anyway. It has further been suggested that declining voter participation,

REPRESENTATIVE DEMOCRATIC GOVERNMENT
A democracy in which representatives are empowered by the people to act on behalf of those represented.

rather than spelling alarm for the future of American democracy, may really reflect a better-informed voting public. According to political scientists William H. Flanigan and Nancy H. Zingale,

> The high rate of turnout in the nineteenth century may not have resulted from political involvement by an interested, well-informed electorate, but on the contrary it may have been possible at all only because of low levels of information and interest. During the last half of the nineteenth century, a largely uninformed electorate was aroused to vote by means of extreme and emotional political appeals. . . . [B]y and large, the parties manipulated the electorate—a manipulation possible because the electorate was not well informed.[11]

Factors Influencing Who Votes

A clear association exists between voting and the following characteristics: age, educational attainment, minority status, income level, and the existence of two-party competition.

1. Age. Look at Table 10-4 where we show the breakdown of voter participation by age group for the 1988 presidential election. It would appear from these figures that age is a strong factor in determining voter turnout on election day. The reported turnout increases as the age groups become older. Greater participation with age is very likely due to the fact that older voters are more settled in their lives, are already registered, and have had more time to experience voting as an expected activity.

2. Educational attainment. Education also influences voter turnout. In general, the more education you have, the more likely you are to vote. This pattern is clearly evident in the 1988 election results, as we can see in Table 10-5. Reported turnout was over 30 percentage points higher for those who have a college education than it was for people who have never been to high school.

3. Minority status and income level. Race is important, too, in determining the level of voter turnout. Whites in 1988 voted at a 59 percent rate, whereas

[11]*Political Behavior of the American Electorate*, 5th ed. (Boston: Allyn and Bacon, 1983), p. 9.

TABLE 10-4
Voting in the 1988 Presidential Election by Age Group (in percent)

Age	Reported Turnout
18–24	36
25–44	54
45–64	68
65 and over	69

SOURCE: Bureau of the Census, reported in *National Journal.*

Young voters learning to use the voting machine.

the African-American turnout rate was 51.5 percent. Differences in income can also lead to differences in voter turnout. Wealthier people tend to be overrepresented in the electorate. In 1988, turnout among whites varied from less than 40 percent of those with annual family incomes under $15,000 to about 70 percent for people whose annual family incomes were $50,000 and over.

4. Two-party competition. Another factor in voter turnout is the extent to which elections are competitive within a state. More competitive states generally have higher turnout rates, although the highest average percentage turnout for the past two decades has been in states in which Republicans were elected to most state offices.

The foregoing statistics reinforce one another. For example, rich, white, educated, elderly Minnesotans vote more often than poor, nonwhite, uneducated, young people in Texas.

Why Citizens Do Not Vote: The Rational Ignorance Effect

Less than 50 percent of the American electorate can correctly identify the names of their members of Congress. Even fewer are able to name their state representatives, and still fewer can tell where their representatives—either state or national—stand on various issues. It should not be surprising then that the number of nonvoters in our society is so great. To understand why, we must understand the incentives confronting the potential voter. If citizens believe their vote will not affect the outcome of an election, then they have little incentive to seek the information they need to cast an intelligent vote. The lack of incentive to obtain costly (in terms of time, attention, and so on)

TABLE 10-5
Voting in the 1988 Presidential Election by Education Level (in percent)

Years of School Completed	Reported Turnout
8 years or less	36.7
9–11 years	41.3
12 years	54.7
More than 12 years	71

SOURCE: Statistical Abstract of the United States, 1990, p. 262.

A voter registration drive to increase the number of potential voters. Would even more voters register if they could do so at home or through the mail?

RATIONAL IGNORANCE EFFECT
When people purposely and rationally decide not to become informed on an issue because they believe that their vote on the issue is not likely to be a deciding one; a lack of incentive to seek the necessary information to cast an intelligent vote.

information about politicians and political issues has been called the **rational ignorance effect.** That term may seem contradictory, but it is not. Rational ignorance involves purposely and rationally deciding *not* to obtain information—to remain ignorant.

If average voters choose to remain rationally ignorant, what determines how they vote when they do vote? According to the rational ignorance theory, voters will simply rely on information that is supplied by candidates and by the mass media. Bits of information picked up from TV news and political advertising, as well as information gleaned from casual conversations with co-workers and friends, will be used as a basis for making a choice among candidates. Few voters will take the time to examine the issues and assess a candidate's likely handling of them (see Critical Perspective, Voting in the Noninformation Age).

Since there is such a low probability that an individual's vote will make a difference, it is understandable why voter turnout is so low. The personal payoffs are low. After all, the probability that a single vote will be decisive is almost zero. Why, then, do even one-third to one-half of U.S. citizens bother to show up at the polls? One explanation is that most citizens receive personal satisfaction from the act of voting. It makes them feel that they are good citizens and that they are doing something patriotic. But that feeling is not overriding. Even among voters who are registered and who plan to vote, if the cost of voting goes up (in time and in convenience), the number of eligible voters will fall. In particular, bad weather on election day means on average a smaller percentage of eligible voters at the polls.

■ LEGAL RESTRICTIONS ON VOTING

Legal restrictions on voter registration have existed since the founding of the nation. Most groups in the United States have been involved in the suffrage issue at one time or another.

Historical Restrictions

In colonial times, only white males who owned property with a certain minimum value were eligible to vote, leaving a far greater number of Americans ineligible to take part in the democratic process. Because many of government's functions are in the economic sphere and concern property rights and the distribution of income and wealth, some of the Founding Fathers felt it was appropriate that only people who had an interest in property should vote on these issues. The idea of extending the vote to all citizens was, according to South Carolina delegate Charles Pinckney, merely "theoretical nonsense." Of paramount concern to the backers of the Constitution was that the government should be as insulated as possible from the shifting electoral will of the population. A restricted vote meant a more stable government. An unrestricted vote would result, as Elbridge Gerry of Massachusetts declared at the Constitutional Convention, in "the evils . . . [which] flow from the excess of democracy."

FRANCHISE
The legal right to vote, extended to African Americans by the Fifteenth Amendment, to women by the Nineteenth Amendment, and to all citizens age eighteen and over by the Twenty-sixth Amendment.

The logic behind this restriction of the **franchise** to property owners was seriously questioned by Thomas Paine in his pamphlet *Common Sense:*

Here is a man who today owns a jackass, and the jackass is worth $60. Today the man is a voter and goes to the polls and deposits his vote. Tomorrow the jackass dies. The next day the man comes to vote without his jackass and cannot vote at all. Now tell me, which was the voter, the man or the jackass?[12]

The writers of the Constitution resolved the issue by allowing the states to decide who should vote. Thus women were allowed to vote in Wyoming in 1870 but not in the entire nation until the Nineteenth Amendment was ratified in 1920.

It wasn't until the Jacksonian era of the 1830s that the common man (but not woman) began to be heralded as the backbone of democracy. Men without property were first given the right to vote in the western states, but by about 1850 most white adult males in virtually all the states could vote without any property qualification. North Carolina was the last state to eliminate its property test for voting—in 1856.

Extension of the franchise to African-American males occurred with the passage of the Fifteenth Amendment in 1870. This enfranchisement was short-lived, however, as the "redemption" of the South by white racists rolled back these gains by the end of the century. As discussed in Chapter 5, only in the 1960s were African Americans, both male and female, able to participate in large numbers in the electoral process. Women received full national voting rights with the Nineteenth Amendment in 1920. The most recent extension of the franchise occurred when the voting age was reduced to eighteen by the Twenty-sixth Amendment in 1971.

Douglas Wilder, the first African American to be elected governor of Virginia.

Current Eligibility and Registration Requirements

Voting requires **registration,** and registration requires satisfying voter qualifications, or legal requirements. These requirements are the following: (1) citizenship, (2) age (eighteen or older), and (3) residence—the duration varying widely from state to state and with types of elections. In addition, most states disqualify mental incompetents, prison inmates, convicted felons, and election-law violators.

Each state has different qualifications for voting and registration. In every state except North Dakota, registration must take place before voting. Also, many states still require a personal appearance at an official building during normal working hours to register.[13] In general, a person must register well in advance of an election, although voters in Maine, Minnesota, Oregon, and Wisconsin are allowed to register up to and on election day.

Some argue that these registration requirements are responsible for much of the nonparticipation in our political process. One study[14] showed that they reduce national voter turnout by about 9 percent. Certainly, since their introduction in the late nineteenth century, registration laws have had the effect of reducing the voting participation of African Americans and immigrants.

There also is a partisan dimension to the debate over registration and non-voting. When Congress considered the National Voter Registration Act of 1989, support among Republican legislators was stronger than had been the case in the past, when Republicans generally feared that an expanded electorate

REGISTRATION
The entry of a person's name onto the list of eligible voters for elections.
Registration requires meeting certain legal requirements such as age, citizenship, and residency.

[12]Thomas Paine, *Common Sense* (London: H. D. Symonds, 1792), p. 28.
[13]Twenty states now allow registration by postcard, however.
[14]Raymond E. Wolfinger and Steven J. Rosenstone, "The Effect of Registration Laws on Voter Turnout," *American Political Science Review* (March 1978), pp. 22–48.

Voting in the Noninformation Age

According to Philip E. Converse, former director of the Institute for Social Research at the University of Michigan, one of the biggest problems facing democracy in the United States is the low level of public information about government and politics. Information is vital to the performance of a democratic system that is dependent on high levels of voter participation and activism. Yet, Converse finds levels of information are declining in spite of the spread of new technologies such as cable television, satellite broadcasting, and computer information services.

The reason for the decline is that information is not "free." Instead, there are real information costs in receiving, absorbing, sorting out, analyzing, reflecting on, storing, and recalling information. Converse explains that the ability and willingness to receive and store political information is directly related to how much information the person already has absorbed. Those who possess little information find what they see and hear unintelligible and tune it out. Those who have a reservoir of information seek out and process new facts about politics.

Low levels of information are one explanation for low voter turnout in the United States. In fact, one might ask why people vote at all. The argument that there is a *payoff* or *direct benefit* to the voter seems untenable if you consider that a single vote in the presidential election equals one one-hundred millionth of the total vote cast. The odds of one vote making a difference in an election are too remote to be considered. Converse reminds us that many citizens vote from habit or a sense of civic duty.

Low information levels and interest result in less voting by the poorly informed and higher turnout among the better informed. However, there is a process by which those with less information can orient themselves to the candidates and issues and make a reasonable choice. They take their cues about issues from friends and co-workers who are informed, from the news media, and from candidate advertising. Party labels, ideological identification as liberal or conservative, or incumbent name are some of the cues that are effective. In a democracy, cue taking is useful and allows for more participation than would otherwise occur. Indeed, although citizen information and voter turnout is relatively low, many argue that it is still sufficient to make a representative democracy work.

In addition, the checks and balances built into our system force parties and leaders to abandon radical positions and propose more moderate policies for the relatively ill-informed voters to support or oppose. Although Converse notes that the centrist quality of American politics adds to the stability of the system, the real reason for the moderate tone of debate is because lack of information forces voters to choose the middle. He says, ". . . voters tend to huddle near the center more as a default of ignorance than by conviction." Indeed, political elites and activists in both political parties often hold more extreme positions than the party identifiers in the general population.

In spite of the low level of public information and motivation to get involved in politics, democracy is "legitimate" in the United States because the system itself invites but does not force people to vote. People understand that they could vote if they felt like it; it's a matter of choice. Moreover, the system is not a "direct democracy" and thus voters select representatives who in turn steer the system regardless of voter turnout. This process is repeated regularly, and people understand that they may change their government and are not stuck permanently with the current leaders or policies. Converse points out that many voters go to the polls to "throw the rascals out." Politicians understand this, fear being labeled the "rascal," and so spend time and effort to understand their constituents' needs whether they voted or not.

Exercise in Critical Thinking

1. If the news media were required to present more information about candidates and their stands on the issues, would voters use the information?

2. Think about the cues that voters might use to sort out the information received through the campaign process. How can the cues be manipulated by the campaign itself?

3. Would voter interest and information seeking increase if political parties and candidates took stronger and more clearly expressed positions on issues?

SOURCE: Philip E. Converse, "Perspectives on the Democratic Process," *ISR Newsletter,* Vol. 16, no. 2.

would help to elect more Democrats. The bill required that states provide voter registration forms as part of their applications for drivers' licenses, that all states allow voters to register by mail, and that voter registration forms be made available at a wider variety of public places and agencies, and prohibited states from purging people's names off the voter registration lists for failing to vote. Election fraud would have been made a federal crime, and it would have become a federal crime to intimidate voters into not casting their ballots.

The question arises as to whether registration is really necessary. If it decreases participation in the political process, perhaps it should be dropped altogether. Still, as those in favor of registration requirements argue, such requirements may prevent fraudulent voting practices, such as multiple voting or voting by noncitizens.

■ HOW DO VOTERS DECIDE?

Political scientists and survey researchers have collected much information about voting behavior. This information sheds some light on which people vote and why people decide to vote for particular candidates. We have already discussed factors influencing voter turnout. Generally, the factors that influence voting decisions can be divided into two groups: socioeconomic and demographic factors, and psychological factors.

Socioeconomic and Demographic Factors

The socioeconomic and demographic factors include, but are not limited to, the following: (1) education, (2) income and **socioeconomic status,** (3) religion, (4) ethnic background, (5) sex, (6) age, and (7) geographic region. These influences all reflect the voter's personal background and place in society. Some have to do with the family into which a person is born: race, religion (for most people), and ethnic background. Others may be the result of choices made throughout an individual's life: place of residence, educational achieve-

DID YOU KNOW?

That on July 1, 1990, forty-eight days after the Nebraska Democratic primary for governor, Ben Nelson was finally declared the winner by the State Board of Conveners (he won by 42 votes out of 89,400 votes cast, which was a margin of only .05 of one percent, making it the closest primary or general election for governor in modern American politics)?

SOCIOECONOMIC STATUS
A category of people within a society who have similar levels of income and similar types of occupations.

Registering eighteen-year-old voters.

ment, or profession. It is also clear that many of these factors are related. People who have more education are likely to have higher incomes and to hold professional jobs. Similarly, children born into wealthier families are far more likely to complete college than children from poorer families. Furthermore, some of these demographic factors relate to the psychological factors—as we shall see.

Education.   More education seems to be highly correlated with voting Republican. Those who leave school earlier rather than later tend to vote Democratic. As can be seen in Table 10-6, 56 percent of college graduates voted

TABLE 10-6
Vote by Groups in Presidential Elections Since 1960 (in percent)

	1960		1964		1968			1972		1976		
	JFK	Nixon	LBJ	Goldwater	Humphrey	Nixon	Wallace	McGovern	Nixon	Carter	Ford	McCarthy
NATIONAL	50.1	49.9	61.3	38.7	43.0	43.4	13.6	38	62	50	48	1
SEX												
Male	52	48	60	40	41	43	16	37	63	53	45	1
Female	49	51	62	38	45	43	12	38	62	48	51	*
RACE												
White	49	51	59	41	38	47	15	32	68	46	52	1
Nonwhite	68	32	94	6	85	12	3	87	13	85	15	*
EDUCATION												
College	39	61	52	48	37	54	9	37	63	42	55	2
High school	52	48	62	38	42	43	15	34	66	54	46	*
Grade school	55	45	66	34	52	33	15	49	51	58	41	1
OCCUPATION												
Professional	42	58	54	46	34	56	10	31	69	42	56	1
White collar	48	52	57	43	41	47	12	36	64	50	48	2
Manual	60	40	71	29	50	35	15	43	57	58	41	1
AGE												
Under 30 years	54	46	64	36	47	38	15	48	52	53	45	1
30–49 years	54	46	63	37	44	41	15	33	67	48	49	2
50 years and older	46	54	59	41	41	47	12	36	64	52	48	*
RELIGION												
Protestants	38	62	55	45	35	49	16	30	70	46	53	*
Catholics	78	22	76	24	59	33	8	48	52	57	42	1
POLITICS												
Republicans	5	95	20	80	9	86	5	5	95	9	91	*
Democrats	84	16	87	13	74	12	14	67	33	82	18	*
Independents	43	57	56	44	31	44	25	31	69	38	57	4
REGION												
East	53	47	68	32	50	43	7	42	58	51	47	1
Midwest	48	52	61	39	44	47	9	40	60	48	50	1
South	51	49	52	48	31	36	33	29	71	54	45	*
West	49	51	60	40	44	49	7	41	59	46	51	1
MEMBERS OF LABOR UNION FAMILIES	65	35	73	27	56	29	15	46	54	63	36	1

*Less than 1 percent.
Note: 1976 and 1980 results do not include vote for minor party candidates.

for Bush in the 1988 election and only 43 percent voted for Dukakis. The relationship is not invariable, however. In 1964, college graduates voted 52 percent for Democrat Johnson and 48 percent for Republican Goldwater. Typically, those with less education are more inclined to vote for the Democratic nominee. In 1984, Mondale received 43 percent and Reagan 57 percent of the vote from high school graduates, whereas those with only a grade-school education voted 51 percent for Mondale and 49 percent for Reagan. The same pattern held in 1988 when 56 percent of the college graduates voted for Bush compared with 43 percent of those who have not completed high school.

TABLE 10-6
Vote by Groups in Presidential Elections Since 1960 (in percent)

	1980			1984		1988	
	Carter	Reagan	Anderson	Mondale	Reagan	Dukakis	Bush
NATIONAL	41	51	7	41	59	45	53
SEX							
Male	38	53	7	36	64	41	57
Female	44	49	6	45	55	49	50
RACE							
White	36	56	7	34	66	40	59
Nonwhite	86	10	2	87	13	86	12
EDUCATION							
College	35	53	10	39	61	43	56
High school	43	51	5	43	57	49	50
Grade school	54	42	3	51	49	56	43
OCCUPATION							
Professional	33	55	10	34	66	40	59
White collar	40	51	9	47	53	42	57
Manual	48	46	5	46	54	50	49
AGE							
Under 30 years	47	41	11	40	60	47	52
30–49 years	38	52	8	40	60	45	54
50 years and older	41	54	4	41	59	49	50
RELIGION							
Protestants	39	54	6	39	61	33	66
Catholics	46	47	6	39	61	47	52
POLITICS							
Republicans	8	86	5	4	96	8	91
Democrats	69	26	4	79	21	82	17
Independents	29	55	14	33	67	43	55
REGION							
East	43	47	9	46	54	49	50
Midwest	41	51	7	42	58	47	52
South	44	52	3	37	63	41	58
West	35	54	9	40	60	46	52
MEMBERS OF LABOR UNION FAMILIES	50	43	5	52	48	57	42

*Less than 1 percent.
Note: 1976 and 1980 results do not include vote for minor party candidates.

SOURCE: *The Gallup Report*, November 1984, p. 32, *New York Times*, November 10, 1988, p. 18.

DID YOU KNOW?

That the sixteen candidates who received public funding in the 1988 presidential primary elections raised $213.8 million and spent $210.7 million in the campaign?

Income and Socioeconomic Class.   If we measure socioeconomic class by profession, then professionals and businesspersons, as well as white-collar workers, tend to vote Republican. Manual laborers, factory workers and especially union members are more likely to vote Democratic. The effects of income are much the same: The higher the income, the more likely it is that a person will vote Republican. Conversely, a much larger percentage of low-income individuals vote Democratic. But there are no hard and fast rules. There are some very poor individuals who are devoted Republicans just as there are some extremely wealthy supporters of the Democratic party. In some recent elections, the traditional pattern did not hold. In 1980, for example, many blue-collar Democrats voted for Ronald Reagan. The 1988 election saw Bush getting 49 percent of the blue-collar vote, a decline of 5 percent from Reagan's 1984 victory.

Religion.   In the United States, Protestants have traditionally voted Republican, and Catholics and Jews have voted Democratic. Like the other patterns discussed, however, these are somewhat fluid. Nixon obtained 52 percent of the Catholic vote in 1972, and Johnson won 55 percent of the Protestant vote in 1964. The Catholic vote was evenly split between Carter and Reagan in 1980, but went heavily for Reagan in 1984. In 1988, Republican candidate Bush obtained more votes from Catholics than did the Democratic candidate Dukakis.

Ethnic Background.   Traditionally, the Irish have voted for Democrats. So too have Slavs, Poles, and Italians. However, Anglo-Saxon and northern European ethnic groups have voted for Republican presidential candidates. These patterns were disrupted in 1980 when Reagan obtained much of his support from several of the traditionally Democratic ethnic groups, with the help of fundamentalist religious groups.

African Americans voted principally for Republicans until Roosevelt's New Deal. Since then they have largely identified with the Democratic party. Indeed, the Democratic presidential candidates have received, on average, more than 80 percent of the African-American vote since 1956.

Sex.   Until recently, there seemed to have been no fixed pattern of voter preference by sex in presidential elections. One year more women than men would vote for the Democratic candidate; another year more men than women would do so. Some political analysts believe that a "gender gap" became a major determinant of voter decision making in the 1980 presidential election. Ronald Reagan obtained 15 percentage points more than Carter among male voters, whereas women gave about an equal number of votes to each candidate. Polls continued to show greater approval ratings of Reagan among men than women. Several reasons have been advanced for this gender gap, including Reagan's refusal to endorse the Equal Rights Amendment, his aggressive promilitary stance (one study indicates that women are less likely than men to favor military action[15]), the "feminization" of families living in poverty, and the increasing number of women in the work force. In 1984, the gender gap amounted to 9 percent nationally, with 64 percent of male voters casting their ballots for Ronald Reagan and 55 percent of the female voters doing the same. The gender gap decreased in 1988 to about 7 percentage points.

[15]Sandra Baxter and Marjorie Lansing, *Women in Politics: The Invisible Majority* (Ann Arbor: University of Michigan Press, 1980), p. 57.

Age. Age clearly seems to relate to an individual's voting behavior. Younger voters have tended to vote Democratic; older voters have tended to vote Republican. It was only the voters under thirty who clearly favored Carter during the Carter-Reagan election in 1980. This trend was reversed in 1984, when voters under thirty voted heavily for Ronald Reagan and again voted Republican in 1988.

Geographical Region. As we noted earlier, the formerly Solid (Democratic) South has crumbled. In 1972, Republican Nixon obtained 71 percent of the southern vote, whereas McGovern only obtained 29 percent. Reagan drew 52 percent of the southern vote in 1980 and 58 percent in 1984.

Democrats still draw much of their strength from large northern and eastern cities. Rural areas tend to be Republican (and conservative) throughout the country except in the South, where the rural vote still tends to be heavily Democratic. On average, the West has voted Republican in presidential elections. Except for the 1964 election between Goldwater and Johnson, the Republicans have held the edge in western states in every presidential election since 1956.

Psychological Factors

In addition to socioeconomic and demographic explanations for the way people vote, there are at least three important psychological factors, which are rooted in attitudes and beliefs held by voters. These are (1) party identification, (2) perception of the candidates, and (3) issue preferences.

Party Identification. With the possible exception of race, party identification has been the most important determinant of voting behavior in national elections. As we pointed out in Chapter 7, party affiliation is influenced by family and peer groups, by age, and by psychological attachment. During the 1950s, independent voters were a little more than 20 percent of the eligible electorate. In the middle to late 1960s, however, party identification began to weaken, and by the 1970s independent voters had become roughly 30 percent of all voters. In 1988, the estimated proportion of independent voters was 33 percent. Independent voting seems to be most concentrated among new voters, particularly among new young voters. Thus we can still say that party identification for established voters is a major determinant in voter choice.

Perception of the Candidates. Another psychological factor, candidate image, seems to be important in a voter's choice for president. We do not know as much about the effect of candidate image as we do about party identification, however, because it is difficult to make systematic comparisons of candidate appeal over time. The evidence is mixed. Data complied by Warren Miller and others[16] show some important differences in the strength of this factor on voter choice from one election to the next. These researchers found that perceptions of *both* candidates were positive in 1952, 1960, and 1976, whereas in 1956 Eisenhower's image was highly favorable, and Stevenson's was neutral. In 1964, very positive ratings for Johnson contrasted with very negative perceptions of Goldwater. Nixon's positive 1968 and 1972 ratings allowed him

DID YOU KNOW?

That the greatest declines in voter turnout between 1984 and 1988 occurred among young voters, the less educated, and minorities?

[16]Warren E. Miller, Arthur H. Miller, and Edward J. Schneider, *American National Election Studies Data Sourcebook* (Cambridge, Mass.: Harvard University Press, 1980), pp. 127, 129; Center for Political Studies 1980 National Election Study.

DID YOU KNOW?

That in the 1988 election, about 15 to 20 percent of all votes cast in Florida, California, and parts of Texas were by absentee ballot?

to defeat his negatively evaluated opponents. In 1980, both Reagan and Carter had negative images. The researchers also determined that, except in 1964 and 1976, Republican candidates were evaluated more favorably by the voters than were the Democratic candidates. To some extent, voter attitudes toward candidates are based on emotions (such as trust) rather than on any judgment about experience or policy. One of the keys to Bush's victory in 1988 was his ability to raise his favorability ratings during the campaign while Dukakis's ratings fell precipitously.

Issue Preferences.   Issues make a difference in presidential and congressional elections. Although personality or image factors may be very persuasive, most voters have some notion of how the candidates differ on basic issues or at least know that they want a change in the direction of government policy.

Historically, economic issues have the strongest influence on voters' choices. When the economy is doing well, it is very difficult for a challenger, particularly at the presidential level, to defeat the incumbent. On the other hand, increasing inflation, a rising rate of unemployment, or a high interest rate is likely to work to the disadvantage of the incumbent. Studies of how economic conditions affect the vote differ in their conclusions: Some indicate that people vote on the basis of their personal economic well-being, whereas other studies seem to show that people vote on the basis of the nation's overall economic health.

Foreign policy issues become more prominent in a time of crisis. Although the parties and candidates differ greatly over policy toward South Africa, for example, foreign policy issues are only truly influential when armed conflict is a possibility. Clearly, public dissension over the war in Vietnam had an effect on elections in 1968 and 1972. In 1980, the Reagan campaign capitalized on recent Soviet initiatives and the Iranian hostage crisis to persuade the voters that the United States was declining in power and respect.

Some of the most heated debates in American political campaigns take place over the social issues of abortion, the role of women, the rights of homosexuals, and prayer in the public schools. In general, presidential candidates would

Governor Michael Dukakis campaigning in a coffee shop. Is the purpose of such a campaign stop to convince two voters or to play to the news cameras?

prefer to avoid such issues because voters who care about these questions are likely to be offended if the candidate does not share their view.

From time to time, drugs, crime, and corruption become important campaign issues. The Watergate affair cost the Republicans a number of congressional seats in 1974, and its aftereffects probably defeated Gerald Ford in 1976. By the end of the Reagan administration in 1988, there were at least three potentially damaging scandals lying in wait for Republican candidates: The individuals charged in the Iran-*contra* affair were about to go to trial, Attorney General Meese faced criticism for assisting friends to get government contracts, and the Defense Department was investigating a number of individuals, in and out of government, for massive profiteering, and bribery in defense contracts. If the president or high officials are involved in truly criminal or outrageous conduct, the issue will undoubtedly influence voters.

All candidates try to set themselves apart from their opposition on crucial issues in order to attract voters. What is difficult to ascertain is the extent to which issues overshadow partisan loyalty or personality factors in the voters' minds. It appears that some campaigns are much more issue oriented than others. Some research has shown that **issue voting** was most important in the presidential elections of 1964, 1968, and 1972, and moderately important in 1980; 1992 remains to be seen.

ISSUE VOTING
Voting for a candidate based on how he or she stands on a particular issue.

GETTING INVOLVED

Voting

In nearly every state, before you are allowed to cast a vote in an election, you must first register. Specific registration laws vary considerably from state to state, and, depending on how difficult state laws make it to register, some states have much higher rates of registration and voting participation than do others.

What do you have to do to register and cast a vote? Most states require that you meet minimum residence requirements. In other words, you must have lived in the state in which you plan to be registered for a specified period of time. You may retain your previous registration, if any, in another state, and you can cast an absentee vote if your previous state permits that. The minimum residency requirement is very short in some states, such as one day in Alabama or ten days in New Hampshire and Wisconsin, but in other states, as much as fifty days (in Arizona or Tennessee) must elapse before you can vote. Other states with voter residency requirements have minimum-day requirements in between these extremes. Twenty states do not have any minimum residency requirement at all.

Nearly every state also specifies a closing date by which you must be registered before an election. In other words, even if you have met a residency requirement, you still may not be able to vote if you register too close to the day of the election. The closing date is different in certain states (Connecticut, Delaware, and Louisiana) for primary elections than for other elections. The closing date for registration varies from election day itself (Maine, Minnesota, Oregon, and Wisconsin) up to fifty days (Arizona). Delaware specifies the third Saturday in October as the closing date.

In most states your registration can be revoked if you do not vote within a certain number of years. This process of automatically "purging" the voter registration lists of nonactive voters happens every two years in about a dozen states, every three years in Georgia, every four years in more than twenty other states, every five years in Maryland and Rhode Island, every eight years in North Carolina, and every ten years in Michigan. Ten states do not require this purging at all.

What you must do to register and remain registered to vote varies from state to state and even from county to county within a state. In general, you must be a citizen of the United States, at least eighteen years old on or before election day, and a resident of the state in which you intend to register.

Using Iowa as an example, you would normally register through the local county auditor. If you move to a new address within the state, you must also change your registration to vote by contacting the auditor. Postcard registrations must be postmarked or delivered to the county auditor no later than the twenty-fifth day before an election. Party affiliation may be changed or declared when you register or reregister, or you may change or declare a party at the polls on election day. Postcard registration forms in Iowa are available at many public buildings, from labor unions, at political party headquarters, at the county auditors' offices, or from campus groups. Mobile registrars may be made available by calling your party headquarters or your county auditor.

For more information on voting registration, you should contact your county or state officials, party headquarters, labor union, or local chapter of the League of Women Voters.

CHAPTER SUMMARY

1. People may choose to run for political office to further their careers, to carry out specific political programs, or in response to certain issues or events. Others are recruited by political parties, interest groups, close friends, or family.

2. The legal qualifications for holding political office are minimal at both the state and local levels, but most segments of the population do not run for office. Holders of political office are predominantly white and male and are likely to be from the professional class.

3. American political campaigns are lengthy and extremely expensive. In the last decade, they have changed from being party-centered to being candidate-centered in response to technological innovations and decreasing party identification.

4. Candidates have begun to rely less on the party and more on paid professional consultants to perform the various tasks necessary to wage a political campaign. The first person hired is a campaign director who then decides how to accomplish the tasks of financing the campaign, gaining maximum media coverage, scheduling campaign events, recruiting assistants for fieldwork, and conducting research.

5. The crucial task of professional political consultants is image building.

6. The campaign organization devises a campaign strategy to maximize the candidate's chances of winning. Whether to emphasize style or substance is a strategic issue.

7. Candidates use public opinion polls to gauge their popularity and to test the mood of the country.

8. The amount of money spent in financing campaigns is steadily increasing. There have been a variety of corrupt practices acts designed to regulate campaign finance. The Federal Election Campaign Acts of 1972 and 1974 instituted major reforms by limiting spending and contributions. Incumbents have benefited from this legislation.

9. The Federal Election Campaign Act of 1974, as amended in 1976, allows corporations, labor unions, and interest groups to set up political action committees (PACs) to raise money for candidates.

10. After the 1968 Democratic convention, the McGovern–Fraser Commission was appointed to study the problems of the primary system. It formulated new rules, which were also adopted by Republicans in many states. These reforms opened up the nomination process for the presidency to all voters.

11. The presidential campaign must follow two strategies. First, primaries must be won state by state within the party. Second, after the national convention and the nomination of one person to carry the party standard, candidates must appeal not only to the party faithful but also to independent voters and to those from the opposing party.

12. A presidential primary is a statewide election to help a political party determine its presidential nominee at the national convention. Almost two-thirds of the states and the District of Columbia have some form of primary. Other states use the caucus method of choosing convention delegates.

13. Different types of presidential primaries include the closed primary, the open primary, the blanket primary, and the run-off primary. Some argue for a single, nationwide presidential primary election to replace the state-by-state system.

14. Delegates from each state, apportioned on the basis of state representation, are sent to the national convention. A credentials committee determines which delegates may participate.

15. The United States uses the Australian ballot, a secret ballot that is prepared, distributed, and counted by government officials.

16. The office-block ballot groups candidates according to office. The party-column ballot groups candidates according to party labels and symbols.

17. To minimize the possibility of voting fraud, the use of a canvassing board to tabulate and certify election returns is common. Each party often appoints poll watchers who may make a challenge if a voter is unqualified or if his or her vote appears invalid.

18. In making a presidential choice on election day, the voter technically does not vote directly for a candidate but chooses between slates of presidential electors. The slate that wins the most popular votes throughout the state gets to cast all the electoral votes for the state. The candidate receiving a majority (270) of the electoral votes wins.

19. It is possible for a candidate to become president without obtaining a majority or plurality of the popular vote.

20. Both the mechanics and the politics of the electoral college have been sharply criticized. There are many proposed reforms, including a direct election where candidates are elected on a popular-vote basis.

21. Voter participation in the United States is low (and declining) compared with that of other countries. Some view the decline in voter turnout as a threat to representative democracy, whereas others believe it simply indicates greater satisfaction with the status quo.

22. There is an association between nonvoting and a person's age, education, minority status, and income level. Another factor is the extent to which elections are competitive within a state.

23. Citizens may purposely and rationally decide not to seek the necessary information they need to cast an intelligent vote because the information is too costly (in terms of time, attention, and so on) to obtain; they may rely instead on information supplied by candidates and through the mass media. Citizens may decide not to vote because they believe that any one person's vote will not make a difference.

24. In colonial times, only white males with a certain minimum amount of property were eligible to vote. The suffrage issue has involved, at one time or another, most groups in the United States.

25. Current voter eligibility requires registration, citizenship, and specified age and residence requirements. Each state has different qualifications. It is argued that these requirements are responsible for much of the nonparticipation in the political process in the United States.

26. Socioeconomic or demographic factors that influence voting decisions include (a) education, (b) income and socioeconomic class, (c) religion, (d) ethnic background, (e) sex, (f) age, and (g) geographic region.

27. Psychological factors that influence voting decisions include (a) party identification, (b) perception of candidates, and (c) issue preferences.

QUESTIONS FOR REVIEW AND DISCUSSION

1. Think about the U.S. senators from your own state. How did each begin in politics? To what extent are they "self starters?" Did either of your senators hold political office before running for the national legislature? What are the major sources of support and campaign funding for each of the senators?

2. What factors have led to the replacement of the old-time politician or political boss by the modern political consultant? Why do such consultants only work for candidates with similar political philosophies as their own? How might this sharing of viewpoints weaken a campaign plan?

3. Suppose you were going to run for election on the Democratic ticket in your community. What demographic groups in the population would you try to recruit as supporters and voters?

4. What is the relationship between the primary elections in the states and the national convention of the political party? Who are the delegates to the national convention and whom do they represent?

5. How would our elections change if we abolished the electoral college and the electoral vote and held a national popular election for president instead?

SELECTED REFERENCES

Paul R. Abramson, John H. Aldrich, and David W. Rohde, *Change and Continuity in the 1988 Elections* (Washington, D.C.: Congressional Quarterly Press, 1990). A solid social-science analysis of the 1988 elections for president and Congress, with thorough analysis of the short-term and long-term forces that influenced the elections.

Larry Bartels, *Presidential Primaries and the Dynamics of Public Choice* (Princeton, N.J.: Princeton University Press, 1987). Studies the primary process and the dynamics that propel one candidate to the nomination.

Bruce Cain, John Ferejohn, and Morris Fiorina, *The Personal Vote: Constituency Service and Electoral Independence* (Cambridge, Mass.: Harvard University Press, 1987). The study assesses the relationship between the elected official and his or her constituents in the United States and Great Britain, analyzing the influence of the constituency on public policy decisions.

M. Margaret Conway, *Political Participation in the United States* (Washington, D.C.: Congressional Quarterly Press, 1985). The nature and extent of participation in American politics. Factors examined include citizens' life experiences, their psychological orientations to politics, the political environment, the legal context in which participation occurs, and the decision process by which citizens evaluate the costs and benefits of participation.

France Fox Piven and Richard A. Cloward, *Why Americans Don't Vote* (New York: Pantheon, 1988). The authors trace the decline in voter turnout to the 19th century and examine the class basis for different levels of voter turnout among Americans.

Stephen A. Salmore and Barbara G. Salmore, *Candidates, Parties, and Campaigns: Electoral Politics in America* (Washington, D.C.: Congressional Quarterly Press, 1989). Identifies the central characteristics of successful and unsuccessful campaigns and discusses the challenges to the role of the political parties and how the parties have responded.

THE MEDIA

WHAT IF . . . WE COULD VOTE WITH OUR VIDEO REMOTE CONTROL?

Imagine the scene. An American family is gathered around the television set watching its favorite sitcom. At the end of the program, still laughing at the antics of the characters, the father, Bob Larsen, announces that it is time to attend to a more serious issue. The president and members of the Congress are going to present their positions on placing a $1 per gallon tax on gasoline to help clean up the environment. Bob, his wife, Leona, and their two children settle back.

The president speaks for about five minutes, followed by leading members of the House and the Senate. Earlier in the week, each of the major networks had shown "specials" on the issue. Several of the cable channels lobbied for the tax by programming hours of nature shows. After keying in her Social Security number on the video remote control, Leona Larsen is cleared to vote on the legislative question flashed on the screen. She enters her decision, pressing "1" for Yes. Bob Larsen enters his identification and chooses "2" for No. Within several hours, the results are known: The gasoline tax is defeated by a combination of voters in rural states and urban areas.

This may seem farfetched, but the technology for voting from the home is already available. With either cable TV lines or telephone connections, it is possible to establish two-way communications using the remote control for the television to enter numbers or letters. Cable companies have already experimented with two-way interactions with their subscribers.

There are a number of pluses to at-home voting. Probably the greatest advantage would be the increase in voter turnout. More people watch the Super Bowl game than vote for president of the United States. By allowing individuals to vote from home, all barriers to accessibility would be eliminated. The handicapped, the aged, and the homemaker with small children, all of whom have difficulty getting to the polls, could vote easily. The college student living in the dormitory would not need to register in the college town. The naturalized citizen who is embarrassed by his weak language skills could vote privately and without worrying about communicating with voting officials.

There would be a number of logistical problems to work out: Only eligible individuals could vote, so some sort of identity code would be necessary; individuals could only vote once, so a checking mechanism would be necessary; and some access would have to be provided for those who lack a television or a remote controller. Finally, we would need to protect the anonymity of each voter.

Of far more importance are the constitutional and political issues. If "remote voting" is legal, would it be restricted only to choosing candidates from lists on the television screen, or, as in the example here, could individuals vote on issues? Some states, like California, regularly list referenda on the ballot, and voters could easily make those decisions by remote choice. But could the Congress of the United States delegate its decision-making power to the voters? The Constitution presently has no provisions for a national referendum, but it could be amended.

Voting by video remote seems to be a logical extension of the media age. But can television convey the quality of information that voters need to make reasonable choices? To what extent will all campaigns and issues become even more saturated with "image" advertising appeals to viewers' emotions? Television is unsurpassed in its ability to convey action and mood, but can it do justice to complex political issues? Would voters be willing to watch programs about public policy and use the information to choose between alternative policies and programs? With evidence suggesting that the least-informed voters make their choices at the last minute and under the influence of media-supplied information, it is likely that television balloting would increase the influence of these voters.

---

1. *Does television have the capacity to produce programs that examine policy issues in depth?*
2. *Can TV educate viewers to political issues without bias or manipulation?*
3. *Would the possibility of voting from home lead to superficial decisions by voters or to higher interest and participation in politics?*

Historian Daniel J. Boorstin said, "Nothing is 'really' real unless it happens on television."[1] It is not surprising that in a Roper poll, when asked which news source they thought was most credible, most Americans chose the national TV news commentators.[2]

Any study of people and politics, including public opinion, political parties, campaigns, elections, and voter behavior, must take as a given the enormous importance that the media have in American politics today. Not only are the newscasters and their programs the most trusted information sources in our society but the media also depend on the political system for much of the news they report. The relationship between the media and politics can best be described as reciprocal; the media need politics and politicians to report on, and political leaders need the media to campaign, to persuade, and to influence. This mutual dependence has sometimes led each party to feel mistreated. Republican leaders frequently complain that the press is too liberal (that is, too critical of Republicans), whereas Democrats argue that the media are controlled by big business (read "Republicans").

> **DID YOU KNOW?**
>
> That the first "wire" story transmitted by telegraph was sent in 1846?

■ THE MEDIA'S FUNCTIONS

The mass media perform a number of different functions in any country. In the United States we can list at least six. Almost all of them can have political implications, and some are essential to the democratic process. These functions are as follows: (1) entertainment, (2) reporting the news, (3) identifying public problems, (4) socializing new generations, (5) providing a political forum, and (6) making profits.

[1]*The Quotable Quotations Book,* ed. Alec Lewis (New York: Cornerstone Library, 1981), p. 283.
[2]*U.S. News & World Report,* February 21, 1983, p. 49.

Network booths at the 1988 Democratic convention.

Satellite vans for the news services covering the convention.

Entertainment

By far the greatest number of radio and television hours are dedicated to entertaining the public. The battle for prime-time ratings indicates how important successful entertainment is to the survival of networks and individual stations. There is no direct linkage between entertainment and politics; however, network dramas often introduce material that may be politically controversial and that may stimulate public discussion. One controversial segment of "L.A. Law" discussed the "right-to-die" of a paralyzed woman. Made-for-TV movies have focused on many controversial topics, including AIDS, incest, and wife-battering.

Reporting the News

The mass media in all their forms—newspapers, radio, television, cable, magazines—have as their primary goal the reporting of news. The media convey words and pictures about events, facts, personalities, and ideas. The protections of the First Amendment are intended to keep the flow of news as free as possible because it is an essential part of the democratic process. If citizens cannot get unbiased information about the state of their community and their leaders' actions, how can they make voting decisions? Perhaps the most incisive comment about the importance of the media was that made by James Madison, who said:

> A people who mean to be their own governors must arm themselves with the power knowledge gives. A popular government without popular information or the means of acquiring it, is but a prologue to a farce or a tragedy or perhaps both.[3]

Identifying Public Problems

The power of information is important, not only in revealing what the government is doing or is doing wrong, but also in determining what the government ought to do—in other words, in setting the public agenda. The mass media identify public problems, such as the scandal of "missing children," and sometimes help to set up mechanisms to deal with them (in this example, the missing children hotline, "Childfind"). American journalists also work in a long tradition of uncovering public wrongdoing, corruption, and bribery and of bringing such wrongdoing to the public's attention. Closely related to this investigative function is that of presenting policy alternatives. Because public policy is often complex and difficult to make entertaining, programs devoted to public policy are not often scheduled for prime-time television. Several networks, however, have produced "white papers" on foreign policy and on other issues.

Socializing New Generations

The media are a major influence on the ideas and beliefs of all adults, but particularly the younger generation and recent immigrants. Through the transmission of historical information (sometimes fictionalized), the presentation of American culture, and the portrayal of all the diverse regions and groups

[3]Quoted in "Castro vs. (Some) Censorship," editorial in the *New York Times,* November 22, 1983, p. 24.

in the United States, the media teach young people and immigrants about what it is to be an American. The extensive coverage of elections is a socializing process for these groups.

Providing a Political Forum

As part of their news function, the media also provide a political forum for leaders and the public. Candidates for office use news reporting to sustain interest in their campaigns, whereas officeholders use the media to gain support for their policies or to present an image of leadership. Presidential trips abroad are an outstanding way for the chief executive to get colorful, positive, and exciting news coverage that makes him look "presidential." The media also offer a way for the citizen to participate in public debate, either through letters to the editor or televised editorials. The question of whether more public access should be provided is discussed later in the chapter.

Making Profits

Most of the news media in the United States are private, for-profit corporate enterprises. One of their goals is to make profits—for employee salaries, for expansion, and for dividends to the stockholders who own the company. Profits are made, in general, by charging for advertising. Advertising revenues are usually directly related to circulation or listener/viewer ratings.

Several well-known outlets are publicly owned—public television stations in many communities and National Public Radio. These operate without commercials and are locally supported and often subsidized by the government and corporations.

Added up, these factors form the basis for a complex relationship among the media, the government, and the public. Throughout the rest of this chapter, we examine some of the many facets of this relationship. Our purpose is to set a foundation for understanding how the media influence the political process.

Walter Cronkite and Dan Rather discuss the 1988 presidential convention. Do Americans depend too heavily on what news personalities tell them, rather than making up their own minds?

> **DID YOU KNOW?**
>
> That in a 1989 public opinion poll, 63 percent of Americans expressed the view that news organizations help to fuel controversies?

HIGHLIGHT

How Much Does a Thirty-Second Commercial Cost?

It's cheaper to campaign in a rural state than in the big city (although it's harder to raise campaign funds), mainly because there are fewer voters to woo. As the chart to the right indicates, a single contribution of $450 would buy a thirty-second commercial for a candidate on the most popular show on television in South Dakota. To buy the equivalent advertising "spot" in New York City would cost $30,000. The extreme variance in advertising costs is di-rectly related to the number of viewers in each market as well as to the competition to buy those precious seconds. It is worth noting that whereas in New York City, residents are used to candidates approaching them through television, in South Dakota, with its relatively small population, candidates had better spend a lot of time meeting people—campaigning only by television would make candidates seem pretty remote to the constituents.

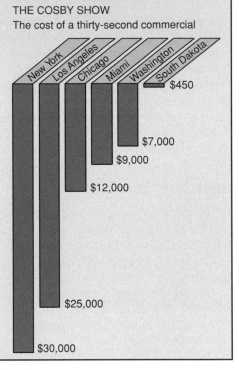

THE COSBY SHOW
The cost of a thirty-second commercial

New York — $30,000
Los Angeles — $25,000
Chicago — $12,000
Miami — $9,000
Washington — $7,000
South Dakota — $450

■ HISTORY OF THE MEDIA IN THE UNITED STATES

Many years ago Thomas Jefferson wrote:

> Were it left to me to decide whether we should have a government without news-papers, or newspapers without a government, I should not hesitate a moment to prefer the latter.[4]

Although the media have played a significant role in politics since the founding of this nation, they were not as overwhelmingly important then as they are today. For one thing, politics was controlled by a small elite who communicated personally. For another, during the early 1800s news traveled slowly. If an important political event occurred in New York, it wasn't known until five days later in Philadelphia; ten days later in Hartford, Connecticut; Baltimore, Maryland; and Richmond, Virginia; and fifteen days later in Boston, Massachusetts. Of course, there were one or more newspapers in each major city and they served some of the functions that newspapers do today. Most of these early newspapers were weeklies, but a few daily publications existed also.

[4]Quoted by Richard M. Clurman in "The Media Learn a Lesson," *New York Times,* December 2, 1983, p. 2-A.

Roughly three thousand newspapers were being published by 1860. Some of these, such as the *New York Tribune,* were mainly sensation-mongers, concentrating on crimes, scandals, and the like. The *New York Herald* specialized in self-improvement and what today would be called practical news. Although sensational and biased reporting often created political divisiveness (this was particularly true during the Civil War), many historians believe the growth of the printed media played an important role in unifying the country.[5] A few printed publications stand out as being instrumental in changing the fate of the nation. As we pointed out in Chapter 2, Thomas Paine's *Common Sense* was not only a best-seller (half a million copies) but also a catalyst for the revolt against the mother country. Later *The Federalist Papers* were instrumental in creating the atmosphere necessary for the ratification of the Constitution.

The Rise of the Political Press

Americans may cherish the idea of a nonpartisan press, but in the early years of the nation's history the number of politically sponsored newspapers was significant. The sole reason for the existence of such periodicals was to further the interests of the politicians who paid for their publication. Printing newspapers was relatively expensive in the 1700s and 1800s, and poor transportation meant they could not be widely distributed. As a consequence, political newspapers had a small clientele who paid a relatively high subscription price.

As chief executive during this period, George Washington has been called a "firm believer" in **managed news.** Although acknowledging that the public had a right to be informed, he felt there were some matters that should be kept secret and that news that might damage the image of the United States should not be published. Washington, however, made no attempt to control the press.

Several political periodicals were partially subsidized by the government. No one seemed to think it was improper for government-paid employees to work on partisan newspapers. Indeed, the change to objectivity on the part of the press that we value so much was not due to any increase in idealism; rather, it was the result of a reduction in the cost of printing newspapers and the consequent rise of the self-supported mass-readership daily.

The Development of Mass-Readership Newspapers

Two inventions led to the development of mass-readership newspapers. The first was the high-speed rotary press; the second was the telegraph. Faster presses meant lower per-unit costs and lower subscription prices. The telegraph meant instant access to news between major cities at a low cost. By 1848, the Associated Press had developed the telegraph into a nationwide apparatus for the dissemination of all types of information on a systematic basic.

Along with these technological changes came a growing population and increasing urbanization. Daily newspapers could be supported by a larger, more urbanized populace, even if the price were only a penny. Finally, the burgeoning, diversified economy encouraged the growth of advertising, which meant that newspapers could obtain additional revenues from merchants who seized on the opportunity to promote their wares to a larger public. The days of dependence on political interests for newspapers were coming to an end.

[5]Richard N. Current, T. Harry Williams, and Frank Freidel, *American History: A Survey* (New York: Alfred A. Knopf, 1979), pp. 299–301.

DID YOU KNOW?

That there are approximately 1,250 full-time radio, TV, and newspaper correspondents in Washington, D.C.?

MANAGED NEWS
Information generated and distributed by the government in such a way as to give government interests priority over candor.

High-speed presses made newspapers cheap and easily available. What effect did this have on politics?

DID YOU KNOW?

That, during World War I, President Wilson established a government propaganda agency that gave out 6,000 press releases and sent 75,000 speakers into communities?

The Popular Press and Yellow Journalism

Students of the history of journalism have noted a change in the last half of the 1800s, not in the level of biased news reporting, but in its origin. Whereas earlier politically sponsored newspapers expounded a particular party's point of view, most mass-based newspapers expounded whatever political philosophy the owner of the newspaper happened to have. William Randolph Hearst thought the United States should go to war against Spain. He was also interested in selling newspapers. Tensions between the United States and Spain grew over a bloody colonial war the Spanish were fighting in Cuba, and Hearst used this episode to launch his anti-Spanish campaign with screaming headlines. When the U.S. battleship *Maine* exploded in Havana harbor at 9:40 P.M. on February 15, 1898, killing 260 officers and soldiers, Hearst and others wrote such inflammatory articles that President William McKinley had little

A cartoon attacking "yellow journalism." William Randolph Hearst (left) and Joseph Pulitzer are lampooned. Is today's emphasis on the personal life of politicians another form of sensationalism?

choice but to go to war. Spain was blamed for the explosion, even though later investigations could not fix responsibility on anyone.[6]

Even if newspaper heads did not have a particular political axe to grind, they often allowed their editors to engage in sensationalism and **yellow journalism.** Exposing the questionable or simply personal activities of a prominent businessperson, politician, or socialite was front-page material. Newspapers then as today made their economic way by maximizing readership, and as the *National Enquirer* shows today, with its more than five million circulation, sensationalism is rewarded by high levels of readership.

YELLOW JOURNALISM
A derogatory term for sensationalistic, irresponsible journalism. Reputedly, the term is short for "Yellow Kid Journalism," an allusion to the cartoon "The Yellow Kid" in the old *New York World,* a paper especially noted for its sensationalism.

The Age of the Electromagnetic Signal

The first scheduled radio program in the United States featured politicians. On the night of November 2, 1920, KDKA-Pittsburgh transmitted the returns of the presidential election race between Harding and Cox. The listeners were a few thousand people tuning in on very primitive, homemade sets.

By 1924, there were nearly 1,400 radio stations. But it wasn't until 8:00 P.M. on November 15, 1926, that the electronic media came into its own in the United States. On that night, the National Broadcasting Company (NBC) debuted with a four-hour program broadcast by twenty-five stations in twenty-one cities. Network broadcasting had become a reality.

Even with the advent of national radio in the 1920s and television in the late 1940s, many politicians were slow to understand the significance of the electronic media. The 1952 presidential campaign involved a real role for TV, starting with the convention during which television coverage helped Eisenhower win the delegate disputes and the nomination. Even though Eisenhower had problems reading a teleprompter that didn't work, his vice presidential running mate put the TV time to good use. Accused of hiding a secret slush fund, Nixon replied to his critics with his famous "Checkers" speech. He denied the attacks, cried real tears, and said the only thing he ever received

[6]John Tebbel, *The Media in America* (New York: Thomas Y. Crowell, 1974), pp. 269–272.

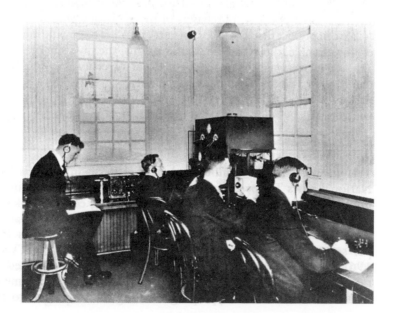

KDKA Radio in Pittsburgh, broadcasting the 1920 presidential election returns.

HIGHLIGHT

Style and Sell in Political Advertising

Political advertising has its fashions. At the birth of political advertising on television—the so-called Paleolithic Age of TV politics—media experts favored a blunt appeal to voters known as the hard sell. In the 1950s, viewers were treated to scenes of straight-faced forthright endorsements of their favorites or candidates commenting on the state of the nation.

This approach was an extention of techniques that were favored in the marketing of commercial products—and that are still reliable standbys in the selling of antacids and other products for which it is deemed an advantage to leave nothing to the viewer's imagination. But political ads have changed. The newer advertising approach, developed in the 1960s, was to create a mood or emotion in the viewer, rather than concentrating on detailed description of the product. Gradually this approach was adopted in political TV advertising as well. The notorious "daisy girl" advertisement of the 1964 presidential campaign used an emotion-provoking series of visual images in an attempt to link Barry Goldwater to the use of nuclear weapons—and frighten voters away from him.

Although few studies demonstrate the superiority of any approach to political ads, the soft sell has been considered effective by media professionals. This genre reached its height in the Reagan media blitz during the 1984 election campaign. Many Reagan ads appeared to be almost apolitical, showing beautiful images of grandfathers playing with grandchildren or well-kept small towns with good-looking young people. The ads were supposed to provoke deeply rooted and extremely positive feelings toward the viewer's family, faith, and country and to link these with the benevolent, smiling president whose name appeared on the screen for the last five seconds of the spot. The use of images and symbols bypassed the viewer's rational consciousness, appealing instead to the emotions and even the subconscious.

By the 1988 presidential campaign, political consultants and media people were growing tired of this "light" approach to promoting candidates. Roger Ailes, who headed George Bush's media team, declared that the electorate "was not going to take any bull," and

Willie Horton's mugshot.

set to work creating a series of aggressive TV commercials emphasizing the weaknesses of Bush's opponent. It was Ailes who publicized the case of Willie Horton, a convicted felon who committed a crime while on an approved furlough from a Massachusetts prison. The furlough was supported by the Democratic presidential candidate, Massachusetts Governor Michael Dukakis. Critics of the ad claimed that it distorted the facts, tried to make Dukakis look like a supporter of crime and, because Willie Horton is an African American, appealed to racial bias. Although serious in tone, the thirty-second commercial differed from the staid commercials of the fifties in its use of memorable—and menacing—imagery. A shot of a revolving door disgorging men in prison uniforms outside penitentiary walls cut away to an unflattering photograph of Governor Dukakis, while a deep and threatening voice recited the litany of Willie Horton's crimes.

The popularity of so-called negative or attack ads grew after Dukakis's resounding defeat in 1988. It is likely, however, that a wide variety of techniques will continue to be employed in the thirty-second political commercial. Ailes, who created the Willie Horton spot, also made commercials for Bush using the feel-good, mood-inducing techniques perfected during the Reagan years. There is no way of knowing what the fashion will be in political advertising for television in 1992.

SPIN
An interpretation of campaign events or election results that is most favorable to the candidate's campaign strategy.

through granting favors such as a personal interview with the candidate. Third, an important task for the scheduler in the campaign is the planning of events that will be photogenic and interesting enough for the evening news. A related goal, although one that is more difficult to attain, is to convince reporters that a particular interpretation of an event is correct. By 1988, the art of putting the appropriate "spin" on a story or event had become highly developed. Each presidential candidate's press advisers tried to convince the journalists that their interpretation of the primary results was correct. For example, Bush's people tried to convince the press that he didn't really expect to win the Iowa caucuses anyway, while the Dole camp insisted that winning the Iowa caucuses was a great and unexpected victory. Journalists began to report on the different spins and how the candidates tried to manipulate campaign news coverage.

Going for the Knock-Out Punch—Presidential Debates

Perhaps of equal importance to paid-for political advertisements is the performance of the candidate in a televised presidential debate. After the first such debate, which took place in 1960, candidates became aware of the great potential of television for changing the momentum of a campaign. In that first meeting, John Kennedy, the young senator from Massachusetts, took on the vice president of the United States, Richard Nixon. Kennedy's fresh, energetic appearance on television gave him an advantage over the vice president who looked tired, unshaven, and haggard. Polls taken by Gallup indicated that 43 percent of the respondents felt that Kennedy was the leader in the race after the first debate. By the end of the third debate, Nixon, who had a slight lead in September, was 3 percentage points behind.[8] What the Kennedy-Nixon debate emphasized was the importance of the candidate's televised image to the campaign.

In general, challengers have much more to gain from debating than do incumbents. Challengers hope that the incumbent may make a mistake in the debate and undermine his "presidential" image. Incumbent presidents are loath to debate the challenger because it puts their opponent on an equal footing with the president. In the Ford-Carter debate of 1976, Gerald Ford, the

[8]Theodore H. White, *The Making of the President 1960* (New York: Atheneum Publishers, 1961), pp. 294–295.

> ### DID YOU KNOW?
>
> That a majority of those who watched the 1960 Kennedy-Nixon debates on TV said Kennedy had won, but a majority of those who listened to them on the radio felt that Nixon did better than Kennedy?

A family watching the Kennedy and Nixon debates on TV, 1960. What candidate qualities are displayed in TV debates?

CRITICAL PERSPECTIVE

What's in the News?

Both politicians and the general citizenry are subject to what seems to be endless coverage of election campaigns. No sooner is the president inaugurated than the networks begin speculating on the potential candidates for the next presidential election, four years away. During the election year itself, coverage of candidates, delegate counts, the convention struggles, and even coverage of the media effort to report on the campaign dominates the news. The question that researchers have tried to answer is to what degree such extensive coverage influences election results. In investigating this question, many researchers have looked carefully at the kind of news actually reported during election campaigns.

Candidates and critics of the media alike charge that the media, particularly television, tend to avoid reporting on the issues of the campaign. If the voters cannot find out what the issue differences are among candidates, how can they make judgments about which candidate would best represent their interests? Research suggests that the criticism is true. Particularly during the primary campaigns, stories about which candidate is winning the "horse race" clearly dominate those concerned with issues. Even later in the campaign, when the media carry more stories oriented toward issues, the focus is often on candidate differences with respect to emotional issues such as abortion rather than foreign policy. The electronic media admit this but say that such reporting is easier.

"Horse race" journalism changes the kind of stories that become news. Because they are looking for excitement and conflict to report to their readers and viewers, reporters and news producers tend to focus on which candidate seems to be ahead and what the daily strategic decisions of each campaign are rather than what the candidates are saying. The language used in such stories is drawn from sports: "the game plan," "clash," "attack," "offense and defense." Reporting on the campaign becomes very similar in style to reporting on the "Road to the Super Bowl." The polling efforts of the candidates and the media themselves add to this emphasis on "who's ahead." By constantly polling the public on the campaign, the networks and major newspapers are creating news about who is currently winning. In the 1976 election, Thomas Patterson divided all of the media stories about the campaign into "substance" stories and "game" stories. He found that 50 to 60 percent of all of the stories concerned the game, whereas only 30 to 35 percent focused on issues, policies, and candidate traits.* In 1980,

*Thomas E. Patterson, *The Mass Media Election* (New York: Praeger, 1980).

another study showed that 67 percent of the stories on CBS news, during the primaries, were "horse race" stories.

This emphasis on who's winning can be explained by the "melodramatic imperative" of the media. Paul Weaver suggests that news stories about the campaign must be affected by the media's need to entertain their audience. The demand for melodrama emphasizes the unusual story, the exciting development, the unfolding of the plot. As Weaver puts it, the story opens "in the snows of New Hampshire; the plot develops, election by election, until it reaches its *denouement* before the national conventions, not as people who are running for elective office, but as figures deeply and totally embroiled in an all-out struggle."**

Accenting the competition between the candidates tends to cast everything they do and say as part of the struggle. Their issue positions, choices of running mates, decisions to campaign on the road or "to stay in the Rose Garden," and relationships with interest groups are all interpreted as decisions with a strategic purpose: to increase the chances of winning. As one of Carter's campaign aides said, "Reporters are . . . telling Americans no candidate takes any position except to enhance his election prospects. It's automatically assumed that nobody can do anything because he believes it."*** Politicians complain that it becomes impossible to get the media to report their policy initiatives; what gets reported are their blunders on the campaign trail. Yet politicians are not blameless here. All too often, their managers plan campaign events with an eye toward getting the best pictures for the evening news. The question that remains is how this emphasis on the strategy of campaigns influences the minds of the voters.

Exercise in Critical Thinking

1. Why do the media and the candidates avoid talking about the issues?
2. To what extent are voters swayed by the "horse race" style of reporting?
3. How do candidates manipulate the media to get better coverage?

**Paul Weaver, "Captives of Melodrama," *New York Times Magazine,* August 29, 1986, p. 6.
***Quoted in David L. Swanson, "And That's the Way It Was?" Television Covers the 1976 Presidential Campaign," *Quarterly Journal of Speech* (October 1977), p. 246.

incumbent, agreed to debate Jimmy Carter because Ford was already running behind in the polls and he hoped to improve his chances through the debate. There is little doubt in most analysts' minds that the 1976 debates helped Carter, the challenger, win the election by a narrow margin.

Aware of the pitfalls of debating, Carter, as the incumbent in 1980, tried to avoid debating with Ronald Reagan and the independent candidate John Anderson. Finally, Reagan and Carter faced off a few days before the election. Both men were skilled debators. Reagan, of course, had thirty years of experience as an actor behind him. His relaxed manner seemed at odds with Carter's denunciation of Reagan as a militaristic hawk. How could a hawk be so genial? Reagan also was able to zero in on the Democratic incumbent's main weakness—the state of the economy.

In 1984, Walter Mondale made another attempt to weaken the public's perception of Reagan by picturing the president as too old for the job and as being unable to deal with the facts of specific policy positions. In the first debate, Mondale's strategy rattled the president, but in the second debate, Reagan played his usual calm, congenial, humorous role, and Mondale was unable to gain any advantage.

Both Bush and Dukakis were considered experienced debaters in 1988 but Dukakis, with his showy intellectual skills, was the one favored to do well. Bush held his own in the first debate and seemed more articulate in the second, thus denying the Massachusetts governor any chance to improve his position through the debate.

The crucial fact about the practice of televising debates is that, although debates are publicly justified as an opportunity for the voters to find out how candidates differ on the issues, what the candidates want is to capitalize on the power of television to project an image. They view the debate as a strategic opportunity to improve their own images or to point out the failings in their opponent. Candidates are very aware that not only is the actual performance important but also the morning-after interpretation of the debate by the news media may play a crucial role in what the public thinks. Regardless of the risks of debating, the potential for gaining votes is so great that candidates will undoubtedly continue to seek televised debates.

DID YOU KNOW?

That Franklin Roosevelt held approximately 1,000 press conferences during his terms as president?

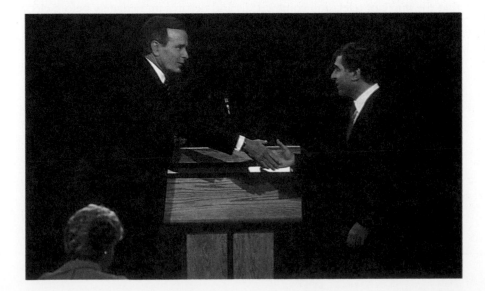

George Bush and Michael Dukakis at the conclusion of the 1988 presidential debates.

Investigating the Government

The mass media not only wield considerable power when it comes to political campaigns but they also can, in one way or another, wield power over the affairs of government and over government officials. Perhaps the most notable example in recent times concerns the activities of *Washington Post* reporters Bob Woodward and Carl Bernstein. Assigned to cover the **Watergate break-in,** these two reporters undertook an investigation that eventually led to the resignation of President Nixon (and later to a best-selling book and a film, *All the President's Men*). Investigative reporting—with its antecedents in the muckraking journalism of the first decades of this century—became increasingly popular, and journalism as a career attracted a new crop of inquisitive, probing reporters intent on going beyond the news by digging for hidden facts. The 1988 presidential primary campaign saw intensive investigation of the private lives of the candidates, as discussed in the Highlight on page 343.

WATERGATE BREAK-IN
The 1972 illegal entry into the Democratic campaign offices engineered by the Nixon reelection campaign.

The Media and Public Attitudes

The question of how much influence the media have on public opinion is difficult to answer. Although one of the media's greatest powers is the ability to shape the public agenda by focusing attention on public problems and on particular political leaders, studies have shown that the media may not have as much power to change the minds of the people as has been thought. Generally, individuals watch television or read newspapers with certain preconceived ideas about political issues and candidates. These attitudes and opinions act as a kind of perceptual screen that blocks out information people find uncomfortable or that does not fit with their own ideas.

Voters watch campaign commercials and news about political campaigns with "selective attentiveness." That is, they tend to watch those commercials that support the candidate they favor and tend to pay attention to news stories about their own candidates. This process of selectivity also affects perceptions of the content of the news story or commercial and whether it is remembered. Apparently, the media are most influential with those persons who have not formed an opinion about political candidates or issues. Studies have shown that the flurry of television commercials and debates immediately before election day has the most impact on those voters who are truly undecided. Few voters change their minds under the influence of the media.

The Media and the Presidency

A love–hate relationship clearly exists between the president and the media. During the administration of John F. Kennedy, the president was seen in numerous photos scanning the *New York Times* and the *Washington Post*, as well as other newspapers, each morning to see how the press tallied his successes and failures. This led to frequent jocular comments about his speed-reading ability.

In the United States the prominence of the president is cultivated by a **White House press corps** that is assigned full time to cover the presidency. These reporters even have a lounge in the White House where they spend their days, waiting for a story to break. Most of the time they simply wait for the daily or twice-daily briefing by the president's **press secretary.** Because of

WHITE HOUSE PRESS CORPS
A group of reporters assigned full time to cover the presidency.

PRESS SECRETARY
The individual responsible for representing the White House before the media. The press secretary writes news releases, provides background information, sets up press conferences, and so on.

HIGHLIGHT

The Private Lives of Public Figures

In the summer of 1987, Craig Whitney, Washington editor of the *New York Times,* sent a letter to all aspirants for the 1988 presidential nomination. In the letter he asked them to provide the *Times* with personal information. He also asked that they waive their privacy rights and allow the *Times* to obtain files from the FBI, through the Freedom of Information Act and from confidential records of House or Senate ethics committees.

This unprecedented intrusion by the media into candidates' private lives followed on the heels of the "Gary Hart Affair," which broke in May of 1987. Democratic presidential frontrunner Senator Gary Hart (Colorado) was rumored for many years to be having extramarital affairs. When asked about these allegations, Hart invited the media to follow him around to see for themselves that there was nothing to the rumors. Acting on a tip, *Miami Herald* reporters flew to Washington, D.C., staked out Hart's townhouse, and observed him in the company of an attractive woman, twenty-nine-year-old Donna Rice, a model and aspiring movie actress. When the story broke, Hart denied any wrong-doing, insisting Rice was just an acquaintance and someone who wanted to work on his presidential campaign. The story further exploded when it was revealed

Gary Hart announces his withdrawal from the 1988 presidential race.

that he had met her before, called her several times, and had gone on a weekend trip with her to the Bahamas aboard a chartered yacht aptly named *Monkey Business.* In the wake of this story, Hart first fought back, then returned to Colorado where he withdrew from the race.

There were rumors about other candidates' infidelity. Jesse Jackson said he would refuse to answer questions about allegations regarding his personal sexual life. In June of 1987, the *Cleveland*

Plain Dealer reported that Ohio Governor Richard F. Celeste, who was considering a presidential candidacy, had been "romantically linked" to three women other than his wife. Governor and Mrs. Celeste refused to comment, saying it was a personal matter.

All of these developments signaled a sharp increase in the intrusion of the media into the private lives of public figures, setting off a lively debate on the rights of the media to explore such allegations. Some argued that this is an appropriate function of the media in a free society in which people have "the right to know" about character issues. Others objected to the media intrusion, noting that some of America's greatest presidents (including Franklin D. Roosevelt and John Kennedy) had extramarital affairs with no apparent adverse consequences for their leadership of the nation. It was also feared that the lack of privacy would discourage many bright, experienced, and valuable persons from presenting themselves as candidates for public office.

Whatever the pros and cons of media investigations, it appears that the precedent has been set for public figures to have, in the future, all aspects of their personality and behavior open to public scrutiny. Some commentators have called this process the "*People* magazining of politics."

the press corps's physical proximity to the president, the chief executive cannot even take a brief stroll around the presidential swimming pool without it becoming news. Perhaps no other nation allows the press such access to its highest government official. Consequently, no other nation has its airwaves and print media so filled with absolute trivia regarding the personal life of the chief executive and his family.

President Franklin D. Roosevelt brought new spirit to a demoralized country and led it through the Great Depression. His radio "**fireside chats**" brought hope to millions. Roosevelt's speeches were masterly in their ability to forge a common emotional bond among his listeners. His decisive announcement in 1933 on the reorganization of the banks calmed a jittery nation and pre-

FIRESIDE CHATS
Warm, informal talks by Franklin D. Roosevelt to a few million of his intimate friends—via the radio. Roosevelt's fireside chats were so effective that succeeding presidents have been urged by their advisers to emulate him by giving more radio and television reports to the nation.

President Franklin D. Roosevelt, the first president fully to exploit the airwaves for his benefit.

vented the collapse of the banking industry that was threatened by a run on banks in which nervous depositors were withdrawing their assets. His famous Pearl Harbor speech, following the Japanese attack on the U.S. Pacific fleet on December 7, 1941 ("a day that will live in infamy"), mobilized the nation for the sacrifices and effort necessary to win World War II.

Perhaps no president exploited the electronic media more effectively than Ronald Reagan. The "great communicator," as he was called, was never more dramatic than in his speech to the nation following the October 1983 U.S. invasion of Grenada. In this address, the president, in an almost flawless performance, appeared to many to have decisively laid to rest the uncertainty and confusion surrounding the event.

The relationship between the media and the president has thus been reciprocal; both institutions have used each other, sometimes positively, sometimes negatively. The presidency and the news media are mutually dependent.

President Bush responds to questions at a press conference.

■ SETTING THE PUBLIC AGENDA

Given that government officials have in front of them an array of problems with which they must deal, the process of setting the **public agenda** is constant. To be sure, what goes on the public agenda for discussion, debate, and ultimately policy action depends on many factors—not the least being each official's personal philosophy.

According to a number of studies, the media play an important part in setting the agenda, as well as in helping government officials to understand society's needs and desires better. W. P. Davison went so far as to claim that diplomats obtain the bulk of their information about what is happening in the world not from other diplomats but from the press.[9]

In recent years, television coverage has brought a number of issues to public attention and, consequently, to the attention of policy makers. Videotaped footage of the refugee camps in Ethiopia was captured by journalists. The painful images of thousands of children starving while relief shipments were stopped by the combatants in the conflict aroused public attention around the globe. Private efforts were mounted by groups and individuals, including the staging of a massive rock concert benefit, called "Live Aid," to raise money for famine relief. Although many foreign policy decision makers were aware of the situation in Ethiopia, media attention caused them to put enough

[9]W. P. Davison, "News and Media and International Negotiation," *Public Opinion Quarterly*, No. 38 (Summer 1974): 174–191.

PUBLIC AGENDA
Issues that are commonly perceived by members of the political community as meriting public attention and governmental action. The media play an important role in setting the public agenda by focusing attention on certain topics.

The Live-Aid concert in Philadelphia. Why did sponsors of this event choose a concert as the way to raise consciousness and funds to relieve famine in Africa?

DID YOU KNOW?

That it has been estimated that the U.S. government retains about 50 percent of the radio broadcast spectrum for government and military uses?

pressure on officials there to allow the shipments of food and medical supplies through to the camps.

Interest groups understand well the power of the media. After campaigning unsuccessfully for years against the tuna industry practice of using fishing nets that also captured dolphins, one group infiltrated a fishing crew and shot video film of the slaughter of hundreds of dolphins. The broadcast of this tape led to public outrage, congressional investigations of the industry, and a self-imposed ban on the practice by the major tuna merchandisers in the United States.

The relationship of the media to agenda setting is complex. Evidence is strong that whatever public problems receive the most media treatment will be cited by the public in contemporary surveys as the most important problems. On the other hand, politicians, whether at home or abroad, are able to manipulate media coverage to control some of its effects as well as exploit the media to press their agendas with the public.

GOVERNMENT REGULATION OF THE MEDIA

The United States has perhaps the freest press in the world. Nonetheless, regulation of the media does exist, particularly of the electronic media. Many aspects of this regulation were discussed in Chapter 4, when we examined First Amendment rights and the press.

The Electronic Media and Government Control

The First Amendment does not mention the electronic media—they didn't exist at that time. For many reasons, the government has much greater control over the electronic media than it does over printed media. Through the Federal Communications Commission (FCC), the number of radio stations has been controlled for many years, in spite of the fact that technologically we could have many more radio stations than now exist. Also, the FCC created a situation in which the three major TV networks have dominated the airwaves. Only recently did the FCC bow to public and political pressure to open up the TV airwaves to all the new technological devices now available. Most FCC rules have dealt with ownership of news media, such as how many stations a network can own.

In general, the broadcasting industry has successfully avoided government regulation of content by establishing its own code. This code consists of a set of rules determined by the National Association of Broadcasters, the lobby for the TV and radio industry, regulating the amount of sex, violence, nudity, profanity, and so forth allowed on the air. It should be noted that abiding by the code is voluntary on the part of networks and stations.

Since 1980, there has been continued public debate over whether the government should attempt to control polling and the "early calling" of presidential elections. On election night in 1980, the networks predicted that Ronald Reagan had been elected before numerous states had closed their polls. In 1984, this controversy over network predictions based on exit polls surfaced again. The concern expressed by many was that voters on their way to vote might not bother since the victor had already been declared. It was feared that the drop in turnout due to these voters would affect state and local races and,

The Parents Musical Resource Center tries to influence rock music lyrics. Should musical groups be censored, or is that a violation of the First Amendment?

because some types of voters such as factory workers are more likely to vote late in the day, the outcomes of elections and referenda might be seriously affected.

In 1984, the networks were careful to say that they would not project winners in any state until the polling places *in that state* were closed. However, with the different time zones and with a concentration of population (and electoral college votes) in the Northeast and Midwest, the networks were able to project a winner by 8:00 P.M., Eastern time, which was 5:00 P.M. on the West Coast.

Some legislators and citizens have called for a ban on exit polls or on releasing them before *all* polling places in the continental United States are closed. Others have called for a federal law establishing a uniform closing time for voting so that voting would end at the same time all over the country, and thus exit polls could not be a factor. In any event, although turnout has been lower than expected in many western states, studies suggest that the early announcement of election results based on exit polls has little effect on election outcomes.

Does National Security Justify Suppression of the News?

On October 25, 1983, the United States, supported by the island nations of Antigua, Barbados, Dominica, Jamaica, St. Lucia, and St. Vincent, invaded the island of Grenada. The purpose of the invasion, as stated by the president, was to rescue Americans on the island following a violent coup d'etat, and to replace a hard-line Marxist government. No advance notice was given to the media on the planned operation. Once the assault on Grenada began, no American reporters were allowed on the island for several days. Reporters who tried to get there on a chartered boat were ordered away by the U.S. forces. The U.S. government claimed that this news blackout was necessary to ensure a surprise attack.

The reaction of the American news media was strong and swift. By denying independent access, the government threatened American freedom and the

Marines take up positions in Panama as part of the operation to capture Manuel Noriega. Should the press be allowed to accompany troops on such missions?

role that the media play in keeping Americans informed. The media and other observers saw the blackout as censorship, and some denounced the military's control of information about the invasion as a blatant propaganda effort.

At the time of the U.S. invasion of Panama in 1989, the Pentagon agreed to send a small pool of reporters to cover the military operation. In fact, the press were allowed into the streets of Panama several hours after the invasion began. The first television pictures sent via satellite showed victorious American troops waving at friendly Panamanians. There were virtually no pictures of deaths and, even several days later, no stories about the civilian casualties in Panama.

The news media were criticized for their coverage of the Panamanian operation on two counts: First, journalists followed the lead of the administration and focused only on the "hunt for Noriega;" and, second, neither the print nor electronic media tried to investigate the question of civilian casualties. The major networks and newspapers claimed that the number of civilian deaths was so problematic, ranging from the American estimate of two hundred to Panamanian reports of more than two thousand, that they felt uncomfortable reporting a story based on such widely varying figures. The invasion of Panama suggests that even if the media are allowed to cover military operations, journalists tend to support the administration's perspective on the event.

MEDIA ACCESS
The public's right of access to the media. The FCC and the courts have gradually taken the stance that citizens do have an access right to the media.

PERSONAL ATTACK RULE
The rule promulgated by the FCC that allows individuals or groups air time to reply to attacks that have previously been aired.

■ THE PUBLIC'S RIGHT TO MEDIA ACCESS

Does the public have a right to **media access?** Both the FCC and the courts have gradually taken the stance that citizens have a right of access to the media, particularly the electronic media. The argument is that the airwaves are public, but, because they are used for private profit, the government has the right to dictate how they are used. It does so in many ways. In addition to the equal time rule for candidates, the FCC has also promulgated the **personal attack rule.** This rule allows individuals (or groups) air time to reply to attacks that have previously been aired. Another rule governing access to the airwaves involves the right of candidates opposed by a station to have time to reply to the station's statements about them.

Technology is giving more citizens access to the electronic media, in particular television. As more and more cable operators have more and more time to sell, some of that time will remain unused and will be available for public access. At the same time such developments as citizens' band radio, video magazines for the millions of videocassette recorder owners, and other technological changes are making the issue of media access by the public less important. The public increasingly has relatively cheap access to the electronic media, although not in the traditional forms.

■ BIAS IN THE MEDIA

Spiro T. Agnew, who resigned the vice presidency during the Nixon administration after having been implicated in a major kickback scheme while governor of Maryland, called the media "nattering nabobs of negativism." Agnew's criticism of the press was very accurate if you talk to conservatives; not so accurate if you talk to liberals. Relatively few objective studies of media bias have been undertaken to allow us to answer the charges. But Richard Hofstadter, in his extensive study of the 1972 presidential campaign,[10] found that the Democratic candidate, George McGovern, received a few percentage points more coverage than did Nixon. However, according to Hofstadter, Nixon received more favorable stories than McGovern. He concluded that there was no general bias in the media presentation of the 1972 presidential campaign.

Some critics of the electronic media continue to point out their perception of the electronic media's alleged antibusiness and progovernment intervention bias. The power of the media and its impact on American society is clearly a controversial and important subject. To what extent the mass media help to clarify issues and to contribute to a more enlightened public, as opposed to distorting and oversimplifying reality, is a topic hotly debated in the United States.

Jonathan Power has said that "the front page is a paper's most precious commodity. It helps set the nation's agenda."[11] If that is the case, then the media have indeed become a force in American politics equal to that of the traditional three branches of government.

> **DID YOU KNOW?**
>
> That Americans generally have an overall favorable view of the news media—82 percent report favorably on network TV news, 80 percent on local TV news, and 77 percent on daily newspapers?

[10]Richard Hofstadter, *Bias in the News* (Columbus: Ohio State University Press, 1976).
[11]*The Quotable Quotations Book,* ed. Alec Lewis (New York: Cornerstone Library, 1981), p. 181.

GETTING INVOLVED

Being a Critical Consumer of the News

Television and newspapers provide an enormous range of choice for Americans who want to keep informed. Still, critics of the media argue that a substantial amount of programming and print is colored either by the subjectivity of editors and producers or by the demands of profit making. Few Americans take the time to become critical consumers of the news, either in print or on the TV screen.

To become a critical news consumer, you must practice reading a newspaper with a critical eye toward editorial decisions. For example, what stories are given prominence on the front page of the paper and which ones merit a photograph? What is the editorial stance of the newspaper? Most American papers tend to have moderate to conservative editorial pages. Who are the columnists given space on the "op-ed" page, the page opposite the paper's own editorial page? For a contrast to most daily papers, occasionally pick up an outright political publication such as the *National Review* and *New Republic* and take note of the editorial positions.

Watching the evening news can be far more rewarding if you look at how much the news depends on "video" effects. You will note that stories on the evening news tend to be no more than three minutes long, stories with excellent videotape get more attention, and considerable time is taken up with "happy talk" or human interest stories that tap the emotions of the audience.

Another interesting study you might make is to compare the evening news with the daily paper on a given date. You will see that the paper is perhaps half a day behind the news but that the print story contains far more information. Head-

lines must take the place of videotape in grabbing your attention.

You can also be a more active consumer by voicing your views and suggestions to the producers of television news or to the editors of newspapers and magazines. These persons are often responsive to criticism and open to constructive suggestions; you might be surprised to find them so accessible.

If you wish to obtain more information on the media and increase your active role as a consumer of the news, you can contact one of the following organizations:

National Association of Broadcasters
1771 N St., N.W.
Washington, D.C. 20036
(202) 293-3500

National Newspaper Publishers Association
970 National Press Bldg.
Washington, D.C. 20045
(202) 662-7324

Accuracy in Media (a conservative group)
1275 K St., N.W., Suite 1150
Washington, D.C. 20005
(202) 371-6710

People for the American Way (a liberal group)
1424 16th St., N.W., Suite 601
Washington, D.C. 20036
(202) 462-4777

CHAPTER SUMMARY

1. The media are enormously important in American politics today. There is a complex and reciprocal relationship among the media, the government, and the public.

2. The media perform a number of functions, including (a) entertainment, (b) news reporting, (c) identifying public problems, (d) socializing new generations, (e) providing a political forum, and (f) making profits.

3. The media have always played a significant role in American politics. However, in the 1800s news traveled slowly and politics was controlled by a small group whose members communicated personally. The high-speed rotary press and the telegraph led to self-supported newspapers and mass readership.

4. In contrast to today's ideal of objective news coverage, in

the early years of this nation many publications were politically sponsored and contained partisan views.

5. The electronic media (television and radio) are growing in significance in the area of communications; new technologies, such as cable TV, are giving broadcasters the opportunity to air more specialized programs.

6. The media wield enormous political power during political campaigns and over the affairs of government and government officials by focusing attention on their actions.

7. Mastering the media is critical in today's political campaigns. This is done through paid-for political announcements and expert management of news coverage.

8. Of equal importance for presidential candidates is how they appear in presidential debates.

9. The media play an important role in setting the public agenda and in getting government officials to understand better the needs and desires of American society.

10. The relationship between the media and the president is close; both have used each other—sometimes positively, sometimes negatively.

11. The media in the United States, particularly the electronic media, are subject to government regulation, although the United States has possibly the freest press in the world. Most FCC rules have dealt with ownership of TV and radio stations.

12. When the United States invaded the island of Grenada on October 25, 1983, the media were not allowed on the island for national security reasons. This blackout raised the question of how the public's "right to know" should be balanced against the need to protect the national interests.

13. Whether the media clarify and enlighten issues or distort them through biased reporting is a hotly debated topic in the United States. Relatively few objective studies have been undertaken, and answers often depend on personal views or ideological orientations.

QUESTIONS FOR REVIEW AND DISCUSSION

1. Explain why the media and political candidates are dependent on each other. Why does this relationship sometimes become antagonistic, especially between the press and the president?

2. Suppose that you are the campaign manager for a U.S. Senate candidate in your state. What kinds of "media events" would you try to set up so that your candidate would get coverage? What meetings, parades, celebrations, and rallies would you have your candidate attend to provide good pictures for TV news? What kinds of assistance could you give to the newspeople to make them generally favorable to your campaign?

3. Compare the coverage of a political event, such as an election, or a speech, such as the State of the Union message, by the newspapers, the news magazines, television, and radio. How are pictures used to convey the story as compared with words? How does "editing" change the content and the effect of such a story?

4. How could the media become more responsive to their readers and viewers? Should there be more opportunities for individual citizens and groups to convey their messages through the media? If there were more opportunities for public access to television, for example, what groups would be most likely to take advantage of them?

5. Should the media be required to provide equal coverage to all of the candidates for an office and for all political parties? Is it fair for the two major political parties to be able to buy or otherwise obtain more coverage in every news medium?

SELECTED REFERENCES

David L. Altheide, *Media Power* (Beverly Hills, Calif.: Sage Publications, 1985). Explores how the mass media, especially television, structure our perceptions, expectations, and actions.

Ronald Berkman and Laura W. Kitch, *Politics in the Media Age* (New York: McGraw-Hill, 1986). Investigates the place of the mass media in the new American political landscape. Examines how the media cover the political world, how the political world uses the media, and effects of the media on political behavior.

Edward Epstein, *News from Nowhere* (New York: Random House, 1973). A critical examination of how television news is produced.

Doris A. Graber, *Media Power in Politics,* 3rd ed. (Washington, D.C.: Congressional Quarterly Press, 1990). This book explores the profound impact of the mass media on the political system. It has both an historical and a topical focus.

Mark Hertsgaard, *On Bended Knee: The Press and the Reagan Presidency* (New York: Random House, 1989). Using over 175 interviews, this interesting book discusses and analyzes the methods used by the Reagan White House public relations staff to manipulate and influence the media and create a favorable image of Reagan as well as generate acceptance of his policies.

Michael Parenti, *Inventing Reality: The Politics of the Mass Media* (New York: St. Martin's Press, 1986). How and why the print and television news media distort important aspects of social and political life. Emphasis is placed on suppression of news, underlying ideological values, mechanisms of information control, media ownership, and the role of newspeople, publishers, advertisers, and the government.

Neil Postman, *Amusing Ourselves to Death: Public Discourse in the Age of Show Business* (New York: Viking, 1985). Postman offers a serious critique of the way television conveys information and how it undermines the public's ability to analyze the news.

William W. Van Alstyne, *Interpretations of the First Amendment* (Durham, N.C.: Duke University Press, 1984). All about the First Amendment and its relationship to the electronic media.

A GLOBAL PERSPECTIVE
JUDICIAL SYSTEMS AROUND THE WORLD

Most of the judicial systems around the world belong to one of two groups—the civil law system or the common law system. These two systems differ in their historical beginnings and in some of their characteristics.

The civil law system grew out of ancient Roman law, which reached its highest development in the Roman Empire in the first and second centuries A.D. Of course, due to the many changes that have occurred over time, modern civil law systems are very different from the ancient Roman system.

Today, the civil law system is in effect in most continental European countries and in the Latin American, African, and Asian countries that were once colonies of those European countries. Japan and South Africa have civil law systems. There are civil law ingredients in the court systems of Islamic countries. Courts in the Soviet Union use a system similar in many ways to the civil law approach. In the United States, the state of Louisiana has in part a civil law system. So, too, do Puerto Rico, Quebec, and Scotland.

Common law systems have their roots in medieval England. The common law was shaped in the courts of the English kings and, beginning in the twelfth century, applied across the nation. The common law was assumed to represent the common customs of all English people. A common law system was adopted in the United States before and after the Revolutionary War. Common law systems exist today in England, Ireland, Canada, Australia, New Zealand, and India.

In a civil law system, the starting point in deciding a controversy is almost always a statute. Decisions made by judges in earlier similar cases (judicial precedents) are supposed to be given no more consideration than the opinions of other legal writers. In reality, however, precedents are widely followed by the courts. In a common law system, legal arguments in a case center around earlier judicial decisions. The idea is that the results in all similar cases should be the same,

King Henry II, originator of the grand jury and circuit courts.

Napoleon Bonaparte, creator of the Napoleonic Code, foundation of modern continental law.

so the arguments concern how similar the case in question is to previous cases and whether the decision should be the same as the decisions in those earlier cases. In recent years, statutes and administrative rules have become increasingly important in common law systems.

The judges in a civil law system take an active role in questioning witnesses and conducting court proceedings, which reduces the role of the attorneys. Because of this dominant role of the judges, these systems are often called "inquisitorial." In a common law system, the attorneys take a more active role, shaping the content and course of cases. That's why common law systems are often called "adversarial." These differences in the roles that judges play are becoming less definite, however, as American judges increasingly act to develop facts and issues in trials.

Courtroom for the Italian trial of the terrorists who hijacked the cruise ship Achille Lauro.

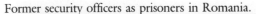

Former security officers as prisoners in Romania.

POLITICAL INSTITUTIONS

CHAPTER 12

THE CONGRESS

CHAPTER CONTENTS

WHAT IF . . . MEMBERS OF CONGRESS WERE LIMITED TO TWO TERMS?

We all know that members of the U.S. House of Representatives serve terms that last for two years, that members of the U.S. Senate serve terms that last for six years, and that both House and Senate members can be reelected indefinitely. In fact, some members of Congress have been able to achieve reelection so easily and often that occasionally they have served for as long as half a century in the national legislature! Most members, of course, serve far less time in office than that, but, once elected, most representatives and senators are hard to dethrone. What might happen, though, if members of the U.S. Congress were limited to serving only, say, two terms (four years in the House or twelve years in the Senate)?

The most obvious impact of the two-term limit would come in the area of seniority. Seniority, or the length of continuous service on the record of a member of Congress in either chamber, is the single most important factor in determining who gets to be the chair of a committee, who becomes a party leader, speaker of the House, or president pro tempore of the Senate, who is influential in floor debate, and who has an easier time getting his or her legislative measures adopted on the floor of Congress. With everyone limited to just two terms in office, distinctions of rank based on seniority would all but vanish, and

other criteria would have to be adopted in order to make it possible to tell the difference between more and less influential members. As was true in the early history of Congress, greater influence would probably go to those who are the best natural leaders because of telegenic magnetism, spellbinding oratorical powers, or intricate knowledge of the rules of procedure. Power on committees would likely become even more diffuse than it is now, and even very young legislators would be in a much better position to make a name for themselves and to pass laws to their liking.

Relationships between Congress and the White House would quite likely be affected, too, by a change to a two-term limit on membership in Congress. Presidents, assuming that their own terms were not changed, would know that they could easily last in office longer than most members of Congress. Hence, they would not have to confront in policy battles with Congress such powerful members as, say, Representative Jamie Whitten from Mississippi, who has been called "the permanent Secretary of Agriculture" owing to his chairing the House

Appropriations Committee's subcommittee on agriculture for many years while presidents and secretaries of agriculture came and went. From the presidential viewpoint, then, the two-term limit would seem to even the odds of success when dealing with members of Congress. From the perspective of Congress, on the other hand, this might increase all the more the power that senators and representatives fear and that has grown in the executive branch since World War II.

From the voters' perspective, it would be very likely that we would all have to get used to an entirely new set of people running for the

House and Senate every few years. That would make it imperative that voters have "cues" about how they might want to vote according to the personalities and issue positions taken by these new sets of candidates. Unless voters are able to educate themselves quickly about new candidates (which seems rather unlikely), it will be up to interest groups and party organizations to make candidates seem either more attractive or less so, depending on how they want us to vote. Even though this might lead to an increased role for private and public organized groups in the process of congressional elections, it is likely that the two-term limit would make it harder to "buy" the roll-call votes of the short-term members of Congress. On the other hand, if a member of Congress knows that she or he will be in office for two terms, what incentive is there to listen to "the folks back home?" One might expect that the limitation on congressional terms will result in elected officials who are less responsive to local constituency pressures and more responsive to their perceptions or their party's perceptions of proper public policy.

---

1. *Would two-term members of Congress be more in touch with the voters?*
2. *In a two-term Congress, what would seniority mean?*

Most Americans spend little time thinking about the Congress of the United States, although polls indicate they have a fairly poor opinion of that institution. The Congress, with its myriad committees, complicated rules and procedures, endless debates, and 535 voting members, is not easy to understand. Furthermore, Congress seems to attack some problems with glacial slowness; for example, writing new trade legislation to improve American competitiveness took more than eighteen months, while other issues, such as Pentagon waste and corruption, prick the attention of Congress only when scandal erupts.

For most citizens, contact with the Congress is measured by the responsiveness of their own representative or senator. If the constituent needs help in dealing with the federal bureaucracy, can the representative help? Did the senator meet with the members of the eighth-grade class from the local school? Does the congressperson come to the district for coffee or open meetings with constituents? What most Americans see of Congress is the work of their own representatives in their home states. The Congress, however, was created to work, not just for the constituents, but for the nation as a whole, and understanding the nature of the institution and the process of lawmaking is an important part of understanding how the policies that shape our lives are made.

■ WHY WAS CONGRESS CREATED?

The founders of the American republic believed that the bulk of the power that would be exercised by a national government should be in the hands of the legislature. As you will recall from Chapter 2, the authors of the Constitution were strongly influenced by their fear of tyrannous kings and powerful, unchecked rulers. They were also aware of how ineffective the confederal Congress had been during its brief existence under the Articles of Confederation.

The leading role envisioned for Congress in the new government is apparent from its primacy in the Constitution. Article I deals with the structure, the

John Lewis, former civil rights worker, was elected to Congress in 1986, representing a state in which he had been denied political participation twenty-five years earlier.

BICAMERALISM
The division of a legislature into two separate assemblies.

powers, and the operation of Congress, beginning in Section I with an application of the basic principle of separation of powers: "All legislative Powers herein granted shall be vested in a Congress of the United States, which shall consist of a Senate and House of Representatives." These legislative powers are spelled out in detail in Article I and elsewhere.

The **bicameralism** of Congress—its division into two legislative houses—was in part an outgrowth of the Connecticut Compromise, which tried to balance the big-state population advantage, reflected in the House, and the small-state demand for equality, which was satisfied in the Senate. Beyond that, the two chambers of Congress also reflected the social class biases of the founders. They wished to balance the interests and the numerical superiority of the common citizen with the property interests of the less numerous businesspeople, landowners, bankers, and merchants. This goal was achieved by providing in Sections 2 and 3 of Article I that the House of Representatives should be elected directly by "the People," whereas the Senate was to be chosen by the elected representatives sitting in state legislatures.

The elected House, then, was to be the common person's chamber, and the nonelected Senate was to be the chamber of the wealthy, similar to the division between the House of Commons and the House of Lords in England. Also, the House was meant to represent people, whereas the Senate was meant to represent the states, in accordance with the intent of the Connecticut Compromise. The issue of who counted as part of "the People" for electing members of the House was left up to the states. As a practical matter, the electorate as defined in state laws originally included only property-owning adult white males. Women, African Americans, the impoverished, many common workers, and Native Americans could not vote for congressional representatives. The logic of separate constituencies and separate interests underlying the bicameral Congress was reinforced by differences in length of tenure. Members of the House were required to face the electorate every two years, whereas senators could serve for a much more secure term of six years—even longer than the four-year term provided for the president. Furthermore, the senators' terms were staggered so that only one-third face election with the House members.

■ THE POWERS OF CONGRESS

The Constitution is both highly specific and extremely vague about the powers that Congress may exercise. The first seventeen clauses of Article I, Section 8, specify most of the **enumerated powers** of Congress—that is, powers expressly given to that body.

ENUMERATED POWERS
The powers specifically granted to the national government by the Constitution. The first seventeen clauses of Article I, Section 8, specify most of the enumerated powers of Congress.

Express Powers

The enumerated powers of Congress include the right to impose taxes and import tariffs, borrow money, regulate interstate commerce and international trade, establish procedures for naturalizing citizens, make laws regulating bankruptcies, coin (and print) money and regulate its value, establish standards of weights and measures, punish counterfeiting, establish post offices and postal roads, regulate copyrights and patents, establish lower federal courts, punish piracy and other illegal acts committed on the high seas, declare war, raise and regulate an army and navy, call up and regulate the state militias to enforce laws, to suppress insurrections, and to repel invasions, and govern the District of Columbia.

The most important of the domestic powers of Congress, listed in Article I, Section 8, are the rights to collect taxes, to spend money, and to regulate commerce, whereas the most important foreign policy power is the power to declare war. Other sections of the Constitution give Congress a wide range of further powers. Generally, Congress is able to establish rules for its own members, to regulate the electoral college, and to override a presidential veto.

Some functions are restricted to only one house. Under Article II, Section 2, the Senate must advise on and consent to the ratification of treaties, and must accept or reject presidential nominations of ambassadors, Supreme Court justices, and "all other Officers of the United States," but may delegate to the president, the courts, or department heads the power to make lesser appointments. Congress may regulate the appellate jurisdiction of the Supreme Court, regulate relations between states, and propose amendments to the Constitution.

The amendments to the Constitution provide yet another source of congressional power. Congress must certify the election of a president and a vice president or itself choose these officers if no candidate has a majority of the electoral vote (Twelfth Amendment), may levy an income tax (Sixteenth Amendment), and determines who will be acting president in case of death or incapacity of the president or vice president (Twentieth Amendment, Sections 3 and 4, and Twenty-fifth Amendment, Sections 2, 3, and 4). In addition, Congress is explicitly given the power to enforce, by appropriate legislation, the provisions of several other amendments.

The Necessary and Proper Clause

Beyond these numerous specific powers, Congress enjoys the right under Article I, Section 8 (the "elastic," or "necessary and proper," clause), "to make all Laws which shall be necessary and proper for carrying into Execution the foregoing Powers [of Article I], and all other Powers vested by this Consti-

> **DID YOU KNOW?**
>
> That under Senate rules, based on the number of voting-age constituents in the state, a senator from New York was entitled to mail 26,960,000 sheets of government-supplied paper in the form of newsletters in 1988?

Senator Joseph Biden chairs the Judiciary Committee hearings on the nomination of Judge David Souter. What is the role of the Senate committee in the nomination of Supreme Court justices?

tution in the Government of the United States, or in any Department or Officer thereof." This vague statement of congressional responsibilities has set the stage for a greatly expanded role for the national government relative to the states and has also constituted, at least in theory, a check on the expansion of presidential powers. By continuing to delegate powers to the executive branch, however, Congress has over time reduced the role it might otherwise play in national and international affairs.

The Constitution provides the foundation of congressional powers. Yet a complete understanding of the role that Congress plays requires a broader study of the functions that the national legislature performs for the American political system.

■ THE FUNCTIONS OF CONGRESS

Congress as an institution of government is expected by its members, by the public, and by other centers of political power to perform a number of functions. Our perceptions of how good a job Congress is doing overall are tied closely to evaluations of whether and how it fulfills certain specific tasks. These tasks include the following:

1. Lawmaking activities
2. Service to constituents
3. Representation of diverse interests
4. Oversight of the manner in which laws are implemented
5. Educating the public about national issues and setting the terms for national debate
6. Resolving conflicts in American society

The Lawmaking Function

LAWMAKING
The process of deciding the legal rules that govern our society. Such laws may regulate minor affairs or establish broad national policies.

LOGROLLING
An arrangement by which two or more members of Congress agree in advance to support each other's bills.

CASEWORK
Personal work for constituents by members of Congress.

The principal and most obvious function of any legislature is **lawmaking**. Congress is the highest elected body in the country charged with making binding rules for all Americans. Lawmaking requires decisions about the size of the federal budget, about issues such as abortion or school busing, and about the long-term prospects for war or peace. This does not mean, however, that Congress initiates most of the ideas for legislation that it eventually considers; the bulk of the bills that Congress acts on originates in the executive branch, and many other bills are traceable to interest groups and political party organizations. Through processes of compromise and **logrolling** (offering to support a fellow member's bill in exchange for that member's promise to support your bill in the future), backers of legislation attempt to fashion a winning majority coalition.

Service to Constituents

Individual members of Congress are expected by their constituents to act as brokers between private citizens and the imposing, often faceless, federal government. **Casework** is the usual form taken by this function of providing service to constituents. The legislator and his or her staff spend a considerable portion of time on casework activity, such as tracking down a missing Social Security check, explaining the meaning of particular bills to people who may

Congressman Romano Mazzoli talking with constituents in Louisville, Kentucky. Do legislators really learn from their constituents or are such chats primarily to win votes?

be affected by them, promoting a local business interest, or interceding with a regulatory agency on behalf of constituents who disagree with proposed bureaucratic rules and regulations. Legislators and analysts of congressional behavior regard this **ombudsman** role as an activity that strongly benefits the members of Congress. A government characterized by a large, confusing bureaucracy and complex public programs offers innumerable opportunities for legislators to come to the assistance of (usually) grateful constituents. Morris Fiorina suggests somewhat mischievously that senators and representatives prefer to maintain bureaucratic confusion in order to maximize their opportunities for performing good deeds on behalf of their constituents:

> Some poor, aggrieved constituent becomes enmeshed in the tentacles of an evil bureaucracy and calls upon Congressman St. George to do battle with the dragon. . . . In dealing with the bureaucracy, the congressman is not merely one vote of 435. Rather, he is a nonpartisan power, someone whose phone call snaps an office to attention. He is not kept on hold. The constituent who receives aid believes that his congressman and his congressman alone got results.[1]

OMBUDSMAN
An individual in the role of hearing and investigating complaints by private individuals against public officials or agencies.

The Representation Function

If constituency service carries with it nothing but benefits for most members of Congress, the function of **representation** is less certain and even carries with it some danger than the legislator will lose his or her bid for reelection. Generally, representation means that the many competing interests in society should be represented in Congress. It follows that Congress should be a body acting slowly and deliberately, whose foremost concern is to maintain a carefully crafted balance of power among competing interests.

REPRESENTATION
The function of Congress as elected officials to represent the views of their constituents.

The Trustee View of Representation. How is representation to be achieved? There are basically two points of view on this issue. The first approach is that

[1]*Congress: Keystone of the Washington Establishment* (New Haven: Yale University Press, 1977), pp. 44–47.

TRUSTEES
The idea that a legislator should act according to his or her conscience and the broad interests of the entire society, often associated with the British statesman Edmund Burke.

INSTRUCTED DELEGATES
The concept that legislators are agents of the voters who elected them and that they should vote according to the views of their constituents regardless of their own personal assessments.

POLITICO
The legislative role that combines the delegate and trustee concepts. The legislator varies the role according to the issue under consideration.

OVERSIGHT
The responsibility Congress has for following up on laws it has enacted to ensure that they are being enforced and administered in the way in which they were intended.

LEGISLATIVE VETO
Provision in a bill reserving to Congress or to a congressional committee the power to reject an act or regulation of a national agency by majority vote; declared unconstitutional by the Supreme Court in 1983.

legislators should act as **trustees** of the broad interests of the entire society and that they should vote against the narrow interests of their constituents as their conscience and their perception of national needs dictate.

The Instructed-Delegate View of Representation.   A view directly opposite to the notion of the legislator as trustee is that the members of Congress should behave as **instructed delegates;** that is, they should mirror the views of the majority of the constituents who elected them to power in the first place. On the surface, this approach is plausible and rewarding. For it to work, however, we must assume that constituents actually have well-formed views on the issues that are decided in Congress and, further, that they have clear-cut preferences about these issues. Neither condition is likely to be satisfied often. Most people generally do not have well-articulated views on major issues, and, among those who do, there frequently is no clear majority position but rather a range of often conflicting minority perspectives.

In a major study of the attitudes held by members of Congress about their proper role as representatives, Roger Davidson found that neither a pure trustee nor a pure instructed-delegate view was held by most legislators. Davidson's sampling of members of Congress showed that about the same proportion endorsed the trustee (28 percent) and delegate (23 percent) approaches to representation, but the clear preference was for the **politico** position—which combines the perspectives of both the trustee and the delegate in a pragmatic mix.[2]

The Oversight Function

Oversight of the bureaucracy is essential if the decisions made by Congress are to have any force. **Oversight** is the process by which Congress follows up on the laws it has enacted to ensure that they are being enforced and administered in the way Congress intended. This is done by holding committee hearings and investigations, changing the size of an agency's budget, and cross-examining high-level presidential nominees to head major agencies. Also, until 1983, Congress could refuse to accede to proposed rules and regulations by resorting to the **legislative veto,** which provided that one or sometimes both chambers of Congress could disapprove of an executive rule within a specified period of time by a simple majority vote and thereby prevent its enforcement. In 1983, however, the Supreme Court ruled that such a veto violated separation of powers because the president had no power to veto the legislative action. Thus the legislative veto was declared unconstitutional.[3]

Senators and representatives increasingly see their oversight function as a critically important part of their legislative activities. In part, oversight is related to the concept of constituency service, particularly when Congress investigates alleged arbitrariness or wrongdoing by bureaucratic agencies. Beyond service to constituents, however, oversight is seen by many legislators, and by political scientists such as Morris Ogul,[4] as a crucial tool for preserving the balance of power between Congress and the executive branch.

[2]*The Role of the Congressman* (New York: Pegasus, 1969), p. 117.
[3]*Immigration and Naturalization Serv. v. Chadha,* 454 U.S. 812 (1983).
[4]Morris S. Ogul, *Congress Oversees the Bureaucracy* (Pittsburgh: University of Pittsburgh Press, 1976), pp. 21–22.

The Public Education Function

Educating the public is a function that is exercised every time Congress holds public hearings, exercises oversight over the bureaucracy, or engages in committee and floor debate on major issues and such topics as political assassinations, aging, drugs, or the concerns of small businesses. In so doing, Congress presents a range of viewpoints on pressing national questions. Congress also decides what issues will come up for discussion and decision; **agenda setting** is a major facet of its public education function.

AGENDA SETTING
The power to determine which public policy questions will be debated or considered by Congress.

The Conflict Resolution Function

Congress is commonly seen as an institution for resolving conflicts within American society. Organized interest groups and representatives of different racial, religious, economic, and ideological interests look on Congress as an access point for airing their grievances and possibly for stimulating government action on their behalf. A logical extension of the representation function, this focus on conflict resolution puts Congress in the role of trying to resolve the differences among competing points of view by passing laws to accommodate as many interested parties as possible. Clearly, this is not always achieved. Every legislative decision results in some winners and some losers. Congress is commonly regarded as the place to go in Washington to get a friendly hearing or a desired policy result. To the extent that Congress does accommodate competing interests, it tends to legitimize the entire political process by all branches of government.

■ HOUSE–SENATE DIFFERENCES

The preceding functions of Congress describe how that body is expected to perform and what it does as a whole. To understand better what goes on in the national legislature, however, we need to examine the effects of bicamer-

Witness testifying on the links between General Manuel Noriega of Panama and the drug trade. What role does Congress play through such investigations?

After African Americans gained the right to vote in 1870, several southern states elected African-American senators and representatives to Congress.

alism, for Congress is composed of two markedly different—although coequal—chambers. Although the Senate and the House of Representatives exist within the same legislative institution, each has developed certain distinctive features that clearly distinguish life on one end of Capitol Hill from conditions on the other (the Senate wing is on the north side of the Capitol building and the House wing is on the south side). A summary of these differences is given in Table 12-1.

Size and Rules

The central difference is simply that the House is much larger than the Senate. There are 435 representatives, plus nonvoting delegates from the District of Columbia, Puerto Rico, Guam, and the Virgin Islands, in the House, compared with just 100 senators. This size difference means that a greater number of formal rules are needed to govern activity in the House, whereas correspondingly looser procedures can be followed in the less crowded Senate. This difference is most obvious in the rules governing debate on the floors of the two chambers.

The Senate normally permits extended debate on all issues that arise before it, whereas the House operates with an elaborate system in which its **Rules Committee** normally proposes time limitations on debate for any bill, and a majority of the entire body accepts or modifies those suggested time limits. As a consequence of its stricter debate time limits, and in spite of its greater size, the House is often able to act on legislation more quickly than the Senate.

RULES COMMITTEE
A standing committee of the House of Representatives that provides special rules under which specific bills can be debated, amended, and considered by the House.

Debate and Filibustering

FILIBUSTERING
In the Senate, unlimited debate to halt action on a particular bill.

According to historians, the Senate tradition of unlimited debate, or **filibustering,** dates back to 1790, when a proposal to move the United States capitol

TABLE 12-1
Differences Between the House and the Senate

House*	Senate*
Members chosen from local districts	Members chosen from an entire state
Two-year term	Six-year term
Originally elected by voters	Originally (until 1913) elected by state legislatures
May impeach (indict) federal officials	May convict federal officials of impeachable offenses
Larger (435 voting members)	Smaller (100 members)
More formal rules	Fewer rules and restrictions
Debate limited	Debate extended
Floor action controlled	Unanimous consent rules
Less prestige and less individual notice	More prestige and media attention
Originates bills for raising revenues	Power to "advise and consent" on presidential appointments and treaties
Local or narrow leadership	National leadership

*Some of these differences, such as the term of office, are provided for in the Constitution, while others, such as debate rules, are not.

from New York to Philadelphia was stalled by such time-wasting tactics. This unlimited debate tradition—which also existed in the House until 1811[5]—is not absolute, however.

Under Senate Rule 22, debate may be ended by invoking **cloture,** or shutting off discussion on a bill. Recently amended in 1975 and 1979, Rule 22 states that debate may be closed off on a bill if sixteen senators sign a petition requesting it and if, after two days have elapsed, three-fifths of the entire

CLOTURE
A method to close off debate and to bring the matter under consideration to a vote in the Senate.

[5]William J. Keefe and Morris S. Ogul, *The American Legislative Process,* 5th ed. (Englewood Cliffs, N.J.: Prentice-Hall, 1982).

Senator Strom Thurmond leaves the chamber after completing his twenty-four-hour-and eighteen-minute filibuster. What is the purpose of the filibuster as a legislative tactic?

DID YOU KNOW?

That you can get information on the status of legislation in either the House or the Senate, whether committee hearings have been held, and the dates of upcoming hearings by calling the Legislative Status Office of Congress, at (202) 225-1772?

membership (sixty votes, assuming no vacancies) vote for cloture. After cloture is invoked, each senator may speak for a maximum of one hour on a bill before a vote is taken.

The Senate made further changes in its filibuster rule in 1979. It extended Rule 22 to provide that a final vote must take place within one hundred hours of debate after cloture has been imposed, and it further limited the use of multiple amendments to stall postcloture final action on a bill.

Prestige

As a consequence of the greater size of the House, representatives generally cannot achieve as much individual recognition and public prestige as can members of the Senate. Senators, especially those who openly express presidential ambitions, are better able to gain media exposure and to establish careers as spokespersons for large national constituencies. To obtain recognition for his or her activities, a member of the House must either survive in office long enough to join the ranks of the leadership on committees or within the party or become an expert on some specialized aspect of legislative policy—such as tax laws, the environment, or education.

Other Differences

Other major differences between the House and the Senate are unrelated to the size of each chamber. The Constitution in Article I provides that members of the House serve shorter terms (two years) than senators (six years). All 435 voting members of the House must run for reelection in November of even-numbered years, but only about one-third of the Senate seats are contested in the same biennial election. Before passage of the Seventeenth Amendment in 1913, all senators were not even elected by direct popular vote; they were instead appointed by state legislatures. The longer term in office generally gives senators more time to act as national leaders before facing the electorate again.

Government institutions are given life by the people who work in them and shape them as political structures. Who, then, are the members of Congress, and how are they elected?

Nancy Landon Kassebaum

■ CONGRESSPERSONS AND THE CITIZENRY—A COMPARISON

Members of the United States Senate and the United States House of Representatives are not typical American citizens (Table 12-2). Members of Congress are, of course, older than most Americans, partly because of constitutional age requirements and party because a good deal of political experience is normally an advantage in running for national office. Members of Congress are also disproportionately white, male, Protestant, and trained in higher-status occupations.

Some recent trends in the social characteristics of Congress should be noted, however. The average age of members of the One Hundred and Second Congress is 53.6 years—a slight increase from an average age of 53 three decades ago. The Protestant domination of Congress has been loosened, with sub-

TABLE 12-2
Characteristics of the 102nd Congress (1991–1993)

	U.S. Population (1980)	House	Senate
Age (Median)	30.6	52.8	57.2
Percent Nonwhite	14.4	8	2
Religion			
Percent church members	60	87	97
Percent Catholic	36.9	28	20
Percent Protestant	55.1	67	65
Percent Jewish	4.3	7.5	8
Percent Female	51.4	6.7	2
Percent College Educated	17.7	93	100
Occupation			
Percent lawyers and judges	0.6	44	61
Percent blue-collar workers	29.7	0	0
Family Income			
Percent of families earning over $50,000 annually	4.4	100	100
Personal wealth			
Percent of population with assets over $1 million	0.7	16	33

stantial increases being made in the representation of Jews and Roman Catholics. "Higher-status" Protestant denominations, notably Episcopalians and Presbyterians, are overrepresented in Congress, whereas Baptists and Lutherans are underrepresented relative to their numbers among American Protestants.

Lawyers are by far the largest occupational group among congresspersons: 61 senators and 183 representatives in the One Hundred and Second Congress reported that they were trained in the legal profession. However, the proportion of lawyers in the House is lower now than at nearly any time in the last thirty years. Members of this Congress reported other previous occupations as follows: 28 in agriculture, 188 businesspersons or banks, 67 educators, 7 engineers, 35 journalists, 3 labor leaders, 5 law enforcement officers, 5 medical doctors, 65 in politics and public service, 3 clergymen, 2 in aeronautics, 2 in the military, 4 in professional sports, and 2 actors (Fred Grandy, R. Iowa, who starred in the series "Love Boat" and Ben Jones, D. Georgia, who acted in the "Dukes of Hazard").

■ CONGRESSIONAL ELECTIONS

The process of electing members of Congress is decentralized. Congressional elections are operated by the individual state governments, which must conform to the rules established by the Constitution and by national statutes. The Constitution states that representatives are to be elected every second year by popular ballot, and the number of seats awarded to each state is to be determined by the results of the decennial census. Each state has at least one

DID YOU KNOW?

That fewer than three in ten people can name the House member from their district and fewer than half can name even one of the two senators from their state?

representative, with most congressional districts having about a half million residents. Senators are elected by popular vote (since the passage of the Seventeenth Amendment) every six years; approximately one-third of the seats are chosen every two years. Each state has two senators. Under Article I, Section 4, of the Constitution, state legislatures are given control over "The Times, Places and Manner of holding Elections for Senators and Representatives"; however, "the Congress may at any time by Law make or alter such Regulations, . . ."

Candidates for Congressional Elections

Candidates for seats in Congress are generally recruited by local political party activists. Potential candidates who are selected or self-selected usually have many of the social characteristics shared by their prospective constituents. Religion, race, and ethnic background are especially important considerations here. Prior political experience may be an important asset, especially in states with strong political parties or restrictive nominating systems.

Reasons for Making the Race.   At least three major factors are important in determining who will run for congressional office and whether party leaders are willing to recruit someone for the race. As discussed by James David Barber,[6] these are *motivation, resources,* and *opportunity.* Motivation means that a candidate must be able to achieve a sense of self-satisfaction from participating in the contest. It also implies that a candidate must project a positive attitude toward electoral politics. Important resources for the campaign include money,

[6] *The Lawmakers: Recruitment and Adaptation to Legislative Life* (New Haven: Yale University Press, 1965), pp. 10–15.

"Please, Hobart, would you kindly confine your speeches about the damned deficit to the floor of the Senate? You've already got my vote."

Drawing by Stan Hunt; © 1984 The New Yorker Magazine, Inc.

PROFILE

Ileana Ros-Lehtinen

"Now it's time for healing. I know there are a lot of people out there who feel alienated."

In a special congressional election in Florida in 1989, the Republican candidate won a seat that had been Democratic for the past forty years and was held much of that time by one person, Claude Pepper. Even more unusual than the change of parties were the characteristics of the victor. Ileana Ros-Lehtinen, a naturalized American citizen who was born in Cuba, defeated a native-born American citizen for the seat.

Ros-Lehtinen left Cuba as a child when her parents fled the Castro regime. During her time in the state legislature, she was known for her service to constituents. Her views are generally conservative; she favors the prolife position on abortion, for example. As a member of Congress, one of the major challenges confronting her will not be ideology, but rather it will be the job of smoothing relations between the Hispanic community and other ethnic groups.

During the campaign, Ros-Lehtinen's Latin American heritage overshadowed most other issues. Her opponent urged voters to keep the congressional position "an American seat." The voting was described as "an ethnic war," with turnout sharply divided along racial and ethnic lines. Such conflict is not new in Miami, which is part of the congressional district Ros-Lehtinen will be serving. Her victory may, however, represent a turning point in the political balance of power between Hispanic and non-Hispanic residents of the area. The election may demonstrate the political effect of the growth in the number of new Americans coming from Latin America and Asia.

The attempt to portray Ros-Lehtinen as un-American was not only ethically questionable but also misleading. She is a conservative Republican who spent seven years in the Florida legislature before running for Congress. Perhaps more important, she beat her opponent by mastering the rules of American democracy—by using a successful campaign strategy and building the necessary organization to implement it. In fact, the national Republican party targeted the Miami district as vulnerable before the campaign began, and hand picked Ros-Lehtinen as the candidate with the best chance of wresting the seat from the Democrats. The issue of Ros-Lehtinen's ethnic heritage was in fact used by both sides in the campaign; it turned out to be an advantage for her.

the political skills of the candidate and of his or her supporters, the ability of the candidate and staff to take time off from their jobs and other commitments, and the candidate's access to the mass media. Opportunity relates to such questions as whether an incumbent is running for office, whether many candidates are contending for the same nomination, how strong the opposition party may be in November, and whether the local party activists form a positive image of the candidate.

The Nomination Process.   Since the early part of the century, control over the process of nominating congressional candidates has been shifting from party conventions—which reformers charged with being corrupt and boss-controlled—to **direct primaries** in which **party identifiers** in the electorate select the candidate who will carry that party's endorsement into the actual

DIRECT PRIMARIES
An intraparty election in which the voters select the candidates who will run on a party's ticket in the subsequent general election.

PARTY IDENTIFIERS
Those who identify themselves with a political party.

DID YOU KNOW?

That Congress is exempt from the Occupational Safety and Health Act, the Freedom of Information Act, the Civil Rights Act of 1964, the Equal Pay Act, the Privacy Act, the Age Discrimination in Employment Act, and the District of Columbia health, fire, safety, and building construction codes, among other laws?

election. All fifty states currently use the direct primary to select party nominees for senator or representative. In general, there are more candidates running and the competition is more intense when a party is strong and a November victory is likely.

Who Wins, and Why?   Most candidates win through the effectiveness of their personal organizations, although sometimes with assistance from the state party organization. It is important to realize that congressional candidates have only a loose affiliation to the party at the national and state level. Even the effects of presidential "coattails," in which a victorious president helps bring into office legislators who would not have won otherwise, are minimal. For example, Richard Nixon's smashing victory over George McGovern in 1972, with 61 percent of the popular vote and 520 out of 538 electoral votes, resulted in a gain of only twelve Republican seats in the House.

In midterm congressional elections—those held between presidential contests—voter turnout falls sharply. In these elections party affiliation of the voters who turn out is a stronger force in deciding election outcomes, and the party controlling the White House normally loses seats in Congress. Table 12-3 shows the pattern for midterm elections since 1942. The result is a fragmentation of party authority and a loosening of ties between Congress and the president.

The 1990 Elections

The 1990 elections proved to be no exception to the historical pattern. In spite of public opinion polls that showed very high levels of dissatisfaction with the inability of the Congress to deal with the budget and with a serious ethics investigation about to begin in the Senate, 96 percent of all the incumbent legislators who sought reelection were returned to the Capitol. Like presidents before him, George Bush took to the campaign trail to increase support for Republican candidates. Also like his predecessors, he had little impact on the results. The Republicans lost nine seats in the House of Representatives and one in the Senate, a relatively modest loss compared to the 26 seats lost in Reagan's first midterm election or the 15 Democratic seats lost at Carter's midterm point.

The strong showing of incumbent legislators in the 1990 election surprised many media commentators who expected that disillusioned voters would "turn the rascals out." Instead the 1990 results affirmed the fact that voters can be very dissatisfied with the Congress as a whole yet remain committed to their own representatives who have worked hard for the interests of their constituents.

The Power of Incumbency

The power of incumbency in the outcome of congressional elections cannot be overemphasized. Table 12-4 shows that the overwhelming majority of representatives and a smaller proportion of senators who decide to run for reelection are successful. This conclusion holds for both presidential election and midterm election years.

David R. Mayhew argues that the pursuit of reelection is the strongest motivation behind the activities of members of Congress.[7] The reelection goal

[7]*Congress: The Electoral Connection* (New Haven: Yale University Press, 1974).

TABLE 12-3
Midterm Losses by the Party of the President: 1942–1990

Seats Lost by the Party of the President in the House of Representatives	
1942	−45 (D)
1946	−55 (D)
1950	−29 (D)
1954	−18 (R)
1958	−47 (R)
1962	− 4 (D)
1966	−47 (D)
1970	−12 (R)
1974	−48 (R)
1978	−15 (D)
1982	−26 (R)
1986	− 5 (R)
1990	− 8 (R)

TABLE 12-4
The Power of Incumbency

	PRESIDENTIAL-YEAR ELECTIONS							MIDTERM ELECTIONS						
	1964	1968	1972	1976	1980	1984	1988	1966	1970	1974	1978	1982	1986	1990
House														
Number of incumbent candidates	397	409	390	384	398	409	409	411	401	391	382	393	393	407
Reelected	344	396	365	368	361	390	402	362	379	343	358	352	385	391
Percentage of total	86.6	96.8	93.6	95.8	90.7	95.4	98.3	88.1	94.5	87.7	93.7	90.1	98.0	96.1
Defeated	53	13	25	16	37	19	7	49	22	48	24	39	8	16
In primary	8	4	12	3	6	3	1	8	10	8	5	10	2	1
In general election	45	9	13	13	31	16	6	41	12	40	19	29	6	15
Senate														
Number of incumbent candidates	33	28	27	25	29	29	27	32	31	27	25	30	28	32
Reelected	28	20	20	16	16	26	23	28	24	23	15	28	21	31
Percentage of total	84.8	71.4	74.1	64.0	55.2	89.6	85	87.5	77.4	85.2	60.0	93.3	75	96.9
Defeated	5	8	7	9	13	3	4	4	7	4	10	2	7	1
In primary	1	4	2	0	4	0	0	3	1	2	3	0	0	0
In general election	4	4	5	9	9	3	4	1	6	2	7	2	7	1

SOURCE: *Statistical Abstract of the United States, 1982–83,* p. 485; *Congressional Quarterly Weekly Report,* 40, (October 30, 1982), 44, no. 45 (November 8, 1986), 46, no. 46 (November 12, 1988), 44, no. 45 (November 10, 1990).

is pursued in three major ways: by *advertising,* by *credit claiming,* and by *position taking.* Advertising involves using the mass media, making personal appearances with constituents, sending newsletters—all to produce a favorable image and to make the incumbent's name a household word. Members of Congress try to present themselves as informed, experienced, and responsive to people's needs. Credit claiming focuses on the things a legislator claims to have done to benefit his or her constituents—by fulfilling the congressional casework function or by supplying material goods in the form of, say, a new post office or a construction project such as a dam or a highway. Position taking refers to explaining why a member of Congress voted the way he or she did and to making public statements of general support for presidential decisions or specific support for positions on key issues such as gun control or anti-inflation policies. Position taking carries with it certain risks, as the incumbent may lose support by disagreeing with the attitudes of large numbers of constituents. Another view, put forward by Richard Fenno, Jr. (see the Critical Perspective) is that members develop a "homestyle" to build support among their constituents.

■ CONGRESSIONAL REAPPORTIONMENT

By far the most complicated aspect of the mechanics of congressional elections is the issue of **reapportionment,** or the allocation of seats in the House to

REAPPORTIONMENT
The redrawing of legislative district lines to accord with the existing population distribution.

At Home with House Members

Although opinion polls have shown for at least a decade that the public does not have great confidence in the Congress, such mistrust does not seem to affect congressional elections. More than 90 percent of members of the House who seek reelection are victorious every two years. This puzzle, that we cheerfully reelect our congresspersons although we don't think much of the institution, has intrigued political scientists for some time.

One explanation of the phenomenon is that many congressional districts have been drawn to be safe for one party. This does not, however, account for the ability of the incumbent to fend off primary challenges from within his or her own party. Similarly, the fact that incumbents gain an advantage at the polls through voter recall of their names does not completely explain incumbent staying power, particularly in an age in which challengers can make extensive use of the media to become well known.

Another explanation relates to the seniority system in Congress. The longer a member of Congress stays in office, the more seniority he or she has, and therefore the more important that person's committee assignments. Ultimately, seniority results in committee chairpersonships. These positions of power are basically the ones that determine the geographic and industry-specific types of federal government spending. Hence, the "folks back home," including interest groups, have an incentive to continue to support a member of Congress in his or her reelection efforts—election after election after election.

An intriguing view of why incumbents do so well with their voters is put forth by Richard Fenno in his book, *Homestyle: House Members in Their Districts.* Fenno believes that political scientists usually focus on what legislators do in Washington, D.C., to the exclusion of what they do back in their districts. To investigate the members at home, he spent more than seven years accompanying congresspersons in their home-district travels. His research suggests that an important key to understanding why incumbents are so successful lies in the development of their respective "homestyles."

By interviewing legislators, their aides, and their constituents, Fenno found that each legislator develops a unique style of dealing with the voters in his or her district. It is rooted first in the legislator's perception of the district: Is it a homogeneous district, or is it heterogeneous in class, race, and economic factors? The legislator then thinks about how he or she "fits" that district. Some representatives are so similar to most of their constituents, having been born and bred in the district, that they feel they understand their constituents' needs intuitively. Others, who do not have a "close fit" to their districts or who have very heterogeneous districts must develop different homestyles.

According to Fenno, each House member develops a "presentational style" for home use that fits his or her personality and the type of district. Some representatives use a person-to-person style that emphasizes personal contact and informality. As one representative put it, "No one will vote against you if you are on a first-name basis." Other representatives choose to emphasize issues or their own personal views, which may mark them as, say, a maverick or a staunch liberal.

The representative must also decide to whom he or she will make this self-presentation. Fenno suggests that each member sees the constituency as a set of concentric rings, with the closest friends and political advisers at the center, then the strongest supporters within the electorate, the reelection constituency, and finally the entire geographical district. The representative has to decide which of the groups needs to be visited or given extra attention. At some time, the representative must make an appeal to each of them to be reelected.

At the heart of the representative's homestyle is the relationship with constituents. Fenno sees the activities at home as building a certain trust between the legislator and the constituents. Since voters must send off the congressperson to vote on issues with which the public is unfamiliar and since voters really do not expect or desire to keep close watch on the legislator, this relationship rests to some extent on the trust built up by House members in their visits home. This trust is a vital ingredient in the ability of incumbents to be reelected time after time.

Exercise in Critical Thinking

1. Why do congresspersons work so diligently at keeping in touch with their constituents?
2. Why do constituents trust their congressional representatives to vote for their interests on hundreds of issues?
3. Why do most Americans know so little about what their representatives do in Washington, D.C.?

Source: Richard F. Fenno, Jr., *Homestyle: House Members in Their Districts* (Boston: Little, Brown, 1978).

each state after each census, and **redistricting,** the redrawing of the boundaries of the districts within each state.[8]

In a landmark six-to-two vote in 1962, the Supreme Court made reapportionment a **justiciable** (that is, a reviewable) **question** in the Tennessee case of *Baker v Carr*[9] by invoking the Fourteenth Amendment principle that no state can deny to any person "the equal protection of the laws." This principle was applied directly in the 1964 ruling, *Reynolds v. Sims,*[10] when the Court held that *both* chambers of a state legislature must be apportioned with equal populations in each district. This "one man, one vote" principle was applied to congressional districts in the 1964 case of *Wesberry v. Sanders,*[11] based on Article I, Section 2, of the Constitution, which requires that congresspersons be chosen "by the People of the several States."

Severe malapportionment of congressional districts prior to *Wesberry* had resulted in some districts containing two or three times the populations of other districts in the same state, thereby diluting the effect of a vote cast in the larger districts. This system had generally benefited the conservative populations of rural areas and small towns and harmed the interests of the more heavily populated and liberal urban areas. In fact, suburban areas have benefited the most from the *Wesberry* ruling, as suburbs account for an increasingly larger proportion of the nation's population and cities include a correspondingly smaller segment of the population.

Although the general issue of reapportionment has been dealt with fairly successfully by the one man, one vote principle, the specific case of **gerrymandering** has not yet been resolved. This term refers to the legislative boundary-drawing tactics used by Elbridge Gerry, the governor of Massachusetts, in the 1812 elections (Figure 12-1). A district is said to have been gerrymandered when its shape is substantially altered by the dominant party in a state legislature to maximize its electoral strength at the expense of the minority party. This can be achieved by either concentrating the opposition's voter support in as few districts as possible or diffusing the minority party's strength by spreading it thinly across many districts.

In 1986, the Supreme Court heard a case that challenged gerrymandered congressional districts in Indiana. The Court ruled for the first time that redistricting for the political benefit of one group could be challenged on constitutional grounds. In this specific case, *Davis v. Bandemer,*[12] the Court did not, however, agree that the districts were unfairly drawn, since it could not be proven that a group of voters would be consistently deprived of its influence at the polls because of the new districts. Figure 12-2 shows a contemporary gerrymander.

REDISTRICTING
Redrawing district lines within the states.

JUSTICIABLE QUESTION
A question that may be raised and reviewed in court.

GERRYMANDERING
The drawing of legislative district boundary lines for the purpose of obtaining partisan or factional advantage. A district is said to be gerrymandered when its shape is manipulated by the dominant party in the state legislature to maximize electoral strength at the expense of the minority party.

■ PAY, PERKS, AND PRIVILEGES

Compared with the average American citizen, members of Congress are well paid. In 1989, annual congressional salaries were increased to $135,000. Hon-

---

[8]For an excellent discussion of reapportionment, see Keefe and Ogul, *The American Legislative Process,* pp. 68–85.
[9]369 U.S. 186.
[10]377 U.S. 533.
[11]376 U.S. 1.
[12]478 U.S. 109.

FIGURE 12-1
The Original Gerrymander

The practice of "gerrymandering"—the excessive manipulation of the shape of a legislative district to benefit a certain incumbent or party—is probably as old as the republic, but the name originated in 1812. In that year the Massachusetts legislature carved out of Essex County a district that historian John Fiske said had a "dragonlike contour." When the painter Gilbert Stuart saw the misshapen district, he penciled in a head, wings, and claws and exclaimed: "That will do for a salamander!"—to which editor Benjamin Russell replied: "Better say a Gerrymander"—after Elbridge Gerry, then governor of Massachusetts.

SOURCE: *Congressional Quarterly's Guide to Congress,* 3rd ed. (Washington, D.C.: Congressional Quarterly Press, 1982), p. 695.

FIGURE 12-2
A Modern Gerrymander

After the 1980 Census, Oklahoma legislators redrew their congressional districts in such a way as to concentrate a large number of Republicans in the strangely shaped Fifth District. By lumping the wealthier suburbs of Oklahoma City with Bartlesville four counties away, they were able to create one Republican district while safeguarding the Democratic majorities in the five other districts.

SOURCE: Michael Barone and Grant Ujifusa, *Almanac of American Politics 1986* (Washington, D.C.: National Journal, 1985).

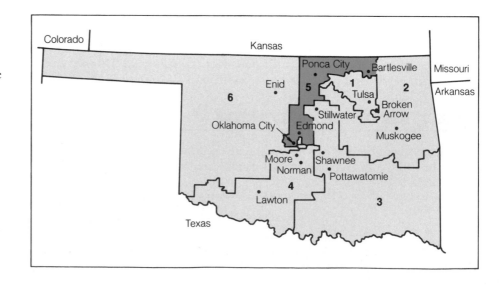

oraria from outside speeches are limited to $26,850 for House members and $35,800 for senators. In addition, legislators elected before 1980 can convert unused campaign funds to their personal use after retirement.

Members of Congress also benefit in other ways from belonging to a select group. They have access to private Capitol Hill gymnasium facilities, get low-cost haircuts, receive free, close-in parking at National and Dulles airports near Washington, and get six free parking spaces in Capitol Hill garages—plus one free outdoor Capitol parking slot. They also avoid parking tickets because of their congressional license plates and are not required to comply with labor laws in dealing with their staffs. They eat in a subsidized dining room and take advantage of free plants from the Botanical Gardens for their offices, free medical care, an inexpensive but generous pension plan, liberal travel allowances, and special tax considerations.

Members of Congress are also granted generous **franking** privileges that permit them to mail newsletters, surveys, and other letters to their constituents. The annual costs of congressional mail has risen from $11 million in 1971 to almost $200 million today. Typically, the costs for these mailings rise enormously during election years.

In recent years, increasingly generous staff support and office costs have also been provided. Each member is assigned office space in one of the three Senate office buildings named after former senators Richard B. Russell (Dem.-Georgia), Everett M. Dirksen (Rep.-Illinois), and Philip A. Hart (Dem.-Michigan) or in one of the three House office buildings named for former Speakers of the House Samuel Rayburn (Dem.-Texas), Joseph Cannon (Rep.-Illinois), and Nicholas Longworth (Rep.-Ohio). Senators are allocated office space based on the populations of their states.

Permanent Professional Staffs

Over forty thousand people are employed in the Capitol Hill bureaucracy.[13] About half of this total consists of personal and committee staff members. The personal staff includes office clerks and secretaries; professionals who deal with media relations, draft legislation, and satisfy constituency requests for service; and staffers who maintain local offices in the member's home district or state. The average Senate office on Capitol Hill employs about thirty staff members, and twice that number work on the personal staff of senators from the most populous states. House office staffs are typically about half as large as those of the Senate. As Figure 12-3 shows, the number of staff members has increased dramatically over the last two decades. With the bulk of those increases coming in assistance to members, some scholars question whether the staff are really advising on legislation or are primarily aiding constituents and gaining votes.

Congress also benefits from the expertise of the professional staff who work in agencies that were created to produce information for members of the House and Senate—resources comparable to those available to the president and the rest of the executive branch. The Congressional Research Service (CRS), a section of the Library of Congress, is an information and fact-finding center for legislators and their assistants. It furnishes a computer-based record of the

FRANKING
A policy that enables members of Congress to send material through the mail by substituting their facsimile signature (frank) for postage.

Delivering constituent mail

[13]Harrison W. Fox, Jr., and Susan Webb Hammond, *Congressional Staffs: The Invisible Force in American Lawmaking* (New York: Free Press, 1977).

FIGURE 12-3
Growth in Congressional Staff, 1955–1989

SOURCE: Ornstein, *Vital Statistics on Congress,* 1989–90.

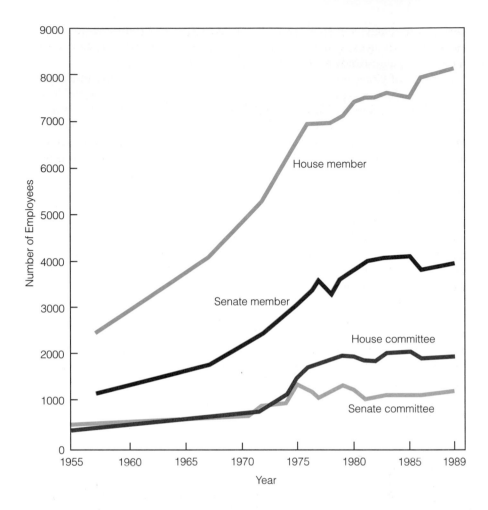

contents and current legislative status of major bills that are under consideration. This record can be reviewed by staff members using computer terminals available in most offices. The General Accounting Office (GAO) audits the spending of money by federal agencies, investigates agency practices, and makes policy recommendations to Congress, especially concerning financial activities of the government. The Office of Technology Assessment (OTA), as yet little used, is designed to evaluate national technology policy in such areas as energy and the environment. The Congressional Budget Office (CBO) advises Congress on the anticipated effect on the economy of government expenditures and estimates the cost of proposed policies.

Privileges and Immunities Under the Law

Members of Congress also benefit from a number of legal privileges and immunities. Under Article I, Section 6, of the Constitution, they "shall in all Cases, except Treason, Felony, and Breach of the Peace, be privileged from Arrest during their Attendance at the Session of their respective Houses, and in going to and returning from the same; and for any Speech or Debate in either House, they shall not be questioned in any other Place." While the arrest immunity clause is not really an important provision today, the "speech or debate" clause means that a member may make any allegations or other statements he or she wishes in connection with official duties and not normally be sued for libel or slander or be otherwise subject to legal action.

■ THE COMMITTEE STRUCTURE

Most of the actual work of legislating is performed by the committees and subcommittees within Congress. With the thousands of bills that are introduced in every session of Congress, no single member can possibly be adequately informed on all the issues that arise. The committee system is a way to provide for specialization or division of the legislative labor. Members of a committee can concentrate on just one area or topic—such as taxation or energy—and develop sufficient expertise to draft appropriate legislation when called for. The flow of legislation through both the House and the Senate is largely determined by the speed with which the members of these committees act on bills and resolutions.

Commonly known as "little legislatures,"[14] committees usually have the final say on pieces of legislation. Committee actions may be overturned on the floor by the full House or Senate, but this is rarely accomplished. Legislators normally defer to the expertise of the chairperson and other members of the committee who speak on the floor in defense of a committee decision. Chairpersons of full committees exercise control over the scheduling of both hearings

[14]This term is from Woodrow Wilson, *Congressional Government* (New York: Meridian Books, 1956 [first published in 1885]).

> **DID YOU KNOW?**
>
> That in 1990, senators and their staff sent more than 2 million pages of Fax messages—20,000 per senator—and printed 422,261,000 pages of material?

Budget Committee meeting. When the television lights are turned off the committee begins to work.

and formal action on a bill and decide which subcommittee will act on legislation falling within their committee's jurisdiction. Committees are very rarely deprived of control over a bill—although this kind of action is provided for in the rules of each chamber. In the House, if a bill has been considered by a standing committee for thirty days, the signatures of a majority (218) of the House membership on a **discharge petition** can pry a bill out of an uncooperative committee's hands. From 1909 to 1990, however, although 909 such petitions were made, only 26 resulted in successful discharge efforts, and of those, 20 passed the House.[15]

Types of Congressional Committees

Over the past two centuries, Congress has created several different types of committees, each of which serves particular needs of the institution.

Standing Committees. By far the most important committees are the **standing committees**—permanent bodies established by the rules of each chamber of Congress that continue from session to session. A list of the standing committees of the One Hundred and Second Congress is presented in Table 12-5. In addition, most of the standing committees have created several subcommittees to carry out their work. In the One Hundred and Second Congress, there were 103 subcommittees in the Senate and 139 in the House.[16]

Each standing committee is given a specific area of legislative policy jurisdiction, and almost all legislative measures are considered by the appropriate standing committees. Because of the importance of their work and the traditional influence of their members in Congress, certain committees are considered to be more prestigious than others. If a congressperson seeks to be influential, he or she will usually aspire to a seat on the Appropriations Committee in either chamber or on the Ways and Means Committee in the House. Significant public policy committees are the House Education and Labor Committee and the Senate Foreign Relations Committee.

Each member of the House serves generally on two standing committees, except when that member sits on the Appropriations, Rules, or Ways and Means Committee—in which case he or she serve on only that one standing committee. Each senator may serve on two major committees and one minor committee (only the Rules and Administration Committee and the Veterans Affairs Committee are considered minor).

Select Committees. A **select committee** is normally created for a limited period of time and for a specific legislative purpose, such as conducting an investigation or study of a public problem such as nutrition or aging. Select committees are disbanded when they have reported to the chamber that created them. They rarely create original legislation.

Joint Committees. A **joint committee** is formed by the concurrent action of both chambers of Congress and consists of members from each chamber. Joint committees, which may be permanent or temporary, have dealt with the economy, taxation, the Library of Congress, and congressional printing operations.

---

[15]*Congressional Quarterly's Guide to Congress,* 3rd ed., p. 426, and authors' update.
[16]*Congressional Directory* (Washington, D.C.: Government Printing Office, 1989–1990).

DISCHARGE PETITION
A procedure by which a bill in the House of Representatives may be forced out of a committee (discharged) that has refused to report it for consideration by the House. The discharge motion must be signed by an absolute majority (218) of representatives and is used only on rare occasions.

STANDING COMMITTEE
A permanent committee within the House or Senate that considers bills within a subject area.

SELECT COMMITTEE
A temporary legislative committee established for a limited time period for a special purpose.

JOINT COMMITTEE
A legislative committee composed of members from both houses of Congress.

Senator Sam Nunn, Chairman of the Senate Armed Services Committee.

Conference Committees.   **Conference committees** are special cases of joint committees that are formed for the purpose of achieving agreement between the House and the Senate on the exact wording of legislative acts when the two chambers pass legislative proposals in different forms. No bill can be sent to the White House to be signed into law unless it first passes both chambers in identical form. Sometimes called the "third house" of Congress, conference committees are in a position to make significant alterations in legislation and frequently become the focal point of policy debates. This was the case, for example, with the passage of the National Energy Act of 1978 and the tax reform legislation of 1986, both of which required long and difficult negotiations in the House–Senate conference committee to reconcile conflicting versions.

The House Rules Committee.   Because of its special "gatekeeping" power over the terms on which legislation will reach the floor of the House of Representatives, the House Rules Committee holds a uniquely powerful position. A special committee rule sets the time limit on debate and determines whether and how the bill may be amended. This practice dates back to 1883.

> **DID YOU KNOW?**
>
> That retiring members of Congress can start collecting a pension at age fifty after twenty years of work or at sixty after ten years of service?

CONFERENCE COMMITTEES
Special joint committees appointed to reconcile differences when bills pass the two houses of Congress in different forms.

TABLE 12-5
Standing Committees of the One Hundred and Second Congress

House Committees	Chair	Senate Committees	Chair
Agriculture	Kika de la Garza, D., Tex.	Agriculture, Nutrition, and Forestry	Patrick Leahy, D., Ver.
Appropriations	Jamie Whitten, D., Miss.	Appropriations	Robert C. Byrd, D., W. Va.
Armed Services	Les Aspin, D., Wis.	Armed Services	Sam Nunn, D., Ga.
Banking, Finance, and Urban Affairs	Henry B. Gonzalez, D., Tex.	Banking, Housing, and Urban Affairs	Donald W. Riegle, Jr., D., Mich.
Budget	Leon Panetta, D., Calif.	Budget	Jim Sasser, D., Tenn.
District of Columbia	Ronald Dellums, D., Calif.	Commerce, Science, and Transportation	Ernest Hollings, D., S.C.
Education and Labor	William Ford, D., Mich.	Energy and Natural Resources	J. Bennett Johnston, D., La.
Energy and Commerce	John Dingell, D., Mich.	Environment and Public Works	Quentin Burdick, D., N.Dak.
Foreign Affairs	Dante Fascell, D., Fla.	Finance	Lloyd Bentsen, D., Tex.
Government Operations	John Conyers, Jr., D., Mich.	Foreign Relations	Claiborne Pell, D., R.I.
House Administration	Charles Rose, D., N.C.	Governmental Affairs	John Glenn, D., Ohio
Interior and Insular Affairs	Morris Udall, D., Ariz.	Judiciary	Joseph Biden, Jr., D., Del.
Judiciary	Jack Brooks, D., Tex.	Labor and Human Resources	Edward Kennedy, D., Mass.
Merchant Marine and Fisheries	Walter Jones, D., N.C.	Rules and Administration	Wendell Ford, D., Ky.
Post Office and Civil Service	William Clay, D., Mo.	Small Business	Dale Bumpers, D., Ark.
Public Works and Transportation	Robert A. Roe, D., N.J.	Veterans Affairs	Alan Cranston, D., Calif.
Rules	Joe Moakley, D., Mass.		
Science and Technology	George E. Brown, Jr., D., Calif.		
Small Business	John J. LaFalce, D., N.Y.		
Standards of Official Conduct	Julian Dixon, D., Calif.		
Veterans' Affairs	G. V. "Sonny" Montgomery, D., Miss.		
Ways and Means	Dan Rostenkowski, D., Ill.		

The members of the Rules Committee have the unusual powers to meet while the House is in session, to have its resolutions considered immediately on the floor, and to initiate legislation on its own.

The Selection of Committee Members

In the House, representatives are appointed to standing committees by the Steering and Policy Committee (for Democrats) and by the Committee on Committees (for Republicans). Committee chairpersons are normally appointed according to seniority.

The rule regarding seniority specifies that majority party members with longer terms of continuous service on the committee will be given preference when committee chairpersons—as well as holders of other significant posts in Congress—are selected. This is not a law but an informal, traditional process. The **seniority system,** although deliberately unequal, provides a predictable means of assigning positions of power within Congress.

The general pattern until the 1970s was that members of the House or Senate who represented **safe seats** would be continually reelected and would eventually accumulate enough years of continuous committee service to enable them to become the chairpersons of their committees—if their party gained control of the appropriate chamber of Congress. Traditionally, this avenue of access to power benefited southern Democrats and midwesterners within the Republican party, who seldom faced serious, organized opposition either in their own party's primaries or during the general election. This resulted in a predominance of committee chairpersons from the more conservative ranks of both political parties.

In the 1970s, a number of reforms in the chairperson selection process somewhat modified the seniority system and introduced the use of a secret ballot in electing House committee chairpersons, as well as a greater dispersal of authority within the committees themselves by establishing rules for the selection of subcommittee chairpersons.

■ THE FORMAL LEADERSHIP

The limited amount of centralized power that exists in Congress is exercised through party-based mechanisms. Congress is organized by party. When the Democratic party, for example, wins a majority of seats in either the House or the Senate, Democrats control the official positions of power in that chamber, and every committee has a Democratic chairperson and a majority of Democratic members. The same process holds when Republicans are in the majority. Every member of Congress, except for occasionally successful independent candidates, was elected through a partisan electoral process. Senators and representatives therefore usually have some sense of loyalty to their party in Congress.

We consider the formal leadership positions in the House and in the Senate separately, but some broad similarities are apparent in the way that leaders are selected and in the ways they exercise power in the two chambers.

Leadership in the House

The House leadership is made up of the speaker, the majority and minority leaders, and the party whips.

SENIORITY SYSTEM
A custom followed in both houses of Congress specifying that members with longer terms of continuous service will be given preference when committee chairpersons and holders of other significant posts are selected.

SAFE SEAT
A district that returns the legislator with 55 percent of the vote or more.

Speaker of the House Tom Foley (D., Washington) and Senate Majority Leader George Mitchell (D., Maine) speak to the press.

The Speaker.   The foremost power holder in the House of Representatives is the **speaker of the House.** The speaker's position is technically a nonpartisan one, but in fact, for the better part of two centuries, the speaker has been the official leader of the majority party in the House. When a new Congress convenes in January of odd-numbered years, each party nominates a candidate for speaker. In one of the very rare instances of perfect party cohesion, all Democratic members of the House ordinarily vote for their party's nominee, and all Republicans support their alternative candidate.

House leadership is exercised primarily by the speaker, the majority leader, the minority leader, and the majority and minority whips. The election of the speaker thus automatically puts the majority party in control of the powers that are available to that office.

The extent of the speaker's power has varied markedly over time. Throughout most of the nineteenth century, speakers had to share power with groups of powerful members or with key committee chairpersons. Beginning about 1890 and continuing through 1910, speakers gradually consolidated their power and exercised such dictatorial powers as controlling all committee appointments and the agenda. In the aftermath of a revolt in 1910 and 1911, however, these extensive powers of the speaker were substantially reduced.

The influence of modern-day speakers is primarily based on their personal prestige, persuasive ability, and knowledge of the legislative process—plus the acquiescence or active support of other representatives. The major formal powers of the speaker include the following:

1. Presiding over meetings of the House
2. Appointing members of joint committees and conference committees
3. Scheduling legislation for floor action
4. Deciding points of order and interpreting the rules with the advice of the House parliamentarian
5. Referring bills and resolutions to the appropriate standing committees of the House

SPEAKER OF THE HOUSE
The presiding officer in the House of Representatives. The speaker is always a member of the majority party and is the most powerful and influential member of the House.

DID YOU KNOW?

That the Constitution does not require that the speaker of the House of Representatives must be an elected member of the House?

A speaker may take part in floor debate and vote, as can any other member of Congress, but recent speakers usually have voted only to break a tie.

In general, the powers of the speaker are related to his or her control over information and communications channels in the House. This is a significant power in a large, decentralized institution where information is a very important resource. With this control over communications, the speaker attempts to ensure the smooth operation of the chamber and to integrate presidential and congressional policies.

In 1975, the powers of the speaker were expanded when the House Democratic caucus gave its party's speaker the power to appoint the Democratic Steering Committee, which determines new committee assignments for House party members.

MAJORITY LEADER OF THE HOUSE
A legislative position held by an important party member in the House of Representatives. The majority leader is selected by the majority party in caucus or conference to foster cohesion among party members and to act as spokesperson for the majority party in the House.

HOUSE MINORITY LEADER
The party leader elected by the minority party in the House.

The Majority Leader.   The **majority leader of the House** has been a separate position since 1899, transferring to a new office a power that had usually been exercised by the chairperson of the Ways and Means Committee. The majority leader is elected by the caucus of party members to foster cohesion among party members and to act as a spokesperson for the party. The majority leader influences the scheduling of debate and generally acts as chief supporter of the speaker. Majority leaders conduct most procedural debate and also much of the substantive debate on the House floor. They are most deeply involved in debates on the important partisan issues that separate Democrats from Republicans. The majority leader cooperates with the speaker and other party leaders, both inside and outside Congress, to formulate the party's legislative program and to guide that program through the legislative process in the House. The majority leader's post is a very prestigious one because of the power and responsibility inherent in the office and also because, at least among Democrats, future speakers are recruited from that position.

Robert H. Michel, Ill., House minority leader.

The Minority Leader.   The **House minority leader** is the losing candidate nominated for speaker by the caucus of the minority party. Like the majority leader, the leader of the minority party has as his or her primary responsibility maintaining cohesion within the party's ranks. As the official spokesperson for the minority party, he or she consults with the ranking minority members of the House committees and encourages them to adhere to the party platform. The minority leader also acts as a morale booster for the generally less well-informed and usually less successful minority and speaks on behalf of the president if the minority party controls the White House. In relations with the majority party, the minority leader consults with both the speaker and the majority leader on recognizing members who wish to speak on the floor, on House rules and procedures, and on the scheduling of legislation. Minority leaders have no actual power in these areas, however.

WHIPS
Assistant floor leaders who aid the majority and minority floor leaders.

Whips.   The formal leadership of each party includes assistants to the majority and minority leaders known as **whips.** These positions have existed throughout this century, and over the past fifty years they have developed into a complex network of deputy and regional whips supervised by the chief party whip. The whips assist the party leader by passing information down from the leadership to party members and by ensuring that members show up for floor debate and recorded votes on important issues. Whips conduct polls among party members about their views on major pieces of legislation, inform the leaders about whose vote is doubtful and whose is certain, and may exert pressure on members to support the leader's position. The Democratic whip was historically appointed by the party leader in consultation with the Democratic speaker, whereas the Republican chief whip has been elected in a party caucus since 1965. Beginning with the One Hundredth Congress, though, the position of House Democratic whip has been filled by a vote of the Democratic caucus. In all, several dozen members take part in this formal effort to maintain party discipline.

Leadership in the Senate

The Senate is less than one-fourth the size of the House. This fact alone probably explains why a formal, complex, and centralized leadership structure is less necessary in the Senate than in the House.

The two highest-ranking formal leadership positions in the Senate are essentially ceremonial in nature. Under the Constitution, the vice president of the United States is the president (that is, the presiding officer) of the Senate and may vote to break a tie. The vice president, however, only rarely is present for a meeting of the Senate. In his absence the Senate elects instead a **president pro tempore.** Ordinarily the member of the majority party with the longest continuous term of service in the Senate, the president pro tem does not have powers analogous to those of the speaker of the House, although he or she does appoint, jointly with the speaker, the director of the Congressional Budget Office. The most junior senators are usually chosen by the president pro tem and the majority leader to chair portions of each day's session.

The real leadership power in the Senate rests in the hands of the **majority floor leader,** the **minority floor leader,** and their respective whips. The majority and minority Senate leaders have the right to be recognized first in debate on the floor and generally exercise the same powers available to the House majority and minority leaders. They control the scheduling of debate on the floor in conjunction with the majority party's Policy Committee, influence the allocation of committee assignments for new members or for senators attempting to transfer to a new committee, influence the selection of other party officials, and participate in selecting members of conference committees. The leaders are expected to mobilize support for partisan legislative initiatives or for the proposals of a president who belongs to the same party. They act as a liaison with the White House when the president is of their party, try to get the cooperation of committee chairpersons, and seek to facilitate the smooth functioning of the Senate through the senators' unanimous consent. Floor leaders are elected by their respective party caucuses.

Leaders of the Senate Democrats potentially have more power than Republican leaders. The Democratic floor leader is also simultaneously chairperson of the Democratic Conference (caucus); the Steering Committee, which makes committee assignments; and the Policy Committee, which schedules legislation for floor action. In contrast, four different Republican senators hold these comparable positions, in a much more decentralized pattern of leadership.

Senate party whips, like their House counterparts, maintain communication within the party on platform positions and try to assure that party colleagues are present for floor debate and important votes. The Senate whip system is far less elaborate than its counterpart in the House, simply because there are fewer members to keep track of.

Representative Newt Gingrich (R., Georgia), often a leader of the conservative Republican legislators.

PRESIDENT PRO TEMPORE
The temporary presiding officer of the Senate in the absence of the vice president.

MAJORITY FLOOR LEADER
The chief spokesperson of the major party in the Senate who directs the legislative program and party strategy.

MINORITY FLOOR LEADER
The party officer in the Senate who commands the minority party's opposition to the policies of the majority party and directs the legislative program and strategy of his or her party.

Robert Dole, Kan., Senate minority floor leader.

A list of the formal party leaders of the One Hundred and Second Congress is presented in Table 12-6.

Party leaders are a major source of influence over the decisions about public issues that senators and representatives must make every day. We consider the nature of partisan and other pressures on congressional decision making in the next section.

■ HOW MEMBERS OF CONGRESS DECIDE

Why congresspersons vote as they do is uncertain. One popular perception of the legislative decision-making process is that legislators take cues from other trusted or more senior colleagues.[17] This model holds that since most members of Congress have neither the time nor the incentive to study the details of most pieces of legislation, they frequently arrive on the floor with no clear idea about what they are voting on or how they should vote. Their decision is simplified, according to the cue-taking model, by quickly checking how key colleagues have voted or intend to vote. More broadly, verbal and nonverbal cues can be taken from fellow committee members and chairpersons, party leaders, state delegation members, or the president.

[17]Donald Matthews and James Stimson, *Yeas and Nays: Normal Decision Making in the U.S. House of Representatives* (New York: John Wiley, 1975).

TABLE 12-6
Party Leaders in the One Hundred and Second Congress

Position	Incumbent	Party/State	Leader Since
House			
Speaker	Tom Foley	D.-Wash.	June, 1989
Majority leader	Richard Gephardt	D.-Mo.	June, 1989
Majority whip	William H. Gray, III	D.-Penn.	June, 1989
Chairperson of the Democratic Caucus	Steny H. Hoyer	D.-Md.	June, 1989
Minority leader	Robert Michel	R.-Ill.	Dec., 1980
Minority whip	Newt Gingrich	R.-Ga.	Mar., 1989
Chairperson of the Republican Conference	Jerry Lewis	R.-Cal.	Jan., 1989
Senate			
President pro tempore	Robert C. Byrd	D.-W. Va.	Jan., 1989
Majority floor leader	George J. Mitchell	D.-Maine	Jan., 1989
Assistant majority leader	Wendell H. Ford	D.-Ky.	Dec., 1990
Secretary of the Democratic Caucus	David Pryor	D.-Ark.	Jan., 1989
Minority floor leader	Robert Dole	R.-Kan.	Jan., 1987
Assistant minority leader	Alan K. Simpson	R.-Wyo.	Jan., 1987
Chairperson of the Republican Conference	Thad Cochran	R.-Miss.	Dec., 1990

SOURCE: *Congressional Directory,* One Hundred and Second Congress.

PROFILE

George Mitchell

"Being majority leader is not an end in itself; it is a means to an end."

George Mitchell, the leader of the Democratic majority in the Senate, faces a dilemma every day. On the one hand, he has the job of getting his fellow Democrats to act as a united group of political partisans against their Republican opponents. On the other hand, he faces the task of reconciling the views of those Democrats with the initiatives of a Republican president. The resulting game of give and take places Mitchell on a tightrope: Senate Democrats expect him vigorously to present and defend the party line, but too vigorous a defense can lead to friction with the opposition and a legislative deadlock.

By temperament, Mitchell appears to be well suited to balance these conflicting demands. Indeed, for much of his adult life Mitchell was not a partisan politician at all, but a federal judge in a district that included his native Maine. The sobriety of that office was a good match for his temperament: Mitchell is a self-made man who rose from the poverty of his immigrant family through hard work and education. In

action as majority leader, Mitchell tends to be matter of fact and to defuse political conflict through understatement. During a potentially bitter fight with a member of his own party, Mitchell told reporters, "Senator Byrd is urging members to vote for him, and I am doing the same."

A knack for hammering out compromises on key bills has won Mitchell praise from his colleagues in both parties. More than any other individual

senator, it was Mitchell who assured passage of the Clean Air bill of 1990 by crafting a workable compromise between the parties. Yet this insistence on taking care of Senate business sometimes brings Mitchell closer to the Republican-controlled administration than some Democratic partisans would like. Indeed, Mitchell has kept his distance from the national Democratic organization, refusing to tailor Democratic strategy in the Senate to the national election strategy of the party.

Mitchell would not have been elected majority leader, however, if his fellow Democrats believed he could not safeguard the party's interest in the Senate. In fact, he has done so by visibly opposing President Bush on several issues that were at the top of the president's legislative agenda. Among these was the administration's proposal to lower the tax on capital gains (profits on the sale of stocks and bonds). Mitchell's position on the issue was classically Democratic, with a twist of the Maine native's own judicial reasoning: The president, he declared, wants to cut taxes for the rich, but will not raise the wages of the poor. The capital gains tax cut failed to pass the Senate, and Mitchell added to his reputation as a leader.

A different theory of congressional decision making places the emphasis on the policy content of the issues being decided and on the desires of a congressperson's constituents and the pressures brought to bear by his or her supporters.[18] The degree of constituency influence on congressional voting patterns depends on the extent to which a state or district is urbanized, the region and state that a member represents, and the blue-collar proportion of the labor force.

Most people who study the decision-making process in Congress agree that the single best predictor for how a member will vote is his or her party membership.[19] Republicans tend to vote similarly on issues, as do Democrats.

[18]Aage R. Clausen, *How Congressmen Decide* (New York: St. Martin's Press, 1973).
[19]David Mayhew, *Party Loyalty Among Congressmen* (Cambridge: Harvard University Press, 1966).

Of course, even though liberals predominate among the Democrats in Congress and conservatives among the Republicans, the parties still may have internal disagreements about the proper direction that national policy should take. This was generally true for the civil rights legislation of the 1950s and 1960s, for example, when the greatest disagreement was within the Democratic party between its conservative southern members and its liberal northern wing.

One way to measure the degree of party unity in Congress is to look at how often a majority of one party votes against the majority of members from the other party. Table 12-7 displays the percentage of all roll-call votes in the House and the Senate when this type of party voting has occurred. Note that party voting occurs at a much higher rate in the House in the odd-numbered years, which happen to be the years when congressional elections are not held.

Regional differences, especially between northern and southern Democrats, may overlap and reinforce basic ideological differences among members of the same party. One consequence of the North–South split among Democrats has been the **conservative coalition** policy alliance between southern Democrats and Republicans. This conservative, cross-party grouping can be counted on to form regularly on votes on controversial issues in Congress. It is usually highly successful.

CONSERVATIVE COALITION
An alliance of Republicans and southern Democrats that can form in the House or the Senate to oppose liberal legislation and support conservative legislation.

■ HOW A BILL BECOMES LAW

Perhaps the best way to understand how a bill becomes a law is to follow the passage of one piece of legislation through the process, in this case the Omnibus Trade and Competitiveness Law of 1988. (Figure 12-4 diagrams the process with two hypothetical bills.) Faced with an ever-increasing trade deficit and the threat of foreign competition, members of Congress, representatives of business and labor, and members of the administration recognized the need for trade legislation in the mid-1980s. Rewriting the current trade laws, however, would be a major task, requiring the time and energy of many of the committees of Congress and the willingness to compromise by all of those concerned.

On January 7, 1987, as soon as the One Hundredth Congress convened, 180 Democratic House members cosponsored a comprehensive trade bill, HR3. It was immediately referred to the House Ways and Means Committee and then to the subcommittee on trade. In the Senate, Democratic Senator Lloyd Bentsen, chair of the Senate Finance Committee, introduced his party's bill into that chamber and it was referred to his committee along with the administration's version, which was introduced by Senator Robert Dole, the minority leader. Consideration of the trade legislation was complicated by the fact that more than one committee had jurisdiction over some parts of the bill, so that the legislation was, in effect, broken up into pieces and worked on separately by different standing committees.

By March 17, the House Ways and Means subcommittee reported a version of the bill to the full committee, which made further changes. The other House committees furnished their work by late April, and the House Rules Committee, which sets the rules for debating bills, put the pieces together to form one bill. Debate in the House was carried out in late April under the rule that only fourteen amendments would be allowed. The comprehensive trade bill passed by a vote of 290–137 on April 30, 1987, and was sent on to the Senate.

TABLE 12-7
Party Voting in Congress
Percentage of all roll calls when a majority of Democratic legislators voted against a majority of Republican legislators.

Year	House	Senate
1989	55.0	35.0
1988	47.0	42.0
1987	64.0	41.0
1986	57.0	52.0
1985	61.0	50.0
1984	47.1	40.0
1983	55.6	43.6
1982	36.4	43.4
1981	37.4	47.8
1980	37.6	45.8
1979	47.3	46.7
1978	33.2	45.2
1977	42.2	42.4
1976	35.9	37.2
1975	48.4	47.8
1974	29.4	44.3
1973	41.8	39.9

SOURCE: *Congressional Quarterly Weekly Report*, Dec. 30, 1989, p. 3546.

FIGURE 12-5
How a Bill Becomes Law

This illustration shows the most typical way in which proposed legislation is enacted into law. The process is illustrated with two hypothetical bills, House bill No. 100 (HR 100) and Senate bill No. 200 (S 200). Bills must be passed by both houses in identical form before they can be sent to the president. The path of HR 100 is traced by a blue line, that of S 200 by a red line. In practice most bills begin as similar proposals in both houses.

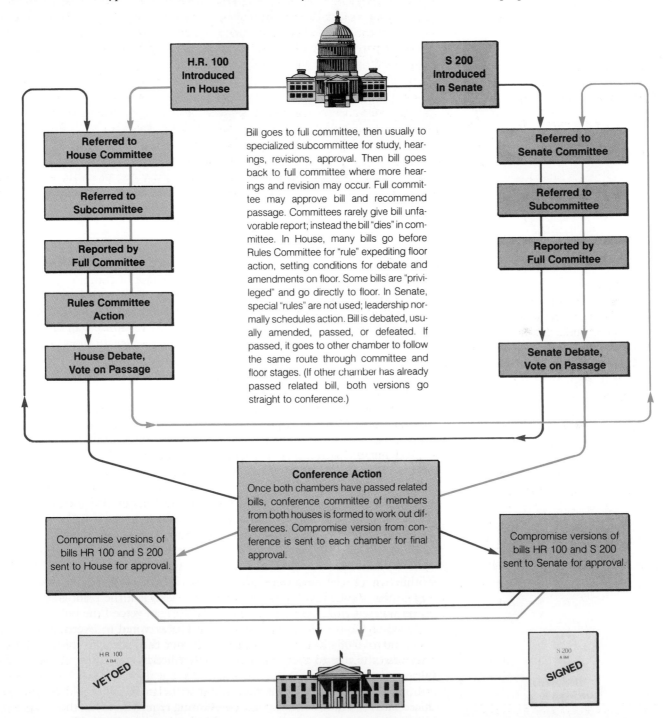

H.R. 100 Introduced in House

S 200 Introduced In Senate

Referred to House Committee

Referred to Subcommittee

Reported by Full Committee

Rules Committee Action

House Debate, Vote on Passage

Bill goes to full committee, then usually to specialized subcommittee for study, hearings, revisions, approval. Then bill goes back to full committee where more hearings and revision may occur. Full committee may approve bill and recommend passage. Committees rarely give bill unfavorable report; instead the bill "dies" in committee. In House, many bills go before Rules Committee for "rule" expediting floor action, setting conditions for debate and amendments on floor. Some bills are "privileged" and go directly to floor. In Senate, special "rules" are not used; leadership normally schedules action. Bill is debated, usually amended, passed, or defeated. If passed, it goes to other chamber to follow the same route through committee and floor stages. (If other chamber has already passed related bill, both versions go straight to conference.)

Referred to Senate Committee

Referred to Subcommittee

Reported by Full Committee

Senate Debate, Vote on Passage

Conference Action
Once both chambers have passed related bills, conference committee of members from both houses is formed to work out differences. Compromise version from conference is sent to each chamber for final approval.

Compromise versions of bills HR 100 and S 200 sent to House for approval.

Compromise versions of bills HR 100 and S 200 sent to Senate for approval.

H.R. 100 A Bill **VETOED**

S 200 A Bill **SIGNED**

Compromise bill approved by both houses is sent to the president, who can sign it into law or veto it and return it to Congress. Congress may override veto by a two-thirds majority vote in both houses; bill then becomes law without president's signature.

Roll-call votes posted in the House. Since electronic voting was instituted, attendance at roll calls has increased. Legislators were quite aware that their absences would also be recorded.

At the same time, eleven Senate committees were working on portions of their own trade bill. All of the committees finished their hearings and "mark-ups" of the bill by mid-June, and the formidable task of combining all of the provisions into one bill fell to the majority leader. Threats of filibusters were made over certain provisions, and the president threatened to veto the bill if changes were not made. Senate debate on its own version began on June 25 and lasted four weeks. As a more informal body, the Senate allows unlimited debate and unlimited amendments as long as the amendments are not for delaying purposes. After considering 160 amendments, the Senate passed the bill on July 21 by a 71–27 vote.

At this point, there were two trade bills—one from the House and one from the Senate. A conference committee, with members representing each house and all of the committees that had worked on the bill, was appointed to iron out the differences between the versions. The unwieldy conference committee, which by now included two hundred legislators, was broken up into seventeen working groups. Following six months of negotiations and hard bargaining, the conference agreed on a bill that still included many controversial provisions. One of the most difficult issues was the provision requiring plants to give sixty-days' notice to workers before closing.

On April 21, 1988, more than fifteen months after the House had begun work on the bill, the conference report was approved by a vote of 312–107. Within a week, the Senate had also approved the conference bill, and it was sent to the president, who had threatened to veto it if the plant-closing provision was retained. On May 24, President Reagan vetoed the bill and it was returned to Capitol Hill. Hours later, the House voted to override the veto by a vote of 308–133, a margin much greater than the two-thirds needed. However, the vote to override in the Senate failed by five votes, and the trade bill was defeated.

Immediately, the speaker announced that the trade bill would be reintroduced into the House without the plant-closing requirement but that a separate bill dealing only with that issue would also be considered. The trade bill,

President Reagan signs the Omnibus Trade Act of 1988, after eighteen months of debate and negotiation in Congress.

without the plant-closing provision, was passed by a House vote of 376–45 in July and by the Senate on August 3 by a vote of 85–11. The lopsided margins of approval meant that a veto could not be effective. Based on the advice of Republican congressional leaders, President Reagan let the bill become law without his signature rather than veto it again.

The passage of the Omnibus Trade bill illustrates a number of points about the legislative process. First, and most obvious, dealing with such a complex issue requires a long time, both to frame the legislation and to negotiate compromises among representatives from different constituencies. It should also be clear that the House, with its greater formality and the power of the speaker, can operate more speedily than the Senate. Finally, the passage of the trade bill demonstrates the working of the checks and balances of the Constitution through the interaction of the president and the Congress.

■ HOW MUCH WILL THE GOVERNMENT SPEND?

The Constitution is extremely clear about where the power of the purse lies in the national government: All money bills, whether for taxing or spending, must originate in the House of Representatives. Today, much of the business of the Congress is concerned with approving government expenditures through the budget process and with raising the revenues to pay for government programs.

From 1922, when Congress required the president to prepare an **executive budget** and to present it to the legislature, until 1974, the congressional budget process was so disjointed that it was difficult to visualize the total picture of government finances. The president presented his budget to Congress in January, it was broken down into thirteen or more appropriations bills, and some time later, after all of the bills were debated, amended, and passed, it was possible to estimate total government spending for the next year.

EXECUTIVE BUDGET

Budget prepared and submitted by the president to Congress.

Frustrated by the president's ability to impound funds and dissatisfied with the entire budget process, Congress passed the Budget and Impoundment Control Act of 1974 to regain some control over the nation's spending. The act required the president to spend the funds that Congress had appropriated, frustrating his ability to kill programs he disapproved of by withholding funds, as Richard Nixon tried to do. The other major accomplishment of the act was to force Congress to examine total national taxing and spending at least twice in each budget cycle.

Preparing the Budget

FISCAL YEAR
The twelve-month period that is used for bookkeeping, or accounting, purposes. Usually the fiscal year does not coincide with the calendar year. For example, the federal government's fiscal year runs from October 1 through September 30.

SPRING REVIEW
Every year, the Office of Management and Budget requires federal agencies to review their programs, activities, and goals, and submit their requests for funding for the next year.

The federal government operates on a **fiscal year** running from October through September, so that fiscal 1992, or FY92, runs from October 1, 1991 through September 30, 1992. Eighteen months before a fiscal year starts, the executive branch begins preparing the budget (Figure 12-5). The Office of Management and Budget (OMB) receives advice from the Council of Economic Advisers (CEA) and the Treasury Department. OMB outlines the budget and then sends it to the various departments and agencies. Bargaining follows, in which, to use only two of many examples, the Department of Health and Human Services argues for more welfare spending, and the armed forces argue for fewer defense spending cuts.

Even though OMB has only six hundred employees, it is known as one of the most powerful agencies in Washington. It assembles the budget documents and monitors the agencies throughout each year. Every year, it begins the budget process with a **spring review,** in which it requires all of the agencies to review their programs, activities, and goals. At the beginning of each summer, the director of OMB sends out a letter instructing agencies to submit

FIGURE 12-6
The Budget Cycle

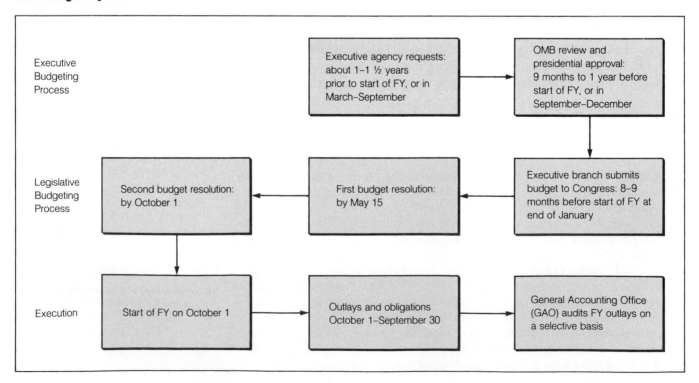

Executive Budgeting Process	Executive agency requests: about 1–1 ½ years prior to start of FY, or in March–September	OMB review and presidential approval: 9 months to 1 year before start of FY, or in September–December
Legislative Budgeting Process	Second budget resolution: by October 1 ← First budget resolution: by May 15	Executive branch submits budget to Congress: 8–9 months before start of FY at end of January
Execution	Start of FY on October 1	Outlays and obligations October 1–September 30	General Accounting Office (GAO) audits FY outlays on a selective basis

their requests for funding for the next fiscal year. By the end of the summer, each agency must submit a formal request to OMB.

In actuality, the "budget season" begins with the **fall review.** At this time, OMB looks at budget requests and in almost all cases routinely cuts them back. Although OMB works within guidelines established by the president, specific decisions are often left to the director and his associates. By the beginning of November, the director's review begins. He meets with cabinet secretaries and budget officers. Time becomes crucial. The budget must be completed by January to go to the printer to be included in the *Economic Report of the President.*

Congress Faces the Budget

In January, nine months before the fiscal year starts, the president takes whatever OMB has finally come up with and submits it to Congress. Then the congressional budgeting process takes over. Congressional committees and subcommittees look at the proposals from the executive branch. The Congressional Budget Office (CBO) advises the different committees on economic matters, just as the OMB and the CEA advise the president. The **first budget resolution** by Congress is supposed to be passed in May. It sets overall revenue goals and spending targets and, by definition, the size of the deficit (or surplus, if that were ever to occur again).

During the summer, bargaining among all the parties involved takes place. Spending and tax laws that are drawn up during this period are supposed to be guided by the May congressional budget resolution. By September, Con-

Congressional budget negotiators meet with the president to discuss alternative proposals. Why, with a Democratic majority in both houses, should the leaders need the Republican president's cooperation?

FALL REVIEW
Every year, after receiving formal federal agency requests for funding for the next fiscal year, the Office of Management and Budget reviews the requests, makes changes, and submits its recommendations to the president.

FIRST BUDGET RESOLUTION
A resolution passed by Congress in May setting overall revenue and spending goals and, hence, by definition, the size of the deficit for the following fiscal year.

DID YOU KNOW?

That less than half of all Americans polled believe that members of Congress have a high personal moral code of conduct or care deeply about the problems of ordinary citizens?

SECOND BUDGET RESOLUTION
A resolution passed by Congress in September that sets "binding" limits on taxes and spending for the next fiscal year beginning October 1.

CONTINUING RESOLUTIONS
Temporary laws that Congress passes when various appropriations bills have not been decided by the beginning of the new fiscal year on October 1.

gress is supposed to pass its **second budget resolution,** one that will set "binding" limits on taxes and spending for the fiscal year beginning October 1. Bills passed before that date that do not fit within the limits of the budget resolution are supposed to be changed.

In actuality, between 1978 and 1990, Congress did not pass a complete budget by October 1. In other words, generally, Congress does not follow its own rules. Budget resolutions are passed late, and when they are passed they are not treated as binding. In each fiscal year that starts without a budget, every agency operates on the basis of **continuing resolutions,** which enable the agencies to keep on doing whatever they were doing the previous year with the same amount of funding. Even continuing resolutions have not always been passed on time.

In the fall of 1990, the voters witnessed the worst budget stalemate since the institution of the new budget process. After President Bush reneged on his pledge of "No new taxes," Republicans battled Democrats in Congress over which taxes to raise. The new fiscal year 1991 budget had to provide enough revenue to begin reducing the federal deficit. A compromise bill crafted by Congressional leaders and representatives of Bush was soundly defeated by majorities of both the Republican and Democratic contingents in the House. Several weeks later, after the president threatened to shut the government down, another budget bill passed, raising taxes on some wealthy Americans and adding to the federal "sin taxes" on cigarettes and alcohol. The budget struggle did little to raise the voters' esteem for Congress or the executive branch.

Although many critics feel that the new budget process is neither efficient nor effective, there is little doubt that focusing on the bottom line has made legislators much more conscious of the federal budget deficit. Furthermore, there is some evidence that members of Congress now see the budget as the most important way to set the nation's agenda. Recent voting patterns in Congress reveal that members of each party are most united on the budget votes, since each party, Democratic and Republican, is fighting for its own preferences in spending.

■ THE QUESTION OF CONGRESSIONAL ETHICS

Ethics is the most serious public relations problem confronting Congress. Perhaps nothing has so tarnished the public's perception of Congress as the revelations concerning the abuse of staff members, the misuse of public funds, and the personal indiscretions of several members of that institution. (The Highlight on Congressional Ethics details some recent investigations of ethical inproprieties by members of Congress.)

Congress's response to revelations of member misconduct has been mixed. The House Democratic caucus in June 1980 voted 160 to 0 to require that chairpersons of committees or subcommittees be stripped of their posts automatically if they have been censured or indicted on a felony charge carrying a prison sentence of at least two years. This rule can be waived, however, by the same caucus.

Public financing of congressional campaigns may offer a partial solution to recurring problems of financial misconduct. Nonetheless, Congress has refused to use tax money or to impose spending limits on its members' campaigns,

HIGHLIGHT

Ethics: Congress Examines Its Own for Improprieties

Misuse of funds, doing political favors, sexual misbehavior. These and other forms of misconduct constitute the domain of congressional ethics—the rules and norms of behavior expected of public figures. Ethics comprise matters of judgment rather than legality.

Congress has always wrestled with matters of ethics. Many congresspersons have been investigated, censured, and otherwise disciplined since the First Congress in 1789 for improprieties including dueling, improper sexual behavior, corruption, and other violations of ethics.

In 1989, both House Speaker Jim Wright (Dem., Texas) and the House majority whip Tony Coelho (Dem., Calif.) resigned from Congress. Wright came under investigation on dozens of charges including influence peddling and violating campaign contribution limits by having supporters buy tens of thousands of dollars worth of a book he wrote that consisted largely of his speeches. Wright's relationship with a Texas businessman who provided the speaker's wife with a car and a job was also judged improper.

Tony Coelho resigned while under investigation for numerous improprieties including involvement in a junk bond deal with convicted financier Michael Milkin. He also accepted favors, including the use of a yacht, and had created a variety of schemes to raise money from political action committees. After quitting Congress, Coelho took a job with a financial company where his knowledge of bonds and stocks was prized.

In 1990, the Senate Ethics Committee held a full investigation of Minnesota Senator Dave Durenberger (Rep.–Minn.). It was the first such Senate hearing since 1981 when Senator Harrison Williams, Jr., Democrat from

Representative Barney Frank (D., Mass.).

New Jersey, was investigated by the panel as part of the ABSCAM case. The Ethics Committee charged that Durenberger received illegal reimbursements for staying in an apartment and that he had backdated the record of his participation in a partnership that owns the condominium. He was also questioned about a book publishing deal that was allegedly a way of obtaining illegal campaign contributions. Durenberger was formally denounced by the full Senate in July, 1990 and ordered to pay restitution for his financial misconduct.

Four cases of sexual misconduct came before the House ethics committee in 1989. Congressman Gus Savage (Dem., Ill.) was accused of fondling a Peace Corps volunteer while he was on an official trip to Africa. Congressman Donald "Buz" Lukens (Rep., Ohio), a Republican, was charged and convicted of having had sex with a sixteen-year-old

girl. He lost his bid for reelection in the 1990 primary. Representative Jim Bates (Dem., Calif.) was accused of sexually harassing women on his staff. The most dramatic case involved Congressman Barney Frank, a liberal Democrat from Massachusetts who disclosed in 1987 that he was a homosexual. Frank admitted that he had bought sex from a male prostitute whom he then hired as a personal assistant. In the weeks following the disclosure, Frank's standing fell dramatically in a poll taken in his Massachusetts district. The House Ethics Committee, however, had difficulty finding a proper strategy for dealing with the scandal and in the spring of 1990 suspended its consideration of the case. Finally, the committee recommended a reprimand for Rep. Frank and, on July 27, 1990, the House of Representatives voted 408 to 18 to reprimand officially Barney Frank for using his office to help his assistant.

even though it adopted such provisions for presidential campaigns in 1974. Part of the campaign-funding problem is illustrated by the former congressman who used leftover campaign funds to make a down payment on a fifty-five-foot houseboat in Florida and to finance a limousine carrying the congressional seal. The practice of diverting unused campaign funds to personal use was outlawed in January 1980, but current members of Congress were exempted from coverage by the law.

The extent of public disenchantment with the state of congressional ethics is suggested by a Gallup poll conducted in early 1980.[20] Seventy-eight percent of a national sample answered yes when asked if they believed "there are senators and representatives now serving in Congress who won election by using unethical and illegal methods in their campaigns." Forty percent of the same sample felt that one-fifth or more of the present members of Congress "got there by using unethical or illegal campaign methods."

■ NEW DIRECTIONS FROM OLD

Winds of an uncertain change have blown through Congress in the last few years. The old seniority system, once a virtually certain path to power through the committee structure, has been eroded. Power has been decentralized and diffused in many respects, most importantly by the growth of subcommittees. The greater number and increased importance of subcommittees has reduced control over information and material resources formerly in the hands of full committee chairpersons and party leaders.

A response to this fragmentation of power in Congress has been the increased importance of the party caucuses, especially on the Democratic side, though this too has meant that party and committee leaders are more answerable to the will of each party member. Numerous mini-caucuses have formed around the specific personal or constituency interests of different members of Congress. These sources of inside lobbying include such groups as the Congressional Black Caucus, the New England Congressional Caucus, the Northeast-Midwest Economic Advancement Coalition, the Congresswomen's Caucus, and the Textile Caucus. These groups have appeared in the House but not yet in the Senate.

Many of the recent changes in Congress resulted from reforms that were intended to "liberalize" the legislative body. However, the decentralization of power and increasing importance of individual members has tended to make compromise more difficult and to slow down the legislative process. The function of lawmaking is sometimes sacrificed to the representation of constituency interests as a consequence of making the Congress more democratic.

[20]*The Gallup Poll 1980* (Wilmington, Del.: Scholarly Resources, 1981), p. 65.

GETTING INVOLVED

How to Be an Intern in Washington, D.C.

John Stuart Mill, the British political philosopher and economist, wrote in the last century, "There are many truths of which the full meaning cannot be realized until personal experience has brought it home." Hundreds of students each year flock to Washington, D.C., for a summer, a semester, or a full year to gain personal experience in one of the myriad institutions of the nation's capital. For those with "Potomac fever," an internship in Washington earning college credit while working is an extraordinary opportunity. If you are interested in a Washington experience, here are some things to keep in mind.

First, make sure you discuss your internship plan with your faculty adviser. He or she will have useful tips. Some colleges have strict rules on who may obtain credit for internships, what preparation is necessary, in what year students are allowed to participate in internships, and other such matters. Internships are most useful if you are in your junior or senior year.

There are several ways to plan an internship: First, contact an existing program such as the Washington Center (514 10th St. N.W., Suite 600, Washington, D.C., 20004, Tel. 202-289-8680). Such an organization will assist you in finding a suitable internship in government, the private sector, business, foundations and nonprofit or volunteer organizations, and in considering other opportunities. "Organized" internship programs will also find you housing and usually provide field trips, special seminars, internship advisers, and other support. Ask if your college or university is affiliated with or has its own Washington program.

Second, find your own internship. There are several avenues for identifying and pursuing opportunities. Contact the local office of your representative or senator, which is usually listed in the telephone directory under "United States Government." Many members of Congress have internship coordinators and large, well-supervised programs. Some may even be able to pay part of your expenses.

Yet another route to finding your own internship is to study carefully one of the many directories on internships, such as the *Directory of Washington Internships,* Society for Internships and Experimental Education, 122 St. Mary's St., Raleigh, N.C. 27605.

Always make sure you explore in detail what a specific job offers. Think carefully about internships that are glorified secretarial jobs for which all you do is typing and filing. Good internships should give you an insider's view on how a profession works. It should furnish some real "hands on" opportunities to do research, deal with the public, learn about legislation, and watch government officials in action.

Remember that most internships are nonpaying. Make sure you understand all the costs involved and arrange for financing through your college, guaranteed student loan, personal savings, or family support.

Finally, keep in mind that there are also internships in most members' district offices close to home. Such jobs may not have the glamour of Washington but they may offer excellent opportunities for political experience.

A very useful booklet with which you should start is: *Storming Washington: An Intern's Guide to National Government,* by Stephen E. Frantzich, available from the American Political Science Association, 1527 N. Hampshire Ave., N.W., Washington, D.C., 20036, Tel. 202-483-2512.

CHAPTER SUMMARY

1. The Founding Fathers, believing the bulk of national power should be in the legislature, set forth the structure, power, and operations of Congress in Article I of the Constitution.

2. Article I, Section 2, of the Constitution says that Congress will consist of two chambers. Partly an outgrowth of the Connecticut Compromise, this bicameral structure established a balanced legislature with the membership in the House of Representatives based on population and the membership in the Senate based on the equality of states.

3. The first seventeen clauses of Article I, Section 8, of the Constitution specify most of the enumerated, or express, powers of Congress, including the right to collect taxes, to spend money, to regulate commerce, and to declare war. Other sections cover a wide range of further powers.

4. Besides its enumerated powers, Congress enjoys the right to "make all Laws which shall be necessary and proper for carrying into Execution the foregoing Powers, and all other Powers vested by this Constitution in the Government of the United States, or in any Department or Officer thereof." This is called the necessary and proper clause.

5. Functions of Congress include (a) lawmaking activities, (b) service to constituents, (c) representation of diverse interests, (d) oversight of the manner in which laws are implemented, (e) educating the public about national issues and setting the terms for national debate, and (f) resolving conflicts.

6. There are 435 members in the House of Representatives compared with 100 senators. Owing to its larger size, there are a greater number of formal rules in the House.

7. The Senate tradition of unlimited debate, or filibustering, dates back to 1790 and has been used over the years to frustrate the passage of bills. Under Senate Rule 22, cloture can be used to shut off debate on a bill.

8. Congressional elections are operated by the individual state governments, which must conform to rules established by the Constitution and national statutes.

9. The process of nominating congressional candidates has shifted from party conventions to the direct primaries currently used in all states.

10. Candidates win through the effectiveness of their personal organizations, often with assistance from the state party organization. They have a loose affiliation with the party at the national level. The overwhelming majority of incumbent representatives and a smaller proportion of senators who run for reelection are successful.

11. The most complicated aspect of the mechanics of congressional elections is reapportionment—the allocation of legislative seats to constituencies. The Supreme Court's one man, one vote rule has been applied to equalize the populations of state legislative and congressional districts.

12. Members of Congress have a personal staff and benefit from the expertise of the professional staff of agencies created to produce information for their use. They enjoy certain legal privileges and immunities.

13. Members of Congress are disproportionately white, male, Protestant, and trained in higher-status occupations, relative to the American population as a whole.

14. Most of the actual work of legislating is performed by committees and subcommittees within Congress. This is the method for dividing legislative, appropriations, and investigatory functions among small, specialized groups.

15. Legislation introduced into the House or Senate is assigned to the appropriate standing committees for review.

16. Select committees are created for a limited period of time for a specific legislative purpose. Joint committees are formed by the concurrent action of both chambers and consist of members from each chamber.

17. Conference committees are special joint committees set up to achieve agreement between the House and the Senate on the exact wording of legislative acts passed by both chambers in different forms.

18. The House Rules Committee sets the rules by which bills may be debated, amended, and considered by the House.

19. The seniority rule specifies that longer-serving members will be given preference when committee chairpersons and holders of other important posts are selected.

20. The foremost power holder in the House of Representatives is the speaker of the House. Other leaders are the House majority leader, the House minority leader, and the majority and minority whips.

21. Formally, the vice president is the presiding officer of the Senate, with the majority party choosing a senior member as the president pro tem to preside when the vice president is absent. Actual leadership in the Senate rests with the majority floor leader, the minority floor leader, and their respective whips.

22. Congresspersons may make decisions by taking cues from trusted party colleagues or by responding to the policy context of issues and the desires of their constituents.

23. A bill becomes law by progressing through both houses of Congress and their appropriate standing and joint committees to the president.

24. The budget process for a fiscal year begins with the preparation of an executive budget by the president. This is reviewed by the OMB and then sent to Congress, which is supposed to pass a final budget by September. Since 1978, Congress has not followed its own time rules.

25. Ethics is the most serious public relations problem facing Congress. Congress's response to member misconduct has been mixed.

QUESTIONS FOR REVIEW AND DISCUSSION

1. Two of the most important functions of Congress are representation and lawmaking. Think of several instances where these two functions present a conflict for an individual legislator. What should a congressperson do if a vote for a cut in defense spending means reducing jobs in a defense plant in his or her district?

2. Why are so many incumbent congresspersons reelected to office? How do they build so much support in their constituencies? Do voters know enough about congressional activity to make an intelligent choice for their representatives?

3. If legislators in Washington are mostly wealthy, well-educated lawyers, how can they know the needs and desires of their constituents? Would Congress be different if there were more women, minorities, and working-class people elected?

4. What functions does the leadership of the parties perform in Congress? Why is the leadership organization important to individual members?

5. Is the process of lawmaking too complicated? Does it give too many opportunities to block needed legislation?

SELECTED REFERENCES

Michael Barone and Grant Ujifusa, *The Almanac of American Politics 1991* (Washington, D.C.: National Journal, 1990). A comprehensive summary of current political information on each member of Congress, his or her state or congressional district, recent congressional election results, key votes and ratings of roll call votes by various organizations, and sources of campaign contributions and records of campaign expenditures.

David W. Brady, *Critical Elections and Congressional Policy Making* (Stanford, Calif.: Stanford University Press, 1988). This book analyzes the House of Representatives during critical periods—the Civil War, the 1890s, and the New Deal—when it legislated major policy changes.

Lawrence C. Dodd and Bruce I. Oppenheimer, *Congress Reconsidered,* 3d ed. (Washington, D.C.: Congressional Quarterly Press, 1985). A collection of essays on recent developments in congressional elections, changes in how Congress operates, committee and subcommittee politics, leadership and party politics, effects on public policy, and relationships with the executive branch.

Richard F. Fenno, Jr., *The Making of a Senator: Dan Quayle* (Washington, D.C.: Congressional Quarterly Press, 1989). The author reports on the career and ambitions of the vice president of the United States when he was a member of the U.S. Senate, with emphasis on senatorial elections and Quayle's adjustment to congressional norms.

Morris P. Fiorina, *Congress: Keystone of the Washington Establishment,* 2nd ed. (New Haven: Yale University Press, 1989). An extensive update to the 1977 original, this book examines the sources of the criticism that unconstrained pursuit of personal goals by members of Congress has resulted in their failure to meet the responsibilities imposed by the nation.

Louis Fisher, *The Politics of Shared Power: Congress and the Executive* (Washington, D.C.: Congressional Quarterly Press, 1981). Operation of the separation of powers doctrine in practice, emphasizing the president's role as legislator, congressional intervention in administrative matters, and the political and constitutional problems in this sharing of power.

John W. Kingdon, *Congressmen's Voting Decisions,* 3rd ed. (Ann Arbor: University of Michigan Press, 1990). This is considered to be one of the best studies of the way members of Congress vote, and includes the roles played in this process by constituents, colleagues, interest groups, the executive branch, and staff.

Norman J. Ornstein, Thomas E. Mann, and Michael J. Malbin, *Vital Statistics on Congress, 1989–1990* (Washington, D.C.: Congressional Quarterly Press, 1990). The authors bring together from various sources information on eight areas related to Congress including data on the members themselves, on elections, campaign finances, budgeting, committees, and so on.

Randall B. Ripley, *Congress: Process and Policy,* 3d ed. (New York: W. W. Norton, 1983). An overview of Congress covering its role in the policy-making environment, historical development, elections, socialization of its members, committees and subcommittees, party leadership, state delegations, ideologically based groups, personal and committee staffs, support agencies, relations with interest groups and constituents, relations with the president and the bureaucracy, access to policy making, and impact on policy.

CHAPTER 13

THE PRESIDENCY

CHAPTER CONTENTS

WHAT IF . . . THE PRESIDENT COULD BE RECALLED?

One year after his election to a second term in office, the president of the United States is faced with an economic crisis that threatens to rival that of the Great Depression of the 1930s. The president, believing that governmental intervention is futile, does nothing. He has not committed "high crimes and misdemeanors," so no grounds for impeachment exist. He is perfectly well, mentally and physically, so he cannot be declared unable to fulfill the duties of office. As the Constitution stands, there is no way to force a president to act or not to act as long as he or she stays within the bounds of law.

In contrast, many states have constitutional provisions that allow for the citizens of the state to petition for an election to recall the state's highest officer, the governor. If sufficient petitions are filed, then the state holds an election to decide whether the governor is removed from office. Proponents of recall provisions feel that the procedure allows citizens the right to remove an executive who no longer represents their views or who is acting in a manner completely contrary to public preferences or who is corrupt. The recall procedure removes this political judgment from the hands of legislators who may be partisan allies of the executive or who fear that use of the impeachment proceeding will lead to similar action against governors of their own party or ideological persuasion at some later date.

The same constraints work to prevent frequent impeachment proceedings against presidents. The evidence of wrongdoing must be so overwhelming that even members of the president's party will feel comfortable charging the chief executive. They must also be assured that their actions will not be perceived as primarily political; otherwise they might be punished themselves at the next election.

A recall procedure for the president could be legitimated by an amendment to the United States Constitution. The procedure might, for example, require the signatures of 10 percent of the voters in three-fourths of the states, easily a total of several million. If the petitions were judged to be valid, a national election would be held to remove the president from office. Presumably, the vice president would assume the chief executive's position until the term expired.

What would the effects of such a recall possibility be? On the positive side, facing a potential recall vote might well make the president more sensitive to the voters' views. The recall provision, together with the investigative media, would also keep presidents aware of the need for high ethical standards for the executive branch. Furthermore, strong public support for a particular policy proposal coupled with the potential of recall could strengthen the president's resolve to fight for the proposal against a recalcitrant

Congress or the Supreme Court.

On the negative side, as a threat, the recall would keep presidents ever mindful of their popularity, thus increasing the pressure to manipulate images and media coverage to raise approval ratings.

The recall could also be seen as a device to weaken the chief executive in the struggle with Congress. The Congress, which cannot be recalled until the next election day, seeing a president under the threat of recall, might hamstring the executive's power through regulations and pork barrel legislation. It would be very tempting for extremely vocal and intense interest groups, such as those both pro- and antichoice for abortion, to attempt recall petition drives to force the president to support their position. The chief executive might have to spend an inordinate amount

of time and energy mollifying such special interests. Finally, it could be argued that the Congress already has enough power through its override of the veto and through the appropriations process to control the president, even on foreign policy issues. The recall, although it might serve to make presidents more responsive in specific and rare situations, might also work to shift the balance of power between the branches of government to the Congress and weaken the president's resources to lead.

---

1. *What kinds of behavior might lead to an attempt to recall the president?*
2. *If the president could be removed from office, should new congressional elections be held to replace the legislative branch at the same time?*
3. *How could the recall be structured to apply pressure to the president without becoming a long-running media event?*

It is ironic that the Founding Fathers, rejecting so emphatically the model of a king, created an office presently invested with authority far beyond that of any surviving king and only to be rivaled by the powers of absolute monarchs.[1]

The writers of the Constitution created the presidency of the United States without any models to draw on. Nowhere else in the world was there a democratically selected chief executive. What the Founders did not want was a king. In fact, given their previous experience with royal governors in the colonies, many of the delegates to the Constitutional Convention wanted to create a very weak executive who could not veto legislation. In part because the delegates knew that George Washington, whose character and integrity were clear, would be the first occupant of the office, they created a chief executive who had enough powers granted in the Constitution to balance those of the Congress.

> **DID YOU KNOW?**
>
> That Thomas Jefferson was the first president inaugurated in Washington, D.C., where he walked to the Capitol from a boarding house, took the oath, made a brief speech in the Senate chamber, and then walked back home?

■ THE PRESIDENT: IMPERIAL OR IMPERILED?

Looking at the presidential office today, it is difficult to imagine that in the last century, many Americans felt that the president had far too little power to deal with the Congress. As commander-in-chief of the world's most powerful military arsenal, negotiator of treaties with other superpowers, head of the largest organization in the nation, chief collector of taxes and law enforcement officer, and chief persuader of public opinion, the president can hardly be seen as weak partner to the Congress.

The powers given to the president in the Constitution have been expanded by congressional legislation, by custom and usage, and by the precedents set by earlier executives. As the United States has taken its place as a global leader, its chief executive has become the most powerful in the world. The debate most often heard in the late twentieth century is whether the president has enough power.

We are all fascinated by presidential power. The power exercised by each president who has held the office has been scrutinized and judged by historians, political scientists, the media, and the public. In the 1950s and 1960s, the nation sought "heroic" presidents in the legacy of Washington, Jackson, Lincoln, and Theodore and Franklin Roosevelt, who would lead the nation to greatness.[2]

In the view of many, President Lyndon Baines Johnson's domestic leadership placed him in the heroic class, but his decision to involve the nation massively in the Vietnam war and his inability to resolve that conflict made many feel that the president was much too powerful. After the nation's experience with President Richard Nixon and the Watergate scandal, Arthur Schlesinger coined the phrase "the imperial presidency" to describe an office that had ignored the constitutional prerogatives of the Congress or the Constitution itself.[3] Reacting to the abuses of the Nixon presidency, Congress reasserted its power, passing the War Powers Act in 1973 and the Budget and Impoundment Act in 1974, both of which limited the president's ability to act. Since that time, some have

Abraham Lincoln, who is usually classified as one of the greatest presidents. What qualities make a president outstanding?

[1]Page Smith, *The Constitution: A Documentary and Narrative History* (New York: William Morrow, 1978), p. 528.
[2]Richard A. Watson and Norman C. Thomas, *The Politics of the Presidency* (Washington, D.C.: Congressional Quarterly, 1988), p. 3.
[3]Arthur Schlesinger, *The Imperial Presidency* (Boston: Houghton Mifflin, 1973).

PROFILE

George Washington

"I do not conceive we can exist long as a nation without having lodged somewhere a power which will pervade the whole union in as energetic a manner as the authority of the state governments extends over the several states."

George Washington was born more than two and a half centuries ago. In spite of voluminous research and the millions of words written about him, he still retains his aura of greatness. Not surprisingly, his contemporaries offered him as much respect as schoolchildren do today.

However, if Washington were alive today and scrutinized with the same standards we use with our contemporary presidents, this aura might be diminished. Consider his reading habits. They certainly weren't as sophisticated as those of John Fitzgerald Kennedy, who, when asked what his ten favorite books were, listed works of biography, history, and politics. Washington, a how-to-do-it expert, enjoyed books about manure and animal husbandry.

Washington was not a world traveler. Indeed, he never went to Europe. He spoke no foreign languages—and he was a poor public speaker. The single outstanding characteristic of his military career was perseverance. It was perseverance that won the Battle of Trenton and brought the Revolution back to life, convincing France to commit herself to the American cause. Military analysts of today, however, do not have high praise for the technical expertise of Washington's military campaign. Crossing the Delaware River, his troops couldn't fire their guns because the powder was soaked by freezing rain. His officers wanted to call off the attack, but his men fought with bayonets. The Battle of Trenton was won because Washington was determined, not because he was a military genius.

In his day, Washington was one of the wealthiest individuals in the nation. He was proud and aristocratic in manner and never attempted to give the impression that he was a great democrat. The story goes that Gouverneur Morris, an old friend and supporter, once put his hand on Washington's shoulder to show his close relationship with the chief executive. Washington removed Morris's hand almost immediately.

Contemporaries of the first president and historians of today agree that Washington had the necessary qualities to be the "father of our country"; Washington was a natural leader. As the chief executive, he organized the administration, maintained dignity in office, and kept the early decisions of the nation free from partisanship.

---

expressed concern that the president has been denied the powers he needs to function as an effective executive. Faced with congressional interference in foreign policy and military affairs, with congressional involvement in the budget process, and with a weakened party system, the imperial president perhaps has become an "imperiled president."[4]

■ WHO CAN BECOME PRESIDENT?

The requirements for becoming president, as outlined in Article II, Section 1, of the Constitution, are not overwhelmingly stringent:

> No person except a natural-born Citizen, or a Citizen of the United States, at the time of the Adoption of this Constitution shall be eligible to the Office of President;

[4]Thomas E. Cronin, "An Imperiled Presidency," in Vincent Davis, ed., *The Post-Imperial Presidency* (New Brunswick, N.J.: Transaction Books, 1980).

neither shall any Person be eligible to that Office who shall not have attained to the Age of 35 Years, and been fourteen Years a Resident within the United States.

The only question that arises about these qualifications relates to the term *natural-born citizen*. Does that mean that only citizens born in the United States and its territories? What about a child born to a U.S. citizen (or to a couple who are U.S. citizens) while visiting or living in another country? Although the question has not been dealt with directly by the Supreme Court, it is reasonable to expect that someone would be eligible if his or her parents were Americans. The first presidents, after all, were not even American citizens at birth, and others were born in areas that did not become part of the United States until later. This issue became important when George Romney,[5] who was born in Chihuahua, Mexico, made a serious bid for the Republican presidential nomination in the 1960s.

The great American dream is symbolized by the statement that "anybody can become president of this country." It is true that in modern times presidents have included a haberdasher (Truman—for a short period of time), a peanut farmer (Carter), and an actor (Reagan). But if you examine Appendix C, you will see that the most common previous occupation of presidents in this country has been the legal profession. Out of forty-one presidents, twenty-four have been lawyers (and many have been wealthy; see the Highlight on well-heeled competitors).

Although the Constitution states that the minimum-age requirement for the presidency is thirty-five years, most presidents have been much older than that when they assumed office. John F. Kennedy, at the age of forty-three, was the youngest elected president, and the oldest has been Ronald Reagan, at age sixty-nine. The average age at inauguration has been fifty-four. There has clearly been a demographic bias in the selection of presidents. All have been male, white, and Protestants, except for John F. Kennedy, a Roman Catholic. Presidents have been men of great stature—like Washington—and men in whom leadership qualities were not so pronounced—such as Warren Harding.

The first cabinet—from left to right: Henry Knox, Thomas Jefferson, Edmund Randolph, Alexander Hamilton, and President George Washington.

■ THE PROCESS OF BECOMING PRESIDENT

Major and minor political parties nominate candidates for president and vice president at the national conventions every four years. The nation's voters do not elect a president and vice president directly, but rather cast ballots for presidential electors who then vote for president and vice president in the electoral college. The electors are chosen from all the states and the District of Columbia.

Since the election is governed by a majority in the electoral college, it is conceivable that someone could be elected to the office of the presidency without having a plurality of the popular vote cast. Indeed, in three cases, candidates won elections even though their major opponents received more popular votes. This occurred in the elections of John Quincy Adams in 1824, Rutherford B. Hayes in 1876, and Benjamin Harrison in 1888. In cases in which there were more than two candidates running for office, many presidential candidates have won the election with less than 50 percent of the total popular votes cast for all candidates—including Abraham Lincoln, Woodrow

[5]Governor of Michigan from 1963 to 1969.

HIGHLIGHT
Well-Heeled Competitors

The 1988 election for president and vice president matched Republicans George Bush and Dan Quayle against Democrats Michael Dukakis and Lloyd Bentsen. As the table indicates, all four men were essentially millionaires.

Bush	Quayle	Dukakis	Bentsen
Net worth **$2.6 million**	Net worth **$50 million+**	Net worth **$464,365**	Net worth **$10 million+**
Income (1987) **$308,400**	Income **$143,944+**	Income **$108,957**	Income **$919,566**
Taxes paid **$86,684**	Taxes paid **not released**	Taxes paid **$25,892**	Taxes paid **$211,411**
Assets	Assets	Assets	Assets
Bush's assets include a $1.5 million house in Kennebunkport, Maine, a $1 million blind trust and a 1973 Cigarette boat worth between $12,000 and $18,000.	Quayle's suburban house in McLean, Va., has a market value of $500,000, and he owns stock in his family's newspaper chain worth more than $250,000.	On his mother's death, Dukakis may inherit half of two separate $1 million trusts set up by his father. His house in Brookline, Mass., is worth $367,400.	Bentsen has a $1 million town house in Washington. Other assets: a condominium, a farm, a ranch and a blind trust worth at least $3.5 million.

SOURCE: *Newsweek,* Aug. 29, 1988.

Wilson, Harry S Truman, John F. Kennedy, and Richard Nixon. (See the Highlight on presidential elections.)

On occasion, the electoral college has failed to give any candidate a majority. At this point, the election is thrown into the House of Representatives, where the president is chosen from among the three candidates having the most electoral college votes. Each state's House delegation has one vote. To win the election, a candidate must receive a majority of the votes that are cast in the House of Representatives. By House rule, each state's vote is given to the candidate preferred by a majority of the state's delegation in the House. In the event that there is a tie within any state's House delegation, that state's vote is not counted.

Only two times in our past has the House had to decide on a president. Thomas Jefferson and Aaron Burr tied in the electoral college in 1800. This happened because the Constitution had not been explicit in indicating which of the two electoral votes was for president and which was for vice president. In 1804, the **Twelfth Amendment** clarified the matter. In 1824, the House had to make a choice among William H. Crawford, Henry Clay, Andrew Jackson, and John Quincy Adams. It chose Adams, even though Jackson had more electoral and popular votes.

What if the House fails to choose a president? Then the vice president, who has been chosen by the electoral college—or, failing that, chosen by the Senate—becomes president. There is no explicit provision in the Twelfth Amendment or elsewhere in the Constitution about what will happen if neither a president

TWELFTH AMENDMENT
An amendment to the Constitution, adopted in 1804, which specifies the separate election of the president and vice president by the electoral college.

Presidential Elections

No president of the United States has ever been elected by a majority of all adults of voting age, even though many presidents have been elected by very large majorities of votes from citizens who actually cast ballots. As you can see from the accompanying table (Table 13-1), Martin Van Buren was elected president by a record low of just 11.4 percent of voting-age Americans in 1836. The proportion of voting-age citizens who have elected presidents has generally increased over time. This has happened largely because of several important extensions of voting rights—the Fifteenth Amendment in 1870, which removed race as a barrier to voting for African-American males; the Nineteenth Amendment in 1920, which enfranchised women; the Twenty-fourth Amendment in 1964, which abolished the poll tax in federal elections; and the Twenty-sixth Amendment in 1971 lowering the minimum voting age to eighteen. Ronald Reagan was reelected in 1984 with the votes of 32.0 percent of Americans of voting age. Lyndon Johnson, in 1964, came the closest of any president in history to being elected by a majority of the voting-age public, and even he gained the votes of less than 40 percent of those who were old enough to cast a ballot.

These results are especially useful to keep in mind whenever a president lays claim to having received a "mandate" from the people to govern the nation. In reality, no president has ever been elected with sufficient popular backing to make this a serious claim.

TABLE 13-1
Popular Votes and Presidential Elections, 1828–1988

Year	Winning Candidate	Percentage of Total Vote	Percentage of Voting-Age Population
1828	Andrew Jackson	56.0	12.4
1832	Andrew Jackson	56.5	11.6
1836	Martin Van Buren	50.8	11.4
1840	William Harrison	52.9	16.9
1844	James Polk	49.5	15.1
1848	Zachary Taylor	47.3	13.5
1852	Franklin Pierce	50.6	13.8
1856	James Buchanan	45.3	13.8
1860	Abraham Lincoln	39.8	12.5
1864	Abraham Lincoln	55.0	13.4
1868	Ulysses Grant	52.8	16.7
1872	Ulysses Grant	55.7	17.8
1876	Rutherford Hayes	47.9	17.8
1880	James Garfield	48.3	17.5
1884	Grover Cleveland	48.5	17.3
1888	Benjamin Harrison	47.9	17.4
1892	Grover Cleveland	46.1	16.1
1896	William McKinley	51.1	18.8
1900	William McKinley	51.7	17.6
1904	Theodore Roosevelt	56.4	16.8
1908	William Taft	51.6	15.4
1912	Woodrow Wilson	41.9	11.7
1916	Woodrow Wilson	49.3	15.8
1920	Warren Harding	60.4	25.6
1924	Calvin Coolidge	54.0	23.7
1928	Herbert Hoover	58.1	30.1
1932	Franklin Roosevelt	57.4	30.1
1936	Franklin Roosevelt	60.8	34.6
1940	Franklin Roosevelt	54.7	32.2
1944	Franklin Roosevelt	53.4	29.9
1948	Harry Truman	49.6	25.3
1952	Dwight Eisenhower	55.1	34.0
1956	Dwight Eisenhower	57.4	34.1
1960	John Kennedy	49.7	31.2
1964	Lyndon Johnson	61.1	37.8
1968	Richard Nixon	43.4	26.4
1972	Richard Nixon	60.7	33.7
1976	Jimmy Carter	50.1	27.2
1980	Ronald Reagan	51.0	26.7
1984	Ronald Reagan	58.7	32.0
1988	George Bush	53.4	26.7

John F. Kennedy's inaugeral.

CHIEF OF STATE
The role of the president as ceremonial head of the government.

CHIEF EXECUTIVE
The role of the president as head of the executive branch of the government.

COMMANDER IN CHIEF
The role of the president as supreme commander of the military forces of the United States and of the state national guard units when they are called into federal service.

CHIEF DIPLOMAT
The role of the president in recognizing foreign governments, making treaties, and making executive agreements.

CHIEF LEGISLATOR
The role of the president in influencing the making of laws.

nor a vice president can be selected by Congress. Failure to select a vice president, however, is very unlikely because the Senate makes its choice with all members voting for one of the top two candidates. A Senate deadlock is still possible. Either a new election could be called or the speaker of the House could succeed to the presidency until the matter could be resolved.

■ THE MANY ROLES OF THE PRESIDENT

The Constitution speaks briefly about the duties and obligations of the president. Based on a terse list of powers and the precedents of history, the presidency has grown into a very complicated job that requires balancing at least five constitutional roles. These are (1) **chief of state,** (2) **chief executive,** (3) **commander in chief** of the armed forces, (4) **chief diplomat,** and (5) **chief legislator** of the United States.[6] Here we examine each of these significant presidential functions, or roles. It is worth noting that one person plays all these roles simultaneously and that the needs of these roles may at times be contradictory.

Chief of State

Every nation has at least one person who is the ceremonial head of state. In most democratic governments, the role of chief of state is given to someone other than the chief executive (see Highlight on filling the ceremonial role). In Britain, for example, the chief of state is the queen. In France, where the prime minister is the chief executive, the chief of state is the president. But in the United States, the president is both chief executive and chief of state. According to William Howard Taft, as chief of state the president symbolizes the "dignity and majesty" of the American people. In his capacity as chief of state, the president engages in a number of activities that are largely symbolic or ceremonial in nature, such as the following:

■ Decorating war heroes
■ Throwing out the first ball to open the baseball season
■ Dedicating parks and post offices
■ Launching charity drives
■ Receiving visiting chiefs of state at the White House
■ Going on official state visits to other countries
■ Making personal telephone calls to congratulate the country's heroes and heroines

Many students of the American political system believe that having the president serve as both the chief executive and the head of state drastically limits the time available to do "real" work. Not all presidents have agreed with this conclusion, however—particularly those presidents who have been able to blend skillfully these two roles with their role as politician. Being chief of state gives the president tremendous public exposure, and when that is positive it helps the president deal with Congress over proposed legislation and increases his chances of being reelected—or getting his party's candidates elected.

[6]One scholar, Clinton Rossiter, has proposed at least five other roles for the president, including party chief, voice of the people, protector of peace, manager of prosperity, and world leader, *The American Presidency,* rev. ed. (New York: Harcourt, Brace, 1960).

HIGHLIGHT

Filling the Ceremonial Role

For decades, scholars have felt that the president of the United States spends far too much time on the duties of chief of state—largely ceremonial tasks such as greeting the Superbowl champions or receiving foreign dignataries. In virtually every other Western nation, the chief of state is a separate position from the chief executive.

In the seven Western European countries headed by royalty, the monarch is considered the chief of state and plays a ceremonial role. In the United Kingdom, for example, Queen Elizabeth represents the state at ceremonial occasions, such as the opening sessions of Parliament, the christening of ships, and receptions for foreign ambassadors. The monarch presides at swearing-in ceremonies for government ministers and other important officials.

In the monarchies of Holland and Norway, the king or queen initiates the process of forming a government after national elections, by determining which parties can combine to rule in

Queen Elizabeth of Great Britain is the chief of state of that nation but she has no political power.

coalition. This process really depends on the results of the election and the

desires of the political parties—but the monarch must certify it.

The majority of European states are not monarchies, but they split the duties of government between prime minister and president. In Switzerland, for example, the president is indirectly elected by the legislature. The president is selected from among members of a governing council, but, once chosen, assumes purely ceremonial duties. In addition to those occasions requiring protocol or exceptional pomp, the president is called on to represent the nation in a symbolic way whenever portentous events require authoritative—but nonpartisan—comment. Such events might include the death of an outstanding citizen or the victory of the national team in a soccer match.

Throughout Western Europe, the pattern is the same: Presidents have ceremonial powers only. The single exception to this rule is France, which has a presidential system giving the head of state real political power.

As chief of state, the president is expected to meet with champions such as the Detroit Pistons. Does he get any advantage from such publicity opportunities?

Barbara Bush takes Millie to visit with senior citizens. What role should the First Lady play in our system, if any?

CIVIL SERVICE
A collective term for the body of employees working for the government. Generally, civil service is understood to apply to all those who gain government employment through a merit system.

APPOINTMENT POWER
The authority vested in the president to fill a government office or position. Positions filled by presidential appointment include those in the executive branch, the federal judiciary, commissioned officers in the armed forces, and members of the independent regulatory commissions.

One effect of the president's role as chief of state is that his life is put on public display day in and day out. Everything the president and the "first family" does has become intensely interesting to the American—and indeed to the world—public. One reason why many Americans are so absorbed by the trivia of presidential activities is that the president is also the personal symbol of the nation, in the same way that kings and queens are. This symbolic role leads to an emotional investment by citizens and explains why, even if the president is not liked by many individuals, they still feel great anxiety when his life is threatened. It seems like a threat to the nation, not just to the person in the office.

Chief Executive

According to the Constitution, "The executive Power shall be vested in a President of the United States of America. . . . He may require the Opinion, in writing, of the principal Officer in each of the Executive Departments, upon any Subject relating to the Duties of their respective Offices . . . and he shall nominate, and by and with the Advice and Consent of the Senate, shall appoint . . . Officers of the United States. . . . He shall take Care that the Laws be faithfully executed, . . ."

As chief executive the president is constitutionally bound to enforce the acts of Congress, the judgments of federal courts, and treaties to which the United States is a signator. To assist in the various tasks of the chief executive, the president has a federal bureaucracy (see Chapter 14), which currently consists of some three million civilian employees and which spends over a trillion dollars per year.

The Powers of Appointment and Removal. Since the president is head of the largest bureaucracy in the United States, you might think that he wields enormous power. The president, however, only nominally runs the executive bureaucracy, for most of its jobs are protected by **civil service.**[7] Therefore, even though the president has **appointment power,** it is not very extensive, being limited to cabinet and subcabinet jobs, federal judgeships, agency heads, and about two thousand lesser jobs. In Table 13-2, we show what percentage of the total employment in each executive department is available for political appointment by the president.

The president's power to remove from office officials who are doing a poor job or who don't agree with the president is not explicitly granted by the Constitution and has been limited. In 1926, however, a Supreme Court decision prevented Congress from interfering with the president's ability to fire those executive-branch officials that the president had appointed with Senate approval.[8]

The ten agencies whose directors the president can remove at any time are as follows:

1. ACTION (coordinates volunteer programs)
2. Arms Control and Disarmament Agency
3. Commission on Civil Rights

---

[7]See pages 458–459 for a discussion of the Civil Service Reform Act.
[8]*Meyers v. United States,* 272 U.S. 52 (1926).

4. Energy Research and Development Agency
5. Environmental Protection Agency (EPA)
6. Federal Mediation and Conciliation Service
7. General Services Administration (GSA)
8. National Aeronautics and Space Administration (NASA)
9. Postal Service
10. Small Business Administration (SBA)

In addition, the president can remove all heads of cabinet departments and all individuals in the Executive Office of the President.

Harry Truman spoke candidly of the difficulties a president faces in trying to control the executive bureaucracy. Upon leaving office, he referred to the problems that Eisenhower, as a former general of the army, was going to have: "He'll sit here and he'll say do this! do that! and nothing will happen. Poor Ike—it won't be a bit like the Army. He'll find it very frustrating."[9]

[9]Quoted in Richard E. Neustadt, *Presidential Power* (New York: John Wiley, 1960), p. 9.

DID YOU KNOW?

That President William Henry Harrison gave the longest inaugural address of any American president lasting two hours? The weather was cold and stormy, Harrison caught a cold, got pneumonia and pleurisy, and died a month later.

TABLE 13-2
Total Employment in Cabinet Departments Available for Political Appointment by the President
How much change can a president make with less than 3/10 of 1 percent of the jobs for his supporters?

Executive Department	Total Number of Employees[1]	Political Appointments Available[2]	Percent
Agriculture	114,361	463	0.40
Commerce	34,302	261	0.76
Defense	1,018,098	549	0.05
Education	5,783	159	2.75
Energy	18,641	170	0.91
Health and Human Services	147,830	234	0.16
Housing and Urban Development	14,921	167	1.12
Interior	73,852	140	0.19
Justice	54,722	364	0.67
Labor	18,795	151	0.80
State	23,795	463	1.95
Transportation	60,946	114	0.19
Treasury	126,421	454	0.36
Veterans	n.a.	n.a.	n.a.
Total	1,712,620	3,689	0.22

[1]1989.
[2]Includes noncareer employees in the Senior Executive Service.

SOURCES: Committee on Post Office and Civil Service, House of Representatives, 96th Congress, 2nd Session, *Policy and Supporting Positions*, November 18, 1980; *Statistical Abstract of the United States, 1989–90*.

The new Air Force One, a 747, was inaugurated in 1990. Why do presidents need specially equipped, luxurious airplanes?

REPRIEVE
The president has the power to grant a reprieve to postpone the execution of a sentence imposed by a court of law; usually done for humanitarian reasons or to await new evidence.

PARDON
The granting of a release from the punishment or legal consequences of a crime; a pardon can be granted by the president before or after a conviction.

The Power to Grant Reprieves and Pardons.   Section 2 of Article II of the Constitution gives the president the power to grant **reprieves** and **pardons** for offenses against the United States except in cases of impeachment. All pardons are administered by the Office of the Pardon Attorney in the Department of Justice. In principle, pardons are granted to remedy a mistake made in a conviction.

The Supreme Court upheld the president's right to reprieve in a 1925 case concerning the pardon granted by the president to an individual convicted of contempt of court.[10] The judiciary had contended that only judges had the authority to convict individuals for contempt of court when court orders were violated and that the courts should be free from interference by the executive branch. The Supreme Court simply stated that the president could reprieve or pardon all offenses "either before trial, during trial, or after trial, by individuals, or by classes, conditionally or absolutely, and this without modification or regulation by Congress."[11] In a controversial decision, President Gerald Ford pardoned former President Richard Nixon for his role in the Watergate Affair before any charges were brought in court.

Commander in Chief

The president, according to the Constitution, "shall be Commander in Chief of the Army and Navy of the United States, and of the militia of the several States, when called into the actual service of the United States." In other words, the armed forces are under civilian, rather than military, control.

Certainly the Founding Fathers had George Washington in mind when they made the president the commander in chief. President Washington was in physical command of the troops that put down the Whiskey Rebellion in 1794. Although we no longer expect our president to lead the troops to battle, presidents as commanders in chief have certainly wielded dramatic power.

[10]*Ex parte Grossman,* 267 U.S. 87 (1925).
[11]Ibid.

Harry Truman made the awesome decision to drop the atomic bomb on Hiroshima and Nagasaki. Lyndon Johnson ordered bombing missions to North Vietnam, and he personally selected the targets. Nixon decided to invade Cambodia in 1970, and Ronald Reagan sent troops to Lebanon and Grenada in 1983 and ordered American fighter planes to attack Libya in 1986 in retaliation for terrorist attacks on American citizens. Bush sent troops to Panama in 1989 and to the Middle East in 1990.

The president is the ultimate decision maker in military matters. Everywhere he goes, so too goes the "football"—a briefcase filled with all the codes necessary to order a nuclear attack. Only the president has the power to order the use of nuclear force.

In his role as commander in chief, the president has probably exercised more authority than in any other role. Constitutionally, Congress has the sole power to declare war, but the president can send the armed forces into a country in situations that are certainly the equivalent of war. When William McKinley ordered troops into Peking to help suppress the Boxer Rebellion in 1900, he was sending them into a combat situation. Harry Truman dispatched troops to Korea as part of a "police action" in 1950. Kennedy, Johnson, and Nixon waged an undeclared war in Vietnam, where 57,000 Americans were killed and 300,000 were wounded. In none of these situations did Congress declare war.

In an attempt to gain more control over such military activities, in 1973 Congress passed a **War Powers Act**—over President Nixon's veto—requiring that the president consult with Congress before sending American forces into action. Once they are sent, the president must report to Congress within forty-eight hours. Unless the Congress has passed a declaration of war within sixty days or has extended the sixty-day time limit, the forces must be withdrawn. The War Powers Act was tested in the fall of 1983 when Reagan requested that troops be left in Lebanon. The resulting compromise was a congressional resolution allowing troops to remain there for eighteen months. Shortly after the resolution was passed, however, more than 240 sailors and marines were

Military aide carrying the "football."

WAR POWERS ACT
A law passed in 1973 spelling out the conditions under which the president can commit troops without congressional approval.

Shortly after the invasion of Kuwait, Bush met with the exiled Emir of Kuwait to discuss the situation. Such a meeting signals the importance of the crisis to other nations.

DID YOU KNOW?

That Theodore Roosevelt was the first president to leave the country on an official trip during his term, the first president to ride in a submarine and an airplane, and the first to have a telephone on his desk?

ADVICE AND CONSENT
The power vested in the U.S. Senate by the Constitution (Article II, Section 2) to give its advice and consent to the president concerning treaties and presidential appointments.

RECOGNITION POWER
The president's power, as chief diplomat, to extend diplomatic recognition to foreign governments.

killed in the suicide bombing of a U.S. military housing compound in Beirut. That event provoked a furious congressional debate over the role American troops were playing in the Middle East, and all troops were withdrawn shortly afterward.

In spite of the War Powers Act, the powers of the president as commander in chief are more extensive today than they were in the past. These powers are closely linked to the president's powers as chief diplomat, or chief crafter of foreign policy.

Chief Diplomat

The Constitution gives the president the power to recognize foreign governments, to make nontreaty agreements with other heads of state, and, with the **advice and consent** of the Senate, to make treaties. In addition, the president nominates ambassadors. As chief diplomat, the president dominates American foreign policy.

Recognition Power.   An important power of the president as chief diplomat is **recognition power,** or the power to recognize—or refuse to recognize—foreign governments. In his role as ceremonial head of state, the president has always received foreign diplomats. In modern times, the simple act of receiving a foreign diplomat has been equivalent to accrediting the diplomat and officially recognizing his or her government. Such recognition of the legitimacy of another country's government is a prerequisite to diplomatic relations or negotiations between that country and the United States.

Deciding when to recognize a foreign power is not always a simple task. The United States, for example, did not recognize the Soviet Union until 1933—sixteen years following the Russian Revolution of 1917. It was only after all attempts—including military invasion of Russia as well as diplomatic isolation—to reverse the effects of that revolution had proved futile that Franklin Roosevelt extended recognition to the Soviet government. U.S. presidents faced a similar problem with the Chinese communist revolution and the emerg-

President Bush meets with President F. W. de Klerk of South Africa.

ence of a new communist government in mainland China. The former government had fled to the island of Taiwan, establishing its headquarters there, and so two rival governments existed—both claiming legitimacy. In December 1978, forty years after the communist victory in China, Jimmy Carter granted official recognition to the People's Republic of China and downgraded diplomatic relations with the rival government of the Republic of China in Taiwan. Nixon's earlier "ping-pong diplomacy"[12] and subsequent trip to China did much to prepare the way for diplomatic recognition of that country by the United States, but Carter's policy nonetheless elicited much criticism from anticommunist hardliners. On April 7, 1979, Carter again used his recognition powers as chief diplomat when he broke diplomatic ties with the revolutionary Khomeini government in Iran.

When Lithuania declared its independence of the Soviet Union in 1990, President Bush was put in a difficult spot. The United States had never recognized the Soviet occupation of the Lithuanian republic after World War II. Should Bush have sent an ambassador as soon as Lithuania declared its freedom? Bush moved cautiously, giving Lithuania moral support but avoiding direct recognition in order to avoid disrupting newly cordial relations with the Soviet Union.

Proposal and Ratification of Treaties.   The president has the sole power to negotiate treaties with other nations. These treaties must be presented to the Senate, where they may be modified and must be approved by a two-thirds

---

[12]The Nixon administration first encouraged new relations with the People's Republic by allowing a cultural exchange of ping-pong teams.

DID YOU KNOW?

That the expression "O.K.," which is used worldwide, was coined in the presidential campaign of 1840 in reference to Martin Van Buren who was called "Old Kinderhook" after his birthplace? His New York supporters formed the "O.K." club and shouted the expression at political rallies and parades.

The Bushes and Gorbachevs prepare to greet guests at a formal dinner. To what extent does it matter if world leaders become personal friends?

DID YOU KNOW?

That more than $125 million has been spent since 1980 to pay living and security expenses for former presidents Nixon, Ford, Carter, and Reagan?

vote. After ratification, the president can approve of the senatorial version of the treaty. Approval poses a problem when the Senate has tacked on substantive amendments or reservations to a treaty, particularly when such changes may require reopening negotiations with the other signatory governments. Sometimes a president may decide to withdraw a treaty if the senatorial changes are too extensive—as Wilson did with the Versailles Treaty in 1919. Wilson felt the senatorial reservations would weaken the treaty so much that it would be ineffective. His refusal to accept the senatorial version of the treaty led to the eventual refusal of the United States to join the League of Nations.

President Carter was more successful in lobbying for the treaties returning the Panama Canal to Panama by the year 2000 and neutralizing the canal. However, he was unsuccessful in his attempts to gain ratification of the Strategic Arms Limitation Talks treaty, known as SALT II. That treaty, which provided for limits on nuclear-armed, long-range bombers and intercontinental ballistic missiles, encountered fierce opposition from Senate conservatives and from the subsequent Reagan administration. The treaty was withdrawn by President Reagan. In 1988, Ronald Reagan succeeded in getting Senate approval of the INF treaty with the Soviet Union, which reduced the intermediate-range missiles of both nations.

EXECUTIVE AGREEMENTS
International agreements made by the president, without senatorial ratification, with heads of foreign states.

Executive Agreements. Presidential power in foreign affairs is greatly enhanced by the use of **executive agreements** made between the president and other heads of state. Such an agreement does not require Senate approval, although the House and Senate may refuse to appropriate the funds necessary to implement it. Whereas treaties are binding on all succeeding administrations, executive agreements are not binding without each new president's consent.

Among the advantages of executive agreements are speed and secrecy. The former is essential during a crisis; the latter is important when the administration fears that open senatorial debate may be detrimental to the best interests of the United States or to the interests of the president. There have been far more executive agreements (about 9,000) than treaties (about 1,300). In 1905,

Carter, Sadat, and Begin signing the Camp David accords, bringing peace between Egypt and Israel. Why would an American president be so involved in the Middle East conflict?

Theodore Roosevelt implemented the Dillingham–Sanchez Protocol, which permitted American control of customs houses in Santo Domingo (now the Dominican Republic), as an executive agreement. In 1970, Richard Nixon did the same in concluding an agreement with the governments of Spain to operate military bases. Franklin Roosevelt used executive agreements to bypass congressional isolationists in trading American destroyers for British Caribbean naval bases and in arranging diplomatic and military affairs with Canada and Latin American nations. Many executive agreements contain secret provisions calling for American military assistance or other support.

Chief Legislator

Constitutionally, the president must recommend to the Congress legislation that he judges necessary and expedient. Not all presidents have wielded their powers as chief legislator in the same manner. President John Tyler was almost completely unsuccessful in getting his legislative programs implemented by Congress. Presidents Theodore Roosevelt, Franklin Roosevelt, and Lyndon B. Johnson, however, saw much of their proposed legislation put into effect.

In modern times, the president has played a dominant role in creating the congressional agenda. In the president's **State of the Union message,** which is required by the Constitution (Article II, Section 3) and given annually, usually in late January shortly after Congress reconvenes, the president as chief legislator presents his program. The message gives a broad, comprehensive view of what the president wishes the legislature to accomplish during its session. It is as much a message to the American people and to the world as it is to Congress, and its impact on public opinion can determine the way Congress responds to the president's agenda.

Getting Legislation Passed.   The president can propose legislation, but Congress is not required to pass any of the administration's bills. How then does the president get those proposals made into law? One way, of course, is to draft the bills that he wants to see passed. But perhaps equally important is the power of persuasion. The president writes to, telephones, and meets with various congressional leaders, makes public announcements to force the weight of public opinion onto Congress in favor of a legislative program, and, as head of the party, exercises legislative leadership through the congresspersons of the president's party.

To be sure, presidents whose party represents a majority in both houses of Congress have an easier time getting their legislation passed than do presidents facing hostile Congresses. But one of the ways in which a president who faces a hostile Congress can still wield power is through the ability to veto legislation.

Saying No to Legislation.   The president has the power to say no through use of the veto,[13] by which the White House returns a bill unsigned to the legislative body with a **veto message** attached. Since the Constitution requires that every bill passed by the House and the Senate must be sent to the president before it becomes law, the president must act on each bill.

[13]*Veto* in Latin means "I forbid."

STATE OF THE UNION MESSAGE
An annual message to Congress in which the president proposes a legislative program. The message is not only to Congress but also to the American people and to the world. It offers the opportunity to dramatize policies and objectives and to gain public support.

VETO MESSAGE
The president's formal explanation of a veto when legislation is returned to the Congress.

President Bush gives the State of the Union Address. Historically have these addresses proved to be significant?

1. If the bill is signed, it becomes law.

2. If the bill is not sent back to Congress after ten congressional working days, it becomes law.

3. The bill can be vetoed and sent back to Congress with a message setting forth objections. The Congress then can change the bill, hoping to secure presidential approval and repass it, or it can simply reject the president's objections by overriding the veto with a two-thirds roll-call vote of the members present in each house.

4. If the president refuses to sign the bill and Congress adjourns within ten working days after the bill has been submitted to the president, the bill is killed permanently for that session of Congress; if Congress wishes the bill to be reconsidered, it must be reintroduced during the following session. This is called a **pocket veto**.

POCKET VETO
A special veto power exercised by the chief executive after a legislative body has adjourned. Bills not signed by the chief executive die after a specified period of time. If Congress wishes to reconsider such a bill, it must be reintroduced in the following session of Congress.

Presidents employed the veto power infrequently until the administration of Andrew Johnson, but it has been used with increasing vigor since then (Table 13-3). The total number of vetoes from George Washington through Ronald Reagan was 2,525, with almost 45 percent of those vetoes being exercised by Franklin Roosevelt, Truman, and Eisenhower.

TABLE 13-3
Presidential Vetoes, 1789–1990
Note that few bills were vetoed until after the Civil War.

Years	President	Regular Vetoes	Vetoes Overridden	Pocket Vetoes	Total Vetoes
1789–1797	Washington	2	0	0	2
1797–1801	J. Adams	0	0	0	0
1801–1809	Jefferson	0	0	0	0
1809–1817	Madison	5	0	2	7
1817–1825	Monroe	1	0	0	1
1825–1829	J. Q. Adams	0	0	0	0
1829–1837	Jackson	5	0	7	12
1837–1841	Van Buren	0	0	1	1
1841–1841	Harrison	0	0	0	0
1841–1845	Tyler	6	1	4	10
1845–1849	Polk	2	0	1	3
1849–1850	Taylor	0	0	0	0
1850–1853	Fillmore	0	0	0	0
1853–1857	Pierce	9	5	0	9
1857–1861	Buchanan	4	0	3	7
1861–1865	Lincoln	2	0	5	7
1865–1869	A. Johnson	21	15	8	29
1869–1877	Grant	45	4	48	93
1877–1881	Hayes	12	1	1	13
1881–1881	Garfield	0	0	0	0
1881–1885	Arthur	4	1	8	12

Ronald Reagan lobbied strenuously for Congress to give another tool to the president—the line-item veto. Reagan saw the ability to veto specific spending provisions as the only way that the president could control overall congressional spending. The line-item veto would require a constitutional amendment. Such an amendment also would need to spell out how Congress could override the veto.

A veto is a clear-cut indication of the president's dissatisfaction with congressional legislation. It is a very effective tool as well, because it denies the legislative power of the Congress. Nonetheless, Congress rarely overrides a regular presidential veto. Consider that two-thirds of the members of each house who are present must vote to override the president's veto in a roll-call vote. This means that if only one-third plus one of the members voting in one of the houses of Congress do not agree to override the veto, the veto holds. Table 13-3 tells us that it wasn't until the administration of John Tyler that Congress overrode a presidential veto. In the first sixty-five years of American federal government history, out of thirty-three regular vetoes, Congress only overrode one, or less than 3 percent. Overall, only about 4 percent of all vetoes have been overridden.

TABLE 13-3 (continued)

Years	President	Regular Vetoes	Vetoes Overridden	Pocket Vetoes	Total Vetoes
1885–1889	Cleveland	304	2	110	414
1889–1893	Harrison	19	1	25	44
1893–1897	Cleveland	42	5	128	170
1897–1901	McKinley	6	0	36	42
1901–1909	T. Roosevelt	42	1	40	82
1909–1913	Taft	30	1	9	39
1913–1921	Wilson	33	6	11	44
1921–1923	Harding	5	0	1	6
1923–1929	Coolidge	20	4	30	50
1929–1933	Hoover	21	3	16	37
1933–1945	F. Roosevelt	372	9	263	635
1945–1953	Truman	180	12	70	250
1953–1961	Eisenhower	73	2	108	181
1961–1963	Kennedy	12	0	9	21
1963–1969	L. Johnson	16	0	14	30
1969–1974	Nixon	26[a]	7	17	43
1974–1977	Ford	48	12	18	66
1977–1981	Carter	13	2	18	31
1981–1989	Reagan	39	9	28	67
1989–1990	Bush	12	0	1	13
Total		1,431	103	952	2,383

[a]Two pocket vetoes, overruled in the courts, are counted here as regular vetoes.

SOURCE: Louis Fisher, *The Politics of Shared Power: Congress and the Executive,* 2d ed. (Washington, D.C.: Congressional Quarterly Press, 1987), p. 30, *Congressional Quarterly Weekly Report,* June 23, 1990, p. 1934.

CONSTITUTIONAL POWERS
The powers vested in the president by Article II of the Constitution.

STATUTORY POWERS
The powers created for the president through laws established by Congress.

EXPRESS POWERS
Constitutional and statutory powers of the president, which are expressly written into the Constitution or into congressional law.

INHERENT POWERS
Powers of the president derived from the loosely worded statement in the Constitution that "the executive power shall be vested in a president" and that the president should "take care that the laws be faithfully executed"; defined through practice rather than through constitutional or statutory law.

FIGURE 13-1
Presidential Support on Congressional Votes 1953–1989
Most presidents have their greatest successes in the first years of their terms in office.
SOURCE: *Congressional Quarterly Weekly Report,* December 30, 1989, p. 3540.

Measuring the Success of a President's Legislative Program. One way of determining a president's strength is to evaluate his success as chief legislator: A strong president is one who has achieved much of his legislative program; a weak president is one who has achieved little. Using these definitions of strong and weak, it is possible to rank presidents according to their legislative success. Researchers do not, however, have a unified view of measuring the success of the president's legislative program. Look at Figure 13-1. Here we show the percentages of presidential victories measured by congressional votes in situations in which the president took a clear-cut position. Based on this information, Kennedy appears to have been the most successful president in recent years. Ford was the least successful. The problem with the data is that they do not indicate how much proposed legislation was subsequently not pursued by the president; nor do they indicate how much legislation the president did not support after knowing it would not be possible to win on the original form of a bill that had been proposed. The data in Figure 13-1 also do not weigh legislative victories and defeats in terms of their importance to the president's overall program.

Other Presidential Powers

The powers of the president just discussed are called **constitutional powers** because their basis lies in the Constitution. In addition, Congress has established by law, or statute, numerous other presidential powers—such as the ability to declare national emergencies. These are called **statutory powers.** Both constitutional and statutory powers have been labeled the **express powers** of the president because they are expressly written into the Constitution or into congressional law.

Presidents also have what have come to be known as **inherent powers.** These depend on the loosely worded statement in the Constitution that "the executive power shall be vested in a president" and that the president should "take care that the laws be faithfully executed." The most common example

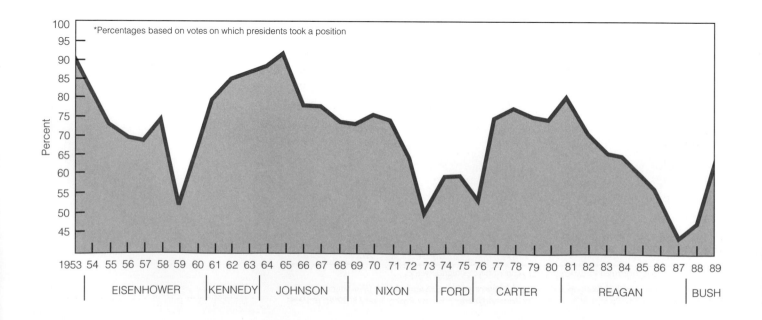

CRITICAL PERSPECTIVE

The President's Personality

The legal powers of the presidency, the relationship among the president and Congress, the courts, and the media, and the challenges of history all determine the success and failure of individuals in the White House. Another set of factors influencing the president's achievements is the chief executive's style, personality, and character.

Probably the best-known scheme for analyzing presidential character is that of political scientist James David Barber. Barber suggests we look at two separate dimensions of personality that manifest themselves in the chief executive and that can be traced to early experiences. These two dimensions are (a) the degree of energy and activity a president puts into the job, and (b) whether the president likes and enjoys the job. These two characteristics can be further broken down: In work energy, the president can be *active* or *passive;* in attitude toward the job, the president can be *positive* or *negative.*

When these dimensions are laid out as a grid (see the accompanying figure), we discover that Barber's presidential character model offers four different types: Active-Positive, Active-Negative, Passive-Positive, and Passive-Negative.

In Barber's view, the Active-Positives make the best presidents because they have high activity levels and are energetic while at the same time relishing the job. They display a zest for presidential tasks, project high levels of self-esteem, tolerate frustration well, and gain a sense of accomplishment from their work. They are flexible and able to laugh at themselves. Franklin Roosevelt, Harry Truman, John Kennedy, Gerald Ford, and Jimmy Carter were all Active-Positives.

On the other hand, Active-Negatives can be ultimately destructive. Although hardworking and dynamic, they receive little pleasure from politics, see the world as full of enemies, are sensitive to criticism, and are excessively serious, even morose. They may compulsively fix their sights on certain objectives, and in their rigidity ruin themselves or endanger the nation. Among the Active-Negatives were Woodrow Wilson, who could not compromise with the Senate on the League of Nations treaty; Herbert Hoover, who refused to face the economic crisis of the Depression; Lyndon Johnson, who became fixated on the Vietnam war; and Richard Nixon, who was destroyed by Watergate.

Passive-Positives enjoy what they are doing, have an upbeat approach to politics, look for approval from others, but have a laid-back approach to the job. They take regular vacations, work shorter hours, and emphasize sociability. William Howard Taft, Warren G. Harding, and Ronald Reagan fall into this group.

Passive-Negatives consider the presidency to be a duty, focus their efforts on carrying out the law, avoid controversy and

---

Presidential Personality

Attitude:
level of enjoyment for the job,
satisfaction, self-esteem, flexibility, humor.

	POSITIVE	NEGATIVE
ACTIVE	**Active-Positive** Flexible, self-confident, enjoys the job, "best" type. Examples: FDR, JFK, Carter	**Active-Negative** Ambitious, driven, high energy but low esteem, feels threatened, "worst" type. Examples: Nixon, LBJ
PASSIVE	**Passive-Positive** Likeable, tolerant, other-directed, little ambition or drive Examples: Taft, Reagan, Harding	**Passive-Negative** Avoids conflict, self-doubting, serves out of duty and responsibility Examples: Eisenhower, Coolidge

Activity Level:
high energy, drive
for accomplishment

Source: James David Barber, *The Presidential Character: Predicting Performance in the White House,* 3d ed. (Englewood Cliffs, N.J.: Prentice-Hall, 1985).

CRITICAL PERSPECTIVE, CONTINUED

conflict, and show little initiative. Recent Passive-Negatives were Calvin Coolidge and Dwight Eisenhower.

Critics of presidential personality studies and Barber's model in particular point out several flaws. First of all, reducing all human behavior to two dimensions is overly simplistic. Such analysis can be criticized as "pop psychology," with little grounding in psychiatry or psychological theory. Second, the possibility exists that presidents may grow and change in office. Finally, even though presidents act as lone individuals, their advisers may well counterbalance their own weaknesses.

Barber's typology does not always seem to match the performance of the presidents he discusses. Kennedy, an Active-Positive, is hard to judge because his death cut short his record. Jimmy Carter, also an Active-Positive, is often considered to have been a weak president. Ronald Reagan, although mellow and prone to vacation, was very active and certainly had more significant accomplishments than his Passive-Positive classifi-

cation would predict. Some critics suggest that Barber selectively chooses evidence on presidential personalities and puts those he likes best in the most favored category. His efforts at analyzing recent presidents may be more subjective than his work with commercial figures.

Attempts such as Barber's to identify presidential character, personality, and the role of the individual in the executive office are impressionistic, but they offer useful insights into the actions of past presidents.

Exercise in Critical Thinking

1. Is Barber's scheme biased by his choices of the best presidents?
2. How can the voting public find out the psychological traits of presidential candidates?
3. To what degree could a candidate try to live up to Barber's ideal type to be elected?

---

of inherent powers are those emergency powers invoked by the president during wartime. Franklin Roosevelt used his inherent powers to relocate the Japanese living in the United States after the bombing of Pearl Harbor.

■ THE PRESIDENT AS PARTY CHIEF AND SUPER POLITICIAN

Presidents are by no means above political partisanship, and one of their many roles is that of chief of party. Although the Constitution says nothing about the function of the president within a political party (the mere concept of political parties was abhorrent to most of the Founding Fathers), today presidents are the actual leaders of their parties.

PATRONAGE
Rewarding faithful party workers and followers with government employment and contracts.

As party leader, presidents choose the national committee chairperson and can try to discipline those party members who fail to support their policies. One way of exerting political power within the party is by the use of **patronage**—appointing individuals to government or public jobs. This power was more extensive in the past, before the establishment of the civil service in 1882 (see Chapter 14), but the president still retains impressive patronage power. As we noted earlier, the president can appoint several thousand individuals to jobs in the cabinet, the White House, and the federal regulatory agencies.

Presidents have a number of other ways of exerting influence as party chief. They may make it known that they will not appoint a particular congressperson's choice for federal judge, unless that member of Congress is more supportive of their legislative program.[14] They may agree to campaign for a particular program or for a particular candidate. The president is often called

---

[14]However, "senatorial courtesy" (see Chapter 12) often puts the judicial appointment in the hands of the Senate.

Bush relaxes fishing in Maine. Is the president's leisure activity really a concern for the media and the nation?

on to mend party fences—which was the reason for John F. Kennedy's trip to Dallas on November 22, 1963, when he was assassinated.

All politicians worry about their constituencies, and so do presidents. Presidents, however, have numerous constituencies. In principle, they are beholden to the entire electorate—the public of the United States—even to those who did not vote. They are certainly beholden to their party constituency because its members put them in office. The presidents' constituencies also include members of the opposing party whose cooperation they need. Finally, the president has to take into consideration a constituency that has come to be called the **Washington community.** It is a community that consists of individuals who—whether in or out of political office—are intimately familiar with the workings of government, that thrives on gossip, and that daily measures the political power of the president.[15]

All of these constituencies are impressed by presidents who maintain a high level of public approval, partly because this is very difficult to accomplish. Presidential popularity, as measured by national polls, gives the president an extra political resource to use in persuading legislators or bureaucrats, who realize that in refusing the president, they may be going against public sentiment. President Reagan showed amazing strength in the public opinion polls for a second-term chief executive. As Figure 13-2 indicates, Reagan's popularity surpassed even that of Eisenhower, who was genuinely admired by many Americans. A Gallup poll of June 1985 showed that President Reagan was also improving his image in history, with the public ranking him as sixth on the list of the nation's greatest presidents, behind Kennedy, Lincoln, Franklin Roosevelt, Truman, and Washington.[16]

The presidential preoccupation with public opinion has been criticized by at least one scholar as changing the balance of national politics. Samuel Kernell proposes that the style of presidential leadership since World War II has changed, partly owing to the influence of television.[17] Presidents frequently

WASHINGTON COMMUNITY
Individuals regularly involved with the political circles in Washington, D.C.

[15]See Richard E. Neustadt, *Presidential Power* (New York: John Wiley, 1960).
[16]*The Gallup Poll, 1985.*
[17]Samuel Kernell, *Going Public: New Strategies of Presidential Leadership,* (Washington, D.C.: Congressional Quarterly Press, 1986).

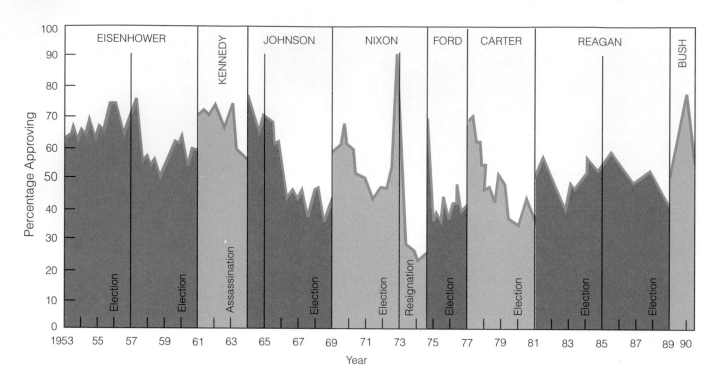

FIGURE 13-2
Public Popularity of Bush and His Predecessors
SOURCE: *Public Opinion,* February/March 1988, pp. 36–39; Gallup Poll, March, 1990, p. 15.

go over the heads of Congress and the political elites, taking their case directly to the people. This strategy, which Kernell dubbed "going public," gives the president additional power through the ability to persuade and manipulate public opinion. By identifying their own positions so clearly, presidents make compromise with the Congress much more difficult and weaken the legislators' positions. Furthermore, Kernell asserts, legislators who follow the president are not rewarded by their constituents, whereas those congresspersons who oppose the president may be punished at the polls. Given the increasing importance of the media as the major source of political information for citizens and elites, presidents will continue to use public opinion as part of their arsenal of weapons to get support from Congress and to achieve their policy goals.

■ THE SPECIAL USES OF PRESIDENTIAL POWER

Presidents have at their disposal a variety of special powers and privileges not available to other branches of the U.S. government. These include (1) emergency powers, (2) executive orders, (3) executive privilege, and (4) impoundment of funds.

Emergency Powers

If you were to read the Constitution, you would find no mention of the additional powers that the executive office may exercise during national emergencies. Indeed, the Supreme Court has indicated that an "emergency does not create power."[18] But it is clear that presidents have used their inherent

[18]*Home Building and Loan Association v. Blaisdell,* 290 U.S. 398 (1934).

powers during times of emergency, particularly in the realm of foreign affairs. The **emergency powers** of the president were first enunciated in the Supreme Court's decision in *United States v. Curtiss-Wright Export Corporation*.[19] In that case, President Franklin Roosevelt, without authorization by Congress, had ordered an embargo on the shipment of weapons to two warring South American countries. The Court recognized that the president may exercise his inherent powers in foreign affairs and that the national government has primacy in foreign affairs.

Examples of emergency powers are abundant, coinciding with real or contrived crises in domestic and foreign affairs. Abraham Lincoln's suspension of civil liberties at the beginning of the Civil War, his calling of the state militias into national service, and his subsequent governance of conquered areas and even of areas of northern states were justified by claims that such actions were essential to preserve the Union. Franklin Roosevelt declared an "unlimited national emergency" following the fall of France in World War II and mobilized the federal budget and the economy for war.

A more recent example occurred when President Harry S Truman authorized the federal seizure of steel plants and their operation by the national government in 1952 during the Korean war. Truman claimed he was using his inherent emergency power as chief executive and commander in chief to safeguard the nation's security, as the ongoing steel mill strike threatened the supply of weapons to the armed forces. The Supreme Court did not agree, saying the president had no authority under the Constitution to seize private property or to legislate such action.[20] According to legal scholars, this was the first time a limit was placed on the exercise of the president's emergency powers.

EMERGENCY POWERS
Inherent powers exercised by the president during a period of national crisis, particularly in foreign affairs.

Executive Orders

Congress allows the president (and his administrative agencies) to issue **executive orders** that have the force of law. These executive orders can do the following: (1) give force to legislative statutes, (2) enforce the Constitution or treaties with foreign nations, and (3) establish or modify practices of executive administrative agencies.

An executive order, then, represents the president's legislative power. The only apparent requirement is that under the Administrative Procedure Act of 1946, all executive orders must be published in the **Federal Register.**

Executive orders have been used to establish some procedures for appointing noncareer administrators, to implement national affirmative action regulations, to restructure the White House bureaucracy, to ration consumer goods and to administer wage and price controls under emergency conditions, to classify government information as secret, and to regulate exports of restricted items. More than thirteen thousand executive orders have been promulgated in a numbered series officially compiled by the State Department, and many more have never been compiled.

EXECUTIVE ORDER
A rule or regulation issued by the president that has the effect of law. Executive orders can implement and give administrative effect to provisions in the Constitution, to treaties, and to statutes.

FEDERAL REGISTER
A publication of the executive branch that prints executive orders, rules, and regulations.

Executive Privilege

Another inherent executive power that has been claimed by presidents involves the ability of the president and his executive officials to refuse to appear before,

---

[19]229 U.S. 304 (1936).
[20]*Youngstown Sheet and Tube Co. v. Sawyer*, 343 U.S. 579 (1952).

DID YOU KNOW?

That our tenth president, John Tyler, had fifteen children?

EXECUTIVE PRIVILEGE
The right of executive officials to refuse to appear before, or to withhold information from, a legislative committee. Executive privilege is enjoyed by the president and by those executive officials accorded that right by the president.

or to withhold information from, Congress or the courts. This is called **executive privilege,** and it relies on the constitutional separation of powers for its basis. Critics of executive privilege believe it can be used to shield from public scrutiny actions of the executive branch that should be open to Congress and to the American public.

Limits to executive privilege went untested until the Watergate affair in the early 1970s when the Supreme Court subpoenaed secret tapes containing Richard Nixon's Oval Office conversations during his tenure at the White House. Nixon refused to turn them over, claiming executive privilege. He argued that "no president could function if the private papers of his office, prepared by his personal staff, were open to public scrutiny." In one of the Court's most famous cases, *United States v. Nixon* (1974),[21] the justices unanimously ruled that Nixon had to hand over the tapes to the Court. Executive privilege could not be used to prevent evidence from being heard in criminal proceedings.

Impoundment of Funds

By law, the president proposes a budget and Congress approves it. But there is no clear-cut constitutional indication that the president, as chief executive, is required by law to *spend* all of the funds appropriated by Congress, and many presidents have not done so. In 1803, Thomas Jefferson deferred a $50,000 appropriation for gunboats. Ulysses Grant returned to the Treasury unspent money for public works. In 1932, Herbert Hoover canceled projects funded by Congress. Franklin Roosevelt deferred spending on a number of appropriations to later fiscal years. Truman didn't spend all the money Congress had allocated for the military, nor did Johnson the money allocated for highway construction, nor did Kennedy the money for weapons systems.

The question came to a head during the Nixon administration after a number of confrontations over this issue between the president and an antagonistic, Democratic-controlled Congress. When Nixon vetoed appropriations bills, Congress often overruled his veto. In retaliation, Nixon impounded the appropriated funds and refused to spend them, claiming that he wanted to reduce overall federal spending. As part of its new Budget and Impoundment Control Act of 1974, Congress required that the president spend all appropriated funds, although Congress gave the president some leeway. A president who is not going to spend all appropriated funds must tell Congress; and only if Congress agrees within forty-five days can the president withhold spending. If the president simply wishes to delay spending, this must be indicated to Congress. If Congress does not agree, it can pass a resolution requiring immediate spending of the appropriated funds. During the time when Congress was deliberating on the budget bill, cities, states, and certain members of Congress sued President Nixon over the impoundment issue. The Supreme Court in 1975 unanimously ruled that the president had to spend money appropriated by Congress because of his obligation to "take care that the laws be faithfully executed."[22]

■ ABUSES OF EXECUTIVE POWER AND IMPEACHMENT

Presidents normally leave office either because their first term has expired and they did not seek (or win) reelection or because, having served two full terms,

[21]318 U.S. 683.
[22]*Train v. City of New York,* 420 U.S. 35 (1975).

they are not allowed to seek reelection (owing to the Twenty-second Amendment, passed in 1951). Eight presidents have left office because of death. But there is still another way for a president to leave office—by **impeachment.** Article I of the Constitution authorizes the House and Senate to remove the president, the vice president, or other civil officers of the United States for crimes of "treason, bribery, or other high crimes and misdemeanors." No one has really defined "high crimes and misdemeanors," but at least twice the Congress and the American public were pretty sure that a president had engaged in them.

The authority to impeach is vested in the House of Representatives, and formal impeachment proceedings are initiated there. The power to try impeachment cases rests with the Senate. In the House, a representative must list the charges against the president, vice president, or other civil officer. The impeachment charges are referred either to the Judiciary Committee or to a special investigating committee. If a majority in the House vote for impeachment, then Articles of Impeachment are drawn up, which set forth the basis for the removal of the executive-branch officer. When the president is on trial, the chief justice of the United States Supreme Court presides over the Senate. A two-thirds vote of the senators present is required for conviction. The only punishment that Congress can mete out is removal from office and disqualification from holding any other federal office. The convicted official, however, is subject to further punishment according to law.

In the history of the United States, no president has ever been impeached and also convicted. The only president who was actually impeached by the House was Andrew Johnson, but he was acquitted by the Senate by the margin of a single vote in 1868. Some argue that Johnson's impeachment was simply a case of partisan politics. Impeachment attempts were made against Tyler (1847), Hoover (1932 and 1933), and Vice President Schuyler Colfax (1873).

The case of Richard Nixon, however, was more serious and certainly less questionable in terms of its political motivation (see the Highlight on Watergate). In 1974, the House was ready to vote on Nixon's impeachment and to send the Articles of Impeachment to the Senate when Nixon resigned.

Nixon leaving the White House after his resignation.

IMPEACHMENT
As authorized by Article I of the Constitution, impeachment is an action by the House of Representatives and the Senate to remove the president, vice president, or civil officers of the United States from office for crimes of "treason, bribery, or other high crimes and misdemeanors."

■ THE EXECUTIVE ORGANIZATION

Gone are the days when presidents answered their own mail, as George Washington did. It wasn't until 1857 that Congress authorized a private secretary for the president to be paid by the federal government. Woodrow Wilson typed most of his correspondence, even though he did have several secretaries. At the beginning of FDR's long tenure at the White House, the entire staff consisted of thirty-seven individuals. It wasn't until the New Deal and World War II that the presidential staff became a sizable organization. Today, the executive organization includes a White House Office staff of about six hundred, including some workers who are part-time and others who are detailed from their departments to the White House. Not all of these employees have equal access to the president, nor are all of them likely to be equally concerned about the administration's political success. The more than 350 employees who work in the White House Office itself are closest to the president. They often include many individuals who worked in the president's campaign. These assistants are most concerned with preserving the president's reputation. Also included in the president's staff are a number of councils and advisory organizations,

Watergate: A Crime of Power?

On June 17, 1972, at 2:30 A.M., five men were arrested in the headquarters of the Democratic National Committee in the Watergate apartment complex in Washington, D.C. It was obvious from the outset that this was no ordinary burglary. The five men, dressed in business suits and wearing surgical gloves, were also found to have in their possession some extraordinary items: two cameras, forty rolls of film, lock picks, pen-sized tear-gas guns, bugging devices, a walkie-talkie, and nearly $2,300 in cash among them. In the following days and months, as investigations of the Watergate break-in continued, a story was pieced together that shocked the nation.

The five men had been searching for documents that would connect Senator George McGovern, the Democratic nominee for president, with Fidel Castro and thereby discredit McGovern in the eyes of the American public. They were also looking for any information the Democratic National Committee might have stumbled on that could prove embarrassing to the Nixon administration.

Six days after the break-in, President Nixon and his White House chief of staff, H. R. (Bob) Halderman, formulated a plan by which the Central Intelligence Agency (CIA) would impede the investigation of the affair that was being undertaken by the Federal Bureau of Investigation.

By early 1973, however, a select Senate committee was established, under the chairmanship of Senator Sam Ervin of North Carolina, to investigate the Watergate affair. During the Senate investigation, information about the White House-sponsored criminal activi-

John Dean testifying at Nixon's impeachment hearing.

ties and subsequent cover-up began to leak out. John Dean, III, President Nixon's legal counsel, eventually told the committee that the president himself was responsible for the cover-up. The committee also learned that the Oval Office conversations had been tape-recorded.

Archibald Cox, the Watergate special prosecutor in charge of legal investigations into the affair, subpoenaed several of the tapes, an action upheld by the federal district and appeals courts. The "Saturday Night Massacre" ensued, in which Nixon fired Cox, and the attorney general and deputy attorney general were both forced to resign because they refused to obey Nixon's orders to fire Cox. Many of Nixon's closest White House aides were indicted in the

scandal, and Nixon himself was named an unindicted co-conspirator by the grand jury. A new special prosecutor and Congress subpoenaed a large number of tapes, which the president refused to make available—except in edited form—to Congress. On July 24, 1974, the U.S. Supreme Court ruled that Nixon had to give up the information requested by the special prosecutor. Three days later, the House Judiciary Committee passed the first of three Articles of Impeachment against President Nixon. On August 9, Nixon resigned, and his vice president, Gerald Ford (who had in turn replaced the first Nixon vice president, Spiro Agnew—who had resigned because it was revealed he had accepted bribes as governor of Maryland), became president.

such as the National Security Council (NSC). Although the individuals who hold staff positions in these offices are appointed by the president, they are really more concerned with their own area than with the president's overall success. The group of appointees who perhaps are least helpful to the president is the cabinet, whose members are each the principal officer of a government bureau.

The Cabinet

Although the Constitution does not include the word *cabinet,* it does state that the president "may require the Opinion, in writing, of the principal Officer in each of the executive Departments." Since our first president there has always been an advisory group, or **cabinet,** to which the president turns for counsel. Originally, the cabinet consisted of only four individuals—the secretaries of state, treasury, and war, and the attorney general. Today the cabinet numbers thirteen secretaries and the attorney general. Table 13-4 shows the chronological growth of the president's cabinet.

The cabinet may consist of more than the secretaries of the various departments. The president at his discretion can, for example, ascribe cabinet rank to his National Security Council adviser, to the ambassador to the United Nations, or to others. Since neither the Constitution nor statutory law requires the president to consult with the cabinet, its use is purely discretionary. Some presidents have relied on the counsel of their cabinets more than others.

DID YOU KNOW?

That John Kennedy was the first president to hold a live television news conference, although Dwight Eisenhower had admitted television cameras to film his press conferences?

CABINET
An advisory group selected by the president to aid him in making decisions. The cabinet presently numbers thirteen department secretaries and the attorney general. Depending on the president, the cabinet may be highly influential or relatively insignificant in its advisory role.

The president meets with the full Cabinet. Would it be possible for Cabinet meetings to really be helpful to the president?

TABLE 13-4
The Cabinet Departments in Order of Their Creation

Department	Function
State (1789)	Foreign policy making and treaties
Treasury (1789)	The federal government's banker
War (1789)	Administration of the Army only (this department was merged with the Department of the Navy and with the addition of the Air Force was called the National Military Establishment in 1947)
Attorney General (1789)	Government's attorney (became the Justice Department in 1870)
Navy (1798)	Administration of the Navy (became part of the National Military Establishment in 1947)
Interior (1849)	Manager of national natural resources, including public lands
Justice (1870)	Government's attorney with attorney general as head
Post Office (1872)	Operation of the mails (became an independent federal agency in 1970)
Agriculture (1889)	Administration of farm programs and, currently, the food stamp program
Commerce and Labor (1903)	Conducts U.S. Census, aids business and labor organizations (split into two separate departments in 1913)
Commerce (1913)	Formerly part of Commerce and Labor
Labor (1913)	Formerly part of Commerce and Labor
Defense (DOD) (1949)	Combined departments of Army and Navy with Air Force added
Health, Education and Welfare (HEW) (1953)	Health and welfare programs, Social Security, and education (split in 1980)
Housing and Urban Development (HUD) (1965)	The nation's public housing program
Transportation (DOT) (1966)	Federally funded highway program and mass transportation
Energy (DOE) (1977)	Research, atomic energy, and overall national energy policy
Health and Human Services (HHS) (1980)	From HEW
Education (1980)	From HEW
Veterans Affairs (1989)	Elevation of Veterans Administration

Eisenhower frequently turned to his cabinet for advice on a wide range of governmental policies—perhaps because he was used to the team approach in solving problems. Other presidents have solicited the opinions of their cabinets and then did what they wanted to do anyway. Lincoln supposedly said—after a cabinet meeting in which a vote was seven nays against his one aye—"Seven nays and one aye, the ayes have it."[23] In general, few presidents have relied heavily on the advice of their cabinet members. Carter thought he could put

---

[23]Quoted in Thomas E. Cronin, *The State of the Presidency,* 2d ed. (Boston: Little, Brown, 1980), p. 11.

John Sununu

President Bush's chief of staff is sometimes called "Snarling Sununu." He is impatient, aggressive, bold, and sometimes even rude. He is also brilliant, with an IQ reported as 180. John Sununu has political savvy and an impressive record as a three-time winner of the governorship of New Hampshire. His unruly hair, rumpled-looking clothes, including a shirttail that often is not tucked in securely, contrasts sharply with his boss President Bush's carefully neat appearance.

Born in Havana, Cuba, in 1939, Sununu's father was a Lebanese American from Boston who was in the import and foreign film distribution business. He grew up in Forest Hills, New York, in a cosmopolitan family that traveled to Europe and spoke and read several foreign languages. Sununu is fluent in Spanish, speaks French, and reads German. He attended MIT, earned a doctorate, taught engineering at Tufts University, and founded an engineering firm.

As so many people in Massachusetts (called "Taxachusetts" by locals) have done, Sununu moved across the border into New Hampshire for lower taxes and a more pleasant living environment. It was here that he first became interested in politics, running for the local planning board and later a seat in the state legislature. He lost races for the state and U.S. Senate, but was elected governor in 1982. New Hampshire has no state personal income or sales taxes, and Sununu managed to balance the state budget without in-

creasing the tax burden on New Hampshire residents, an accomplishment that reinforced the antitax perspective he was later to bring to the Bush White House.

In New Hampshire, Sununu gained a reputation as a hands-on, aggressive administrator. He computerized the inefficient state government so that, allegedly, even in his own bedroom he could bring up on his computer all manner of statistics related to New Hampshire finances, expenditures, and other facts. The business boom of the 1980s allowed him to spend generously on new health programs, parks, prisons, and other services. Although a conservative Republican, he also believed in an activist and leadership-oriented government, and he played that role as governor.

In 1988, George Bush lost the Iowa caucuses to Senator Bob Dole of Kansas. Bush's chances for getting the Republican nomination and reaching the White House were slipping. Sununu, who was in charge of the Bush campaign in New Hampshire, convinced Bush to change his campaign style, first, by reaching out to the public and projecting a more friendly, folksy image and, second, by attacking Dole in a series of powerful advertisements and speeches warning people that Dole was a "taxer" who would dip into people's pockets if he were president. The strategy worked. Bush won New Hampshire, regained his momentum, and became president.

Sununu wanted to be chosen as Bush's vice presidential running mate and was disappointed when that job went to Dan Quayle. But as president, Bush would need a tough fighter for his programs and someone who would act as a lightning rod for any negative reactions of Congress, the media, and the public on controversial issues and positions, thus protecting the president. Bush asked Sununu to serve as White House chief of staff, a job that he has relished.

Although Sununu's influence within the Bush administration cannot be measured precisely, it is noteworthy that Bush's first Supreme Court nominee was a New Hampshire judge, David Souter, known by Sununu.

his cabinet to good use and held regular cabinet meetings for the first two years of his tenure. Then he fired three cabinet members and forced two others to resign while reorganizing his "inner government." He rarely met with the members of his cabinet thereafter. In recent years, the growth of other parts of the executive branch has rendered the cabinet relatively insignificant as an advisory board to the president.

KITCHEN CABINET
The informal advisers to the president.

Often a president will use a **kitchen cabinet** to replace the formal cabinet as a major source of advice. The term *kitchen cabinet* originated during the presidency of Andrew Jackson, who relied on the counsel of close friends who often met with him in the kitchen of the White House. A kitchen cabinet is a very informal group of advisers who may or may not be otherwise connected with the government, such as Reagan's trusted California coterie.

It is not surprising that presidents only reluctantly meet with their cabinet heads. Often the departmental heads are more responsive to the wishes of their own staffs or to their own political ambitions than they are to the president. They may be more concerned with obtaining resources for their departments than with helping presidents achieve their goals. So there is often a strong conflict of interest between presidents and their cabinet members. It is likely that formal cabinet meetings are held more out of respect for the cabinet tradition than for their problem-solving value.

The Executive Office of the President

When President Franklin Roosevelt appointed a special committee on administrative management, he knew it would determine that the president needed help. Indeed, the committee proposed a major reorganization of the executive branch. Congress did not approve the entire reorganization, but it did create the **Executive Office of the President (EOP)** to provide staff assistance for the chief executive and to help coordinate the executive bureaucracy. Since that time, a number of agencies have been created to supply the president with advice and staff help. These are as follows:

EXECUTIVE OFFICE OF THE PRESIDENT (EOP)
Established by President Franklin D. Roosevelt by executive order under the Reorganization Act of 1939. It currently consists of nine staff agencies that assist the president in carrying out major duties.

- White House Office (1939)
- Council of Economic Advisers (1946)
- National Security Council (1947)
- Office of the United States Trade Representative (1963)
- Council on Environmental Quality (1969)
- Office of Management and Budget (1970)
- Office of Science and Technology Policy (1976)
- Office of Administration (1977)
- Office of Policy Development (1977)

WHITE HOUSE OFFICE
The personal office of the president which tends presidential political needs and manages the media.

CHIEF OF STAFF
Directs the White House Office and advises the president.

The White House Office. One of the most important of the agencies within the EOP is the **White House Office,** which includes most of the key personal and political advisers to the president. Among the jobs held by these aides are legal counsel to the president, secretary, press secretary, and appointments secretary. Often the individuals who hold these positions are recruited from the president's campaign staff, and their duties, mainly protecting the president's political interests, are similar to campaign functions. In some administrations, one member of the White House Office is named **chief of staff.** This person, who is responsible for coordinating the office, is one of the president's chief advisers. Some chiefs of staff, such as Donald Regan during the Reagan administration, have been criticized for keeping the president too isolated, while others have been praised for facilitating compromise within the administration.

Employees of the White House Office have been both envied and criticized. The White House Office, according to most ex-staffers, grants its employees access and power. They are able to use the resources of the White House to contact virtually anyone in the world by telephone or cable, as well as to use the influence of the White House to persuade legislators and citizens. Because of this influence, staffers are often criticized for overstepping the bounds of the office. It is the appointments secretary who is able to grant or deny access to the president to senators, representatives, and cabinet secretaries. It is the press secretary who grants access to any information about the president to the press and television journalists. White House staff are closest to the president and may have considerable influence over the administration's decisions. Often, when presidents are under fire for their decisions, the staff is accused of keeping the chief executive too isolated from criticism or help. Presidents insist that they will not allow the staff to become too powerful, but, given the difficulty of the office, each president eventually turns to staff members for loyal assistance and protection.

Several other of the nine offices within the EOP are especially important.

Council of Economic Advisers (CEA). The Employment Act of 1946 created a three-member **Council of Economic Advisers** to advise the president on economic matters. Their advice serves as the basis for the president's annual economic report to Congress. Each of the three members is appointed by the president and can be removed at will. In principle the CEA was also created to advise the president on economic policy, but for the most part CEAs have functioned to prepare the annual report.

Office of Management and Budget (OMB). The **Office of Management and Budget** was originally the Bureau of the Budget, created in 1921 in the Department of the Treasury. Recognizing the importance of this agency, President Franklin Roosevelt moved it into the White House Office in 1939. Nixon reorganized the Bureau of the Budget in 1970 and changed its name to reflect its new managerial function. It is headed by a director who must make up the annual federal budget that the president presents to Congress each January for approval (which is rarely forthcoming without months of haggling over changes). In principle, the director of the OMB has broad fiscal powers in planning and estimating various parts of the federal budget, as all agencies must submit their proposed budget to OMB for approval. In reality, it is not so clear that the OMB truly can affect the greater scope of the federal budget. The director's job may be more important as a clearinghouse for legislative proposals initiated in the executive agencies.

National Security Council (NSC). The **National Security Council** is a link between the president's key foreign and military advisers and the president. Its members consist of the president, the vice president, and the secretaries of state and defense, plus other informal members. The NSC has the resources of the National Security Agency (NSA) at its disposal in giving counsel to the president. Included in the NSC is the president's special assistant for

---

DID YOU KNOW?

That every president from William Henry Harrison to John Kennedy who was elected on the first year of a new decade died in office (Harrison was elected in 1840, Lincoln in 1860, Garfield in 1880, McKinley in 1900, Harding in 1920, Roosevelt in 1940, and Kennedy in 1960)?

COUNCIL OF ECONOMIC ADVISERS (CEA)
A staff agency in the Executive Office that advises the president on measures to maintain stability in the nation's economy. Established in 1946, the council develops economic plans and budget recommendations for maintaining the nation's "employment, production, and purchasing power" and helps the president prepare an annual economic report to Congress.

OFFICE OF MANAGEMENT AND BUDGET (OMB)
A division of the Executive Office created by executive order in 1970 to replace the Bureau of the Budget. OMB's main functions are to assist the president in preparing the annual budget, to clear and coordinate all departmental agency budgets, to help set fiscal policy, and to supervise the administration of the federal budget.

NATIONAL SECURITY COUNCIL (NSC)
A staff agency in the Executive Office established by the National Security Act of 1947. The NSC advises the president on domestic and foreign matters involving national security.

national security affairs. Nixon had Henry Kissinger in this post; Carter had the equally visible Zbigniew Brzezinksi. In the Reagan years, staff members of the NSC, including Lieutenant Colonel Oliver North and Admiral John Poindexter, became involved in an illegal plan to aid the contras in Nicaragua (see Highlight, The Tower Commission . . .).

■ THE VICE PRESIDENCY

Vice presidents usually have not been overly ecstatic about their position. FDR's vice president for his first two terms, John Nance Garner, said that "the vice presidency isn't worth a pitcher of warm spit." Harry Truman, himself FDR's last vice president, was even more forthright: "[Vice presidents] were about as useful as a cow's fifth tit." Walter Mondale, Carter's hard-working vice president and one of the few who truly took an active role in the executive branch, said, "They know who Amy is, but they don't know me." He was referring to Carter's grammar school-aged daughter.

The Vice President's Job

The Constitution doesn't give much power to the vice president. The only formal duty is to preside over the Senate—which is rarely necessary. This obligation is fulfilled when the Senate organizes and adopts its rules and when the vice president is needed to decide a tie vote. In all other cases, the president pro tempore manages parliamentary procedures in the Senate. The vice president is expected only to participate informally in senatorial deliberations, if at all.

Traditionally, vice presidents have been chosen by presidential nominees to balance the ticket or to reward or appease party factions. If a presidential nominee is from the North, it is not a bad idea to have a vice presidential nominee who is from the South or the West. If the presidential nominee is from a rural state, perhaps someone with an urban background would be most

Vice President Dan Quayle addresses Asian Americans on behalf of the president.

The Tower Commission and the Iran-Contra Investigations

The risks created by unchecked Presidential advisors were made clear in the Iran-contra affair. The Reagan administration was shaken by the revelation that government officials had sold weapons to Iran in return for Iranian promises to help negotiate the release of American and other hostages held by pro-Iranian terrorist groups in the Middle East. Profits from these arms sales had then been used to finance operations of the *contras* in Nicaragua who were attempting to overthrow the Sandinista government there.

These efforts began to unravel after an American C123K cargo plane carrying guns and other weapons to the *contras* was shot down over Nicaragua on October 5, 1986. The Justice Department launched a full-scale investigation by the FBI into the Iran weapons shipments. President Reagan announced on the same day the appointment of the President's Special Review Board, chaired by former Republican Texas Senator John G. Tower and including former Secretary of State and former Democratic Maine Senator Edmund S. Muskie, and former National Security Adviser Brent Scowcroft. This special review board, which became known as the Tower Commission, was charged with studying the role of the National Security Council in the scandal.

In early March 1987, the Tower Commission released its report on what had come to be called variously the Iran-Contra affair, "Iran-scam," "Iranamok," or "Contragate." The report concluded that Reagan had let his emotional commitment to obtain release of the hostages overrule better judgment, faulted him for failing to conduct a forceful review of the programs once they were under way, and determined that the president's aides had manipulated him and had made their own private foreign policy through a process of lying, surreptitiously diverting arms-

deal profits, and trying to cover up the scandal.

The Tower Commission did not give detailed answers to basic questions such as exactly who had approved and who had knowledge of the Iran and *contra* dealings, when the relevant decisions had been made, or whether any illegal activities had indeed taken place. The joint congressional hearings on the affair, however, supplied dramatic and contradictory testimony on these and other questions. It became clearer that control over the general policy in this regard and control over operational details had rested with National Security Adviser John Poindexter and with his aide, Marine Lieutenant Colonel Oliver North, rather than with the Central Intelligence Agency. A former Air Force general, Richard Secord, had been instrumental in assisting North's execution of the plan.

Oliver North, who testified under a congressional grant of immunity, argued that Congress did not have a right to oversee the activities in which he was engaged and did not even have the right to know what he was up to.

Testimony from Richard Secord revealed some details behind the shipments of arms to the *contras*. North's secretary, Fawn Hall, testified about the shredding of important documents, while Former National Security Adviser John Poindexter argued before the committee that it had been necessary to preserve the secret nature of the operation from a probing Congress.

North, Poindexter, Secord, and an arms dealer were all indicted on charges including conspiracy to divert government funds to buy arms for the *contras*. North was convicted on three counts but found innocent on five charges by a jury that reportedly felt he was the "fall guy" for those higher up. However, a federal court overturned one of North's convictions in July, 1990 because he had been granted immunity for his congressional testimony. Poindexter was convicted and sentenced to six months in prison.

What remains unresolved in how Presidential aides can be controlled and how presidents can be held responsible for what their aides do.

DID YOU KNOW?

That David Atchison, president pro tempore of the Senate in 1849, was briefly president of the United States because Zachary Taylor refused to be sworn into office on a Sunday and that Atchison spent most of his term asleep?

suitable as a running mate. Presidential nominees who are strongly conservative or strongly liberal would do well to have vice presidential nominees who are more in the middle of the political road.

Vice presidents have infrequently become elected presidents in their own right. John Adams and Thomas Jefferson were the first to do so. Then Martin Van Buren was elected president in 1836 after he had served as Jackson's vice president. Nixon became president in 1968, having been Eisenhower's vice president eight years earlier. In 1988, George Bush was elected to the presidency after eight years as Ronald Reagan's vice president.

The job of the vice president is certainly not time consuming, even when the president gives some specific task to the vice president. Typically, vice presidents spend their time supporting the president's activities. All of this changes, of course, if the president becomes disabled or dies in office.

Presidential Succession

Eight vice presidents have become president because of the death of the president. John Tyler, the first, took over William Henry Harrison's position after only one month. No one knew whether Tyler should simply be a caretaker until a new president could be elected three and a half years later or whether he actually should be president. Tyler assumed that he was supposed to be the chief executive and he acted as such—although he was commonly referred to as "His Accidency." On all occasions since then, vice presidents taking over the position of the presidency because of the incumbent's death have assumed all the presidential powers.

Reagan assassination attempt of March 31, 1981.

But what should a vice president do if a president becomes incapable of carrying out necessary duties while in office? When Garfield was shot in 1888, he stayed alive for two and a half months. What was Vice President Chester Arthur's role?

This question was not addressed in the original Constitution. Article II, Section 1, says only that "in the case of the removal of the president from office, or of his death, resignation, or inability to discharge the powers and duties of the said office, the same shall devolve on the vice president." There have been many instances of presidential disability. When Eisenhower became ill a second time in 1958, he entered into a pact with Nixon providing that the vice president could determine whether the president was incapable of carrying out his duties if the president could not communicate. Kennedy and Johnson entered into similar agreements with their vice presidents. Finally, the **Twenty-fifth Amendment** was passed in 1967, establishing procedures in case of presidential incapacity.

The Twenty-fifth Amendment

According to the Twenty-fifth Amendment, when the president believes he is incapable of performing the duties of office, he must inform the Congress in writing. Then the vice president serves as acting president until the president can resume his normal duties. In cases where the president is unable to communicate, a majority of the cabinet, including the vice president, can declare that fact to Congress. Then the vice president serves as acting president until the president resumes his normal duties.

If a dispute arises over the president's ability to discharge his normal functions, a two-thirds vote of Congress is required to decide whether the vice president shall remain acting president or whether the president shall resume his duties.

Although President Reagan did not formally invoke the Twenty-fifth Amendment during his surgery for the removal of a cancerous growth in his colon on July 13, 1985, he followed its provisions in temporarily transferring power to the vice president, George Bush. At 10:32 A.M., before the operation began, Reagan signed letters to the speaker of the House and the president pro tem of the Senate directing that the vice president "shall discharge those powers and duties in my stead commencing with the administration of anesthesia to me. . . ." In early evening of that same day, Reagan transmitted another letter to both officials announcing that he was again in charge. During this period, Vice President Bush signed no bills and took no actions as acting president. Although the Reagan administration claimed that the president's action set no precedents, most legal experts saw his acts as the first official use of the Twenty-fifth Amendment.

When the Vice Presidency Becomes Vacant

The Twenty-fifth Amendment also addresses the issue of how the president should fill a vacant vice presidency. Section 2 of the amendment simply states, "Whenever there is a vacancy in the office of the vice president, the president shall nominate a vice president who shall take office upon confirmation by a majority vote of both houses of Congress." This is exactly what occurred when Nixon's vice president, Spiro Agnew, resigned in 1973 because of his alleged

TWENTY-FIFTH AMENDMENT
An amendment to the Constitution adopted in 1967 that establishes procedures for filling vacancies in the two top executive offices and that makes provisions for situations involving presidential disability.

Spiro Agnew, Vice President 1969–1973.

TABLE 13-5
Line of Succession to the Presidency of the United States

1. Vice president.
2. Speaker of the House of Representatives.
3. Senate president pro tempore.
4. Secretary of State.
5. Secretary of the Treasury.
6. Secretary of Defense.
7. Attorney General.
8. Secretary of the Interior.
9. Secretary of Agriculture.
10. Secretary of Commerce.
11. Secretary of Labor.
12. Secretary of Health and Human Services.
13. Secretary of Housing and Urban Development.
14. Secretary of Transportation.
15. Secretary of Energy.
16. Secretary of Education.
17. Secretary of Veterans Affairs.

receipt of construction contract kickbacks during his tenure as governor of Maryland. Nixon turned to Gerald R. Ford as his choice for vice president. After extensive hearings, both houses confirmed the appointment. Then when Nixon resigned on August 9, 1974, Ford automatically became president and nominated as his vice president Nelson Rockefeller. Congress confirmed Ford's choice. For the first time in the history of the country, both the president and the vice president were individuals who were not elected to their positions.

The question of who shall be president if both the president and vice president die is answered by the Succession Act of 1947. If the president and vice president die, resign, or are disabled, the speaker of the House will act as president, after resigning from congress. Next in line is the president pro tempore of the Senate, followed by the cabinet officers in order of creation of the department (see Table 13-5).

■ IS THE POWER OF THE PRESIDENCY INCREASING OR DECREASING?

After the Watergate scandal in 1972 and immediately following the end of the Vietnam war, many people feared that the American presidency had become far too powerful. As commander in chief, the president could engage U.S. military forces anywhere in the world; control over the budget process established authority over Congress and the executive agencies; and the constant expansion of the Executive Office of the President provided better information and assistance than that available to the other branches of government.

Congressional response to this augmented presidential power was quite striking. Among the techniques forged by Congress to maintain a balance of power with the president were the War Powers Act of 1973, which required the president to consult with Congress before committing American troops; the Budget and Impoundment Control Act of 1974, which restrained the president's power to impound funds; and the Case–Zablocki Act of 1972, which required secret executive agreements to be reported to Congress with safeguards for the sake of security. Congress also resorted more frequently to the legislative veto to control presidential policy making.

The ability of President Reagan to get his first tax plan and budget passed in 1981 by a Democratic House suggests that the balance of power has not swung too heavily to Congress. Reagan reaffirmed the power of the president as commander in chief with his use of military forces in Lebanon and Central America and against Libya. He convinced the Congress to support aid for the *contras* in Nicaragua and to work for and complete serious tax reform.

President Bush sent troops to Panama and the Middle East, vetoed almost a dozen bills without an override, and remained strong during the first two years of his presidency. Congress still has not found a way to restrain the president.

GETTING INVOLVED

Influencing the Presidency

O n June 14, 1990, James Baker, the secretary of state, rebuked Israel for not responding to the U.S. peace plan to resolve the Israeli–Palestinian conflict, saying, "When you're serious about peace, call us. The phone number is 202-456-1414." In the next twenty-four hours, the White House switchboard received about eight thousand calls.

If you wish to contact the president, that switchboard is open twenty-four hours a day. If you ask for the president, you will be directed to the appropriate department or to the Comment line. If you call the Comment line (202-456-7639), an operator will take down your comment or question and forward it to the president's office.

Expressions of public support or opposition are important either to legitimize the administration's actions or to voice disapproval. Although you will probably not have the opportunity to express your personal opinions directly to the pres-

ident, your views and those of others who think the same way can be brought to his attention. If you strongly agree with, or oppose, certain actions taken by the president, call the White House or write, addressing your letter to:

The President of the United States
The White House
1600 Pennsylvania Ave., N.W.
Washington, D.C. 20500

Another way to communicate your views to the executive branch is to write a letter to the editor of a major newspaper. The White House clips letters from newspapers across the country to provide a digest of public opinion for the president and the presidential staff.

CHAPTER SUMMARY

1. The office of the presidency of the United States, combining the functions of chief of state and chief executive, is unique.

2. Of the two opposing views at the Constitution Convention, one favored a weak executive who would carry out the will of the legislature and the other favored a strong, independent executive. The office of the presidency was molded by the desires of the latter. Modern scholars debate whether the president is too strong or not strong enough.

3. Requirements for becoming president, outlined in Article II, Section 1, of the Constitution, concern age, citizenship, and residence.

4. U.S. voters select a president and vice president by casting ballots for presidential electors who in turn cast their ballots in the electoral college.

5. Constitutional powers of the president are set forth in Article II of the Constitution. These include the roles of chief of state, chief executive, commander in chief, chief diplomat, and chief legislator.

6. As chief of state, the president is the ceremonial head of the government of the United States.

7. As chief executive, the president is constitutionally bound to enforce the acts of Congress, the judgments of federal courts, and treaties to which the United States is a signatory. The president has the power of appointment and the power to grant reprieves and pardons.

8. As commander in chief of the armed forces, the president

exercises a vast array of war powers and is the ultimate decision maker in military matters.

9. As chief diplomat, the president makes treaties (with the advice and consent of the Senate), recognizes foreign governments, and nominates and receives ambassadors. The president can make executive agreements with other heads of state without senatorial approval.

10. The role of the president as chief legislator includes recommending legislation to Congress, exercising veto power, and informally influencing Congress to pass presidentially sponsored legislation. The evaluation of presidents' success is based to a large extent on their success or failure as chief legislator.

11. The Constitution provides that every bill passed by the House and Senate must be sent to the president before it becomes law. The president has the option to veto the bill and send it back to Congress with a message setting forth any objections. Congress can change the bill and repass it or override the veto with a two-thirds roll-call vote.

12. The president has statutory powers, or those written into law by Congress, and inherent powers, which are defined by practice.

13. Although it is not set forth in the Constitution, the president is the leader of his political party as well as a politician serving numerous constituencies. Presidents have learned to use popular support to further their programs.

14. The special powers of the president include emergency

powers, executive orders, executive privilege, and impoundment of funds.

15. Abuses of executive power are dealt with by Article I of the Constitution, which authorizes the House and Senate to remove the president, the vice president, or civil officers of the United States for crimes of "treason, bribery, or other high crimes and misdemeanors."

16. The primary function of the White House staff is to protect the president's programs and reputation.

17. The cabinet, an advisory group selected by the president to aid him in making decisions, today includes thirteen department secretaries and the attorney general. Its use and membership are determined by tradition and at the discretion of the president.

18. The Executive Office of the President was established by Franklin D. Roosevelt by executive order in 1939. The components have changed over the years; today the major staff agencies include the Office of Management and Budget, the White House Office, the Council of Economic Advisers, the National Security Council, the Office of Policy Development, the Office of the United States Trade Representative, the Council on Environmental Quality, the Office of Science and Technology Policy, and the Office of Administration.

19. The vice president is the constitutional officer assigned to preside over the Senate and to assume the presidency in case of the death, resignation, removal, or disability of the president. The vice president participates informally in the Senate, voting only when a tie occurs. Vice presidents have traditionally been chosen to balance the party ticket or to reward or appease party functions.

20. The Twenty-fifth Amendment, passed in 1967, established procedures to be followed in case of presidential incapacity and when filling a vacant vice presidency.

QUESTIONS FOR REVIEW AND DISCUSSION

1. The roles of the president often require difficult decisions. What should the president do when Congress sends him a law that violates his own party platform? Think of other situations when the political needs of the president may not be consistent with national needs.

2. The president is frequently seen as the chief legislator of the nation. How much power does he have to get laws passed? What restraints does the Congress have on this role?

3. What is the process for impeaching the president? Can a president be impeached for political reasons—that is, by offending enough members of Congress?

4. Why has the Executive Office of the President grown so dramatically in the last quarter century? Does the existence of so many advisory and staff offices really assist the president in his job?

SELECTED REFERENCES

James D. Barber, *The Presidential Character: Predicting Performance in the White House,* 3rd ed. (Englewood Cliffs, N.J.: Prentice-Hall, 1985). A major typology of the personal traits of presidents and the consequences of how we are governed.

John Hart, *The Presidential Branch* (Elmsford, N.Y.: Pergamon Press, 1987). This book traces the history of the Executive Office from 1857 to the present, analyzing the role of staff power, accountability, and the importance of the Executive Office in the post-Watergate period.

Samuel Kernell, *Going Public: New Strategies of Presidential Leadership* (Washington, D.C.: Congressional Quarterly Press, 1986). This fascinating book explores how presidents have increasingly bypassed the traditional process of bargaining with Congress and have "gone public" with presidential priorities in an effort to bring direct public pressure on Congress.

Peggy Noonan, *What I Saw at the Revolution* (New York: Random House, 1990). The author of this book, President Reagan's favorite speechwriter who also wrote for George Bush's campaign (coining such phrases as "a kinder, gentler nation," "a thousand points of light," and "Read my lips: no new taxes") provides a unique and often very funny perspective on the Reagan presidency and its cast of characters.

Raymond Tatalovich and Byron Daynes, *Presidential Power in the United States* (Monterey, Calif.: Brooks/Cole, 1983). An authoritative book summarizing the research on presidential power and action.

John Tebbel and Sara Miles Watts, *The Press and the Presidency* (New York: Oxford University Press, 1985). From Washington to Reagan, this book explores the delicate relationship between the White House and the media, with special emphasis on presidential manipulation of the mass media and implications for the First Amendment.

THE BUREAUCRACY

WHAT IF . . . ALL INDEPENDENT AGENCIES HAD TO MAKE A PROFIT?

The federal government is big. It employs millions of individuals. It provides millions of services to Americans every day. As you will read in this chapter, the federal bureaucracy consists of the fourteen departments in the executive branch, independent regulatory agencies, government corporations, and so-called independent executive agencies. The last two categories include the National Aeronautics and Space Administration (NASA), the Tennessee Valley Authority (TVA), the U.S. Postal Service, and AMTRAK—the nation's nationalized passenger railroad system.

Currently, there is no legal requirement that independent agencies and government corporations make a profit. Indeed, one might suspect that the legal requirement was the reverse—that they must lose money—because they always do. For example, AMTRAK has been losing billions of dollars a year for a number of years. The U.S. Postal Service routinely loses billions of dollars a year. NASA normally doesn't sell its satellite-launching services and manned space flights, so the little that it spends is recovered.

What if independent agencies and government corporations had to make a profit each year? What if a law were passed that required such agencies to charge enough money for their services to cover all of their costs? Now to make this

scenario somewhat more realistic, we will assume that each government agency and corporation is given a certain number of years until it has to be profitable, say, five years.

The first thing that would happen is that certain government agencies and corporations would have to start charging user fees for the services they render to the public. Those agencies that are already charging user fees would have to raise them significantly. The Tennessee Valley Authority—if forced to take account of the true costs of all its operations— would have to raise the price of electricity to its customers. The U.S. Postal Service would have to raise its rates probably more than it already plans to. The Small Business Administration would have to charge small businesses for any services rendered. The National

Mediation Board would have to bill unions and businesses for its mediation services in labor-management disputes.

But what about those agencies that weren't put into existence with the idea of charging for their services? Well, they would have to rethink their charter. NASA would basically have to become a commercial satellite-launching operation. It might even advertise throughout the world. It would have to refocus its efforts away from big, bold plans such as a manned space station to more mundane operations such as communication satellites.

Something else might have to happen on the cost side with all government independent agencies and corporations. They might actually have to be run like

private businesses. Managers would be required under law to contain costs to enable such agencies to make a profit. The U.S. Postal Service, for example, would be run more like Federal Express. U.S. postal workers, who are now part of a very strong union, would find postal management much less willing to accept union demands for higher wages. After all, the profit requirement means keeping costs down, and labor is one of the largest costs in the Postal Service budget.

Nationwide, the requirement that independent agencies and corporations make a profit would certainly lead to the elimination of a large number of them. Many publicly offered services in the arts, medical care, welfare, science, and technology would disappear. Other services, now being furnished at bargain rates, would become much more expensive and would reflect more accurately the true cost to the nation of providing those services. Some groups would undoubtedly be hurt. The American taxpayer in general, however, would certainly see smaller federal budget deficits and less federal government spending.

1. *What government agencies and corporations would be good candidates for the requirement that they turn a profit?*
2. *Why should some government agencies never be required to turn a profit?*

One day a president of the United States smelled a rat. Actually, he thought he smelled a dead mouse that had died behind a wall near the Oval Office. Since the president was expecting some important visitors, he demanded that the mouse be removed. His staffers called the General Services Administration (GSA), the independent agency that is responsible for the maintenance of the White House. The bureaucrats at the GSA claimed that the dead mouse in the White House was not their problem; after all, they had just fumigated for mice. They reasoned that the mouse must have come in from the outside and therefore was under the jurisdiction of the Department of the Interior. But when the bureaucrats at Interior were contacted, they refused to respond, claiming that their jurisdiction ended where the White House walls began.

The irate president demanded to see the responsible individuals from both agencies. He wanted action—and eventually he got it. A special interagency task force was formed to remove the dead mouse from the White House.

A tale of fiction? Unfortunately not. The president in question was Jimmy Carter, and the irony was that Carter had campaigned only months earlier on a platform promising to streamline the federal bureaucracy. Carter had not been alone. In the last thirty years, almost every presidential candidate has at one time or another promised to do "something" about the bureaucracy.

■ CONTROLLING THE FEDERAL BUREAUCRACY

How successful have all these presidential candidates been at controlling, containing, or altering the federal bureaucracy once they have taken office? The answer is easy—not very successful at all. Reagan claimed he was going to eliminate both the Department of Education and the Department of Energy. He did neither and added the Department of Veterans Affairs. Bush may add a Department of the Environment.

Presidents have been virtually powerless to affect significantly the structure and operation of the federal bureaucracy. It has been called the "fourth branch of government," even though you will find no reference to the bureaucracy in the original Constitution or in the twenty-six amendments that have been passed since 1787. But Article II, Section 2, of the Constitution gives the president the power to appoint "all other officers of the United States, whose appointments are not herein otherwise provided for," and Article II, Section 3, states that the president "shall take care that the laws be faithfully executed, and shall commission all the officers of the United States." Constitutional scholars believe that the legal basis for the bureaucracy rests on these two sections in Article II.

Presidents have not only found it almost impossible to change the bureaucracy but, more seriously, they have also found that departments and agencies are often able to obstruct the president's own goals. Franklin Roosevelt complained of ideological and personal opposition from cabinet departments during his tenure:

> The Treasury is so large and far-flung and ingrained in its practices that I find it is almost impossible to get the action and results that I want. . . . But the Treasury is not to be compared with the State Department. You should go through the experience of trying to get any changes in the thinking, policy and action of the career diplomats and then you'd know what a real problem was. But the Treasury and the State Department put together are nothing compared with the Na-a-vy.[1]

[1]Quoted in Marriner Eccles, *Beckoning Frontiers* (New York: Alfred A. Knopf, 1951), p. 336.

DID YOU KNOW?

That the federal government in 1990 spent $150 million each hour, twenty-four hours per day?

It soon becomes clear to new administrations that real power in the executive branch lies at least as much with bureaucrats and cabinet officers as it does with the White House. Resistance to John Kennedy's New Frontier was led by "the feudal barons of the permanent government, entrenched in their domains and fortified by their sense of proprietorship."[2] The Nixon administration encountered social service interests within the government "dominated by administrators ideologically hostile to many of the directions of the Nixon administration in the realm of social policy."[3]

Two questions raised by such comments are What is a bureaucracy? and How did it become so powerful?

■ THE NATURE OF BUREAUCRACY

BUREAUCRACY
A large organization that is structured hierarchically to carry out specific functions.

A **bureaucracy** is the name given to a large organization that is structured hierarchically to carry out specific functions. Generally, most bureaucracies are characterized first and foremost by an organization chart. According to the German sociologist Max Weber, bureaucracies share certain qualities. Every person who works in the organization has a superior to whom he or she reports. The units of the organization are divided according to specialization and the expertise of the employees. There are elaborate rules that everyone in the organization is expected to accept and follow. Finally, tasks are supposed to be done in a neutral manner, that is, for the sake of the organization rather than for personal gain.[4]

Bureaucracy is not always consistent with democratic principles. Weber concluded that bureaucracy transforms people from social beings and whole persons to organizational cogs. Hierarchical position, job specialty, and rules set the standards for behavior. The organization grinds on, ignoring the personal feelings of its members. Bureaucracy can cause individuals to doubt the value of their opinions and inhibit their expression. "Specialists without spirit," Weber called bureaucrats. But he also believed that there is no realistic alternative. A bureaucracy coordinates an enormous work force responsible for thousands of programs. Without hierarchy, specialization, and rules, the work would not get done.

We should not think of bureaucracy as unique to government. Any large corporation or university can be considered a bureaucratic organization. The fact is that the handling of complex problems requires a division of labor. Individuals must concentrate their skills on specific, well-defined aspects of a problem and depend on others to solve the rest of it.

But public or government bureaucracies differ from private organizations in some important ways. Unlike a private corporation such as General Motors, public bureaucracies do not have a single set of leaders such as GM's board of directors. Although the president is the chief administrator of the federal system, all bureaucratic agencies are subject to the desires of Congress for their funding, staffing, and, indeed, for their continued existence. Furthermore, public bureaucracies supposedly serve the citizen rather than the stockholder.

[2]Arthur Schlesinger, Jr., *A Thousand Days* (Boston: Houghton Mifflin, 1965), p. 981.
[3]Joel Aberbach and Bert Rockman, "Clashing Beliefs Within the Executive Branch," *American Political Science Review*, 70, no. 2 (June 1976), pp. 456–468.
[4]Max Weber, *Theory of Social and Economic Organization*, ed. Talcott Parsons (New York: Oxford University Press, 1974).

In a sense each American has a right to feel that he or she should control the bureaucracy. Perhaps it is this aspect of government organization that makes citizens hostile toward government employees when they experience inefficiency and red tape. One other important difference is that government bureaucracies are not organized to make a profit. Rather they are supposed to perform their functions as efficiently as possible to conserve the taxpayers' dollars. These characteristics, together with the prevalence and size of the government bureaucracies, make them an important factor in American life.

DID YOU KNOW?

That 114 million individual income tax returns were filed in 1990?

■ THE SIZE OF THE BUREAUCRACY

In 1789, the new government's bureaucracy was miniscule. There were three departments—State (with nine employees), War (with two employees), and Treasury (with thirty-nine employees). This bureaucracy was still small in 1798 when the secretary of state had seven clerks and spent a total of $500 (about $4,950 in 1991 dollars) on stationery and printing. In that year the Appro-

Internal Revenue Service employees sorting returns.

FIGURE 14-1
**Federal Agencies and Their Re-
spective Numbers of Civilian
Employees**

SOURCE: *Statistical Abstract of the United States,
1990.*

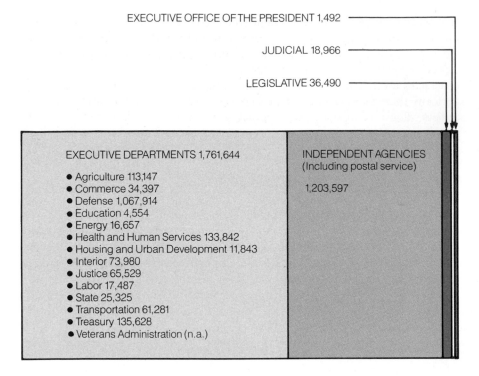

EXECUTIVE OFFICE OF THE PRESIDENT 1,492

JUDICIAL 18,966

LEGISLATIVE 36,490

EXECUTIVE DEPARTMENTS 1,761,644

- Agriculture 113,147
- Commerce 34,397
- Defense 1,067,914
- Education 4,554
- Energy 16,657
- Health and Human Services 133,842
- Housing and Urban Development 11,843
- Interior 73,980
- Justice 65,529
- Labor 17,487
- State 25,325
- Transportation 61,281
- Treasury 135,628
- Veterans Administration (n.a.)

INDEPENDENT AGENCIES
(Including postal service)

1,203,597

FIGURE 14-2
**Growth in Government Employ-
ment on Federal, State, and Local
Levels**

By the 1980s, there were more local
government employees than federal and
state employees.

SOURCE: *Department of Commerce, 1990;* 1991
data are estimates.

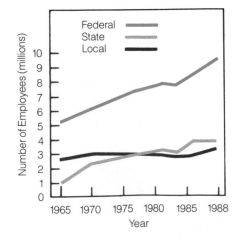

priations Act allocated $1.4 million to the War Department (or $13.5 million
in 1991 dollars).[5]

Times have changed, as we can see in Figure 14-1, which lists the various
federal agencies and the number of employees in each. Excluding the military,
3.2 million government employees constitute the federal bureaucracy. That
number has remained relatively stable for the last several decades. It is somewhat deceiving, however, because there are many others working directly or
indirectly for the federal government as subcontractors or consultants, and in
other capacities.

But the figures for federal government employment are only part of the
story. Figure 14-2 shows the growth in government employment on federal,
state, and local levels. Since 1950, this growth has been mainly at the state
and local levels, so that if all government employees are counted, 9.7 percent
of the entire civilian population over age sixteen works directly for the government. If we include the military, about 14 percent of the entire labor force
is employed directly by government.

The costs of the bureaucracy are commensurately high and growing. The
share of the gross national product taken up by government spending was
only 8.5 percent in 1929, but today it exceeds 40 percent.

■ THE ORGANIZATION OF THE FEDERAL BUREAUCRACY

Within the federal bureaucracy are a number of different types of government
agencies and organizations. Figure 14-3 outlines the several bureaucracies

[5]Leonard D. White, *The Federalists: A Study in Administrative History 1789–1801* (New York: The Free
Press, 1948).

within the executive branch as well as the separate organizations that provide services to the Congress, to the courts, and to the president directly. In Chapter 13, we discussed those agencies that are considered to be part of the Executive Office of the President.

The executive branch, which employs most of the bureaucrats, has four major types of bureaucratic structures. They are (1) cabinet departments, (2) independent executive agencies, (3) independent regulatory agencies, and (4) government corporations. Each has a distinctive relationship to the president, and some have unusual internal structures, overall goals, and grants of power.

Cabinet Departments

The fourteen **cabinet departments** are the major service organizations of the federal government. They can also be described in management terms as **line organizations.** This means they are directly accountable to the president and are responsible for performing functions of government such as printing money or training troops. These departments were created by Congress when the

CABINET DEPARTMENTS
The fourteen departments of the executive branch (State, Treasury, Defense, Justice, Interior, Agriculture, Commerce, Labor, Health and Human Services, Housing and Urban Development, Education, Energy, Transportation, and Veterans Affairs).

LINE ORGANIZATION
Government or corporate units that provide direct services or products for the public.

FIGURE 14-3
Organization Chart of the Federal Government
SOURCE: *U.S. Government Manual, 1989–90.*

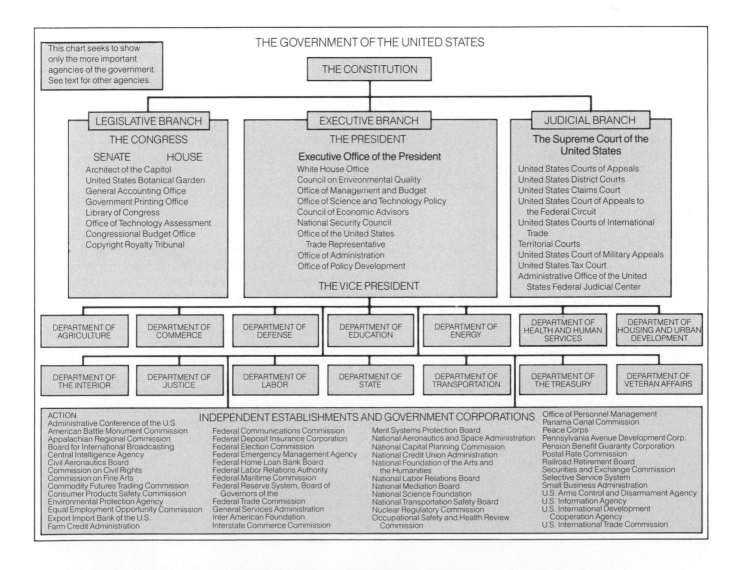

PROFILE

Carla A. Hills

"My objective is to get the world's trading system open so that entrepreneurs, wherever they are located, can sell and buy and expand trade without government interference."

The official title of the U.S. trade representative is ambassador extraordinary and plenipotentiary. That exalted title is held by Carla A. Hills who, at fifty-six, was appointed by President Bush to handle this challenging and sensitive position. Her responsibilities are to pry open foreign markets and look after U.S. business interests overseas.

A graduate of Stanford University and Yale University Law School, she worked as an assistant U.S. attorney in Los Angeles and then formed her own law firm with her husband, Roderick. At the end of the Nixon presidency, she and her husband moved to Washington to work for the Justice Department. In the Ford administration she became the third woman in U.S. history to hold a cabinet post when she was confirmed as secretary of housing and urban development (HUD).

Her past has not been devoid of potential scandal. When she was in private law practice in 1985 she represented D.R.G., a large mortgage lender. In that year she paid a visit to the secretary of HUD, Samuel R. Pierce, Jr. Pierce renewed a loan guarantee for D.R.G. in spite of the fact that the company had received an unfavorable report. During the 1989 congressional investigations of HUD scandals, Carla Hills's role in the D.R.G. matter was scrutinized. Although Congress found nothing illegal, the controversy received widespread negative press coverage.

Carla Hills has a reputation of being a hard-working, rational, and meticulous professional who puts in fourteen-hour days and spends weekends at the office. In spite of the fact that she indicated to President Ford that she wasn't interested in an appointment to the U.S. Supreme Court, Washington insiders insist that she is high on the list of potential Republican appointees for the nation's highest court.

need for each arose. The first department to be created was State and the most recent one was Veterans Affairs, established in 1988. A president might ask that a new department be created or an old one abolished, but has no power to do so without legislative approval from Congress.

Each department is headed by a secretary and several levels of under-secretaries, assistant secretaries, and so on. Presidents theoretically have considerable control over the cabinet departments because they are able to appoint or fire all of the top officials. As Franklin Roosevelt suggested, however, even cabinet departments do not always respond to the president's wishes. One reason for the frequent unhappiness of presidents with their departments is that the entire bureaucratic structure below the top political levels is staffed by permanent employees, many of whom are committed to established programs or procedures and who resist change. As we can see from Table 14-1, each cabinet department employs thousands of individuals, only a handful of whom are under the control of the president.

Some observers have grouped the cabinet departments according to their closeness to the chief executive. Several of the departments—State, Defense, Justice, and Treasury—are known as the "inner" departments, since they primarily serve the president and their secretaries are often those who are closest politically and personally to the Oval Office. The other departments are sometimes classified as "outer" because their functions deal more with domestic constituency groups and thus their goals may differ from those of the president. Very large and complex departments such as Defense, Health and Human Services, and Housing and Urban Development have been called "holding companies" because of the multitude of agencies and interests that are combined within one organization. Such complex departments tend to suffer from internal conflicts as one bureau tries to expand its functions or budget at the expense of another.

The cabinet departments are by far the most important sectors within the federal bureaucracy. The fourteen cabinet departments combined account for more than 2.03 million employees, or fully 64 percent of the civilian federal bureaucracy. In terms of spending, the Department of Defense and the Department of Health and Human Services together account for 63 percent of all federal outlays.

Independent Executive Agencies

Independent executive agencies are bureaucratic organizations that have a single function. They are not located within a department and report directly to the president who appoints their chief officials. When a new federal agency is created—the Environmental Protection Agency, for example—a decision is made by the president and Congress about where it will be located in the bureaucracy. In this century, presidents have often asked that a new organization be kept separate or independent rather than added to an existing department. This is a political decision, which may focus public attention on the new agency by putting it closer to the White House to keep the new group out of a department that may in fact be hostile to its creation. Two major independent agencies are the following:

General Services Administration (GSA). This independent agency was established in 1949 to centralize purchasing for the federal government and the management of its property and records. The GSA is headed by an administrator, appointed by the president with Senate approval, who has the responsibility for procuring, supplying, and transporting the property and services of all the executive agencies. The administrator of the GSA also is in charge of the acquisition and management of federally owned or leased property, the disposal of service property, and the management of all records. The GSA has more than thirty thousand employees.

Since the GSA is the business arm of the federal government, it has implied powers of oversight. For example, as the major government contractor in the construction industry and elsewhere, it implements national policy by requiring contractors to prove they are complying with Equal Employment Opportunity legislation. It also oversees spending. The GSA has uncovered a number of overcharges and other procurement irregularities in government each year. In one case, a single Defense Department employee was discovered to have falsified more than 3,300 forms and embezzled some $1.8 million in medical funds.

National Aeronautics and Space Administration (NASA). This independent government agency was established in 1958 by the National Aero-

---

DID YOU KNOW?

That the Internal Revenue Service (IRS), with 125,000 employees, is the largest federal law-enforcement agency?

INDEPENDENT EXECUTIVE AGENCY
A federal agency having a single function that is not part of a cabinet department but reports directly to the president.

TABLE 14-1
Employment in the Executive Branch

Agriculture	113,147
Commerce	34,397
Defense	1,067,947
Education	4,554
Energy	16,657
Environmental Protection Agency	13,141
Health and Human Services	133,842
Housing and Urban Development	11,843
Interior	73,980
Justice	65,529
Labor	17,487
National Aeronautics and Space Administration	21,682
State	25,325
Transportation	61,281
Treasury	135,628
Veterans Affairs	231,486

SOURCE: *Statistical Abstract of the United States, 1990.*

Explosion of the space shuttle, *Challenger*. How did that tragedy change the behavior of those working in NASA?

nautics and Space Act. Its primary purpose is to explore the peaceful use of space, and as such it is responsible for building, testing, and operating space vehicles. NASA has four divisions: (1) the Office of Manned Space Flights, (2) the Office of Space Science and Applications, (3) the Office of Advanced Research and Technology, and (4) the Office of Tracking and Data Acquisition. In its early years, NASA at times had extremely large budgets, particularly during its efforts to put a person on the moon. (See the Highlight on one of NASA's more costly ventures.)

Shuttle crew members display a model of the Hubble Space Telescope before the launch. Investigations of the telescope's flaws after its deployment suggested that bureaucratic practices at NASA may have contributed to the problem. How can government bureaucracies best be managed to avoid such problems?

HIGHLIGHT

How an $8 Billion Space Station Will Cost $120 Billion

Scientists' study of space sounds like a good idea. Congress decided to take on the task with a space station for which it agreed to pay $8 billion in 1984. Today, the estimated cost is over $120 billion when operating and other expenses are counted. If President Bush's desire to send Americans to the Moon and Mars is included, the final tally may be as high as $200 billion.

Going from $8 billion to $120 billion is in part a demonstration of how the bureaucracy can make sure that projects become bigger and bigger. According to the White House official in charge of NASA's budget, NASA's talk about a stripped-down model never got off the drawing boards. By 1990, NASA had spent $4 billion and didn't have one nut or bolt to show for it. In response to criticisms, NASA officials maintained that the price of the space station may be high, but that it was a "fair" price for the scientific and commercial benefits that it promises.

A former NASA director in the early 1980s had to concede that the space station idea was put forth simply as a way to keep the agency in business because otherwise NASA would run out of a mission. NASA immediately rejected the less costly Soviet method of putting up small, self-contained units that could be linked together. It wanted one big unit that could only work when it was fully assembled. According to two critics of the project, Ronald D. Brunner and Radford Byerly Jr. of the University of Colorado, the latter plan was simply put forth "to meet NASA's own institutional needs and to secure program approval and survival."

By 1986, NASA said that the cost of the project would be $16 billion. That same year the National Academy of Sciences estimated the cost at $30 billion. In May 1988, the General Accounting Office (GAO) pointed out that it would cost almost $3 billion annually to operate the station, or $81 billion over its thirty-year lifetime.

By the beginning of the 1990s, Congress had delayed funding the station and pushed back its completion date to 1999. NASA reestimated construction costs at close to $40 billion.

It seems, though, that no matter what the cost, the space station will probably move forward to some level of completion. Why? It will happen by the sheer power of political momentum. "It's going to get built," said a spokesperson for the Federation of American Scientists. "When you've got all those employees and contractors, and that big an operation at stake, a project has to be more obviously preposterous than the station in order not to happen."[*]

[*]*New York Times,* June 10, 1990, sec. Y, p. 16.

Independent Regulatory Agencies

The **independent regulatory agencies** are typically responsible for a specific type of public policy. Their function is to make and implement rules and regulations in a particular sector of the economy to protect the public interest. The earliest such agency was the Interstate Commerce Commission (ICC), which was established in 1887 when Americans began to seek some form of government control over the rapidly growing business and industrial sector. This new form of organization, the independent regulatory commission, was supposed to make technical, nonpolitical decisions about rates, profits, and rules that would be for the benefit of all and that did not require congressional legislation. In the years that followed the creation of the ICC, other agencies were formed to regulate aviation (the Civil Aeronautics Board, CAB), communication (the Federal Communications Commission, SEC), nuclear power (the Nuclear Regulatory Commission, NRC), and so on.

The regulatory commissions are administered independently of all three branches of government. Since they were set up because Congress felt it was unable to handle the complexities and technicalities required to carry out specific laws in the public interest, the regulatory commissions in fact combine some functions of all three branches of government—executive, legislative,

INDEPENDENT REGULATORY AGENCY
An agency outside the major executive departments charged with making and implementing rules and regulations to protect the public interest.

DID YOU KNOW?

That the secret U.S. government intelligence fund, which finances the Central Intelligence Agency (CIA) as well as intelligence activities in other departments, exceeds $35 billion per year?

and judicial. They are legislative in that they make rules that have the force of law. They are executive in that they provide for the enforcement of those rules. They are judicial in that they decide disputes involving the rules they have made (primarily through administrative law judges, discussed in more detail in Chapter 15).

Regulatory commission members are appointed by the president with the consent of the Senate, although they do not report to the president. By law, the members of regulatory commissions cannot all be from the same political party. The president can influence regulatory agency behavior by appointing people of his party or those who share his philosophy when vacancies occur, in particular when the chair is vacant.

The most important independent regulatory agencies, in order of their creation, are as follows:

1. Interstate Commerce Commission (1887)
2. Federal Reserve System (1913)
3. Federal Trade Commission (1914)
4. Federal Deposit Insurance Corporation (1916)
5. Farm Credit Administration (1933)
6. Federal Communications Commission (1934)
7. Securities and Exchange Commission (1934)
8. National Labor Relations Board (1935)
9. Civil Aeronautics Board (1940, terminated January 1, 1985)
10. Equal Employment Opportunity Commission (1964)
11. Environmental Protection Agency (1970)
12. Consumer Product Safety Commission (1972)

All told, the independent regulatory agencies employ roughly eighty thousand civilians directly. A number of bureaus and sections within cabinet departments also function as regulatory agencies, such as the Occupational Safety and Health Administration (OSHA), which is part of the Department of Labor, and the Food and Drug Administration, which is part of the Department of Health and Human Services.

Over the last several decades, some observers have concluded that these agencies, although nominally independent of the three branches of the federal government, may in fact not always be so. They contend that many independent regulatory commissions have been "captured" by the very industries and firms that they were supposed to regulate. The results have been less competition rather than more, higher prices rather than lower ones, and less choice rather than more choice for consumers.

ERA OF DEREGULATION
The early 1980s, characterized by deregulation of several industries including trucking, air transport, and banking.

Not surprisingly, the 1980s have been called the **era of deregulation.** An important part of Reagan's 1980 campaign was his promise to reduce the regulation of American business. But deregulation had already started before Reagan was elected. President Carter pushed for and obtained the Motor Carrier Deregulation Act of 1978. He also appointed a chairperson of the Civil Aeronautics Board who waged a war against the regulation of airline tariffs and routes. The result has been the almost complete deregulation of the airline industry. The CAB ceased to exist on January 1, 1985.

Since the late 1970s, there has been relatively little additional congressionally mandated deregulation—except perhaps in the banking industry, in conformity with the Depository Institutions Deregulation and Monetary Control Act of 1980. Again, this deregulation was initiated before Reagan's election in 1980.

PROFILE

Antonia Coello Novello

Surgeon General C. Everett Koop was constantly in the news. He seemed to make the headlines wherever he went, whatever his current mission. Even his resignation was controversial. His successor in the surgeon general's office, Antonia Coello Novello, however, did not appear to be following in Dr. Koop's footsteps, at least during her first few months on the job. Dr. Novello, a native of Puerto Rico, received her medical degree in pediatrics from the University of Puerto Rico School of Medicine in 1970. She also earned a masters degree in public health from Johns Hopkins University in 1982. Along with her experience as a professor of pediatrics at Georgetown University, Dr. Novello has also served as medical adviser to Senator Orrin Hatch for the U.S. Senate Committee on Labor and Human Resources. Before being appointed surgeon general, Novello was deputy director of the National Institute of Child Health and Human Development, for which she specialized in pediatric AIDS.

Novello has a reputation as a conscientious but unaggressive administrator. Observers therefore expect that she will not make headlines with the same regularity as her predecessor, Dr. Koop. Not surprisingly, given President Bush's stand on the subject, Dr. Novello is a foe of abortion. The White House reportedly made a point of

checking the position of all prospective nominees to the surgeon general's office on this subject. While claiming it was not a "litmus test," President Bush did make sure that his new surgeon general supported the White House view.

On the question of cigarette smoking, Antonia Novello appears to have picked up the gauntlet where Dr. Koop dropped it. In her first meeting as the head of a federal committee on smoking, Novello joined other top health officials in urging states to enforce laws barring cigarette sales to minors. If current smoking rates continue, according to Novello, about five million of the children now living in the United States will die of a smoking-related disease. "That alarming statistic should be enough to raise this issue to the top of the public agenda," she stated. It does appear that Antonia Novello will champion her causes, but we should not expect to find her written up in the media with the regularity of Dr. Koop. Novello's style is very different from that of her predecessor.

Between 1970 and 1980, expenditures by regulatory agencies grew from $1.6 billion to a high of $6.8 billion, but since then such expenditures have grown much more slowly. Moreover, the number of regulatory personnel has declined from 131,500 in 1980 to an estimated 119,600 in 1990.

Deregulation has not been entirely successful. In perhaps the most conspicuous example, when restrictions were lifted on how savings and loan institutions could invest their depositors' savings, many institutions invested in highly risky business ventures. By 1990, bad investments, fraud, and insider abuse had resulted in failures of an estimated one thousand savings and loan institutions at a cost to taxpayers of an estimated $500 billion. Calls for reregulation have mounted (see this chapter's Critical Perspective).

Government Corporations

The newest form of bureaucratic organization to be adopted in the United States is the **government corporation.** Although the concept is borrowed

GOVERNMENT CORPORATION
An agency of government that administers a quasibusiness enterprise. Used when an activity is primarily commercial, produces revenue for its continued existence, and requires greater flexibility than permitted for departments.

CRITICAL PERSPECTIVE

Should There Be Reregulation?

A notable phenomenon of complex, modern society is the widespread participation of government in the economy. The most common form in the United States is the regulation of business—a major function of the federal bureaucracy. Regulation has gone through phases from protecting and promoting business to protecting consumers and the environment *from* business.

The form of regulation may be economic, through controlling prices that regulated enterprises are allowed to charge, or social, through stipulating conditions affecting public welfare across all industries. Social regulation has as its aim a better quality of life for all through a less-polluted environment, better working conditions, and safer and better products. For example, the Food and Drug Administration (FDA) helps protect against impure and unsafe foods, drugs, cosmetics, and other potentially hazardous products. The Consumer Products Safety Commission (CPSC) specifies minimum standards for consumer products in order to reduce "unreasonable" risk of injury. The Occupational Safety and Health Administration (OSHA) protects workers against work-related injuries and illnesses.

In the late 1970s, the mood of the country and of Washington decision makers began to turn against "overregulation" and "big government." The trend toward deregulation started with the Airline Deregulation Act of 1978. That act reduced route restrictions and decontrolled prices. The Depository Institutions Deregulation and Monetary Control Act of 1980 phased out deposit interest ceilings, lowered the prices of financial services, allowed savings and loans institutions to make commercial and consumer loans, and allowed all depository institutions to offer checking-type accounts. The railroads were deregulated to some extent under the Staggers Rail Act of 1980, as were the buses under the Bus Regulatory and Reform Act of 1982. Trucking saw many of its restrictions eliminated by the Motor Carrier Act of 1980.

Deregulation has had benefits and costs, as do all changes in public policy. The benefits have been lower prices to consumers who use the services of the trucking, airline, and long-distance telephone industries. In the banking industry, one result of deregulation has been higher yields for small savers. But not everybody has benefited. In the airline industry, many individuals, particularly business travelers, often end up paying a relatively higher price for short trips on less heavily traveled routes than before deregulation in 1978. In general, customers in high-cost airline markets have had to pay more because under a deregulated industry structure no *cross-subsidization*

Inside the air traffic control tower at New Orleans. Controllers argue that budget cut-backs may reduce air safety. How can decisions about vital services best be made?

exists. Cross-subsidization occurs whenever price is below cost in one market and the losses are covered by the profits of another market within the same industry.

Additionally, deregulation has yielded intense competition. This competition has increased the number of bankruptcies, for example, in the airline industry. Certainly, the deregulation of the savings and loan industry created a number of problems leading to a financial crisis of unprecedented proportion (a topic covered in Chapter 16). Moreover, employees in newly deregulated industries have often seen their salaries cut or their jobs disappear.

The 1990s may be the era of reregulation, that is, reapplying some of the regulatory apparatus that existed before deregulation. On the face of it, certain industries seem to cry out for reregulation, in particular, the airline industry and the banking industry. Consider the airline industry. Everybody seems to believe that flights are late, the food is unspeakable, passengers are packed in like sardines, and luggage will never arrive on time. Also, and perhaps more important, the common perception is that safety has deteriorated.

The data don't necessarily confirm these casual views of what has happened in the airlines since 1978. With respect to safety, for example, fatal accidents per 100,000 departures have decreased almost 75 percent. There are more fatal accidents, that is certain. But there are many many more passengers flying today than before 1978 because prices are so much lower. During the decade after the deregulation of airlines, fatal accidents per million miles traveled declined almost 60 percent. Believe it or not, it is safer to fly today than it was in the 1970s.

What about passenger complaints? From 1979 to 1991, complaints have fallen almost 50 percent. Now we are not talking about the absolute number of complaints but about the *percentage* of passengers complaining.

What about air fares? Even though some air fares are higher, particularly for people not staying over a Saturday, the average air fare per passenger mile has fallen by more than 25 percent since 1978. If we take account of inflation during this period, the real reduction in air fares is closer to 40 percent. Not surprisingly, airlines are carrying twice as many passengers as they were in 1978.

These facts do not necessarily mean we don't need some reregulation. The issue is complicated but certainly not one-sided. That is to say, deregulation has brought with it costs and benefits and neither the costs nor the benefits are so obviously out of line with each other that we can categorically call for more or less regulation.

Exercise in Critical Thinking

1. Who would benefit most from reregulation of the airline industry, and why?
2. Why do some industries seem to need regulation and others not?
3. What types of individuals would be the best regulators of an industry?

from the world of business, distinct differences exist between the public and private types.

A private corporation has shareholders who elect a board of directors, who in turn choose the corporate officers, such as president and vice president. When a private corporation makes a profit, it must pay taxes (unless it avoids them through various legal loopholes), and it either distributes part or all of the after-tax profits to shareholders as dividends or plows them back into the corporation to make new investments.

A government corporation has a board of directors and managers, but it doesn't have any stockholders. We cannot buy shares of stock in a government corporation. If the government corporation makes a profit, it does not distribute the profit as dividends. Also, if it makes a profit, it does not have to pay taxes; the profits remain in the corporation.

Three of the major federal government corporations are as follows:

Tennessee Valley Authority (TVA). Created in 1933, TVA is run by a three-person board that is appointed by, and is directly responsible to, the president. The general manager of TVA reports to that board. TVA operates a Tennessee River control system and also generates power for a seven-state region and for the U.S. atomic and space programs. TVA has sold electricity at relatively low rates compared with rates charged by privately owned electric utilities. As such, its rates have been deemed the "yardstick" by which the fairness of other electricity rates are measured. Critics of TVA claim, however, that the yardstick concept is misguided since TVA does not have to pay federal or state taxes. TVA has about forty-five thousand employees.

U.S. Postal Service. The history of the mail service in the United States dates back to the colonial era when King William of England granted Thomas Neale a patent to set up and maintain a postal system. When Neale died in 1707, the British government took control of the postal service. In 1753, Benjamin Franklin and William Hunter were appointed by the British gov-

DID YOU KNOW?

That the Postal Service delivered more than 160 billion pieces of mail in 1990, which is about 640 pieces per person?

ernment as joint postmasters general in the colonies. The Articles of Confederation gave Congress the exclusive control over the mails.

The Constitution, in Article I, Section 8, expressly gives Congress the power to establish post offices. In 1789, Congress exercised this power and created the Office of Postmaster General within the Treasury Department. Then, in 1792, a Post Office Department was created. In 1829, the postmaster general under President Jackson sat as a member of the cabinet, although it wasn't until 1872 that the Post Office Department officially became part of the executive branch. The post office remained as part of the cabinet until 1970, when President Nixon signed the Postal Reorganization Act. Currently, the U.S. Postal Service is managed by a presidentially appointed, bipartisan board of governors and by a postmaster general and deputy postmaster general selected by the board.

The U.S. Postal Service is by far the largest of the government corporations, employing about 800,000 workers (see Highlight on personnel and other problems of the Postal Service). The reorganization of the post office into the U.S. Postal Service did not change its unprofitable status. In 1986, despite opposition from the Reagan administration, Congress approved legislation that included almost $1 billion in subsidies for postage rates for nonprofit organizations, newspapers, and other special categories of mail. Subsidizing these rates has always been popular with Congress, although it undercuts the goal of self-sufficiency for the postal service.

AMTRAK.   This railway service, administered by the National Railroad Passenger Corporation, was created in 1970 to help provide an integrated, balanced national and intercity rail passenger service network. It currently controls about 23,000 miles of track, serves 505 stations, employs 18,500 persons, and in 1990 carried more than 23 million people.

AMTRAK was created in response to a declining number of U.S. rail passengers and deteriorating quality of railroad service. Its main objectives have been to renovate track, replace outdated equipment, streamline and reduce revenue-losing routes, and in general elevate U.S. passenger rail service to a position similar to that existing in Europe. Although it is far from reaching that goal, the overall performance is impressive. In 1990, AMTRAK maintained on-time performance 70 percent of the time—better than many other types of public transportation.

AMTRAK, however, has never been able to generate enough revenue to pay for the improvements. Subsidies for the service were set at $800 million in 1990, about the same level as in 1985.

Some of the other government corporations include the Federal Deposit Insurance Corporation, which insures bank deposits; CONRAIL, which is a freight rail service; and the Export-Import Bank, which loans money for foreign trade.

AMTRAK service.

■ STAFFING THE BUREAUCRACY

There are two groups of people whom we may call bureaucrats: political appointees and civil servants. As noted earlier, the president is able to make political appointments to most of the top jobs in the federal bureaucracy as well as to appoint ambassadors to the most important foreign posts. All of

The U.S. Postal Service—Job Stress and Inefficiency

The figure is 162 billion. That's the estimate for the number of pieces of mail moved by 800,000 U.S. Postal Service employees in a year. In spite of automation, each letter is handled by fourteen people. As in some industries, automation has brought increased work-related stress. A postal clerk sitting at a machine has roughly one second to read the address and punch in on a keyboard the first three digits of the ZIP code. The machine translates the numbers into a bar code symbol stamped on the letter, which can then be sorted automatically by mail-carrier route.

The pressure to increase efficiency and cost effectiveness have led to labor-related conflicts. The weight of each mail carrier's bag is one of the most frequent sources of complaints, especially during the Christmas season. Required overtime is another. In San Diego, California, for example, almost half of the 800-plus carrier routes require more than an eight-hour shift to complete. Each year there are over 150,000 grievance procedures waged against workers who break the numerous work rules. Disciplinary actions exceed 70,000 per year. In addition, carriers have to contend with dog bites, muggings, dangerous neighborhoods and buildings, inclement weather, and other hazards.

Violence between workers and supervisors has increased—over 100 workers attack their supervisors each year and vice versa. One letter carrier in Escondido, California went on a shooting spree with a rifle, killing two coworkers, his wife, and himself. A Boston mail handler stole an airplane and strafed Boston neighborhoods with an AK-47 assault rifle. A mail handler shot a supervisor and wounded three others.

Postal workers sort the mail.

In Edmond, Oklahoma, an enraged postal worker killed fourteen coworkers and then killed himself. It's hard to say whether these incidents are caused by the high-stress environment and poor personnel relations or whether they are simply random occurrences among a very large group of workers.

On the public side, critics stress the inefficiencies of the organization. It takes as long for a letter to get from Miami to Boston as it does to drive there by car. According to the Postal Service itself, it takes longer to deliver a first-class letter today than it did in the 1960s. The service has lost most of its package business to companies like United Parcel Service because of high postal rates, slow and unreliable delivery, and high rates of damage. Com-

plaints about first-class mail delivery service rose a phenomenal 35 percent in the summer of 1989. (Private companies are not allowed to compete with the Postal Service in delivering first-class letters because of a law called the Private Express Statute.)

Postal Service costs are rising one and a half times faster than the rate of inflation. Rates are expected to rise continually during the 1990s. In fiscal year 1990, the service was expected to lose over $1.5 billion. Almost 85 percent of the Postal Service's $40 billion in revenues go to wages, salaries, and benefits. The average annual wage and benefits level in 1990 was $42,500, which is high for a semiskilled work force.

One proposed solution envisions a radically changed organization. Economics professor Douglas K. Adie recommends that change be accomplished through three mechanisms: (1) *deregulation* of mail service similar to the deregulation of transportation and communications; (2) *divestiture* of the U.S. Postal Service into several smaller entities, such as was done with AT&T; and (3) *privatization*, by literally selling stock and turning over the company, which is now government owned, to private investors and thus turning it into several private-sector corporations. This, Adie argues, would lead to competition and therefore better service.

The history of the U.S. Postal Service demonstrates that the challenges of effective governmental service is the same as in the private sector—good management, sound personnel policy, client satisfaction, cost effectiveness, and productivity.

(SOURCE: *Time*, 12-25, 1989; Douglas K. Adie, "Privatization of the United States Postal Service," *National Forum*, Spring 1990, pp. 17–20.)

DID YOU KNOW?

That the U.S. Postal Service with almost 800,000 employees is the largest civilian employer in the United States?

NATURAL ARISTOCRACY
A small ruling clique of the state's "best" citizens, whose membership is based on birth, wealth, and ability. The Jeffersonian era emphasized rule by such a group.

Cartoon satire on the spoils system.

SPOILS SYSTEM
The awarding of government jobs to political supporters and friends; generally associated with President Andrew Jackson.

MERIT SYSTEM
The selection, retention, and promotion of government employees on the basis of competitive examinations.

the jobs that are considered "political plums" and that usually go to the politically well connected are listed in *Policy and Supporting Position,* published by the Government Printing Office after each presidential election. This has been informally (and correctly) called "The Plum Book." The rest of the individuals who work for the national government belong to the civil service and got their jobs through a much more formal process.

A Short History of the Federal Civil Service

When the federal government was formed in 1789, it had no career public servants, but rather consisted of amateurs who were almost all Federalists. When Jefferson took over as president, he found that few in his party were holding federal administrative jobs, so he fired more than one hundred officials, replacing them with members of the so-called **natural aristocracy**—that is, with his own Jeffersonian Republicans. For the next twenty-five years, a growing body of federal administrators gained experience and expertise, becoming in the process professional public servants. These administrators stayed in office regardless of who was elected president. The bureaucracy had become a self-maintaining, long-lived element within government.

To the Victor Belongs the Spoils.   When Andrew Jackson took over the White House in 1828, he could not believe how many appointed officials (appointed before him, that is) were overtly hostile toward him and his Democratic party. The bureaucracy—indeed an aristocracy—considered itself the only group fit to rule. But Jackson was a man of the people, and his policies were populist in nature. As the bureaucracy was reluctant to carry out his programs, Jackson did the obvious: He fired federal officials—more than had all his predecessors combined. The **spoils system**—an application of the principle that to the victor belongs the spoils—reigned. The northeastern aristocrats were out and the common folk were in. The spoils system was not, of course, a Jacksonian invention. Thomas Jefferson too had used this system of patronage in which the boss, or patron, rewards his workers for the job they did in getting him elected.

In addition to putting his own people on the federal payroll, Jackson decided to reorganize the bureaucracy in order to ensure that his policies were carried out. During his eight years in office, almost every department and bureau was restructured.[6]

The Civil Service Reform Act of 1883.   Jackson's spoils system survived for a number of years, but it became increasingly corrupt. Also, the size of the bureaucracy increased by 300 percent between 1851 and 1881. Reformers began to examine the professional civil service that was established in several European countries, which operated under a **merit system**—in which job appointments were based on competitive examinations. The cry for civil service reform began to be heard more loudly.

The ruling Republican party was divided in its attitude toward reform, the "stalwart" faction opposing reform of any sort. When President James A. Garfield, a moderate reformer, was assassinated in 1881 by a disappointed office seeker, Charles J. Guiteau, the latter was heard to shout "I am a stalwart,

[6]Matthew A. Crenson, *The Federal Machine: Beginnings of a Bureaucracy in Jacksonian America* (Baltimore, Md.: Johns Hopkins University Press, 1975).

The assassination of President Garfield by a disappointed office seeker. What effect did this event have on presidential appointments?

and Arthur is president now!" He was correct: Chester A. Arthur, a stalwart vice president, became president. Ironically, it was under the stalwart Arthur that civil service reform actually occurred—partly as a result of public outrage over Garfield's assassination. The movement to replace the spoils system with a permanent career civil service had the cause that would carry it to victory.

In 1883, the **Pendleton Act**—the **Civil Service Reform Act**—was passed, bringing to a close the period of Jacksonian spoils. The act established the principle of employment on the basis of open competitive examinations and created the **Civil Service Commission** to administer the personnel service. However, only 10 percent of federal employees were covered by the merit system. Later laws, amendments, and executive orders increased the coverage to more than 90 percent of the federal civil service.

The Supreme Court put an even heavier lid on the spoils system in *Elrod v. Burns* in 1976 and *Branti v. Finkel* in 1980. In those two cases, the Court used the First Amendment to forbid government officials from discharging or threatening to discharge public employees solely for not being supporters of the political party in power, unless party affiliation is an appropriate requirement for the position involved. Additional curbs on political patronage were added in *Rutan v. Republican Party of Illinois* in 1990. The Court ruling effectively prevents the use of partisan political considerations as the basis for hiring, promoting, or transferring most public employees. An exception was permitted, however, for senior policy positions, which usually go to officials who will support the programs of the elected leaders.

The Hatch Act of 1939.   The growing size of the federal bureaucracy created the potential for political manipulation. In principle, a civil servant is politically neutral. But civil servants certainly know that it is politicians who pay the bills through their appropriations and that it is politicians who decide about the growth of agencies. In 1933, when President Franklin D. Roosevelt set up his New Deal, a virtual army of civil servants was put on board to staff the numerous new agencies that were created to cope with the problems of the

PENDLETON ACT (CIVIL SERVICE REFORM ACT OF 1883)
This law, as amended over the years, remains the basic statute regulating federal employment personnel policies. It established the principle of employment on the basis of merit and created the Civil Service Commission to administer the personnel service.

CIVIL SERVICE COMMISSION
The central personnel agency of the national government created in 1883.

DID YOU KNOW?

That the federal government owns one-third of the land in the United States (744 million acres), an area the size of all the states east of the Mississippi River plus Texas?

HATCH ACT (POLITICAL ACTIVITIES ACT)
This 1939 act prohibits the use of federal authority to influence nominations and elections or the use of rank to pressure federal employees to make political contributions. It also prohibits civil service employees from active involvement in political campaigns.

Great Depression. Because the individuals who worked in these agencies owed their jobs to the Democratic party, it seemed natural for them to campaign for Democratic party candidates. The Democrats controlling Congress in the mid-1930s did not object. But in 1938, a coalition of conservative Democrats and Republicans took control of the Congress and forced through the **Hatch Act**—the **Political Activities Act**—of 1939.

The main provision of this act is that civil service employees cannot take an active part in the political management of campaigns. It also prohibits the use of federal authority to influence nominations and elections and outlaws the use of bureaucratic rank to pressure federal employees to make political contributions.

In 1972, a federal district court declared the Hatch Act prohibition against political activity to be unconstitutional. The U.S. Supreme Court, however, reaffirmed the challenged portion of the act in 1973, stating that the government's interest in preserving a nonpartisan civil service was so great that the prohibitions should remain.[7]

In June 1990, Congress passed legislation that would have significantly changed the Hatch Act by allowing three million federal civil service and postal employees to organize voter registration drives, hold office in political party organizations, and serve as delegates to presidential nominating conventions. The act also would have allowed the solicitation of campaign funds from coworkers on behalf of federal employee union political action committees (PACs). Opponents of the legislation argued that it would significantly weaken the Hatch Act, politicize the bureaucracy, and erode public trust in government. President Bush vetoed the legislation, saying that he didn't want to change a law that has "successfully insulated the federal service from the undue political influence that would destroy its essential political neutrality." Congress failed to override the veto. Some of Bush's critics argued that his veto was purely political, pointing out that a majority of federal civil servants are Democrats.

The Carter Reforms

The Civil Service Commission worked well, according to many students of the bureaucracy. But a persistent group of reformers felt it had taken on too many tasks. President Carter, a particularly concerned critic, worked out a reform package with his head of the Civil Service Commission, political scientist Allen K. Campbell. Among the reforms they proposed, and that were finally adopted by Congress in its reform bill passed on October 13, 1978, was one splitting the Civil Service Commission into the Office of Personnel Management (OPM) and the Merit Systems Protection Board (MSPB).

The Office of Personnel Management. In charge of hiring for most of the federal agencies, the members of OPM are appointed by the president and confirmed by the Senate. Among the elaborate rules that OPM has established for hiring, promotion, and firing is one requiring competitive examinations for most civil service jobs. Assuming an applicant passes that examination, she or he is then sent to an agency that has a job with skills that fit the applicant's own. For each federal agency job that is open, the OPM uses the "rule of

[7]*United States Civil Service Commission v. National Association of Letter Carriers,* 413 U.S. 548 (1973).

three," sending three names to the agency for consideration. In general, the agency has to hire someone on this list.

Within the civil service, each individual hired is assigned a general schedule, or GS, rating (Table 14-2). In 1990, the salary range extended from $9,619 to $86,682 (but Congress limits it to $70,800).

The Merit Systems Protection Board.   The Merit Systems Protection Board was created as an independent agency with an independent staff, whose goal is to protect the integrity of the federal merit system. The MSPB undertakes studies of the merit system. It hears charges of wrongdoing and appeals of adverse agency actions against civil servants. It can order corrective and disciplinary action against executive agencies (or employees—but that is rare). The MSPB also has an independent legal staff, which investigates prohibited personnel practices and can prosecute officials who violate civil service rules and regulations.

The Senior Executive Service.   Another major reform of the civil service that President Carter obtained in the 1978 Civil Service Reform Act was the creation of a **Senior Executive Service (SES)**, a corps of about 8,500 high-level administrators and managers. The purpose of establishing the SES was to award top-ranking civil servants for superior performance by making those who choose to join eligible for substantial cash bonuses.

Risk and reward go hand in hand, however, so that anybody who joins the SES has less job tenure and can be transferred more easily within an agency or to another agency. But the lure of cash bonuses for merit has apparently been sufficient to outweigh the decreased job security. Of those eligible to join the SES (approximately seven thousand), 98.5 percent did join—a far greater number than had been anticipated.[8]

■ CURRENT ATTEMPTS AT BUREAUCRATIC REFORM

As long as federal bureaucracy exists, there will continue to be attempts to make it more open, efficient, and responsive to the needs of the American citizen. The most important actual and proposed reforms in the last few years include grade banding, sunshine and sunset laws, privatization and more protection to so-called whistle-blowers.

Grade Banding

The 1978 Civil Service Reform Act encouraged, among other things, merit pay experiments in the federal government. The China Lake Naval Weapons Center began an experiment in merit pay in 1980. The practice, called "grade banding," consists of grouping similar occupations together and combining from two to four GS pay levels into broader "pay bands" or "grade bands." This allows supervisors to have more flexibility in offering starting salaries, rewarding persons for excellence with incentive raises, and penalizing poor performers with low or no pay raises. This can all be done without reclassifying positions into higher GS levels, a process that is cumbersome and that cannot be used to reward individual cases.

[8]Office of Personnel Management, Government Printing Office, *Civil Service Reform: A Report on the First Year* (Washington, D.C.: January 1980), p. 5.

SENIOR EXECUTIVE SERVICE (SES)
A corps of about 8,500 high-level government administrators created in 1978 to provide rewards and incentives for top-ranking civil servants.

TABLE 14-2
GS Ratings and Their Respective Minimum Salaries, 1990

GS-1	$ 9,619
GS-2	10,816
GS-3	11,802
GS-4	13,248
GS-5	14,822
GS-6	16,521
GS-7	18,358
GS-8	20,333
GS-9	22,458
GS-10	24,732
GS-11	27,172
GS-12	32,567
GS-13	38,727
GS-14	45,763
GS-15	53,830
GS-16	63,135
GS-17	73,958*
GS-18	86,682*

*These rates are applicable to the "super grade" officers but have been limited by Congress to $70,800.

SOURCE: *Current Salary Schedules of Federal Officers and Employees* (Washington, D.C., U.S. Government Printing Office, 1990).

Social worker interviewing a client.

Sunshine Laws

GOVERNMENT IN THE SUNSHINE
ACT
Requires that all multiheaded federal
agencies conduct their business regularly
in public session.

In 1976, Congress enacted the **Government in the Sunshine Act.** It required
for the first time that all multiheaded federal agencies—about fifty of them—
hold their meetings regularly in public session. The bill defined *meetings* as
almost any gathering, formal and informal, of agency members—including
conference telephone calls. The only exceptions to this rule of openness are
discussions of matters such as court proceedings or personnel problems, and
these exceptions are specifically listed in the bill.

Sunset Laws

SUNSET LEGISLATION
A law requiring that an existing program
be regularly reviewed for its effectiveness
and terminated unless specifically
extended as a result of this review.

A potential type of control on the size and scope of the federal bureaucracy
is **sunset legislation,** which would place government programs on a definite
schedule of congressional consideration. Unless Congress specifically reau-
thorized a particular federally operated program at the end of a designated
period, it would automatically be terminated; that is, its sun would set.

The idea of sunset legislation was first suggested by Franklin D. Roosevelt
when he created the plethora of New Deal agencies. His assistant, William O.
Douglas, recommended that each agency's charter should include a provision
allowing for its termination in ten years. Only an act of Congress could re-
vitalize it. Obviously, FDR's and Douglas's proposal was never adopted. It
wasn't until 1976 that a state legislature—Colorado's—adopted sunset legislation for state regulatory commissions, giving them a life of six years before
their sun set. Today thirty-five states have some type of sunset law.

In 1978, the Senate passed legislation that would require review of most
federal programs every ten years, but since then the House has not passed its
own version of the Senate bill.

Privatization

PRIVATIZATION, or CONTRACTING
OUT
The replacement of government paid-for
products and services by private firms.

One approach to bureaucratic reform is **privatization,** or **contracting out.**
Privatization involves replacing government services with services from the

private sector. For example, the government might contract with private firms to operate prisons. Supporters argue that some services could be provided more efficiently by the marketplace. Another privatization scheme is to furnish vouchers to clients in lieu of services. For example, it has been proposed that instead of federally supported housing assistance, the government offer vouchers that recipients could use to "pay" for housing in privately-owned buildings. Privatization also includes selling government assets. The Reagan administration proposed selling the naval petroleum reserve oil fields at Elk Hills, California, and Teapot Dome, Wyoming, to private companies. Another proposal is that AMTRAK passenger rail service be sold to private business or to states or local governments.

Helping Out the Whistle Blowers

The term **whistle blower** as applied to the federal bureaucracy has a special meaning; it is someone who blows the whistle on a gross governmental inefficiency or illegal action. One of the most famous whistle blowers is A. Earnest Fitzgerald, who worked for the Defense Department as a cost analyst. In 1968, Fitzgerald went before a congressional committee, claiming that the Lockheed C-5A transport plane had cost more than Congress had appropriated for it. He also pointed out that the plane was not worth the money. Upon close scrutiny, his accusations proved to be accurate, but Mr. Fitzgerald was fired. A court ordered the Defense Department to give him back his job, and a later decision awarded him $350,000 in back pay and damages.[9]

In 1982, another whistle-blower, George Spanton, working as a $50,000-a-year Pentagon auditor, accused Pratt-Whitney Aircraft of overcharging the federal government $150 million. His reward for whistle blowing was a bitter struggle with his own superiors at the Pentagon's Defense Contract Audit Agency. Spanton's boss tried to get him transferred to another job within the agency, but Spanton filed an appeal with the Merit Systems Protection Board charging that the transfer was in retaliation for his "candid audits." The special counsel to the board supported Spanton and even filed disciplinary charges against Spanton's superiors.

Congress included some protection for whistle blowers in the 1978 Civil Service Reform Act. Specifically, that act prohibits reprisals against whistle blowers by their superiors, and it set up the Merit Systems Protection Board as part of this protection. There is little evidence, though, that potential whistle blowers truly have received much improved protection. An attempt by Congress to increase that protection was vetoed by President Reagan in 1988.

Many federal agencies also have toll-free hot lines that employees can use to report, anonymously, bureaucratic waste and inappropriate behavior. About 35 percent of all calls are followed up. Some result in dramatic savings for the government. The General Accounting Office hot line was reported to have generated $26 million in savings in 1989 alone. Further, excluding crank calls, the hot line received more than ten thousand calls during that period, which resulted in three hundred cases of conviction or reprimand.

WHISTLE BLOWER
Someone who brings to public attention gross governmental inefficiency or an illegal action.

George Spanton.

[9]Kenneth Bredemeier, "Tapes Show Nixon Role in Firing of Earnest Fitzgerald," *Washington Post,* March 7, 1979.

■ BUREAUCRATS AS POLITICIANS AND POLICY MAKERS

The bureaucracy and its individual employees are supposed to be nonpolitical, but we have seen that political activity is natural within the bureaucratic setting. Although the majority of persons working for an organization are not likely to be politically active, we cannot say that their agencies and departments are politically neutral. The civil service as a whole is interested in survival and expansion because that is how its members stay employed. Each agency and department is also interested in survival and expansion, which means they are constantly, if quietly, battling each other for a share of the budget and to retain or expand their functions and staff. Every agency attempts to gain the good will of the White House and of the Congress for these ends.

The various bureaucratic agencies of the federal government are specifically prohibited from lobbying Congress directly. Nonetheless, bureaus and agencies have developed a number of techniques to help them gain political support. Each organization generally maintains a congressional information office, which specializes in helping members of Congress by supplying requested information or solving casework problems. The Defense Department has earned a reputation for being able to create good publicity for itself and thus support on Capitol Hill. When Congress began to consider seriously the prospect of cutting costs by reducing or eliminating expenditures on the B-2 Stealth bomber, the air force held highly visible flying demonstrations of the radically designed aircraft, which had until that time been kept under wraps, supposedly in the interests of national security. Even the secretaries of the departments are expected to lobby the president for support of their budget and programs. This kind of politicking from people whom the president appointed to support his own objectives can lead to considerable tension between the White House and the departments.

Theories of **public administration** once assumed that bureaucracies do not make policy but only implement the laws and policies promulgated by the president and legislative bodies. A more realistic view of the role of the bu-

PUBLIC ADMINISTRATION
The science of managing public organizations.

The Stealth Bomber.

reaucracy in policy making, which is now held by most bureaucrats and elected officials, is that the agencies and departments of government play important roles in policy making. Many government rules, regulations, and programs are in fact initiated by the bureaucracy, based on its expertise and scientific studies. How a law passed by Congress is eventually translated into concrete action—from the forms to be filled out to decisions about who gets the benefits—is usually determined within each department. Even the evaluation of whether a policy achieved its purpose is usually based on studies that are commissioned and interpreted by the agency administering the program.[10]

We can try to understand the bureaucracy's policy-making role by examining what has been called the "**iron triangle.**"

The Iron Triangle

Consider the bureaucracy within the Department of Agriculture. It consists of 113,147 individuals working directly for the federal government and thousands of other individuals who, directly or indirectly, work as contractors, subcontractors, or consultants to the department. Now consider that there are various interest, or client, groups that are concerned with what the federal government does for farmers. These include the American Farm Bureau Federation, the National Cattleman's Association, the National Milk Producers Association, the Corn Growers Association, and the Citrus Growers Association. Finally, go directly to Congress and you will see that there are two major committees concerned with agriculture in the House and in the Senate: the House Committee on Agriculture and the Senate Committee on Agriculture, Nutrition, and Forestry, each of which has seven subcommittees.

Figure 14-4 is a schematic view of the iron triangle. This triangle, or subgovernment, is an alliance of mutual benefit among some unit within the bureaucracy, its interest or client group, and committees or subcommittees of Congress and their staff members. The workings of the iron triangle are complicated, but well established in almost every subgovernment.

Consider again the Department of Agriculture. The secretary of agriculture is nominated by the president (and confirmed by the Senate) and is nominally the boss of the Department of Agriculture. But that secretary cannot even buy a desk lamp if Congress does not approve the appropriations for Agriculture's budget. Within Congress, the responsibility for considering the Department of Agriculture's request for funding belongs first to the House and Senate Appropriations committees and to the Agriculture subcommittees under them. The members of those committees, most of whom represent agricultural states, have been around a long time. They have their own ideas about what is appropriate for the Agriculture Department's spending. They have their own program concepts. They carefully scrutinize the ideas of the president and the secretary of agriculture.

Finally, the various interest groups—including producers of farm chemicals and farm machinery, consumer groups, agricultural cooperatives, grain dealers, and exporters—have vested interests in whatever the Department of Agriculture does and in whatever Congress lets the Department of Agriculture do. Those interests are well represented by the lobbyists who crowd the halls of Congress. Many lobbyists have been working for agricultural pressure groups

[10]See, for example, Francis E. Rourke, ed., *Bureaucratic Power in National Politics* (Boston: Little, Brown, 1965).

IRON TRIANGLE
The three-way alliance among legislators, bureaucrats, and interest groups to make or preserve policies that benefit their respective individual interests.

FIGURE 14-4
The Iron Triangle

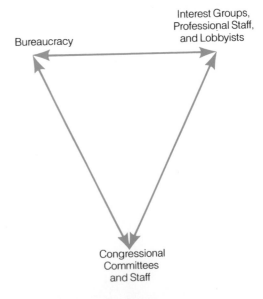

Bureaucracy

Interest Groups, Professional Staff, and Lobbyists

Congressional Committees and Staff

for decades. They know the congressional committee members and Agriculture Department staff extremely well and routinely meet with them. Industry representatives may be named to administrative positions in the Department of Agriculture, or they may be former bureaucrats. When the president or others propose policies that benefit or harm the natural interests or constituents of groups of the triangle, they present a united front either to pass or to oppose such legislation.

Such iron triangles—of which there are many, not only on Capitol Hill, but also in state capitols—at times have completely thwarted efforts by the president to get the administration's programs enacted.

Congressional Control of the Bureaucracy

Is the bureaucracy so strong that Congress cannot control it? Some cynics say yes. But others point out that Congress has a variety of controls over the federal bureaucracy, including the ultimate control—the purse, or the appropriations check. One could reasonably argue that the power of the purse has not been used very often. After all, the real size of the federal administrative budget has increased many times since, say, World War II. In some instances, Congress may control the bureaucracy by cutting off its funds, but in general it does not. Since bureaucrats know their continued funding is a function of previous funding, they make every effort to assure that previous funding is completely spent. Actually, they make sure that any fiscal year's funding is completely spent down to the last penny. If it were not spent, Congress might not provide at least the same amount of funding for the following fiscal year.

Some argue that Congress has encouraged bureaucratic growth by formulating laws that are vague—but vague for a reason. One observer claims that Congress ultimately creates credit for itself by creating an ever-larger bureaucracy with increasingly ill-defined goals:

> Legislation is drafted in very general terms, so some agency, existing or newly established, must translate a vague policy mandate into a functioning program, a process that necessitates the promulgation of numerous rules and regulations and, incidentally, the trampling of numerous toes. At the next stage, aggrieved and/or hopeful constituents petition their Congressman to intervene in the complex . . . decision processes of the bureaucracy. The cycle closes when the Congressman lends a sympathetic ear, piously denounces the evils of bureaucracy, intervenes in the latter's decisions, and rides a grateful electorate to even more impressive electoral showings. Congressmen take credit coming and going.[11]

If there is any truth to this statement, the probability of our seeing a reduction in the bureaucracy in our lifetimes is quite small.

[11]Morris P. Fiorina, *Congress: Keystone of the Washington Establishment* (New Haven, Conn.: Yale University Press, 1977), p. 49.

GETTING INVOLVED

What Does the Government Know About You?

The federal government collects billions of pieces of information on tens of millions of Americans each year. These are stored in files and gigantic computers and often are exchanged between agencies. You probably have at least several federal records (for example, those in the Social Security Administration, the Internal Revenue Service, and, if you are male, the Selective Service).

The 1966 Freedom of Information Act requires that the federal government release, on your request, any identifiable information it has in the administrative agencies of the executive branch. This information can be about you or about any other subject; however, ten categories of material are exempted (classified material, confidential material dealing with trade secrets, internal personnel rules, personal medical files, and the like). To request material, you must write the Freedom of Information Act officer directly at the agency in question (let's say the Department of Education). You must also have a relatively specific idea about the document or information you wish to obtain.

A second law—the Privacy Act of 1974—gives you access specifically to information the government may have collected about you. This is a very important law because it allows you to review your records on file with federal agencies (for example, with the Federal Bureau of Investigation) and to check those records for possible inaccuracies. Cases do exist in which two people with similar or the same names have had their records confused. In some cases, innocent persons have had criminal records from someone else erroneously inserted in their files.

If you wish to look at any records or find out if an agency has a record on you, write to the Agency Head or Privacy Act Officer, address it to the specific agency, state that "under the provisions of the Privacy Act of 1974, 5 U.S.C. 522a, I hereby request a copy of (or access to) . . .," and then describe the record you wish to investigate.

If you have trouble finding out about your records or wish to locate an attorney in Washington, D.C., to help you with this matter, you can contact:

Lawyer Referral Service
Washington Bar Association
1819 H St., N.W., Suite 300
Washington, D.C. 20036
202-223-1484

CHAPTER SUMMARY

1. Although not directly referred to in the Constitution, the functions of the "fourth branch" of government are implied in Article II, Sections 2 and 3.

2. In theory, bureaucracies are defined by hierarchical organizational charts with clear lines of authority and division of labor.

3. Although government employment at the federal level has remained relatively stable in the past several decades, it has increased at the state and local levels. A large percentage of the labor force is employed directly or indirectly by the government.

4. There are four major types of government organizations in which the federal bureaucrats are employed: (1) cabinet departments, (2) independent executive agencies, (3) independent regulatory agencies, and (4) government corporations.

5. The fourteen cabinet departments are the major service organizations of the federal government. They are directly accountable to the president and are responsible for performing broad governmental functions.

6. There are numerous independent agencies that report directly to the president and have a single function. One example is the General Services Administration, established in 1949 to centralize the purchasing and management of property.

7. Regulatory agencies, also independent of the cabinet departments, are charged with making and implementing rules and regulations designed to protect the public interest. Their functions combine executive, legislative, and judicial powers.

8. Major government corporations include the Tennessee Valley Authority, the U.S. Postal Service, and AMTRAK.

9. The federal bureaucracy has a long history, originating with the Jefferson administration's first permanent government organization. In 1828, President Andrew Jackson instituted the spoils system and replaced Jefferson's "elite" with his own political allies.

10. In 1883, Congress passed the Civil Service Reform Act, which was intended to make ability rather than personal or party loyalty the criterion for choosing federal workers. It established the merit system and created the Civil Service Commission to administer personnel services.

11. The Hatch Act of 1939 prohibits civil service employees from taking an active part in political campaigns and prohibits the use of federal authority to influence nominations and elections.

12. President Carter's reform package split the Civil Service Commission into the Office of Personnel Management and the Merit Systems Protection Board. The OPM is the hiring agency, and the MSPB investigates personnel practices.

13. President Carter's 1978 Civil Service Reform Act created the Senior Executive Service to provide rewards and incentives to top-ranking civil servants for superior performance.

14. Current attempts at bureaucratic reform include grade banding, or grouping similar occupations and combining GS pay levels to allow supervisors more flexibility in personnel dealings; sunshine laws, for establishing "openness" in government operations; sunset laws, for placing government programs on a definite schedule of congressional consideration; privatization, or contracting out; and encouraging individual reporting of bureaucratic wrongdoing and waste.

15. The alliance of congressional committees, bureaucratic agencies, and interest groups that influences policy making has been called "the iron triangle."

16. The ultimate control that Congress has over bureaucracy is the appropriations process.

QUESTIONS FOR REVIEW AND DISCUSSION

1. Why did the federal bureaucracy grow so tremendously in the twentieth century? Why has it remained relatively stable in recent decades while the state and local bureaucracies continue to grow?

2. Although Congress often attacks the bureaucracy as overgrown and inefficient, it has done little to reform it. Why is Congress unlikely to make major reforms in the bureaucracy?

3. Tales of $5,000 screwdrivers being purchased by the army abound. Who is responsible for such inefficiencies? What role do private interests play in making the government inefficient?

4. If you were on a government commission to streamline the federal bureaucracy, how would you reorganize the departments, independent agencies, and regulatory commissions? Could some of these organizations be combined so that the president would have more direct control over them? Or would you grant them more independence from the president's authority?

SELECTED REFERENCES

Cole Blease Graham, Jr., and Steven W. Hays, *Managing the Public Organization* (Washington, D.C.: Congressional Quarterly Press, 1986). This book distinguishes sharply between private and public sector management and thoroughly explores such practical topics as planning, organization, staffing, co-ordination, reporting, budgeting, and evaluation.

David Burnham, *A Law Unto Itself: The IRS and the Abuse of Power* (New York: Random House, 1990). A very critical study of the role of the Internal Revenue Service, the largest, most powerful, and least accountable enforcement agency in the federal government.

David Lowery and William D. Berry, *Government Growth in the United States* (New York: Praeger, 1986). An excellent effort to review past explanations of government growth and then test empirically the reasons for growth of government in the United States in the post-World War II era.

Kenneth J. Meyer, *Politics and the Bureaucracy: Policymaking in the Fourth Branch of Government* (Monterey, Calif.: Brooks/Cole, 1986). The impact of bureaucracy on policy making (as opposed to simple policy implementation) is explored in this book. Includes suggestions on how to channel, structure, and control bureaucratic policy making.

Dennis D. Riley, *Controlling the Federal Bureaucracy* (Philadelphia: Temple University Press, 1987). An analysis of the power of the bureaucracy and its relationship to other political institutions.

Bernard Rosen, *Holding Government Bureaucracies Accountable* (New York: Praeger, 1984). The principal focus of this book is the question of accountability of the bureaucracy to the executive, legislative, and judicial branches of government and to interest groups and citizens, with suggestions on how such accountability can be strengthened.

CHAPTER 15

THE JUDICIARY

CHAPTER CONTENTS

WHAT IF . . . FEDERAL JUDGES WERE ELECTED?

It is commonly argued that the federal judiciary is, and many say ought to be, insulated from the fierce winds of politics. The notion of a Supreme Court justice having to go out to the populace to attempt to save his or her job on the Court every few years would be unseemly to many Americans.

While there certainly is a lot to be said for having the federal courts act impartially, it must be kept in mind that judges in most states have long been elected.

Many state judicial officers would not be in power except by the will of the voters. Even appointed judges, such as the justices on the U.S. Supreme Court, are nominated to office through the highly political apparatus of presidential appointment, followed by either the confirmation or rejection of that nomination by the U.S. Senate. Moreover, judges on the federal courts are not necessarily out of tune with changing political attitudes.

There is the general sense among judicial experts, as expressed pointedly by the humorist Finley Peter Dunne, that "'th' Supreme Court follows th' iliction returns." In fact, the surest way to get a federal judiciary

that is to your liking politically is to vote for presidents and U.S. senators who have taken campaign positions in support of hiring judges with certain specific views on major issues. The federal courts, in this sense, have always been part of the electoral process.

What might happen if we did elect federal judges, up to and including the Supreme Court? One possibility is that the public's wishes, as measured, for example, in public opinion polls or in national referenda on key issues, could be put into effect more rapidly and more certainly. If strong majorities of the public were to favor, say, a federal flag-burning law or an end to legalized abortion, then that is the way that the courts might be expected to rule. However, the uneven track record of Congress and the presidents of the United States in translating popular will into public policy suggests that success through this process is not at all assured.

Another real possibility is that the federal judiciary would become as thoroughly influenced by special interest groups (such as large corporations, labor unions, or ideologically motivated political action committees) as the Congress and the presidency. That would undoubtedly increase the cost of the electoral process overall, as judi-

cial candidates would be added to those running for legislative and executive office who seek millions of dollars from organized interests. It may even happen that judges would run on "tickets" with candidates for the presidency or for other offices, so that when you voted for a new team in the White House you also would be voting for a set of judges.

Think, too, about what might happen if your judicial

candidates lost and you, as, say, a registered Republican, were in court against a Democrat and had to have your case argued before a panel of Democratic judges. The federal judicial system as it is currently constituted is, of course, not always fair or free of bias; nonetheless, the chances that overt partisanship might enter into the administration of justice may increase the likelihood of decisions that are arbitrary and capricious or vindictive against the losing party.

Keep in mind, though, that many of the decisions that are made by judges are about obscure clauses in tax laws, bureaucratic regulations, or other complicated points regarding statutes and rules that even expert lawyers can't disentangle. Voters would not pay attention to these arcane arguments and would probably vote much as they do for congressional representatives or U.S. senators, with the candidate's party label (if the elections are partisan), personality, and name recognition deciding most elections.

---

1. *Who might benefit if federal judges were popularly elected?*
2. *Is it possible for any judiciary to be free of political motivation?*
3. *How does public opinion currently affect judicial behavior?*

We have just examined a hypothetical federal judiciary in which judges and justices were elected rather than appointed. Of course, the federal judiciary is 100 percent appointed in the United States, but that does not mean the judicial branch of the federal government is apolitical. Indeed, our courts play a larger role in making public policy than in any other country in the world today. As Alexis de Tocqueville, the nineteenth-century French commentator on American society, noted, "Scarcely any political question arises in the United States that is not resolved, sooner or later, into a judicial question."[1] Our judiciary forms part of our political process. The instant judges interpret the law, they become actors in the political arena—policy makers working within a political institution. As such, the most important political force within our judiciary is the United States Supreme Court. Because of its preeminence, we devote the major portion of this chapter to it. The remainder of the chapter is devoted to the lower federal courts and the state court system.

■ THE FOUNDATION OF AMERICAN LAW: THE COURTS AND *STARE DECISIS*

Because of its colonial heritage, most of American law is based on the English legal system. In 1066, the Normans conquered England, and William the Conqueror and his successors began the process of unifying the country under their rule. One of the ways they did this was to establish the King's Court,

[1]Alexis de Tocqueville, *Democracy in America* (New York: Schocken Books, 1961).

Swearing in the jury.

COMMON LAW
Judge-made law that originated in England from decisions shaped according to prevailing custom. Decisions were reapplied to similar situations and gradually became common to the nation. Common law forms the basis of legal procedures in the American states.

PRECEDENT
A court rule bearing on subsequent legal decisions in similar cases. Judges rely on precedents in deciding cases.

STARE DECISIS
"To stand on decided cases." The policy of courts to follow precedents established by the decisions of the past.

or *Curia Regis.* Before the conquest, disputes had been settled according to local custom. The King's Court sought to establish a common or uniform set of rules for the whole country. As the number of courts and cases increased, the more important decisions of each year were gathered together and recorded in yearbooks. Judges settling disputes similar to ones that had been decided before used the yearbooks as the basis for their decisions. If a case was unique, judges had to create new laws, but they based their decisions on the general principles suggested by earlier cases. The body of judge-made law that developed under this system is still used today and is known as the **common law.**

The practice of deciding new cases with reference to former decisions, that is, according to **precedent,** became a cornerstone of the English and American judicial system and is embodied in the doctrine of *stare decisis* ("to stand on decided cases").

The rule of *stare decisis* performs many useful functions. First, it helps the courts to be more efficient. It would be time consuming if each judge had to establish reasons for deciding what the law should be for each case brought before the court. If other courts have confronted the same issue and reasoned through the case carefully, their opinions can serve as guides.

Second, *stare decisis* makes for a more uniform system. All courts try to follow precedent, and thus different courts will often use the same rule of law. (Some variations occur, however, because different states and regions follow different precedents.) Also, the rule of precedent tends to neutralize the personal prejudices of individual judges to the degree that they feel obliged to use precedent as the basis for their decision.

Finally, the rule makes the law more stable and predictable than it otherwise would be. If the law on a subject is well settled, someone bringing a case to court can usually rely on the court to make a decision based on what the law has been.

Sometimes a court will depart from the rule of precedent because it has decided that the precedent is no longer valid—for example, that changes in technology, business practice, or society's attitudes require a change in the law. But judges are reluctant to overrule precedent, and whether they do so will depend on the case, the number and prestige of prior decisions, the degree of social change that has occurred, and the identity of the deciding court. (The Supreme Court of the United States, when deciding a constitutional question, is the highest authority in the land and is therefore freer to reverse the direction of the law than a lower court.)

Sometimes there is no acceptable precedent on which to base a decision, or there are conflicting precedents. In these situations, a court will (1) refer to past decisions that may be similar to the current case and decide the case by reasoning through analogy; (2) look at social factors—changes in the status of women, for example—that might influence the issues involved; and (3) consider what the fairest result would be.

Cases that overturn precedent often receive a lot of publicity, and it might seem that they are fairly common. In reality, the overwhelming majority of cases are decided according to the rule of *stare decisis.*

■ MORE RECENT SOURCES OF LAW

Today, courts have sources other than precedent to consider when making their decisions. These sources are described in the following pages.

Constitutions

The constitutions of the federal government and the states set forth the general organization, powers, and limits of government. The U.S. Constitution is the supreme law of the land. A law in violation of the Constitution, no matter what its source, may be declared unconstitutional and thereafter cannot be enforced. Similarly, the state constitutions are supreme within their respective borders (unless they conflict with the U.S. Constitution or laws and treaties made in accordance with it).

Statutes and Administrative Regulations

Statutes enacted by Congress and the state legislatures are a source of law. Ordinances passed by cities, counties, and other local political bodies are also included. Rules and regulations issued by **administrative agencies** are another source. Legislative bodies and administrative agencies have assumed an ever-increasing share of lawmaking. Today, much of the work of courts consists of interpreting these laws and regulations and applying them to circumstances in cases before the courts.

Judicial Review

The process for deciding whether a law is contrary to the mandates of the Constitution is known as **judicial review.** The power of judicial review is nowhere mentioned in the U.S. Constitution. Rather, this judicial power was first established in the famous case of *Marbury v. Madison* (see Highlight in this section), which determined that the Supreme Court had the power to decide that a law passed by Congress violated the Constitution:

> It is emphatically the province and duty of the Judicial Department to say what the law is. Those who apply the rule to a particular case, must of necessity expound and interpret that rule. If two laws conflict with each other, the courts must decide on the operation of each.[2]

The Supreme Court has ruled parts or all of acts of Congress to be unconstitutional only 138 times in its history through 1987. State laws, however, have been declared unconstitutional by the Court much more often—about 1,000 times (see Table 15-1). Most of these rulings date from the period after the Civil War, before which time only two acts of Congress were declared unconstitutional. There have been two periods of relatively extensive use of the process of judicial negation—from 1921 to 1940, when a conservative Court upheld private interests over public statutes, and in the 1960s and 1970s, when more liberal justices upheld individual and group rights to racial and political equality.

A recent significant case of judicial review was the ruling by the Supreme Court in 1983 that outlawed the practice of the *legislative veto* by which one or both chambers of Congress could overturn decisions made by the president or by executive agencies.[3] This single declaration of unconstitutionality affected several dozen separate statutes and reinforced the Court's position as an enforcer of the separation of powers principle.

[2]5 U.S. (1 Cranch) 137 (1803).
[3]*Immigration and Naturalization Service v. Chadha*, 462 U.S. 919 (1983).

JUDICIAL REVIEW
The power of the courts to declare acts of the executive, legislative, and judicial branches unconstitutional. First established in *Marbury v. Madison.*

ADMINISTRATIVE AGENCIES
Agencies that usually form part of the executive branch, plus independent regulatory agencies and independent agencies; for example, the Federal Trade Commission, the Securities and Exchange Commission, and the Federal Communications Commission.

TABLE 15-1
Number of Supreme Court Rulings of Unconstitutionality

Decade	Congress	State Legislatures
1789–1800	0	0
1801–1810	1	2
1811–1820	0	6
1821–1830	0	8
1831–1840	0	2
1841–1850	0	9
1851–1860	1	9
1861–1870	7	22
1871–1880	4	39
1881–1890	4	43
1891–1900	5	29
1901–1910	9	36
1911–1920	8	99
1921–1930	15	131
1931–1940	14	74
1941–1950	2	49
1951–1960	7	53
1961–1970	20	138
1971–1980	16	83
1981–1987	15	101
TOTAL	138	932

SOURCE: Library of Congress, *The Constitution of the United States of America: Analysis and Interpretation* (Washington, D.C.: Government Printing Office, 1986), pp. 1883–2093, and *1988 Supplement,* pp. S127–S141.

HIGHLIGHT

Judicial Review—Marbury v. Madison (1803)

In the edifice of American public law, the *Marbury v. Madison* decision in 1803 can be viewed as the keystone of the constitutional arch. The story is often told, and for a reason—it shows how seemingly insignificant cases can have important and enduring results.

Consider the facts behind *Marbury v. Madison*. John Adams had lost his bid for reelection to Thomas Jefferson in 1800. Adams, a Federalist, thought the Jeffersonian Republicans (Anti-Federalists) would weaken the power of the national government by asserting states' rights. He also feared the Anti-Federalists' antipathy toward business. During the final hours of Adam's presidency, he worked feverishly to "pack" the judiciary with loyal Federalists by giving what came to be called "midnight appointments," just before Jefferson took office.

All of the judicial commissions had to be certified and delivered. The task of delivery fell on Adam's secretary of state, John Marshall. Out of the fifty-nine midnight appointments, Marshall

John Marshall.

delivered only forty-two. He assumed that the remaining seventeen would be sent out by Jefferson's new secretary of state, James Madison. Of course, the new administration refused to cooperate in packing the judiciary: Jefferson refused to deliver the remaining commissions. William Marbury, along with three other Federalists to whom the

James Madison.

commissions had not been delivered, decided to sue. The suit was brought directly to the Supreme Court seeking a **writ of mandamus,** authorized by the Judiciary Act of 1789.

As fate would have it, the man responsible for the lawsuit, John Marshall, had stepped down as Adam's secretary of state only to become chief

---

WRIT OF MANDAMUS
An order issued by a court to compel performance of an act.

It is interesting to contrast the power of the Supreme Court in this country with the equivalent court's lack of power in the British system. In Britain, Parliament is supreme. No court may strike down a law that it passes. The only obstacles that prevent Parliament from acting contrary to the unwritten constitution of Britain are the opinions of the citizens and the consciences of its members.

Although the United States is not alone in having a Supreme Court with the power of judicial review—there are sixty other nations that have something resembling judicial review—the United States is the one country in which such power is truly effective in practice.

■ OUR COURT SYSTEM TODAY

The United States has a dual court system. There are state courts and federal courts. Each of the fifty states, and the District of Columbia, has its own fully developed, independent system of courts. The federal court system derives its power from the U.S. Constitution, Article III, Section 1. Both the federal and state court systems have several tiers of authority. Figure 15-1 shows the

---

HIGHLIGHT

Judicial Review—Marbury v. Madison (1803)

justice. He was now in a position to decide the case for which he was responsible.* Marshall was faced with a dilemma: If he ordered the commissions delivered, the new secretary of state could simply refuse. The Court had no way to compel action because it has no police force. Also, Congress was controlled by the Jeffersonian Republicans. It might impeach Marshall for such an action.** But if Marshall simply allowed Secretary of State Madison to do as he wished, the Court's power would be severely eroded.

Marshall stated for the unanimous Court that Jefferson and Madison had acted incorrectly in refusing to deliver Marbury's commission. However, Marshall also stated that the highest court did not have the power to act as a

*Today any justice who has been involved in the issue before the Court would probably disqualify himself or herself because of a conflict of interest.
**In fact, in 1805, Congress did impeach Supreme Court Justice Samuel Chase, a Federalist, though he was not convicted. The charge was abusive behavior under the Sedition Act.
***3 U.S. (3 Dallas) 171, (1796).

court of **original jurisdiction** in this particular case, because the section of the law that gave it original jurisdiction was unconstitutional. The Judiciary Act of 1789 specified that the Supreme Court could issue writs of mandamus as part of its original jurisdiction, but Marshall pointed out that Article III of the Constitution, which spelled out the Supreme Court's original jurisdiction, did not mention writs of mandamus. In other words, Congress did not have the right to expand the Court's jurisdiction, so this section of the Judiciary Act of 1789 was unconstitutional and hence void.

The decision avoided a showdown between the Federalists and the Jeffersonian Republicans. The power of the Supreme Court was enlarged: "A law repugnant to the Constitution is void."

Was the Marshall Court's assumption of judicial review power justified by the Constitution? Whether or not it was, *Marbury v. Madison* confirmed a doctrine that was part of the legal tradition of the time. Indeed, judicial review was

a major premise (although not articulated) on which the movement to draft constitutions and bills of rights was ultimately based, as well as being part of the legal theory underlying the Revolution of 1776. During the decade before the adoption of the federal Constitution, cases in at least eight states involved the power of judicial review. Also, the Supreme Court had considered the constitutionality of an act of Congress in *Hylton v. United States,*** in which Congress's power to levy certain taxes was challenged. But since that particular act was ruled constitutional, rather than unconstitutional, this first federal exercise of true judicial review was not clearly recognized as such.

In any event, since Marshall masterfully fashioned a decision that did not require anyone to do anything, there was no practical legal point to challenge. It still stands today as a judicial and political masterpiece.

---

components of the federal and state judiciary. On the federal side are ninety-six U.S district courts, which are the basic **trial courts** in the federal system. The majority of cases that are appropriately within the **jurisdiction** of the federal courts start here.[4]

There are other federal trial courts. These have special, or limited, jurisdiction. They include the tax courts, which decide cases involving taxpayers' challenges to tax assessments, and the bankruptcy courts, which interpret and apply the federal bankruptcy laws. The U.S. Claims Court hears lawsuits against the government based on the Constitution, federal laws, and contracts. The Claims Court also decides cases concerning salaries of public officials, payment of money to persons unjustly imprisoned for federal crimes, and some Native American claims. The Court of International Trade hears cases involving taxes on imported merchandise.

When cases that have been decided in a federal trial court are appealed, they usually go to one of the judicial circuit courts of appeals, the boundaries of which are outlined in Figure 15-2 (or to the federal circuit court of appeals). Under normal circumstances, the decisions of the courts of appeals are final,

ORIGINAL JURISDICTION
The authority of a court to hear a case in the first instance.

TRIAL COURTS
Those courts in which most cases usually begin, where questions of fact are examined.

JURISDICTION
The authority of a court to decide certain cases. All courts do not have the authority to decide all cases. Where a case arises and what its subject matter is are two jurisdictional factors.

---

[4]The jurisdiction of the federal courts is limited by Article III, Section 2, of the U.S. Constitution.

FIGURE 15-1
Our Dual Judicial System
*Other special courts within the federal system are the U.S. tax court, U.S. bankruptcy court, court of international trade, and claims court.

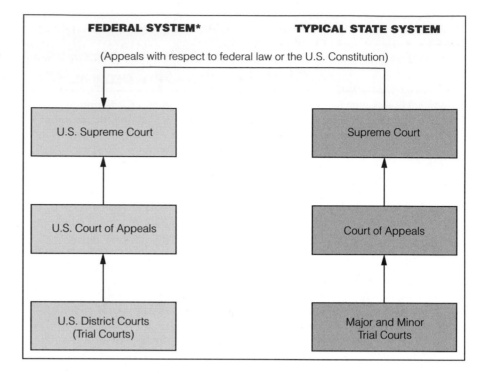

but appeal to the United States Supreme Court is possible. At the top of the federal judiciary is the Supreme Court of the United States. According to the language of Article III of the U.S. Constitution, there can only be one Supreme Court, with all other courts in the federal system "inferior" to it.

A typical state system, shown on the right-hand side of Figure 15-1, also has three tiers. At the bottom, we see minor and major trial courts, where the majority of cases originate. Some of these cases require juries—that is, people selected to hear the evidence and decide questions of fact. The number of jurors may vary, although in most states twelve is the number. In most states, jury verdicts must be unanimous. If jurors cannot agree, a new trial is held or the case is dropped. In the middle of the figure are one or more state **appellate courts,** often called intermediate courts. These courts only hear appeals from the trial courts. And every state has its highest court, usually called a supreme court.[5] The decision of each state's highest court on all questions of state law is final. It is only when issues of federal law are involved that a state's highest court can be overruled by the Supreme Court of the United States.

APPELLATE COURTS
Those courts that review decisions reached by lower courts.

■ THE EARLY YEARS OF THE SUPREME COURT

Alexander Hamilton, writing in *The Federalist Papers,* No. 78, believed that the Supreme Court would be the "least dangerous branch" of the federal government because it had no enforcement powers, nor could it raise money— the other two branches had to cooperate with it and the public had to accept its decisions, or the Supreme Court would be superfluous.

[5]In New York, Maryland, and the District of Columbia, it is called the court of appeals. In West Virginia, it is called the supreme court of appeals. In Massachusetts and Maine, it is called the supreme judicial court.

In its earliest years, it appeared that Hamilton's prediction would come true. The first Supreme Court chief justice, John Jay, resigned to become governor of New York because he thought the Court would never play an important role in American society. The next chief justice, Oliver Ellsworth, quit to become envoy to France. In 1801, when the federal capital was moved to Washington, somebody forgot to include the Supreme Court in the plans: It met in the office of the clerk of the Senate until 1935.

Of the total number of cases that are decided each year, those reviewed by the Supreme Court represent less than one-half of 1 percent. Included in these, however, are decisions that profoundly affect our lives—even issues of life and death. In recent years, the U.S. Supreme Court has dealt with capital punishment, affirmative action programs, abortion, busing, and pornography.

DID YOU KNOW?

That George Washington appointed more Supreme Court justices (ten, including three who served as chief justice) than any other president?

■ WHICH CASES REACH THE SUPREME COURT?

Many people are surprised to learn that in a typical case there is no absolute right of appeal to the United States Supreme Court. The Supreme Court is given original, or trial court, jurisdiction in a small number of situations. Under Article III, Section 2, Paragraph 2, the Supreme Court has original jurisdiction in all cases affecting foreign diplomats and in all cases in which a state is a party. The Eleventh Amendment, passed in 1798, removed from the

FIGURE 15-2
Geographical Boundaries of Federal Circuit Courts

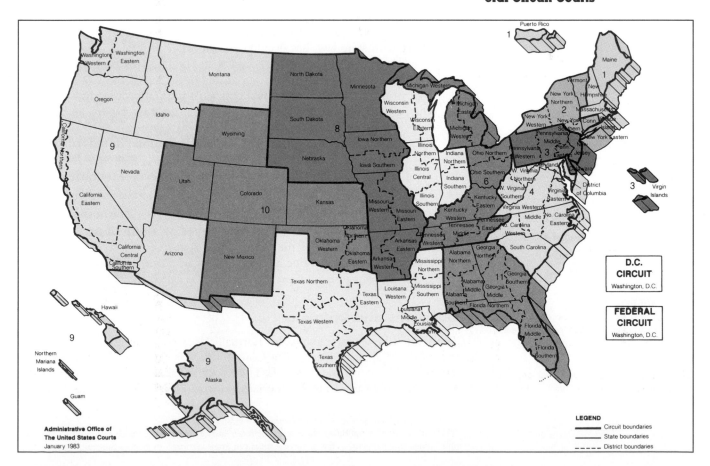

DID YOU KNOW?

That the chief justice of the
United States has the same salary
as the vice president?

WRIT OF CERTIORARI
An order issued by a higher court to a
lower court to send up the record of a
case for review. It is the principal vehicle
for U.S. Supreme Court review.

RULE OF FOUR
A U.S. Supreme Court procedure
requiring four affirmative votes to hear
the case before the full Court.

ORAL ARGUMENTS
The verbal arguments presented in person
by opposing counsel.

judicial power of the United States suits commenced by, or prosecuted against, citizens of another state or by citizens or subjects of any foreign state. Therefore, the Supreme Court today rarely acts as a court of original jurisdiction. In all other cases, its jurisdiction is appellate "with such Exceptions, and under such Regulations as the Congress shall make." Appellate jurisdiction involves the authority of the Court to review decisions of a lower court.

Writ of Certiorari

With a **writ of certiorari,** the Supreme Court orders a lower court to send it the record of a case for review. A party can petition the Supreme Court to issue a writ of certiorari. Typically, however, only petitions that raise the possibility of important constitutional questions or problems of statutory interpretation are granted writs of certiorari. Within these limits, the granting of certiorari (or "cert," as it is popularly called) is done entirely at the discretion of the Court and seems to depend on factors such as who the petitioners are, the kinds of issues, and the ideologies of the individual justices.

The following situations indicate when the Court will issue a writ, although they are not a limit on the Court's discretion:

1. When a state court has decided a substantial federal question that has not been determined by the Supreme Court before or the state court has decided it in a way that is probably in disagreement with the trend of the Supreme Court's decisions.
2. When two federal courts of appeals are in disagreement with each other.
3. When a federal court of appeals has decided an important state question in conflict with state law, has decided an important federal question not yet addressed by the Court but which should be decided by the Court, has decided a federal question in conflict with applicable decisions of the Court, or has departed from the accepted and usual course of judicial proceedings.
4. When a federal court of appeals holds a state statute to be invalid because it violates federal law.
5. When the highest state court holds a federal law invalid or upholds a state law that has been challenged as violating a federal law.
6. When a federal court holds an act of Congress unconstitutional and the federal government or one of its employees is a party.

Most petitions for writs of certiorari are denied. A denial is not a decision on the merits of a case, nor does it indicate agreement with the lower court's opinion. (The judgment of the lower court remains, however.) Therefore, denial of the writ has no value as precedent.[6] The Court will not issue a writ unless at least four justices approve of it. This is called the **rule of four.**[7]

Decisions and Opinions

The United States Supreme Court normally does not hear any evidence, as is true with all appeals courts. The Court's decision in a case is based on the abstracts, the record, and the briefs. The attorneys can present **oral arguments,** after which the case is taken under advisement. When the Court has reached

[6]*Singleton v. Commissioner of Internal Revenue,* 439 U.S. 940 (1978).
[7]The "rule of four" is modified when seven or fewer justices participate, which occurs from time to time. When that happens, as few as three justices can grant certiorari to go to a full-scale appeal.

a decision, the decision is written. It contains the **opinion** (the Court's reasons for its decision), the rules of law that apply, and the judgment. In general, the Court will not **reverse** findings of fact unless the findings are unsupported or contradicted by the evidence. Rather, it will review the record for errors of law. If the Supreme Court feels that a reversible error was committed during the trial or that the jury was improperly instructed, the judgment will be reversed. Sometimes the case will be **remanded** (sent back to the court that originally heard the case) for a new trial or other proceeding. In many cases, the decision of the lower court is **affirmed,** resulting in enforcement of that court's judgment or decree.

The Court's written opinion is sometimes brief and unsigned; this is called a *per curiam* opinion. Often it is long and signed by all those justices who agree with it. Usually, when the chief justice is in the majority, he will write the opinion or assign it to another justice who agrees with him. Whenever the chief justice is in the minority, the senior justice on the majority side decides who writes the opinion.

There are four types of written opinions for any particular case decided by the Supreme Court. When all justices unanimously agree on an opinion, the opinion is written for the entire Court (all the justices) and can be deemed a **unanimous opinion.** When there is not a unanimous opinion, a **majority opinion** is written, outlining the views of the majority of the justices involved in the particular case. Often one or more justices who feel strongly about making or emphasizing a particular point that was not made or emphasized in the unanimous or majority written opinion will write a **concurring opinion.** That means the justice writing the concurring opinion agrees with the conclusion given in the unanimous or majority written opinion (concurs) but for different reasons. Finally, in other than unanimous opinions, one or more dissenting opinions are usually written by those justices who did not agree with the majority. The **dissenting opinion** is important because it often forms the basis of the arguments used years later that cause the Court to reverse the previous decision and establish a new precedent.

Group-Sponsored Litigation and the Supreme Court

In Chapter 8, we discussed the role of interest groups in the United States. Interest groups play an important role in our judicial system, because they **litigate**—bring to trial—most cases of race or sex discrimination and virtually all civil liberties cases, as well as more than one-third of criminal cases and those involving business matters. In 1928, for example, interest groups filed **amicus curiae briefs** in fewer than 2 percent of the cases decided by the Supreme Court, but more than 50 percent are accompanied by such briefs today.

Interest groups see litigation as a political strategy complementing other activities, such as helping individuals favorable to the groups' causes to be elected to Congress or to the presidency. There are numerous litigating organizations today, such as the Washington Legal Foundation, the Capital Legal Foundation, and the Pacific Legal Foundation (which normally seek pro-business judicial outcomes), and the Center for the Study of Responsive Law and the Public Interest Research Group (which normally seek proconsumer and proenvironment judicial outcomes). The interest group (or the litigating organization it supports) will directly challenge a law or administrative ruling

OPINION
The statement by a judge or a court of the decision reached in a case tried or argued before them. It expounds the law as applied to the case and details the reasons on which the judgment was based.

REVERSE
To annul or make void a judgment on account of some error or irregularity.

REMAND
To send a case back to the court that originally heard it.

AFFIRM
To declare that a judgment is valid and right and must stand.

UNANIMOUS OPINION
Agreement of all judges on the same opinion or determination.

MAJORITY OPINION
The views of the majority of the judges.

CONCURRING OPINION
An opinion, prepared by a judge who supports the decision of the majority of the court, but wants to make or clarify a particular point or to voice disapproval of the grounds on which the decision was made.

DISSENTING OPINION
A separate opinion in which a judge dissents from the conclusion reached by the majority of the court and expounds his or her own views about the case.

LITIGATE
To engage in a legal proceeding.

AMICUS CURIAE BRIEFS
Latin for "friend of the court"; refers here to persons or groups not parties to a case, but who have an interest in its outcome. These briefs are documents filed with the court that contain legal arguments for a particular desired outcome in a case.

HIGHLIGHT

Do Students Lose Their First Amendment Rights at the Schoolhouse Door?

In May 1983, Robert Reynolds, the principal of Hazelwood East High School near St. Louis, Missouri, ordered that two articles scheduled to appear in the school-sponsored student newspaper be deleted. One article dealt with student pregnancy, the other with the effects of parents' divorces on Hazelwood High students. The principal argued that the articles didn't properly protect student identities and dealt with subjects not suitable for younger students. He also asserted his right to censor the paper.

Three students working on the paper, *The Spectrum,* sued, arguing that their First Amendment right to free expression had been violated. After a **bench trial,** the U.S. District Court for the Eastern District of Missouri held that the students' First Amendment

rights had not been violated. The court argued that school officials may restrain a student's speech when this seems "reasonable" and when it is related directly to a school activity.

The case was appealed, and the U.S. Court of Appeals for the Eighth Circuit reversed the decision. The court held that the newspaper was a public forum because it was intended as a "conduit for student viewpoint" and that school officials were entitled to censor only if the publication could have resulted in a lawsuit against the school.

On a writ of certiorari, the United States Supreme Court, in *Hazelwood School District v. Cathy Kuhlmeier,* on January 13, 1988, reversed the court of appeals' ruling by a vote of five to three. Justice Byron White, writing for the majority, argued that "school offi-

cials may impose reasonable restrictions on the speech of students, teachers, and other members of the school community." The majority also noted that student rights "are not automatically coextensive with the rights of adults in other settings."

In his dissent, Justice William Brennan (joined by Justices Marshall and Blackmun) said the decision might make public schools into "enclaves of totalitarianism . . ."

This Supreme Court decision prompted several state legislatures to consider writing specific state laws spelling out student rights and in some cases granting student publications specific privileges against such censorship.

The figure at right shows how this case got to the Supreme Court:

Question: Was the action by the principal a violation of the student editors' First Amendment rights?

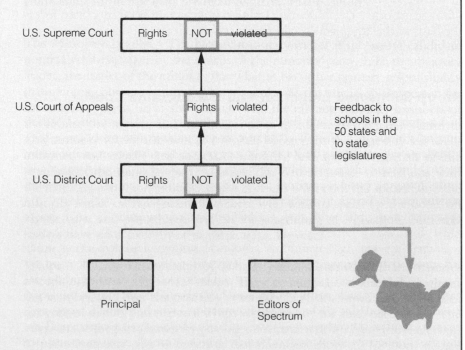

and take it to court. Alternatively, such a group may have an individual test a law in court while the interest group lends financial and legal support to the case.

Sometimes interest groups will start a **class-action suit** in which whatever the court decides will affect all members of a class "similarly situated." Significant recent class-action suits involved individuals suffering injuries associated with use of the Dalkon shield, individuals suffering from asbestos-related injuries, and individuals claiming injuries associated with automobiles, tampons, and chemicals such as formaldehyde, DES, and Agent Orange.

Sometimes interest-group-sponsored challenges to legislation will not be heard by the Supreme Court because the Court decides that a **political question** is involved.

Refusing to Hear a Case—Political Questions

The Supreme Court (and other courts, too) will only hear what are called **justiciable disputes,** which are ones that arise out of actual cases and can be settled by legal methods. When the Court deems a dispute to be a "political question," it will refuse to rule under the doctrine of political questions. Basically, any dispute deemed a political question by the Supreme Court is one that it declares should be decided by the executive branch, or the legislative branch, or those two branches together. For many years, for example, the Supreme Court refused to rule on the constitutionality of laws concerning legislative apportionment, even when they resulted in grossly obvious gerrymandering (see Chapter 12). It was not until 1962 in *Baker v. Carr*[8] that the doctrine of political questions was put aside. No political scientist or legal expert has been able to develop a consistent definition of "political questions" that applies to all of the reasoning of the Court.

After a Decision Is Reached

President Andrew Jackson was once supposed to have said after Chief Justice John Marshall made an unpopular decision[9] that "John Marshall has made his decision; now let him enforce it." This purported quote goes to the heart of **judicial implementation,** or whether court decisions are actually translated into policy and thereby affect the behavior of individuals, businesspersons, police personnel, and the like. The Court does not have the executive power to implement its decisions, nor does it have control of the budget to pay for such implementation when government funds are required. Other units of government have to carry out the Court's decisions.

That means the process of judicial implementation may take time or it may never occur at all. Prayers were banned in public schools in 1962, yet it was (and is still) widely known that the ban was ignored in many southern districts. After the Court ordered schools to desegregate "with all deliberate speed" in 1955,[10] the inflammatory rhetoric against desegregation expounded by the governor and state legislators in Little Rock, Arkansas, encouraged citizens to take the law into their own hands. A riot broke out in 1957, and the

BENCH TRIAL
Trial before a judge, without a jury.

CLASS-ACTION SUIT
A lawsuit filed by an individual seeking damages for "all persons similarly situated."

POLITICAL QUESTION
An issue that the Court believes should be decided by the executive or legislative branches.

JUSTICIABLE DISPUTES
Disputes that raise questions about the law and are appropriate for resolution before a court of law.

JUDICIAL IMPLEMENTATION
The way in which court decisions are translated into policy.

[8]369 U.S. 186 (1962).
[9]*Cherokee Nation v. Georgia,* 30 U.S. (5 Pet.) (1831).
[10]*Brown v. Board of Education of Topeka,* 349 U.S. 294 (1955).

president finally decided to act. President Eisenhower federalized the state's national guard, which quelled the riot.

Initially, the media reporting on Supreme Court decisions provide the most widespread information about what the Court has decided. Often, though, such paraphrased information may be inaccurate. The consumer population of Supreme Court decisions somehow has to become aware of its new-found rights (or the stripping of existing rights). For example, the Supreme Court in *Miranda v. Arizona*[11] in 1966 set guidelines for police questioning of suspects (see Chapter 4). It has been estimated that it took seventeen months before all of the police departments around the country were aware of the decision, and it certainly took even longer for suspected criminals to be aware that they should be "read their Miranda rights."

The Supreme Court at Work

The Supreme Court, by law, begins its regular annual term on the first Monday in October and usually adjourns in late June or early July of the next year. Special sessions may be held after the regular term is over, but only a few cases are decided in this way. More commonly, cases are carried over until the next regular session.

The Court hears oral arguments on Monday, Tuesday, Wednesday, and sometimes Thursday, usually for seven two-week sessions scattered from the first week in October to the end of April or the first week in May. Recesses

[11]384 U.S. 436 (1966).

The Supreme Court chamber.

are held between periods of oral argument to allow the justices to consider the cases and handle other Court business. Oral arguments run from 10 A.M. to noon and again from 1 to 3 P.M., with thirty minutes for each side unless special exception is granted. All statements and the justices' questions are tape recorded during these sessions. Unlike most courts, lawyers addressing the Supreme Court can be questioned by the justices at any time during oral argument.

Deciding a Case: Private Research.   All of the crucial work on accepted cases is done through private research and reflection. Each justice is entitled to four law clerks, recent graduates of law schools, who undertake much of the research and preliminary drafting necessary for the justice to form an opinion. It is sometimes suspected that because of their extensive assistance, the law clerks form a kind of junior court in themselves, deciding the fate of appeals and petitions to the Court. Some disgruntled lawyers have even suggested that the Senate no longer confirm the appointment of justices but rather the appointment of law clerks. Such criticism is probably too harsh. Clerks do help in screening the large volume of petitions and in the preliminary research work for cases under review, but the justices make the decisions.

Deciding a Case: The Friday Conference.   Each Friday during the annual Court term, the justices meet in conference to discuss cases then under consideration and to decide which new appeals and petitions the Court will accept. These conferences take place in the oak-paneled chamber and are strictly private—no stenographers, tape recorders, or video cameras are allowed. There used to be two pages in attendance who waited on the justices while they were in conference, but fear of information leaks caused the Court to stop this practice.[12]

In the justices' conference, certain procedures are traditionally observed. On entering the room, each justice shakes hands with all present. The justices then sit by order of seniority around a large, rectangular table. Each case is discussed by each justice in that order, with the chief justice starting the discussion. The chief justice determines the order in which the cases are called, guides the discussion generally, and in most cases sets the tone for a case.

Starting with the Court of John Marshall, after each discussion a vote was taken in reverse order of seniority. Today, the justices seldom vote formally. Rather, the chief justice gets a sense of what the majority wants by listening to the justices' individual arguments. When each conference is over, the chief justice, if he is in the majority, will assign the writing of opinions. When the chief justice is not in the majority, the most senior justice in the majority assigns the writing. Since 1965, decisions have been announced on any day that they are ready to be released. They are usually presented orally, in summary form, in open session by the author of the decision. Other views may be stated by members who have written concurring or dissenting opinions. Cases that are brought on petition or appeal to the Court are scheduled for an oral argument or denied a hearing in a written "orders list" released on Mondays. After the necessary editing and the publication of preliminary prints, the official Court decision is placed in the *United States Reports,* the official record of the Court's decisions, which is available in most college libraries.

DID YOU KNOW?

That only four American presidents, William Henry Harrison, Zachary Taylor, Andrew Johnson, and Jimmy Carter, appointed no Supreme Court justices?

---

[12]Even though it turned out that one supposed information leak came from lawyers making educated guesses.

■ THE SELECTION OF FEDERAL JUDGES: POLITICS AGAIN

Federal judges are all appointed. The Constitution, in Article II, Section 2, states that the president selects the justices of the Supreme Court with the advice and consent of the Senate.[13] Congress has provided the same procedure for staffing other federal courts. That means that the Senate and the president jointly decide who shall be a federal judge no matter what the level.

Nominating Judicial Candidates

Judicial candidates for federal judgeships are suggested to the president by the Department of Justice, senators, other judges, the candidates themselves, and bar associations and other interest groups.

Since the Truman administration, the American Bar Association, through its Committee on the Federal Judiciary, furnishes the president with evaluations of those individuals being considered. No president is required to refer any nominees to the committee, but most presidents have done so.

The nomination process—no matter how the nominees are obtained—always works the same way: The president does the actual nomination, transmitting the name to the Senate. The Senate then either confirms or rejects. To reach a conclusion, the Senate Judiciary Committee (operating through subcommittees) invites testimony, both written and oral, at its various hearings. In the case of federal district court judgeship nominations, a practice used in the Senate, called **senatorial courtesy,** is a constraint on the president's freedom to appoint whomever he chooses. Senatorial courtesy allows a senator of the president's political party to veto a judicial appointment in his or her state.

Nominating Candidates for Federal District Courts and Courts of Appeals

There are approximately 700 important federal judgeships in the United States, including over 500 district court judgeships and 160 appellate judgeships. Once appointed to such a judgeship, a person holds that job for life. Judges serve until they resign or retire voluntarily. Federal judges may be removed through impeachment although such action is extremely rare. See the Highlight on p. 485 for two recent cases. The selection of such judges is highly political. During the Reagan years, more than 50 percent of the sitting federal judges were appointed by that administration.

District Court Judgeship Nominations. Although the president nominates federal judges, the nomination of district court judges typically originates with a senator or senators of the president's party from the state in which there is a vacancy. If the Committee on the Federal Judiciary of the American Bar Association deems the nominee unqualified, as a matter of senatorial courtesy the president will discuss with the senator or senators who originated the nomination whether the nomination should be withdrawn. Also, when a nom-

SENATORIAL COURTESY
In the case of federal district court judgeship nominations, a Senate tradition allowing a senator of the president's political party to veto a judgeship appointment in his or her state simply by indicating that the appointment is personally "obnoxious." At that point, the Senate may reject the nomination or the president may withdraw consideration of the nominee.

---

[13]The terms *justice* and *judge* are two designations given to judges in various courts. All members of the U.S. Supreme Court are referred to as justices. In most appellate courts, the formal title given to the judge is justice also, although the converse is true in the state of New York.

HIGHLIGHT

Removing a Federal Judge by Impeachment

When U.S. District Judge Alcee Hastings was impeached by the Senate on a charge of conspiracy to obtain a bribery, he became only the sixth federal official in history to be removed from office by impeachment. Judge Hastings was accused of plotting to obtain a $150,000 bribe and lying about this to a jury, which in 1983 had acquitted him. Hastings was Florida's first African-American federal district judge.

This caused many African-American leaders to charge that race played a role in Hastings's impeachment.

Two weeks after the Hastings case, the Senate impeached U.S. District Court judge Walter Nixon, Jr. on charges of lying to a federal grand jury. Nixon was convicted of charges that he told a grand jury he didn't discuss a marijuana charge with a district county attorney in Mississippi. The county at-

torney was prosecuting a case against the son of Wyley Fairchild, a friend of Judge Nixon. Nixon had obtained a very profitable oil and gas investment with the help of Fairchild.

These two cases raised the specter of political impeachment but, since each judge was charged with a federal offense, the impeachments proceeded and the judges were removed.

---

ination is politically unacceptable to the president, he will consult with the appropriate senator or senators to indicate his displeasure and to seek an alternative candidate.

Courts of Appeals Appointments.   Although there are many fewer courts of appeals appointments than district court appointments, they are more important because federal appellate judges handle more important matters, at least from the point of view of the president, and therefore presidents take a keener interest in the nomination process for such judgeships. Also, appointments to the United States courts of appeals have become "stepping stones" to the Supreme Court. Typically, the president culls the Circuit Judge Nominating Commission's list of nominees for potential candidates. The president may also use this list to oppose senators' recommendations that may be politically unacceptable to him.

■ SUPREME COURT APPOINTMENTS AND IDEOLOGY

The nomination of Supreme Court justices belongs solely to the president. That is not to say the president's nominations are always confirmed, however. In fact, almost 20 percent of presidential nominations for the Supreme Court have been either rejected or not acted on by the Senate. Numerous acrimonious battles over Supreme Court appointments have ensued when the Senate and the president have not seen eye to eye about political matters. The U.S. Senate had a long record of refusing to confirm the president's judicial nominations from the beginning of Jackson's presidency in 1829 to the end of Grant's presidency in 1877. During a fairly long period of relative acquiescence on the part of the Senate to presidential nominations, from 1894 until 1968, only three nominees were not confirmed. From 1968 through 1983, however, there were two rejections of presidential nominees to the highest court. Both were Nixon appointees—G. Harold Carswell and Clement Haynsworth. Both were from the South because Nixon wanted to shore up his southern support. Both were rejected because of questions about their racial attitudes. In addition,

Drawing by D. Reilly; © 1990 The New Yorker Magazine, Inc.

"I think it's high time we had an enigma on the Supreme Court."

Supreme Court Justice Anthony M. Kennedy.

one of Lyndon Johnson's nominations was not acted on, and his choice for chief justice in 1968—Abe Fortas, a member of the Court—was withdrawn after a question arose during confirmation hearings involving Fortas's association with an industrialist convicted of securities irregularities. That problem resulted in Fortas's eventual resignation from the Court.

President Reagan found two of his nominees for a Supreme Court vacancy rejected by the Senate. Both were sitting judges on the courts of appeals. In 1987, he first nominated Robert Bork, who faced sometimes caustic grilling by the Senate on his views of the Constitution. His nomination was rejected. Next Reagan nominated Douglas Ginsburg, who ultimately withdrew his nomination when the press reported information about his alleged social use of marijuana during the 1970s. Finally, the Senate approved Reagan's third choice, Anthony M. Kennedy.

Ideology plays an important role in the president's choices for the Supreme Court (and the lower federal courts, too), and ideology plays a large role in the Senate's confirmation hearings. There has been an extremely partisan distribution of presidential appointments to the federal judiciary. In the almost two hundred years of the U.S. Supreme Court's history, fewer than 13 percent of the justices nominated by a president have been from an opposing political party.

■ WHO BECOMES A SUPREME COURT JUSTICE?

The makeup of the federal judiciary is far from typical of the American public. Table 15-2 summarizes the background of all of the 106 Supreme Court justices to 1991. In general, the justices' partisan attachments have been mostly the same as those of the president who appointed them. There have been some exceptions, however. Nine nominal Democrats have been appointed by Re-

TABLE 15-2
Background of Supreme Court Justices to 1991

	Number of Justices (106 = Total)
Occupational Position before Appointment	
Private legal practice	25
State judgeship	21
Federal judgeship	25
U.S. Attorney General	7
Deputy or Assistant U.S. Attorney General	2
U.S. Solicitor General	2
U.S. Senator	6
U.S. Representative	2
State governor	3
Federal executive posts	10
Other	3
Religious Background	
Protestant	84
Roman Catholic	9
Jewish	5
Unitarian	7
No religious affiliation	1
Age on Appointment	
Under 40	5
41–50	30
51–60	57
61–70	14
Political Party Affiliation	
Federalist (to 1835)	13
Democrat Republican (to 1828)	7
Whig (to 1861)	2
Democrat	42
Republican	42
Educational Background	
College graduate	90
Not a college graduate	16
Sex	
Male	105
Female	1
Race	
Caucasian	105
Other	1

SOURCES: Congressional Quarterly, *Congressional Quarterly's Guide to the U.S. Supreme Court* (Washington, D.C.: Congressional Quarterly Press, 1979); *Congressional Quarterly's Guide to Government, Spring 1983* (Washington, D.C., 1982), pp. 108–109; John J. Cound, "The Justices of the Supreme Court in Historical Perspective" in John E. Nowak, Ronald D. Rotunda, and J. Nelson Young, *Constitutional Law,* 3d ed. (St. Paul: West Publishing Co., 1986), pp. 1104–1112; Leon Friedman and Fred L. Israel, eds., *The Justices of the United States Supreme Court, 1789–1969: Their Lives and Major Opinions,* 4 vols. (New York: Chelsea House, 1969); *Information Please Almanac, 1983,* pp. 633–635.

publican presidents, three Republicans by Democratic presidents, and one Democrat by Whig President John Tyler.[14]

[14]Actually, Tyler was a member of the Democratic party who ran with Harrison on the Whig ticket. When Harrison died, much to the surprise of the Whigs, Tyler—a Democrat—became president, although they tried to call him "acting president." Thus there are historians who quibble over the statement that Tyler was a Whig.

As you will note, the most common occupational background of the justices has been private legal practice or state or federal judgeships at the time of their appointment. Those ten justices who were in federal executive posts at the time of their appointment held the high offices of secretary of state, comptroller of the treasury, secretary of the navy, postmaster general, secretary of the interior, chairman of the Securities and Exchange Commission, and secretary of labor. In the "other" category in the table are two justices who were professors of law (including Taft, a former president), and one justice who was a North Carolina state employee with responsibility for organizing and revising the state's statutes.

Most justices were in their fifties when they assumed office, although two were as young as thirty-two and one as old as sixty-six. The average age of newly sworn justices is about fifty-three.

Note also that the great majority of justices have had a college education. By and large, those who didn't attend college or receive a degree lived in the late eighteenth and early nineteenth centuries when a college education was much less common than it is today. In recent years, degrees from such schools as Yale, Harvard, Columbia, and other prestigious institutions have been typical. It is interesting that many of the earlier college-educated justices did not hold their degrees in law. In fact, it was not until 1957 that all the then-current members of the Court were graduates of law schools.

The religious background of Supreme Court justices is strikingly untypical of that of the American population as a whole, even making allowances for changes over time in the religious composition of the nation. Catholics (and certain Protestant denominations, notably Baptists and Lutherans) have been underrepresented, whereas Protestants in general (Episcopalians, Presbyterians, Methodists, and others), as well as Unitarians, have been overrepresented among the justices. Typically, there has been a "Catholic seat" on the Court, with interruptions, and a "Jewish seat" existed without a break from 1916 until 1969, when Fortas resigned.

Justice David Souter, confirmed as a member of the Supreme Court in October, 1990.

■ THE REHNQUIST COURT

William H. Rehnquist (see Profile) became the sixteenth chief justice of the Supreme Court in 1986 after fifteen years as an associate justice. He was known as a strong anchor of the Court's conservative wing. With Rehnquist's appointment as chief justice, it seemed to observers that the Court would necessarily become more conservative. In the past, Rehnquist had dissented from numerous majority opinions. His views on individual liberties seemed to favor a strong state, because the Constitution, according to him, had as its purpose a government that would have direct authority over individuals. Proponents of civil liberties feared that the Rehnquist Court would eventually erode many of those liberties that the previous Courts under Earl Warren (1953–1969) and Warren Burger (1969–1986) had established or maintained.

In 1990 the Rehnquist Court ruled on several extremely important matters that raised the question of the direction in which the court was moving ideologically and caused renewed speculation about the impact on the court if one or more of the aging and ill justices should die or resign and be replaced with Bush appointees. That is precisely what did happen during the summer of 1990, when William Brennan resigned from the Court and President Bush nominated as his replacement David Souter, a judge from New Hampshire.

PROFILE

Chief Justice Rehnquist

"It is basically unhealthy to have so much authority concentrated in a small group of lawyers who have been appointed to the Supreme Court and enjoy virtual life tenure."

O n Tuesday, June 17, 1986, Warren Burger, chief justice of the Supreme Court, announced that he would retire after seventeen years of service. President Ronald Reagan named Supreme Court Justice William Rehnquist to replace Burger as chief justice. Rehnquist had been on the Supreme Court since 1971, when he was nominated by Richard Nixon. Since that time, he has been viewed as one of the Court's most conservative members. He faced a hard chief justice confirmation fight in the Senate because of his conservative views. The Senate ultimately approved his nomination by the smallest margin in the history of the U.S. Senate.

His background includes a B.A. from Stanford University, a master's degree in political science from Harvard, and a degree from Stanford Law School where he graduated first in his class in 1952. He clerked for Supreme Court Justice Robert Jackson in 1952 and 1953 and then practiced law in Arizona, where in 1964 he worked on conservative Barry Goldwater's presidential campaign. Under the Nixon administration in 1969, he became a deputy attorney general and, later, head of the Department of Justice, Office of Legal Counsel, from which he successfully defended the government's program of secret surveillance of anti-Vietnam war groups in the United States.

On many issues, Rehnquist is an almost doctrinaire conservative. For example, he has been the leader in the Court conservatives' efforts to narrow the interpretation of defendants' rights in criminal cases. In recent decisions, he has dissented forcefully when the Court reaffirmed women's rights to abortion and wrote a strong decision upholding Missouri's restrictions on abortion rights.

Personal acquaintances say that Rehnquist is affable and friendly, with great skills at interpersonal relations. One University of Virginia law professor has indicated that he is one of the brightest justices ever to sit on the bench because he writes with style, force, and assurance, as no one else has in recent times. "It is hard to match his agility in shaping a record and marshalling arguments to reach a conclusion."

Professor of Law A. E. Dick Howard, University of Virginia, quoted in *U.S. News & World Report*, June 30, 1986, p. 18.

On June 25, 1990, the court ruled that states may require teenagers to notify both parents before obtaining an abortion, as long as the state provides the possibility of a judicial hearing for pregnant young women who don't want to tell their parents. This ruling in two cases, one from Ohio and the other from Minnesota, was seen as a further restriction on a woman's right to choice. The ruling was extremely significant because when the judgment was handed down, thirty-two states had laws on the books requiring some form of parental notification and several states were considering such laws.

In the Ohio ruling, the conservative majority of the Court was joined by Justice John Paul Stevens for a six-to-three vote. The Court upheld the Ohio law requiring unmarried women under the age of eighteen either to notify one parent or obtain a judge's permission before getting an abortion. In the Minnesota case, the court on a five-to-four vote upheld what at that point was the nation's strictest law, requiring notification of both parents but also pro-

Supreme Court Justice Antonin Scalia.

viding the option of a judicial hearing. Because of the addition of more conservative appointees during the Reagan administration, there no longer appears to be a majority which views abortion as a fundamental constitutional right.

The mood and direction of the Court was also revealed in a so-called "right to die case." By a vote of five to four, the Court ruled that the state of Missouri can sustain the life of a woman who has been in a complete coma (a "persistent vegetative state") for over seven years because her family could not demonstrate with "clear and convincing evidence" that the woman, Nancy Cruzan, would have wanted her treatment terminated. However, all the justices except Antonin Scalia supported in their written arguments the principle that, as part of the "liberty" guaranteed by the Fourteenth Amendment's due process clause of the Constitution, a person has the right to refuse unwanted medical treatment. This was the first time the court had addressed that issue.

The case is particularly fascinating because just weeks earlier, Dr. Jack Kevorkian provided Mrs. Janet Adkins, a fifty-four-year-old woman suffering from Alzheimer's disease, with access to an intravenous device he had invented which allowed her to commit suicide. The justices' opinions do not appear to endorse suicide per se or helping a person commit suicide. However, the ruling will no doubt affect cases such as that of Dr. Kevorkian.

■ JUDICIAL ACTIVISM AND JUDICIAL RESTRAINT

JUDICIAL ACTIVISM
A doctrine advocating an active role for the Supreme Court in enforcing the Constitution and in using judicial review. An activist Court takes a broad view of the Constitution and involves itself in legislative and executive matters by altering the direction of activities of Congress, state legislatures, and administrative agencies.

JUDICIAL RESTRAINT
A doctrine holding that the Court should rarely use its power of judicial review or otherwise intervene in the political process.

Judicial scholars like to characterize different Supreme Courts and different Supreme Court justices as being either activist or restraintist. Those advocating the doctrine of **judicial activism** believe that the Court should use its power to alter the direction of the activities of Congress, state legislatures, and administrative agencies. Those advocating the doctrine of **judicial restraint** believe the Court should use its powers of judicial review only rarely. In other words, whatever popularly elected legislatures decide should not be thwarted by the Supreme Court so long as such decisions are not unconstitutional.

During the early years of the nation, the Supreme Court certainly was in no position to exercise judicial activism. Indeed, in *The Federalist Papers,* Alexander Hamilton stated that "the judiciary is beyond comparison the weakest of the three departments of power." The Supreme Court during its first decade justified that remark, because it handled few matters and decided only one important case.

Alexis de Tocqueville, an astute French observer of American institutions in the early nineteenth century, appreciated the position of the Court in the American constitutional system, however. He stated that "the supreme court is placed higher than any known tribunal. . . . The peace, the prosperity, and the very existence of the Union are vested in the hands of the seven [now nine] Federal judges."

The difference between activist judges and those who exercise restraint is not the same as the difference between political liberals and conservatives. In the early 1930s, for example, the Supreme Court was activist and conservative, ruling that much regulation of business was unconstitutional. In the later 1930s, however, the Court became restrained and liberal, ruling that similar business regulation was constitutional.

In the 1950s and 1960s, the Court was activist and liberal. Many of the Court's critics believed it should have exercised more restraint. They criticize

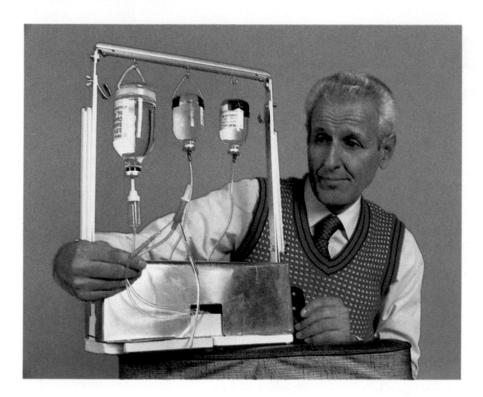

Dr. Jack Kevorkian shows his machine for allowing patients to choose to die rather than face continued pain or illness. How can a society control the availability of such methods?

the first *Brown* decision in 1954 (see Chapter 5) on the grounds that the highest court settled a problem that should have been resolved by Congress or have been left to the states. Critics of the current courts call them "mini-legislatures." They argue, for example, that in *Baker v. Carr*[15] the federal courts wrongly exercised jurisdiction over the issue of state legislative districting plans and that the U.S. Supreme Court had no right to intervene in such a state matter.

Another activist decision in the 1970s was *Roe v. Wade,*[16] in which the Supreme Court gave women the right to an abortion during the first and second trimesters of pregnancy, thereby striking down state statutes permitting abortions only in special cases. Recent Supreme Court decisions have indicated an unmistakable change in the Court's attitude toward civil rights (see Chapter 5). Some critics fear that the current Court, with its conservative majority, will become increasingly activist in this and other areas in the 1990s (see this chapter's Critical Perspective).

The question of judicial activism in closely linked to the actual constraints on our judicial system. We examine these next.

■ WHAT CHECKS OUR COURTS?

Our judicial system is probably the most independent in the world. But the courts do not have absolute independence, for they are part of the political

[15]369 U.S. 186 (1962).
[16]410 U.S. 113, rehearing denied 410 U.S. 959 (1973).

CRITICAL PERSPECTIVE

Will the Federal Judiciary Become More Conservative?

I n the Supreme Court term that ended in June 1990, the liberal wing of the court was virtually neutralized. Legal experts agreed that on ideological issues where liberal and conservative alignment can be measured, the court divided four to five on the conservative side. The liberal justices as of 1990 were William Brennan, eighty-four, Thurgood Marshall, eighty-one, Harry Blackmun, eighty-one, and John Stevens, seventy. The Supreme Court, wrote the *Wall Street Journal* in its June 28, 1990 summary of the session is "now firmly headed in a conservative direction," as can be seen in the table below on the right.

When there *were* liberal decisions, they simply tended to confirm existing policy or rulings rather than break new ground and thus merely slowed down the conservative trend. That was true, for example, in the Court's striking down the flag desecration law, which was based on a similar ruling a year earlier on a Texas law. It was also the case with the ruling that upheld Federal Communications Commission preference programs to help minorities and women obtain broadcast licenses.

With the retirement of Justice Brennan after the close of the 1990 Spring term, President George Bush had an opportunity to make an appointment to the Court. Bush, however, has proven to be a much less ideological conservative than Ronald Reagan. Indeed, Bush in the 1960s and 1970s was considered a relatively moderate-to-liberal Republican. His nomination of New Hampshire judge David Souter to replace Brennan led to some impassioned arguments by leaders of civil rights and women's groups that he was insensitive to their views and their groups' needs, particularly on the issue of abortion.

Recent Supreme Court rulings on business and economic issues are also significant. The Court's decisions in these areas will have a multibillion dollar impact on corporations (pension funds and anticompetitive mergers), as well as on state and federal government tax revenues.

Exercise in Critical Thinking
1. On what basis is the classification of "conservative" and "liberal" made as these labels are applied to Supreme Court justices?
2. If the Bush administration is able to place more conservatives on the Court, what aspects of the American socio-economic-political landscape will likely change, and why?
3. Which groups will benefit most from a more conservative Court and which groups will be hurt the most?

VOTING BLOCS IN THE SUPREME COURT
This chart shows the different voting blocs of five justices and how often they voted together in the Supreme Court's 5–4 decisions. Classifying cases as "5–4" involves some subjective judgments in cases in which the five votes were achieved through multiple opinions.

Conservative-Voting Blocs	
Rehnquist, White, O'Connor, Scalia, Kennedy	17
Rehnquist, Stevens, O'Connor, Scalia, Kennedy	2
Rehnquist, White, Blackmun, O'Connor, Scalia	1
Rehnquist, White, Blackmun, O'Connor, Kennedy	1
Rehnquist, White, Stevens, O'Connor, Scalia	1
Rehnquist, White, Stevens, O'Connor, Kennedy	1
Rehnquist, White, Stevens, Scalia, Kennedy	1

Liberal-Voting Blocs	
Brennan, White, Marshall, Blackmun, Stevens	7
Brennan, Marshall, Blackmun, Stevens, O'Connor	1
Brennan, Marshall, Blackmun, Scalia, Kennedy	1
Brennan, Marshall, Blackmun, Stevens, Kennedy	1
Brennan, Marshall, Stevens, O'Connor, Scalia	1
Rehnquist, Brennan, White, Marshall, Stevens	1

SOURCE: *Wall Street Journal*, June 28, 1990, p. B1.

process. Political checks limit the extent to which courts can exercise judicial review and engage in an activist policy. These checks are exercised by the legislature, the executive, other courts, and the public.

Legislative Checks

Courts may make rulings, but often the legislatures at local, state, and federal levels are required to appropriate funds to carry out the court's rulings. When such funds are not appropriated, the court in effect has been checked. A court, for example, may decide that prison conditions must be improved. Then a legislature has to find the funds to carry out such a ruling.

Courts' rulings can be overturned by constitutional amendments at both the federal and state levels. Many of the amendments to the U.S. Constitution check the state courts' ability to allow discrimination, for example. Recently, though, proposed constitutional amendments created by a desire to reverse courts' decisions on school prayer and abortion have failed.

Finally, legislatures can pass new laws to overturn courts' rulings. This may happen particularly when a court interprets a statute in a way that Congress disapproves or when a court finds no relevant statute to apply in certain cases. The legislature can then pass a new statute to negate the court's ruling.

Executive Checks

Presidents have the power to change the direction of the Supreme Court and the federal judiciary, for the president can appoint new judges who in principle have philosophies more in line with that of the administration. Also, a president, governor, or mayor can refuse to enforce courts' rulings. Recall President Andrew Jackson's comment in response to the Marshall ruling that a state could not pass laws governing Indians on their own territory: "John Marshall has made his decision. Now let him enforce it."

The Rest of the Judiciary

Higher courts can reverse the decisions of lower courts. Lower courts can put a check on higher courts, too. The Supreme Court of the United States, for example, cannot possibly hear all the cases that go through the lower courts. Lower courts can and have ignored, directly or subtly, Supreme Court decisions by deciding in the other direction in particular cases. Only if a case goes to the Supreme Court can the Court correct the situation.

The Public Has a Say

History has shown members of the Supreme Court that if its decisions are noticeably further ahead than, or at odds with, a national consensus, it will lose its support and some of its power. Perhaps the best example was the Dred Scott decision of 1857 in which the Supreme Court held that slaves were not

DID YOU KNOW?

That among the 106 persons who have served on the Supreme Court from 1789 to 1991, only one, Thurgood Marshall, has been black and only one, Sandra Day O'Connor, has been a woman?

citizens of the United States, nor were they entitled to the rights and privileges of citizenship. The Court ruled, in addition, that the Missouri Compromise banning slavery in the territories was unconstitutional. Most observers contend that the Dred Scott ruling contributed to making the Civil War inevitable.

Observers of the court system believe that because of the sense of self-preservation of the judges, they are forced to develop a sense of self-restraint. Some observers even argue that this sense of self-restraint is more important than the other checks just discussed.

GETTING INVOLVED

Changing the Legal System

Although impressed by the power of judges in American government, Alexis de Tocqueville stated:

> The power is enormous, but it is clothed in the authority of public opinion. They are the all-powerful guardians of a people which respects law; but they would be impotent against public neglect or popular contempt.*

The court system may seem all-powerful and too complex to be influenced by one individual, but its power nonetheless depends on our support. A hostile public has many ways of resisting, modifying, or overturning rulings of the court. Sooner or later a determined majority will prevail. Even a determined minority can make a difference. As Hamilton suggested in *The Federalist Papers,* No. 1, the people will always hold the scales of justice in their hands, and ultimately all constitutional government depends on their firmness and wisdom.

One example of the kind of pressure that can be exerted on the court system began with a tragedy. On a spring afternoon in 1980, thirteen-year-old Cari Lightner was hit from behind and killed by a drunk driver while walking in a bicycle lane. The driver turned out to be a forty-seven-year-old man with two prior drunk-driving convictions. He was at that time out on bail for a third arrest. Cari's mother, Candy, quit her job as a real estate agent to form MADD (Mothers Against Drunk Driving) and launched a personal campaign to stiffen penalties for drunk-driving convictions.

The organization grew to 20,000 members with 91 regional offices and a staff of 160. Outraged by the estimated 26,000 lives lost every year because of drunk driving, the group not only seeks stiff penalties against drunk drivers but also urges police, prosecutors, and judges to crack down on such violators. MADD, by becoming involved, has gotten results. Owing to its efforts and the efforts of other citizen-activist groups,

Democracy in America, vol. 1 (New York: Schocken Books, 1961), p. 166.

many states have responded with stronger penalties and deterrents. If you feel strongly about this issue and want to get involved, contact the following:

MADD
5330 Primrose, Suite 146
Fair Oaks, CA 95628
916-966-6233

Several other organizations have been formed by people who want to change or influence the judicial system. A few of them are as follows:

Legal Defense Research Institute
733 N. Van Buren
Milwaukee, WI 53202
414-272-5995

HALT—An Organization of Americans for Legal Reform
201 Massachusetts Ave., NE
Suite 319
Washington, D.C. 20002
205-546-4258

National Legal Center for the Public Interest
1101 17th St., NW
Washington, D.C. 20036
202-296-1683

If you want information about the Supreme Court, contact the following by telephone or letter:

Clerk of the Court
The Supreme Court of the United States
1 First St., NE
Washington, D.C.
202-393-1640

CHAPTER SUMMARY

1. Because of its colonial heritage, most American law is based on the English legal system.

2. The body of judge-made law based on decisions in earlier cases is known as common law.

3. The doctrine of *stare decisis* means that judges attempt to follow precedents established by decisions of the past. The doctrine helps courts to be more efficient, uniform, and stable.

4. The U.S. Constitution is the supreme law of the land. State constitutions are supreme within their respective borders.

5. The process of deciding whether a law is contrary to the mandates of the Constitution is known as judicial review. This judicial power, first established in *Marbury v. Madison* (1803), is not often exercised.

6. For a court to exercise valid authority, it must have jurisdiction over the case.

7. The federal court system is a three-tiered model consisting of (a) trial courts, (b) intermediate courts of appeals, and (c) the Supreme Court.

8. Article III of the Constitution establishes the boundaries of federal judicial power. Federal courts are normally restricted to so-called federal questions.

9. In its earliest years, the Supreme Court was considered the "least dangerous" branch of the federal government because it has no enforcement powers and it cannot raise money.

10. The Supreme Court rarely acts as a court of original jurisdiction. In all other cases, its jurisdiction is appellate. The normal procedure for bringing a case before the Supreme Court is by writ of certiorari.

11. The Supreme Court conveys its decisions in written form. The decision contains the opinion (the Court's reason for its decision), the rules of law that apply, and the judgment.

12. Many interest groups either start litigation or file *amicus curiae* briefs in favor of a particular side in a case. There are numerous conservative and liberal litigation organizations of a public nature that operate today. Some of these organizations, as well as specific interest groups, may start class action suits to benefit all members of a class similarly situated.

13. The Supreme Court (and other courts, too) hears only justiciable disputes arising out of actual cases that can be settled by legal methods. Whenever the Court deems a dispute to be a political question, it will refuse to rule on it.

14. Because the Supreme Court has no police force or "power of the purse," it has to rely on the executive branch, judges on lower courts, police personnel, and other public officials for judicial implementation.

15. The president appoints federal judges with the advice and consent of the Senate. The nomination of district court judges typically originates with a senator or senators of the president's party from the state in which there is a vacancy.

16. Almost 20 percent of presidential nominations for the Supreme Court have been either rejected or not acted on because of partisan considerations, lack of professional qualifications, or disagreement on important policy issues.

17. The makeup of the federal judiciary is far from typical of the American public. Most judges are white, male, Protestant, over age fifty, and college educated.

18. Supreme Courts are characterized as either activist or restraintist. Those advocating judicial activism believe the Court should use its power to alter the direction of the activities of Congress, state legislatures, and administrative agencies. Those advocating judicial restraint believe the Court should use its power of judicial review only rarely.

19. Ronald Reagan appointed William H. Rehnquist as the nation's sixteenth chief justice and added other conservatives to the Supreme Court, including Sandra O'Connor, Anthony Kennedy, and Antonin Scalia. Many of the conservative trends started under the Burger Court may continue under Rehnquist, as the Rehnquist Court has proven itself to be conservative in many areas.

20. There are numerous checks on our courts. They include (a) legislative checks, (b) executive checks, (c) checks by the rest of the judiciary, and (d) checks by the public.

QUESTIONS FOR REVIEW AND DISCUSSION

1. Define "judicial review." Does the Supreme Court "legislate" using this power? In what areas has the Court made major policy decisions by judicial review?

2. An old political saying declares that "the Supreme Court follows the election returns." What factors in the nomination process, the decision process, and the power of the Court make this true?

3. What are the benefits of being a member of the federal judiciary? Why is this such a sought-after position? How would you go about planning a career in the judicial branch?

4. Why is it possible for the law to change radically within a few decades? For example, after World War II, the Communist party was illegal, women were barred from many activities in our society, and the races were legally segregated in many parts of the country. All of those conditions are now legally reversed, mostly due to Court decisions. How does the Court shape our ideas of what is right or what is fair?

SELECTED REFERENCES

Henry J. Abraham, *The Judiciary: The Supreme Court and the Governmental Process,* 7th ed. (Needham Heights, Mass.: Allyn & Bacon, 1987). A classic textbook that treats in much more detail virtually every aspect in the chapter you have just read.

Alan Barth, *Prophets with Honor: Great Dissents and Great Dissenters in the Supreme Court* (New York: Alfred A. Knopf, 1974). Six cases in which dissenting justices had their views vindicated years later when the Court reversed itself.

Sheldon Goldman and Thomas P. Jahnige, *The Federal Courts as a Political System,* 3d ed. (New York: Harper and Row, 1985). Using the systems analysis approach, this book examines inputs, conversions, outputs, feedback, and other processes in a dynamic investigation of the complicated interrelationships of the federal courts' "political system."

William Lasser, *The Limits of Judicial Power: The Supreme Court and American Politics* (Chapel Hill: University of North Carolina Press, 1989). The author examines the role of the Supreme Court in shaping American politics, especially the question of judicial activism and what limits are placed on it.

Leonard W. Levy, *Original Intent and the Framers' Constitution* (New York, Macmillan, 1988). The author examines the strict constructionist versus the loose constructionist point of view with respect to what the Supreme Court should do.

David Neubauer, *America's Courts and the Criminal Justice System,* 3d ed. (Pacific Grove, Calif.: Brooks/Cole, 1988). This book thoroughly covers the major issues facing the criminal courts today including the death penalty, victims' rights, the insanity defense, and the exclusionary rule.

David O'Brien, *Storm Center: The Supreme Court and American Politics,* 2nd ed. (New York: W. W. Norton, 1990). This book treats the controversy surrounding the role of the federal judiciary within the United States' political system.

Lawrence Tribe, *God Save this Honorable Court* (New York: Random House, 1985). A critical review of the Supreme Court written by an outspoken liberal legal scholar.

Bob Woodward and Scott Armstrong, *The Brethren: Inside the Supreme Court* (New York: Simon and Schuster, 1979). A detailed, behind-the-scenes account of Supreme Court decision making on cases dealing with abortion, busing, the Nixon tapes, and obscenity.

A GLOBAL PERSPECTIVE
GLOBAL PUBLIC POLICY MAKING

Everything depends on everything else. A cliché, but perhaps more of a reality in today's world then ever before. The decisions of the public policy makers in Washington, D.C., affect not only Americans but everyone else as well. Sometimes the same is true for our state policy makers. For example, the inability of state and federal government to curtail pollution in the United States has contributed to the problem of acid rain. The continued pollution of our atmosphere creates high-sulfur-content rain that destroys lakes and forests, not just in the United States but in Canada, too. The coal-fired electric power plants, the factories, and the cars in America's northeast corridor are causing fish to die and forests to turn brown and lifeless in remote parts of Canada.

The policies of each sovereign government with respect to nuclear power plant safety are of global proportions. Improper supervision, lack of controls, outdated equipment—any of these can lead to a nuclear meltdown at a power plant. This is exactly what happened in the Soviet Union at Chernobyl in 1986. This tragedy not only affected Soviet citizens but also individuals living as far away as Western Europe who suffered from the radiation. Safety of nuclear power plants is a global, not a local, issue.

Public health policies in each individual nation affect the well-being of all other nations. A case in point is acquired immune deficiency syndrome, or AIDS. The

Clearcutting the Amazon rain forest.

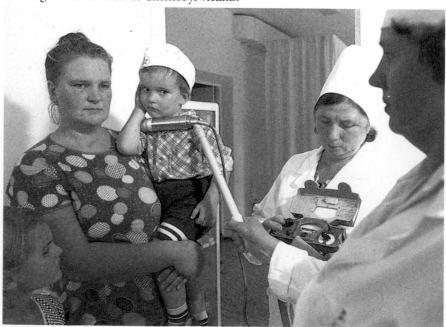

Checking radiation levels in Chernobyl victims.

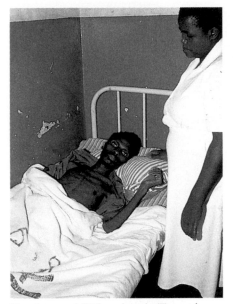

Treating an AIDS patient in Tanzania.

worldwide transmission of this deadly disease has occurred in part because of certain nations' inability to reduce the spread of the disease within their own borders. In parts of Africa, for example, some villages have been swept by AIDS epidemics that have affected more than 30 percent of their populations—men, women, and children. Public health facilities in these areas are practically nonexistent. In parts of the Soviet Union and Romania, the spread of AIDS has been dramatic. Why? Because in those countries, sterile needles for routine shots and intravenous medication procedures are unavailable. The policies in those countries and elsewhere that have resulted in rapid increases in the

number of people infected with the AIDS virus affect everyone—including Americans. When AIDS was first discovered, Americans firmly believed that it was a problem mainly on the African continent; then it was considered a problem mainly associated with homosexual men; then intravenous drug users were included. Now we know the truth—AIDS is a global problem encompassing all demographic groups which everyone has to be concerned about.

A nation's drug policies—whether certain drugs are legal or illegal—has a great impact on other nations. Cocaine and the opiates have been illegal in the United States since 1914, which has led to high prices for those drugs and a subsequent incentive

for poor nations in Latin America and Southeast Asia to provide the products. U.S. drug policies particularly affect the economies of Peru, Bolivia, and Colombia, because they are the main growing and processing centers for coca leaves and cocaine. In the past, U.S. foreign policy with respect to Turkey was guided almost exclusively by this country's attempt to stop the production of the raw materials necessary for heroin processing.

Perhaps no other product typifies the worldwide economy more than oil. Petroleum and petroleum-based products are used throughout the entire world. Crude oil is produced in the North Sea, in the Mideast, in South America, and elsewhere, and shipments of crude oil are

Surveying the coca fields in Peru.

Saudi Arabian oil refinery

made twenty-four hours a day, again virtually everywhere in the world. When one country decides to do something about the "oil situation," policy makers in the United States react. The invasion of Kuwait by Iraq in the summer of 1990, and the threat of a significant percentage of the world production of crude oil being under the control of one person, Saddam Hussein, brought an immediate response from President Bush, the United Nations Security Council, Japan, and many other nations. The foreign policies of the United States may not be completely dictated by our economic interests, but certainly economics plays a large part today since the virtual disappearance of the cold war between the United States and the Soviet Union. Global oil politics—for better or for worse—are here to stay.

The vision of one world includes the potential for huge benefits—improved living conditions, communications, and hope that, together, the more-than-150 nations in the world can prevent planetary disaster. But achieving this potential means that we must recognize the increased interrelationship among all countries—one that requires a global sensitivity on the part of all policy makers.

PUBLIC POLICY

POLITICS OF ECONOMIC POLICY MAKING

WHAT IF . . . THE U.S. DEFAULTED ON THE NATIONAL DEBT?

The United States's national, or public, debt exceeds $2 trillion. It doubled during the eight years of the Reagan administration. Even today, the federal government is adding to the size of the public debt to the tune of anywhere from $100 to $300 billion a year, depending on who is doing the measuring.

Families often go into debt. Indeed, a typical family goes into debt to purchase a house or buy a car. Businesses go into debt, too. Even the most successful and highly profitable corporations in the United States carry debt at all times. In other words, owing money is the American way of life—in the household, in the corporate world, and in government.

Households that take on too much debt find they have difficulty making their payments. When a household misses a few months of payments on a credit account at a local department store, for example, its credit dries up. A bad mark on the household's credit rating will make it more difficult to get credit in the future. If a household misses its payments on a mortgage, something more serious can occur—the mortgage can be foreclosed and the family can lose its house.

Businesses that get into financial trouble sometimes are unable to make payments on loans they have taken out. Even the Donald Trumps of the world sometimes run into a cash

squeeze and have to renegotiate interest payments owed on large debts. When a business doesn't come up with the money it owes to at least pay interest payments, its credit line will be eliminated. In the worst scenario, the business will default on its debt and the business's creditors will force it into bankruptcy.

What if the U.S. government defaulted on the public debt? Certainly, such an event is not impossible. After all, many governments throughout the world have refused to make payments on their own public debt. In the last two decades, some governments have refused to make interest payments (let alone payments on principal) on hundreds of billions of dollars of debt they owe to American, British, and French banks. What if the U.S. did the same with the national debt—that is, simply refused to make the interest payments due on more than $2 trillion that is owed,

not only to Americans but to foreigners?

The first thing that would happen is that the solid-gold platinum-quality highest credit rating of the federal government would drop abruptly. Foreigners would no longer purchase U.S. Treasury bonds at auction. Most certainly, the federal government would no longer be able to finance the deficit that it accrues every year by spending more than it receives in tax dollars. Federal government spending would have to drop dramatically overnight. Many social programs and those related to defense would have to be cut off in midstream.

Another grave consequence is that the American public would lose faith in the federal government's monetary soundness. The market value of all government debt would fall because debt holders would have no notion

about when the government would pay the interest it owes on its debt. These debt holders—numbering in the tens of millions of Americans—would see their wealth fall also. They in turn would invest less and consume less, leading probably to a serious recession if not another Great Depression.

Finally, if the U.S. government defaulted on its public debt, the economies of other western nations would be severely damaged. Much of the debt is held by Japanese, German, and other foreign investors—individual, corporate, and governmental. Defaults by the United States would shake confidence in all financial markets, perhaps leading to a world-wide depression.

Is there a guarantee that the U.S. government would never default on its public debt? The answer is yes. The main guarantee is the taxing power of the federal government. It can always raise taxes to pay for the interest on the public debt. As long as the citizenry is willing to continue to pay taxes, the federal government is not about to default on the public debt.

---

1. *What do you think happened in countries in which the government did default on its public debt?*
2. *Since we owe much of the public debt to ourselves, why would it matter if the federal government defaulted on the public debt?*

At this point in our text we begin to analyze public policy, or the substance of what government does. In particular, we examine national economic policies (Chapter 16), domestic programs (Chapter 17), and foreign policies (Chapter 18). But before we start, we must look at the national policy-making process. How does a problem such as the crisis in the U.S. savings and loan industry get solved? The first thing that has to happen, of course, is for people to be aware of the problem. Policy makers can obtain information on such problems from nationally published statistics. Sometimes policy makers simply have to open their local newspaper to find out that a problem is brewing. This was exactly the situation with the savings and loan problem during virtually all of the 1980s.

Policy makers certainly weren't aware of an impending S & L crisis before 1980. After all, for the previous forty years, very few savings and loan associations—called thrifts in the banking industry—had failed. All this changed in 1980 when 35 thrifts insured by a quasi-governmental agency failed. The number of failures the following year reached 453.[1] With thrift failures running about 500 a year, year in and year out, the public started to get worried. Could the agency that insured deposits (the Federal Savings and Loan Insurance Corporation, or FSLIC) handle the problem? Members of Congress were increasingly being asked this question. The industry was also sending lobbyists (principally from the United States League of Savings Institutions) to Congress to argue that "something" had to be done. Senators and representatives began worrying that massive failures in the S & L industry might lead to a banking panic in the entire United States and might even threaten our international banking status. Proposed bills were put into the legislative hopper. The first result was the 1987 Competitive Banking and Quality Act, which provided for $10.8 billion over three years to help the beleaguered Federal Savings and Loan Insurance Corporation. That turned out to be a drop in the bucket. Thrift industry lobbyists argued that much more was needed. One of the first national problems that the Bush administration had to deal with was the rescue

[1]This number includes outright failures and also those thrifts that couldn't cover their ongoing expenses.

The son of the president, Neal Bush, testifies before Congress on the savings and loan scandal. As a director of Silverado Savings and Loan in Denver, Bush was charged with approving loans that brought personal gain for himself.

DID YOU KNOW?

That at the beginning of 1991, the federal government had over thirty-five thousand real-estate properties worth $50 billion which it was offering for sale as part of its takeover of failing savings and loan institutions, making it the biggest real-estate agent in the world?

of depositors in failed savings and loans. With backing of the administration and intense lobbying by the thrift industry, the Financial Institution Reform, Recovery, and Enforcement Act of 1989 was passed. Depositors breathed a sign of relief and so did the owners of failing thrifts. What remained to be seen was the total cost, a point we turn to shortly.

The problem, the reaction to the problem, and the solution all form part of public policy in the United States. No matter how simple or how complex the problem, those who make policy follow a number of steps. The following section outlines the policy-making process and evaluates its effectiveness.

■ THE POLICY-MAKING PROCESS

How does a nation or state become aware of a problem that governments need to address, and how is a solution arrived at? Based on observation, we can divide the process of policy making into at least five steps:

1. *Agenda building: The issue must get on the agenda.* This occurs through crises, technological change, or mass media campaigns, as well as through strong political personalities. In the case of the savings and loan crisis, members of Congress whose constituents were the managers and owners of savings and loan associations, especially those in trouble, urged congressional action. Congresspersons who received numerous letters and phone calls from concerned depositors in savings and loans associations also urged action.

2. *Agenda formulation: The proposals are discussed among government officials and the public.* Such discussions may appear in the press, on television, in the halls of Congress, and in scholarly journals. Congress holds hearings, the president voices his views, and the topic may become a campaign issue.

3. *Agenda adoption: A specific strategy is chosen from among the proposals discussed.* That is, Congress must enact legislation, or executive departments must write new regulations, or courts must interpret past policy differently. Much of the congressional year, for example, in 1988–89, was taken up by work on the thrift bailout bill. After much debate, a bill was passed and the president signed it.

4. *Agenda implementation: Government action must be implemented by bureaucrats, the courts, police, and individual citizens.* Every law requires someone to carry it out. In the case of the Thrift Bailout Act, Congress dissolved the Federal Savings and Loan Insurance Corporation and created in its place the Savings Association Insurance Fund (SAIF). In addition, the Resolution Trust Corporation (RTC) was created with the purpose of taking over about five hundred failing savings and loan associations and selling their assets. Then Congress had to fund the RTC, which it did initially with $50 billion. The task of the RTC was easier assigned than done. The RTC will be engaged in selling thrifts and trying to recover assets for the next decade.

5. *Agenda evaluation: Increasingly after a policy is implemented, groups undertake policy evaluation.* Groups both inside and outside government perform studies to show what actually happened after a policy was instituted. Such policy evaluations do not always lead anywhere, though, because proponents of the program tend to exaggerate the positive benefits, whereas critics tend to exaggerate the lack of benefits or any negative side effects. Nonetheless, the test of any program is, more and more, its outcome rather than its content. Presidential commissions are often appointed after an obvious failure or crisis

in a program, such as the NASA *Challenger* explosion on January 28, 1986. In our example of the Thrift Bailout Act, evaluation will be difficult because it will take years for the legislation to be completely effected (if it ever is).

It is worth noting that, although the flow of the policy process is well understood, there are competing models of how that process works and to whose benefit. Table 16-1 lists a number of competing models of the policy-making process and gives a brief summary of each.

ECONOMIC POLICY MAKING

Nowhere are the principles of public policy making clearer than in the area of economic decisions undertaken by our federal government. The president and Congress (and to a growing extent the judiciary) are constantly faced with economic choices. Consider some of them:

1. Should more federal funds be spent on helping the homeless?
2. Should Congress pass laws restricting foreigners' ability to buy U.S. companies and real estate?
3. Should more be spent on health care, and consequently less on other programs?
4. Should the federal government require welfare recipients to seek work or engage in additional training?

TABLE 16-1
Selected Models of the Policy-Making Process

1. *The Bureaucratic Politics Model:* In the bureaucratic politics model, the relative power of the large bureaucracies in Washington determines which policy becomes part of the national agenda and which is implemented. This theory of American politics is based on the struggle among competing interest groups.

2. *The Power Elite, or Elitism, Model:* Powerful economic interests determine the outcome of policy struggles, according to the power elite, or elitism, model. The rich, and those who know the rich, determine what gets done. More importantly, the power elite decides what items do *not* get on the public agenda and which items get removed if they are already on it.

3. *The Marxist Model:* Closely aligned with the power elite model is the Marxist model of public policy-making in which the ruling class institutes public policy, often at the expense of the working class.

4. *The Incrementalist Model:* Public policy evolves through small changes or adjustments, according to this model. Consequently, policy makers examine only a few alternatives in trying to solve national problems. A good public policy decision is made when there is agreement among contesting interests, and agreement is obtained most easily when changes are minimal.

5. *The Rationalist Model:* This model, sometimes thought of as a pure textbook abstraction, hypothesizes a rational policy maker who sets out to maximize his or her own self-interest, rather than determining what the public, or collective, interest might be. Rational policy makers will rank goals and objectives according to their benefit to the policy maker. Such a model is often viewed as an alternative to the incrementalist model.

6. *The Systems Model:* The most general, and perhaps the most ambitious, approach to modeling public policy making is a systems approach, in which policy is a product of the relationships between the institutions of government and the socioeconomic-political environment. Such a model has (a) inputs from public opinion and crises, (b) a political process involving legislative hearings, debates, court deliberations, party conventions, and so on, (c) a set of policy outputs consisting of legislation, appropriations, and regulations, and (d) policy outcomes, which may provide, for example, more job security, less unemployment, more research on AIDS, and so on.

POLICY TRADE-OFFS
The cost to the nation of undertaking any one policy in terms of all of the other policies that could have been taken; for example, an increase in the expenditures on one federal program means a reduction in expenditures on another program, or an increase in federal taxes.

In each of these cases, policy makers cannot have clear-cut answers to their public policy questions. Each policy action carries with it a cost and a benefit known to analysts as a **policy trade-off.** The costs are typically borne by one group and the benefits enjoyed by another group.

The Savings and Loan Bailout

Consider the thrift bailout bill. Assume that you are a congressional representative from a state that has a large number of potential savings and loan failures—Texas, for example. You know that unless you get Congress to pass the bailout bill, many of your constituents will lose all that they invested in many of your state's savings and loan associations. You know that your state will be adversely affected by a large number of thrift failures. When the bill is passed, you can breathe a sigh of relief, for you have just helped out your state and many of the investors in its savings and loan associations. In general, the beneficiaries of this act have been the managers and shareholders in poorly run thrifts throughout the country. To a lesser extent, depositors in those thrifts have benefited, although it is not certain how much. After all, their deposits were insured up to $100,000 each. Had the government decided simply to honor those commitments—and nothing else—then very few depositors would have suffered.

We know who benefited from the Thrift Bailout Act. But somebody has to pay—that is true for every policy action. That somebody, in this case, is the American taxpayer. Although a tiny fraction of the bailout will be paid by higher insurance fees assessed against savings and loan associations, the lion's share of the money will come from taxpayers. The question, of course, is how much.

FIGURE 16-1
Breakdown of the Thrift Bailout (estimates of the government's major costs through the year 2029.)
SOURCE: General Accounting Office

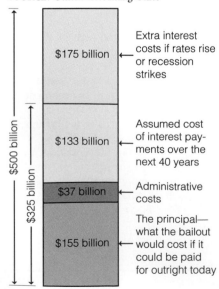

The True Cost of the Savings and Loan Bailout

When the thrift bailout bill was debated in Congress, $50 billion seemed like a reasonable figure for the bailout cost. When the bill was finally passed, the "official" tab was raised to $165 billion. The most current estimate is closer to $500 billion. That means that every man, woman, and child in the United States has committed $2,000 in federal taxes to bail out the nation's thrifts. Figure 16-1 shows this breakdown.

Interest-Group Legislation: The Distribution of Costs and Benefits

We now know that each man, woman, and child may pay up to $2,000 for the savings and loan bailout, but this information was certainly not readily available, at least not to the public and maybe not even to the members of Congress when the bill was debated during the 1988–89 session. All U.S. taxpayers are vaguely aware that government actions cost something, but rarely do they know exactly how much.

On the benefit side, the savings and loan industry had a much better idea of how much it was going to gain from a congressional bailout bill. Through its United States League of Savings Institutions, it lobbied heavily for congressional action. Not surprisingly, more than 160 thrift-industry political action committees (PACs) contributed large amounts of money to congressional candidates—at least $4.5 million during the 1986 and 1988 congressional elections. More than $1 million of those contributions went to members of the House and Senate banking committees. The chairman of House Banking Committee, Henry Gonzalez (D.-Texas) said that "everything the industry has wanted, Congress has rolled over and given to them."

Even if the American public fully realized the individual costs associated with legislation such as the thrift bailout bill, would it devote much time, effort, or money to stopping that legislation? The answer is probably not. But as we just pointed out, those who would clearly benefit from that legislation would and did donate time and money to making sure it passed. It's always easier for interest groups specifically affected by legislation to raise money for candidates and incumbents who will continue to promote and vote for it.

A general rule of special interest-group legislation is: *The more widespread the costs and the more narrowly focused the benefits of government economic policy making, the more of such policy making we will see.* Indeed, that has been the history of much of our economic legislation at the federal, state, and local levels. (See the Critical Perspective for an evaluation of the solution to our banking crisis.)

DID YOU KNOW?

That the first income tax law was passed in 1862 to support the Civil War, but was eliminated in 1872 only to be brought back in 1913 by the Sixteenth Amendment to the Constitution, which gave Congress permanent authority to pass such a tax?

■ MORE LESSONS IN POLITICS: TAXES AND SUBSIDIES

We can extend our political analysis of government economic activities by examining the areas of taxes and **subsidies** (negative taxes). Let's begin with the premise that in the world of taxes and subsidies, *for every action on the part of the government, there will be a reaction on the part of the public.* Eventually, the government will react with another action, followed by the public's further reaction. The **action-reaction syndrome** is a reality that has plagued government policy makers since before the beginning of the Republic.

SUBSIDIES
Negative taxes; usually payments to producers given on a per-unit basis according to the amount of production of a particular commodity.

ACTION-REACTION SYNDROME
For every action on the part of government, there is a reaction on the part of the affected public. Then the government attempts to counter the reaction with another action, which starts the cycle all over again.

The Tax Code, Tax Rates, and Tax Loopholes

An examination of the U.S. Tax Code, encompassing thousands of pages, thousands of sections, and thousands of subsections, gives you some indication that our tax system is not very simple. The 1986 Tax Reform Act was supposed to simplify it somewhat, but once you understand the action-reaction principle of taxation, you can predict that whatever simplification occurred in 1986 will be undone over time.

People are not assessed a lump-sum tax each year; each family doesn't just pay $1,000 or $10,000 or $20,000. Rather, individuals and businesses pay taxes based on tax rates. (Table 16-2 shows the 1990 tax rates for individuals.

TABLE 16-2
1991 Tax Rates for Individuals

SINGLE PERSONS		MARRIED COUPLES	
Marginal Tax Bracket	Marginal Tax Rate	Marginal Tax Bracket	Marginal Tax Rate
Up to $20,349	15%	Up to $33,999	15%
$20,350–$49,300	28	$34,000–$82,150	28
Above $49,300	31	Above $82,150	31

Have We Solved Our Banking Crisis?

You have learned about the politics of the thrift bailout. You have learned about the costs and the benefits. But have we solved the banking crisis? The answer is probably no. There is a fundamental defect in the way in which the federal government insures deposits in the banking industry, not only for savings and loans, but for all depository institutions whether they be banks, savings banks, or credit unions.

The government in effect insures most deposits in the United States up to $100,000. Thrifts and banks have to pay a small insurance premium. The amount they pay is the same, no matter how risky the investments the savings and loan or bank undertakes. This would be equivalent to your being able to purchase auto insurance for the same price whether you lived in the middle of the countryside where there is little theft and few accidents or in the middle of a major city where theft and accidents are common. The result is that some savings and loan associations and banks have decided to make risky, but high-paying, investments. Many times those risky, high-paying investments don't pan out—and the thrift or bank gets in trouble. But the depositors don't have to worry because of deposit insurance.

To understand this risk-taking behavior, put yourself in the position in which you are offered a million dollars to take to Las Vegas. In one situation, the offer requires that in order to share in any profits, you have to share in the losses. In another situation, the offer simply states that you will share in any profits, but won't have to pay any losses. Don't you think your behavior would be different depending on which offer you received? Undoubtedly, if you had the second offer you would be much more reckless, choosing to play those games of chance that had huge jackpots but also very little probability of winning. Your behavior with respect to risk depends on how much you have to pay for any bad luck.

The same has been true in the banking industry. The managers of thrifts and banks, when faced with potential losses, decided to "take the trip to Las Vegas and go for broke." In the banking industry, that's equivalent to loaning out money for very high-risk ventures and charging very high interest rates. In effect, the managers of thrifts and banks who do this pay little of the cost if those high-risk, high-yielding investments go bad, but reap substantial rewards if they turn out well. Since most of them have gone bad, we have had numerous failures every year in the thrift and banking industry.

Because the Thrift Bailout Act of 1989 basically did not change the incentives facing the managers and owners of thrifts and banks, we predict more trouble in the future. Unless the cost of deposit insurance is higher when riskier investments are undertaken by thrifts and banks, many of them will continue to act recklessly. Be prepared for future bailout bills similar to the one that just cost you $2,000.

The banking industry is not the only one that is in trouble, and will continue to be in trouble, because of deposit insurance. The federal government also is backing another $5 trillion of loans. (That was not a typo; the word is indeed *tr*illion.) The government guarantees mortgage money for buying farms through the Farmers' Home Administration. It guarantees $320 billion of mortgages for low- and middle-income people through its Federal Housing Authority (FHA), which is part of the Department of Housing and Urban Development (HUD). It guarantees student loans, and it guarantees loans to veterans. Virtually all of these programs are in trouble. The FHA is losing billions a year. The Farmers' Home Administration has 50 percent of its guaranteed loans in default. Defaults on guaranteed veterans' loans are running at several billion dollars a year.

The worst is probably yet to come with bailouts of government-insured deposits and loans in the United States.

Exercise in Critical Thinking

1. Why couldn't the federal government simply watch more closely over the managers of savings and loan associations to prevent them from making risky investments?
2. Why do you think Congress did not address the basic problem with the structure of deposit insurance in the Thrift Bailout Act?
3. Is the analogy to gambling in Las Vegas appropriate? Why or why not?

HIGHLIGHT

The $50 Billion Headache

Toward midnight on April 15 of every year, post offices throughout the country fill up with anxious patrons. American taxpayers are attempting to beat the deadline for filing the previous year's tax returns. Although each taxpayer may complain about paying taxes, there is more cost to our tax system than what we pay. There is a cost in time and, of course, time is money. The average household spends about twenty-three hours preparing its tax return. The average value of such labor is about $385. Multiply that times 110 million individual tax returns and you get $42.35 billion of time. But that's not all. Households pay an average of $60 to accountants and tax preparers. That adds another $6.6 billion in expenses, for a total of about $50 billion per year.

Before the 1986 Tax Reform Act, individuals faced a total of fifteen separate possible tax rates on taxable income.) The higher the tax rate—the action on the part of government—the greater the public's reaction to that tax rate. Again, it's all a matter of costs and benefits. If the tax rate on all the income you make is 15 percent, that means that any method you can use to reduce your taxable income by $1 saves you 15 cents in tax liabilities that you owe the federal government. Therefore, those individuals paying a 15 percent rate have a relatively small incentive to avoid or evade paying taxes. But consider individuals who were faced with a tax rate of 91 percent in the early 1960s. They had a tremendous incentive to find legal ways to reduce their taxable incomes. For every dollar of income that was somehow deemed nontaxable, the taxpayer would reduce tax liabilities by 91 cents.

So, individuals and corporations facing high tax rates will always react by making concerted attempts to get Congress to add **loopholes** in the tax law that allow them to reduce their taxable incomes. Loopholes are defined as legal methods of avoiding taxes. When the Tax Code imposed very high tax rates

LOOPHOLES
Legal methods by which individuals and businesses are allowed to reduce the tax liabilities owed to the government.

A citizen calculates her income taxes.

PROFILE

Dan Rostenkowski

"When you get a growing resentment about paying taxes, you get a problem with compliance."

Mention tax reform or deficit reduction, and the name Dan Rostenkowski will come up. The Democratic chairman of the powerful House Ways and Means Committee is best known for work on tax reform in the 1980s and, more recently, for a bold plan to reduce the federal deficit. Although a Democrat, "Rosty" has worked closely with the Bush and Reagan administrations on domestic tax issues.

An alumnus of the late Chicago mayor Richard Daley's political machine, Rostenkowski has been a member of Congress for more than thirty years. He has never forgotten his Chicago roots, and has received much publicity for his charitable donations to local Illinois organizations, such as the Polish Museum of America. (Its holdings, incidentally, include a bust of Dan Rostenkowski.)

Before his election to the House of Representatives, Rostenkowski served as a member of the Illinois General Assembly. He was originally elected to Congress with the help of Mayor Daley, whose support he won by convincing Daley that younger men were needed to build seniority and break the southern-Democrats' hold on committee chairmanships.

Rostenkowski is probably best known to the general public for his stand on tax reform during the Reagan administration. At one point, during a televised rebuttal of a Reagan speech, Rostenkowski asked everyone to write R-O-S-T-Y, Washington, D.C., to express their views on tax reform. He felt that "any reform is better than the current law." In an interview with *U.S. News and World Report,* Rostenkowski complained that it was unfair that his kids paid about a third of their income in taxes, while at the same time some very wealthy people "aren't paying a dime and living very comfortably."

Along with his congressional successes, Rostenkowski has also had his share of failures. One recent temporary failure was his fight against the Bush-supported capital gains tax rollback. When President Bush proposed the rollback, Rostenkowski responded, "I'm not about to tell the wage earners in Chicago that they should pay a higher rate than the stockbrokers." In the fight over capital gains, Rostenkowski lost control of his committee (which he later regained) and was therefore frozen out of some key decisions.

Rostenkowski's surprise for the 1990s was a deficit reduction proposal that advocated both stiff taxes on gasoline and other special items and sharp cuts in spending for domestic social programs. His motives, however, have been under heavy scrutiny. Some observers see Rostenkowski as a fiscal moderate, who has always supported the need for budget reform. His latest proposal, they believe, was made partly for its shock value and as a call to action. Other observers, more cynical in outlook, hypothesize that he wants to regain some power after the capital gains struggle and retire in a few years. A successful deficit package would allow him to leave office on a high note.

Whatever his reasons, no one can doubt that Dan Rostenkowski is one of the top persuaders in Congress. Although not known as a great orator, he persuades his colleagues by bargaining, by trading favors, by the idea of "If I do this, will you do that?" It's an old, familiar style—and it works.

on high incomes, it also provided for more loopholes. There were special provisions that enabled investors in oil and gas wells to reduce their taxable income. There were loopholes that allowed people to shift income from one year to the next. There were loopholes that allowed individuals to form corporations outside the United States in order to avoid some taxes completely. The same principles apply as with other interest groups. As long as one group of taxpayers sees a specific benefit from getting the law changed and that benefit means a lot of money per individual, the interest group will aggressively support lobbying activities and the election and reelection of members of Congress who will push for special loopholes. In other words, if there's enough benefit to be derived from influencing tax legislation, such influence will be forthcoming from the affected parties.

Will the Tax System Stay "Simple"?

After 1986, the federal Tax Code was simplified for some people. Our prediction, however, is that it will not remain simple. All we need do is look at the action–reaction syndrome and apply it to the future in an economy that is running large deficits. The federal government deficit has exceeded $100 billion a year since 1982. The administration and Congress are faced with the need to raise taxes or cut the growth of federal government spending, or both. Although federal government spending growth may drop a bit, we can surmise that new taxes will be levied in the 1990s, as already happened in 1990.

Here is the likely scenario. Congress will initially "fiddle" with the Tax Code by first removing certain remaining loopholes and **tax preferences** and by increasing certain "painless" taxes, such as the **excise taxes** on cigarettes and on gasoline. But then there will be increased pressure to "soak the rich." So a hue and cry will be raised to solve our deficit problem by increasing taxes on richer Americans. We will then see the tax rate on higher incomes ratcheting upward. The political appeal of increasing tax rates on higher-income-earning Americans will probably be too great to pass up. But then the action-reaction syndrome will come into play. As tax rates go up, those who are affected will spend more time and effort to get Congress to legislate special exceptions, exemptions, loopholes, and the like, so that the full impact of such tax-rate increases will not be felt by richer Americans. Within less than a decade, we predict that the U.S. Tax Code will be more complicated than it was before the Tax Reform Act of 1986. The 1990 Tax Act confirms this.

And Now the Question of Subsidies

Subsidies are just negative taxes. Instead of paying taxes to the governments, you receive money. Subsidies to farmers are often based on amount of output. Dairy producers, beekeepers, peanut farmers, corn farmers, and others have received direct subsidies from the federal government. As a form of negative taxes, the politics of subsidies follows the action-reaction syndrome. If a subsidy is provided to farmers, they will farm more land, buy more fertilizer, and increase output. If a subsidy is given to oil producers by offering investors in oil production tax breaks, more resources will flow into oil production. If a subsidy is offered to new industry in the form of reduced taxes if such industry moves into a particular state, other things remaining the same, more industry will move into that state than would otherwise.

The main thing to remember about subsidies is that they take away government dollars that could be spent elsewhere and induce the private sector to funnel more resources into the subsidized activity. When there were numerous tax benefits to investing in oil exploration, more resources in the United States flowed to oil exploration than would have otherwise. Today the same is true for the amount of resources that flow to subsidized agricultural pursuits, subsidized manufacturing activities, and the like.

DID YOU KNOW?

That on April 15, 1991, it is estimated that Americans paid $510 billion in 1990 individual income taxes?

TAX PREFERENCES
Another name for loopholes, or reduced taxes, legally mandated by Congress for particular activities, individuals, or businesses.

EXCISE TAXES
A tax on certain commodities, such as liquor and tobacco, levied on their manufacture or sale within a country.

FISCAL POLICY
Changes in government spending or taxes to alter national economic variables such as the rate of unemployment.

MONETARY POLICY
Changes in the amount of money in circulation to alter credit markets, employment, and the rate of inflation.

■ THE POLITICS OF MONETARY AND FISCAL POLICY

Changes in the Tax Code sometimes form part of an overall fiscal policy change. **Fiscal policy** is defined as the use of changes in government expenditures and taxes to alter national economic variables, such as the rate of inflation, the rate of unemployment, the level of interest rates, and the rate of economic growth. The federal government also has under its control **monetary policy,** defined as changes in the amount of money in circulation so as to affect interest rates, credit markets, the rate of inflation, and employment. Fiscal policy is the domain of Congress and the president, whereas monetary policy, as we shall see, is much less under the control of Congress and the president because the monetary authority, the Federal Reserve System—the Fed—is an independent agency not directly controlled by either Congress or the president.

Fiscal Policy in Theory and in Reality

The theory behind fiscal policy changes is relatively straightforward: When the economy is going into a recession—a period of rising unemployment—the federal government should stimulate economic activity by increasing government expenditures or by decreasing taxes (or both). When the economy is becoming overheated with rapid increases in employment and rising prices—a condition of inflation—fiscal policy should become contractionary, reducing government expenditures and increasing taxes. That particular view of fiscal policy became popular during the 1960s and was an outgrowth of the economic theories of the English economist John Maynard Keynes. Keynes's ideas, published during the Great Depression of the 1930s (see Highlight in this section), influenced the economic policy makers guiding President Franklin Delano Roosevelt's New Deal. **Keynesian economics** has not turned out to be as simple as expected, though. Starting in 1969, the United States economy entered a period of simultaneously rising prices and rising unemployment—called **stagflation.** In such a situation, applying a fiscal policy stimulus is not so obviously appropriate.

KEYNESIAN ECONOMICS
An economic theory named after English economist John Maynard Keynes, which gained prominence during the Great Depression of the 1930s. Typically associated with the use of fiscal policy to alter national economic variables, for example, increased government spending during times of economic downturns.

STAGFLATION
A period during which the rate of inflation is increasing simultaneously with an increase in the rate of unemployment.

Unemployment benefits line.

HIGHLIGHT

The Great Depression, 1929–1941

On October 24, 1929, commonly called "Black Thursday," the New York Stock Exchange suffered through the first of a series of steep declines that made the nation and much of the world aware that a major economic catastrophe was in progress. From 1929 to 1933, the nation's unemployment rate shot up from 3.2 percent to an astronomical 25.2 percent, and income per person (in then current dollars) fell from $846 to $442. Public and private construction fell by nearly three-fourths, the business failure rate increased by 50 percent, and thousands of banks and hundreds of thousands of business firms closed by the time the Depression hit bottom in 1933.

In this climate of nearly total economic collapse, Republican President Herbert Hoover was voted out of office and replaced by the "New Deal" Democratic administration of Franklin Roosevelt. Roosevelt promised aid to farmers, public development of electric power, a balanced federal budget, and government regulation of private economic power, which many people blamed for causing the Depression. He temporarily closed the nation's banks to thwart depositors' panicky withdrawal of funds and implemented measures to economize on government spending. Under his prodding, Congress enacted a bold series of relief measures.

Congress passed legislation in 1933 to create the Federal Emergency Relief Administration, which gave money to state relief agencies; the Civilian Conservation Corps (CCC), which employed as many as 500,000 young men at a time in flood control and reforestation work; the Agricultural Adjustment Administration (AAA), which aimed to raise farm prices and farmers' incomes

Wall Street during the stock market crash.

through farm commodity subsidies; the Public Works Administration (PWA) to encourage building and construction; the National Recovery Administration (NRA) to regulate labor and fair trade practices; the Tennessee Valley Authority (TVA) to provide flood control, energy, and regional planning for a large segment of lower-income Americans living in Appalachia; and the Securities and Exchange Commission (SEC) to regulate stock market practices. Other legislation established maximum hours of work, minimum wages, guarantees of labor-management collective bargaining, and abolition of child labor in interstate commerce.

In 1935, the Social Security Act was passed and the Works Progress Admin-istration (WPA) was created. The WPA employed more than two million workers.

Subsequent opposition from the Supreme Court and from conservative Republicans and many southern Democrats in Congress limited the effectiveness of these and other programs of Roosevelt's New Deal. The Depression and its direct economic and political consequences effectively ended by 1941, as the United States rebuilt its industrial base for a wartime economy. Clearly, however, many of the political and economic institutions of today, as well as the debate over their usefulness, can be traced to these events of the Great Depression and the political responses to that crisis.

HIGHLIGHT

No More Pennies; No More Dollar Bills?

Every year the U.S. Mint produces approximately twelve *billion* new pennies, and Americans promptly lose, store, mutilate, or otherwise dispose of half of them—that's six billion pennies rattling around people's dressers, jackets, car floors, and penny jars.

These days there is "serious interest" in the U.S. penny in Washington, D.C. The penny has its supporters and opponents. James Benfield is the founder and only paid employee of the Coin Coalition, an organization intent on getting rid of the penny. "The penny's a nuisance," he says. Michael Brown opposes abolition of the smallest U.S. currency unit, arguing that rounding off the price of things would cost the U.S. consumer over half a billion dollars each year. Brown is a spokesman for the organization Americans for Common Cents. Americans for Common Cents is backed by the zinc industry (the penny is 97 percent zinc), as well as the manufacturers of the penny blanks (which are stamped out as pennies) and U.S. coin collectors.

This excitement about pennies was stimulated by the Senate Banking Committee's "coinage reform," an effort to pinpoint needed changes in U.S. cur-

rency. The hottest issue is the movement to create a one-dollar coin and do away with the one-dollar bill. This idea is supported by the U.S. vending machine industry (including video arcades), the American Council for the Blind, the copper industry, the convenience store industry, and the mass transit business. It is opposed by the ink and paper industry which supplies these ingredients for the printing of paper currency.

The reason behind the anti-dollar-bill

movement is that handling such bills manually, including straightening and unfolding them, arranging them right side up, and counting them, is a very expensive and time-consuming process. Also, the U.S. Treasury spends over $300 million each year shredding and replacing worn-out one-dollar bills. It is difficult for visually impaired people to identify the dollar bill. Dollar coins in vending machines and mass transit turnstiles would be convenient and reduce the handling of smaller coins and making change. The same factors also account for the convenience-store support of a dollar coin. The copper industry supports the proposed copper dollar for obvious reasons.

In 1979, a one-dollar coin, the Susan B. Anthony, was introduced in the United States but failed to gain public acceptance. Now the strategy is to introduce a coin dollar and phase out entirely the paper dollar, thus forcing Americans to use the coin. This was successfully done in Canada in 1987 with the Loon dollar coin. A 1990 Gallup poll showed that 62 percent of Americans support abolishing the penny but only 15 percent support abolishing the dollar bill in favor of a dollar coin.

Lags in Policy. Another problem with fiscal policy is that even under the best of circumstances, from the time the economy needs fiscal stimulus—say, at the start of a recession—to the time that any fiscal stimulus is forthcoming, there might be a lag of several years. First, there is a lag between the time a recession starts and when policy makers know that it has started. Next, there is a lag between that time and when policy makers actually decide that fiscal policy should be expansionary. Finally, there is another lag between the time fiscal policy is put into action and when it has its desired effects.

The Reality of the Federal Budgeting Process. Even if we knew when recessions were beginning the instant they started, the federal budgeting process precludes quick reactions. We examined in Chapter 12 the complexity of the federal budgeting process in which no single agency is responsible for the amorphous concept called fiscal policy. The budget authority is divided between the president and Congress; moreover, budget policy serves many other

Richard Darman, Director of the Budget for the Bush administration.

goals besides low inflation, low unemployment, and higher economic growth. Indeed, the so-called national goals of full employment, price stability, and economic growth as outlined, for example, in the Full Employment Act of 1946, often carry little weight in the real budgetary process within Congress. Taxing and spending decisions are made in dozens of subcommittees dominated by interest group and client politics.

Monetary Policy: Politics and Reality

The theory behind monetary policy is relatively straightforward, also. In periods of recession and high unemployment, stimulate the economy by expanding the rate of growth of the money supply (defined loosely as currency plus checking-account balances, plus other types of account balances that generally serve as money). An easier money policy is supposed to lower interest rates and induce consumers to spend more and producers to invest more. With rising inflation, do the reverse: Reduce the rate of growth of the amount of money in circulation. Interest rates should rise, choking off some consumer spending and some business investment. But the world is never so simple as the theory we use to explain it. If the nation experiences stagflation—rising inflation *and* rising unemployment—expansionary monetary policy will lead to even more inflation. Ultimately, the more money there is in circulation, the higher prices will be.

The Monetary Authority—the Federal Reserve System. Congress established our modern central bank, the Federal Reserve, in 1913. It is governed by a Board of Governors consisting of seven individuals, including the very powerful chair. All of the governors, including the chair, are nominated by the president and approved by the Senate. Their appointments are for fourteen years. Through the Federal Reserve System, or Fed, and the **Federal Open Market Committee (FOMC),** decisions about monetary policy are made thirteen times a year. The Board of Governors of the Federal Reserve System is independent. The president can "jawbone" the board and Congress can

FEDERAL OPEN MARKET COMMITTEE (FOMC)
The most important body within the Federal Reserve System, the FOMC decides how monetary policy should be carried out by the Federal Reserve.

A meeting of the Board of Governors of the Federal Reserve.

threaten to merge the Fed with the Treasury, but as long as the Fed retains its independence, its chairperson and governors can do what they please. Hence, talking about "the president's monetary policy" or "Congress's monetary policy" is inaccurate. To be sure, the Fed has, on occasion, yielded to presidential pressure, and for a while the Fed's chairman felt constrained to follow a congressional resolution requiring him to report monetary targets over each six-month period. But now, more than ever, the Fed remains one of the truly independent sources of power in the government.

Monetary Policy and Lags.   Monetary policy does not suffer from the same lengthy time lags as fiscal policy because the Fed can, within a very short period, put into effect any policy it decides. Nonetheless, researchers have estimated that it takes almost fourteen months for a monetary policy change to become effective, measured from the time the economy either slows down or speeds up too much to the time the economy feels the policy change.[2] This means that by the time monetary policy goes into effect, a different policy might be appropriate.

The Fed's Record.   Federal Reserve monetary policy, in principle, is supposed to be countercyclical. The economy goes through so-called business cycles, made up of recessions (and sometimes depressions) when unemployment is high, and boom times when unemployment is low and businesses are straining capacity. For the Fed to "ride against the wind," it must create policies that go counter to business activity. Researchers, examining the evidence since 1914, have uniformly concluded that, on average, the Fed's policy has turned out to be procyclical. That is, by the time the Fed started pumping money into the economy, it was time to do the opposite; by the time the Fed started reducing the rate of growth of the money supply, it was time for it to start increasing it. Perhaps the Fed's biggest procyclical blunder occurred during

[2]Robert Gordon, *Macroeconomics,* 4th ed. (Boston: Little, Brown, 1987), p. 423.

the Great Depression. Many economists believe that what would have been a severe recession turned into the Great Depression in the 1930s because the Fed's action resulted in almost a one-third decrease in the amount of money in circulation. It has also been argued that the rapid inflation experienced in the 1970s was the direct result of the Fed increasing the rate of growth of the money supply too much. In addition, some observers of Federal Reserve policy claim that former head of the Fed Paul Volker created one of the worst recessions since the Great Depression in 1981–82 when he caused the Fed to engage in extremely restrictive monetary policy. Others argue that he needed to do so to "break inflation's back." In fact, inflation did slow down to almost zero during the middle of the 1980s.

■ REFLECTIONS ON THE PUBLIC DEBT AND BIG DEFICITS

We've already talked about deficit spending and the fact that the federal government has run a deficit in every year except two since 1960. Every time a budget deficit occurs, the federal government issues debt instruments in the form of **U.S. Treasury bonds.** The sale of these bonds to corporations, private individuals, pension plans, foreign governments, foreign businesses, and foreign individuals adds to the **public,** or **national, debt,** defined as the total amount owed by the federal government. Table 16-3 shows what has happened to the net public debt through time. It would seem that the nation is increasingly mortgaging its future. But this table does not take into account two important variables: inflation and increases in population. In Figure 16-2, we correct the public debt for inflation and increases in population. The per capita public debt in so-called **constant dollars** (dollars corrected for inflation) reached its peak, as you might expect, during World War II and fell steadily thereafter until the mid-1970s. Since then, except for a reduction in 1980, it has continued to rise. If we are not careful, it will exceed (in per capita constant-dollar terms) what it was during World War II. Politicians and the public alike are concerned.

Is the Public Debt a Burden?

We often hear about the burden of the public debt. Some argue that the government is eventually going to go bankrupt, but that, of course, cannot happen. As long as the government has the ability to pay for interest payments on the public debt through taxation, it will never go bankrupt. What happens is that when Treasury bonds come due, they are simply "rolled over." That is, if a $1 million Treasury bond comes due today, the U.S. Treasury pays it off and sells another $1 million bond.

What about the interest payments? Interest payments are paid by taxes, so what we are really talking about is taxing some people to pay interest to others who loan money to the government. This cannot really be called a burden to all of society. There is one hitch, however. Not all of the interest payments are paid to Americans. An increasing amount is paid to foreigners, because foreigners own almost 15 percent of the public debt, raising the fear of too much foreign control of U.S. assets. So it is no longer that we "owe it all to ourselves."

DID YOU KNOW?

That the per capita national debt was only $2.06 in 1860?

U.S. TREASURY BONDS
Evidences of debt issued by the federal government. Similar to corporate bonds, but issued by the U.S. Treasury.

PUBLIC, OR NATIONAL, DEBT
The total amount of debt incurred by the federal government since the beginning of the nation.

CONSTANT DOLLARS
Dollars corrected for inflation; dollars expressed in terms of purchasing power for a given year.

TABLE 16-3
Net Public Debt of the Federal Government

Year	Total (billions of current dollars)
1940	$ 42.7
1945	235.2
1950	219.0
1960	237.2
1970	284.9
1980	709.3
1985	1,499.5
1986	1,736.2
1987	1,888.1
1988	2,050.2
1989	2,177.8
1990	2,339.2
1991	2,467.7*

*Estimate

SOURCE: U.S. Office of Management and Budget

DID YOU KNOW?

That perhaps as much as $200 billion in federal tax revenues are lost each year to the so-called underground economy?

PUBLIC DEBT FINANCING
Government spending more than it receives in taxes and paying for the difference by issuing U.S. Treasury bonds, thereby adding to the public debt.

FIGURE 16-2
Per Capita Public Debt of the United States in Constant 1982 Dollars
If we correct the public debt for intergovernmental borrowing, the growth in the population, and changes in the price level (inflation), we obtain a graph that shows the per capita net public debt in the United States expressed in constant 1982 dollars reaching its peak during World War II and then dropping consistently until about 1975. In the last fifteen years, however, it has risen steadily and is starting to approach World War II levels.

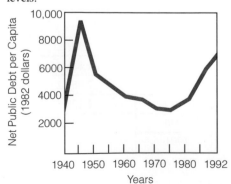

Another factor is also important. Even though we are paying interest to ourselves for the most part, the more the federal government borrows, the greater the percentage of the federal budget that is committed to interest payments. The ever-increasing portion of the budget committed to interest payments reduces the federal government's ability to purchase public goods in the future, such as more parks. In 1976, interest costs to the government were less than 9 percent of total federal outlays. The estimate for 1992 is almost 20 percent. Indeed, if you wish to do a simple projection of current trends, some time in the next century the federal government will be spending almost 100 percent of its budget on interest payments! This, of course, will not occur, but it highlights the problem of running larger and larger deficits and borrowing more and more money to cover them.

The Problem of "Crowding Out"

Although it may be true that we owe the public debt to ourselves (except for what is owed to foreigners), another issue is involved in having a large public debt that is made up of a series of annual federal government budget deficits. Each time the federal government runs a deficit, we know that it must go into the financial marketplace and borrow the money. This process in which the U.S. Treasury sells U.S. Treasury bonds is called **public debt financing.** Public debt financing in effect "crowds out" private borrowing. Consider that to borrow, say, $100 billion, the federal government must bid for loanable funds in the marketplace just as any business does. It bids for these loanable funds by offering to pay higher interest rates. Consequently, interest rates are increased when the federal government runs large deficits and goes out to borrow money to cover them. Higher interest rates can stifle or slow business investment, which reduces the rate of economic growth.

■ BALANCING THE BUDGET: A CONSTITUTIONAL AMENDMENT OR GRAMM–RUDMAN?

Some argue that the way not to have deficits is to have a constitutional convention to draft a balanced-budget amendment to the U.S. Constitution. Two-thirds of the state legislatures need to petition the Congress for a convention to be called. To date, the required number of legislative petitions has not been filed. Perhaps as an alternative to a constitutional amendment for balancing the budget, in December 1985, Congress passed the Gramm–Rudman–Hollings Act, also known as the Balanced Budget and Emergency Deficit Control Act of 1985. Its goal was to reach a balanced budget by fiscal year 1991. The act mandated progressive annual cuts in the deficit—a series of automatic, across-the-board spending cuts designed to achieve a balanced budget by the specified year. Half of the cuts would come from domestic programs, the other half from defense. At a minimum, the Gramm–Rudman–Hollings Act has increased the visibility of deficits as a political issue. Nonetheless, deficits persist, indicating that Congress is not making the necessary painful choices.

Originally, the Office of Budget and Management and the Congressional Budget Office were required to issue an annual joint report estimating the size of the deficit. Whenever congressional and presidential action failed to

HIGHLIGHT

Are Republicans the Fiscal Conservatives?

From 1929 through 1990, the U.S. government had only thirteen budget surpluses, totaling $67.1 billion, and forty deficits, totaling over $2 trillion. An interesting question is whether Democratic or Republican administrations run higher deficits. Typically, Republicans are known as fiscal conservatives, and we would therefore expect Republican administrations to run fewer and lower federal budget deficits than Democratic administrations. Such is not the case. The Hoover, Eisenhower, Nixon, Ford, Reagan, and Bush administrations have had four surpluses and twenty-four deficits. Democrats Roosevelt, Truman, Kennedy, Johnson,

and Carter produced five surpluses and twenty-seven deficits.

The real test, though, is in the cumulative budget deficits over each president's term, expressed as a proportion of total output of goods and services. The accompanying table shows the average cumulative budget deficit as a proportion of total national output of goods and services since Hoover. If we eliminate the World War II years under Roosevelt, whom do you call a fiscal conservative?

(right) Cumulative Budget Deficits as a Proportion of Total National Output of Goods and Services

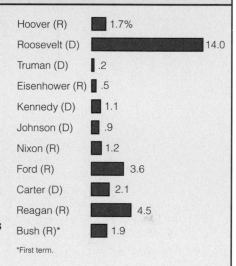

Hoover (R)	1.7%
Roosevelt (D)	14.0
Truman (D)	.2
Eisenhower (R)	.5
Kennedy (D)	1.1
Johnson (D)	.9
Nixon (R)	1.2
Ford (R)	3.6
Carter (D)	2.1
Reagan (R)	4.5
Bush (R)*	1.9

*First term.

meet the deficit targets, the General Accounting Office (GAO), an agency of Congress, would issue a report to the president containing specific reductions in program expenditures that would be necessary to meet the Gramm–Rudman deficit targets. This particular aspect of the legislation immediately came under attack and was challenged in the courts. In 1986, the Supreme Court ruled that the GAO could not order spending cuts because that would constitute a violation of the separation of powers.[3] Since the GAO is a congressional agency and its head can be removed by Congress, the Supreme Court ruled that the GAO director cannot exercise executive powers. Spending cuts mandated by Gramm–Rudman can only be instituted by congressional vote and agreement by the president. In other words, neither the president nor Congress can pass on the onerous task of reducing government spending without being held accountable.

After the passage of Gramm–Rudman, the federal government failed for two years to comply with its target deficit reductions. Congress then passed a revised act requiring that the 1988 deficit be no higher than $144 billion and that it drop to zero by 1993. Congress failed to meet the required deficit reductions for the first four years of the revised act. In 1990 a second revised Gramm-Rudman set of targets was proposed, allowing for an over $200 billion deficit in 1991 (*excluding* the cost of the savings and loan bailout).

In any event, the deficit is probably much bigger than actually is reported. Each year, in an effort to make the amount of red ink look smaller, Congress takes more and more government outlays out of the official federal budget and puts them in a category called "off-budget items." For example, all the

[3]*Bowsher v. Synar*, 478 U.S. 714 (1986).

TABLE 16-4
The Deficit, With Or Without Social Security, Excluding the Savings and Loan Bailout (in billions of dollars)

Fiscal Year	With Social Security Surplus	Without Social Security Surplus
1990	$220	$278
1991	253	319
1992	262	336
1993	170	253
1994	56	154
1995	29	143

Note: Deficit projections exclude spending on thrift industry bailout.

SOURCE: *Congressional Budget Office, December, 1990.*

TABLE 16-5
How the Public Wants the Federal Budget Deficit Reduced

By raising taxes on alcoholic beverages	72%
By raising taxes on cigarettes	72
By raising the income-tax rate for the wealthiest from 28 to 33 percent	71
By instituting an oil import fee	43
By raising taxes on energy consumption	33
By raising federal taxes on gasoline	24

SOURCE:*Time/CNN* Telephone Opinion Survey, May 21, 1990.

operating losses of the U.S. Postal Service have been removed from the official U.S. government budget. Much of the cost of borrowing money to pay for the Thrift Bailout Act will not show up on the official government budget. Indeed, off-budget federal spending is growing much more rapidly than the official on-budget spending that you read about in newspapers and magazines.

Even the reductions made officially to the federal deficit each year are overstated, as can be seen in Table 16-4. The federal government is collecting more in Social Security taxes than it currently is paying out in Social Security benefits. The remainder is supposed to be invested in a type of trust fund to provide for the extremely large Social Security benefit payments that will have to be made toward the beginning of the twenty-first century when the current crop of baby boomers retires and the United States reaches zero population growth. In other words, Congress is creating a huge multitrillion dollar commitment to pay retirees tomorrow with the excess taxes it is collecting for Social Security today. At the same time, it is applying the excess Social Security taxes to the general treasury and thereby, on paper, reducing the budget deficit.

As can be seen in Table 16-5, the public had strong ideas about how to reduce the deficit. In 1990, Congress raised income taxes on the rich and raised the excise tax on gasoline, plus did a variety of other things to trim the deficit. Nonetheless, it continued to grow in 1991.

GETTING INVOLVED

The Importance of Government in Your Life

In this chapter, we have talked about the federal budgetary process as a complex system that involves many players. The ultimate test of the effectiveness of the federal budgetary process is how it affects each individual American. One way for you to take stock of how the federal government affects your life is as follows: (1) List what you have as assets. (2) List what you do during the day as activities. Then note the extent to which government is involved in your life—and at what cost. The emphasis should always be on the services that must be paid for, either directly or indirectly.

Consider the following example:

1. Rode bicycle to class—highway usage. How are the highways paid for? Who paid for them?

2. Checked out book from public library—Who paid for that library? Who owns it?
3. Received student loan—a subsidy from the government. Who ultimately paid for it?
4. Went to class—On average, in the United States, taxpayers pay approximately 70 percent of the cost of higher education and students and their families directly pay only 30 percent.
5. Got groceries—How much of the meat was government inspected?

Where else did government intervene?

CHAPTER SUMMARY

1. The five steps in the policy process are agenda building, agenda formulation, agenda adoption, agenda implementation, and agenda evaluation.

2. There are numerous models of the policy-making process, including (1) the bureaucratic politics model, (2) the power elite model, (3) the Marxist model, (4) the incrementalist model, and (5) the rationalist model.

3. Every policy action carries with it a cost and a benefit. Typically, costs are borne by one group, while benefits are enjoyed by another group.

4. In the example of the thrift industry bailout, the main beneficiaries are the managers and shareholders in poorly run thrifts throughout the country. The costs are borne by all of the electorate.

5. In general, interest group legislation is effective because the benefits are enjoyed by a narrow group of well-defined individuals, whereas the costs are spread across everyone in the nation. Therefore, those who will benefit are able to band together to pay lobbyists and the like to support special-interest legislation. Those who bear the costs, that is, all taxpayers, will not spend the time or money to fight such legislation because even if they win, they will not notice a big difference in their spendable income.

6. Whenever individuals and businesses face high tax rates, they will expend resources to get legislators to give them tax loopholes, enabling them to reduce their taxable incomes legally.

7. Subsidies are a type of negative tax in which the government gives money to individuals and businesses. For example, some

farmers obtain subsidies based on the total amount of production of corn or wheat. Some manufacturers obtain subsidies on the basis of how much they have produced.

8. Fiscal policy is the use of changes in government expenditures and taxes to alter national economic variables, such as the rate of inflation or unemployment. Monetary policy is defined as changes in the amount of money in circulation so as to affect interest rates, credit markets, the rate of inflation, and employment.

9. Fiscal policy was made popular by the English economist John Maynard Keynes, whose ideas influenced Franklin Delano Roosevelt's New Deal legislation as well as the fiscal policies of the government during the 1960s.

10. Keynesian fiscal policy economics usually involves increasing government spending during recession periods and increasing taxes during overheated inflationary boom periods.

11. Keynesian fiscal policy economics does not work well during periods of stagflation, defined as simultaneously rising unemployment and inflation.

12. The problem with fiscal policy and monetary policy is the lag between the time a problem occurs in the economy, when policy changes can be implemented, and when such changes are actually felt in the economy.

13. The track record of the Federal Reserve System—our central monetary authority—in countering excessive swings in economic activity has not been consistent. Some critics of the Federal Reserve System argue that it was responsible for worsening the Great Depression in the 1930s because it allowed for a one-third reduction in the amount of money in circulation. They

also contend that the Federal Reserve was responsible for the serious inflation we had in the 1970s because it allowed the money supply to increase too rapidly.

14. Whenever the federal government spends more than it receives, it runs a deficit. The deficit is met by United States Treasury borrowing. This adds to the public debt of the federal government. Although the public debt has grown dramatically, when corrected for increases in population and inflation, it fell from the end of World War II to the middle of the 1970s. Since then, it has increased almost to its previous level at the height of World War II.

15. One problem with annual federal government budget deficits is that when the Treasury goes out to borrow money to pay for them, it increases interest rates, thereby crowding out private investment because private investors are unwilling to pay the higher cost of borrowing money.

16. The Gramm-Rudman-Hollings Balanced Budget and Emergency Deficit Control Act of 1985 was passed in an attempt to force the federal government to balance its budget by government fiscal year 1991. A revised plan called for a balanced budget by 1993. Yet a second revision calls for a balanced budget no earlier than 1996.

QUESTIONS FOR REVIEW AND DISCUSSION

1. How much influence do you think that the president or Congress has over monetary policy?

2. Does the manner in which the federal government obtains its spending power from the private sector to finance its activities matter to you? That is, do you as an individual care whether the federal government taxes you for the full amount of its expenditures every year, or runs a deficit?

3. How can Congress pass a law requiring it to balance the federal budget and not comply with its own legislation?

SELECTED REFERENCES

Benjamin Friedman, *Day of Reckoning: The Consequences of American Economic Policy* (New York: Random House, 1990). An interesting analysis of the impact of Reaganomics on the American economy and suggestions for new economic policies in the post-Reagan era that will repair the damage the author feels was done during that period.

Milton Friedman and Walter Heller, *Monetary versus Fiscal Policy* (New York: Norton, 1969). A classic presentation of the pros and cons of monetary and fiscal policy given by a noninterventionist (Friedman) and an advocate of federal government intervention in the economy (Heller).

William Greider, *Secrets of the Temple: How the Federal Reserve Runs the Country* (New York: Simon & Schuster, 1987). An insider's view of how our nation's monetary authority—the Fed—actually conducts its policy-making business. Readable and fascinating.

Denise E. Markovich and Ronald E. Pynn, *American Political Economy: Using Economics with Politics* (New York: Brooks/Cole, 1988). An integrated overview of how political decision-making affects economics and how economic conditions help shape politics.

Roger LeRoy Miller and Daniel K. Benjamin, *The Economics of Macro Issues,* 6th ed. (St. Paul, Minn.: West Publishing Company, 1989). This short paperback consists of 29 topical chapters examining the major issues facing economic policy makers today. Lively, up to date, and easily understood.

Kevin Phillips, *The Politics of Rich and Poor: Wealth and the American Electorate* (New York: Random House, 1990). The author, a well-known student of election politics, analyzes the changing distribution of income and wealth in the United States, primarily as a result of Reagan administration policies that favored the rich. Phillips predicts that populist, liberal policies favoring the middle- and lower-income groups will become a major political force in the 1990s.

The President's Council of Economic Advisers, *Economic Report of the President* (Washington, D.C.: Government Printing Office, annually). This volume contains a wealth of details concerning current monetary and fiscal policy and what is happening to the economy.

Grover Starling, *Strategies for Policymaking* (Chicago: The Dorsey Press, 1988). In graphics and text, the author presents a detailed outline of the policy-making process, including the key elements in the relationship between policy making and policy analysis. He also examines the interdisciplinary aspects of policy analysis.

John F. Witte, *The Politics and Development of the Federal Income Tax* (Madison: University of Wisconsin Press, 1985). The author presents the history of our federal tax system and the politics of special-interest legislation with respect to tax policy.

CHAPTER CONTENTS

WHAT IF . . . FEDERAL TROOPS WERE USED TO STOP DRUGS?

In 1990, the news on drug use in the United States was bad. Kids under ten years of age were making $100 a day as lookouts for drug sellers. A successful "crack" dealer in New York City was making as much as $3,000 a day! It was estimated that a teen using crack could spend as much as $20,000 a year on the habit. Much of this expense was paid for by robbery, prostitution, and other crime. Campaigns to "Just Say NO!" to drugs were ineffective. The spread of the deadly AIDS virus rapidly accelerated through needle sharing by drug users. Tens of thousands of infants born to addicted mothers were themselves addicted. Many of these infants were also mentally retarded and would become wards of the state.

In Washington, D.C., Southern California, and other areas, drug-related gang violence erupted into street shootouts in which innocent bystanders were killed. Teenage drug dealers began carrying high-tech weapons. Local law enforcement agencies increasingly appeared helpless to deal with the drug situation. Drug dealers were often better armed and equipped than law-enforcement personnel.

Up to now, federal law has prohibited the use of the military for drug enforcement. What if, to stem the growing drug problem in the United States, the armed forces were used to stop drugs at home and abroad?

First of all, this would represent a major shift in law enforcement from the local community, which is now principally responsible, to the federal government. For some drug-fighting operations it would put states and local communities under the jurisdiction of military commanders, the Pentagon, and the White House (the president is commander in chief). The fundamental structure of American federalism would be changed.

Second, some high-crime and drug areas, especially in larger cities such as New York, Miami, Washington, D.C., and Los Angeles, might be turned into battlegrounds. Military searches, soldiers patrolling with M-16 rifles in full combat gear, small tanks and armored personnel carriers driving down Main Street, assaults on "crack houses" and other drug-dealing centers by military units could become common viewing on the evening news.

Third, to control transporting and distributing drugs, special checkpoints would probably be set up on highways. Vehicles might be subject to search. Students going home for Christmas break, families on summer vacation, truckers, and traveling salespersons, all would be subject to long delays along interstate highways and other roads.

Fourth, the American Civil Liberties Union (ACLU) and other organizations would immediately file lawsuits arguing that people's civil liberties were violated by the "militarization" of U.S communities. Moreover, the constitutionality of using the U.S. armed forces for prolonged (perhaps permanent), routine, domestic law enforcement would be raised.

Fifth, there would certainly be military incidents along the U.S.–Mexico border, over which a substantial proportion of drugs flows. These would probably damage U.S. relations with its southern neighbor. In an extreme case, the U.S. military might conduct extensive operations against foreign drug growers, manufacturers, and shippers. This might mean the virtual large-scale military invasion of parts of Colombia, Bolivia, Peru, Thailand, Lebanon, and other major sources of drugs.

The use of military forces in fighting drugs was already developing in the 1980s. In May 1988, Congress voted almost $500 million in funds that would require the president to deploy the U.S. military, including the National Guard and the reserves, to stop the flow of drugs into the United States. The U.S. Coast Guard had already been actively involved in the fight against drug smuggling. This new measure brought the U.S. military directly into a law enforcement capacity. Its primary mission was to "seal the U.S. border" to drug smugglers.

In December, 1989, United States troops invaded a sovereign nation, Panama, in an effort to capture an indicted drug dealer, General Manuel Noriega, the leader of Panama. Although the United States also hoped to install a democratic regime in Panama by toppling Noriega's government, the action was the first use of the military to carry out our drug policy within the borders of another country without that nation's consent.

Clearly, using the military to combat drugs could signify a major shift in U.S. law enforcement and more generally in the nature of American federalism.

---

1. *How would a shift of drug enforcement power to the federal government affect the operations of local law enforcement officials?*
2. *Would a federal effort be likely to end the drug problem?*
3. *How serious would the infringement of individual rights be? Would the benefit be worth the cost?*

Economic policy making is only one dimension of domestic public policy which can be thought of as all of the laws, policies, and government actions that affect life in the United States. The span of domestic policies is enormous, ranging from such relatively simple laws as the 65 m.p.h. speed limit on interstate highways to the complex issues of environmental protection. Some domestic policies such as social security are formulated and implemented entirely by the federal government. More common are policies like those we discuss in this chapter—drug enforcement, environmental protection, and education—that involve coordination of efforts by state, federal, and local governments.

The United States is not a planned society; no national plan identifying all needed policy areas exists. Policies are created by governments to meet public problems as they arise and as the public demands government action. Often such demands are amplified or, in some cases, originated by interest groups as noted in Chapters 8 and 16. In other cases, such as dealing with the AIDS epidemic or acid rain, the problem has forced itself onto the public agenda. Rather than try to analyze many major areas in brief in this chapter, we will focus on four major policy problems currently facing the United States. These four policy domains—drug regulation, environmental protection, the AIDS epidemic, and the American educational system—will provide examples of the policy-making process, the complexities of formulating and implementing policies, and the impact of policies nationally and, in some cases, internationally.

■ AMERICA'S WAR ON DRUGS

In public opinion surveys over the last five years, one concern remains constant—America's growing illicit drug problem. At times, the political response to the public's concern has bordered on hysteria. In 1989, then federal drug czar William Bennett told reporters that he favored shooting down suspected drug-trafficking airplanes, fining casual users $10,000 and putting them in jail, and creating military-style boot camps to hold convicted drug users.

Drug abuse is a problem that politicians from both parties have embraced. No politician can go wrong by advocating a more comprehensive and effective antidrug policy. Before we examine the extent of the government's drug policy today and the effectiveness of the government's war on drugs, let's first look at its origins.

A Short History of Legislation

Before 1845, there was little legislation anywhere in the United States regulating the use of **psychoactives,** a term that applies to all drugs that affect the psyche, or mind, including alcohol, nicotine, caffeine, marijuana, opiates, cocaine and its derivatives, amphetamines, and other drugs. In 1845, New York banned the public sale of liquor, only to repeal the law two years later. From 1875 to 1914, twenty-seven states and cities banned opium smoking.

The Harrison Narcotics Act. Current legislation owes its origins to the Harrison Narcotics Act of 1914. Before that time, opium, morphine, and cocaine were legally and cheaply available without prescriptions at drugstores,

PSYCHOACTIVES
All substances having a profound or significant effect on mental processes, such as alcohol, nicotine, caffeine, cocaine, the opiates, methamphetamine, and the like.

DID YOU KNOW?

That 61 percent of Americans identified drug abuse as the nation's greatest overall problem, almost one-third of American adults know someone who uses cocaine, and over eight million Americans have used cocaine in the past year?

in grocery stores, and through the mail. The 1914 Harrison Act put controls on the sale of opium, morphine, heroin, and coca-leaf derivatives. Although initially passed as a law for the orderly marketing of those drugs (particularly in larger quantities), the Harrison Act soon became the basis for strict controls on the users and sellers of the controlled drugs.

The first federal law against marijuana was not the Harrison Act, for that drug was left completely out of that legislation. It wasn't until 1937 that the federal government banned the sale and use of marijuana.

Prohibition.   In 1919, the Eighteenth Amendment to the U.S. Constitution ushered in the era of Prohibition. For fourteen years it was illegal in the United States to manufacture, transport, or consume intoxicating beverages, defined as any beverage with more than .05 percent alcohol content by volume. In 1933, Prohibition was repealed with the ratification of the Twenty-first Amendment. This era in the United States's history of regulating psychoactive substances is described in the Critical Perspective.

Current Controlling Legislation.   A variety of federal laws were enacted modifying the Harrison Act of 1914. In 1942, the Opium Poppy Control Act was passed. The Boggs Act of 1951 presented a list of mandatory sentences for the possession and sale of certain illegal drugs. The Narcotics Control Act of 1956 provided the death penalty for selling heroin to minors.

All previous legislation was combined into the Controlled Substances Act (CSA) of 1970, which now, along with its amendments, is the controlling legislation. The CSA was amended by the Controlled Substances Penalties Act in 1984, the Anti-drug Abuse Act of 1986, and the Omnibus Drug Bill of 1988. In summary, the controlling federal CSA makes it a crime to sell, possess, or use a wide variety of drugs, including all opiates and their derivatives; all derivatives of coca leaves, including cocaine and crack cocaine; marijuana; and virtually all hallucinogens such as LSD and all amphetamines ("speed"). Consistent with legislation in much of the world, the United States's drug legislation has nothing to say about the two most-used psychoactives—alcohol and nicotine.

The Size of the Problem

The use of illegal psychoactives is widespread in the United States. There are an estimated 500,000 heroin addicts. Ten to 20 million people have used cocaine or its derivatives, of which 200,000 to 2 million are addicts or abusers (depending on which source of data one accepts). Ten to 20 million Americans use marijuana, at least occasionally. Amphetamines, hallucinogens, and "designer" drugs are used by an increasing number of Americans, although the total subpopulation of regular users is apparently relatively small.

The number of deaths associated with heroin and cocaine use varies between two and four thousand per year. With respect to heroin alone, most of those deaths are due to AIDS contracted through the sharing of contaminated needles.

The incidences of robbery, violence, and murders associated with illicit drugs are hard to estimate. In some major cities, authorities estimate that over one-half of the homicides are drug related, typically due to "turf" wars and drug deals gone awry. In many cities, drug users steal and commit assaults in order to obtain money to satisfy their expensive habits.

CRITICAL PERSPECTIVE

Prohibition in Retrospect: Can We Learn Any Lessons?

On January 16, 1920, Secretary of State Bainbridge Colby certified that, effective at midnight, the Eighteenth Amendment to the U.S. Constitution was the law of the land. That amendment prohibited "the manufacture, sale, transportation, importation, or exportation of intoxicating liquors for beverage purposes," thus beginning the era known as Prohibition. Prohibition was the first *federal* effort at regulating the drinking behavior of Americans. State governments had had the power to regulate liquor consumption since the inception of our country. By the early twentieth century, some states had prohibited alcohol statewide. By 1920, thirty-three of the forty-eight states were, to varying degrees, "dry" states.

Simply passing a law was one thing; making it turn into reality was another. The supply of alcohol did decrease in the United States after 1920, but certainly not disappear completely. During Prohibition, a bottle of gin that sold for $1 in Ontario, Canada, was worth $6 if successfully marketed across the river in Detroit. Bootleggers were in their heyday. Five hundred cases of scotch whiskey legally imported from Britain into Canada cost about $50,000 per load, in today's dollars. Smuggled across the border into Detroit and sold by the bottle at retail, the whiskey was worth approximately $500,000, in today's dollars. Trucked to New York or Chicago and sold by the drink in any of a hundred speakeasies, the whiskey would fetch over $1 million, in today's dollars. Profits like those attracted numerous people who were willing to risk fines and jail.

Organized crime grew rapidly during this period. Bloody hijackings of booze-laden trucks became sufficiently common that bootleggers began moving liquor across the borders only in heavily armed convoys. In New York City alone, there were more than one thousand gangland murders during Prohibition, most of them believed to be related to bootlegged liquor. The infamous St. Valentine's Day Massacre in 1929, in which Al Capone's men machine-gunned six members of the Bugs Moran gang, was simply part of Capone's efforts to consolidate control over the Chicago liquor market.

Nationwide, the murder rate hit record levels, rising to 25 percent above the years preceding 1920. When Prohibition was repealed in 1933, the murder rate declined for eleven consecutive years. In 1933, the last year of Prohibition, there were more than twelve thousand homicides and almost eight thousand assaults with firearms; within eight years after the repeal of Prohibition, both figures had declined by more than one-third. The Thompson machine gun—Capone's favorite—reigned supreme. It took the repeal of Prohibition to dethrone it.

The economics of Prohibition were such that it was more profitable to produce higher-alcohol-content hard liquor than beer. Moreover, it was easier to hide hard liquor with higher alcohol content per measure than it was to hide beer. Overall, Prohibition managed to reduce per-capita alcohol consumption by about 30 percent. Consumption of beer, however, was reduced by more than 90 percent. Few bootleggers or drinkers were willing to assume the legal risk of bothering with beer. Wine consumption also dropped sharply when Prohibition was instituted. The higher alcohol content of wine, though, made it a more appealing product for both suppliers and consumers. Thus, wine consumption soon began to rise again, and by the time of repeal it was greater than it had been before Prohibition. Also, by the mid-1920s, the consumption of hard liquor had risen to levels above those observed before 1920. During the last five years of Prohibition, the per-capita consumption of hard liquor was higher than at any time during the sixty years before or since!

When a good is made illegal, it becomes more difficult for consumers to punish suppliers who behave irresponsibly or maliciously. During Prohibition, consumers of alcohol often did not know exactly what they were buying or where to find the supplier the next day if they were dissatisfied. Fly-by-night operators sometimes adulterated liquor with methyl alcohol, like that used in portable cooking stoves. In extremely small concentrations, the result was to make watered-down booze taste like it had more "kick." In only slightly higher concentrations, the methyl alcohol blinded or even killed the unsuspecting consumer. Not surprisingly, during Prohibition the death rate from acute alcohol poisoning was more than thirty times higher than it is today. During 1927 alone, twelve thousand people died from acute alcohol poisoning, and many thousands more were blinded by contaminated booze.

At 3:32 P.M. (mountain time) on December 5, 1933, the results were announced: The people of Utah had voted in favor of the Twenty-first Amendment to the U.S. Constitution, repealing Prohibition. Citizens across the land celebrated on that day, for Utah was the last of the thirty-six states needed to ratify the amendment. America's "liquor wars" were over. Within days, the bootleggers and rumrunners were out of business.

Exercise in Critical Thinking
1. What are the similarities between the fourteen years of Prohibition and the current war on drugs?
2. What are the difficulties always faced by a government attempting to make certain activities illegal?
3. What were the costs and the benefits of Prohibition?

Four thousand kilograms of marijuana are seized by drug agents. Given the ease of growing this plant, are such seizures very effective in limiting illegal sales and use?

Drug Arrests, Prisons, and Courts. Current attempts at stopping drug sales and use have resulted in over 1.1 million drug-related arrests per year. Of those, however, only 20 percent are for drug trafficking. The remaining 80 percent are for simple drug possession, and most of those arrests are for possession of marijuana.

Not surprisingly, the U.S. prison population has been growing more rapidly in the last few years than at any time in our history. In 1990 alone, prison populations increased at five times the average annual rate for the previous fifty years. Prisons are overcrowded today, forcing many authorities to release dangerous prisoners before the end of their sentence. If current growth rates in the total prison population continue, we will see a doubling of that population every five years. In 1994, it will be 1.4 million; in 1999, 2.8 million; and by 2009 it will exceed 11 million. The annual cost of building, maintaining, and operating prisons is about $25 billion a year. By the year 2009, that annual cost will have risen to $400 billion if current trends continue.

The courts have also become victims of the increased number of drug arrests. Court calendars are overflowing. Because of speedy-trial statutes for criminal cases, virtually all drug cases get on the docket before civil cases. Civil lawsuits—those involving private parties rather than the state—take up to five years to get to court. In some jurisdictions, virtually all cases being heard are drug cases.

The Political Response to the Drug Problem

As noted earlier, Congress has responded to the increased illegal drug problem by passing amendments to the Controlled Substance Act of 1970 in 1984, 1986, and 1988. Before these amendments, a "war on drugs" had been waged by the Nixon administration. In 1971, President Nixon declared that drugs were "America's public enemy number one." He repeated his statement the following year. In 1973, Nixon announced that "we have turned the corner on drug addiction in America." In fact, of course, nothing was further from the truth.

The Bush administration immediately created a "drug czar" position, to which William Bennett, formerly secretary of education under President Reagan, was appointed. In 1989, Bennett and the Bush administration published the much-heralded *National Drug Control Strategy*. George Bush's covering letter to the speaker of the House stated that

> America's fight against epidemic illegal drug use cannot be won on any single front alone; it must be waged *everywhere*—at every level of Federal, State, and local government and by every citizen and every community across the country.

Bush called this strategy a "comprehensive blueprint" for a new direction and effort—and for success in the near- and long-term future. It proposed a variety of new measures and increased expenditures for the federal Drug Enforcement Administration (DEA). The total package that Congress approved in 1989 was $8.2 billion, up from $2.2 billion five years before. In total, federal, state, and local drug enforcement costs are estimated to be between $20 and $30 billion per year.

Drugs, the Military, and Foreign Policy

The raw materials for cocaine currently are grown in the Andes in Bolivia and Peru and are processed mainly in Colombia. The United States government has increased its effort at stopping the supply of cocaine at its source. Also, the government used the alleged drug dealing of former Panamanian strongman Manuel Noriega as a reason to invade Panama in December 1989. Recently, the U.S. Air Force has devoted an increasing number of its AWACS long-distance reconnaissance planes to the war on drugs in South America and at U.S. borders. The U.S. Army, while initially disavowing its ability to help in the war on drugs, agreed in 1989 that it could do so. This is not surprising, considering that the U.S. armed forces' long-term budgets are threatened with severe reductions because of the winding down of the Cold War and the reduced threat of Soviet military power. In addition, the CIA,

DID YOU KNOW?

That a Harvard University researcher reported in 1990 that nearly 2.2 million Americans use cocaine each week, more than twice the number previously estimated by the federal government?

William Bennett, former director of the federal drug war, presents his report to the media.

An anti-drug unit in Colombia destroys coca plants. To what extent should the United States be involved in the drug efforts of other nations?

which until 1990 had also stated its intention not to get involved in the war on drugs, has now agreed that it, too, can take part. Its motive is the same as that of the armed forces.

Critics of the government's attempt at stopping cocaine at its source point out some obvious facts. First, the raw ingredient of cocaine—coca leaves—can be grown virtually anywhere between the Tropic of Cancer and the Tropic of Capricorn. In South America alone, there are 2.5 *million* square miles available for coca production. Only .04 percent—1,000 square miles—are currently being used. The percentage of available land used for marijuana production is even less, because marijuana can be grown anywhere on the globe (even in Antarctica) provided there is a warm closet with a "grow" light.

Additionally, the economic situation facing Peruvian peasants is such that it will be virtually impossible for any coca eradication or crop substitution effort to succeed. The cultivation of coca yields ten to one hundred times more in annual income than the peasants could earn from growing any other crop.

Critics of America's foreign drug interdiction efforts point out the similarities between the U.S. government's current forays into Latin-American jungles and its forays into the jungles of Vietnam in the early 1960s. The American anti-communist crusade foundered against the strength of Vietnamese nationalism. The American crusade against drugs is likely to founder against the grinding poverty of the region's peasantry and urban underclass and the private armies of criminal drug lords and armed guerrilla liberation movements.

The Future of America's Drug Policy

There are basically three major views of U.S. drug policy. The laissez-faire, or libertarian, view argues for complete legalization of drugs. At the other end of the spectrum is the view that what is needed is even harsher penalties, a greater enforcement effort, and higher expenditures for that effort. The middle view calls for increased education and regulation, with perhaps even the decriminalization of certain "soft" drugs such as marijuana. Already, ten states have decriminalized the possession of small amounts of marijuana for personal use. One state, Alaska, had decriminalized the growing of small amounts of marijuana for personal use until 1990.

Certainly, the evidence shows that the results of the drug war to date have not been encouraging in reducing the amount of criminal activity associated with illegal drugs. A much-heralded and heavily publicized crackdown in late 1989 on Washington, D.C. drug dealers yielded virtually no reduction in drug use, drug trafficking, or drug crimes. Indeed, one year after the crackdown, then drug czar William Bennett was forced to admit that the policy had been a failure. Murders in Washington, D.C. had increased.

DID YOU KNOW?

That many push-button pay telephones in the Minneapolis–St. Paul area were replaced as a means of reducing drug trafficking, because the electronic pagers that drug dealers commonly use to conduct their business can send and receive messages through touch-tone phones but will not work with dial phones?

■ ENVIRONMENTAL POLICY

When the supertanker *Exxon Valdez* struck Bligh Reef in the pristine, frigid waters of Prince William Sound in Alaska, on March 24, 1989, it caused the worst oil spill in North American history: a quarter of a million barrels of crude oil (more than ten million gallons). Within a week, the oil slick covered almost 1,000 square miles, killing and maiming marine animals, fish, and migratory birds in its path. Within four weeks the slick had grown to 1,600 square miles and threatened wildlife living hundreds of miles to the southwest of the accident site. By the end of the summer of 1989, Exxon Corporation had already spent more than $1 billion on cleanup efforts, but probably recovered less than one-fourth of the crude oil that had escaped from the hold of the *Valdez*.

Oil spill disasters in the United States and elsewhere serve as constant reminders that human actions may create unwanted side effects—often the

An army of workers attempts to clean up the oil spill from the Exxon Valdez on Alaska beaches. How can such disasters be avoided if we continue our dependence on oil for energy?

Nuclear waste in Washington.

destruction of the environment and the ecology (the total pattern of environmental relationships). Every day, humans, through their actions, emit pollutants into the air and the water. Each year, the world atmosphere receives twenty million metric tons of sulfur dioxide, eighteen million metric tons of ozone pollutants, and sixty million metric tons of carbon monoxide.

The Government's Response to Pollution Problems

Government has been responding to pollution problems since before the American Revolution, when the Massachusetts Bay Colony issued regulations to try to stop the pollution of Boston Harbor. In the nineteenth century, states passed laws controlling water pollution after scientists and medical researchers convinced most policy makers that dumping sewage into drinking and bathing water caused disease. At the national level, the Water Pollution Control Act of 1948 provided research and assistance to the states for pollution control efforts, but little was done. In 1952, the first state air pollution law was passed in Oregon. The federal Air Pollution Control Act of 1955 gave some assistance to states and cities. Table 17-1 describes the major environmental legislation in the United States.

The National Environmental Policy Act.   The year 1969 marked the start of the most concerted national government involvement in pollution problems. In that year, the conflict between oil exploration interests and environmental interests literally erupted when a Union Oil Company's oil well six miles off the coast of Santa Barbara, California, exploded, releasing 235,000 gallons of crude oil. The result was an oil slick covering an area of eight hundred square miles, that washed up on the city's beaches and killed plant life, birds, and fish. Hearings in Congress revealed that the Interior Department did not know which way to go in the energy-environment trade-off. Congress did know, however, and passed the National Environmental Policy Act in 1969. This landmark legislation established, among other things, the Council for Environmental Quality (CEQ). Also, it mandated that an **environmental impact statement (EIS)** be prepared for every recommendation or report on legislation or major federal action that significantly affected the quality of the environment. The act gave citizens and public interest groups concerned with the environment a weapon against unnecessary and inappropriate use of our resources by government.

ENVIRONMENTAL IMPACT STATEMENT (EIS)
As a requirement mandated by NEPA, EISs must show the costs and benefits of major federal actions that could significantly affect the quality of the environment.

The Creation and Trading of Pollution Rights

One solution to environmental problems that actually has been put into effect is the creation and trading of pollution rights. For many years, governments have charged individuals and firms for the right to pollute. In some municipalities, for example, you can, for a fee, dispose of garbage in the city dump. In the past three decades, the concept of marketing pollution rights has been expanded. The Environmental Protection Agency (EPA) has even made a halfhearted attempt to create a marketplace for the buying and selling of pollution rights.

NATIONAL AIR QUALITY STANDARDS (NAQSs)
Standards concerning air quality for sulfur dioxide and other pollutants that are city or region specific and defined by the rules and regulations of the EPA following the passage of the 1963 federal Clean Air Act.

The 1963 federal Clean Air Act, through the rules and regulations of the EPA, presents localities with specified permitted pollution levels, called **national air quality standards (NAQSs)**. Since the air in most metropolitan

TABLE 17-1
Major Federal Environmental Legislation

1899 Refuse Act Made it unlawful to dump refuse into navigable waters without a permit. A 1966 court decision made all industrial wastes subject to this act.

1955 Federal Water Pollution Control Act Set standards for treatment of municipal water waste before discharge. Revisions to this act were passed in 1965 and 1967.

1963 Clean Air Act Assisted local and state governments in establishing control programs and coordinated research.

1965 Clean Air Act Amendments Authorized establishment of federal standards for automobile exhaust emissions, beginning with 1968 models.

1965 Solid Waste Disposal Act Provided assistance to local and state governments for control programs and authorized research in this area.

1965 Water Quality Act Authorized the setting of standards for discharges into waters.

1967 Air Quality Act Established air quality regions, with acceptable regional pollution levels. Required local and state governments to implement approved control programs or be subject to federal controls.

1969 National Environmental Policy Act Established the Council for Environmental Quality for the purpose of coordinating all federal pollution control programs. Authorized the establishment of the Environmental Protection Agency to implement CEQ policies on a case-by-case basis.

1970 Clean Air Act Amendments Authorized the Environmental Protection Agency to set national air pollution standards. Restricted the discharge of six major pollutants into the lower atmosphere. Automobile manufacturers were required to reduce nitrogen oxide, hydrocarbon, and carbon monoxide emissions by 90 percent (in addition to the 1965 requirements) during the 1970s. Set aircraft emission standards. Required states to meet deadlines for complying with EPA standards. Authorized legal action by private citizens to require EPA to carry out approved standards against undiscovered offenders.

1972 Federal Water Pollution Control Act Amendments Set national water quality goal of restoring polluted water to swimmable, fishable waters by 1983.

1972 Pesticide Control Act Required that all pesticides used in interstate commerce be approved and certified as effective for their stated purpose. Required certification that they were harmless to humans, animal life, animal feed, and crops.

1974 Clean Water Act Originally called the Safe Water Drinking Act, this law set (for the first time) federal standards for water suppliers serving more than twenty-five people, having more than fifteen service connections, or operating more than sixty days a year.

1976 Resource Conservation and Recovery Act Encouraged conservation and the recovery of resources. Put hazardous waste under government control. Disallowed the opening of new dumping sites. Required that all existing open dumps be closed or upgraded to sanitary landfills by 1983. Set standards for providing technical, financial, and marketing assistance to encourage solid waste management.

1977 Clean Air Act Amendments Postponed the deadline for automobile emission requirements.

1980 Comprehensive Environmental Response, Compensation, and Liability Act Established a "superfund" to clean up toxic waste dumps.

1990 Clean Air Act Amendments Provides for precise formulas for new gasoline to be burned in the smoggiest cities; further reduction in carbon monoxide and other exhaust emissions in certain areas that still have dangerous ozone levels in the year 2003; and a cap on total emissions of sulfur dioxide from electricity plants; new restrictions on toxic pollutants.

areas does not come close to meeting NAQSs, it would seem that no further economic industrial growth would be allowed in many urban areas. To get around the problem, the EPA approved an **offset policy** requiring a company wishing to build a plant to work out a corresponding reduction in pollution with another plant in the same area. The EPA has even suggested that a pollution rights bank be set up to act as a clearinghouse.

Pollution Credits. As an alternative, some commentators have suggested that the government set uniform emission standards and allow companies that beat the standards to accumulate and sell **pollution credits.** Companies that fail to meet the standards would be able to buy them. Clearly, companies building newer plants find it relatively cheaper to install pollution control equipment than do companies with older plants that have to be retrofitted. The older plants would be able to buy the pollution credits to avoid adopting expensive antipollution measures. Assuming a high enough standard, pollution

OFFSET POLICY
A method in which a company wishing to build a plant in a polluted area works out an agreement with another plant in the same area for that other plant to reduce its pollutants.

POLLUTION CREDITS
Unused "units" of pollutants that a company has to its credit for a specific plant. In certain instances, these pollution credits can be sold to other companies to allow those other companies to emit more than the standard amount of pollutants.

overall would still decrease. One estimate by Senators Timothy E. Wirth of Colorado and John Heinz of Pennsylvania is that the annual benefit to the economy would be $3 billion for sulfur dioxide emissions alone.

Problems With Pollution Credits.   One major problem with a system of buying and selling pollution credits is that pollution "hot spots" may develop. Ground-level air quality could actually worsen in some areas. This would be the case if the firms buying the pollution credits are concentrated in one particular area and the ones selling them are in different areas.

There is an additional problem of measuring the amount of pollution. Each company's pollution credit would be dependent on an EPA-certified ambient air certificate. This calculation is subject to error and, of course, fraud.

The Trading of Pollution Rights

Among the many proposals offered by the Bush administration to clean up our environment, one was to harness market forces by expanding the offset principle nationwide. For example, during the second half of the 1990s, owners of 107 of the nation's most pollution-producing electric utility plants would be required to bring down their emission levels for sulfur dioxide. The utilities themselves would decide how this is to be done. During this period, the EPA would set up a market in emission credits. Phase 2 of the Bush plan would start in the year 2000 and would apply to an additional 200 to 300 electric utility plants. At this point, the utilities would begin to buy and sell credits to one another with little restriction.

Smog blankets a valley in California. What measures is the public prepared to take to really reduce air pollution?

The initial price of pollution rights would be about equal to the incremental cost of pollution reduction, somewhere between $1,000 and $2,000 a ton at current prices. Environmentalists will also have a right to buy pollution credits for the purpose of retiring them, forcing down the level of legally permissible air pollution.

The Latest Government Response: The Clean Air Act Amendments

In 1990, amendments to the 1970 Clean Air Act were passed—over a thousand pages of regulations of American industrial emissions.

One innovative aspect of this act is that Congress has mandated precise formulas for new less-polluting gasoline that must be used in the smoggiest cities. Also, the act requires that if by the year 2003 certain cities still have dangerous ozone levels, pollution emissions standards for automobiles in those cities must be drastically reduced. The emission of potential cancer-causing air toxins was greatly limited. Additionally, the act places severe restrictions on the total emissions of sulfur dioxide from electric utilities.

Can Voluntarism Help?

Many concerned environmentalists argue that not only private individuals but also business management could voluntarily help solve, or at least reduce, our pollution problems by cutting back on pollution-causing practices. The problem is that "nice-guy" environmentalists who voluntarily pay to abate pollution end up at a competitive disadvantage in our very competitive marketplace. The concerned environmentalist–business manager will be dealt with harshly by the marketplace. In a competitive situation, there is constant pressure to minimize costs. That is why pollution occurs in the first place. Managers will attempt to produce everything they wish to sell at the lowest possible cost. If they can get away with not paying for using certain resources, such as the clean air and water into which they dump their pollutants, they will do so.

Should we conclude that cleaning up or avoiding pollution would cost too much? Not really. Any statement that cleaning up our environment costs too much is missing the point. The costs of pollution always exist. The question is who should bear the costs.

Global Warming

One of the most pressing concerns around the world is the threat of global warming. Not too many years ago, however, most commentators and scientists were worried about a new ice age. In the June 24, 1974, issue of *Time* magazine, for example, the editor said that "the atmosphere has been growing gradually cooler for the past three decades. The trend shows no indication of reversing." Dr. Reid Bryson, writing in *People* magazine on October 24, 1980, stated that "the overall cooling trend is unmistakable, and in coming years it will profoundly affect agriculture, geopolitics, and human survival worldwide." As late as May 12, 1983, the editors of *Rolling Stone* declared:

> For years now, climatologists have foreseen a trend toward colder weather—long range, to be sure, but a trend as inevitable as death. . . . according to one theory, all it would take is a single cold summer to plunge the earth into a sudden apocalypse of ice.

By 1990, however, scientists had decided that the earth was warming. According to the National Academy of Sciences, "global environmental change [global warming] may well be the most pressing international issue of the next century" and "the future welfare of human society is . . . at risk."

Some observers believe there is a silver lining in the cloud of global warming. James R. Udall, a frequent contributor to *Audubon*, *National Wildlife*, and *Sierra* magazines, wrote:

> A century from now historians may conclude that the threat of global warming was the best thing that ever happened to the environment. Humanity has an enormous investment in a stable climate, and global warming gives us a compelling, selfish, economic incentive to change patterns of energy use that have proved so harmful to the environment.[1]

The Greenhouse Effect and Global Warming

GREENHOUSE EFFECT
The trapping of heat within the earth's atmosphere as a result of pollution caused largely by the burning of fossil fuels and emissions of carbon dioxide.

The **greenhouse effect** is the trapping of heat inside the earth's atmosphere as a result of pollution caused largely by the burning of fossil fuels and the emission of carbon dioxide (CO_2). The process is accelerated by deforestation and the burning of trees in places such as the Amazon rain forest.

There are still deep disagreements among scientists on the extent and nature of the global warming phenomenon and the greenhouse effect. It probably will take several more years before hard evidence is available that the earth indeed is warming.

However, some of the most reliable computer models of the world's climate, such as one at the National Center for Atmospheric Research, suggest that if the current rate of the greenhouse effect continues, by the year 2050 the earth's temperature will rise by three to nine degrees Fahrenheit. The change in temperature would precipitate ecological changes that in turn would result in dramatic social, economic, and political upheavals. The icecaps would melt, coastal water levels would rise, flooding many cities, forests would die, some

[1]"Global Warming: Diplomacy's Next Great Challenge," *Phi Kappa Phi Journal*, Winter, 1990, p. 36.

Destruction of the Brazilian rain forest may contribute to global warming.

PROFILE

Manuel Lujan

"If one little piece of our public trust is desecrated, we all suffer from it."

For many years the Department of the Interior was one of the quietest federal agencies, controlling the federal public lands and national parks. However, during the Reagan administration, two successive Secretaries of that department—James Watts and Donald Hodel—managed to push the department into the national spotlight. Both secretaries espoused the conservative philosophy of Mr. Reagan, supporting the commercial development of public lands and opposing many claims of environmentalists. Although he has a reputation for being a congenial moderate on environmental issues, Manuel Lujan, Bush's Secretary of the Interior may not be able to escape the controversies that now seem inherent to the job.

One of eleven children, Lujan was raised in the village of San Ildefonso, near Santa Fe, New Mexico. After completing college and beginning a career in his father's insurance agency, Lujan became active in Republican party politics. In 1968, he upset the incumbent congressman to become the Representative from the First District of New Mexico. His constituency included Santa Fe, Albuquerque, and most of the northeastern third of the state. As the first Hispanic Republican in the House of Representatives, Lujan was frequently showcased by the party, especially at national conventions.

After twenty years in the House, he rose to the position of senior Republican on the House Interior and Insular Affairs Committee and vice chairman of the House Science, Space, and Technology Committee. Known as a consensus builder and good listener, he compiled a moderate record on environmental issues. Although he had supported the 1970 Clean Air Act and the 1980 Alaska Lands Act, Lujan was considered pro-business on issues of timber and oil drilling. In 1988, he announced his retirement from Congress, saying that, "I see so many of my colleagues stay too long. After twenty years, it's time to come home."

Lujan had been passed over twice by Ronald Reagan for the job at Interior. When George Bush asked him to serve in the Cabinet, Lujan accepted the position. Environmentalists objected to his pro-business tendencies, but members of the House supported his appointment, noting that he was well-known to them and should be easy for legislators to work with.

Two months after taking office, Manuel Lujan faced his first crisis: the *Exxon Valdez* oil spill in Alaska. Since that time, a series of decisions have kept the amiable secretary in the spotlight. He angered environmentalists with his approval of California water contracts, but placed the national park and wilderness system off-limits to mining. In the summer of 1990, he announced the decision of the department to declare the spotted owl an endangered species. Although Lujan expressed deep concern over the impact of the designation for the timber industry, the department proceeded with plans to cease timber operations in the old-growth forests that provide habitat for the bird.

Given the strength of public support for preservation of the environment, it is unlikely that Lujan will have many easy decisions in his years at the Department of the Interior.

geographic areas would become desert, and, in others, farmland and crops would be severely stressed.

The rise in sea levels by the year 2100 would put most of the Netherlands, Bangladesh, and Egypt under water. New Orleans, New York, Venice, Bangkok, and other cities would be devastated. Florida south of Palm Beach, including Miami and Key West, would disappear under the Atlantic Ocean.

Most experts now agree that the greenhouse effect may well pose one of the most serious challenges to U.S. and world leaders in the coming three decades—and that the problem must be addressed on a global scale. The revelation of terrible environmental devastation in Eastern Europe, and China and India's continued reliance on coal as a major energy source, indicate the urgency of the issue as well as some of the difficulties in reaching solutions. Of course, because the United States, with 5 percent of the world's population, produces 23 percent of the world's CO_2, so the responsibility of American leadership is clear.

Perhaps most daunting is the fact that only drastic reductions in the use of fossil fuels and the use of alternate energy will slow down, stop, and perhaps reverse the damage already done. Those energy sources are not currently cost-effective and safe (nuclear energy for example), and new, clean energy sources and technologies have yet to be devised, much less put on line for use.

The Government's Response to the Global Warming Threat

The federal government has responded to the threat of global warming. For example, the Environmental Protection Agency is still requiring ever-improved gas mileage ratings and pollution controls for newly-produced automobiles sold in the United States. The argument is that we must reduce the amount of carbon dioxide spewed into the air because of the threat of global warming and the possible destruction of the ozone layer. Although legislation to raise fuel efficiency levels generally has been met with strong opposition from corporate interests and their political allies, events which threaten to reduce fuel supplies—such as the Iraqi invasion of Kuwait in 1990—provide new impetus to the need for enhanced efficiency.

Ozone

The ozone layer shields the earth from excessive ultraviolet radiation from the sun, which causes skin cancer, cataracts, and suppression of the human immune system, as well as harming crops and wildlife.

In 1990, scientists discovered that the ozone layer is being destroyed much faster than previously thought—a 10 percent reduction since 1987 over Europe and North America. Over the polar regions, especially Antarctica, the loss has been 50 percent, causing "holes" in the ozone shield. Industrial chemicals that contain chlorine—chloroflurocarbons (CFC), halons, carbon tetrachloride, methyl chloroform—are thought to be the principal culprits in destroying the ozone molecules. These chemicals are used extensively in refrigeration equipment and as a propellant for aerosol sprays.

Fifty-six nations signed a treaty in Montreal, Canada, in 1987 that requires them to reduce the production and use of chloroflurocarbons by 50 percent by the year 2000. However, new data has increased pressure for a more rapid elimination of this and other ozone-depleting chemicals. The United States, Japan, the Soviet Union, and several other countries support the complete elimination of chloroflurocarbons by the end of this century and have agreed to give economic and technical assistance to developing nations that switch to alternative chemicals.

Federal law in the United States now requires special disposal and handling of equipment containing ozone-reducing chemicals that might leak into the atmosphere, and reduction of CFC in widely used consumer products such as aerosol sprays. It remains to be seen whether the damage to the ozone layer and the earth's atmosphere can be reduced.

Once declared an endangered species, the spotted owl became the center of controversy in the northwest United States. Should the owl be saved by limiting the cutting of timber in that region if the cost is thousands of jobs for the lumber industry?

■ THE AIDS EPIDEMIC

By the time you read this, almost 100,000 Americans will have died from AIDS (acquired immunodeficiency syndrome). At least 1 million more have been infected with the HIV virus, which causes AIDS.[2] The economic and social costs of the AIDS epidemic in the United States are large, but not as great as in many other parts of the world. As many as half of the populations of major cities in Africa, for example, have been infected with the virus. AIDS is a worldwide problem and one that is not about to disappear.

The Global Epidemic

In 1984, scientists first identified the virus that causes AIDS. At that time, fewer than 4,500 Americans had been stricken. Today, more than 3,000 cases of AIDS are reported every month in this country. As can be seen in Figure 17-1, the worldwide situation is deteriorating. The estimate for 1992 is that 800,000 people will have developed AIDS worldwide and 8 million people will have contracted the virus that causes it. By the year 2000, about 6 million people will be sick and 30 million more will be infected. A third of the population in some parts of Africa are infected by the AIDS virus.

In the United States, 5 to 12 percent of pregnant women in the Bronx are infected with the virus, as well as 25 percent of young men surveyed in Newark, New Jersey. Although, initially the U.S. epidemic was concentrated in major cities, among intravenous drug users and gay men, that pattern is changing. As the epidemic matures, America's smallest cities are seeing an increase in cases. The transmission of AIDS will, by the year 2000, be primarily through heterosexual activity in most industrial countries, according to Dr. James Chin, an epidemiologist in charge of AIDS surveillance at the World Health Organization.

[2]The virus attacks the immune system, leaving its victim exposed to a host of diseases against which the body has no defense.

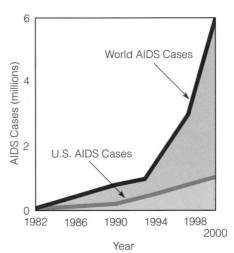

FIGURE 17-1
AIDS: Global Epidemic
Most of the 1 million infected in the United States will be sick by 2000; worldwide, six times that many will be afflicted.
SOURCE: *Newsweek,* July 18, 1990.

Demonstrators at an AIDS conference in Montreal try to raise global awareness of the disease.

HIGHLIGHT

The Ryan White Story

"Ryan has helped us understand the truth about AIDS, and he's shown all of us the strength and bravery of the human heart." This quote by President Bush summed up the feeling of the nation as it mourned the death of Ryan White, the boy who had come to symbolize the struggle against AIDS. Ryan White was a hemophiliac, and contracted AIDS through a blood transfusion. Ryan captured the heart of the nation during his unsuccessful fight to continue attending public school in his hometown of Kokomo, Indiana. Under pressure, the Whites left Kokomo and found acceptance in Cicero, Indiana. His bravery and cheerfulness throughout his illness brought him the attention of rock stars, politicians, and other celebrities. Michael Jackson and Elton

Ryan White

John, who both attended Ryan's funeral, were just two of the many lives touched by Ryan White.

Many people viewed Ryan as a major spokesperson for AIDS victims. He showed that people with AIDS can still lead full, productive lives and need not be feared or avoided. Ryan's story and his inspiration have made people more aware of the sad consequences of discriminating against AIDS victims.

Ryan White left high school during his senior year because of failing health and died four months later, in April 1989, at the age of eighteen. The memory of his heroic struggle against AIDS remains. In the words of former president Ronald Reagan, "We owe it to Ryan to open our hearts and minds to those with AIDS. We owe it to Ryan to be compassionate, caring, and tolerant toward those with AIDS, their families and friends."

Medically, there have been some successes. After all, no one had heard of AIDS when doctors started describing the syndrome in 1981. Since then researchers have identified the human immunodeficiency virus (HIV) and also learned how it infects cells and destroys the immune system. During the 1980s, a diagnostic test was developed, safer blood supplies were made available, and some treatments—notably the drugs AZT and pentamidine that have prolonged AIDS patients' lives—made available.

The initial response of the medical community and the government to the problem of AIDS was not only slow but also political. Gay men and Haitians are the two high-risk groups that were first targeted. These are not people who generate rapid and favorable government response in the form of research and treatment funds. Some conservatives and traditional religious groups even asserted that this disease was a punishment by God for immoral behavior.

Outraged at the slowness and apparent hostility of government, the gay and lesbian community began to mobilize politically. Rallies, news conferences, and a strategy for inducing wider societal concern about the condition, as well as support for programs to find a cure, were launched. By the mid-1980s, a concerted effort was made to demonstrate that AIDS was a threat to all Americans, not just to high-risk groups. This became dramatically clear when AIDS-contaminated blood was identified as the source of infection of persons falling outside the high-risk groups.

By the late 1980s, AIDS had been taken up as a cause by celebrities Elizabeth Taylor and others. A huge quilt embroidered with the names of AIDS victims was assembled and displayed in many cities throughout the country. Massive demonstrations were organized in Washington, D.C. and elsewhere. The media lent its support to the pressure for AIDS research and treatment, while public service television ads depicted white, middle-class, nongay men and women with AIDS (the lowest-risk group). After much prodding, Congress began to fund AIDS research, treatment, and education programs. The surgeon general prepared and mailed to every U.S. household a booklet with information on AIDS and its prevention and advocated sex education and the use of condoms.

By 1990, some public health experts began to argue that money for AIDS was now so abundant that it was threatening research and treatment for other major public health problems, including cancer, heart disease, and Alzheimer's disease. In 1990, the House voted $4 billion over a four-year period for treating AIDS and almost $1.5 billion for AIDS research. AIDS activists have disputed these numbers, citing $1.6 billion as the four-year figure and pressing for continued increases in funding.

Meanwhile, statistics indicated that AIDS was still most likely to be a major problem for intravenous drug users, persons engaged in anal sex, and people linked to these two groups (for example, prostitutes who use intravenous drugs can spread it to their clients who spread it to other women; bisexual men can pass it on to other men and women; and pregnant women with AIDS can infect their unborn children). Particularly disturbing was the discovery in 1990 that many younger gay men (over 45 percent in one study) were engaged in unsafe sex—anal intercourse without condoms. Moreover, AIDS was also showing up in adolescents, drug users not using intravenous drugs (but using crack cocaine and alcohol), and women. Surgical workers and other medical professionals exposed to blood were also shown to be increasingly at risk. Even dentists began to wear surgical gloves, as did law-enforcement persons exposed to contaminated needles or to bleeding crime victims or criminals.

Studies to check the effectiveness of providing free needles or bleach to disinfect the needles of intravenous drug users (who often share contaminated needles) were conducted with private funds because federal law prohibited the use of money for these purposes.

Radical AIDS advocacy groups, such as ACT UP, increased their protests, interrupting the 1990 AIDS conference in San Francisco and completely drowning out the speech by U.S. Secretary of Health and Human Services Dr. Louis Sullivan, and refusing to reject violence against property as a strategy to call attention to the AIDS problem. Other groups have bypassed the very slow U.S. Federal Drug Administration (FDA) procedures for testing and licensing new drugs and are testing on their own drugs and medication that can help reduce the symptoms or prolong the lives of AIDS sufferers. Pressure from AIDS activists on the FDA have produced some changes in the procedures for allowing the experimental use of promising drugs before licensing.

Whatever the level of effort, no single government initiative is going to solve the AIDS crisis. It will require a concerted international attack.

■ THE CRISIS IN AMERICAN EDUCATION

Recently, President George Bush outlined six national goals for education to be met by the year 2000:

1. Every American child must start school prepared to learn, sound in body, and sound in mind.

2. The high school graduation rate in the United States must increase to at least 90 percent.
3. All students in grades four, eight, and twelve will be tested for progress in critical subjects.
4. American students must rank first in the world in achievement in mathematics and science.
5. Every adult must be a skilled, literate worker and citizen, able to compete in a global economy.
6. Every school must be drug-free and offer a disciplined environment conducive to learning.

To achieve these goals in less than a decade will not be easy. In a standardized math test given to thirteen-year-olds in six countries, Koreans performed the best and Americans the worst, trailing Spain, Great Britain, Ireland, and Canada. In spite of this poor showing, when asked whether "I am good at mathematics," 68 percent of American students answered yes. Comparatively poor test results by American school children were found for geography and some other subjects as well.

Is More Spending the Answer?

There is a debate going on about the extent to which more spending can help in attaining President Bush's goals. Table 17-2 shows that the United States is almost at the top in instructional spending per student throughout the world. Nonetheless, the United States lags behind most industrialized countries in student achievement.

Even more telling is the relationship between spending and achievement as measured by average SAT scores. Combined SAT scores peaked at a little less than 1,000 (out of a possible 1,600) in the early 1960s, as seen in Figure 17-2. While public school expenditures per pupil (corrected for inflation) continued to rise, SAT scores fell to about 900 in the mid-1970s and remained approximately the same though the entire 1980s. Between 1972 and 1981, the number of high school seniors scoring above 600 (out of a possible 800) on the verbal portion of the SAT dropped by 70 percent (in 1990 this number remained nearly 30 percent below the 1972 average).

In the 1980s, most states poured money into schools to boost salaries and improve teaching. The student-teacher ratio in public elementary and secondary schools fell from 27.5:1 in 1949 to 17.4:1 by 1990. The student-administrative staff ratio in public elementary and secondary schools fell dramatically from almost 20:1 in 1949 to just over 9:1 by 1990.

Indeed, the last statistic highlights one important aspect of increased spending on public education in the United States. Although we are spending more and more money on our public schools, the teachers are not, in general, getting it. Teachers' salaries as a proportion of operating budgets have been declining for decades, falling from 55 percent in 1959 to only 40 percent in 1990. Although a portion of the increased overhead (administrative expenses) is going for librarians and guidance counselors, much of it has been characterized as contributing to bureaucratic bloat.

If More Money Won't Improve Education, What Will?

Other solutions than increasing public expenditures have been offered to solve America's education crisis. These include more freedom to choose schools and a voucher system.

TABLE 17-2
How Much Do Governments Spend Per Student?
Instructional expenditures (pre-K through 12th grade)*

Switzerland	$3,683	1985
United States	3,310	1985
Sweden	3,214	1985
Canada	3,192	1985
Denmark	3,089	1986
Norway	2,900	1985
Luxembourg	2,596	1983
Austria	2,497	1985
West Germany	2,253	1985
Belgium	2,234	1985
France	1,996	1984
Australia	1,995	1985
Britain	1,897	1984
Netherlands	1,860	1984
Japan	1,805	1985

*Based on the Organization for Economic Cooperation and Development's 1985 purchasing power parities index.
SOURCE: *U.S. Department of Education.*

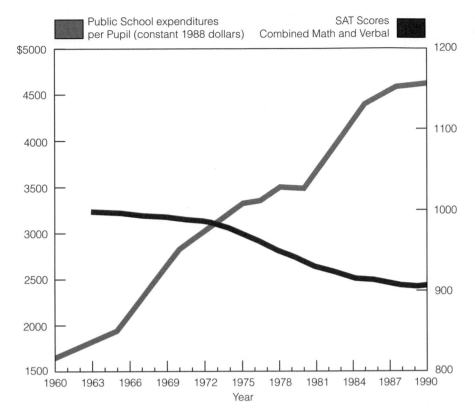

FIGURE 17-2
Expenditures vs. SAT scores

Freedom of Choice.   Some proponents of change in American education argue that the current system does not allow enough freedom of choice. That is, parents are not allowed to send their children to the school of their choice unless they are willing to pay twice—once in property taxes for public education and again in the form of private school tuition. If parents were able to choose among schools for their children, proponents of choice say, schools would be stimulated to improve their performance in order to compete successfully for students.

The Minnesota Experiment In 1985, the governor of Minnesota proposed that juniors and seniors in public schools be permitted to receive all or part of their last two years of high school in colleges and vocational schools, with state monies following them to pay their tuition, lab fees, and book fees. The governor also recommended that families be allowed to send their children to public schools outside their home districts, as long as the receiving districts had room and the movement did not harm desegregation efforts. Despite vigorous opposition to the proposals by teachers' unions, school boards, and superintendents' groups, four laws allowing greater freedom of educational choice have been passed in Minnesota.

   Since 1985, more than ten thousand students have taken advantage of the program permitting them to take college courses while still in high school. Many of them have higher grade-point averages in those courses than do the regular college freshman students. The program has attracted hundreds of students who had dropped out of high school due to boredom or frustration. Moreover, many participants are, thanks to the new program, the first in their families to attend college.

DID YOU KNOW?

That in 1989, the state government of New Jersey took control of the 28,000-student Jersey City school system because the district was deemed corrupt, mismanaged, filled with patronage, and academically unsound?

The experiment seems to have stimulated many high schools to improve their programs. Between 1985 and 1990, the number of advanced-placement courses offered by Minnesota high schools quadrupled—without any new mandates or dollars targeted for this purpose. Also, more than fifty high schools have been spurred on to establish cooperative programs with colleges and universities that let them offer college courses right in the high schools.

Minnesota has passed two other laws. Students at any level who don't succeed in one junior or senior high school are allowed to attend a school outside their district. Several thousand students have taken advantage of this plan—about half of them high school dropouts. Another law is phasing in a plan to enable Minnesota students in all grades to attend school outside their districts, subject to space and racial balance. During the first year after the law's passage, about four thousand students applied for transfers.

The East Harlem Experiment In 1974, East Harlem ranked dead last among New York City's thirty-two community school districts. Only 15 percent of its students read at or above their grade level. By 1990, the East Harlem school district ranked sixteenth in New York City. More than 65 percent of its students read at or above grade school level. Today, East Harlem—one of the poorest areas of New York—has a waiting list of teachers wishing to work there.

This change began in 1974, when the administrators of the East Harlem school district decided to permit curriculum choice. Teachers could choose curriculums and programs they thought would provide the best educational products. Students and parents were allowed to choose from among those products the ones best suited for their preferences and educational objectives. Along the way, some schools did a poor job and failed to attract "new customers." They have closed their doors. Other schools offered popular, effective programs that have been replicated successfully elsewhere in the district. The program was so successful that the East Harlem educators decided in 1985

An urban school yard. What kinds of changes are needed to strengthen education in the United States?

to assume responsibility for a neighborhood high school with a graduation rate of 7 percent. Its graduation rate now exceeds 90 percent and almost all of its graduates go on to some kind of postsecondary education.

Increased Parental Involvement Part of the reason, apparently, why educational choice works is because choice secures the involvement of parents in the education process. Parent involvement in private schools has always been high, according to supporters of choice. A recent study by James S. Coleman showed that "the estimated effect of attending a Catholic school is about an extra year's achievement over a two-year period."[3] In recent years, Chicago has radically decentralized control over local schools in an effort to increase parental involvement in that city's crisis-plagued educational system.

Vouchers.   Another proposed solution to the United States's declining public school educational achievement is the use of vouchers. In this system, the state would grant a specified amount of money in the form of a voucher for each student in the state. The parent could then use the voucher at any bona fide public or private school. Although the voucher idea has been around for decades, it has been vigorously opposed, particularly by teachers' unions and public school administrators. The voucher system was used after World War II and the Korean war for college education for veterans—the so-called G.I. Bill. The G.I. Bill allowed for a certain amount of money to be applied to tuition and other expenses at virtually any college or university in the United States. So far, however, the voucher system has not been used on a wide scale for primary or secondary school-aged children.

■ THE CHALLENGE OF POLICYMAKING IN A COMPLEX WORLD

As these four cases illustrate, making public policy today is a difficult and exasperating task. Perhaps the least controversial of the four domestic policy domains examined in this chapter is education, yet even this policy problem involves federal, state, and local public authorities. In addition, citizens have very strong feelings about government decisions that affect their children and their communities. In the cases of AIDS and the environment, the policy problem is not confined to American society, much less to one state or locality. Only through the cooperative efforts of many nations and the development of new technologies can these problems be addressed adequately. Finally, the United States has spent billions of dollars and used troops with little impact on the drug problem. At the heart of this issue is the question of what causes the demand for illegal substances. Until that question is better understood, it is unlikely that any strategy, either punitive or preventative will be successful in reducing the drug trade. Like most public policy issues, these four require political decisions that balance the interests of those affected, deal with moral choices of human beings, and respect the processes outlined in the Constitution.

[3]James S. Coleman, *Do Students Learn More in Private Schools Than in Public Schools?* (Tallahassee, Fl.), Madison Institute for Public Policies Studies, 1990.

Working for a Clean Environment

Energy undoubtedly will be among the more important domestic issues in the coming decades. Ultimately, every energy policy involves environmental questions. Not only is this issue central to our everyday lives, but also, it is argued, the fate of the planet may hang in the balance of today's decisions made about energy production and environmental protection. To make things more complicated, these parallel struggles of coping with energy problems and preserving our environment tend to work at cross-purposes. In the pursuit of secure and abundant energy, the interests of clean air, water, and land—as well as people—are sometimes sacrificed.

Over all decisions about nuclear energy hang memories of Three Mile Island, Chernobyl, continuous low-level radiation, the hazards of radioactive waste, and the threat of worldwide proliferation of nuclear weapons. Reliance on oil raises the problem of continuing pollution and of committing the economic well-being of the nation to decisions of other nations. Increasing reliance on coal means encouraging an industry that is hazardous to its workers, as well as increasing the possibility of severe environmental damage through acid rain and global warming.

When objectives clash, difficult political trade-offs must be made. To a large group of environmentalists in this country, the choice is clear. Through citizen action groups, environmentalists have challenged the government on these and other issues. They argue that if we want to improve or even preserve our quality of life, we must stop environmental degradation.

Although these diverse groups work on a host of issues from solar power to mass transit and from wildlife preservation to population control, they are bound by certain commonly held beliefs. Brock Evans describes the traditional goals of the environmental movement:

> We have always sought the highest quality management of public lands for the full spectrum of multiple uses, so that the lands will not be abused but will be passed on to the future intact and not ravaged by short-term exploitation.
> We have always sought special reservations of our finest scenic vistas, our superlative natural and historic wonders, the remnants of once-vast wilderness . . . because they are part of our culture, history, and traditions, too.
> We have always sought the highest degree of protection for our native wildlife in parks, refuges, and wilderness areas, and through high-quality management . . . so that future generations as well as our own can enjoy this abundance.*

*Brock Evans, "The Environmental Community: Response to the Reagan Administration Program," delivered to the National Symposium on Public Lands and the Reagan Administration, Denver, Colorado, November 19, 1981, and published in *Vital Speeches*, February 1, 1982, p. 231.

If you feel strongly about these issues and want to get involved, contact the following groups:

Environmental Defense Fund
1616 P St., N.W.
Washington, D.C. 20036

Environmental Policy Institute
218 D St., S.E.
Washington, D.C. 20003

Friends of the Earth
537 Seventh St., N.E.
Washington, D.C. 20003

Greenpeace USA
1611 Connecticut Ave., N.W.
Washington, D.C. 20009

Izaak Walton League of America
1701 N. Fort Meyer Dr.
Arlington, VA 22209

League of Conservation Voters
320 Fourth St., N.E.
Washington, D.C. 20002

National Audubon Society
1130 Fifth Ave.
New York, NY 10038

National Parks Conservation Association
1701 Eighteenth Street, N.W.
Washington, D.C. 20009

National Wildlife Federation
1325 Massachusetts Ave., N.W.
Washington, D.C. 20036

Natural Resources Defense Fund
11350 New York Ave., N.W.
Washington, D.C. 20005

Sierra Club
730 Polk St.
San Francisco, CA 94109

Wilderness Society
1400 Eye Street, N.W.
Washington, D.C. 20005

CHAPTER SUMMARY

1. The first comprehensive national legislation that outlawed the use of opium, morphine, and cocaine was the Harrison Narcotics Act of 1914. The sale and use of marijuana was banned in 1937.

2. In 1919, the Eighteenth Amendment to the U.S. Constitution prohibited the manufacture and sale of alcoholic beverages. During the era of Prohibition, alcohol consumption was reduced somewhat, but the amount of hard liquor consumed actually increased during the fourteen years of Prohibition. Organized crime got its foothold during this period. Murder rates increased. Death from acute alcohol poisoning reached a maximum.

3. The dominant federal legislation on all drugs in the Controlled Substances Act (CSA) of 1970, amended in 1984, 1986, and 1988. It is a federal crime to sell, possess, or use any opiates or their derivatives, cocaine or its derivatives, marijuana, and all hallucinogens and amphetamines.

4. The current war on drugs has clogged the courts and the jails. If current trends continue, the prison population will double every five years and reach eleven million (from its current one million) by 2009. The cost of building, maintaining, and operating prisons will rise to $400 billion per year from its current $25 billion.

5. President Nixon started a war on drugs in 1971 and declared that we had turned the corner on drug addiction in 1973. The Bush administration created a "drug czar" position and pushed Congress to increase funding fourfold in its first two years. In spite of total government spending of $20 to $30 billion per year on drug enforcement, the problem remains serious.

6. Because of reduced tensions with the Soviet Union, potential military and intelligence budgets are threatened. Consequently, the armed services and the CIA have agreed to take part in the war on drugs.

7. Pollution problems continue to plague the United States and the world. The federal government's first environmental legislation was passed in 1899 with the Refuse Act. Since then, at least fifteen significant federal acts have been passed.

8. The National Environmental Policy Act of 1969 established the Council of Environmental Quality. That act also mandated that environmental impact statements (EISs) be prepared for all legislation or major federal actions that significantly affect the quality of the environment.

9. The Environmental Protection Agency has set permitted pollution levels in various cities. These are called national air quality standards (NAQSs).

10. We cannot expect voluntarism on the part of manufacturers in a competitive society to help reduce pollution. An environmental-oriented business manager will be dealt with harshly by the marketplace.

11. Although in the 1970s the threat of a new ice age seemed to be most in the news, by the 1990s the threat of global warming had taken over. The U.S. government's response has been to participate in several international conferences and to agree to limit the use of fluorocarbons as refrigerants and in other commercial uses.

12. The AIDS epidemic in some parts of the world has grown more rapidly than in the United States.

13. After a slow start in allocating money for AIDS research and treatment, the government has stepped up its efforts in both areas, including allowing the FDA to release promising drugs for experimental use before licensing.

14. More spending on education does not seem to be the answer to improved educational achievement. Expenditures per pupil have risen dramatically since 1960, yet SAT scores leveled off a decade and a half ago. Student-teacher ratios have dropped and so have student-administrative staff ratios.

15. One suggestion for improving education is to allow more choice. This may be done through allowing parents to send their children to any school within a certain district or by giving them vouchers that can be used in any qualified school.

QUESTIONS FOR REVIEW AND DISCUSSION

1. What are the arguments for and against drug legalization?

2. Contrast the current status of alcohol and nicotine and how they are controlled with the control of other psychoactives.

3. "We pay for pollution in one way or another." Analyze this statement.

4. What groups in society would be against a voucher system for primary and secondary education in the United States, and why? What groups would be in favor, and why?

5. In this chapter, you learned that there is a disproportionate amount of federal spending on AIDS research, in contrast to, for example, the amount of money spent on heart disease research. Nonetheless, many groups still maintain that the federal government is doing too little and too late. What are the arguments to support this view? What are the arguments against it?

SELECTED REFERENCES

Forest Chisman and Alan Pifer, *Government for the People—The Federal Social Role* (New York, W. W. Norton, 1988). This book analyses what the appropriate role of the federal government is in providing social welfare in America.

Robert Crandal et al., eds., *Regulating the Automobile* (Washington, D.C., Brookings Institution, 1986). The automobile is a source of pleasure and pollution. The authors of the various papers in this volume examine the fact and fiction of air pollution caused by automobiles.

Matthew A. Crenson, *The Un-Politics of Air Pollution* (Baltimore, Md., Johns Hopkins University Press, 1971). This twenty-year old treatise on air pollution still presents some insights into the problem and the politics surrounding it.

Henry J. Erin, ed., *Setting National Priorities: 1990 and Beyond* (Washington, D.C., Brookings Institution, 1990). An important book which explains and evaluates the options for U.S. domestic policy in the 1990s.

Robert A. Leone, *Who Profits: Winners, Losers, and Government Regulation* (New York, Basic Books, 1986). The author analyzes the question of who obtains the benefits and who pays the costs of different types of government regulation including environmental regulation.

Roger LeRoy Miller, et al., *The Economics of Public Issues,* 8th ed. (New York, Harper Collins Publishers, 1990). Chapters 4, 9, 18, 19, 20, 22, 25, 28, and 29 are especially useful. The authors use short three-to-seven-page essays to explain the purely economic aspects of numerous social problems including the war on drugs, the environment, and education.

Roger LeRoy Miller and Daniel K. Benjamin, *Retaking America: The Citizens' Solution to the War on Drugs* (New York, Basic Books, Inc., 1991) A complete analysis of America's past and present drug policies; plus a new solution, *The Constitutional Alternative,* to the drug problem.

Isaac Turiel, *Indoor Air Quality and Human Health* (Palo Alto, Calif.: Stanford University Press, 1985). Most analysis of air pollution focuses on air outside of the home. This author looks at air inside the home.

Margaret Weir et al., eds., *The Politics of Social Policy in the United States* (Princeton, N.J., Princeton University Press, 1988). In this book you will read a series of excellent papers on different aspects of federal social policy in the United States.

FOREIGN AND DEFENSE POLICY

WHAT IF . . . THE UNITED STATES AND THE SOVIET UNION BECAME ALLIES?

The iron curtain has been lifted. All of Western Europe, including what used to be East Germany, has formed one economic union. The nations of the Pacific Rim (Japan, Korea, the Philippines, Thailand, and Malaysia) exercise increasing economic clout and, in some instances, political control of smaller nations in Southeast Asia. Since the United States and the Soviet Union came to an agreement on the reduction of forces in Europe, the limiting of missiles for purely defensive purposes, and the elimination of most of their respective nuclear arsenals, the two superpowers have become simply two among many powerful nations. With the world no longer divided between East and West, both nations have turned to their own pressing economic problems and to finding solutions to conflicts in other regions that threaten world stability.

The Soviet Union and the United States first sign an economic assistance and co-operation treaty that gives each priority in the other's trade policies. A massive exchange of educators, scientists, and industrial engineers takes place. American capital is invested in the Soviet Union. Then, the two nations sign a mutual defense pact which specifies that an attack on either will bring military responses from both the Soviet and the American forces. Finally, the leaders of both nations agree to consult with each other before intervening in conflicts in

the world's "hot spots" and to cooperate in the hunt for terrorists and purveyors of weapons to such groups.

What would such an alliance between the two great post-World War II powers do to the state of world politics? Together, the two nations would have more economic and human resources than any other nation or combination of nations except China and India, both of which, however, lack the technological development and educational level of the United States and the Soviet Union. Each of the nations would have the geographic position and military might to control large areas of the globe, preventing attacks against itself or its ally. Their combined economic might would immediately set up an economic rivalry with the European Community (EC) and the nations of the Pacific Rim. The United States would buy its needed petroleum and other raw materials from the Soviet Union, ending its dependence on the nations of the Middle East.

For the two allies, the question of how to direct military spending would be resolved. Massive armaments to defend against each other could be eliminated and attention paid to sophisticated defensive capabilities and rapid deployment forces for smaller conflicts. If the Soviet Union and the United States truly coordinated their efforts, it would be very difficult for aggressor groups to obtain weaponry from either side such as the way Iraq did during the 1980s.

During the cold war, each of the two superpowers was dominant in its own sphere, with the United States exerting influence over much of the Western world and the Soviet Union controlling internal and external affairs of the nations of Eastern Europe as well as directing the policies of some other allies. Faced with political instability in Africa and the Middle East, the Soviet Union and the United States might decide that the world would be a safer place if they set the rules. As allies, the two nations might move to become the "superpolice" of the world, working to control threatening conflicts wherever they occur.

How would the world react to such allied domination? The nations of the European Community and of Eastern Europe, feeling be-

trayed by their former allies, would probably attempt to establish their freedom from influence by the superpowers. Similarly, Japan and China might simply refuse to accept such a role for the two superpowers. Although the third-world nations might continue to use the United Nations as a forum for debate, the alliance between former enemies and the rise of other major players either could make that international organization superfluous or, supported by the United States and the Soviet Union, it could exert real power.

Several other long-range possibilities exist: A new order might be built without the threat of major war and with the capacity to solve problems such as global warming and hunger, or new divisions might arise between Northern and Southern hemispheres or between the nations with a Western heritage and those of Eastern cultures. It also may be that the alliance would have little power over world affairs as nationalistic, ethnic, and sectarian passions undermine peace-building attempts.

---

1. *What would be the major sources of conflict in the world if the United States and the Soviet Union became true allies?*
2. *Could the Soviet Union and the United States trust each other enough to cooperate militarily in the long run?*
3. *How might the European Community or Japan attempt to thwart such an alliance?*

If Americans did not have so much faith in what they see on television, they might have thought that the world was turning upside-down. The Soviet president strolls down American streets shaking hands with eager citizens, and then addresses the faculty of the School of Business at Stanford University. The Berlin Wall is carted away. The two Germanies become one. Democratic elections are epidemic: They are held throughout Eastern Europe, in Nicaragua, and in the Soviet Union. Nelson Mandela is freed and travels around the world seeking help to end apartheid in South Africa.

Five years ago, these events were not in the realm of possibility. Thus, it should not be surprising that the United States did not have policies in place to deal with any of them. The Bush administration seemed to be following a "one-day-at-a-time" strategy with regard to the Soviet Union and Eastern Europe and to be avoiding any intervention in the affairs of nations previously in the Soviet bloc. As long as there were no negative consequences, most Americans generally approved of this nonpolicy. In fact, the United States was not alone in its inaction. The nations of Western Europe watched from the sidelines as the two Germanies decided to unite and calmly worked out the details.

Yet, the United States is a global power. Whether the nation faces peace or war, instability in Eastern Europe or economic competition, United States interests require the carrying out of foreign policy.

■ WHAT IS FOREIGN POLICY?

As its cultural, military, and economic interdependence with the other nations of the world has increased, it has become even more important for the United States to establish and carry out foreign policies to deal with external situations

Germans celebrate the unification of the two Germanies.

FOREIGN POLICY
A nation's external goals and the techniques and strategies used to achieve them.

DIPLOMACY
The total process by which states carry on political relations with each other; settling conflicts among nations by peaceful means.

ECONOMIC AID
Assistance to other nations in the form of grants, loans, or credits to buy American products.

TECHNICAL ASSISTANCE
Sending experts with technical skills in agriculture, engineering, or business to aid other nations.

FOREIGN POLICY PROCESS
The steps by which external goals are decided and acted on.

NATIONAL SECURITY POLICY
Foreign and domestic policy designed to protect the independence and political and economic integrity of the United States; policy that is concerned with the safety and defense of the nation.

NATIONAL SECURITY COUNCIL (NSC)
A board created by the 1947 National Security Act to advise the president on matters of national security.

DIPLOMACY
The total process by means of which states carry on political relations with each other; settling conflicts among nations by peaceful means.

and to carry out its own national goals. By **foreign policy,** we mean both the goals the government wants to achieve in the world and the techniques and strategies to achieve them. For example, if one national goal is to achieve stability in Eastern Europe and to encourage the formation of democratic governments there, U.S. foreign policy in that area may be carried out with the techniques of **diplomacy, economic aid, technical assistance,** or military intervention. Sometimes foreign policies are restricted to statements of goals or ideas, such as helping to end world poverty, whereas at other times foreign policies are comprehensive efforts to achieve particular objectives.

United States foreign policy is established through the **foreign policy process,** which usually originates with the president and those agencies that provide advice on foreign policy matters. Foreign policy formulation is often affected by congressional action and national public debate.

National Security Policy

As one aspect of overall foreign policy, **national security policy** is designed primarily to protect the independence and the political integrity of the United States. It concerns itself with the defense of the United States against actual or potential (real or imagined) enemies, domestic or foreign.

U.S. national security policy is based on determinations made by the Department of Defense, the Department of State, and a number of other federal agencies, including the **National Security Council (NSC).** The NSC acts as an advisory body to the president, but it has increasingly become a rival to the State Department in influencing the foreign policy process. This was particularly evident when it was revealed, in November 1986, that the Reagan administration had largely by-passed the Department of State (and Congress) in using the NSC to direct sales of U.S. military equipment to Iran.

Diplomacy

Diplomacy is another aspect of foreign policy, but it is not coterminous with it. Diplomacy involves all of a nation's external relationships, from routine diplomatic communications to summit meetings among heads of state. More specifically, diplomacy refers to the settling of disputes and conflicts among nations by peaceful methods. Diplomacy is the set of negotiating techniques by which a nation attempts to carry out its foreign policy.

Diplomacy may or may not be successful, depending on the willingness of the parties to negotiate. After years of fruitless disarmament talks, the United States and the Soviet Union moved swiftly to agreement on the Intermediate Range Nuclear Force (INF) Treaty to limit and destroy certain weapons. In contrast, efforts to negotiate a solution to the Palestinian–Israeli conflict have proved so far to be unsuccessful.

■ MORALITY VERSUS REALITY IN FOREIGN POLICY

From the earliest years of the republic, Americans have felt that their nation had a special destiny. The American experiment in democratic government and capitalism would provide the best possible life for men and women and be a model for other nations. As the United States assumed greater status as a power in world politics, Americans came to believe that the nation's actions on the world stage should be guided by its own political and moral principles. As Harry Truman stated the premise, "The United States should take the lead in running the world in the way that it ought to be run."

This view of America's mission has led to the adoption of many foreign policy initiatives that are rooted in **moral idealism,** a philosophy that sees the world as fundamentally benign and other nations as willing to cooperate for the good of all.[1] In this perspective, nations should come together and agree to keep the peace, as President Woodrow Wilson proposed for the League of Nations. Nations should see the wrong in violating the human rights of ethnic or religious minorities and should work to end such injustice. Many of the foreign policy initiatives taken by the United States have been based on this idealistic view of the world, but few of these actions have been very successful. The Peace Corps, originated by John Kennedy in 1961, is one example of an effort to spread American good will and technology that has achieved some of its goals. In contrast, efforts to influence events in Vietnam, Nicaragua, and El Salvador have been less successful. President Jimmy Carter tried to make human rights the most important priority in his foreign policy, but failed. Foreign policy based on moral imperatives is often unsuccessful because it assumes that other nations agree with American views of morality and politics.

In opposition to the moral perspective is what we might call **political realism.** Realists see the world as a dangerous place in which each nation strives for its own survival and interests. Foreign policy decisions must be based on a cold calculation of what is best for the United States without regard for morality. Realists believe that the United States must be prepared militarily to defend itself because all other nations are, by definition, out to improve their own situation. A strong defense will show the world that the United

[1]Charles W. Kegley, Jr., and Eugene Wittkopf, *American Foreign Policy, Pattern and Process,* 3rd ed., (New York: St. Martin's Press, 1987) p 73.

Jim Baker, Secretary of State.

MORAL IDEALISM
A philosophy that sees all nations as willing to cooperate and agree on moral standards for conduct.

POLITICAL REALISM
A philosophy that sees each nation acting principally in its own interest.

Peace Corps worker in Ecuador. Is the Peace Corps working for idealistic or realistic goals or both?

DID YOU KNOW?

That American troops occupied Haiti from 1915 to 1934?

States is willing to protect its interests. The practice of political realism in foreign policy allows the United States to sell weapons to military dictators who will support its policies, to support American business across the globe, and to repel terrorism through the use of force. Political realism, for example, leads to a policy of never negotiating with terrorists who take hostages, since such negotiations simply will lead to the taking of more hostages.

It is important to note that the United States has never been guided by only one of these principles. Instead, both moral idealism and political realism undergird foreign policy decisions. George Bush faced this tension when the Soviet republic of Lithuania declared its independence in 1990. Although the United States supported Lithuania's claim on moral principle, carefully stating that the United States had never recognized the Soviet annexation of Lithuania in 1940, realism demanded that Bush not intervene overtly in the affairs of the Soviet Union.

■ WHO MAKES FOREIGN POLICY?

Is foreign policy made by the president, by the Congress, or by joint executive and congressional action? There is no easy answer to this question because, as constitutional authority Edwin S. Corwin once observed, the Constitution created an "invitation to struggle" between the president and Congress for control over the foreign policy process. Let us look first at powers given to the president by the Constitution.

President Franklin D. Roosevelt signs the declaration of war against Japan on December 8, 1941.

Constitutional Powers of the President

The Constitution confers on the president broad powers that are either explicit or implied in key constitutional provisions. Article II vests the executive power of the government in the president. The presidential oath of office given in Article II, Section 1, requires that the president must "solemnly swear" to "preserve, protect and defend the Constitution of the United States."

In addition, and perhaps more importantly, Article II, Section 2, designates the president as "Commander in Chief of the Army and Navy of the United States." Starting with Abraham Lincoln, all presidents have interpreted this authority dynamically and broadly. Indeed, since the Washington administration, the United States has been involved in at least 125 undeclared wars that were conducted under presidential authority. In 1846, President Polk provoked Mexico into a war. Theodore Roosevelt sent the navy on a cruise around the world (presumably to impress Japan with the nation's naval power). Before entering World War II, Franklin Roosevelt ordered the navy to "shoot on sight" German submarines that appeared in the Western Hemisphere security zone. Truman personally made the decision to drop atomic bombs on Japan. It was also Truman who ordered American armed forces in the Pacific to enter into North Korea's conflict with South Korea. Eisenhower threatened China and North Korea with nuclear weapons if the Korean peace talks were not successfully concluded. From Eisenhower through Nixon, chief executives increasingly embroiled the United States in a war in Vietnam.

Article II, Section 2, of the Constitution also gives the president the power to make treaties, provided that two-thirds of the senators present concur. Presidents mostly have been successful in getting treaties through the Senate.

President Bush hosts the economic summit in Houston, Texas. How much power do the leaders of the economic powers have to stabilize the world economy?

In addition to these formal treaty-making powers, the president makes use of **executive agreements** (discussed in Chapter 13). Since the Second World War, executive agreements have accounted for almost 95 percent of the understandings reached between the United States and other nations.

Executive agreements have a long and significant history. Franklin Roosevelt made his destroyer base deal with Great Britain in 1940 by executive agreement. More significant in their long-term effects were the several agreements he reached with the U.S.S.R. and other countries, especially at Yalta and Potsdam, during the Second World War. The government of South Vietnam and the government of the United States, particularly under Eisenhower, Kennedy, and Johnson, made a series of executive agreements in which the United States promised support. All in all, between 1946 and 1991, over eight thousand executive agreements with foreign countries were made. There is no way to get an accurate count because perhaps several hundred of these agreements have been secret.

An additional power conferred on the president in Article II, Section 2, is the right to appoint ambassadors, other public ministers, and consuls. In Section 3 of that article, the president is given the power to recognize foreign governments through receiving their ambassadors.

EXECUTIVE AGREEMENT
A binding international obligation made between chiefs of state without legislative sanction.

Informal Techniques of Presidential Leadership

Other broad sources of presidential power in the American foreign policy process are tradition, precedent, and the president's personality. The president can employ a host of informal techniques that give the White House overwhelming superiority within the government in foreign policy leadership.

First, the president has access to information. More information is available to the president from the CIA, the State Department, and the Defense Department than to any other governmental authority. This carries with it the ability to make quick decisions—and that ability is used often.

Second, the president is a legislative leader who can influence the amount of funds that are allocated for different programs. For example, presidents can

DID YOU KNOW?

That including the Civil War, more than one million American soldiers have been killed in the nation's wars?

try, as both Reagan and Carter did, to increase defense spending and decrease nondefense spending.

Third, the president can influence public opinion. President Theodore Roosevelt once said:

> People used to say to me that I was an astonishingly good politician and divined what the people are going to think. . . . I did not "divine" how the people were going to think; I simply made up my mind what they ought to think and then did my best to get them to think it.[2]

Presidents are without equal in this regard, partly because of their ability to command the media. Depending on their skill in appealing to patriotic sentiment (and sometimes fear), they can make people think that their course in foreign affairs is right and necessary. Public opinion seems to be impressed often by the president's decision to make a national commitment abroad. Presidents normally, although certainly not always, receive the immediate support of the American people when reacting to (or creating) a foreign policy crisis.

George Bush used his leadership resources on foreign policy issues to bolster his own popularity. By explaining the December 20, 1989, invasion of Panama as an effort to capture the leader of Panama and alleged drug dealer, Manuel Noriega, he garnered wide approval. His first meeting with Soviet President Gorbachev in Malta, which overcame the barrier of stormy seas, and Gorbachev's visit to the United States in May 1990, added to Bush's image as a foreign policy leader.

Finally, the president can commit the nation morally to a course of action in foreign affairs. Because the president is the head of state and the leader of one of the most powerful nations on earth, once the president has made a commitment for the United States, it is difficult for Congress or anyone else to back down on that commitment.

[2]Sidney Warren, *The President as World Leader* (New York: McGraw-Hill, 1964), p. 23.

Bush and Gorbachev meet at the Malta summit.

Sources of Foreign Policy Making Within the Executive Branch

There are at least four sources of power in foreign policy making within the executive branch, in addition to the president. These are: (1) the Department of State, (2) the National Security Council, (3) the intelligence community and informational programs, and (4) the Department of Defense.

The Department of State.   In principle, the State Department is the executive agency that is most directly concerned with foreign affairs. It supervises U.S. relations with the nearly two hundred independent nations around the world and with the United Nations and other multinational groups, such as the Organization of American States (OAS). It staffs embassies and consulates throughout the world. It has about 24,000 employees. This may sound impressive, but it is small compared with, say, the Department of Health and Human Services with its 140,000 employees. Also, the State Department had an annual operating budget of only $3.8 billion in fiscal year 1991—the smallest budget of the cabinet-level departments.

Newly elected presidents usually tell the American public that the new secretary of state is the nation's chief foreign policy adviser. Nonetheless, the State Department's preeminence in foreign policy has declined rather dramatically since World War II. The State Department's image within the White House Executive Office and Congress (and even other governments) is quite poor—a slow, plodding, bureaucratic maze of inefficient, indecisive individuals. There is even a story about how Soviet Premier Nikita Khruschev urged President Kennedy to formulate his own views rather than to rely on State Department officials who, according to Khruschev, "specialized in why something had not worked forty years ago."[3] In any event, since the days of Franklin Roosevelt, the State Department has been bypassed and often ignored when crucial decisions are made.

[3]Theodore C. Sorensen, *Kennedy* (New York: Harper and Row, 1965), pp. 554–555.

Secretary of State James Baker and the former Soviet counterpart, Eduard Shevardnadze, sign arms reduction accords. Can the two superpowers truly control the development and use of armaments?

NEGATIVE CONSTITUENTS
U.S. citizens who openly oppose
government foreign politics.

It is not surprising that the State Department has been overshadowed in foreign policy. It has no natural domestic constituency as does, for example, the Department of Defense, which can call on defense contractors for support. Instead, the State Department has what might be called **negative constituents**—U.S. citizens who openly oppose American foreign policy. Also, within Congress, the State Department is often looked on as an advocate of unpopular, costly foreign involvement. It is often called "the Department of Bad News."

The National Security Council.   The job of the National Security Council (NSC), created by the National Security Act of 1947, is to advise the president on the integration of "domestic, foreign, and military policies relating to the national security." Its larger purpose is to provide policy continuity from one administration to the next. As it has turned out, the NSC—consisting of the president, the vice president, the secretaries of state and defense, the director of emergency planning, and often the chairman of the joint chiefs of staff and the director of the CIA—is used in just about any way the president wants to use it. Eisenhower made frequent use of the NSC. Kennedy convened it infrequently and on an informal basis. When Nixon was elected, he decided to reestablish the NSC as the principal forum for presidential examination of foreign policy issues. During the Reagan administration, the NSC played a central role in funneling private aid to the *contra* forces in Central America and in arranging the arms deal with Iran, although the agency is not supposed to play an operational role in foreign policy.

The role of national security adviser to the president seems to fit the wearer. Some advisers have come into conflict with heads of the State Department. Henry A. Kissinger, Nixon's flamboyant and aggressive national security adviser, rapidly gained ascendancy over William Rogers, the secretary of state, in foreign policy. When Carter became president, he appointed Zbigniew Brzezinski as national security adviser, who openly competed with Secretary of State Cyrus Vance (who apparently had little power). In contrast, Bush's close friendship with James Baker, his secretary of state, appeared to put the cabinet officer clearly in charge of foreign policy.

INTELLIGENCE COMMUNITY
The government agencies involved in
gathering information about the
capabilities and intentions of foreign
governments and engaging in covert
activities to further American foreign
policy aims.

The Intelligence Community.   No discussion of foreign policy would be complete without some mention of what is generally known as the **intelligence community.** This consists of the forty or more government agencies or bureaus that are involved in intelligence activities—informational and otherwise. On January 24, 1978, President Carter issued Executive Order 12036 in which he formally defined the official major members of the intelligence community. They are as follows:

1. Central Intelligence Agency (CIA)
2. National Security Agency (NSA)
3. Defense Intelligence Agency (DIA)
4. Offices within the Department of Defense
5. Bureau of Intelligence and Research in the Department of State
6. Federal Bureau of Investigation (FBI)
7. Army intelligence
8. Air Force intelligence
9. Department of the Treasury
10. Drug Enforcement Administration (DEA)
11. Department of Energy

The CIA was created as part of the National Security Act of 1947. The National Security Agency and the Defense Intelligence Agency were created by executive order. Until recently, Congress voted billions of dollars for intelligence activities with little knowledge of how the funds were being used. Only twice did the intelligence activities of the agency attract public attention. In 1960, an American U-2 spy plane was shot down over the Soviet Union and its pilot, Gary Powers, captured. Eisenhower at first denied that the U-2 was a spy plane but later admitted that the United States was indeed taking aerial reconnaissance photos of the Soviet Union. Again, in 1961, when the Bay of Pigs invasion of Cuba failed, even though Kennedy took the blame, it was clear that he had been misled by the CIA.

Intelligence activities consist mostly of overt information gathering as well as covert actions. Covert actions, as the name implies, are done secretly, and rarely does the American public find out about them. In the late 1940s and early 1950s, the CIA covertly subsidized anticommunist labor unions in Western Europe. The CIA covertly aided in the overthrow of the Mossadegh regime in Iran, which allowed the restoration of the shah in 1953. The CIA helped to overthrow the Arbenz government of Guatemala in 1954 and apparently was instrumental in destabilizing the Allende government in Chile from 1970 to 1973.

During the mid-1970s, the "dark side" of the CIA was at least partly uncovered when the Senate, under Senator Frank Church (Idaho), undertook an investigation of its activities. One of the major findings of the Senate Select Committee on Intelligence was that the CIA had routinely spied on American citizens domestically—a strictly prohibited activity. Consequently, the CIA came under the scrutiny of six, and later eight, oversight committees within Congress, which restricted the scope of its activity. However, by 1980, the CIA regained much of its lost power to engage in covert activities. In the early 1990s, as the relationship with the Soviet Union eased, the attention of the CIA and other agencies began to turn from military to economic intelligence.

In addition to intelligence activities, U.S. foreign policy also makes use of propaganda and information programs. The United States Information Agency (which for a while was called the United States International Communication Agency) is part of an attempt to spread information and propaganda throughout the world on behalf of the American government. One of its major efforts is the Voice of America, a worldwide radio network that broadcasts news and information from an American point of view. Under the Reagan administration, this activity was expanded. In 1983, Congress passed a bill authorizing Radio Marti to transmit specifically to Cuba. A televised version (TV Marti) was approved later.

The Department of Defense. The Department of Defense (DOD) was created in 1947 to bring all of the various activities of the American military establishment under the jurisdiction of a single department headed by a civilian secretary of defense. At the same time, the joint chiefs of staff, consisting of the commanders of each of the military branches and a chairman, was created to formulate a unified military strategy. The DOD is huge. It has more than one million civilian employees and more than two million military personnel. It has an annual budget that in fiscal year 1991 was over $314 billion. Since much of this budget is spent on contracts with civilian firms, it is not surprising that a somewhat symbiotic relationship has developed between civilian defense contractors and the DOD.

DID YOU KNOW?

That the CIA is estimated to employ more than sixteen thousand individuals, with about five thousand in the clandestine services?

The Pentagon.

Because the Pentagon is unlikely to want any lessening of its power, the Department of Defense responds to the president's foreign policy initiatives in light of its own goals. However, the branches of the military often differ in their points of view, weakening the department's political influence.

■ LIMITING THE PRESIDENT'S POWER

One of the major outcomes of the Vietnam war was a new interest in the balance of power between Congress and the president on foreign policy questions. Sensitive to public frustration over the long and costly war and angry at Richard Nixon for some of his other actions as president, Congress attempted to establish some limits on the power of the president in setting foreign and defense policy. In 1973, Congress passed the War Powers Act over President Nixon's veto, limiting the president's use of troops in military action without congressional approval (see Chapter 13). Most presidents, however, have not interpreted the "consultation" provisions of the act as meaning that Congress should be consulted before military action is taken. Instead, Ford, Carter, Reagan, and Bush have ordered troop movements and then informed congressional leaders. Critics note that it is quite possible for a president to commit troops to a situation from which the nation could not withdraw without incurring heavy losses, whether or not Congress is consulted.

In recent years, Congress has also exerted its authority to limit or deny the president's requests for military assistance to Angolan rebels and to the government of El Salvador, for new weapons such as the B-1 bomber, and for weapons sales through a legislative veto over sales greater than $50 million (although recent court decisions have left the veto technique in doubt). In general, Congress has been far more cautious in supporting the president when military involvement of American troops is possible.

At times the Congress can take the initiative in foreign policy. In 1986, the Congress initiated and passed a bill instituting economic sanctions against South Africa to pressure that nation into ending apartheid. President Reagan vetoed the bill, but the veto was overridden by large majorities in both the House and the Senate.

DID YOU KNOW?

That U.S. diplomats, troops, and other federal employees in Lebanon, Afghanistan, Colombia, Peru, and the Philippines are given "hazardous duty" pay, which adds 15 percent to their normal salary?

■ DOMESTIC SOURCES OF FOREIGN POLICY

The making of foreign policy is often viewed as a presidential prerogative because of the president's constitutional power in that area and the resources of the executive branch which the president controls. Foreign policy positions are also influenced by a number of other nongovernmental agents, including elite and mass opinion, the military-industrial complex, and U.S. multinational business enterprises.

Elite and Mass Opinion

Public opinion influences the making of U.S. foreign policy through a number of channels. Elites in American business, education, communication, labor, and religion try to influence presidential decision making through several strategies. Some individuals, such as former Secretary of State Henry Kissinger and former President Richard Nixon, have a longstanding interest in foreign policy and have been active in government service. They may be asked to advise the president privately. Several elite organizations, such as the Council on Foreign Relations and the Trilateral Commission, work to increase international cooperation and to influence foreign policy through conferences, publications, and research.

The members of the American elite establishment also exert influence on foreign policy through the general public by encouraging debate over foreign policy positions, by publicizing the issues, and by use of the media. Generally, the efforts of the president and the elites are most successful with a segment of the population that is called the **attentive public.** This sector of the mass public, which probably totals 10 to 20 percent of all citizens, is more interested in foreign affairs than most Americans. These Americans are also likely to transmit their opinions to the less-interested members of the public through conversation and local leadership.

ATTENTIVE PUBLIC
That proportion of the general public that pays attention to foreign policy issues.

The Military–Industrial Complex

Civilian fear of "the generals" and the relationship between the defense establishment and arms manufacturers dates back many years. In the 1930s, Franklin Roosevelt raised the specter of mammoth improper military influence in the domestic economy. On the eve of a Senate investigation of the munitions industry, he said that the arms race was a "grave menace . . . due in no small measure to the uncontrolled activities of the manufacturers and the merchants

MILITARY–INDUSTRIAL COMPLEX
The mutually beneficial relationship between the armed forces and defense contractors.

DID YOU KNOW?

That the United States exported more than $18 billion in arms in 1989?

of the engines of destruction and it must be met by the concerted actions of the people of all nations."

Eisenhower's Warning.   During his eight years in office, the former five-star general of the army experienced firsthand the kind of pressure that could be brought against him and other policy makers by arms manufacturers. Eisenhower determined to give the country a solemn and, as he saw it, necessary warning of the consequences of this influence. On January 17, 1961, in his last official speech, he said:

> In the councils of government, we must guard against the acquisition of unwarranted influence, whether sought or unsought, by the military-industrial complex. The potential for the disastrous rise of misplaced power exists and will persist. . . . Only an alert and knowledgeable citizenry can compel the proper meshing of the huge industrial and military machinery of defense with our peaceful methods and goals, so that security and liberty may prosper together.[4]

A Symbiotic Relationship.   The Pentagon has supported a large sector of our economy through defense contracts, in addition to supplying retired army officers as key executives to large defense-contracting firms.

The military establishment also has a powerful political arm. The Department of Defense employs almost 350 lobbyists on Capitol Hill; it maintains some 2,850 public relations representatives in the United States and in foreign countries. As the Soviet Union and the United States worked to conclude treaties reducing their armaments, the Pentagon and defense contractors began to reassess their roles and look for new directions and programs to avoid huge cutbacks in military spending.

■ THE MAJOR FOREIGN POLICY THEMES

Although some observers might suggest that United States foreign policy is inconsistent and changes with the current occupant of the White House, the long view of American diplomatic ventures reveals several major themes underlying that policy. In the early years of the nation, presidents and the people generally agreed that the United States should avoid foreign entanglements and concentrate instead on its own development. From the beginning of the twentieth century until today, the theme has been increasing global involvement, with the United States taking an active role in assisting the development of other nations, dominating the world economy, and in some cases acting as a peacemaker. The other major theme of the post–World War II years was the containment of communism. In the following brief review of American diplomatic history, these three themes predominate.

The Formative Years: Avoiding Entanglements

United States foreign policy dates back to the colonial uprising against the British Crown. The Declaration of Independence formalized the colonists' desired break from Britain. Then, on September 3, 1783, the signing of the Treaty of Paris not only ended the eight-year War of Independence but also

[4]Congressional Quarterly, *Almanac* (Washington, D.C.: Congressional Quarterly Press, 1961), pp. 938–939.

accorded to the United States recognition as an independent nation by the rest of the world. In addition, the Treaty of Paris probably helped to reshape the world, for the American colonies were the first to secure independence against a "superpower."

Foreign policy was largely negative during the formative years. Remember that the new nation was operating under the Articles of Confederation. The national government had no right to levy and collect taxes, no control over commerce, no right to make commercial treaties, and no power to raise an army (the army was dismantled in 1783). Its lack of international power was clear when the United States was unable to obtain American hostages that had been seized in the Mediterranean by Barbary pirates, but ignominiously had to purchase the hostages in a treaty with Morocco.

The Founding Fathers had a basic mistrust of corrupt European governments. George Washington said it was the United State's policy "to steer clear of permanent alliances," and Thomas Jefferson echoed this sentiment when he said America wanted peace with all nations but "entangling alliances with none." This was also a logical position at a time when the United States was so weak militarily that it could not directly influence European development. It chose instead to believe that the United States would set a moral standard that Europe could follow. Moreover, being protected by oceans that took weeks to traverse certainly allowed the nation to avoid entangling alliances. During the 1700s and 1800s, the United States generally stayed out of European conflicts and politics.

Nineteenth-Century Isolationism

The United State's role as a world power began in the early 1800s, nonetheless. President James Monroe, in his message to Congress on December 2, 1823, stated that this country would not accept foreign intervention in the Western Hemisphere. In return, the United States would not meddle in European internal affairs. The **Monroe Doctrine** was the underpinning of the United

DID YOU KNOW?

That the United States invaded and occupied part of Russia in 1919?

MONROE DOCTRINE
The policy statement included in President Monroe's 1823 annual message to Congress, which set out three principles: (1) European nations should not establish new colonies in the Western Hemisphere, (2) European nations should not intervene in the affairs of independent nations of the Western Hemisphere, and (3) the United States would not interfere in the affairs of European nations.

A 1912 painting shows President James Monroe explaining the Monroe Doctrine to a group of government officials. Essentially, he made the Western Hemisphere the concern of the United States.

PERIOD OF ISOLATIONISM
A period of abstaining from an active role in international affairs or alliances, which characterized most of the nineteenth century.

INTERVENTIONISM
Involvement in foreign affairs; actions directed at changing or preserving the internal political arrangements of other nations.

States' isolationist foreign policy throughout the nineteenth century—the **period of isolationism.** More recently, however, the Monroe Doctrine, among other things, was used to justify the invasion of Grenada in the Caribbean in October, 1983.

The Beginning of Interventionism and World War I

Although the nineteenth century was not completely devoid of American **interventionism** in the rest of the world, it was a relatively quiet period in terms of foreign involvement. In 1812, the United States went to war with Great Britain over the ostensible issue of the British navy preying on American commerce. In 1846, President James K. Polk provoked Mexico into war with the United States when he ordered the army to occupy disputed territory along the Rio Grande River. As a result of the Mexican War, the United States acquired New Mexico, Arizona, California, and other western lands.

But the real end of isolationism started with the Spanish-American War in 1898. Winning that war gave the United States possession of Guam, Puerto Rico, and the Philippines (which gained independence in 1946). Although the United States returned to a policy of isolationism following the Spanish-American War, it lasted only for a brief time—until World War I (1914–1918). Still, reluctant to entangle this country with European internal politics, the United States didn't enter the war until late. In his reelection campaign of 1916, President Woodrow Wilson ran on the slogan, "He kept us out of war." Nonetheless, on April 6, 1917, the United States declared war on Germany because it was evident to Wilson that, without help, the Allies would be defeated and that American property and lives, already under attack, would be increasingly endangered. Wilson also sought to promote American democratic ideals in Europe and to end international aggression through the United States' entry into the war.

In the 1920s, the U.S. did indeed go "back to normalcy," as President Warren G. Harding urged it to do. U.S. military forces were largely disbanded, defense spending dropped to about 1 percent of GNP, and the nation once more retreated into isolationism. International power politics ceased to be an issue in U.S. foreign policy—if, in fact, the country can be said to have had a foreign policy.

The Era of Internationalism

Isolationism was permanently shattered and relegated to its place in history by the bombing of the U.S. naval base at Pearl Harbor, Hawaii, on December 7, 1941. The surprise attack by the Japanese resulted in the deaths of 2,403 American servicemen and the wounding of 1,143 others. Eighteen warships were sunk or seriously damaged, and 188 planes were destroyed at the airfields. Tales of the horrors experienced by the wounded survivors quickly reached American shores. The American public was outraged. President Roosevelt asked Congress to declare war on Japan immediately, and the United States entered World War II.

This unequivocal response was certainly due to the nature of the provocation. American soil had not been attacked by a foreign power since the burning of Washington, D.C., by the British in 1814. World War II marked a permanent change in American foreign policy. It also produced a permanent change in

Stalin, Roosevelt, and Churchill at Yalta, February 4–11, 1945.

the size of the American government. Except for brief periods during the Civil War and World War I, defense spending had been a fairly trivial part of the gross national product. By the end of World War II in 1945, defense spending had increased to almost 40 percent of GNP. The number of United States overseas military bases increased from three at the beginning of 1940 to almost 450 by the end of World War II. National security had become a priority item on the federal government's agenda.

The United States was the only country to emerge from World War II with its economy intact, and even strengthened. The Soviet Union, Japan, Italy, France, Germany, Britain, and a number of minor participants in the war were all economically devastated. The United States was also the only country to have control over operational nuclear weapons. President Harry S Truman had personally made the decision to use two atomic bombs to end the war with Japan on August 6 and August 9, 1945. (Historians still dispute the necessity of this action, which ultimately killed more than 100,000 Japanese civilians and left an equal number permanently injured.) The United States had truly become the world's superpower. In the Critical Perspective on page 568, the components of power are discussed.

The atomic bomb explodes over Nagasaki on August 9, 1945.

The Cold War

The United States had become an uncomfortable ally of the Soviet Union after the latter had been invaded by Hitler. Soon after the war ended, relations between the Soviets and the West deteriorated. The Soviets wanted a weakened Germany, and to achieve this they insisted that the country be divided in two,

CRITICAL PERSPECTIVE

Bound To Lead? Hard Versus Soft Power

Is the United States in decline? Not according to Joseph S. Nye, Jr., director of the Center for Science and International Affairs, professor of government at Harvard University, and author of *Bound to Lead: The Changing Nature of American Power.*[*]

Power is the ability to do things, control others, and get others to do what they otherwise would not do. **Hard,** or **command, power,** by which nations have been evaluated in the past, has generally meant the ability to invade or force others to accept a nation's superiority or even military hegemony. This military power has depended in part on sufficient natural resources, on a strong economy, and on the application and development of science and technology. In the current period of history, Nye and others argue, military power and force have become extremely costly.

A second form, **soft,** or *cooptive,* **power**—getting others to *want* what you want—may be the wave of the future. This type of power is based on the attractiveness of a nation's economic, cultural, social, ideological, and political ideas and examples, that is, the model it presents for other nations to replicate or from which to borrow, which Nye calls a "universal culture." It is also based on national cohesion and on influence in international institutions.

Nye cites the establishment of liberal global economic institutions such as the International Monetary Fund (IMF) and the General Agreement on Tariffs and Trade (GATT) as examples of how other nations were sold on a principle that conformed to U.S. long-term interests through soft power. According to Nye, "The universalism of a country's culture and its ability to establish a set of favorable rules and institutions that govern areas of international activity are a critical source of power. These soft sources of power are becoming more important in world politics at the end of this century."[**]

Some observers see the decline of U.S. hard power and feel that the world is about to enter the "Japanese era" or the "Asian century" because of the economic growth and strength of Japan and other Asian nations. Nye argues that Japan, while economically strong, is ill suited as a world leader because its culture is so insular, one-dimensional, and impenetrable. Moreover, Japan has not developed a presence in international institutions. Others point to "multipolarity," with the Soviet Union, China, and Europe assuming world power roles at the expense of the United States. Each of these countries or regions, Nye argues, has its weaknesses in either or both of the three soft-power and four hard-power areas (see accompanying table). The Soviet Union is ethnically conflict ridden and economically a shambles, Europe is not yet unified, and China is a developing country with many liabilities.

The United States, on the other hand, is still able to compete successfully in the four hard-power areas—it enjoys abundant natural resources, is and will remain a major military power, has a stable and revitalized economy, and, in spite of false

[*]New York: Basic Books, 1990.

[**]Joseph S. Nye, Jr., "Still in The Game," *World Monitor,* March 1990, p. 46–47.

Weighing Today's Sources of Power

SOURCE: Joseph S. Nye, Jr., "Still in the Game," *World Monitor,* March 1990, p. 47.

		UNITED STATES	SOVIET UNION	EUROPE	JAPAN	CHINA
HARD POWER	**Basic Resources**	STRONG	STRONG	STRONG	Medium	STRONG
	Military	STRONG	STRONG	Medium	Weak	Medium
	Economic	STRONG	Medium	STRONG	STRONG	Medium
	Science/Technology	STRONG	Medium	STRONG	STRONG	Weak
SOFT POWER	**National Cohesion**	STRONG	Weak	Weak	STRONG	STRONG
	Universal Culture	STRONG	Medium	STRONG	Medium	Medium
	International Institutions	STRONG	Medium	STRONG	Medium	Medium

---

CRITICAL PERSPECTIVE, CONTINUED

impressions, has continued to invest in science and technology, especially in areas that will be crucial on the communications frontier. For example, a U.S. company is planning to launch a new global telephone communication system based on low-orbiting satellites and small, individual telephone units that can send or receive telephone calls from anywhere in the world by directly beaming up to and down from the individual phone to one of the twenty-six satellites.

On the soft-power side, in addition to its major role in international institutions, the multicultural and multiracial richness and experience of the United States and the absorptive capacity of American culture is a unique asset. Of all the world powers, only the United States offered South African leader Nelson Mandela the experience of a rich African-American culture. Whenever a Latin American leader visits the United States, he or she may be received by tens of thousands of Hispanic Americans. The same holds true for Europeans, Asians, and Middle Easterners. It is presumably no accident that American music, clothing, food, and other consumer commodities

have spread around the globe, symbols of a modern, free, and futuristic society.

Nye also suggests that, in the twenty-first century, economic interdependence and global efforts to solve problems such as AIDS, pollution, drugs, terrorism, and so forth will weaken the individual power of any single state. Those countries with institutions, culture, and processes suitable for the soft (and sometimes perhaps also hard) global leadership challenges will be the leaders of the next century. He feels that the United States is well suited for that role.

Exercise in Critical Thinking

1. Why may the concept of hard power mean less in the future than it has meant in the past?
2. To what extent does soft-power "image building" create effective leadership in the world?
3. What will prevent the Soviet Union and China from effectively using soft-power techniques to gain world hegemony?

with East Germany becoming a buffer on their west. Little by little, the Soviets helped to install communist governments in Eastern European countries, which collectively became known as the **Soviet bloc.** In response, the United States encouraged the rearming of Western Europe. The "**cold war**" had begun.[5]

In Fulton, Missouri, on March 5, 1946, Winston Churchill, in a striking metaphor, declared that from the Baltic to the Adriatic seas "an iron curtain has descended across the [European] continent." The term **iron curtain** became even more appropriate when the Soviets built a wall separating East Berlin from West Berlin on August 17–18, 1961.

Containment: A New Foreign Policy

In 1947, a remarkable article was published in *Foreign Affairs*. The article was signed by "X." The actual author was George F. Kennan, chief of the policy-planning staff for the Department of State. The doctrine of **containment** set forth in the article became—according to many—the Bible of Western foreign policy. "X" argued that whenever and wherever the Soviets could successfully challenge Western institutions, they would do so. He recommended that our policy toward the Soviets be "firm and vigilant containment of Russian expansive tendencies."[6]

The containment theory was enunciated quite clearly in the **Truman Doctrine,** which was part of President Harry S Truman's historic address to Congress on March 12, 1947. In that address, he announced that the United States must help countries where a communist takeover seemed likely, and he

SOVIET BLOC
The Eastern European countries which used to have communist regimes.

COLD WAR
The ideological, political, and economic impasse that existed between the United States and the Soviet Union following World War II.

IRON CURTAIN
The term used to describe the division of Europe between the Soviet Union and the West. Popularized by Winston Churchill in a speech portraying Europe as being divided by an iron curtain, with the nations of Eastern Europe behind the curtain and increasingly under Soviet control.

CONTAINMENT
U.S. diplomatic policy adopted by the Truman administration to "build situations of strength" around the globe to contain communist power within its existing boundaries.

TRUMAN DOCTRINE
The policy adopted by President Harry Truman in 1947 to halt communist expansion in southeastern Europe.

[5]See John Lewis Gaddis, *The United Nations and the Origins of the Cold War* (New York: Columbia University Press, 1972).
[6]Mr. X., "The Sources of Soviet Conduct," *Foreign Affairs,* July 1947, p. 575.

The United Nations building. How important has the United Nations been in promoting world peace? How important is the United Nations to the interests of the United States?

proposed the Greek–Turkish aid program specifically to counter Soviet influence in the eastern Mediterranean. He put the choice squarely before Congress—it either supported those measures required to preserve peace and security abroad or it would risk widespread global instability and perhaps World War III.[7]

During the cold war, there was never any direct military confrontation between the United States and the Soviet Union. Rather, confrontations among "client" nations were used to carry out the policies of the superpowers. Only on occasion did the United States directly enter into a conflict in a significant way. Two such occasions were in Korea and Vietnam.

In 1950, North Korean troops were embroiled in a war with South Korea. President Truman asked for and received a Security Council order from the United Nations for the North Koreans to withdraw. The Soviet Union was absent from the council on that day and did not participate in the discussion. Truman then authorized the use of American forces in support of the South Koreans. For the next three years, American troops were engaged in a land war in Asia—the war became a stalemate and a political liability to President Truman. One of Dwight Eisenhower's major 1952 campaign promises was to end the Korean war—which he did. An armistice was signed on July 27, 1953. However, American troops have been stationed in South Korea ever since.

[7]*Public Papers of the Presidents of the United States: Harry S Truman, 1947* (Washington, D.C.: Government Printing Office, 1963), pp. 176–180.

U.S. involvement in Vietnam began shortly after the end of the Korean conflict. When the French army in Indochina was defeated by the communist forces of Ho Chi Minh and the two Vietnams were created in 1954, the Americans assumed the role of supporting the South Vietnamese government against the communist North. John Kennedy sent 16,000 "advisers" to help South Vietnam, and, after Kennedy's death, Lyndon Johnson greatly increased the scope of that support. American forces in Vietnam at the height of the U.S. involvement totaled more than 500,000 troops. Over 56,000 Americans were killed and more than 300,000 were wounded in the conflict. The debate over the United States' presence in Vietnam divided the American electorate and spurred congressional efforts to limit the ability of the president to commit forces to armed combat. After a peace treaty was signed in 1973 and the prisoners of war were returned, the United States seemed unclear about its national security goals and its commitment to the old containment view of dealing with communism.

DID YOU KNOW?

That since 1963, the United States has conducted underground tests of more than four hundred nuclear weapons, whereas the U.S.S.R. has conducted more than three hundred such tests?

Confrontation in a Nuclear World

Nuclear power has spread throughout the world. The United States, the Soviet Union, India, China, Britain, France, and several other countries all have the capability of detonating nuclear bombs. It is estimated that the two super-powers have had enough nuclear bombs to destroy everyone at least twice and maybe three times. Obviously, confrontation between the United States and the Soviet Union could have taken on world-destroying proportions. Perhaps the closest we came to such a confrontation was the Cuban missile crisis in 1962. For thirteen days, the United States and the Soviets were close to nuclear war. The Soviets had decided to place offensive missiles ninety miles off the American coast in Cuba. On October 14, 1962, an American U-2 spy plane photographed the missile site being built. Immediately, the executive committee of the National Security Council met to discuss ways to get the missiles out of Cuba before they became operational. President Kennedy and his advisers rejected the possibility of armed intervention, setting up a naval blockade around the island instead. When Soviet vessels, apparently carrying nuclear warheads, appeared near Cuban waters, the tension reached its height. After intense negotiations between Washington and Moscow, the Soviet ships turned around on October 25, and on October 28 the Soviet Union announced the withdrawal of its missile operations from Cuba. In exchange, the United States agreed not to invade Cuba.

A Period of Détente

The French word **détente** means a relaxation of tensions between nations. By the end of the 1960s, it was clear that some efforts had to be made to reduce the threat of nuclear war between the United States and the Soviet Union. The Soviet Union had gradually begun to catch up in the building of strategic nuclear delivery vehicles in the form of bombers and missiles, thus balancing the nuclear scales. In the parlance of nuclear strategy, both nations had acquired **mutual assured-destruction (MAD)** capabilities. Theoretically, this meant that, if the forces of both nations were approximately equal, neither would chance a war with each other.

DÉTENTE
A French word meaning relaxation of tension. Characterizes U.S.–Soviet policy as it developed under President Nixon and Henry Kissinger. Stresses direct cooperative dealings with cold war rivals but avoids ideological accommodation.

MUTUAL ASSURED DESTRUCTION (MAD)
A theory that if the United States and the Soviet Union had extremely large and invulnerable nuclear forces that were somewhat equal, then neither would chance a war with the other.

ANTIBALLISTIC MISSILES (ABMs)
A defense system designed to protect targets by destroying the attacking airplanes or missiles before they reach their destination.

MULTIPLE, INDEPENDENTLY TARGETABLE, WARHEADS (MIRVs)
Multiple warheads carried by a single missile but directed to different targets.

FIRST-STRIKE CAPABILITIES
The launching of an initial strategic nuclear attack before the opponent has used any strategic weapons.

STRATEGIC ARMS LIMITATION TREATY (SALT I)
A treaty between the United States and the Soviet Union to stabilize the nuclear arms competition between the two countries. SALT I talks began in 1969 and agreements were signed on May 26, 1972.

The development of **antiballistic missiles (ABMs)** made the balance unstable. With ABMs, each side could shoot down the other's intercontinental nuclear warhead missiles. The United States also began to put **multiple, independently targetable warheads (MIRVs)** on a single missile, making it impossible for any ABM defensive system to eliminate completely the possibility of nuclear attack. This policy expanded nuclear **first-strike capabilities** without requiring the production of new missiles. These developments in weapons technology made arms control negotiations to reduce the possibility of war imperative.

As the result of protracted negotiations, in May 1972, the United States and the Soviet Union signed the **Strategic Arms Limitation Treaty (SALT I)**. That treaty "permanently" limited the development and deployment of the ABM, and it limited for five years the number of offensive missiles each country could deploy. The treaty negotiations were only one part of the détente policy developed by Secretary of State Henry Kissinger and President Nixon. Kissinger felt that with the two superpowers becoming equal in weaponry, the best hope for avoiding war was to increase contacts between the two nations, thus creating economic, social, and scientific relationships that would reduce tensions. Under the Kissinger–Nixon policy, new scientific and cultural exchanges were arranged with the Soviets, and new opportunities for Jewish emigration out of the Soviet Union were arranged.

The policy of détente was not limited to relationships with the Soviet Union. Seeing an opportunity to capitalize on increasing tensions between the Soviet

President Nixon signs the SALT I Treaty, the first cold war agreement with the Soviets, in 1972. What was its long-run impact?

PROFILE

Colin Powell

"If we listened to some military men, there would never be a step toward peace."

Colin Powell wears more brass on his shoulders than anyone else in the U.S. Army. As chairman of the joint chiefs of staff, Powell is the nation's highest military commander. In exercising full authority over all the branches of the armed forces, Powell answers to no one, with the exception of the president.

A true American success story, Powell grew up in Harlem, in New York's African-American ghetto. His parents were poor Jamaican immigrants who had a dream of success for their son. That success was achieved by way of the army, which Powell joined through the Reserve Officers' Training Corps (ROTC) while attending the City College of New York. Commissioned as a second lieutenant in 1958, Powell served as a field officer in Vietnam, where he was seriously wounded. On his return to the states, Powell attended the army's Command and General Staff College, and graduated second in his class. Returning to combat duty in Vietnam, Powell obtained a series of promotions and decorations for bravery.

Powell entered the governmental loop in 1972 as a White House fellow—one of a select group of military officers assigned to duties in civilian government. He worked with Caspar Weinberger in the Office of Management and Budget. When Weinberger became secretary of defense under President Reagan, Powell became the secretary's military adviser.

In 1987, the scandal over the sale of missiles to Iran decimated the intelligence community. The top personnel of the National Security Council resigned. President Reagan asked Powell to be the new chairman of the NSC, and he served in that capacity until the end of the president's term, in 1989.

The election of 1988 that brought George Bush to power also brought a new head of the NSC—Air Force General Brent Scowcroft. Powell was asked to stay on with the new administration as chairman of the joint chiefs. The fourth general's star on Powell's shoulder that came with the job is another honor among many for a man who has achieved success in life through service.

Powell's image became a familiar one during the U.S. military buildup in the Middle East in 1990.

Union and the People's Republic of China, Kissinger secretly began negotiations to establish a new relationship with that nation. After some minor cultural exchanges, President Nixon eventually visited the People's Republic and set the stage for the formal diplomatic recognition of that country during the Carter administration. Again, the new relationship was intended to increase cultural, economic, and scientific exchanges with the Chinese in order to reduce tensions.

Historians will certainly mark the late 1970s as threatening détente. Communist military activities increased. The Soviets intervened in Afghanistan on December 27, 1979. The Carter administration, unilaterally and without consulting Congress, retaliated by restricting grain sales to the Soviet Union and by prohibiting Americans from participating in the Olympic Games that were to be held in Moscow in 1980. Beginning in December 1981, the Polish communist regime, backed by the Soviets, crushed the growing Solidarity labor union movement—which had demanded extensive economic, social, and political freedoms—and established martial law.

DID YOU KNOW?

That the U.S. military stockpiled $30 billion worth of unneeded supplies and equipment, including a thirteen-thousand-year supply of a particular part for an F-14 fighter aircraft?

MX missiles.

President Reagan, coming into office in 1981, at first took a hard line against the Soviets, proposing the strategic defense initiative (SDI), or Star Wars, in 1983. Reagan and others in his administration argued that the program would deter nuclear war by shifting the emphasis of defense strategy from offensive to defensive weapons systems. Critics of the program, however, believed it would simply make the arms race more intense, be very expensive, and probably would not be technically feasible. Early public opinion polls on the issue suggested that the public was closely divided on the merits of the Star Wars proposal.

In November 1985, President Reagan and Mikhail Gorbachev, the Soviet leader, held summit talks in Geneva. The two men agreed to reestablish cultural and scientific exchanges and to continue the arms control negotiations. Progress towards an agreement had been slow. Although the United States, the other NATO nations, and the Soviet Union agreed to new measures to reduce the possibility of accidental hostilities in 1986, no new nuclear arms treaty was signed. A second Gorbachev–Reagan meeting in Reykjavik, Iceland in October 1986 came close to achieving an agreement on massive reductions in, and possibly the elimination of, strategic nuclear weapons. A confused postsummit climate, however, left both sides irritated and charging that the other nation's policy makers were not negotiating in good faith.

In the year following the Reykjavik summit, representatives of the United States and the Soviet Union continued work on an arms reduction agreement. Although there were setbacks throughout the year, the negotiations resulted in an historic agreement signed by Reagan and Gorbachev in Washington, D.C., on December 8, 1987. The terms of the Intermediate-Range Nuclear Force (INF) Treaty, listed in Table 18-1 require the superpowers to dismantle a total of four thousand intermediate-range missiles within the first three years of the agreement. The verification procedures allow each nation to keep a team of inspectors on the other nation's soil and to conduct up to twenty short-notice inspections of the disassembly sites each year. The Senate ratified the treaty in a vote of ninety-three to five on May 27, 1988, and the agreement was formally signed by Mr. Reagan and Mr. Gorbachev during the Moscow summit.

George Bush continued the negotiations with the Soviets after he became president, meeting with Gorbachev first in Malta and then in the United States. The goal of both nations was to reduce the number of nuclear weapons and the number of armed troops in Europe. However, the developments in Eastern Europe, the drive by the Baltic republics for independence, and the unification of Germany complicated the negotiations.

■ CHALLENGES IN WORLD POLITICS

As the two superpowers continue to negotiate arms reductions and to open new exchanges between their citizens, U.S. foreign policy still must face other global problems. Some of these issues are regional in nature and require solving very long-term conflicts that threaten world stability. Other issues, such as terrorism and the interdependency of the world economy, require determination and cooperation among many nations.

TABLE 18-1
Provisions of the INF Treaty

Missiles Eliminated

Land-based medium-range missiles (range: 621 to 3,418 miles) and launchers eliminated over three years.

Land-based shorter-range missiles (range: 311 to 621 miles) and launchers eliminated within eighteen months.

Under the treaty, the Soviet Union will destroy 1,752 medium-and shorter-range missiles based on its territory and in Eastern Europe. The United States will be required to destroy 867 medium-and shorter-range missiles in Western Europe.

Flight tests of the missiles to be eliminated are banned. Neither side may produce any stages or launchers for those missiles. Nuclear material from warheads and guidance systems may be retained when the missiles are scrapped.

Each party is to notify the other of the number, type, and location of systems to be eliminated, as well as dates.

Methods of Destruction

Missiles are to be destroyed by such means as crushing and burning. In the first six months, each side could eliminate 100 medium-range missiles by launching them unarmed, to be destroyed on impact.

On-Site Inspections

Thirty days after the treaty went into force, each side could conduct inspections at missile bases and support installations to verify data provided by the other side. Inspections can also be conducted after bases or support installations are eliminated, and as missiles and launchers are destroyed. For thirteen years, each side may conduct "short notice" inspections at agreed locations: twenty a year for the first three years, fifteen a year for the next five years, and ten a year for the last five years.

Spy Satellites

Neither side may interfere with the other's ability to monitor compliance by satellite.

Senate Condition

The Senate specified that its approval of the agreement was based on the current understanding between the administration and the Senate on interpretation of the treaty's terms and that the accord could not be reinterpreted later.

DID YOU KNOW?

That poison gases, such as nerve and blood gas, and chemical weapons that use bacteria, viruses, and toxins, including bubonic plague and anthrax agents, are likely to replace nuclear weapons as the greatest threat to world peace?

Regional Conflict

One of the regions that has traditionally been of great interest to the United States is Central America (Figure 18-1). In 1823, President Monroe declared a special U.S. interest in the region and, in the twentieth century, the Caribbean was known as an "American lake." The nations of Central America have suffered poverty and turmoil for most of their existence, with the exception of Costa Rica. In an attempt to restore order and to protect American property and lives, the United States has intervened militarily in Central America on many occasions. This interventionist policy did not build much affection for the United States among Central American nations. In the 1980s, the United States began a serious involvement in at least three Central American states: in El Salvador, where the right-wing government was under attack from leftist terrorist groups; in Nicaragua, where the United States backed the *contras* in their attempt to overthrow the pro-Soviet Sandinista government; and in

FIGURE 18-1
Countries of Central America

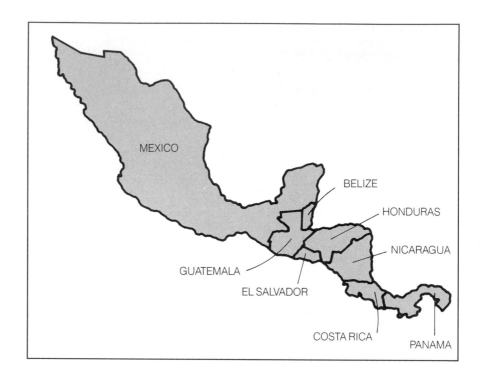

Panama, where the military leader, General Manuêl Noriega, an indicted drug trafficker, refused to leave office.

The Bush administration faced a rapidly changing situation in Central America. When Noriega refused to resign the presidency under pressure of economic sanctions on Panama, Bush ordered military forces into that nation to capture and arrest Noriega for drug dealing (see Highlight in this section). Although Noriega surrendered and was returned to the United States for trial, the invasion killed a large number of Panamanian civilians and leveled many blocks

United States soldier patrolling in part of Panama City that was destroyed during the conflict. What factors limit U.S. effectiveness in achieving its goals in such interventions in other nations?

HIGHLIGHT

Is It OK to Endanger the Life of a Foreign Head of State?

It took a U.S. invasion to remove General Manuel Noriega from power in Panama in December 1989. General Noriega was seized by U.S. forces and brought to the United States to stand trial in an American court on drug and money-laundering charges. After the invasion, the United States installed the civilian winners of the May 1989 election which Noriega had annulled. The Noriega affair exemplifies the complexities of foreign and national security policy.

The CIA recruited Noriega when he was a young Panamanian officer in the 1950s and put him on its payroll. Throughout the '60s, '70s, and early '80s, Noriega served as an intelligence source for the CIA. Noriega passed on information about Cuba's Fidel Castro, with whom he had extensive dealings,

about radicals in various Latin American armed forces, about the Colombian drug cartel, and, after the 1979 revolution, about the Sandinistas in Nicaragua. But Noriega was a double-dealer, not only helping the United States in its war against the Nicaraguan Marxists during the 1980s by training and arming the U.S.-backed *contra* rebels, but also supplying arms and information to the Marxist Nicaraguan government. He turned in some minor Colombian drug dealers but was implicated in alleged drug activities himself, and is assumed to have protected and even given safe haven to some of Colombia's Medellin cocaine cartel bosses. He is also alleged to have passed on *to* Castro as much information as he got *from* Castro to give to the United States.

By 1989, the United States wanted

Noriega out. But because of a presidential executive order issued by Gerald Ford (and reissued by all subsequent presidents), the United States could not support any action that might lead to the death of a foreign head of state. In 1989, Panamanian military officers tried to overthrow Noriega. Their aborted effort and Noriega's brutal reprisals led Congress and the president to reach an understanding that liberalized the interpretation of the executive order. Until it is changed or reinterpreted again, the U.S. president is presumably empowered to act in the interest of the United States *even when this may lead to the death of a foreign head of state*. This represents a major revision of U.S. foreign policy principles and one that may be tested again in Iraq.

of the capital, Panama City. While most Panamanians were glad to be rid of Noriega, the invasion worsened the country's economic problems.

The situation in El Salvador went from bad to worse. Five Jesuit faculty at a leading Salvadoran university and their housekeeper were massacred, possibly by a squad detailed by the rightist military. The United States continued to support the regime, although the administration expressed outrage at the murders and demanded, to no avail, that the perpetrators be found and brought to trial. In contrast, Nicaragua held elections and the Marxist president, Daniel Ortega, lost to Violetta Chamorro, well-known publisher of the opposition newspaper *La Prensa*. Chamorro assumed office and most of the *contras* surrendered their arms, at least temporarily.

The United States has also played a role in the Middle East. As a longtime supporter of Israel, the United States has undertaken to persuade the Israelis to agree to some kind of negotiations with the Palestinians who live as refugees within the occupied territories of the state of Israel. The conflict, which has been ongoing since 1948, is extremely hard to resolve, because it requires the Arab states of the region to recognize Israel's right to exist and requires Israel to make some settlement with the Palestinian Liberation Organization (PLO), which Israel regards as a terrorist organization, that has launched attacks on Israel from within and outside its borders. Further east, in the Persian Gulf, the Iran–Iraq war lasted ten years before the combatants agreed to a cease-fire and the conflict, which had destabilized the region, ended. Most analysts attributed the cease-fire to the high cost of the war for Iran. In December 1988, the U.S. began talking directly to the PLO.

U.S. Response to Iraq's Invasion of Kuwait

U.S. carrier on patrol near Saudi Arabia.

On August 2, 1990, the Middle East became the setting for a major challenge to the authority of the United States and its ability to buy oil from its allies there. President Saddam Hussein of Iraq initially sent more than 100,000 troops into the neighboring oil sheikdom of Kuwait, occupying the entire nation. The government of Kuwait fled the country. In addition, Iraqi troops took up positions on the Kuwaiti-Saudi Arabian border, close to the oil fields that are the key to the Saudis' wealth.

Within less than two days, President George Bush took the position that the annexation of Kuwait must not be tolerated by the Western world and that the oil fields of Saudi Arabia must be protected. At the formal request of the king of Saudi Arabia, American troops were dispatched to set up a defensive line at the Kuwaiti border. In addition, the president announced an economic boycott of Iraq (supported by the United Nations) and sent American carrier groups to seal off the Iraqi ports, thus cutting off shipments of oil.

Although the NATO alliance did not respond as an institution to this threat to the oil supply, individual nations including England, France, and Canada sent ships to assist. Following a vote at an Arab summit meeting, Egypt and Morocco sent troops to join the U.S. and Saudi forces in the desert. The Security Council of the United Nations voted economic sanctions against Iraq and the Soviet Union stopped its arms shipments to Hussein. One of the major concerns of all nations involved in this situation was the fate of Westerners who were caught within Iraq or Kuwait when the invasion began.

In the weeks following the invasion, American troops, planes and ships were moved to Saudi Arabia. The United Nations Security Council vowed to enforce

American tanks on maneuvers in Saudi Arabia.

an economic embargo against Iraq. Although Hussein did permit Western and other non-Iraqi women and children to leave Kuwait and Iraq, he refused to negotiate any terms for leaving Kuwait.

Eastern Europe, a region that had been extremely stable while under Soviet domination, suddenly became an unknown quantity in United States policy. With the decision of the Soviet Union to allow free elections and non-Marxist governments in Eastern Europe, these nations began separate paths to democratic states with mixed or market-oriented economies. As indicated in the Highlight in this section, some nations moved immediately to democratic elections; some struggled first to repair damaged economies, and others attempted to deal with ethnic tensions within their populations.

The Global Economy

Although the United States derives only about 10 percent of its gross national product from world trade, it is deeply dependent on the world economy. The stock market crash of 1987 showed how closely other markets watch the

> **DID YOU KNOW?**
>
> That by December 31, 1992, the twelve members of the European Community (which includes Germany, England, France, and other Western European states) will have created a single economic market of 322 million people, making it the developed world's largest market?

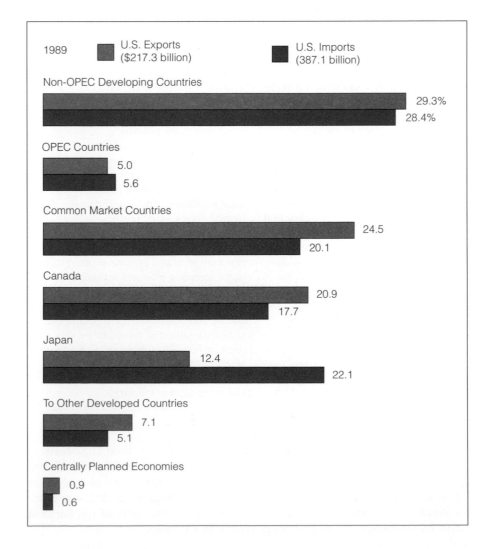

1989   U.S. Exports ($217.3 billion)   U.S. Imports (387.1 billion)

Non-OPEC Developing Countries
29.3%
28.4%

OPEC Countries
5.0
5.6

Common Market Countries
24.5
20.1

Canada
20.9
17.7

Japan
12.4
22.1

To Other Developed Countries
7.1
5.1

Centrally Planned Economies
0.9
0.6

FIGURE 18-2
U.S. Exports and Imports, 1989
SOURCE: U.S. Department of Commerce.

HIGHLIGHT

Is Japan the Problem?

According to a *New York Times*/CBS News poll, the percentage of Americans expressing negative feelings about Japan has significantly increased. A quarter of Americans surveyed said their feelings about Japan are "generally unfriendly." Older Americans with memories of World War II are more likely to have negative feelings toward Japan, but nearly 20 percent of younger persons now also have an unfavorable view. There were few regional differences, but more affluent and better-educated people were somewhat more friendly toward Japan.

Several factors appear to explain this growing trend. The first is the well-publicized Japanese investments in the United States, such as the purchase of Rockefeller Center in New York and Columbia Pictures by Japanese investors. High property values in Japan have made U.S. prices seem cheap, and the Japanese have invested heavily in U.S. real estate in many parts of the country. They have even bought some small private colleges, such as Westmar College in Le Mars, Iowa, as well as prime waterfront homes in Honolulu. Japanese millionaires and corporations have also dominated art auctions, spending enormous sums on paintings and other art which is then transferred to Japanese collections or corporate headquarters for display. All these activities have fed American anxiety that Americans are losing control over their own country and culture.

Second, the end of the cold war with the Soviet Union has freed Americans from the fear of communism and, ac-

cording to experts, has allowed people to become more aware of slipping American economic strength and preeminence. The Japanese have been very protectionist, making it difficult for American business to export its products to Japan. At the same time, Japanese products have become highly visible in the United States, competing with, and sometimes even monopolizing, parts of the American market. This pressure on U.S. companies has aggravated fears of rising unemployment as U.S. firms lay off workers.

Third, racial motives and cultural stereotypes have reinforced these feelings. The Japanese are seen as cunning, aggressive, and themselves racists. Comments by Japanese politicians, in part blaming U.S. minorities, especially African Americans and Hispanics, for many problems in the United States, were widely reported in the American media.

A flurry of new books has depicted Japan as an economic threat and even as a potential military adversary. Steven Schlosstein's *The End of the American Century*[*] argues that a newly militarized Japan could use its power against the United States. George Friedman and Meredith LeBard, in *The Second U.S.-Japanese War,*[*] suggest that there is a good chance of a U.S.-Japanese con-

[*]Albert J. Alletzhauser, *The House of Nomura: The Inside Story of the Legendary Japanese Financial Dynasty,* New York Arcade Publishers, 1990; Pat Choate, *Agents of Influence,* New York: Alfred A. Knopf, 1990; George Friedman and Meredith LeBard, *The Second U.S.-Japanese War,* New York: St. Martin's Press, 1991; Steven Schlosstein, *The End of the American Century,* New York, Contemporary Books, 1989.

flict, including armed conflict, in the next twenty years. Friedman says, "It's not so much a rise in militarism, but a rise in arrogance, a sense that now they'll show the world what they can do. The question is what they will do when they are thwarted, if we cut off their supply of oil, for instance." Pat Choate charges in *Agents of Influence* that Japan spends over $350 million a year trying to influence American public opinion to favor Japanese interests and is even financing American political parties. *The House of Nomura: The Inside Story of the Legendary Japanese Financial Dynasty,* by Albert J. Alletzhauser, which hit the number one spot on *The Times of London* best-seller list, paints a very negative picture of the world's largest brokerage firm and alleges that its power has come in part from connections with Japanese organized crime and politicians.

Blaming Japan has begun to worry American politicians and economists because they see in it the potential for increased protectionism and anti-free trade sentiment. This could damage the United States, since Japanese investment in the United States and growing demand for U.S. products in Japan are generally seen as a positive economic factor, creating jobs and making available capital to finance U.S. industry and government. Moreover, high-quality and moderately priced Japanese and other imported products are desired by the U.S. consumer. U.S.–Japanese joint ventures are bringing together the best of the two countries and creating new industries.

economic situation of the United States and, conversely, how U.S. markets follow those of London and Japan. Furthermore, since the 1980s the United States has become a debtor nation, meaning that we owe more to foreigners than foreigners owe to us. The reason for this is a huge trade deficit and the willingness of foreign individuals and nations to finance part of the national debt by purchasing United States government securities.

Because the United States imports more goods and services than it exports, it has a net trade deficit. These imports include BMWs, Sonys, Toshibas, and Guccis, as well as cheaper products such as shoes manufactured in Brazil and Yugo cars from Yugoslavia. As Figure 18-2 shows, our biggest deficit is with Japan. Because of the strength of the dollar over the last decade and high production costs, the United States has not been able to sell enough products overseas to reduce the trade deficit. One of the major items on the domestic political agenda for 1988 was a major trade bill designed to create incentives for other nations to buy U.S. goods and to place some restrictions on imports. It was signed into law by President Reagan in August 1988.

No one, in the United States or Western Europe, can predict how "Europe 1992" will affect world trade. With the European Community scheduled to become one economic "nation" on December 31, 1992, some expect Europe to close some markets to outside powers. Others see united Europe as a market opportunity for American and multinational corporations.

> **DID YOU KNOW?**
>
> That the largest trading partner of the United States is Canada?

Terrorism

The hijacking of TWA flight 847 on June 21, 1985, illustrated both the complexities of foreign policy and the frustration that terrorism causes for officials and the general public. An American plane bearing mostly American passengers returning from vacations abroad was selected by terrorists to be held hostage for the return of more than seven hundred Moslem prisoners held by the Israelis. The terrorists chose an American target, knowing that the United States had influence over the Israeli government but would be reluctant to exercise it, thus embarrassing both the United States and Israel. The situation was made even more difficult by the delicacy of the diplomatic and military conditions in Beirut, where the plane and thirty-nine of its hostages spent two weeks. It appeared impossible to rescue the hostages regardless of the size and capability of the U.S. defense establishment because the hostages were scattered throughout civilian homes in the city. Any military action would surely kill innocent Lebanese and endanger the Americans. The hostages were placed under the protection of the Amal militia and their leader, Nabih Berri, who receives his political support from President Assad of Syria. Negotiations among all parties finally freed the hostages seventeen days after the hijacking.

After the seizure of the *Achille Lauro,* an Italian cruise ship, and the attack on the Rome airport, the United States acted forcefully against terrorists. On April 14, 1986, at 12:13 P.M., fifty-seven U.S. aircraft, including refueling tankers and F-111 bombers, left England on a southwest course that took them along the coast of France, Portugal, and Spain, through the Straits of Gibraltar, and into the Mediterranean Sea. This trip of 2,800 miles was necessary because France had refused to allow the U.S. aircraft to fly the direct route over French territory.

Once in the Mediterranean, they were joined by fourteen aircraft launched from the U.S. aircraft carriers *Coral Sea* and *America,* which had been positioned off the coast of Libya. This combined air strike force then quickly made its way to land, guided by the most sophisticated radar and communications systems in the U.S. arsenal. At 7:00 P.M., they struck at numerous targets in and around the Libyan capital of Tripoli and the city of Benghazi.

The Reagan administration chose to launch this armed strike against Libya

Marilyn Klinghoffer, wife of the murdered American hostage, leaving the *Achille Lauro*. What steps can the United States take to prevent terrorism?

Colonel Gadaffi of Libya.

because its leader, Colonel Gadaffi, had become the most visible and vocal supporter of terrorist activity against the United States.

After the raid, the United States was widely criticized in the European press, which pointed out that Syria was as heavily implicated in recent terrorist activity as was Libya. Europeans also feared that the United States would force Gadaffi to retaliate, probably within Europe. The British public generally disapproved the decision by Margaret Thatcher to allow the American planes to take off from British bases. Although critical, many European nations tightened their own security efforts and deported many Libyans and other Middle Eastern citizens who may have been connected to terrorist activity. For the short run, terrorist activities declined and Colonel Gadaffi remained subdued.

The Iranian Connection

Beginning in 1984, terrorist groups operating in Beirut, Lebanon, began to kidnap American and European citizens and hold them hostage. The groups responsible for these kidnappings often tried to negotiate for the release of fellow terrorists held in prison by other nations. The official United States policy was the same as that of other nations: No negotiations should be held because it would encourage further terrorist activities. Numerous religious and other world leaders tried to persuade the terrorist groups to release their captives. One of the most prominent among these was Terry Waite, an emissary of the archbishop of Canterbury, who later was taken hostage himself.

Mr. Waite's efforts appeared to be instrumental in the release of Rev. Benjamin Weir, in September 1985. Nine months later, a Catholic priest, Father Martin Jenco, was released and returned to the United States. The third hostage to be released was David Jacobson, an official of the American University in Beirut, who was freed on November 2, 1986, just before the American elections. Terrorists claimed to have killed a fourth hostage, William Buckley, who was said to be the CIA chief in Beirut. This killing was later confirmed. Two other Americans remained captives: Terry Anderson, an American correspondent, and Thomas Sutherland, the dean of agriculture at the American University of Beirut.

Two days after the 1986 election, news stories suggested that the United States had sent a private envoy, Robert McFarlane, who had previously served as national security adviser to Mr. Reagan, on secret missions to Iran to negotiate a deal for the hostages. Within a few days, it became known that the United States had been involved in arms shipments to Iran in return for improved relations with that nation and help in freeing the hostages. Mr. Reagan, in a televised address, acknowledged the strategy, saying that he had authorized the transfer of small shipments of arms to Teheran, even though the United States had imposed a ban on any arms shipments to that nation since 1980.

Oliver North testifying before Congress.

As the story unfolded, it became more complex and more politically damaging to the Reagan presidency. The money for the arms shipments was, evidently, deposited in Swiss bank accounts which were controlled by a member of the National Security Council staff, Colonel Oliver North, and by a retired officer, Major General Richard Secord. The profit from the arms sales was to be used for aiding the *contra* forces in Nicaragua. These funds were possibly used to buy armaments for that rebel force during the months when the Congress had forbidden any military assistance to the *contras*. The president quickly dismissed Oliver North from his staff as well as National Security Adviser Admiral John M. Poindexter, who had known about the *contra* funds. Both men sought protection under the Fifth Amendment in their first appearances at congressional committees.

Congressional hearings showed that the plan to aid the *contras* was kept from the secretary of state and from the secretary of defense, although the role of the CIA was not as certain. The immediate political reaction to the disclosure of the scheme was an enormous 21 percentage-point drop in the president's public approval rating. Both houses of Congress as well as the FBI launched investigations into the transactions and the president asked for the appointment of a special prosecutor to look into any wrongdoing.

In 1988 the special prosecutor returned grand jury indictments against North, Poindexter, and two private citizens.

In early 1989, Oliver North was convicted on only two of the nineteen charges against him. After the trial, jurors stated that they felt North was taking the blame for his superiors. In a surprising decision, the judge put North on probation, requiring him to pay a fine of $150,000 and to perform 1,200 hours of community service but keeping the former officer out of prison. On appeal, North's convictions were overturned because he had been granted immunity by Congress. In 1990, Poindexter was found guilty and sentenced to a jail term of six months, but the overturning of North's convictions also gave Poindexter grounds for appeal.

■ FACING THE UNCERTAIN WORLD

In one sense, the United States is well positioned to plan and implement foreign policy in a world that is changing at a rate faster than at any other time since the conclusion of World War II. The United States is economically strong, militarily powerful, and politically stable. Furthermore, the Congress

Ferment in Eastern Europe

As these brief summaries of political change indicate, each nation in Eastern Europe seems to be following its own path to reform.

Albania: Communist Albania, with strong ties to China, was formerly the most isolated of the Eastern European nations. The Albanian parliament approved the right of residents to travel outside the country in May 1990. The practice of religion will also receive greater toleration than in the past. The Albanian government has indicated that it wants to normalize diplomatic relations with the United States and the Soviet Union.

Bulgaria: After reformists in the communist government sacked dictator Todor Zhivkov in 1989, open elections for parliament were held for the first time in fifty years. The reformed Communist party beat fledgling liberal and nationalist parties by a wide margin.

Czechoslovakia: Free elections brought former dissident Vaclav Havel to the presidency. Havel asked the United States for increased investment during a state visit in 1990. The government has asked the Soviet Union to remove all its troops from Czech soil.

East Germany: The Christian Democrats, conservatives with strong ties to the West German party, won the elections of 1990; the country was governed by a coalition including the leftist Social Democrats. Monetary union with West Germany was agreed and the process of unifying the two economies began on July 1, 1990 and was completed on Oct. 3, 1990; common election occurred on December 2, 1990.

Hungary: The right-of-center Christian party, which is philosophically related to the Christian Democrats of Western Europe, beat the more liberal Free Democrats in parliamentary elections. The Hungarian government called for the removal of all Soviet troops from the country, and declared its intention to leave the Warsaw Pact.

Poland: The Solidarity government was placed under stress by Lech Walesa's decision to seek the presidency of the country. His disagreements with the government were shared by many Poles, who were suffering under severe economic dislocations as the result of a rapid conversion of the economy from state control to a free market.

Romania: Free elections resulted in victory for former communist Ion Iliescu. Iliescu's National Front is composed of former communist officials, a fact that has provoked overt opposition. The election campaign was marked by violence; miners wielding clubs beat up dissidents who were protesting Iliescu's victory.

Soviet Union: Boris Yeltsin was elected president of the Russian Republic, and promptly declared that its laws take precedence over those of the central (Soviet) government. The secessionist declarations of the Baltic republics were joined by assemblies in most of the 15 Soviet republics.

Yugoslavia: Strife among Yugoslavia's many ethnic groups continued. Within the seven republics, pressures for secession from the central government grew. Free elections for local governments were held, with mixed results.

HIGHLIGHT

DID YOU KNOW?

That only 34 percent of Americans say that trade with Japan is good for the U.S. economy?

and the president are not deeply divided over the direction of the United States. It appears as if the United States will not aggressively promote democracy and capitalism in the world by means of economic aid and military intervention unless, as in the case of Central America, the nations are in its own "back yard." In fact, the United States finds itself in the curious position of needing to assist the Soviet Union, its cold war adversary, in that nation's quest for economic and political reform. Such assistance may take the form, in part, of *not* extending aid to the Baltic republics or *not* interfering in the affairs of the Eastern European nations.

The United States has strong resources and a stable regime. It remains to be seen whether the American people and their leaders have the patience and motivation to pursue a foreign policy of restrained leadership and economic competitiveness. The future shape of world politics will require these characteristics to deal with the period of extreme change that lies ahead.

GETTING INVOLVED

Working for Human Rights

I n many countries throughout the world, human rights are not protected to the extent that they are in the United States. In some nations, people are imprisoned, tortured, or killed because they oppose the current regime. In other nations, certain ethnic or racial groups are oppressed by the majority population. In nations such as Ethiopia, where drought has caused starvation among millions of people, international efforts to send food relief to the refugee camps has been hampered by the civil war that rages within that country.

What can you do to work for the improvement of human rights in other nations? One way is to join one of the many national and international organizations listed here that attempt to keep watch over human rights violations. By publicizing human rights violations, these organizations try to pressure nations into changing their tactics. Sometimes such organizations are able to apply enough pressure and cause so much embarrassment that selected individuals may be freed from prison or allowed to emigrate. One of the major goals of U.S. foreign policy, for example, has been to compel the Soviet Union to allow those who wish to emigrate to do so.

Another way to work for human rights is to keep informed about the state of affairs in other nations and to write personally to those governments or to their embassies asking them to cease these violations. Again, most of the organizations listed here have newsletters or other publications to keep you aware of developments in other nations.

If you want to receive general information about the position of the United States on human rights violations, you could begin by writing to:

U.S. Department of State
Bureau of Human Rights and Humanitarian Affairs
U.S. Department of State, Room 7802
Washington, D.C. 20520

The following organizations are best known for their watchdog efforts in countries that violate human rights for political reasons. These include both leftist and rightist regimes.

Amnesty International U.S.A.
304 W. 58th St.
New York, NY 10017

American Friends Service Committee
1501 Cherry St.
Philadelphia, PA 19102

Clergy and Laity Concerned
198 Broadway
New York, NY 10038

The following organizations are primarily concerned with the human rights violations that take place in Eastern-bloc nations, including the Soviet Union:

Freedom House
Wilkie Memorial Building
20 W. 40th St.
New York, NY 10018

Helsinki Watch
36 W. 44th St.
New York, NY 10036

Union of Councils for Soviet Jews
1411 K St., N.W., Suite 402
Washington, D.C. 20005

If you are specifically interested in working against apartheid in South Africa, you might contact:

United Nations Centre Against Apartheid
U.S. Plaza
New York, NY 10017

CHAPTER SUMMARY

1. Foreign policy includes national goals and the techniques used to achieve them. National security policy, which is one aspect of foreign policy, is designed to protect the independence and the political and economic integrity of the United States. Diplomacy involves the nation's external relationships and is an attempt to resolve conflict without resort to arms.

2. Sometimes U.S. foreign policy is based on moral idealism, the belief that the world can be improved and that it is the duty of the United States to lead in this effort. Other times, its policies stem from political realism, the belief that the world is a dangerous place and that every nation must do what it can to survive.

3. The formal power of the president to make foreign policy derives from the Constitution, which makes the president responsible for the preservation of national security and designates the president as commander in chief or the army and navy. Presidents have interpreted this authority broadly. They also have the power to make treaties and executive agreements.

4. The president also has a host of informal techniques that give the White House overwhelming superiority in foreign policy leadership.

5. In principle, the State Department is the executive agency most directly involved with foreign affairs. In the last several administrations, it has often been bypassed, however.

6. The National Security Council advises the president on the integration of "domestic, foreign, and military policies relating to national security." Presidents' use of the NSC has varied.

7. The intelligence community consists of forty or more government agencies engaged in intelligence activities varying from information gathering to covert actions.

8. The Department of Defense was created in 1947 to bring under the jurisdiction of a single department headed by a civilian secretary of defense all of the various activities of the American military establishment.

9. In response to presidential actions in the Vietnam war, Congress attempted to establish some limits on the power of the president in foreign policy by passing the War Powers Act in 1973.

10. In addition to governmental sources, U.S. foreign policy is influenced by a number of nongovernmental sources, including the elite establishment, attentive members of the public, and business interests.

11. Civilian concern about the relationship between the defense establishment and arms manufacturers dates back to the 1930s. In 1961, President Eisenhower cautioned the nation to beware of the military–industrial complex in his famous farewell address to the nation.

12. The DOD has been criticized for too close a relationship with prime defense contractors.

13. Three major themes have guided U.S. foreign policy. In the early years of the nation, isolationism was the primary focus. With the start of the twentieth century, this view gave way to global involvement. Since World War II, the major goal has been containing communism and the influence of the Soviet Union.

14. During the 1700s and 1800s, the United States had little international power and generally stayed out of European conflicts and politics.

15. The nineteenth century has been called the period of isolationism. The Monroe Doctrine of 1823 stated that the United States would not accept foreign intervention in the Western Hemisphere and would not meddle in European affairs.

16. The end of the period of isolationism started with the Spanish–American War of 1898. The first major entanglement in European politics began when the United States entered World War I on April 6, 1917.

17. Following the signing of the Treaty of Versailles in 1919, the United States once more retreated into isolationism, rejecting membership in the League of Nations and largely disbanding its military forces.

18. World War II marked a permanent change in American foreign policy. The United States was the only country to emerge from the war with its economy intact and the only country with operating nuclear weapons.

19. Soon after the war ended, the uncomfortable alliance between the United States and the Soviet Union broke up and the cold war began. A policy of containment, which assumed an expansionist Soviet Union, was enunciated in the Truman Doctrine.

20. Since the spread of nuclear weapons throughout the world, we have entered an era of limited wars. The closest the United States has come to a nuclear confrontation was during the Cuban missile crisis in 1962.

21. Following the frustrations of the Vietnam war and the apparent arms equality of the United States and the Soviet Union, the United States was ready for détente. As the arms race escalated, arms control became a major foreign policy issue.

22. The late 1970s marked the end of the period of détente. As Reagan began formulating his foreign policy, it was evident that the American public was ready to sanction a stronger military stance if it could be convinced that national interests were directly involved.

23. Although President Reagan established a tough stance toward the Soviet Union in the first term of his administration, the second term saw serious negotiations toward arms reduction, culminating with the signing of the Intermediate-Range Nuclear Forces Treaty at the Moscow summit in 1988. Negotiations toward further arms reductions continued in the Bush administration.

24. One very serious threat to world stability is the persistence of regional conflicts in such areas as Central America and the Middle East.

25. The United States is deeply dependent on the world economy, as shown by the vulnerability of its stock market to world forces, its debtor nation status, and its huge trade deficit.

26. Terrorism continues to be a powerful force, which the United

States struggles to deal with diplomatically and militarily. One response, which resulted in a major scandal and possible criminal liability, was the secret plan to use the proceeds of arms sales to Iran to fund the military activities of the *contra* forces in Nicaragua.

QUESTIONS FOR REVIEW AND DISCUSSION

1. Some critics have argued that the United States alternates between internationalism and isolationism, never quite able to decide whether to take a leadership role. What historical experiences might account for this indecisiveness? What would be the consequences for American citizens and for the world community if the United States did withdraw from world affairs?

2. Which branches and agencies of the national government are influential in making foreign policy? Think of at least one issue or foreign policy question on which the Departments of State and Defense would be likely to hold different views. What are the sources of power in foreign policy decision making that would determine which department might be more influential?

3. Foreign economic policy is increasingly important, not only for the United States, but also for its allies and for the less-developed nations. Should economic policy be used as a tool to serve other foreign policy goals, as in the earlier grain embargo against the Soviet Union, or should economic policy only serve the cause of American prosperity?

4. The majority of Americans favor negotiations for a nuclear freeze. Why is it so difficult for the two superpowers to begin these negotiations? To what extent do domestic political concerns within each nation affect these negotiations?

SELECTED REFERENCES

Cecil V. Crabb, Jr., and Pat M. Holt, *Invitation to Struggle: Congress, the President and Foreign Policy* (Washington, D.C.: Congressional Quarterly Press, 1980). A well-presented analysis of the conflict between Congress and the president in the foreign policy arena.

Jean-Claude Derian, *America's Struggle for Leadership in Technology* (Cambridge, Mass.: MIT Press, 1990). This is a very in-teresting and important book which analyzes the role government has played and can play in stimulating successful technological innovation and business practices among corporations. It compares Japan, the United States, and Europe and discusses the role of U.S. defense spending.

Richard E. Feinberg, *The Intemperate Zone: The Third World Challenge to U.S. Foreign Policy* (New York: W. W. Norton, 1983). This excellent study analyzes the implications of a more assertive and active third world.

Raymond L. Garthoff, *Détente and Confrontation: American-Soviet Relations from Nixon to Reagan* (Washington, D.C.: Brookings Institution, 1985). Both Soviet and U.S. foreign policy perspectives are examined from 1969 to 1984 to help readers understand the development of the most powerful factor in U.S. foreign policy and draw conclusions about the future of U.S.-Soviet relations.

Shintaro Ishihara, *The Japan That Can Say No* (New York: Simon & Schuster, 1990). The author, a Japanese legislator and former member of the government, argues, in one of the most controversial books on Japan and the United States to be published so far, that Japan has a technological advantage over the United States, is a rising power while the United States is in decline, and should no longer defer to the United States.

Saul Landau, *The Dangerous Doctrine: National Security and U.S. Foreign Policy* (Bolder, Colo.: Westview Press, 1988). This book traces and sharply critiques the history of "national security" as a justification for U.S. policy overseas from Truman through the Reagan administration, using excellent case studies to illustrate the issue.

James M. McCormick, *American Foreign Policy and American Values* (Itasca, Ill.: F. E. Peacock, 1985). An up-to-date, comprehensive discussion of the foundations and principles of U.S. foreign policy.

John Mueller, *Retreat From Doomsday: The Obsolescence of Major War* (New York: Basic Books, 1990). The author argues that the likelihood of nuclear war has declined, not just because of the fear of nuclear annihilation, but also because people have changed, learned from past mistakes, and become more civilized.

U.S. Foreign Policy: The Reagan Imprint (Washington, D.C.: Congressional Quarterly Press, 1986). This is a very compact and fact-filled compendium of current American foreign policy, with special focus on regional issues, arms control, international trade, and economics.

A GLOBAL PERSPECTIVE
THE URBAN WORLD

From the time that people began to develop large, settled communities after the end of the last Ice Age, there has been a dramatic increase in the proportion of humans who live in urban areas. Today, urban areas around the world provide a combination of the very best and the very worst living conditions imaginable. In Medellín, Colombia, for example, the world's highest murder rate per capita has been the product of massive drug-related violence, yet Medellín is a beautiful, delightful city with a wonderful climate. Cairo, Egypt, is choked with smog and with rush-hour traffic that includes animals and buses, private cars, taxis, bicycles, and pedestrians. Other cities, such as Paris; Rome; Lagos, Nigeria; and Washington, D.C., also are notorious for their traffic problems. Barcelona, Spain, on the other hand, is considered to be Europe's most livable city because of its climate, wide boulevards, pedestrian malls, and sidewalk cafés. In contrast, Mexico City often has air pollution rates ten times higher than is safe for humans to breathe.

The role of government in creating policy initiatives and directing resources can make a difference in determining the quality of life that cities are able to offer their inhabitants. Whether cities are safe, good places to raise a family, and centers of vibrant social and cultural life, or whether they are crime-infested, populated with a huge urban under-

Camel drivers in Egypt.

class, and dirty and smelly depends largely on how local and national governments deal with (or create) the problems that cities confront.

It is important to understand that when we talk about cities these days, the biggest cities and those that are growing the fastest are mostly in Asia, Africa, and Latin America. For example, Cairo was estimated in 1990 to have a population of 13 million. Calcutta has about 10 million people, Bombay's population is over 8 million, Istanbul has nearly 6 million, Jakarta has over 7.5 million, Karachi over 5 million, São Paulo over 10 million, Shanghai 12 million, and Beijing over 9 million. Mexico City, which is probably the most populous urban area in the world, had at least 21 million people according to a 1990 census; it is estimated that it will have between 25 million and 30 million by early in the twenty-first century. In contrast, the largest city in the United States, New York, has just over 7 million population.

Clearly, the problems of urban living are already enormous in developing countries and will increase as population growth con-

Smog shrouds a monument in Mexico City.

People crowd the streets in Shanghai, China.

tinues to be concentrated in these countries. We can expect their burgeoning populations to become increasingly desperate for jobs, better living conditions, and education for their children, drawing them inexorably to the overcrowded slums—the favellas and barrios—of the cities of Asia, Africa, and Latin America. All this will increase demands on already overstretched and often broke governments. It also will lead to greater demands on the handful of developed donor countries, including the United States, to provide badly needed aid. The extent to which the U.S. *will* help, and how much it *can* help, remains unanswered.

Traffic jam in Jakarta, Indonesia.

STATE AND LOCAL POLITICS

CHAPTER 19

STATE AND LOCAL GOVERNMENT

CHAPTER CONTENTS

WHAT IF . . . SOME STATES OUTLAWED SMOKING?

The hazards of smoking have been an important component of public debate over health and consumer issues at least since the first scientific study linking smoking and lung cancer was published in 1939. On January 1, 1966, federal law mandated health-warning labels for all cigarette packages, and, since January 2, 1971, cigarette advertising has been banned on radio and television. Federal laws and laws in some states, as well as policies adopted by some corporations, have transformed many public and private recreational and work environments into smoke-free spaces. Smoking on virtually all domestic airline flights has been banned, and many insurance companies provide favorable rates on life and car insurance premiums to nonsmokers.

Thus far, however, the act of smoking itself is perfectly legal, just so long as people do not light up where it is specifically prohibited. What might happen, though, if some states were to make smoking completely illegal?

One thing that is practically certain, based on past attempts to outlaw alcohol, fireworks, or harmful drugs, is that compliance with such laws would be far from total. Cigarettes and other smoking materials would be smuggled into states that had declared their ownership or consumption to be illegal.

Entrepreneurs would ensure the survival of a smokers' subculture by fulfilling the demand for tobacco products, which certainly would not end with the criminalization of smoking. Some smokers undoubtedly would attempt to engage in open resistance, and cautionary images of people being fined and possibly imprisoned for the act of lighting up would appear on the nation's television screens. Law enforcement would likely be strained severely in attempts to enforce the antismoking laws. People's homes, government offices, and businesses might be raided by the police in search of illicit smoking materials. A smokers' civil rights movement would quite likely arise, and the nation's legislatures, courts, and political executives probably would be embroiled in efforts by pro- and antismoking forces to enforce or change the laws.

If the ban on smoking really were successful, we might expect to have a lower rate of smoking-related health problems, such as lung cancer and emphysema. Hospitals might have fewer patients, insurance premiums might fall, and there might be less pressure on state and national budgets to finance

expensive medical treatment. With smoking-related diseases reduced, the nation's medical agenda might shift more toward AIDS, breast cancer, or stroke prevention and the problems of aging.

Of course, serious political and economic problems would be almost inevitable in states where large numbers of people in the tobacco-related farm, manufacturing, and service sectors would be thrown out of work. The major tobacco-producing states—such as North Carolina, Virginia, or Kentucky—probably would see many incumbent office-holders voted out of power and new political forces emerging to replace the tobacco interests.

If some states successfully adopted antismoking stat-

utes, one result might be effective national action to do the same. This is what happened when congressionally mandated health-warning labels on cigarette packages were adopted following such action by New York, Massachusetts, California, and other states.

It should be kept in mind, however, that at least one previous attempt to ban smoking through state legislation failed. Social reformers launched a campaign to enact anticigarette laws in nine southern and western states before World War I. By 1929, however, increased advertising, women's political emancipation, and illegal liquor consumption acted, together with other social forces, to blunt that early movement to prohibit cigarette consumption by adults.

---

1. *What is the difference between cigarette smoking and other activities detrimental to one's health?*
2. *Since we know that smoking causes lung and heart disease, what forces have prevented legislation banning this activity?*
3. *Can some states effectively act against smoking if others do not?*

The national government was created by design, and thirteen states had of necessity to be included in the system, as did the relatively large number of local units of government in 1787. But the rest of the units—other states, cities, townships, special districts—were all created later, willy-nilly, in response to irresistible political and economic demands in Congress and in the state legislatures . . . there was no stopping their creation. And the process, below the state level at least, has not yet come to a halt. The same pressures that have always been present are still at work to bring new local units of government into existence.

With no foreordained plan from which to build, and no clear guidelines to help the old and the new units adjust to one another (how would such a plan and such guidelines have been drawn up?), so many contenders for power produce a great deal of overlapping, duplication, and conflict, as well as waste of effort and resources.[1]

The United States has more separate governmental units than most other countries in the world. When political scientists use the term *hyperpluralism,* they often point to the existence of the over eighty thousand separate governmental units in the United States to demonstrate the concept. **Hyperpluralism** is an exaggerated form of **pluralism** in which government is so decentralized and authority so fragmented that it doesn't get anything done. It may seem that way, particularly at the local level, but actually the over eighty thousand governments in the United States, minus the federal government and the fifty state governments, do most of what people think government does—provide education, police protection, public health facilities, and the like. Indeed, most individuals come into contact with government workers only at the state and local levels. Although government employment at the federal level has held steady in recent years, at the state and local level the number of civilian employees in government has been increasing—from 9.9 percent of the entire civilian work force in 1963 to 12.8 percent in 1990. In 1990, over 13.5 million American civilians worked directly for state and local governmental units, and millions of others worked indirectly for—or were contractors and consultants to—state and local governments. Just from a prac-

HYPERPLURALISM
An exaggerated form of pluralism in which government is so decentralized and authority so fragmented that it doesn't get anything done.

PLURALISM
A political doctrine in which autonomous groups in society actively compete in the decision-making process for resources and services.

[1]Richard H. Leach, *American Federalism* (New York: W. W. Norton, 1970), pp. 47–48.

Local disaster: the aftermath of an earthquake.

TABLE 19-1
State Expenditures (in percentages)
Education is the largest category of state spending and local spending.

Education	26.66
Public welfare	21.04
Highways	15.51
Health and hospitals	10.28
Interest on general debt	4.32
Natural resources	3.80
Corrections	2.46
Financial administration	2.03
General control	1.67
Social insurance administration	1.63
Police	1.48
General public building	.59
Air transportation	.30
Housing and urban renewal	.28
Water transport and terminals	.24
Libraries	.10
Other	7.61

SOURCE: Tax Foundation, *Facts and Figures on Government Finance, 1990.*

GENERAL SALES TAX
A tax levied as a proportion of the retail price of a commodity at the point of sale.

PROPERTY TAX
A tax on the value of real estate; limited to state and local governments and a particularly important source of revenue for local governments.

tical point of view, a knowledge of how these governments operate is relevant for every citizen, for they are the governments that every citizen must deal with almost on a daily basis.

■ STATE AND LOCAL GOVERNMENT SPENDING

Examining the spending habits of a household often gives relevant information about the personalities and priorities of the household members. Examination of the expenditure patterns of state and local governments likewise can be illuminating. In Table 19-1, we show state expenditures for the latest fiscal year for which data are available. In Table 19-2, we show the same data for local governments. There is a clear-cut pattern. State and city expenditures are concentrated in the areas of education, public welfare, highways, health, and police protection. Education is the biggest category of expenditure, particularly at the local level. Contrast this expenditure pattern with the federal government, which allocates only about 4 percent of its budget to education.

■ PAYING FOR STATE AND LOCAL GOVERNMENT

In 1990, state and local expenditures totaled about $800 billion. These expenditures had to be paid for somehow. Until the twentieth century, almost all state and local expenditures were paid for by state and local revenues raised within state borders. Starting in the twentieth century, however, federal grants to state and local governmental units began to pay some of these costs. In the year 1902, federal grants to state and local governments accounted for 0.7 percent of state and local revenues. By 1990, they accounted for 14 percent.

State and local governments in general are very willing to accept federal money. Indeed, they have entire staffs who devote all of their time to obtaining grants. For obvious reasons politicians usually prefer to obtain money through federal, rather than direct state or local, taxation.

Tax Revenue

Figure 19-1 (a) shows the percentages of taxes in various categories raised by state governments and Figure 19-1 (b) gives the same information for local governments. By far the most important tax at the state level is the **general sales tax,** and at the local level, the **property tax.** Whereas the federal government obtains more than 43 percent of its total revenues from the personal income tax, states obtain only about 13 percent this way. In 1990, there were still eight states that did not have a personal income tax. Other taxes assessed by states include corporate income taxes, and fees, permits, and licenses at both the state and local government level, as well as death and gift taxes at the state level. (See this chapter's Critical Perspective for a discussion of the changing pattern of state and local tax revenues.)

A tremendous amount of variation exists in state and local taxes collected. Look at the average taxes collected per person for all the states in Table 19-3. This table shows that among the states levying the highest taxes are Alaska, New York, and the District of Columbia. Those levying the lowest taxes are Arkansas, Mississippi, and Alabama.

Nontax Revenue

Nontax revenue includes funds granted to state and local governments and transfer payments by the federal government. These funds provide nearly 15 percent of state and local government income. The grants are not always without "strings," however. Federal programs in such areas as education, highway construction, health care, and law enforcement may dispense cash subject to certain conditions. For example, the funds may be used only for a specific purpose or only if matching funds are contributed.

Profits generated by publicly operated businesses is another source of revenue for state and local governments. Publicly operated businesses include toll roads and bridges and water, electric power, and mass transportation systems. More than a third of the states sell liquor through state-operated stores that earn profits. Other state-operated businesses include Washington's ferries and North Dakota's commercial banks. Some states receive lease payments for public lands, and some cities rent space in publicly owned buildings.

Other nontax revenue sources include interest on loans and investments and court fines. In the 1980s, state-run lotteries became an increasingly popular way to raise money. In 1990, nearly two-thirds of the states and the District of Columbia sponsored lotteries. It is expected that the other states will follow.

■ THE U.S. CONSTITUTION AND THE STATES

We live in a federal system in which there are fifty separate state governments and one national government. The U.S. Constitution gives a broad range of powers to state governments. It also prohibits state governments from engaging in certain activities. The U.S. Constitution never explicitly stated what the states actually may do. Rather, state powers were simply reserved, or residual—states may do anything they are not prohibited from doing by the Constitution or anything that is not expressly in the realm of the national government.

TABLE 19-2
Local Expenditures (in percentages)

Education	44.88
Public welfare	7.06
Health and hospitals	6.78
Highways	5.66
Police	5.08
Interest on general debt	3.84
Sewerage	3.72
General control	2.58
Fire protection	2.44
Parks and recreation	2.42
Housing and urban renewal	1.80
Sanitation (other than sewerage)	1.44
Financial administration	1.26
General public building	1.25
Corrections	.89
Air transportation	.76
Libraries	.72
Natural resources	.64
Water transport and terminals	.30
Parking facilities	.21
Other	6.27

SOURCE: Tax Foundation: *Facts and Figures on Government Finance, 1990.*

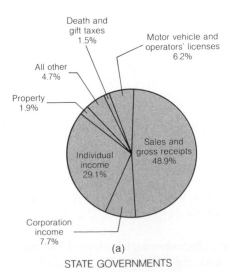

(a)
STATE GOVERNMENTS

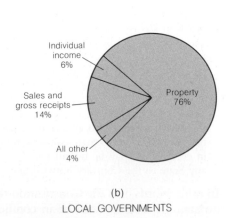

(b)
LOCAL GOVERNMENTS

FIGURE 19-1
Taxes Raised by State and Local Governments
States are generally dependent on sales taxes while towns and cities depend on property taxes.
SOURCE: *Book of the States, 1989–1990*, p. 234.

TABLE 19-3
Total 1989 State and Local Tax Collections, per Capita

Alaska	$3,604.68	Pennsylvania	1,627.48
D.C.	3,339.28	Oregon	1,602.24
New York	2,934.04	Ohio	1,568.54
Connecticut	2,280.78	Nebraska	1,557.47
Hawaii	2,258.58	Montana	1,538.27
New Jersey	2,216.86	Florida	1,521.96
Massachusetts	2,160.26	Texas	1,495.50
Maryland	2,092.82	North Carolina	1,494.72
Minnesota	2,076.44	Georgia	1,491.00
Wyoming	2,045.97	New Mexico	1,472.07
California	1,948.47	New Hampshire	1,471.99
Wisconsin	1,888.76	Utah	1,459.64
Michigan	1,883.92	Indiana	1,440.97
Vermont	1,863.31	Oklahoma	1,402.07
Delaware	1,853.54	North Dakota	1,389.22
Rhode Island	1,837.34	Missouri	1,371.54
Maine	1,831.72	South Carolina	1,337.37
Washington	1,782.68	Louisiana	1,328.70
Illinois	1,781.69	South Dakota	1,321.09
U.S. average	**1,772.43**	Kentucky	1,271.00
Arizona	1,690.47	Idaho	1,259.92
Virginia	1,686.85	Tennessee	1,242.08
Colorado	1,685.61	West Virginia	1,211.75
Kansas	1,676.27	Alabama	1,141.58
Iowa	1,656.85	Arkansas	1,112.56
Nevada	1,655.37	Mississippi	1,087.73

SOURCE: *Taxpayers' Federation of Illinois*, reported in *Crain's Chicago Business*, July 2, 1990, p. F21.

POLICE POWER
Authority to promote and safeguard the health, morals, safety, and welfare of the people.

The major reserved powers of the states are the powers to tax, spend, and regulate intrastate commerce, or commerce within a given state. The states also have general **police power,** meaning they can impose their will on their citizens in the areas of safety (through, say, traffic laws), health (immunizations), welfare (child-abuse laws), and morals (censorship of pornographic materials).

Restrictions on state and local governmental activity are implied by the Constitution in Article VI, Paragraph Two:

> This Constitution, and the Laws of the United States, which shall be made in Pursuance thereof; and all Treaties made, or which shall be made, under the Authority of the United States, shall be the Supreme Law of the Land; and the Judges in every State shall be bound thereby, any Thing in the Constitution or Laws of any State to the Contrary notwithstanding.

In other words, it is the Constitution that is the supreme law of the land, and no state or local law can be in conflict with the Constitution or with laws

CRITICAL PERSPECTIVE

Did the Tax Revolt Really Happen?

In 1978, California's famous (or infamous, as some would say) Proposition 13 rolled back property taxes. This "tax-revolt referendum" spawned a host of other no-new-tax movements through the nation. They often succeeded in holding traditional taxes at bay, according to one researcher, John Herbers, writing in *Governing* magazine. But, Herbers points out, this type of tax revolt is flawed for several reasons.

First, there is no free lunch. If people want more highways, fire protection, police, schools, and parks, as well as other amenities and services, they have to pay for them.

Second, antitax movements such as Proposition 13 haven't really reduced revenues to state and local governments. In California, state and local governments raised $1,321 per person during the 1979–1980 fiscal year. Ten years later, in spite of Proposition 13, revenues raised had risen by 87.7 percent to $2,480 per person.

Third, it has become clear that the continued growth of government revenues, even after tax freezes or rollbacks, has been due to a shift in revenue sources. Traditional taxes may not be raised at the state and local level, but increased **user fees** for parks, pools, and other services, as well as for trust funds for highways and education, are now common. States have also sold more bonds to raise money. In California, for example, in the decade after the passage of Proposition 13, fees and charges increased in California from $335 per capita to $707, an increase of more than 100 percent.

If Americans want a high level of public service, they will have to pay for it. Government will have to find the necessary revenues. So-called tax revolts call attention to tax burdens and in so doing may help produce more frugality and cost effectiveness in local and state government. They will also, however, stimulate the search for new tax revenues. Witness, for example, the passage of Proposition 111 in California in 1990. Voters in June of that year were faced with a variety of revenue-raising propositions. Proposition 111 called for a doubling of the gasoline tax to 18 cents per gallon to be used for improving the state's roads, bridges, and mass-transit system. More states will probably employ such revenue-producing tactics; that is, they will target specific state or local projects and ask the voters to agree to pay taxes just for those projects. This, of course, lets the taxpayer decide what he or she is willing to pay for. No longer are state governments given carte blanche to raise general taxes and make decisions about how to spend those taxes.

In any event, overall state and local taxes are clearly on the rise. Look at the accompanying figure. Here you see that the

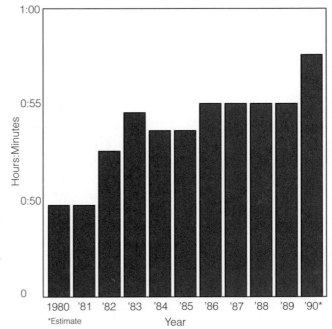

Paying for State and Local Taxes:
The average American spends two hours and forty-five minutes of every eight-hour workday earning enough to pay taxes. The largest share goes to the federal government and is about the same now as it was ten years ago. But the amount of time put in to pay state and local tax bills has grown noticeably. The time spent each day working for the state and local tax man is shown above.
SOURCE: Tax Foundation, Washington, D.C.

average American spends almost one full hour a day earning enough to pay state and local taxes.

Exercise in Critical Thinking

1. Does it matter to you as a taxpayer the method by which state and local governments obtain their revenues?
2. Is there a natural limit to the amount of taxes Americans are willing to pay?
3. In some states, voters have approved large bond issues to pay for new schools, storm, water, and sewer facilities, and so on. Is there any difference to the taxpayer whether such goods are paid for directly by taxes or indirectly by bond issues?

*Source: John Herbers, "Read My Lips: The Tax Revolt Hasn't Had All That Much Impact," *Governing*, April 1990, p. 11.

The Massachusetts gun law is an example of the police power of the states. What are some other police powers? What is the legal source of such powers?

made by the national Congress or by treaties entered into by the national government. Judicially, the U.S. Supreme Court has been the final arbiter of those conflicts arising between the national government and state governments.

■ STATE CONSTITUTIONS

The U.S. Constitution is a model of brevity, although at the cost of specificity. State constitutions, however, typically are models of excessive length and detail. The U.S. Constitution has endured for two hundred years and has been amended only twenty-six times. State constitutions are another matter. Louisiana has had eleven constitutions; Georgia, nine; South Carolina, seven; and the states of Alabama, Florida, and Virginia, six. The number of amendments that have been submitted to voters borders on the absurd. For example, by 1989, the citizens of Alabama had been asked to approve 656 amendments—of which they adopted 452. Table 19-4 offers comparative information on state constitutions.

Why Are State Constitutions So Long?

According to historians, the length and mass of detail of many state constitutions reflects the loss of popular confidence in state legislatures between the end of the Civil War and the early 1900s. During that period, forty-two states adopted or revised their constitutions. Those constitutions that were adopted before or after are shorter and contain fewer restrictions on the powers of state legislatures. Another, equally important, reason for the length and detail of state constitutions is that state constitution makers apparently have had a difficult time distinguishing between constitutional and statutory law. Does the Louisiana constitution need an amendment to declare Huey Long's birthday a legal holiday? Is it necessary for the constitution of South Dakota to authorize a cordage and twine plant at the state penitentiary? Does the Alabama constitution have to include a thirteen-and-a-half-page amendment establishing the "Alabama Heritage Trust Fund"? Does Article XX of the California constitution need to discuss the tax-exempt status of the Huntington Library and Art Gallery? The U.S. Constitution contains no such details. It leaves to the legislature the nuts-and-bolts activity of making specific statutory laws.

There is another reason for the lengthiness of state constitutions. They are basically political documents that attempt to reflect the desires and needs of various groups within a state.

The Constitutional Convention and the Constitutional Initiative

Two of the several ways to effect constitutional changes are the state constitutional convention and the constitutional initiative. As of 1990, at least 232 state constitutional conventions had been used to write an entirely new constitution or to attempt to amend an existing one. A unique feature of the constitutions of seventeen states is the **constitutional initiative**.[2] An initiative allows citizens to place a proposed amendment on the ballot without calling a constitutional convention. The number of signatures required to get a constitutional initiative on the ballot varies from state to state; it is usually between 5 and 10 percent of the total number of votes cast for governor in the last election. The states where the initiative process has been used most frequently are California and Oregon. Relatively few initiative amendments are approved by the electorate.

■ THE STATE EXECUTIVE BRANCH

All state governments in the United States have executive, legislative, and judicial branches. Here the similarity ends. State governments do not always have strong executive branches. Also, as we have noted, in some states citizens can initiate legislation.

A Weak Executive

During the colonial period, governors were appointed by the Crown and had the power to call the colonial assembly into session, recommend legislation, exercise veto power, and dissolve the assembly. The colonial governor acted as commander in chief of each colony's military forces, and the governor was head of the judiciary.

[2]These states are as follows: Arizona, Arkansas, California, Colorado, Florida, Illinois, Massachusetts, Michigan, Missouri, Montana, Nebraska, Nevada, North Dakota, Ohio, Oklahoma, Oregon, and South Dakota.

DID YOU KNOW?

That the governors of all but three states (New Hampshire, Rhode Island, and Vermont) serve four-year terms in office?

CONSTITUTIONAL INITIATIVE
An electoral device whereby citizens can propose a constitutional amendment through petitions signed by the required number of registered voters.

Ann Richards, elected governor of Texas in the 1990 election.

TABLE 19-4
General Information on State Constitutions

State or Other Jurisdiction	Number of Constitutions*	Dates of Adoption	Effective Date of Present Constitution	Estimated Length (number of words)	Number of Amendments Submitted to Voters	Adopted
Alabama 6		1819, 1861, 1865, 1868, 1875, 1901	Nov. 28, 1901	174,000	656	452
Alaska 1		1956	Jan. 3, 1959	13,000	28	20
Arizona 1		1911	Feb. 14, 1912	28,876(a)	187	104
Arkansas 5		1836, 1861, 1864, 1868, 1874	Oct. 30, 1874	40,720(a)	156	71(b)
California 2		1849, 1879	July 4, 1879	33,350	756	449
Colorado 1		1876	Aug. 1, 1876	45,679	227	108
Connecticut 4		1818(c), 1965	Dec. 30, 1965	9,564	24	23
Delaware 4		1776, 1792, 1831, 1897	June 10, 1897	19,000	(d)	115
Florida 6		1839, 1861, 1865, 1868, 1886, 1968	Jan. 7, 1969	25,100	63	41
Georgia 10		1777, 1789, 1798, 1861, 1865, 1868, 1877, 1945, 1976, 1982	July 1, 1983	25,000(a)	11 (e)	10
Hawaii . . . . 1(f)		1950	Aug. 21, 1959	17,453(a)	85	77
Idaho 1		1889	July 3, 1890	21,500	183	103
Illinois 4		1818, 1848, 1870, 1970	July 1, 1971	13,200	7	3
Indiana 2		1816, 1851	Nov. 1, 1851	9,377(a)	65	36
Iowa 2		1846, 1857	Sept. 3, 1857	12,500	48	45(g)
Kansas 1		1859	Jan. 29, 1861	11,865	107	80(g)
Kentucky 4		1792, 1799, 1850, 1891	Sept. 28, 1891	23,500	54	26
Louisiana 11		1812, 1845, 1852, 1861, 1864, 1868, 1879, 1898, 1913, 1921, 1974	Jan. 1, 1975	36,146(a)	24	15
Maine 1		1819	March 15, 1820	13,500	181	153(h)
Maryland 4		1776, 1851, 1864, 1867	Oct. 5, 1867	41,134	227	195
Massachusetts 1		1780	Oct. 25, 1780	36,690(a,i)	141	116
Michigan 4		1835, 1850, 1908, 1963	Jan. 1, 1964	20,000	41	15
Minnesota 1		1857	May 11, 1858	9,500	203	109
Mississippi 4		1817, 1832, 1869, 1890	Nov. 1, 1890	23,500	124	54
Missouri 4		1820, 1865, 1875, 1945	March 30, 1945	42,000	100	62
Montana 2		1889, 1972	July 1, 1973	11,866(a)	17	10

*The constitutions referred to in this table include those Civil War documents customarily listed by the individual states.

(a) Actual word count.

(b) Eight of the approved amendments have been superseded and are not printed in the current edition of the constitution. The total adopted does not include five amendments that were invalidated.

(c) Colonial charters with some alterations served as the first constitutions in Connecticut (1638, 1662) and in Rhode Island (1663).

(d) Proposed amendments are not submitted to the voters in Delaware.

(e) Estimated length of the printed constitution, which includes only provisions of statewide applicability. Local amendments comprise most of the total constitution.

(f) As a kingdom and a republic, Hawaii had five constitutions.

(g) The figure given includes amendments approved by the voters and later nullified by the state supreme court in Iowa (three), Kansas (one), Nevada (six), and Wisconsin (two).

(h) The figure does not include one amendment approved by the voters in 1967 that is inoperative until implemented by legislation.

TABLE 19-4
General Information on State Constitutions (Continued)

State or Other Jurisdiction	Number of Consti- tutions*	Dates of Adoption	Effective Date of Present Constitution	Estimated Length (number of words)	Number of Amendments Submitted to Voters	Adopted
Nebraska........... 2		1866, 1875	Oct. 12, 1875	20,048(a)	276	183
Nevada 1		1864	Oct. 31, 1864	20,770	165	100(g)
New Hampshire 2		1776, 1784	June 2, 1784	9,200	271(j)	141(j)
New Jersey 3		1776, 1844, 1947	Jan. 1, 1948	17,086	48	36
New Mexico........ 1		1911	Jan. 6, 1912	27,200	213	104
New York.......... 4		1777, 1822, 1846, 1894	Jan. 1, 1895	80,000	270	203
North Carolina 3		1776, 1868, 1970	July 1, 1971	11,000	30	24
North Dakota 1		1889	Nov. 2, 1889	31,000	208(k)	119(k)
Ohio 2		1802, 1851	Sept. 1, 1851	36,900	241	142
Oklahoma.......... 1		1907	Nov. 16, 1907	68,800	254(l)	114(l)
Oregon 1		1857	Feb. 14, 1859	25,965	347	174
Pennsylvania........ 5		1776, 1790, 1838, 1873, 1968(m)	1968(m)	21,675	24(m)	19(m)
Rhode Island 2		1842(c)	May 2, 1843	19,026(a,i)	84	44
South Carolina...... 7		1776, 1778, 1790, 1861, 1865, 1868, 1895	Jan. 1, 1896	22,500(n)	628(o)	454(o)
South Dakota....... 1		1889	Nov. 2, 1889	23,300	178	92
Tennessee 3		1796, 1835, 1870	Feb. 23, 1870	15,300	55	32
Texas 5		1845, 1861, 1866, 1869, 1876	Feb. 15, 1876	62,000	430	283
Utah 1		1895	Jan. 4, 1896	17,500	121	73
Vermont 3		1777, 1786, 1793	July 9, 1793	6,600	206	49
Virginia............ 6		1776, 1830, 1851, 1869, 1902, 1970	July 1, 1971	18,500	19	16
Washington 1		1889	Nov. 11, 1889	29,400	139	76
West Virginia....... 2		1863, 1872	April 9, 1872	25,600	96	59
Wisconsin 1		1848	May 29, 1848	13,500	161	118(g)
Wyoming 1		1889	July 10, 1890	31,800	90	51
American Samoa 2		1960, 1967	July 1, 1967	6,000	13	7
No. Mariana Islands........... 1		1977	Oct. 24, 1977	—	—	—
Puerto Rico 1		1952	July 25, 1952	9,281(a)	6	6

(i) The printed constitution includes many provisions that have been annulled. The length of effective provisions is an estimated 24,122 words (12,490 annulled) in Massachusetts and 11,399 words (7,627 annulled) in Rhode Island.

(j) The constitution of 1784 was extensively revised in 1792. Figures show proposals and adoptions since 1793, when the revised constitution became effective.

(k) The figures do not include submission and approval of the constitution of 1889 itself and of Article XX; these are constitutional questions included in some counts of constitutional amendments and would add two to the figure in each column.

(l) The figures include one amendment submitted to and approved by the voters and subsequently ruled by the supreme court to have been illegally submitted.

(m) Certain sections of the constitution were revised by the limited constitutional convention of 1967–68. Amendments proposed and adopted are since 1968.

(n) Of the estimated length, approximately two-thirds is of general statewide effect; the remainder is local amendments.

(o) Of the 628 proposed amendments submitted to the voters, 130 were of general statewide effect and 496 were local; the voters rejected 83 (12 statewide, 71 local). Of the remaining 543, the General Assembly refused to approve 100 (22 statewide, 78 local), and 443 (96 statewide, 347 local) were finally added to the constitution.

Source: Book of the States, 1988–89, p. 14–15.

DID YOU KNOW?

That the Supreme Court ruled, by a five-to-four vote, in 1980, that the nation's cities and counties enjoy no legal immunity when they violate someone's federal civil rights?

Not surprisingly, when the colonies revolted against English rule, that revolt centered on the all-powerful colonial governors. When the first states were formed after the Declaration of Independence, hostility toward the governor's office assured a weak executive branch and an extremely strong legislative branch. By the 1830s, the state executive office had become more important. Since Jackson's presidency, all governors (except in South Carolina) have been elected directly by the people. Simultaneously, there was an effort to democratize state government by popularly electing other state government officials as well.

Under the tenets of Jacksonian democracy, the more public officials who are elected (and not appointed), the more democratic (and better) the system. The adoption of the long ballot (see Chapter 10) was a result. Even today, some states have numerous state offices with independently elected officials. Michigan, for example, has thirty-six. The problem with the long ballot is that the direct election of so many executive officials means it is likely that no one will have much power because each official is working to secure his or her own political support. Only if the elected officials happen to be able to work together cohesively can they get much done.

In some states, the voters have at times chosen a governor from one political party and a lieutenant governor from another. This happened, for example, in California in 1978, in Missouri in 1980, and in Iowa in 1982 and 1986. These situations can result in making the governor unwilling to leave the state in order to keep the lieutenant governor from exerting power during his or her travels.

Reforming the System

Most states follow the practice of electing numerous executive officials. Nonetheless, governors have exercised the authority of their office with increasing frequency in recent years. Governors have become a significant force in legislative policy making. The governor, in theory, enjoys the same advantage that the president has over Congress in his or her ability to make policy decisions and to embody these in a program for the state legislative body to act on. How the governor exercises this ability often depends on his or her powers of charm and persuasion. A strong personality can make for a strong executive office.

Reorganization of the state executive branch to achieve greater efficiency has been attempted numerous times and in many states. In the 1950s, thirty-five states created their own reorganization commissions, patterned after the national commission on organization of the executive branch of the national government that was chaired by former President Hoover. Their administrative reforms typically involved compressing numerous, fragmented governmental agencies into more hierarchical and streamlined systems to increase efficiency or to end obsolete agencies.

There are many obstacles to reorganizing state executive branches. Voters do not want to lose their ability to influence politics directly. Both the voters and the legislators are fearful that reorganization will concentrate too much authority in the hands of the governor. Finally, many believe that numerous governmental functions, such as control of the highway program, should remain administrative rather than political.

HIGHLIGHT

Buffalo Commons

Should parts of 10 Great Plains states (see map), covering an area of roughly 139,000 square miles of land (one and a half times the size of California), 109 counties, and 400,000 people, be turned into the world's largest national park? "Yes," according to Frank Popper and Deborah Epstein Popper, two professors from Rutgers University in New Jersey.

The area, named the Buffalo Commons, would include most of the western parts of North and South Dakota, western Nebraska, eastern Montana, parts of Kansas, Oklahoma, and Texas, and several parts of Colorado, New Mexico, and Wyoming. This region has seen a sharp decline in population and economic activity. Some counties have lost over half their population since 1930 and now have four people or less per square mile, plus a sharp increase in both the median age and the poverty level of people remaining, and extremely low construction rates (as little as $50 per capita). Services such as doctors, ministers, schools, airline service, and even grocery stores are disappearing. In some places people drive fifty miles to buy a loaf of bread and one hundred miles to go shopping. By the year 2020, almost two-thirds of the plains states farms will have vanished.

The idea proposed by the Poppers is to allow the area to revert slowly to its original state, with a repopulation by the original animal inhabitants, including the buffalo, over the next thirty years. "We don't foresee a Mad Max, total-desolation scenario but rather a gradual pullback by the private sector, and then nature taking its course. . . ." says Frank Popper.

The area would then be turned into a massive land-use project, administered by a consortium of private groups and public agencies. It would include tourism, recreational areas, and retirement

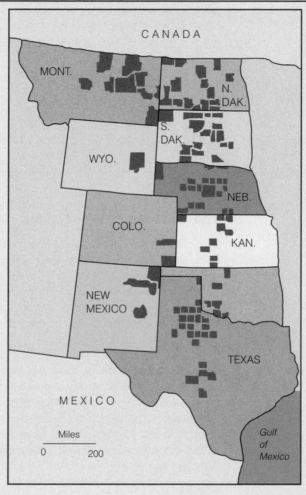

The Proposed Buffalo Commons
The dark brown areas in the map represent the proposed Buffalo Commons which would affect ten states and cover about 139,000 square miles.

communities in and near the boundaries of the Commons. The Commons probably would also contain U.S. Defense Department missile installations, oil-drilling rigs, Native American reservations, and other selected activities.

The Poppers argue that the region in question is not suited for agriculture. The early practice of wide-open animal and human migration changed when pioneer settlers began intensive farming in the nineteenth century. The dry, treeless, and fragile environment is sub-

ject to high winds, extreme temperatures, and drought. In the 1980s, the region was battered by depletion of water resources, loss of farms, and massive out-migration. The Poppers argue that the area was never suitable for farming, and thus should be allowed to revert to its natural ecologic state—a wide-open, natural plains "commons."

The Poppers' proposal has triggered an intense national debate over land use. The idea for the Commons grew out of a university land use exercise and

---

HIGHLIGHT

a scholarly article in the journal *Planning*. There are now both supporters and opponents. Joseph Luther of the University of Nebraska said, "Frank [Popper] represents Europe, the East, Harvard, federal interference—everything the good people of the Plains want to get away from, like my ancestors did, as early as the 1790's . . . No, we will fight the Poppers, all the way."

But there is a growing, worldwide renewal of the concept of commons and cooperatively managed public lands. This movement includes environmental initiatives, such as setting aside most of the Brazilian Amazon jungle as a preserve, saving rainforests and plains in Costa Rica, Kenya, and Southeast Asia, and restoring the Black Forest in Germany and other wooded areas in Europe. In the United States, smaller areas such as Central Park in New York City and the famous Boston Commons (created in 1634) are examples of this type of land use.

A great deal of the plains land is already controlled by government in the form of national parks, repossesed farmland, nature conservancies, private wildlife refuges, the Department of Agriculture Conservation Reserve, state parks and preserves, and so on.

How much would the Buffalo Commons cost? "Billions, but still less expensive than current farm subsidies," according to Frank Popper.
SOURCE: *New York Times*, June 24, 1990.

The Governor's Veto Power

The veto power of the president of the United States gives him immense leverage. Simply the threat of a presidential veto often means that legislation will not be passed by Congress. In some states, governors have stronger veto power than in others, but in some states governors have no veto power at all. Some states give the governor veto power but give him or her only five days in which to exercise it. About twenty states give the governor a pocket veto power (see Chapter 13).

ITEM VETO
The power exercised by the governors of most states to veto particular sections or items of an appropriations bill, while signing the remainder of the bill into law.

In forty-three states, the governor has some form of **item veto** power on appropriations. If the governor in such a state does not particularly like one item, or line, in an appropriations bill, he or she can veto that item. In twelve states, the governor can reduce the amount of the appropriation, but not completely. Nineteen states give governors the ability to use the item veto on more than just appropriations. Contrast this power with that of the president, who must veto the entire piece of legislation or leave it intact.

Off-Year Election of Governors

Increasingly, state elected officials, including the governor, are isolating themselves from national politics. They have been able to do this because of the tendency of states to elect their governors and other executive officials in off-presidential election years. For example, in 1988, fully thirty-six states did not have gubernatorial elections. In 1920, only twelve states did not have gubernatorial elections in that presidential election year.

The purpose behind this shift has been to weaken the influence of national politics over state politics. For example, if a Democratic candidate for governor is running during a presidential election year when the Democratic candidate for president is obviously going to achieve a landslide victory, the Democratic gubernatorial candidate also has a much better chance of winning.

Although this argument certainly has validity, there is a cost to such isolation from presidential politics. The cost is less voter participation in statewide elections. On average, only 65 percent of the voters who vote during the presidential election years vote during off-presidential election years.

PROFILE

David Dinkins

"The best way to survive is to be well trained."

Beset by chronic racial tensions, and a notorious crime rate, New Yorkers elected an understated, unflappable African-American as mayor in 1989. In the process, they seemed to repudiate the memory of the colorful and sometimes inflammatory former mayor, Edward Koch. To win the mayor's seat, Dinkins first had to beat Koch in the Democratic primary, and then defeat a Republican challenger, Rudolph Giuliani, in the general election. In so doing, Dinkins became the first African-American mayor in New York City's history.

Dinkins won by stressing both the need for racial harmony, and the need to get tough on crime. His platform tacked together individual themes dear to the city's African-American and white residents. The mayor's critics said it was long on generalities but short on specific solutions to the problems of crime, housing, and drugs. However, Dinkins gathered enough support from jittery whites to supplement his base in the African-American community; the result was victory.

For the sixty-three year old former president of the city's borough of Manhattan, political survival will depend on his ability to turn his campaign rhetoric into reality. Given the magnitude of the city's problems, Dinkins style of leadership tends to seem low-key. Dinkins' personal reserve stems in part from his political background: he is a consummate organization man.

Dinkins made his career in the organizational politics of New York City's

Harlem. After growing up in Trenton, NJ, he attended Howard University and then completed law school. During the nineteen fifties, he climbed up the ladder in the Harlem political club which was headed by his father-in-law, J. Raymond Jones. One of the keys to his success in Harlem ward politics was a talent for not rocking the organizational boat. His years of loyalty to the African-American Democratic establishment was rewarded in 1965; the Democratic organization slated him to run for the New York state Assembly in 1965. He served one term in the Assembly, and then lost a series of elections for city office. Eventually, he was elected the borough President of Manhattan in 1985, using the office as a springboard for his successful mayoral bid four years later.

Dinkins, as a political moderate, has given many New Yorkers reassurance that the atmosphere of interracial distrust may be soothed. Ultimately, however, Dinkins' political skills will be stretched as he tries to cope with a string of exceptional problems. His survival may depend on more than good training: inspiration, boldness, and the willingness to take risks may be required of him.

The State Legislature

Although there has been a move in recent years to increase the power of governors, state legislatures are still an important force in state politics and state governmental decision making. The task of these assemblies is to legislate on such matters as taxes and the regulation of business and commerce, school systems and the funding of education, and welfare payments. Allocation of funds and program priorities are vital issues to local residents and communities, and conflicts between regions within the state or between the cities and the rural areas are common.

State legislatures have been criticized for being less professional and less effective than the U.S. Congress. It is true that state legislatures sometimes spend their time considering trivial legislation (such as the official state pie in Florida), and lobbyists often have too much influence in state capitals. At the same time, state legislators are often given few resources to work with. In many states, legislatures are limited to meeting only part of the year, and in some the pay is a disincentive to real service. In at least eight states, state legislators are paid under $10,000 per year. A complete list of state legislators' salaries, as well as other characteristics of state legislatures, is given in Table 19-5.

We have seen earlier how a bill becomes law in the U.S. Congress. A similar process occurs at the state level. Figure 19-2 traces "how an idea becomes a

TABLE 19-5
Characteristics of State Legislatures

	Seats in Senate	Length of Term	Seats in House	Length of Term	Years Sessions Are Held	Salary*
Alabama	35	4	105	4	annual	$ 10(d)
Alaska	20	4	40	2	annual	22,140
Arizona	30	2	60	2	annual	15,000
Arkansas	35	4	100	2	odd	7,500**
California	40	4	80	2	even	40,816
Colorado	35	4	65	2	annual	17,500
Connecticut	36	2	151	2	annual	16,760
Delaware	21	4	41	2	annual	23,282
Florida	40	4	120	2	annual	21,684
Georgia	56	2	180	2	annual	10,000
Hawaii	25	4	51	2	annual	27,000
Idaho	42	2	84	2	annual	30(d)
Illinois	59	—‡	118	2	annual	35,661
Indiana	50	4	100	2	annual	11,600
Iowa	50	4	100	2	annual	16,600
Kansas	40	4	125	2	annual	52(d)
Kentucky	38	4	100	2	even	100(d)
Louisiana	39	4	105	4	annual	16,800**
Maine	35	2	151	2	even	7,500***
Maryland	47	4	141	4	annual	25,000
Massachusetts	40	2	160	2	annual	30,000
Michigan	38	4	110	2	annual	45,450
Minnesota	67	4	134	2	odd	26,395
Mississippi	52	4	122	4	annual	10,000
Missouri	34	4	163	2	annual	22,414

*Salaries annual unless otherwise noted as (d), per day, or (b), biennium.
**Plus per diem.
****For odd year; $3,733 for even year.
‡Terms vary from two to four years.
***For odd year; $4,000 for even year.
†Unicameral legislature.
$Per week.

SOURCE: Adapted from *Book of the States*, 1989–90 (Lexington, Ky.: Council of State Governments, 1990).

law" in the Florida legislature. Similar steps are followed in other states (note that Nebraska has a unicameral legislature, so there is no second chamber process).

Legislative Apportionment

Drawing up legislative districts—state as well as federal—has long been subject to gerrymandering—creative cartography designed to guarantee that one political party maintains control of a particular voting district (see Chapter 12).

TABLE 19-5
Characteristics of State Legislatures (continued)

	Seats in Senate	Length of Term	Seats in House	Length of Term	Years Sessions Are Held	Salary*
Montana	50	—‡	100	2	odd	52.13(d)
Nebraska†	49	4	—	—	annual	12,000
Nevada	21	4	42	2	odd	104(d)
New Hampshire	24	2	400	2	annual	200(b)
New Jersey	40	—‡	80	2	annual	35,000
New Mexico	42	4	70	2	annual	75(d)
New York	61	2	150	2	annual	57,500
North Carolina	50	2	120	2	odd	11,124
North Dakota	53	4	100	2	odd	90(d)
Ohio	33	4	99	2	annual	31,659
Oklahoma	48	4	101	2	annual	32,000
Oregon	30	4	60	2	odd	11,868
Pennsylvania	50	4	203	2	annual	47,000
Rhode Island	50	2	100	2	annual	5(d)
South Carolina	46	4	124	2	annual	10,000
South Dakota	35	2	70	2	annual	4,267
Tennessee	33	4	99	2	odd	16,500
Texas	31	4	150	2	odd	7,200**
Utah	29	4	75	2	annual	65(d)
Vermont	30	2	150	2	odd	6,750
Virginia	40	4	100	2	annual	18,000
Washington	49	4	98	2	annual	17,900
West Virginia	34	4	100	2	annual	6,500
Wisconsin	33	4	99	2	annual	32,239
Wyoming	30	4	64	2	annual	75(d)

*Salaries annual unless otherwise noted as (d), per day, or (b), biennium.
**Plus per diem.
****For odd year; $3,733 for even year.
‡Terms vary from two to four years.
***For odd year; $4,000 for even year.
†Unicameral legislature.
§Per week.

SOURCE: Adapted from *Book of the States*, 1989–90 (Lexington, Ky.: Council of State Governments, 1990).

DID YOU KNOW?

That the first African-American mayors of big cities were Richard G. Hatcher of Gary, Indiana, and Carl B. Stokes of Cleveland, both elected in 1967?

In Figure 19-3 we see a particularly bizarre example—the proposed sixty-ninth Assembly District for the State of California, drawn up by the California legislature to create a Democratic district in Orange and Los Angeles counties.

The Supreme Court indicated in 1962 that malapportioned state legislatures violate the equal protection clause of the Fourteenth Amendment.[3] In a series of cases that followed, the Court held that legislative districts must be as nearly equal as possible in terms of population, and the grossest examples of state legislative malapportionment were eliminated.[4] The Burger Court, however, allowed "benevolent, bipartisan gerrymandering" in certain states. Indeed, in 1977, the Supreme Court held that the state had an obligation imposed under the 1965 Voting Rights Act to draw district boundaries to maximize minority legislative representation.[5]

On June 27, 1990, the Los Angeles, California, County Board of Supervisors voted three to two to reshape one of the five districts in the county into a Hispanic majority district (the current supervisor from that district voted against the move). The board made its decision a short time before the 3 P.M. deadline set by Federal District Court Judge David Kenyon for such a re-drawing of the district. Judge Kenyon ruled earlier that after the 1980 census, the district was drawn in such a way as to split the Hispanic population into several districts, thus violating the Voting Rights Act. Judge Kenyon said that if the supervisors failed to correct the problem, he would redraw the district himself.

Does the issue of malapportionment matter? Some researchers believe it does. One study concluded that "reapportionment is making differences in

FIGURE 19-2
How an Idea Becomes a Law
SOURCE: Allen Morris, *The Florida Handbook 1983–1984*, 19th ed. (Tallahassee, Fl.: Peninsular Publishing Co., 1983), pp. 84–85.

[3]In *Baker v. Carr,* 369 U.S. 186 (1962).
[4]*Reynolds v. Sims,* 377 U.S. 533 (1964) and other cases.
[5]*United Jewish Organizations of Williamsburg v. Cary,* 430 U.S. 144 (1977).

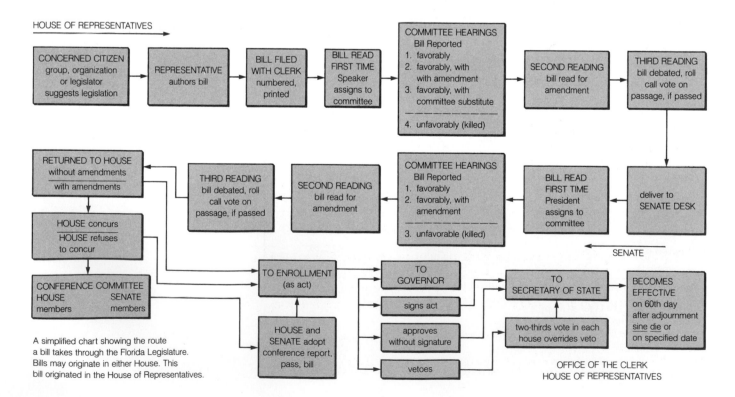

HOUSE OF REPRESENTATIVES

A simplified chart showing the route a bill takes through the Florida Legislature. Bills may originate in either House. This bill originated in the House of Representatives.

state spending in the direction of less discrimination against metropolitan areas."[6] But others, including political scientist Thomas Dye, have concluded that "on the whole, the policy choices of malapportioned legislatures are not noticeably different from the policy choices of well-apportioned legislatures."[7] Dye was particularly referring to state public policies on health, education, highways, welfare, and taxation.

Direct Democracy: The Initiative, Referendum, and Recall

There is a major difference between the legislative process as outlined in the U.S. Constitution and the legislative process as outlined in the various state constitutions. Many states exercise a type of direct democracy through the initiative, the referendum, and the recall—procedures that allow voters directly to control the government.

The Initiative.   This technique lets citizens bypass legislatures by proposing new statutes or changes in government for citizen approval. Most states that have citizen legislative initiative require that the **initiative** backers circulate a petition to place the issue on the ballot and that a certain percentage of the registered voters in the last gubernatorial election sign the petition. Twenty-one states use the legislative initiative, typically those states where political parties are relatively weak and where nonpartisan groups are strong. Some major initiatives that have been passed include a 1980 Washington state ban on out-of-state nuclear waste, a 1982 Massachusetts requirement that voters approve any future nuclear plant construction, and the adoption of laws requiring refunds on beverage cans and bottles in Maine and Michigan in 1976.

The Referendum.   The **referendum** is similar to the initiative, except that the issue (or constitutional change) is proposed first by the legislature and then directed to the voters for their approval. The referendum is most often used for approval of local school bond issues and for amendments to state constitutions. In a number of states that provide for the referendum, a bill passed by the legislature may be suspended by obtaining the required number of voters' signatures on petitions. A statewide referendum election is then held, and if the majority of the voters disapprove of the bill, it is no longer valid.

The referendum was not initially intended for regular use, and indeed it has been used infrequently in the past. Its opponents argue that it is an unnecessary check on representative government and that it weakens legislative responsibility. In recent years, the referendum has become increasingly popular as citizens have attempted to control their state and local governments. Interest groups have been active in sponsoring the petition drives necessary to force a referendum. Thirty-six states provided for the referendum as of 1990.

The Recall.   The right of citizens to recall, or remove, elected officials is not frequently exercised. A recent example was the case of Evan Meacham, former governor of Arizona, who was charged by his opponents with alleged racism, sexism, and corruption in the late 1980s. Meacham, after being removed from

**FIGURE 19-3
Proposed Sixty-ninth Assembly District in California**
SOURCE: Gordon E. Baker, "Redistricting in the Seventies: The Political Thicket Deepens," *National Civic Review* (June 1972), p. 281.

INITIATIVE
A procedure whereby voters can propose a law or a constitutional amendment.

REFERENDUM
An electoral device whereby legislative or constitutional measures are referred by the legislature to the voters for approval or disapproval.

[6]H. George Fredrickson and Yong Hyo Cho, "Sixties' Reapportionment: Is It Victory or Delusion?" *National Civic Review* (February 1971), p. 78.
[7]Thomas R. Dye, "Malapportionment and Public Policy in the States," *Journal of Politics* 27 (August 1965), p. 599.

Campaign signs in support of
California referenda.

office, was convicted of bribery and other misdemeanors he had committed while in office.

Recall is a provision written into the constitutions of fifteen states. It allows voters to remove elected state officials, including the governor, before the expiration of their term of office. In the case of judges, the recall can terminate a lifetime appointment.

Citizens begin the recall process by circulating petitions demanding a state-wide vote to remove the offending officeholder. The number of signatures required to bring about the election ranges from 10 to 40 percent of the last vote for the office in question. If the required number of signatures is obtained, the question of whether to remove the incumbent is decided in a general election.

Only fifteen states sanction the recall, about the same number that permit laws to be passed by direct citizen initiative (without the necessity of action by the state legislature). These states are Alaska, Arizona, California, Colorado, Georgia, Idaho, Kansas, Louisiana, Michigan, Montana, Nevada, North Dakota, Oregon, Washington, and Wisconsin.

All but two of these states lie west of the Mississippi; none of them is in the South. The distribution of these states supports the idea that different regions of the country have distinctive political cultures, or commonly held beliefs about how politics should be conducted. It is probably not a coincidence that most of the states that permit the removal of state officials also permit the passage of laws by initiative—that is, the ability of citizens to place proposed laws on a ballot and submit them to a popular vote without the intervention of the state legislature.

The recall and initiative are examples of "pure democracy," in which the people as a whole vote directly on important issues. Such measures are distinct in theory and in practice from the norms of "representative democracy," in which people are supposed to govern only indirectly, through elected representatives.

RECALL
A procedure enabling voters to remove an elected official from office before his or her term has expired.

■ THE STATE JUDICIARY

Each of the fifty states, as well as the District of Columbia, has its own separate court system (which is in addition to the federal courts—see Chapter 15). Figure 19-4 shows a hypothetical model of the state court system. It appears quite similar to the model of the federal court system, with its three levels of courts—trial courts, intermediate courts of appeal, and a supreme court. Again, the trial courts are of two types: those having limited jurisdiction and those having general jurisdiction.[8] Cases heard before these courts can be appealed to the state appellate court and ultimately to the state supreme court.

State courts confront severe problems of underfunding and overwork. Lack of funds—due to an increased case load, inflation, and fiscal conservatism in state governments—has slowed down, and occasionally even threatened to shut down, operations. State courts annually process about 140 million cases, three-quarters of which involve traffic offenses and about 10 percent of which involve alleged criminal activity. Short on judicial personnel and delayed by often complex cases with lengthy appeals, the state courts are often unable to function efficiently or fairly. The consequence is all too often a resort to plea-bargained convictions or a denial of justice to plaintiffs in civil and criminal cases.

The state courts of last resort are usually called simply supreme courts, although they are also labeled the supreme judicial court (Maine and Massachusetts), the court of appeals (Maryland and New York), the court of criminal appeals (Oklahoma and Texas, which also have separate supreme courts for appeals in noncriminal cases), or the supreme court of appeals (West Virginia). Judges for these highest courts may be chosen either at large from the state as a whole or by judicial district. Chief justices may be chosen by the public in an election, by fellow justices, by gubernatorial appointment with or without legislative approval, by a judicial nominating commission, by seniority, by rotation, or by the legislature. Terms of the chief justice and associate justices range from six years to life, though typically a limit of a certain number of years is set.

All states have major trial courts, commonly called circuit courts, district courts, or superior courts. The number of judges and their terms in office vary widely. Many, though not all, states have intermediate appellate courts between the trial courts of original jurisdiction and the court of last resort. These are usually called courts of appeal. Salaries of state judges also vary widely, but higher pay is given to appellate and supreme court members.

■ HOW LOCAL GOVERNMENT OPERATES

Local governments are difficult to describe because of their great dissimilarities and because, if we include municipalities, counties, towns, townships, and special districts, there are so many of them. We limit the discussion here to the most important types and features of local governments.

The Legal Existence of Local Government

The U.S. Constitution makes no mention of local governments. Article IV, Section 4, states that "the United States shall guarantee to every State in this

[8]See Chapter 15 for a definition of these terms.

DID YOU KNOW?

That nine states have no minimum age and fourteen states have no U.S. citizenship requirements for a person to run for governor?

FIGURE 19-4
The State Court System

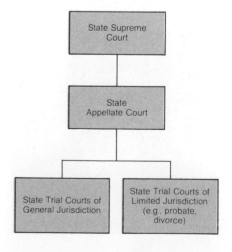

DID YOU KNOW?

That the first woman to become governor of a state was Mrs. Nellie Taylor Ross, in 1925 in Wyoming?

DILLON'S RULE
The narrowest possible interpretation of the legal status of local governments, outlined by Judge John F. Dillon, who in 1911 stated that a municipal corporation can exercise only those powers expressly granted by state law.

COOLEY'S RULE
The view that cities should be able to govern themselves, presented in an 1871 decision by Michigan Judge Thomas Cooley.

MUNICIPAL HOME RULE
The power vested in a local unit of government to draft or change its own charter and to manage its own affairs.

HOME RULE CITY
A city with a charter allowing local voters to frame, adopt, and amend their own charter.

GENERAL LAW CITY
A city operating under general state laws that apply to all local government units of a similar type.

Towing cars in an exercise of city authority.

Union a Republican Form of Government. . . ." Actually, then, the states do not even have to have local governments. Consequently, every local government is a creature of the state. The state can create a local government and the state can terminate the right of a local government to exist. Indeed, states have often abolished entire counties, school districts, cities, and special districts. Since World War II, almost twenty thousand school districts have gone out of existence as they were consolidated with other school districts.

Since the local government is the legal creature of the state, does that mean the state can dictate everything the local government does? For many years that seemed to be the case. The narrowest possible view of the legal status of local governments follows **Dillon's rule,** outlined by John F. Dillon in his *Commentaries on the Law of Municipal Corporations.* He stated that municipal corporations may possess only powers "granted in express words . . . [that are] necessarily or fairly implied in or incident to the powers expressly granted."[9] Cities governed under Dillon's rule have been dominated by the state legislature. Those communities wishing to obtain the status of a municipal corporation have simply petitioned the state legislature for a charter. The charter has typically been extremely narrow.

In a revolt against state legislative power over municipalities, the home rule movement began. It was based on **Cooley's rule,** derived from an 1871 decision by Michigan Judge Thomas Cooley[10] stating that cities should be able to govern themselves. Since 1900, about four-fifths of the states have allowed **municipal home rule,** but only with respect to local concerns—for which no statewide interests are involved. A municipality must choose to become a **home rule city;** otherwise, it operates as a **general law city.** In the latter case, the state makes certain general laws relating to cities of different sizes, which are designated as first-class cities, second-class cities, or towns. Once a city by virtue of its population receives such a ranking, it follows the general law put down by the state. Only if it chooses to be a home rule city can it avoid such state government restrictions. In most states, only cities with populations of 2,500 or more can choose home rule.

Local Governmental Units

There are four major types of local governmental units: municipalities, counties, towns and townships, and special districts.

Municipalities. As of 1990, there were about nineteen thousand municipalities within the fifty states. Almost all municipalities are fairly small cities. Only about five hundred cities have populations over fifty thousand, and only six municipalities (Chicago, Detroit, Houston, Los Angeles, New York, and Philadelphia) have populations over a million. In 1990, all the municipalities combined spent about $130 billion—primarily for water supply and other utilities, police and fire protection, and education. More than half of municipal tax revenues come from property taxes. Municipalities rely very heavily on financial assistance from both the federal and state governments.

[9]John F. Dillon, *Commentaries on the Law of Municipal Corporations,* 5th ed. (Boston: Little, Brown, 1911), I, Sec. 237.
[10]*People v. Hurlbut,* 24 Mich. 44 (1871).

State laws ban smoking in certain areas.

Counties. The difference between a **county** and a municipality is that a county may not be created at the behest of its inhabitants. The state sets up counties on its own initiative to serve as a political extension of the state government. Counties apply state law and administer state business at the local level. Counties are not municipal corporations, even though in some states the law treats counties as involuntary, quasimunicipal corporations.

County governments, of which there are almost three thousand within the United States, vary from Los Angeles County, California, with eight million people, to Loving County, Texas, with less than one hundred people. San

COUNTY
The chief government unit set up by the state to administer state law and business at the local level. Counties are drawn up by area, rather than by rural or urban criteria.

A recycling program in Portland, Oregon. Which policy problems may be most successfully tackled by local governments?

DID YOU KNOW?

That New Hampshire has the largest number of state legislators (four hundred House members and twenty-four senators) of any state?

Bernardino County, California, has more than twenty thousand square miles—half the size of Pennsylvania—but Bristol County, Rhode Island, comprises only twenty-five square miles.

County governments' responsibilities include zoning, building regulations, health, hospitals, parks, recreation, highways, public safety, justice, and record keeping. Typically, when a municipality is established within a county, the county withdraws most of its services from the municipality; for example, the municipal police force takes over from the county police force. County governments are extremely complex entities, a product of the era of Jacksonian democracy and its effort to bring government closer to the people. There is no easy way to describe their operation in summary form. Indeed, the county has been called by one scholar "the dark continent of American politics."[11]

NEW ENGLAND TOWN
Combines the roles of city and county into one governmental unit in the New England states.

TOWN MEETING
The governing authority of a town. Qualified voters may participate in the election of officers and in the passage of legislation.

Towns and Townships.   A unique governmental creation is the **New England town**—not to be confused with the word *town* used as just another name for a city. In Maine, Massachusetts, New Hampshire, Vermont, and Connecticut, the unit called the town combines the roles of city and county into one governing unit. A New England town typically consists of one or more urban settlements and the surrounding rural areas. Consequently, counties have little importance in New England. In Connecticut, for example, they are simply geographic units.

From the New England town comes the tradition of the annual **town meeting,** at which direct democracy was—and continues to be—practiced.

Expressing opinions in a town meeting.

[11]Henry S. Gilbertson, *The County, the "Dark Continent of American Politics"* (New York: National Short Ballot Association, 1917).

Each resident of a town is summoned to the annual meeting at the town hall. Those who attend levy taxes, pass laws, elect town officers, and appropriate money for different activities.

Normally, few residents show up for town meetings today unless a high-interest item is on the agenda or unless family members want to be elected to office. The town meeting takes a day or more, and few citizens are able to set aside such a large amount of time. Because of the declining interest in town meetings, many New England towns have adopted a **town manager system,** in which the voters simply elect three **selectpersons** who then appoint a professional town manager. The town manager in turn appoints other officials.

Townships operate somewhat like counties. Where they exist there may be several dozen within a county, and they perform the same functions that the county would do otherwise. Indiana, Iowa, Kansas, Michigan, Minnesota, New Jersey, New York, Ohio, Pennsylvania, and Wisconsin all have numerous townships. A township is not the same thing as a New England town because it is meant to be a rural government rather than a city government. Moreover, it is never the principal unit of local government—as are New England towns. The boundaries of most townships are based on federal land surveys of the 1780s, which mapped the land into six-mile squares called townships. They were then subdivided into thirty-six blocks of one square mile each called sections. Along the boundaries of each section a road was built.

Although townships have few functions left to perform in many parts of the nation, they are still politically important in others. In some metropolitan areas, townships are the political unit that provides most public services to residents who live in suburban **unincorporated areas.**

Special Districts.   The most numerous form of local government is the special district, which includes school districts. In 1990, there were about 44,300 special districts, of which slightly less than 15,000 were school districts. Special districts are one-function governments which are usually created by the state legislature and governed by a board of directors (Figure 19-5). After school districts, districts for fire protection are the most numerous. There are also districts for mosquito control, cemeteries, and numerous other concerns. Special districts may be called authorities, boards, corporations—and even districts.

One important feature of special districts is that they cut across geographical and governmental boundaries. Sometimes special districts cut across state lines, as does, for example, the Port of New York Authority, which was established by an **interstate compact** between New Jersey and New York. A mosquito control district may cut across both municipal lines and county lines. A metropolitan transit district may provide bus service to dozens of municipalities and to several counties.

Except for school districts, the typical citizen is not very aware of most special districts. Indeed, most citizens don't know who furnishes their weed control, mosquito control, water, or sewage control. Part of the reason for the low profile of special districts is that most special district administrators are appointed, not elected, and therefore receive little public attention.

Consolidation of Governments

With approximately eighty thousand separate and often overlapping governmental units within the United States, the trend in recent years toward con-

---

DID YOU KNOW?

That California spent almost $400,000 for a three-year study on "self-esteem" among Californians that was undertaken by the California Task Force to promote self-esteem and personal and social responsibility?

TOWN MANAGER SYSTEM
Form of city government in which voters elect three selectpersons who then appoint a professional town manager, who in turn appoints other officials.

SELECTPERSONS
The governing group of a town.

TOWNSHIP
Rural units of government based on federal land surveys of the American frontier in the 1780s. They have declined significantly in importance.

UNINCORPORATED AREAS
Areas not located within the boundaries of municipalities.

INTERSTATE COMPACT
An agreement between two or more states to cooperate on a policy or problem such as sharing water resources. It must first be approved by Congress.

FIGURE 19-5
**Special Districts According to
Their Function**

SOURCE: *Statistical Abstract of the United
States, 1990.*

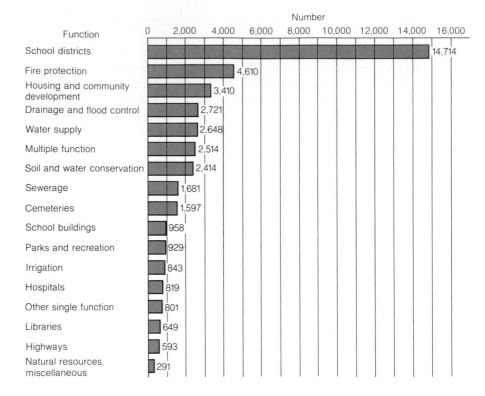

Function	Number
School districts	14,714
Fire protection	4,610
Housing and community development	3,410
Drainage and flood control	2,721
Water supply	2,648
Multiple function	2,514
Soil and water conservation	2,414
Sewerage	1,681
Cemeteries	1,597
School buildings	958
Parks and recreation	929
Irrigation	843
Hospitals	819
Other single function	801
Libraries	649
Highways	593
Natural resources, miscellaneous	291

CONSOLIDATION
The union of two or more governmental
units to form a single unit.

FUNCTIONAL CONSOLIDATION
The cooperation of two or more units of
local government in providing services to
their inhabitants.

**COUNCILS OF GOVERNMENTS
(COGs)**
Voluntary organizations of counties and
municipalities concerned with areawide
problems.

solidation is understandable. **Consolidation** is defined as the union of two or
more governmental units to form a single unit. Typically, a state constitution
or a state statute will designate consolidation procedures.

Consolidation is often recommended for metropolitan-area problems, but
to date there have been few consolidations within metropolitan areas. The
most successful consolidations have been **functional consolidations**—particularly of city and county police, health, and welfare departments. In some
cases, functional consolidation is a satisfactory alternative to the complete
consolidation of governmental units. The most successful form of functional
consolidation was started in 1957 in Dade County, Florida. The county, now
called Metro, is a union of twenty-six municipalities. Each municipality has
its own governmental entity, but the county government operates under a
home rule charter. The county, or Metro, has authority to furnish water,
planning, mass transit, and police services and to set minimum standards of
performance. The governing body of Metro is an elected thirteen-member
board of county commissioners, which appoints a county manager and an
attorney.

A special type of consolidation is **councils of government (COGs),** voluntary organizations of counties and municipalities that attempt to tackle
areawide problems. More than two hundred COGs have been established,
mainly since 1966. The impetus for their establishment was and continues to
be federal government grants. COGs are an alternative means of treating major
regional problems that various communities are unwilling to tackle on a consolidated basis either by true consolidation of governmental units or by functional consolidation.

The power of COGs is advisory only. Each member unit simply selects its
council representatives who report back to the unit after COG meetings.

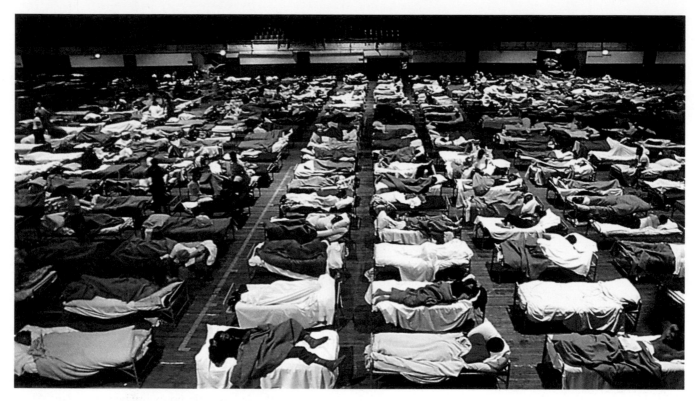

Homeless in a shelter.

Nonetheless, today there are several COGs that have begun to have considerable influence on regional policy. These include the Metropolitan Washington Council of Governments, the Supervisors' Inter-County Commission in Detroit, and the Association of Bay Area Governments in San Francisco.

How Municipalities Are Governed

We can divide municipal representative governments into four types: (1) the commission plan, (2) the council-manager plan, (3) the mayor-administrator plan, and (4) the mayor-council plan.

The Commission Plan.   This form of municipal government consists of a commission of three to nine members who have both legislative and executive powers. The salient aspects of the commission plan are as follows:

1. Executive and legislative powers are concentrated in a small group of individuals, who are elected at large on a (normally) nonpartisan ballot.
2. Each commissioner is individually responsible for heading a particular municipal department, such as the department of public safety.
3. The commission is collectively responsible for passing ordinances and controlling spending.
4. The mayor is selected from the members of the commission (an office that is only ceremonial).

The commission plan, originating in Galveston, Texas, in 1901, had its greatest popularity during the first twenty years of this century. It appealed

DID YOU KNOW?

That, in 1979, a liberal group of Texas state senators called "the Killer Bees" hid from the leadership and the Texas Rangers for five days to thwart a quorum needed to pass a bill they opposed? (The bill died.)

to municipal government reformers, who looked on it as a type of business organization that would eliminate the problems that they believed to be inherent in the long ballot and in partisan municipal politics. Unfortunately, vesting both legislative and executive power in the hands of a small group of individuals means that there are no checks and balances on administration and spending. Also, since the mayoral office is ceremonial, there is no provision for strong leadership. Not surprisingly, only about one hundred cities today use the commission plan—Tulsa, Salt Lake City, Mobile, Topeka, and Atlantic City are a few of them.

The Council–Manager Plan. In this form of municipal government, a city council appoints a professional manager who acts as the chief executive. He or she typically is called the city manager. In principle, the manager is there simply to see that the general directions of the city council are carried out. The important features of the council–manager plan are as follows:

1. A professional trained manager can hire and fire subordinates and is responsible to the council.
2. The council or commission consists of five to seven members, elected at large on a nonpartisan ballot.
3. The mayor may be chosen from within the council or from outside, but he or she has no executive function. As with the commission plan, the mayor's job is largely ceremonial. The city manager works for the council and not the mayor (unless, of course, the mayor is part of the council).

Today, about two thousand cities use the council–manager plan. About one-third of the cities with populations above 5,000 and about one-half of the cities with populations above 25,000 operate with this type of plan. Only four large cities of more than 500,000—Cincinnati, Dallas, San Antonio, and San Diego—have adopted the plan.

The major defect of the council–manager scheme, as with the commission plan, is that there is no single, strong political executive leader. It is therefore not surprising that large cities rarely use such a plan.

The Mayor-Administrator Plan

The **mayor-administrator plan** is often used in large cities where there is a strong mayor. It is similar to the council-manager plan you just learned about except that the political leadership is vested in the mayor. The mayor is an elective chief executive. He or she appoints an administrative officer whose function is to free the mayor from routine administrative tasks, such as personnel direction and budget supervision.

The Mayor-Council Plan

The mayor-council form of municipal government is the oldest and most widely used. The mayor is an elected chief executive and the council is the legislative body. Virtually all councils are unicameral except in Everett, Massachusetts. There are typically five to nine members of the council except in very large cities, such as Chicago, which has 50 members. Council members are popularly elected for terms as long as six, but normally four, years.

The mayor-council plan can either be a strong-mayor type or a weak-mayor type.

The Strong Mayor-Council Plan.   In the **strong mayor-council plan,** the mayor is the chief executive and has virtually complete control over hiring and firing employees, as well as preparing the budget. The mayor exercises strong and positive leadership in the formation of city policies.

The Weak Mayor-Council Plan.   This plan completely separates executive and legislative functions. The mayor is elected as chief executive officer; the council is elected as the legislative body. This traditional separation of powers allows for checks and balances on spending and administration.

About 50 percent of American cities use some form of the mayor-council plan. Most recently the mayor-council plan has lost ground to the council-manager plan in small and middle-sized cities.

Machine versus Reform in City Politics

For much of the later nineteenth and early twentieth centuries, many major cities were run by "the machine." The machine was an integrated political organization in which each city block within the municipality had an organizer, each neighborhood had a political club, each district had a leader, and all of these parts of the machine had a boss—such as Richard Daley in Chicago, Edward Crump in Memphis, or Tom Pendergast in Kansas City. The machine became a popular form of city political organization in the 1840s, when the first waves of European immigrants came to the United States to work in urban factories. Those individuals, often lacking the ability to communicate in English, needed help; and the machine was created to help them.[12] The urban machine drew on the support of the dominant ethnic groups to forge a strong political institution that was able to keep the boss (usually the mayor) in office year after year.

The machine was oiled by **patronage**—rewarding faithful party workers and followers with government employment and contracts. The party in power was often referred to as the patronage party.[13] Loyal voters were rewarded with deliveries of Thanksgiving turkeys or coal at Christmas in return for their continued support for machine candidates. The power of the machine lay in its ability to control votes, and the votes of new immigrants from Europe or from rural America were especially crucial.

According to sociologist Robert Merton,[14] the machine offered personalized assistance to the needy, helped to establish local businesses, opened avenues of upward social mobility for the underprivileged, and afforded a locus of strong political authority and responsibility. More critical of the political machine are Edward Banfield and James Wilson, who argue that

> machine government is, essentially, a system of organized bribery. The destruction of machines . . . permit[s] government on the basis of appropriate motives, that is, public-regarding ones. In fact it has other highly desirable consequences—especially greater honesty, impartiality, and (in routine matters) efficiency.[15]

[12]See Harvey W. Zorbaugh, *The Gold Coast and the Slum: A Sociological Study of Chicago's Near North Side* (Chicago: University of Chicago Press, 1929).

[13]See, for example, Harold F. Gosnell, *Machine Politics: Chicago Model* (Chicago: University of Chicago Press, 1937).

[14]*Social Theory and Social Structure* (Glencoe, Ill.: Free Press, 1957), pp. 71–81.

[15]Edward C. Banfield and James Q. Wilson, *City Politics* (New York: Vintage Books, 1963), p. 125.

DID YOU KNOW?

That Xavier Suarez was elected as the first Cuban-born mayor of Miami in 1985?

PATRONAGE
Rewarding faithful party workers and followers with government employment and contracts.

Precinct worker in a local election calling on a voter.

When the last of the big city bosses, Mayor Richard Daley of Chicago, died in December 1976, with him died an era that had lasted well over one hundred years. The big city machine began to be in serious trouble in the 1960s, when community activists organized to work for municipal government. Soon a government of administrators rather than politicians began to appear. Fewer offices were elective; more were appointive—presumably filled by professionals who had no political axes to grind, payoffs to make, or patrons to please.

Switching from a political to an administrative form of urban government was a way to break up the centralized urban political machine. In some cities, the results have been beneficial to most citizens. In others, decentralization has gone so far that there is no strong leader who can pull together discordant factions to create and follow a coherent policy. Consequently, in cities with a greatly decentralized government typified by numerous independent commissions and boards, a lot that should be done doesn't get done, particularly when an areawide problem is involved. This is an especially severe problem for less economically privileged people, who used to be able to rely on machine-sponsored activities and on the machine's political clout to help them compete against more well-to-do citizens for a share of the city's services. Reform is in some ways a middle-class preoccupation, whereas the less advantaged may find themselves better served by machine politics.

GETTING INVOLVED

Organizing in Your Community

The political arena is filled with issues that concern you. What government does or fails to do in the areas of education, health, employment, and crime affects you, your family, and your friends. Your sense of adventure, concern, curiosity, or injustice may urge you to take an active part in the government of a society with which you might not be particularly content. Yet getting involved on the national level may seem complicated, and national issues may not be of immediate concern. You may not even know exactly where you stand on many of those issues.

However, every week decisions are being made in your community that directly affect your local environment, transportation, education, health, employment, rents, schools, utility rates, freedom from crime, and overall quality of life. The local level is a good place to begin discovering who you are politically.

Another forum in which you may wish to participate involves boycotts.

According to *Boycott News,* there are currently over three hundred boycotts of products, services, and companies in the United States. These are generally carried out by local individuals and organizations pursuing a cause and a set of values. There are many different boycotts, including:

■ Grapes, lettuce, and wines, as a protest over unfair labor practices, poor working conditions of farm workers, and pesticide contamination of migrant workers and food crops
■ Ground beef and certain fast-food restaurants that allegedly buy imported beef from cattle raised on land where rainforests were cut down and turned into pastures
■ Coffee from El Salvador, in protest against human rights abuses allegedly committed by coffee growers against peasants
■ Cosmetic companies whose products have been tested on live laboratory animals
■ Companies that discriminate against women and minorities in their hiring and promotion policies
■ Companies that invest in, or do business with, the white minority apartheid government of South Africa
■ Diamonds from South Africa
■ Companies that support abortion or prochoice programs and activities
■ Companies that produce films that are offensive to religious groups
■ Furriers and stores that sell animal furs
■ Disposable diapers whose plastic liners are not biodegradable
■ Circuses and other entertainment that features performing-animal acts
■ Airlines, bus companies, and other businesses that are embroiled in labor disputes
■ Companies that pollute the air, water, or soil and that produce products harmful to the earth's ozone shield
■ Manufacturers and exporters of armaments and weapons

For more information, contact *National Boycott Newsletter,* 6506 28th Ave., N.E., Seattle, WA 98115.

CHAPTER SUMMARY

1. The United States has more separate governmental units than most other countries in the world.
2. State and local expenditures are concentrated in the areas of education, public welfare, highways, health, and police matters.
3. Starting in the twentieth century, federal grants began to pay for part of the cost of state and local governmental units.
4. The most important tax at the state level is the general sales tax and at the local level the property tax. There is tremendous variation in the rate of state and local taxation.
5. The 1970s and 1980s saw numerous tax revolts, one of the most famous of which was California's Proposition 13. Critics of limiting state taxes point out that such restrictions may undermine essential programs, such as police protection and schools.
6. The Constitution does not explicitly indicate what the states may do, but does say that no state or local law can be in conflict with the Constitution or with national laws. The major reserved powers of the states are to tax, spend, regulate intrastate commerce, and exercise police power.
7. State constitutions are generally lengthy and frequently amended. Seventeen states permit constitutional initiatives allowing citizens to place a proposed amendment on the ballot.
8. All state governments have executive, legislative, and judicial branches, but differ from national government in many important ways.
9. Most states follow the practice of electing numerous executive officials, but governors have become a significant force in legislative policy making in recent years. Reorganization of the executive branch for greater efficiency has been attempted in numerous states.
10. Because most states elect governors in off-presidential election years, state officials are more able to isolate themselves from

national politics. This practice also has meant less voter participation in these years.

11. Most state governors have some form of veto power, especially of specific items in an appropriations bill.

12. Legislatures usually hold the bulk of state governmental power. Their main task is to legislate on such matters as taxes, education, welfare, and regulation of business and commerce.

13. Malapportionment was the rule rather than the exception within the states until 1962, when the Supreme Court ruled that malapportioned state legislatures violated the equal protection clause of the Fourteenth Amendment. The Burger Court allowed "benevolent, bipartisan gerrymandering" in certain states.

14. Many states exercise a type of direct democracy through the initiative, the referendum, and the recall.

15. Each state has a separate court system, which is similar to the model of the federal court system with its three levels of courts—trial courts, intermediate courts of appeal, and a supreme court.

16. There is no mention of local governments in the U.S. Constitution. Thus each local government is a creature of the state.

17. For many years, the legal status of local governments was based on Dillon's rule that municipal corporations may possess only powers expressly granted by state law.

18. The view that cities should be able to govern themselves was presented in an 1871 decision by Michigan Judge Thomas Cooley. Since 1900, about four-fifths of the states have allowed municipal home rule, but only with respect to local concerns.

19. The four major types of local governmental units are municipalities, counties, towns and townships, and special districts.

20. Recent years have seen a trend toward consolidation of governments—the union of two or more governmental units to form a single unit—to cope with metropolitan-area problems.

21. Municipal representative governments are of four types: the commission plan, the council–manager plan, the mayor–administrator plan, and the mayor–council plan. About 50 percent of American cities use some form of mayor–council plan. Most recently, the mayor–council plan has lost ground to the council–manager plan in small and middle-sized cities.

22. The urban machine derived its power from immigrant groups to whom it gave jobs and services. The machines began in the 1840s and endured until the 1970s. Cities then began switching from a political to an administrative form of government as a way to break up the centralized urban political machine.

QUESTIONS FOR REVIEW AND DISCUSSION

1. One of the main thrusts of the new federalism was to cut back *federal* spending on social programs. The philosophy underlying this effort is that the people and the states can decide for themselves whether they want these programs to continue. What factors are likely to influence *state* decisions about financing social programs?

2. What are some of the features of state governments that give

greater control to the voters? To what extent do these features limit the flexibility and effectiveness of state government?

3. The structures and practices of state governments vary widely, revealing many adaptations of the national institutions. What reasons can you give for the unique features of state governments?

4. Some people suggest that the reason we have more than eighty thousand local governmental units is that Americans fear placing too much power in any centralized structure. What are some of the advantages and disadvantages of having multiple governments, particularly within one urban area? What functions of government would be easiest to consolidate? Which functions do you think the voters are least likely to grant to any form of metro government or centralized authority?

SELECTED REFERENCES

Edward C. Banfield and James Q. Wilson, *City Politics* (New York: Vintage Books, 1963). A classic on competing interests and ideas in city life.

Richard D. Bingham, *State and Local Government in an Urban Society* (New York: Random House, 1986). An excellent and detailed discussion of the institutions, processes, and policy issues of state and local government, including valuable and interesting short case studies.

Bernard J. Frieden and Lynne B. Sagalyn, *Downtown Inc.* (Cambridge, Mass.: MIT Press, 1990). This book is an interesting history of the efforts American cities have made in the past forty years to reverse downtown decay, including the senseless failures as well as the successful commercial projects that have helped cities and residents regain jobs, retail business, tourism, and other revitalizing benefits.

A. Lee Fritschler, *Smoking and Politics: Policymaking and the Federal Government,* 3rd ed. (Englewood Cliffs, N.J.: Prentice-Hall, 1983). A detailed analysis of the smoking issue referred to at the beginning of this chapter.

Sanford D. Horwitt, *Let Them Call Me Rebel: Saul Alinsky, His Life and Legacy* (New York: Alfred A. Knopf, 1990). This biography pieces together the views of many people who knew the legendary community activist and organizer Saul Alinsky, who died in 1972.

Mike Royko, *Boss: Richard J. Daley of Chicago* (New York: Signet Books, 1971). The personal and social forces of the Chicago Democratic party machine and the leadership of its famous mayor.

G. Alan Tarr and Mary C. A. Porter, *State Supreme Courts in State and Nation* (New Haven, Conn.: Yale University Press, 1988). An examination of the role of state supreme courts. Gives insights into state politics.

Jack Treadway, *Public Policymaking in the American States* (New York: Praeger, 1985). This book is an extensive literature review of more than 120 studies and provides the reader with an excellent overview of the mix of government, politics, and the socioeconomic environment and its implications for state policy making.

THE DECLARATION OF INDEPENDENCE

IN CONGRESS, JULY 4, 1776.

A Declaration by the Representatives of the United States of America, in General Congress assembled. When in the Course of human Events, it becomes necessary for one People to dissolve the Political Bands which have connected them with another, and to assume among the Powers of the Earth, the separate and equal Station to which the Laws of Nature and of Nature's God entitle them, a decent Respect to the Opinions of Mankind requires that they should declare the causes which impel them to the Separation.

We hold these Truths to be self-evident, that all Men are created equal, that they are endowed by their Creator with certain unalienable Rights, that among these are Life, Liberty, and the Pursuit of Happiness—That to secure these Rights, Governments are instituted among Men, deriving their just Powers from the Consent of the Governed, that whenever any Form of Government becomes destructive of these Ends, it is the Right of the People to alter or to abolish it, and to institute new Government, laying its Foundation on such Principles, and organizing its Powers in such Forms, as to them shall seem most likely to effect their Safety and Happiness. Prudence, indeed, will dictate that Governments long established should not be changed for light and transient Causes; and accordingly all Experience hath shewn, that Mankind are more disposed to suffer, while Evils are sufferable, than to right themselves by abolishing the Forms to which they are accustomed. But when a long Train of Abuses and Usurpations, pursuing invariably the same Object, evinces a Design to reduce them under absolute Despotism, it is their Right, it is their Duty, to throw off such Government, and to provide new Guards for their future Security. Such has been the patient Sufferance of these Colonies; and such is now the Necessity which constrains them to alter their former Systems of Government. The History of the present King of Great-Britain is a History of repeated Injuries and Usurpations, all having in direct Object the Establishment of an absolute Tyranny over these States. To prove this, let Facts be submitted to a candid World.

He has refused his Assent to Laws, the most wholesome and necessary for the public Good.

He has forbidden his Governors to pass Laws of immediate and pressing Importance, unless suspended in their Operation till his Assent should be obtained; and when so suspended, he has utterly neglected to attend to them.

He has refused to pass other Laws for the Accommodation of large Districts of People, unless those People would relinquish the Right of Representation in the Legislature, a Right inestimable to them, and formidable to Tyrants only.

He has called together Legislative Bodies at Places unusual, uncomfortable, and distant from the Depository of their Public Records, for the sole Purpose of fatiguing them into Compliance with his Measures.

He has dissolved Representative Houses repeatedly, for opposing with manly Firmness his Invasions on the Rights of the People.

He has refused for a long Time, after such Dissolutions, to cause others to be elected; whereby the Legislative Powers, incapable of Annihilation, have returned to the People at large for their exercise; the State remaining in the mean time exposed to all the Dangers of Invasion from without, and Convulsions within.

He has endeavoured to prevent the Population of these States; for that Purpose obstructing the Laws for Naturalization of Foreigners; refusing to pass others to encourage their Migrations hither, and raising the Conditions of new Appropriations of Lands.

He has obstructed the Administration of Justice, by refusing his Assent to Laws for establishing Judiciary Powers.

He has made Judges dependent on his Will alone, for the Tenure of their offices, and the Amount and payment of their Salaries.

He has erected a Multitude of new Offices, and sent hither Swarms of Officers to harrass our People, and eat out their Substance.

He has kept among us, in Times of Peace, Standing Armies, without the consent of our Legislatures.

He has affected to render the Military independent of, and superior to the Civil Power.

He has combined with others to subject us to a Jurisdiction foreign to our Constitution, and unacknowledged by our Laws;

giving his Assent to their Acts of pretended Legislation:

For quartering large Bodies of Armed Troops among us:

For protecting them, by a mock Trial, from Punishment for any Murders which they should commit on the Inhabitants of these States:

For cutting off our Trade with all Parts of the World:

For imposing Taxes on us without our Consent:

For depriving us, in many cases, of the Benefits of Trial by Jury:

For transporting us beyond Seas to be tried for pretended Offences:

For abolishing the free System of English Laws in a neighbouring Province, establishing therein an arbitrary Government, and enlarging its Boundaries, so as to render it at once an Example and fit Instrument for introducing the same absolute Rule into these Colonies:

For taking away our Charters, abolishing our most valuable Laws, and altering fundamentally the Forms of our Governments:

For suspending our own Legislatures, and declaring themselves invested with Power to legislate for us in all Cases whatsoever.

He has abdicated Government here, by declaring us out of his Protection and waging War against us.

He has plundered our Seas, ravaged our Coasts, burnt our towns, and destroyed the Lives of our People.

He is, at this Time, transporting large Armies of foreign Mercenaries to compleat the works of Death, Desolation, and Tyranny, already begun with circumstances of Cruelty and Perfidy, scarcely paralleled in the most barbarous Ages, and totally unworthy the Head of a civilized Nation.

He has constrained our fellow Citizens taken Captive on the high Seas to bear Arms against their Country, to become the Executioners of their Friends and Brethren, or to fall themselves by their Hands.

He has excited domestic Insurrections amongst us, and has endeavoured to bring on the Inhabitants of our Frontiers, the merciless Indian Savages, whose known Rule of Warfare, is an undistinguished Destruction, of all Ages, Sexes and Conditions.

In every state of these Oppressions we have Petitioned for Redress in the most humble Terms: Our repeated Petitions have been answered only by repeated Injury. A Prince, whose Character is thus marked by every act which may define a Tyrant, is unfit to be the Ruler of a free People.

Nor have we been wanting in Attentions to our British Brethren. We have warned them from Time to Time of Attempts by their Legislature to extend an unwarrantable Jurisdiction over us. We have reminded them of the Circumstances of our Emigration and Settlement here. We have appealed to their native Justice and Magnanimity, and we have conjured them by the Ties of our common Kindred to disavow these Usurpations, which, would inevitably interrupt our Connections and Correspondence. They too have been deaf to the Voice of Justice and of Consanguinity. We must, therefore, acquiesce in the Necessity, which denounces our Separation, and hold them, as we hold the rest of Mankind, Enemies in War, in Peace, Friends.

We, therefore, the Representatives of the UNITED STATES OF AMERICA, in General Congress Assembled, appealing to the Supreme Judge of the World for the Rectitude of our Intentions, do, in the Name, and by the Authority of the good People of these Colonies, solemnly Publish and Declare, That these United Colonies are, and of Right ought to be, Free and Independent States; that they are absolved from all Allegiance to the British Crown, and that all political Connection between them and the State of Great-Britain, is and ought to be totally dissolved; and that as Free and Independent States, they have full Power to levy War, conclude Peace, contract Alliances, establish Commerce, and to do all other Acts and Things which Independent States may of right do. And for the support of this declaration, with a firm Reliance on the Protection of divine Providence, we mutually pledge to each other our lives, our Fortunes, and our sacred Honor.

CONSTITUTION OF THE UNITED STATES OF AMERICA*

We the People of the United States, in Order to form a more perfect Union, establish Justice, insure domestic Tranquility, provide for the common defence, promote the general Welfare, and secure the Blessings of Liberty to ourselves and our Posterity, do ordain and establish this Constitution for the United States of America.

The Preamble declares that "We the people" are the authority for the Constitution (unlike the Articles of Confederation which derived its authority from the states). The Preamble also sets out the purposes of the Constitution.

ARTICLE I. (LEGISLATIVE BRANCH)

Section 1. All legislative Powers herein granted shall be vested in a Congress of the United States, which shall consist of a Senate and House of Representatives.

Section 2. The House of Representatives shall be composed of Members chosen every second Year by the People of the several States, and the Electors in each State shall have the Qualifications requisite for Electors of the most numerous Branch of the State Legislature.

Each state has the power to decide who may vote for members of Congress. Within each state, those who may vote for state legislators may also vote for members of the House of Representatives (and, under the Seventeenth Amendment, for U.S. Senators). When the Constitution was written, nearly all states limited voting rights to white male property owners or taxpayers at least twenty-one years old. Subsequent amendments granted voting power to African-American men, all women, and eighteen-year-olds.

No Person shall be a Representative who shall not have attained to the Age of twenty five Years, and been seven Years a Citizen of the United States, and who shall not, when elected, be an Inhabitant of that State in which he shall be chosen.

Representatives [and direct Taxes][1] shall be apportioned among the several States which may be included within this Union, according to their respective Numbers [which shall be determined by adding to the whole Number of free Persons, including those bound to Service for a Term of Years, and excluding Indians not taxed, three fifths of all other Persons].[2] The actual Enumeration shall be made within three Years after the first Meeting of the Congress of the United States, and within every subsequent Term of ten Years, in such Manner as they shall by Law direct. The Number of Representatives shall not exceed one for every thirty Thousand, but each State shall have at Least one Representative; and until such enumeration shall be made, the State of New Hampshire shall be entitled to chuse three, Massachusetts eight, Rhode Island and Providence Plantations one, Connecticut five, New York six, New Jersey four, Pennsylvania eight, Delaware one, Maryland six, Virginia ten, North Carolina five, South Carolina five, and Georgia three.

A state's representation in the House is based on the size of its population. Population is counted in each decade's census, after which Congress reapportions House seats. Since early in this century, the number of seats has been limited to 435.

When vacancies happen in the Representation from any State, the Executive Authority thereof shall issue Writs of Election to fill such Vacancies.

The "Executive authority" is the state's governor. When a vacancy occurs in the House, the governor calls a special election to fill it.

---

*The spelling, capitalization, and punctuation of the original have been retained here. Brackets indicate passages that have been altered by amendments to the Constitution.
[1]Modified by the Sixteenth Amendment.
[2]Modified by the Fourteenth Amendment.

The House of Representatives shall chuse their Speaker and other Officers; and shall have the sole Power of Impeachment.

The power to impeach is the power to accuse. In this case, it is the power to accuse members of the executive or judicial branches of wrongdoing or abuse of power. Once a bill of impeachment is issued, the Senate holds the trial.

Section 3. The Senate of the United States shall be composed of two Senators from each State [chosen by the Legislature thereof],[3] for six Years; and each Senator shall have one Vote.

Immediately after they shall be assembled in Consequence of the first Election, they shall be divided as equally as may be into three Classes. The Seats of the Senators of the first Class shall be vacated at the Expiration of the second Year, of the second Class at the Expiration of the fourth Year, and of the third Class at the Expiration of the sixth Year, so that one third may be chosen every second Year [and if Vacancies happen by Resignation, or otherwise, during the Recess of the Legislature of any State, the Executive thereof may make temporary Appointments until the next Meeting of the Legislature, which shall then fill such Vacancies].[4]

One-third of the Senate's seats are open to election every two years (unlike the House, all of whose members are elected simultaneously).

No Person shall be a Senator who shall not have attained to the Age of thirty Years, and been nine Years a Citizen of the United States, and who shall not, when elected, be an Inhabitant of that State for which he shall be chosen.

The Vice President of the United States shall be President of the Senate, but shall have no Vote, unless they be equally divided.

The Senate shall chuse their other Officers, and also a President pro tempore, in the Absence of the Vice President, or when he shall exercise the Office of President of the United States.

The Senate shall have the sole Power to try all Impeachments. When sitting for that Purpose, they shall be on Oath or Affirmation. When the President of the United States is tried, the Chief Justice shall preside: And no Person shall be convicted without the Concurrence of two thirds of the Members present.

The Senate conducts trials of officials that the House impeaches. The Senate sits as a jury, with the Vice President presiding if the President is not on trial.

Judgment in Cases of Impeachment shall not extend further than to removal from Office, and disqualification to hold and enjoy any Office of honor, Trust, or Profit under the United States: but the Party convicted shall nevertheless be liable and subject to Indictment, Trial, Judgment, and Punishment, according to Law.

On conviction on impeachment charges, the Senate can only force an official to leave office and prevent him or her from

holding another office in the federal government. The individual can still be tried in a regular court, however.

Section 4. The Times, Places and Manner of holding Elections for Senators and Representatives, shall be prescribed in each State by the Legislature thereof; but the Congress may at any time by Law make or alter such Regulations, except as to the Places of chusing Senators.

Congress set the Tuesday after the first Monday in November in even-numbered years as the date for Congressional elections. In states with more than one seat in the House, Congress requires that representatives be elected from districts within each state. Under the Seventeenth Amendment, senators are elected at the same places as other officials.

[The Congress shall assemble at least once in every Year, and such Meeting shall be on the first Monday in December, unless they shall by Law appoint a different Day.][5]

Section 5. Each House shall be the Judge of the Elections, Returns, and Qualifications of its own Members, and a Majority of each shall constitute a Quorum to do Business; but a smaller Number may adjourn from day to day, and may be authorized to compel the Attendance of absent Members, in such Manner, and under such Penalties as each House may provide.

Each House may determine the Rules of its Proceedings, punish its Members for disorderly Behaviour, and, with the Concurrence of two thirds, expel a Member.

Each House shall keep a Journal of its Proceedings, and from time to time publish the same, excepting such Parts as may in their Judgment require Secrecy; and the Yeas and Nays of the Members of either House on any question shall, at the Desire of one fifth of those Present, be entered on the Journal.

The journals of the two houses are published at the end of each session of Congress.

Neither House, during the Session of Congress, shall, without the Consent of the other, adjourn for more than three days, nor to any other Place than that in which the two Houses shall be sitting.

Section 6. The Senators and Representatives shall receive a Compensation for their Services, to be ascertained by Law, and paid out of the Treasury of the United States. They shall in all Cases, except Treason, Felony and Breach of the Peace, be privileged from Arrest during their Attendance at the Session of their respective Houses, and in going to and returning from the same; and for any Speech or Debate in either House, they shall not be questioned in any other Place.

[3]Repealed by the Seventeenth Amendment.
[4]Modified by the Seventeenth Amendment.
[5]Changed by the Twentieth Amendment.

Treason is defined in Article III, Section 3. A felony is any serious crime. A breach of the peace is any indictable offense less than treason or a felony. Members cannot be arrested for anything they say in speeches or debates in Congress.

No Senator or Representative shall, during the Time for which he was elected, be appointed to any civil Office under the Authority of the United States, which shall have been created, or the Emoluments whereof shall have been encreased during such time; and no Person holding any Office under the United States, shall be a Member of either House during his Continuance in Office.

During the term for which a member was elected, he or she cannot concurrently accept another federal government position.

Section 7.   All Bills for raising Revenue shall originate in the House of Representatives; but the Senate may propose or concur with Amendments as on other Bills.

Every Bill which shall have passed the House of Representatives and the Senate, shall, before it become a Law, be presented to the President of the United States; If he approve he shall sign it, but if not he shall return it, with his Objections to the House in which it shall have originated, who shall enter the Objections at large on their Journal, and proceed to reconsider it. If after such Reconsideration two thirds of that House shall agree to pass the Bill, it shall be sent together with the Objections, to the other House, by which it shall likewise be reconsidered, and if approved by two thirds of that House, it shall become a Law. But in all such Cases the Votes of both Houses shall be determined by Yeas and Nays, and the Names of the Persons voting for and against the Bill shall be entered on the Journal of each House respectively. If any Bill shall not be returned by the President within ten Days (Sundays excepted) after it shall have been presented to him, the Same shall be a Law, in like Manner as if he had signed it, unless the Congress by their Adjournment prevent its Return in which Case it shall not be a Law.

When Congress sends the President a bill, he or she can sign it, and it becomes law, or send it back to the house in which it originated. If it is sent back, a two-thirds majority of each house must pass it again for it to become law. If the President neither signs it nor sends it back within ten days, it becomes law anyway, unless Congress adjourns in the meantime.

Every Order, Resolution, or Vote to which the Concurrence of the Senate and House of Representatives may be necessary (except on a question of Adjournment) shall be presented to the President of the United States; and before the Same shall take Effect, shall be approved by him, or being disapproved by him, shall be repassed by two thirds of the Senate and House of Representatives, according to the Rules and Limitations prescribed in the Case of a Bill.

The President must either sign or veto everything that Congress passes, except votes to adjourn and resolutions not having the force of law.

Section 8.   The Congress shall have Power To lay and collect Taxes, Duties, Imposts and Excises, to pay the Debts and provide for the common Defence and general Welfare of the United States; but all Duties, Imposts and Excises shall be uniform throughout the United States;

Duties are taxes on imports and exports. Impost is a generic term for tax. Excises are taxes on the manufacture, sale, or use of goods.

To borrow Money on the credit of the United States;

To regulate Commerce with foreign Nations, and among the several States, and with the Indian Tribes;

To establish a uniform Rule of Naturalization, and uniform Laws on the subject of Bankruptcies throughout the United States;

To coin Money, regulate the Value thereof, and of foreign Coin, and fix the Standard of Weights and Measures;

To provide for the Punishment of counterfeiting the Securities and current Coin of the United States;

To establish Post Offices and post Roads;

Post roads include all routes over which mail is carried—highways, railways, waterways, and airways.

To promote the Progress of Science and useful Arts, by securing for limited Times to Authors and Inventors the exclusive Right to their respective Writings and Discoveries;

To constitute Tribunals inferior to the supreme Court;

Congress has the authority to set up all federal courts, except the Supreme Court, and to decide what cases those courts will hear.

To define and punish Piracies and Felonies committed on the high Seas, and Offences against the Law of Nations;

Congress has the authority to prohibit the commission of certain acts outside U.S. territory and to punish certain violations of international law.

To declare War, grant Letters of Marque and Reprisal, and make Rules concerning Captures on Land and Water;

Letters of marque and reprisal authorized private parties to capture and destroy enemy ships in wartime. Since the mid-nineteenth century, international law has prohibited letters of marque and reprisal, and the U.S. has honored the ban.

To raise and support Armies, but no Appropriation of Money to that Use shall be for a longer Term than two Years;

To provide and maintain a Navy;

To make Rules for the Government and Regulation of the

land and naval Forces;

To provide for calling forth the Militia to execute the Laws of the Union, suppress Insurrections and repel Invasions;

The militia is known today as the National Guard. Both Congress and the President have the authority to call the National Guard into federal service.

To provide for organizing, arming, and disciplining the Militia, and for governing such Part of them as may be employed in the Service of the United States, reserving to the States respectively, the Appointment of the Officers, and the Authority of training the Militia according to the discipline prescribed by Congress;

To exercise exclusive Legislation in all Cases whatsoever, over such District (not exceeding ten Miles square) as may, by Cession of particular States, and the Acceptance of Congress, become the Seat of the Government of the United States, and to exercise like Authority over all Places purchased by the Consent of the Legislature of the State in which the Same shall be, for the Erection of Forts, Magazines, Arsenals, dock-Yards, and other needful Buildings;—And

Congress established the District of Columbia as the national capital in 1791. Virginia and Maryland had granted land for the District, but Virginia's grant was returned because it was believed it would not be needed. Today, the District is 69 miles square.

To make all Laws which shall be necessary and proper for carrying into Execution the foregoing Powers, and all other Powers vested by this Constitution in the Government of the United States, or in any Department or Officer thereof.

This clause—the Necessary and Proper Clause, or the Elastic Clause—grants no specific power, and thus it can be stretched to fit different circumstances. It has allowed Congress to adapt the government to changing needs and times.

Section 9. The Migration or Importation of such Persons as any of the States now existing shall think proper to admit, shall not be prohibited by the Congress prior to the Year one thousand eight hundred and eight, but a Tax or duty may be imposed on such Importation, not exceeding ten dollars for each Person.

"Persons" referred to slaves. Congress outlawed the slave trade in 1808.

The privilege of the Writ of Habeas Corpus shall not be suspended, unless when in Cases of Rebellion or Invasion the public Safety may require it.

A writ of habeas corpus is a court order directing a sheriff or other public officer who is detaining another person to "produce the body" of the detainee so the court can assess the legality of the detention.

No Bill of Attainder or ex post facto Law shall be passed.

A bill of attainder is a law that inflicts punishment without a trial. An ex post facto law is a law that inflicts punishment for an act which was not illegal when it was committed.

[No Capitation, or other direct, Tax shall be laid, unless in Proportion to the Census or Enumeration herein before directed to be taken.][6]

A capitation is a tax on a person. A direct tax is a tax paid directly to the government, such as a property tax. This clause was intended to prevent Congress from levying a tax on slaves per person and thereby taxing slavery out of existence.

No Tax or Duty shall be laid on Articles exported from any State.

No Preference shall be given by any Regulation of Commerce or Revenue to the Ports of one State over those of another: nor shall Vessels bound to, or from, one State, be obliged to enter, clear, or pay Duties in another.

No Money shall be drawn from the Treasury, but in Consequence of Appropriations made by Law; and a regular Statement and Account of the Receipts and Expenditures of all public Money shall be published from time to time.

Federal funds can be spent only as Congress authorizes. This is a significant check on the President's power.

No Title of Nobility shall be granted by the United States: And no Person holding any Office of Profit or Trust under them, shall, without the Consent of the Congress, accept of any present, Emolument, Office, or Title, of any kind whatever, from any King, Prince, or foreign State.

Section 10. No State shall enter into any Treaty, Alliance, or Confederation; grant Letters of Marque and Reprisal; coin Money; emit Bills of Credit; make any Thing but gold and silver Coin a Tender in Payment of Debts; pass any Bill of Attainder, ex post facto Law, or Law impairing the Obligation of Contracts, or grant any Title of Nobility.

Prohibiting state laws "impairing the Obligation of Contracts" was intended to protect creditors. (Shays's Rebellion—an attempt to prevent courts from giving effect to creditors' legal actions against debtors—occurred only one year before the Constitution was written.)

No State shall, without the Consent of the Congress, lay any Imposts or Duties on Imports or Exports, except what may be absolutely necessary for executing its inspection Laws; and the net Produce of all Duties and Imposts, laid by any State on Imports or Exports, shall be for the Use of the Treasury of the

---

[6]Modified by the Sixteenth Amendment.

United States; and all such Laws shall be subject to the Revision and Controul of the Congress.

No State shall, without the Consent of Congress, lay any Duty of Tonnage, keep Troops, or Ships of War in time of Peace, enter into any Agreement or Compact with another State, or with a foreign Power or engage in War, unless actually invaded, or in such imminent Danger as will not admit of delay.

A duty of tonnage is a tax on ships according to their cargo capacity

ARTICLE II. (EXECUTIVE BRANCH)

Section 1. The executive Power shall be vested in a President of the United States of America. He shall hold his Office during the Term of four Years, and, together with the Vice President, chosen for the same Term, be elected, as follows.

Each State shall appoint, in such Manner as the Legislature thereof may direct, a Number of Electors, equal to the whole Number of Senators and Representatives to which the State may be entitled in the Congress; but no Senator or Representative, or Person holding an Office of Trust or Profit under the United States, shall be appointed an Elector.

The "Electors" are more commonly known as the "electoral college."

[The Electors shall meet in their respective States, and vote by Ballot for two Persons, of whom one at least shall not be an Inhabitant of the same State with themselves. And they shall make a List of all the Persons voted for, and of the Number of Votes for each; which List they shall sign and certify, and transmit sealed to the Seat of the Government of the United States, directed to the President of the Senate. The President of the Senate shall, in the Presence of the Senate and House of Representatives, open all the Certificates, and the Votes shall then be counted. The Person having the greatest Number of Votes shall be the President, if such Number be a Majority of the whole Number of Electors appointed; and if there be more than one who have such Majority, and have an equal Number of Votes, then the House of Representatives shall immediately chuse by Ballot one of them for President; and if no Person have a Majority, then from the five highest on the List the said House shall in like Manner chuse the President. But in chusing the President, the Votes shall be taken by States, the Representation from each State having one Vote; A quorum for this Purpose shall consist of a Member or Members from two thirds of the States, and a Majority of all the States shall be necessary to a Choice. In every Case, after the Choice of the President, the Person having the greater Number of Votes of the Electors shall be the Vice President. But if there should remain two or more who have equal Votes, the Senate shall chuse from them by Ballot the Vice President.][7]

The Congress may determine the Time of chusing the Electors, and the Day on which they shall give their Votes; which Day shall be the same throughout the United States.

Congress set the Tuesday after the first Monday in November every fourth year as the date for choosing electors. The electors cast their votes on the Monday after the second Wednesday in December of that year.

No person except a natural born Citizen, or a Citizen of the United States, at the time of the Adoption of this Constitution, shall be eligible to the Office of President; neither shall any Person be eligible to that Office who shall not have attained to the Age of thirty five Years, and been fourteen Years a Resident within the United States.

[In Case of the Removal of the President from Office, or of his Death, Resignation or Inability to discharge the Powers and Duties of the said Office, the same shall devolve on the Vice President, and the Congress may by Law provide for the Case of Removal, Death, Resignation or Inability, both of the President and Vice President, declaring what Officer shall then act as President, and such Officer shall act accordingly, until the Disability be removed, or a President shall be elected.][8]

The President shall, at stated Times, receive for his Services, a Compensation, which shall neither be encreased nor diminished during the Period for which he shall have been elected, and he shall not receive within that Period any other Emolument from the United States, or any of them.

Before he enter on the Execution of his Office, he shall take the following Oath or Affirmation: "I do solemnly swear (or affirm) that I will faithfully execute the Office of President of the United States, and will to the best of my Ability, preserve, protect and defend the Constitution of the United States."

Section 2. The President shall be Commander in Chief of the Army and Navy of the United States, and of the Militia of the several States, when called into the actual Service of the United States; he may require the Opinion, in writing, of the principal Officer in each of the executive Departments, upon any Subject relating to the Duties of their respective Offices, and he shall have Power to grant Reprieves and Pardons for Offences against the United States, except in Cases of Impeachment.

The President's clemency powers extend only to federal cases. In those cases, he or she may grant a full or conditional pardon, or reduce a prison term or fine.

He shall have Power, by and with the Advice and Consent of the Senate, to make Treaties, provided two thirds of the Senators present concur; and he shall nominate, and by and with the Advice and Consent of the Senate, shall appoint Ambassadors, other public Ministers and Consuls, Judges of the supreme Court, and all other Officers of the United States, whose Appointments are not herein otherwise provided for, and which shall be established by Law; but the Congress may by Law vest the Appoint-

[7]Changed by the Twelfth Amendment.
[8]Modified by the Twenty-Fifth Amendment.

ment of such inferior Officers, as they think proper, in the President alone, in the Courts of Law, or in the Heads of Departments.

The President shall have Power to fill up all Vacancies that may happen during the Recess of the Senate, by granting Commissions which shall expire at the end of their next Session.

Section 3. He shall from time to time give to the Congress Information of the State of the Union, and recommend to their Consideration such Measures as he shall judge necessary and expedient; he may, on extraordinary Occasions, convene both Houses, or either of them, and in Case of Disagreement between them, with Respect to the Time of Adjournment, he may adjourn them to such Time as he shall think proper; he shall receive Ambassadors and other public Ministers; he shall take Care that the Laws be faithfully executed, and shall Commission all the Officers of the United States.

Annually, the President reports on the State of the Union to Congress, recommending legislative measures, and proposes a federal budget.

Section 4. The President, Vice President and all civil Officers of the United States, shall be removed from Office on Impeachment for, and Conviction of, Treason, Bribery, or other high Crimes and Misdemeanors.

ARTICLE III. (JUDICIAL BRANCH)

Section 1. The judicial Power of the United States, shall be vested in one supreme Court, and in such inferior Courts as the Congress may from time to time ordain and establish. The Judges, both of the supreme and inferior Courts, shall hold their Offices during good Behaviour, and shall, at stated Times, receive for their Services a Compensation, which shall not be diminished during their Continuance in Office.

Section 2. The judicial Power shall extend to all Cases, in Law and Equity, arising under this Constitution, the Laws of the United States, and Treaties made, or which shall be made, under their Authority;—to all Cases affecting Ambassadors, other public Ministers and Consuls;—to all Cases of admiralty and maritime Jurisdiction;—to Controversies to which the United States shall be a Party;—to Controversies between two or more States; [—between a State and Citizens of another State;—][9] between Citizens of different States;—between Citizens of the same State claiming Lands under Grants of different States, [and between a State, or the Citizens thereof, and foreign States, Citizens or Subjects.][10]

In all Cases affecting Ambassadors, other public Ministers and Consuls, and those in which a State shall be a Party, the supreme Court shall have original Jurisdiction. In all the other Cases before mentioned, the supreme Court shall have appellate Jurisdiction, both as to Law and Fact, with such Exceptions, and under such Regulations as the Congress shall make.

The Trial of all Crimes, except in Cases of Impeachment,

shall be by Jury; and such Trial shall be held in the State where the said Crimes shall have been committed; but when not committed within any State, the Trial shall be at such Place or Places as the Congress may by Law have directed.

Section 3. Treason against the United States, shall consist only in levying War against them, or, in adhering to their Enemies, giving them Aid and Comfort. No Person shall be convicted of Treason unless on the Testimony of two Witnesses to the same overt Act, or on Confession in open Court.

The Congress shall have Power to declare the Punishment of Treason, but no Attainder of Treason shall work Corruption of Blood, or Forfeiture except during the Life of the Person attainted.

Congress has provided that the punishment for treason ranges from a minimum of five years in prison and/or a $10,000 fine to a maximum of death, but the U.S. has never executed a person for treason. No "Attainder of Treason shall work Corruption of Blood" prohibits punishment of the traitor's heirs.

ARTICLE IV. (RELATIONS AMONG THE STATES)

Section 1. Full Faith and Credit shall be given in each State to the public Acts, Records, and judicial Proceedings of every other State. And the Congress may by general Laws prescribe the Manner in which such Acts, Records and Proceedings shall be proved, and the Effect thereof.

Section 2. The Citizens of each State shall be entitled to all Privileges and Immunities of Citizens in the several States.

A citizen of a state has the same rights and privileges as the citizens of another state in which he or she happens to be.

A Person charged in any State with Treason, Felony, or other Crime, who shall flee from Justice, and be found in another State, shall on Demand of the executive Authority of the State from which he fled, be delivered up, to be removed to the State having Jurisdiction of the Crime.

[No Person held to Service or Labour in one State, under the Laws thereof, escaping into another, shall, in Consequence of any Law or Regulation therein, be discharged from such Service or Labour, but shall be delivered up on Claim of the Party to whom such Service or Labour may be due.][11]

Section 3. New States may be admitted by the Congress into this Union; but no new State shall be formed or erected within the Jurisdiction of any other State; nor any State be formed by the Junction of two or more States, or Parts of States, without the Consent of the Legislatures of the States concerned as well as of the Congress.

---

[9]Modified by the Eleventh Amendment.
[10]Modified by the Eleventh Amendment.
[11]Repealed by the Thirteenth Amendment.

The Congress shall have Power to dispose of and make all needful Rules and Regulations respecting the Territory or other Property belonging to the United States; and nothing in this Constitution shall be so construed as to Prejudice any Claims of the United States, or of any particular State.

Section 4.   The United States shall guarantee to every State in this Union a Republican Form of Government, and shall protect each of them against Invasion; and on Application of the Legislature, or of the Executive (when the Legislature cannot be convened) against domestic Violence.

ARTICLE V. (METHODS OF AMENDMENT)

The Congress, whenever two thirds of both Houses shall deem it necessary, shall propose Amendments to this Constitution, or on the Application of the Legislatures of two thirds of the several States, shall call a Convention for proposing Amendments, which, in either Case, shall be valid to all Intents and Purposes, as part of this Constitution, when ratified by the Legislatures of three fourths of the several States, or by Conventions in three fourths thereof, as the one or the other Mode of Ratification may be proposed by the Congress; Provided that no Amendment which may be made prior to the Year One thousand eight hundred and eight shall in any Manner affect the first and fourth Clauses in the Ninth Section of the first Article; and that no State, without its Consent, shall be deprived of its equal Suffrage in the Senate.

ARTICLE VI. (NATIONAL SUPREMACY)

All Debts contracted and Engagements entered into, before the Adoption of this Constitution shall be as valid against the United States under this Constitution, as under the Confederation.

During the Revolutionary War and the years of the Confederation, Congress borrowed large sums. This clause pledged that the new federal government would assume those financial obligations.

This Constitution, and the Laws of the United States which shall be made in Pursuance thereof; and all Treaties made, or which shall be made, under the Authority of the United States, shall be the supreme Law of the Land; and the Judges in every State shall be bound thereby, any Thing in the Constitution or Laws of any State to the Contrary notwithstanding.

The Senators and Representatives before mentioned, and the Members of the several State Legislatures, and all executive and judicial Officers, both of the United States and of the several States, shall be bound by Oath or Affirmation, to support this Constitution; but no religious Test shall ever be required as a Qualification to any Office or public Trust under the United States.

ARTICLE VII. (RATIFICATION)

The Ratification of the Conventions of nine States shall, be suf-ficient for the Establishment of this Constitution between the States so ratifying the Same.

Done in Convention by the Unanimous Consent of the States present the Seventeenth Day of September in the Year of our Lord one thousand seven hundred and Eighty seven and of the Independence of the United States of America the Twelfth. IN WITNESS whereof we have hereunto subscribed our Names,

Go. WASHINGTON
Presid't. and deputy from Virginia

Attest
WILLIAM JACKSON
Secretary

Thos. FitzSimons
Jared Ingersoll
James Wilson.
Gouv. Morris

DELAWARE
Geo. Read
Gunning Bedfordjun
John Dickinson
Richard Basset
Jaco. Broom

NEW HAMPSHIRE
John Langdon
Nicholas Gilman

MASSACHUSETTS
Nathaniel Gorham
Rufus King

MARYLAND
James McHenry
Dan of St. Thos. Jenifer
Danl. Carroll.

CONNECTICUT
Wm. Saml. Johnson
Roger Sherman

VIRGINIA
John Blair
James Madison Jr.

NEW YORK
Alexander Hamilton

NORTH CAROLINA
Wm. Blount
Richd. Dobbs Spaight.
Hu. Williamson

NEW JERSEY
Wh. Livingston
David Brearley.
Wm. Paterson.
Jona. Dayton

SOUTH CAROLINA
J. Rutledge
Charles Cotesworth
Pinckney
Charles Pinckney
Pierce Butler.

PENNSYLVANIA
B. Franklin
Thomas Mifflin
Robt. Morris
Geo. Clymer

GEORGIA
William Few
Abr. Baldwin

Articles in addition to, and amendment of the Constitution of the United States of America, proposed by Congress and ratified by the Legislatures of the several states, pursuant to the Fifth Article of the original Constitution.

Amendment I. [12]   Congress shall make no law respecting an establishment of religion, or prohibiting the free exercise thereof; or abridging the freedom of speech, or of the press; or the right of the people peaceably to assembly, and to petition the Government for a redress of grievances.

[12]The first ten amendments were passed by Congress on September 25, 1789, and were ratified on December 15, 1791.

These guarantees, like the others in the Bill of Rights (the first ten amendments), are not absolute—each may be exercised only with regard to the rights of other persons.

Amendment II.   A well regulated militia, being necessary to the security of a free State, the right of the people to keep and bear arms, shall not be infringed.

Amendment III.   No Soldier shall, in time of peace be quartered in any house, without the consent of the owner, nor in time of war, but in a manner to be prescribed by law.

Before the Revolutionary War, it had been common British practice to quarter soldiers in colonists' homes.

Amendment IV.   The right of the people to be secure in their persons, houses, papers, and effects, against unreasonable searches and seizures, shall not be violated, and no warrants shall issue, but upon probable cause, supported by oath or affirmation, and particularly describing the place to be searched, and the persons or things to be seized.

Amendment V.   No person shall be held to answer for a capital, or otherwise infamous crime, unless on a presentment or indictment of a Grand Jury, except in cases arising in the land or naval forces, or in the militia, when in actual service in time of war or public danger; nor shall any person be subject for the same offence to be twice put in jeopardy of life or limb; nor shall be compelled in any criminal case to be a witness against himself, nor be deprived of life, liberty, or property, without due process of law; nor shall private property be taken for public use, without just compensation.

There are two types of juries. A grand jury considers physical evidence and the testimony of witnesses, and decides whether there is sufficient reason to bring a case to trial. A petit jury hears the case at trial and decides it. "[F]or the same offence to be twice put in jeopardy of life or limb" means to be tried twice for the same crime.

Amendment VI.   In all criminal prosecutions, the accused shall enjoy the right to a speedy and public trial, by an impartial jury of the State and district wherein the crime shall have been committed, which district shall have been previously ascertained by law, and to be informed of the nature and cause of the accusation; to be confronted with the witnesses against him; to have compulsory process for obtaining witnesses in his favor, and to have the assistance of counsel for his defence.

Amendment VII.   In Suits at common law, where the value in controversy shall exceed twenty dollars, the right of trial by jury shall be preserved, and no fact tried by jury, shall be otherwise re-examined in any Court of the United States, than according to the rules of the common law.

Amendment VIII.   Excessive bail shall not be required,

nor excessive fines imposed, nor cruel and unusual punishments inflicted.

Amendment IX.   The enumeration in the Constitution, of certain rights, shall not be construed to deny or disparage others retained by the people.

Amendment X.   The powers not delegated to the United States by the Constitution, nor prohibited by it to the States, are reserved to the States respectively, or to the people.

Amendment XI—(Ratified on February 7, 1795).   The Judicial power of the United States shall not be construed to extend to any suit in law or equity, commenced or prosecuted against one of the United States by Citizens of another State, or by Citizens or Subjects of any Foreign State.

This amendment has been interpreted to mean that a state cannot be sued in federal court by one of its citizens, by a citizen of another state, or by a foreign country.

Amendment XII—(Ratified on June 15, 1804).   The Electors shall meet in their respective states, and vote by ballot for President and Vice-President, one of whom, at least, shall not be an inhabitant of the same State with themselves; they shall name in their ballots the person voted for as President, and in distinct ballots the person voted for as Vice-President, and they shall make distinct lists of all persons voted for as President, and of all persons voted for as Vice-President, and of the number of votes for each, which lists they shall sign and certify, and transmit sealed to the seat of the government of the United States, directed to the President of the Senate;—The President of the Senate shall, in the presence of the Senate and House of Representatives, open all the certificates and the votes shall then be counted;—The person having the greatest number of votes for President, shall be the President, if such number be a majority of the whole number of Electors appointed; and if no person have such majority, then from the persons having the highest numbers not exceeding three on the list of those voted for as President, the House of Representatives shall choose immediately, by ballot, the President. But in choosing the President, the votes shall be taken by States, the representation from each State having one vote; a quorum for this purpose shall consist of a member or members from two-thirds of the States, and a majority of all States shall be necessary to a choice. [And if the House of Representatives shall not choose a President whenever the right of choice shall devolve upon them, before the fourth day of March next following, then the Vice-President shall act as President, as in the case of the death or other constitutional disability of the President.][13]—The person having the greatest number of votes as Vice-President, shall be the Vice-President, if such number be a majority of the whole number of Electors appointed, and if no person have a majority, then from the two highest numbers on the list, the Senate shall choose the Vice-President;

[13]Changed by the Twentieth Amendment.

a quorum for the purpose shall consist of two-thirds of the whole number of Senators, and a majority of the whole number shall be necessary to a choice. But no person constitutionally ineligible to the office of President shall be eligible to that of Vice-President of the United States.

The original procedure set out for the election of President and Vice President in Article II, Section 1, resulted in a tie in 1800 between Thomas Jefferson and Aaron Burr. It was not until the next year that the House of Representatives chose Jefferson to be President. This amendment changed the procedure by providing for separate ballots for President and Vice President.

Amendment XIII—(Ratified on December 6, 1865).

Section 1. Neither slavery nor involuntary servitude, except as a punishment for crime whereof the party shall have been duly convicted, shall exist within the United States, or any place subject to their jurisdiction.

Some slaves had been freed during the Civil War. This amendment freed the others and abolished slavery.

Section 2. Congress shall have power to enforce this article by appropriate legislation.

Amendment XIV—(Ratified on July 9, 1868).

Section 1. All persons born or naturalized in the United States, and subject to the jurisdiction thereof, are citizens of the United States and of the State wherein they reside. No State shall make or enforce any law which shall abridge the privileges or immunities of citizens of the United States; nor shall any State deprive any person of life, liberty, or property, without due process of law; nor deny to any person within its jurisdiction the equal protection of the laws.

Under this provision, states cannot make or enforce laws that take away rights given to all citizens by the federal government. States cannot act unfairly or arbitrarily toward or discriminate against any person.

Section 2. Representatives shall be apportioned among the several States according to their respective numbers, counting the whole number of persons in each State, excluding Indians not taxed. But when the right to vote at any election for the choice of electors for President and Vice President of the United States, Representatives in Congress, the Executive and Judicial officers of a State, or the members of the Legislature thereof, is denied to any of the male inhabitants of such State, being [twenty-one][14] years of age, and citizens of the United States, or in any way abridged, except for participation in rebellion, or other crime, the basis of representation therein shall be reduced in the proportion which the number of such male citizens shall bear to the whole number of male citizens twenty-one years of age in such State.

Section 3. No person shall be a Senator or Representative in Congress, or elector of President and Vice President, or hold any office, civil or military, under the United States, or under any State, who having previously taken an oath, as a member of Congress, or as an officer of the United States, or as a member of any State legislature, or as an executive or judicial officer of any State, to support the Constitution of the United States, shall have engaged in insurrection or rebellion against the same, or given aid or comfort to the enemies thereof. But Congress may by a vote of two-thirds of each House, remove such disability.

This provision forbade former state or federal government officials who had acted in support of the Confederacy during the Civil War from holding office again. It limited the President's power to pardon those persons. Congress removed this "disability" in 1898.

Section 4. The validity of the public debt of the United States, authorized by law, including debts incurred for payment of pensions and bounties for services in suppressing insurrection or rebellion, shall not be questioned. But neither the United States nor any State shall assume or pay any debt or obligation incurred in aid of insurrection or rebellion against the United States, or any claim for the loss or emancipation of any slave, but all such debts, obligations and claims shall be held illegal and void.

Section 5. The Congress shall have power to enforce, by appropriate legislation, the provisions of this article.

Amendment XV—(Ratified on February 3, 1870).

Section 1. The right of citizens of the United States to vote shall not be denied or abridged by the United States or by any State on account of race, color, or previous condition of servitude.

Section 2. The Congress shall have power to enforce this article by appropriate legislation.

Amendment XVI—(Ratified on February 3, 1913).
The Congress shall have power to lay and collect taxes on incomes, from whatever source derived, without apportionment among the several States, and without regard to any census or enumeration.

Amendment XVII—(Ratified on April 8, 1913). The Senate of the United States shall be composed of two Senators from each State, elected by the people thereof, for six years; and each Senator shall have one vote. The electors in each State shall have the qualifications requisite for electors of the most numerous branch of the State legislatures.

When vacancies happen in the representation of any State in the Senate, the executive authority of such State shall issue writs of election to fill such vacancies: *Provided*, That the legislature of

[14]Changed by the Twenty-Sixth Amendment.

any State may empower the executive thereof to make temporary appointments until the people fill the vacancies by election as the legislature may direct.

This amendment shall not be so construed as to affect the election or term of any Senator chosen before it becomes valid as part of the Constitution.

Amendment XVIII—(Ratified on January 16, 1919).

Section 1. After one year from the ratification of this article the manufacture, sale, or transportation of intoxicating liquors within, the importation thereof into, or the exportation thereof from the United States and all territory subject to the jurisdiction thereof for beverage purposes is hereby prohibited.

Section 2. The Congress and the several States shall have concurrent power to enforce this article by appropriate legislation.

Section 3. This article shall be inoperative unless it shall have been ratified as an amendment to the Constitution by the legislatures of the several States, as provided in the Constitution, within seven years from the date of the submission hereof to the States by the Congress.[15]

Amendment XIX—(Ratified on August 18, 1920).

The right of citizens of the United States to vote shall not be denied or abridged by the United States or by any State on account of sex.

Congress shall have power to enforce this article by appropriate legislation.

Amendment XX—(Ratified on January 23, 1933).

Section 1. The terms of the President and Vice President shall end at noon on the 20th day of January, and the terms of Senators and Representatives at noon on the 3d day of January, of the years in which such terms would have ended if this article had not been ratified; and the terms of their successors shall then begin.

Section 2. The Congress shall assemble at least once in every year, and such meeting shall begin at noon on the 3d day of January, unless they shall by law appoint a different day.

Section 3. If, at the time fixed for the beginning of the term of the President, the President elect shall have died, the Vice President elect shall become President. If a President shall not have been chosen before the time fixed for the beginning of his term, or if the President elect shall have failed to qualify, then the Vice President elect shall act as President until a President shall have qualified; and the Congress may by law provide for the case wherein neither a President elect nor a Vice President elect shall have qualified, declaring who shall then act as President, or the manner in which one who is to act shall be selected, and such person shall act accordingly until a President or Vice President shall have qualified.

Section 4. The Congress may by law provide for the case of the death of any of the persons from whom the House of Representatives may choose a President whenever the rights of choice shall have devolved upon them, and for the case of the death of any of the persons from whom the Senate may choose a Vice President whenever the right of choice shall have devolved upon them.

Section 5. Sections 1 and 2 shall take effect on the 15th day of October following the ratification of this article.

Section 6. This article shall be inoperative unless it shall have been ratified as an amendment to the Constitution by the legislatures of three-fourths of the several States within seven years from the date of its submission.

Amendment XXI—(Ratified on December 5, 1933).

Section 1. The eighteenth article of amendment to the Constitution of the United States is hereby repealed.

Section 2. The transportation or importation into any State, Territory, or possession of the United States for delivery or use therein of intoxicating liquors, in violation of the laws thereof, is hereby prohibited.

Section 3. This article shall be inoperative unless it shall have been ratified as an amendment to the Constitution by conventions in the several States, as provided in the Constitution, within seven years from the date of the submission hereof to the States by the Congress.

Amendment XXII—(Ratified on February 27, 1951).

No person shall be elected to the office of the President more than twice, and no person who has held the office of President, or acted as President, for more than two years of a term to which some other person was elected President shall be elected to the office of President more than once. But this Article shall not apply to any person holding the office of President when this Article was proposed by the Congress, and shall not prevent any person who may be holding the office of President, or acting as President, during the term within which this Article becomes operative from holding the office of President or acting as President during the remainder of such term.

Amendment XXIII—(Ratified on March 29, 1961).

Section 1. The District constituting the seat of Government of the United States shall appoint in such manner as the Congress may direct:

A number of electors of President and Vice President equal to the whole number of Senators and Representatives in Congress to which the District would be entitled if it were a State, but in no event more than the least populous State; they shall

---

[15]The Eighteenth Amendment was repealed by the Twenty-First Amendment.

be in addition to those appointed by the States, but they shall be considered, for the purposes of the election of President and Vice President, to be electors appointed by a State; and they shall meet in the District and perform such duties as provided by the twelfth article of amendment.

Section 2.   The Congress shall have power to enforce this article by appropriate legislation.

Amendment XXIV—(Ratified on January 23, 1964).

Section 1.   The right of citizens of the United States to vote in any primary or other election for President or Vice President, for electors for President or Vice President, or for Senator or Representative in Congress, shall not be denied or abridged by the United States, or any State by reason of failure to pay any poll tax or other tax.

Section 2.   The Congress shall have power to enforce this article by appropriate legislation.

Amendment XXV—(Ratified on February 10, 1967).

Section 1.   In case of the removal of the President from office or of his death or resignation, the Vice President shall become President.

Section 2.   Whenever there is a vacancy in the office of the Vice President, the President shall nominate a Vice President who shall take office upon confirmation by a majority vote of both Houses of Congress.

Section 3.   Whenever the President transmits to the President pro tempore of the Senate and the Speaker of the House of Representatives his written declaration that he is unable to discharge the powers and duties of his office, and until he transmits to them a written declaration to the contrary, such powers and duties shall be discharged by the Vice President as Acting President.

Section 4.   Whenever the Vice President and a majority of either the principal officers of the executive departments or of such other body as Congress may by law provide, transmit to the President pro tempore of the Senate and the Speaker of the House of Representatives their written declaration that the President is unable to discharge the powers and duties of his office, the Vice President shall immediately assume the powers and duties of the office as Acting President.

Thereafter, when the President transmits to the President pro tempore of the Senate and the Speaker of the House of Representatives his written declaration that no inability exists, he shall resume the powers and duties of his office unless the Vice President and a majority of either the principal officers of the executive department or of such other body as Congress may by law provide, transmit within four days to the President pro tempore of the Senate and the Speaker of the House of Representatives their written declaration that the President is unable to discharge the powers and duties of his office. Thereupon Congress shall decide the issue, assembling within forty-eight hours for that purpose if not in session. If the Congress, within twenty-one days after receipt of the latter written declaration, or, if Congress is not in session, within twenty-one days after Congress is required to assemble, determines by two-thirds vote of both Houses that the President is unable to discharge the powers and duties of his office, the Vice President shall continue to discharge the same as Acting President; otherwise, the President shall resume the powers and duties of his office.

Amendment XXVI—[(Ratified on July 1, 1971)].

Section 1.   The right of citizens of the United States, who are eighteen years of age or older, to vote shall not be denied or abridged by the United States or by any State on account of age.

Section 2.   The Congress shall have power to enforce this article by appropriate legislation.

THE PRESIDENTS OF THE UNITED STATES

	Term of Service	Age at Inauguration	Political Party	College or University	Occupation or Profession
1. George Washington	1789–1797	57	None		Planter
2. John Adams	1797–1801	61	Federalist	Harvard	Lawyer
3. Thomas Jefferson	1801–1809	57	Democratic-Republican	William and Mary	Planter, Lawyer
4. James Madison	1809–1817	57	Democratic-Republican	Princeton	Lawyer
5. James Monroe	1817–1825	58	Democratic-Republican	William and Mary	Lawyer
6. John Quincy Adams	1825–1829	57	Democratic-Republican	Harvard	Lawyer
7. Andrew Jackson	1829–1837	61	Democrat		Lawyer
8. Martin Van Buren	1837–1841	54	Democrat		Lawyer
9. William H. Harrison	1841	68	Whig	Hampden-Sydney	Soldier
10. John Tyler	1841–1845	51	Whig	William and Mary	Lawyer
11. James K. Polk	1845–1849	49	Democrat	U. of N. Carolina	Lawyer
12. Zachary Taylor	1849–1850	64	Whig		Soldier
13. Millard Fillmore	1850–1853	50	Whig		Lawyer
14. Franklin Pierce	1853–1857	48	Democrat	Bowdoin	Lawyer
15. James Buchanan	1857–1861	65	Democrat	Dickinson	Lawyer
16. Abraham Lincoln	1861–1865	52	Republican		Lawyer
17. Andrew Johnson	1865–1869	56	Nat'l. Union[†]		Tailor
18. Ulysses S. Grant	1869–1877	46	Republican	U.S. Mil. Academy	Soldier
19. Rutherford B. Hayes	1877–1881	54	Republican	Kenyon	Lawyer
20. James A. Garfield	1881	49	Republican	Williams	Lawyer
21. Chester A. Arthur	1881–1885	51	Republican	Union	Lawyer
22. Grover Cleveland	1885–1889	47	Democrat		Lawyer
23. Benjamin Harrison	1889–1893	55	Republican	Miami	Lawyer
24. Grover Cleveland	1893–1897	55	Democrat		Lawyer
25. William McKinley	1897–1901	54	Republican	Allegheny College	Lawyer
26. Theodore Roosevelt	1901–1909	42	Republican	Harvard	Author
27. William H. Taft	1909–1913	51	Republican	Yale	Lawyer
28. Woodrow Wilson	1913–1921	56	Democrat	Princeton	Educator
29. Warren G. Harding	1921–1923	55	Republican		Editor
30. Calvin Coolidge	1923–1929	51	Republican	Amherst	Lawyer
31. Herbert C. Hoover	1929–1933	54	Republican	Stanford	Engineer
32. Franklin D. Roosevelt	1933–1945	51	Democrat	Harvard	Lawyer
33. Harry S Truman	1945–1953	60	Democrat		Businessman
34. Dwight D. Eisenhower	1953–1961	62	Republican	U.S. Mil. Academy	Soldier
35. John F. Kennedy	1961–1963	43	Democrat	Harvard	Author
36. Lyndon B. Johnson	1963–1969	55	Democrat	Southwest Texas State	Teacher
37. Richard M. Nixon	1969–1974	56	Republican	Whittier	Lawyer
38. Gerald R. Ford‡	1974–1977	61	Republican	Michigan	Lawyer
39. James E. Carter, Jr.	1977–1981	52	Democrat	U.S. Naval Academy	Businessman
40. Ronald W. Reagan	1981–1989	69	Republican	Eureka College	Actor
41. George H. W. Bush	1989–	64	Republican	Yale	Businessman

*Church preference; never joined any church.

†The National Union Party consisted of Republicans and War Democrats. Johnson was a Democrat.

**Inaugurated Dec. 6, 1973, to replace Agnew, who resigned Oct. 10, 1973.

‡Inaugurated Aug. 9, 1974, to replace Nixon, who resigned that same day.

§Inaugurated Dec. 19, 1974, to replace Ford, who became President Aug. 9, 1974.

	Religion	Born	Died	Age at Death	Vice President	
1.	Episcopalian	Feb. 22, 1732	Dec. 14, 1799	67	John Adams	(1789–1797)
2.	Unitarian	Oct. 30, 1735	July 4, 1826	90	Thomas Jefferson	(1797–1801)
3.	Unitarian*	Apr. 13, 1743	July 4, 1826	83	Aaron Burr	(1801–1805)
					George Clinton	(1805–1809)
4.	Episcopalian	Mar. 16, 1751	June 28, 1836	85	George Clinton	(1809–1812)
					Elbridge Gerry	(1813–1814)
5.	Episcopalian	Apr. 28, 1758	July 4, 1831	73	Daniel D. Tompkins	(1817–1825)
6.	Unitarian	July 11, 1767	Feb. 23, 1848	80	John C. Calhoun	(1825–1829)
7.	Presbyterian	Mar. 15, 1767	June 8, 1845	78	John C. Calhoun	(1829–1832)
					Martin Van Buren	(1833–1837)
8.	Dutch Reformed	Dec. 5, 1782	July 24, 1862	79	Richard M. Johnson	(1837–1841)
9.	Episcopalian	Feb. 9, 1773	Apr. 4, 1841	68	John Tyler	(1841)
10.	Episcopalian	Mar. 29, 1790	Jan. 18, 1862	71		
11.	Methodist	Nov. 2, 1795	June 15, 1849	53	George M. Dallas	(1845–1849)
12.	Episcopalian	Nov. 24, 1784	July 9, 1850	65	Millard Fillmore	(1849–1850)
13.	Unitarian	Jan. 7, 1800	Mar. 8, 1874	74		
14.	Episcopalian	Nov. 23, 1804	Oct. 8, 1869	64	William R. King	(1853)
15.	Presbyterian	Apr. 23, 1791	June 1, 1868	77	John C. Breckinridge	(1857–1861)
16.	Presbyterian*	Feb. 12, 1809	Apr. 15, 1865	56	Hannibal Hamlin	(1861–1865)
					Andrew Johnson	(1865)
17.	Methodist*	Dec. 29, 1808	July 31, 1875	66		
18.	Methodist	Apr. 27, 1822	July 23, 1885	63	Schuyler Colfax	(1869–1873)
					Henry Wilson	(1873–1875)
19.	Methodist*	Oct. 4, 1822	Jan. 17, 1893	70	William A. Wheeler	(1877–1881)
20.	Disciples of Christ	Nov. 19, 1831	Sept. 19, 1881	49	Chester A. Arthur	(1881)
21.	Episcopalian	Oct. 5, 1829	Nov. 18, 1886	57		
22.	Presbyterian	Mar. 18, 1837	June 24, 1908	71	Thomas A. Hendricks	(1885)
23.	Presbyterian	Aug. 20, 1833	Mar. 13, 1901	67	Levi P. Morton	(1889–1893)
24.	Presbyterian	Mar. 18, 1837	June 24, 1908	71	Adlai E. Stevenson	(1893–1897)
25.	Methodist	Jan. 29, 1843	Sept. 14, 1901	58	Garret A. Hobart	(1897–1899)
					Theodore Roosevelt	(1901)
26.	Dutch Reformed	Oct. 27, 1858	Jan. 6, 1919	60	Charles W. Fairbanks	(1905–1909)
27.	Unitarian	Sept. 15, 1857	Mar. 8, 1930	72	James S. Sherman	(1909–1912)
28.	Presbyterian	Dec. 29, 1856	Feb. 3, 1924	67	Thomas R. Marshall	(1913–1921)
29.	Baptist	Nov. 2, 1865	Aug. 2, 1923	57	Calvin Coolidge	(1921–1923)
30.	Congregationalist	July 4, 1872	Jan. 5, 1933	60	Charles G. Dawes	(1925–1929)
31.	Friend (Quaker)	Aug. 10, 1874	Oct. 20, 1964	90	Charles Curtis	(1929–1933)
32.	Episcopalian	Jan. 30, 1882	Apr. 12, 1945	63	John N. Garner	(1933–1941)
					Henry A. Wallace	(1941–1945)
					Harry S Truman	(1945)
33.	Baptist	May 8, 1884	Dec. 26, 1972	88	Alben W. Barkley	(1949–1953)
34.	Presbyterian	Oct. 14, 1890	Mar. 28, 1969	78	Richard M. Nixon	(1953–1961)
35.	Roman Catholic	May 29, 1917	Nov. 22, 1963	46	Lyndon B. Johnson	(1961–1963)
36.	Disciples of Christ	Aug. 27, 1908	Jan. 22, 1973	64	Hubert H. Humphrey	(1965–1969)
37.	Friend (Quaker)	Jan. 9, 1913			Spiro T. Agnew	(1969–1973)
					Gerald R. Ford**	(1973–1974)
38.	Episcopalian	July 14, 1913			Nelson A. Rockefeller§	(1974–1977)
39.	Baptist	Oct. 1, 1924			Walter F. Mondale	(1977–1981)
40.	Disciples of Christ	Feb. 6, 1911			George H. W. Bush	(1981–1989)
41.	Episcopalian	June 12, 1924			J. Danforth Quayle	(1989–)

FEDERALIST PAPERS #10 AND #51

#10

Among the numerous advantages promised by a well-constructed Union, none deserves to be more accurately developed than its tendency to break and control the violence of faction. The friend of popular governments never finds himself so much alarmed for their character and fate as when he contemplates their propensity to this dangerous vice. He will not fail, therefore, to set a due value on any plan which, without violating the principles to which he is attached, provides a proper cure for it. The instability, injustice, and confusion introduced into the public councils have, in truth, been the mortal diseases under which popular governments have everywhere perished, as they continue to be the favorite and fruitful topics from which the adversaries to liberty derive their most specious declamations. The valuable improvements made by the American constitutions on the popular models, both ancient and modern, cannot certainly be too much admired; but it would be an unwarrantable partiality to contend that they have as effectually obviated the danger on this side, as was wished and expected. Complaints are everywhere heard from our most considerate and virtuous citizens, equally the friends of public and private faith and of public and personal liberty, that our governments are too unstable, that the public good is disregarded in the conflicts of rival parties, and that measures are too often decided, not according to the rules of justice and the rights of the minor party, but by the superior force of an interested and overbearing majority. However anxiously we may wish that these complaints had no foundation, the evidence of known facts will not permit us to deny that they are in some degree true. It will be found, indeed, on a candid review of our situation, that some of the distresses under which we labor have been erroneously charged on the operation of our governments; but it will be found, at the same time, that other causes will not alone account for many of our heaviest misfortunes; and, particularly, for that prevailing and increasing distrust of public engagements and alarm for private rights which are echoed from one end of the continent to the other. These must be chiefly, if not wholly, effects of the unsteadiness and injustice with which a factious spirit has tainted our public administration.

By a faction I understand a number of citizens, whether amounting to a majority or minority of the whole, who are united and actuated by some common impulse of passion, or of interest, adverse to the rights of other citizens, or the permanent and aggregate interests of the community.

There are two methods of curing the mischiefs of faction: the one, by removing its causes; the other, by controlling its effects.

There are again two methods of removing the causes of faction: the one, by destroying the liberty which is essential to its existence; the other, by giving to every citizen the same opinions, the same passions, and the same interests.

It could never be more truly said than of the first remedy that it was worse than the disease. Liberty is to faction what air is to fire, an aliment without which it instantly expires. But it could not be a less folly to abolish liberty, which is essential to political life, because it nourishes faction than it would be to wish the annihilation of air, which is essential to animal life, because it imparts to fire its destructive agency.

The second expedient is as impracticable as the first would be unwise. As long as the reason of man continues fallible, and his is at liberty to exercise it, different opinions will be formed. As long as the connection subsists between his reason and his self-love, his opinions and his passions will have a reciprocal influence on each other; and the former will be objects to which the latter will attach themselves. The diversity in the faculties of men, from which the rights of property originate, is not less an insuperable obstacle to a uniformity of interests. The protection of these faculties is the first object of government. From the protection of different and unequal faculties of acquiring property, the possession of different degrees and kinds of property immediately results; and from the influence of these on the sentiments and views of the respective proprietors ensues a division of the society into different interests and parties.

The latent causes of faction are thus sown in the nature of man; and we see them everywhere brought into different degrees of activity, according to the different circumstances of civil society. A zeal for different opinions concerning religion, concerning government, and many other points, as well of speculation as of practice; an attachment to different leaders ambitiously contending for pre-eminence and power; or to persons of other descriptions whose fortunes have been interesting to the human passions, have, in turn, divided mankind into parties, inflamed them with mutual animosity, and rendered them much more disposed to vex and oppress each other than to co-operate for their common good. So strong is this propensity of mankind to fall into mutual animosities that where no substantial occasion presents itself the most frivolous and fanciful distinctions have been sufficient to kindle their unfriendly passions and excite their most violent conflicts. But the most common and durable source of factions has been the various and unequal distribution of property. Those who hold and those who are without property have ever formed distinct interests in society. Those who are creditors, and those who are debtors, fall under a like discrimination. A landed interest, a manufacturing interest, a mercantile interest, a moneyed interest, with many lesser interests, grow up of necessity in civilized nations, and divide them into different classes, actuated by different sentiments and views. The regulation of these various and interfering interests forms the principal task of modern legislation and involves the spirit of party and faction in the necessary and ordinary operations of government.

No man is allowed to be a judge in his own cause, because his interest would certainly bias his judgment, and, not improbably, corrupt his integrity. With equal, nay with greater reason, a body of men are unfit to be both judges and parties at the same time; yet what are many of the most important acts of legislation but so many judicial determinations, not indeed concerning the rights of single persons, but concerning the rights of large bodies of citizens? And what are the different classes of legislators but advocates and parties to the causes which they determine? Is a law proposed concerning private debts? It is a question to which the creditors are parties on one side and the debtors on the other. Justice ought to hold the balance between them. Yet the parties are, and must be, themselves the judges; and the most numerous party, or in other words, the most powerful faction must be expected to prevail. Shall domestic manufacturers be encouraged, and in what degree, by restrictions on foreign manufacturers? are questions which would be differently decided by the landed and the manufacturing classes, and probably by neither with a sole regard to justice and the public good. The apportionment of taxes on the various descriptions of property is an act which seems to require the most exact impartiality; yet there is, perhaps, no legislative act in which greater opportunity and temptation are given to a predominant party to trample on the rules of justice. Every shilling with which they overburden the inferior number is a shilling saved to their own pockets.

It is in vain to say that enlightened statesmen will be able to adjust these clashing interests and render them all subservient to the public good. Enlightened statesmen will not always be at the helm. Nor, in many cases, can such an adjustment be made at all without taking into view indirect and remote considerations, which will rarely prevail over the immediate interest which one party may find in disregarding the rights of another or the good of the whole.

The inference to which we are brought is that the *causes* of faction cannot be removed and that relief is only to be sought in the means of controlling its *effects*.

If a faction consists of less than a majority, relief is supplied by the republican principle, which enables the majority to defeat its sinister views by regular vote. It may clog the administration, it may convulse the society; but it will be unable to execute and mask its violence under the forms of the Constitution. When a majority is included in a faction, the form of popular government, on the other hand, enables it to sacrifice to its ruling passion or interest both the public good and the rights of other citizens. To secure the public good and private rights against the danger of such a faction, and at the same time to preserve the spirit and the form of popular government, is then the great object to which our inquiries are directed. Let me add that it is the great desideratum by which alone this form of government can be rescued from the opprobrium under which it has so long labored and be recommended to the esteem and adoption of mankind.

By what means is this object attainable? Evidently by one of two only. Either the existence of the same passion or interest in a majority at the same time must be prevented, or the majority, having such coexistent passion or interest, must be rendered, by their number and local situation, unable to concert and carry into effect schemes of oppression. If the impulse and the opportunity be suffered to coincide, we well know that neither moral nor religious motives can be relied on as an adequate control. They are not found to be such on the injustice and violence of individuals, and lose their efficacy in proportion to the number combined together, that is, in proportion as their efficacy becomes needful.

From this view of the subject it may be concluded that a pure democracy, by which I mean a society consisting of a small number of citizens, who assemble and administer the government in person, can admit of no cure for the mischiefs of faction. A common passion or interest will, in almost every case, be felt by a majority of the whole; a communication and concert results from the form of government itself; and there is nothing to check the inducements to sacrifice the weaker party or an obnoxious individual. Hence it is that such democracies have ever been spectacles of turbulence and contention; have ever been found incompatible with personal security or the rights of property; and have in general been as short in their lives as they have been violent in their deaths. Theoretic politicians, who have patronized this species of government, have erroneously supposed that by reducing mankind to a perfect equality in their political rights, they would at the same time be perfectly equalized and assimilated in their possessions, their opinions, and their passions.

A republic, by which I mean a government in which the scheme of representation takes place, opens a different prospect and promises the cure for which we are seeking. Let us examine the points in which it varies from pure democracy, and we shall comprehend both the nature of the cure and the efficacy which it must derive from the Union.

The two great points of difference between a democracy and a republic are: first, the delegation of the government, in the latter, to a small number of citizens elected by the rest; secondly, the greater number of citizens and greater sphere of country over which the latter may be extended.

The effect of the first difference is, on the one hand, to refine and enlarge the public views by passing them through the medium of a chosen body of citizens, whose wisdom may best discern the true interest of their country and whose patriotism and love of justice will be least likely to sacrifice it to temporary or partial considerations. Under such a regulation it may well happen that the public voice, pronounced by the representatives of the people, will be more consonant to the public good than if pronounced by the people themselves, convened for the purpose. On the other hand, the effect may be inverted. Men of factious tempers, of local prejudices, or of sinister designs, may, by intrigue, by corruption, or by other means, first obtain the suffrages, and then betray the interests of the people. The question resulting is, whether small or extensive republics are most favorable to the election of proper guardians of the public weal; and it is clearly decided in favor of the latter by two obvious considerations.

In the first place it is to be remarked that however small the republic may be the representatives must be raised to a certain number in order to guard against the cabals of a few; and that however large it may be they must be limited to a certain number in order to guard against the confusion of a multitude. Hence, the number of representatives in the two cases not being in proportion to that of the constituents, and being proportionally greatest in the small republic, it follows that if the proportion of fit characters be not less in the large than in the small republic, the former will present a greater option, and consequently a greater probability of a fit choice.

In the next place, as each representative will be chosen by a greater number of citizens in the large than in the small republic, it will be more difficult for unworthy candidates to practise with success the vicious arts by which elections are too often carried; and the suffrages of the people being more free, will be more likely to center on men who possess the most attractive merit and the most diffusive and established characters.

It must be confessed that in this, as in most other cases, there is a mean, on both sides of which inconveniencies will be found to lie. By enlarging too much the number of electors, you render the representative too little acquainted with all their local circumstances and lesser interests; as by reducing it too much, you render him unduly attached to these, and too little fit to comprehend and pursue great and national objects. The federal Constitution forms a happy combination in this respect; the great and aggregate interests being referred to the national, the local and particular to the State legislatures.

The other point of difference is the greater number of citizens and extent of territory which may be brought within the compass of republican than of democratic government; and it is this circumstance principally which renders factious combinations less to be dreaded in the former than in the latter. The smaller the society, the fewer probably will be the distinct parties and interests composing it; the fewer the distinct parties and interests, the more frequently will a majority be found of the same party;

and the smaller the number of individuals composing a majority, and the smaller the compass within which they are placed, the more easily will they concert and execute their plans of oppression. Extend the sphere and you take in a greater variety of parties and interests; you make it less probable that a majority of the whole will have a common motive to invade the rights of other citizens; or if such a common motive exists, it will be more difficult for all who feel it to discover their own strength and to act in unison with each other. Besides other impediments, it may be remarked that, where there is a consciousness of unjust or dishonorable purposes, communication is always checked by distrust in proportion to the number whose concurrence is necessary.

Hence, it clearly appears that the same advantage which a republic has over a democracy in controlling the effects of faction is enjoyed by a large over a small republic—is enjoyed by the Union over the States composing it. Does this advantage consist in the substitution of representatives whose enlightened views and virtuous sentiments render them superior to local prejudices and to schemes of injustice? It will not be denied that the representation of the Union will be most likely to possess these requisite endowments. Does it consist in the greater security afforded by a greater variety of parties, against the event of any one party being able to outnumber and oppress the rest? In an equal degree does the increased variety of parties comprised within the Union increase this security. Does it, in fine, consist in the greater obstacles opposed to the concert and accomplishment of the secret wishes of an unjust and interested majority? Here again the extent of the Union gives it the most palpable advantage.

The influence of factious leaders may kindle a flame within their particular States but will be unable to spread a general conflagration through the other States. A religious sect may degenerate into a political faction in a part of the Confederacy; but the variety of sects dispersed over the entire face of it must secure the national councils against any danger from that source. A rage for paper money, for an abolition of debts, for an equal division of property, or for any other improper or wicked project, will be less apt to pervade the whole body of the Union than a particular member of it, in the same proportion as such a malady is more likely to taint a particular county or district than an entire State.

In the extent and proper structure of the Union, therefore, we behold a republican remedy for the diseases most incident to republican government. And according to the degree of pleasure and pride we feel in being republicans ought to be our zeal in cherishing the spirit and supporting the character of federalists.

#51

To what expedient, then, shall we finally resort, for maintaining in practice the necessary partition of power among the several departments as laid down in the Constitution? The only answer that can be given is that as all these exterior provisions are found to be inadequate the defect must be supplied, by so contriving the interior structure of the government as that its several constituent parts may, by their mutual relations, be the means of keeping each other in their proper places. Without presuming to undertake a full development of this important idea I will hazard a few general observations which may perhaps place it in a clearer light, and enable us to form a more correct judgment of the principles and structure of the government planned by the convention.

In order to lay a due foundation for that separate and distinct exercise of the different powers of government, which to a certain extent is admitted on all hands to be essential to the preservation of liberty, it is evident that each department should have a will of its own; and consequently should be so constituted that the members of each should have as little agency as possible in the appointment of the members of the others. Were this principle rigorously adhered to, it would require that all the appointments for the supreme executive, legislative, and judiciary magistracies should be drawn from the same fountain of authority, the people, through channels having no communication whatever with one another. Perhaps such a plan of constructing the several departments would be less difficult in practice than it may in contemplation appear. Some difficulties, however, and some additional expense would attend the execution of it. Some deviations, therefore, from the principle must be admitted. In the constitution of the judiciary department in particular, it might be inexpedient to insist rigorously on the principle: first, because peculiar qualifications being essential in the members, the primary consideration ought to be to select that mode of choice which best secures these qualifications; second, because the permanent tenure by which the appointments are held in that department must soon destroy all sense of dependence on the authority conferring them.

It is equally evident that the members of each department should be as little dependent as possible on those of the others for the emoluments annexed to their offices. Were the executive magistrate, or the judges, not independent of the legislature in this particular, their independence in every other would be merely nominal.

But the great security against a gradual concentration of the several powers in the same department consists in giving to those who administer each department the necessary constitutional means and personal motives to resist encroachments of the others. The provision for defense must in this, as in all other cases, be made commensurate to the danger of attack. Ambition must be made to counteract ambition. The interest of the man must be connected with the constitutional rights of the place. It may be a reflection on human nature that such devices should be necessary to control the abuses of government. But what is government itself but the greatest of all reflections on human nature? If men were angels, no government would be necessary. If angels were to govern men, neither external nor internal controls on government would be necessary. In framing a government which is to be administered by men over men, the great difficulty lies in this: you must first enable the government to control the governed; and in the next place oblige it to control itself. A dependence on the people is, no doubt, the primary control on the government; but experience has taught mankind the necessity of auxiliary precautions.

This policy of supplying, by opposite and rival interests, the defect of better motives, might be traced through the whole system of human affairs, private as well as public. We see it particularly displayed in all the subordinate distributions of power, where the constant aim is to divide and arrange the several offices in such a manner as that each may be a check on the other—that the private interest of every individual may be a sentinel over the public rights. These inventions of prudence cannot be less requisite in the distribution of the supreme powers of the State.

But it is not possible to give to each department an equ power of self-defense. In republican government, the legislative authority necessarily predominates. The remedy for this inconveniency is to divide the legislature into different branches; and to render them, by different modes of election and different principles of action, as little connected with each other as the nature of their common functions and their common dependence on the society will admit. It may even be necessary to guard against dangerous encroachments by still further precautions. As the weight of the legislative authority requires that it should be thus divided, the weakness of the executive may require, on the other hand, that it should be fortified. An absolute negative on the legislature appears, at first view, to be the natural defense with which the executive magistrate should be armed. But perhaps it would be neither altogether safe nor alone sufficient. On ordinary occasions it might not be exerted with the requisite firmness, and on extraordinary occasions it might be perfidiously abused. May not this defect of an absolute negative be supplied by some qualified connection between this weaker department and the weaker branch of the stronger department, by which the latter may be led to support the constitutional rights of the former, without being too much detached from the rights of its own department?

If the principles on which these observations are founded be just, as I persuade myself they are, and they be applied as a criterion to the several State constitutions, and to the federal Constitution, it will be found that if the latter does not perfectly correspond with them, the former are infinitely less able to bear such a test.

There are, moreover, two considerations particularly applicable to the federal system of America, which place that system in a very interesting point of view.

First. In a single republic, all the power surrendered by the people is submitted to the administration of a single government; and the usurpations are guarded against by a division of the government into distinct and separate departments. In the compound republic of America, the power surrendered by the people is first divided between two distinct governments, and then the portion allotted to each subdivided among distinct and separate departments. Hence a double security arises to the rights of the people. The different governments will control each other, at the same time that each will be controlled by itself.

Second. It is of great importance in a republic not only to guard the society against the oppression of its rulers, but to guard one part of the society against the injustice of the other part. Different interests necessarily exist in different classes of citizens. If a majority be united by a common interest, the rights of the minority will be insecure. There are but two methods of providing against this evil: the one by creating a will in the community independent of the majority—that is, of the society itself; the other, by comprehending in the society so many separate descriptions of citizens as will render an unjust combination of a majority of the whole very improbable, if not impracticable. The first method prevails in all governments possessing an hereditary or self-appointed authority. This, at best, is but a precarious security; because a power independent of the society may as well espouse the unjust views of the major as the rightful interests of the minor party, and may possibly be turned against both parties. The second method will be exemplified in the federal republic of the United States. Whilst all authority in it will be derived from and dependent on the society, the society itself will be broken into so many parts, interests and classes of citizens, that the rights of individuals, or of the minority, will be in little danger from interested combinations of the majority. In a free government the security for civil rights must be the same as that for religious rights. It consists in the one case in the multiplicity of interests, and in the other in the multiplicity of sects. The degree of security in both cases will depend on the number of interests and sects; and this may be presumed to depend on the extent of country and number of people comprehended under the same government. This view of the subject must particularly recommend a proper federal system to all the sincere and considerate friends of republican government, since it shows that in exact proportion as the territory of the Union may be formed into more circumscribed Confederacies, or States, oppressive combinations of a majority will be facilitated; the best security, under the republican forms, for the rights of every class of citizen, will be diminished; and consequently the stability and independence of some member of the government, the only other security, must be proportionally increased. Justice is the end of government. It is the end of civil society. It ever has been and ever will be pursued until it be obtained, or until liberty be lost in the pursuit. In a society

under the forms of which the stronger faction can readily unite and oppress the weaker, anarchy may as truly be said to reign as in a state of nature, where the weaker individual is not secured against the violence of the stronger; and as, in the latter state, even the stronger individuals are prompted, by the uncertainty of their condition, to submit to a government which may protect the weak as well as themselves; so, in the former state, will the more powerful factions or parties be gradually induced, by a like motive, to wish for a government which will protect all parties, the weaker as well as the more powerful. It can be little doubted that if the State of Rhode Island was separated from the Confederacy and left to itself, the insecurity of rights under the popular form of government within such narrow limits would be displayed by such reiterated oppressions of factious majorities that some power altogether independent of the people would soon be called for by the voice of the very factions whose misrule had proved the necessity of it. In the extended republic of the United States, and among the great variety of interests, parties, and sects which it embraces, a coalition of a majority of the whole society could seldom take place on any other principles than those of justice and the general good; whilst there being thus less danger to a minor from the will of a major party, there must be less pretext, also, to provide for the security of the former, by introducing into the government a will not dependent on the latter, or, in other words, a will independent of the society itself. It is no less certain than it is important, notwithstanding the contrary opinions which have been entertained, that the larger the society, provided it lie within a practicable sphere, the more duly capable it will be of self-government. And happily for the *republican cause*, the practicable sphere may be carried to a very great extent by a judicious modification and mixture of the *federal principle*.

Publius
(James Madison)

HOW TO DO RESEARCH IN POLITICAL SCIENCE

You are expected to complete a political science research project for your class and present the results in a paper. Research, you have learned, is a tool of science. At first you may ask, what is there about politics that is "scientific"? You can't study people the way you do rats in a maze, nor can you conduct experiments in the same manner as in the biology lab. Yet much of what we know today about how political processes work, and especially about how people act in political situations, is the result of scientific research. For the modern political scientist, the acts of voters, the decisions of presidents and Supreme Court justices, and the policy decisions of state and municipal governments are data to be analyzed according to the methods of science.

I. The Scientific Approach to Politics

When you conduct a research project, it is essential to adhere to certain rules of *epistemology*. Epistemology has to do with *how* we know what we think is true, and the answer to this question lies in whether our work is valid and reliable. A research result is *valid* if it tells you something that actually is true, and it is *reliable* if your or other researchers could reproduce the same results (or at least get approximately the same findings). Validity and reliability are the two hallmarks of the scientific method, which is applied to political science research as much as it is to other scientific research.

How do you know when your results are valid and reliable? The validity of your findings is difficult to establish, buy your results are more likely to be valid if you follow these steps in the research process:

1. Formulate a fairly narrow problem to research in such a way that you can make a conclusion based on empirical evidence, that is, evidence based on observation or experience.
2. Set up one or more concrete research hypotheses, which are statements about what you expect to find from your observations.
3. Put together a research design, or a strategy for getting your observations (which might involve doing a sample survey, ob- serving a city council meeting, or gathering information from an almanac or a computer file.
4. Find an appropriate way to measure the key pieces of infor- mation, or data, that you need in order to determine whether your research hypotheses are supported by the factual evidence of your observations.
5. Go out and collect the data.
6. Conduct a careful analysis of the data that you have gathered (usually with appropriate statistical procedures).
7. Make some general conclusions about whether the data tend to support your research hypotheses.

This list of procedures makes empirical research in political science look very mechanical. In part, it is. However it takes intuition and clear thinking to decide how to study political phenomena. There are certain pitfalls to be avoided in analyzing data.

Pitfalls to Avoid. For one thing, you must show that there is some meaningful relationship, or covariation, between or among the variables on which you have collected information. For ex- ample, before you claim that Republicans tend to be in higher- income brackets, you must be able to show that the percentage of people who are Republicans is greater among those who have incomes over, say, $50,000 a year than the percentage of Re- publicans you find among those with incomes under $50,000 a year. The simple fact that you find this pattern of covariation, by itself, though, doesn't necessarily mean that income is what really causes people to choose political sides. It turns out that people's income level is closely related to how much education they have, what kind of job they hold (medical doctors make more money than secretaries), and even how old they are and whether they are married. In other words, you must attempt to eliminate possibly spurious relationships, that is, explanations that don't take into account the complex relationships among variables.

Sometimes empirical covariation can be completely misleading. You probably remember the old story about how storks bring babies. Well, it really is true that birthrates in Europe are higher when storks are busy with their own nesting activities. This empirical fact, however, doesn't mean that the storks bring human babies with them; it just means that there is a similar pattern of human and stork behavior. As another example, you can easily find that the more fire trucks that go to fight a fire, the greater is the amount of damage from the fire. Does sending more fire trucks actually cause the fire to be worse? Of course not. Rather, the correct conclusion would be that a bigger fire requires that more trucks be called in to help fight it, and the bigger fire also produces more property damage. The covariation between the number of fire trucks and the amount of damage is spurious, because both of those variables are affected by the severity of the fire.

The fire truck example also brings us to another point of caution—deciding what "causes" what. You might be led astray in your conclusions if you aren't careful about the order of causal patterns. The fact that you took an examination in your American government course before you went to the polls and voted a straight Democratic ticket doesn't mean that your course (or the exam) caused you to vote that way. Such an incorrect conclusion would be an example of the *post hoc ergo propter hoc* (after, and therefore because of) fallacy. As another example, consider the relationship between your decision to protest ROTC on your campus and your parent's views on whether it is legitimate for people to engage in protest behavior. What "causes" what here? Assume your parents in general support public protests. Does your parents general approval of protesting tend to determine whether your participate in the protest, or does your protesting gradually intensify your parents view. Or could your behavior and their attitudes be mutually "casual"? Probably, the fact that you grew up under your parents' influence (not that you listened to or did everything they said) meant that you absorbed their tolerance for protest behavior. They had a much better chance to influence your behavior than you had a chance to influence their attitudes. In other words, it is important to take into consideration the *time ordering* of the variables that you might measure. In general, a later event logically is not able to "cause" an earlier event. Still, there likely is some tendency for parents to modify their previous views if they can be persuaded that your way of doing things politically is legitimate.

How to Increase Reliability   For your results to be valid, they must first be reliable. Whether your conclusions are reliable depends on how carefully you designed the study to take into account random variation from what otherwise might be observed. There are four different ways to test for reliability in your work.

1. Measure everything a second time. This is called the **test–retest method.**
2. Measure the same phenomenon in more than one way. This is the **parallel forms method** for assessing reliability.
3. Split your sample of observations into two groups and see if the results correspond closely. This is the **split-half method.**

4. Conduct an **item analysis,** which entails looking at the degree to which any one item that you have measured relates to the entire set of results. Any variable that doesn't fit closely with the overall pattern may need to be thrown out, or at least be re-measured. (Incidentially, this is precisely what many university instructors do when they prepare computer analyses for the results of a multiple-answer examination).

II. CHOOSING A TOPIC

Choosing a topic is the most important decision you'll make. Avoid being too broad ("Civil Rights in the U.S."). Avoid being too current (you will find almost nothing published and little analysis on the subject). Your freedom to choose will depend on the instructions you have received. In any case, make sure the topic fits the course. Be specific and focused. Consider the data or variables you will need to complete your project, keeping in mind the need to present valid and reliable facts. Also pick a subject that interests and even excites you. Your research will be more fun and your written report more lively if your heart is really in the project.

III. WRITING THE PAPER

After you have read the pamphlet that accompanies your text entitled, *Handbook on Critical Thinking and Writing in American Politics,* you are ready to start.

Begin with an outline. It is your road map, so, for most research papers, make sure you cover at least the following:

Title page (title, your name, class, date.)

1. Introduction (what you plan to do).
2. Problem statement or thesis (what you plan to prove; why this is an important topic).
3. Body of project (logically arranged discussion of facts; interpretation/analysis of the information).
4. Conclusion (what generalizations or overall insights you have gained from the study. Make sure these relate back to 2).
5. Endnotes or footnotes.
6. Appendix (put tables, charts, and other material here that are important to the paper but are not directly relevant in the body of the study).
7. Sources (bibliography).

Other Tips: Take notes on index cards or a yellow pad. Write down the complete citation, including page numbers of material. You may think it will be easy to do that later but it won't! The book or magazine may be gone, checked out, or missing. You may forget where it was. Label cards or pages so you can sort and organize them to fit the structure of your project.

Try to Be Objective.   Let the facts lead you to conclusions. DON'T start with a conclusion (or bias) and then look for facts to prove you are right!

Type Your Paper. Make sure you number all pages. Cite sources, especially quotations or close paraphrasing. DON'T PLAGIARIZE (in other words, don't use ideas, analysis, or conclusions from other sources and pretend they are your own).

IV. WHERE TO FIND INFORMATION

Where to find information quickly and efficiently in every researcher's goal. The following are excellent places to start:

We assume that you are familiar with the card catalog in your library and know how to search for books and other items indexed there. However, you will want to ge beyond books (perhaps the subject is too recent for books or no one has quite focused on the subject the way you plan to approach it). You should also be familiar with the *Reader's Guide to Periodical Literature,* which cites material in popular periodicals such as *Time* and *People* magazines.

The Public Affairs Information Service (PAIS) publishes the *PAIS Bulletin,* which is an index (cumulated each year) with diverse citations on public affairs including books, journals, government documents, periodicals, fliers, and pamphlets.

Facts on File may be helpful in pinpointing and succinctly informing you about an event or person in the news. Its index is very complete and cross referenced. The *New York Times Index* is an annotated reference to the articles and stories that have appeared in the nation's complete newspaper, the *New York Times.*

The periodicals section of your library should have what we call *scholarly journals.* These are research-oriented publications in which political scientists report the results of their studies. Look for articles on your topic in *ABC POL SCI A Bibliography of Contents; Political Science and Government, Santa Barbara, CA: American Bibliographical Center, Clio Press.* This index is published five times a year and leads you to nearly 300 periodicals.

Familiarize yourself with some of the following scholarly journals: *The American Political Science Review, The Journal of Politics, Comparative Politics, Political Science Quarterly, The Western Political Quarterly, The American Journal of Political Science, Polity, Foreign Affairs, Presidential Studies Quarterly, Public Administration Review.*

For public opinion one of the most widely used sources of the *Gallup Opinion Index.*

The *Congressional Quarterly Weekly Report (CQWR)* is absolutely essential for every researcher. It comes to your library every week, is indexed, and is bound by volume every year. This source contains useful information on members of Congress, issues, scandals, political action committees, legislation, international affairs, and other material related to Congress. Tables and charts are excellent sources of information.

The *National Journal* covers material similar to the *CQWR.*

The *Supreme Court Reporter* (West Publishing) is one of the best-annotated sources of Supreme Court cases. It provides detailed information about the case and background as well as reference to other relevant cases.

The *Book of the States* is the authoritative source on the structure of state government, statistics, finances, and other information about the fifty states. This is published every two years.

The *Encyclopedia of Associations* is a multivolume source of information on organizations. You will be amazed at the number and diversity of organized groups, associations, and other organizations that exist. The *Encyclopedia* tells you the objectives, organizations, budget, membership, names of officers, address, and telephone numbers.

V. USING GOVERNMENT PUBLICATIONS

One of the best sources of information for research is the U.S. government, the largest publisher in the world. There are federal government publications for virtually every research topic. Because of the sheer volume, only specially designated *depository libraries* receive most of these publications. As your librarian where the nearest one is located. Remember that you can obtain this material through interlibrary loan.

Federal publications include statistics; congressional material including hearings, pamphlets, and bulletins; technical reports; presidential statements and documents; court rulings; and agency-specific publications. To find this material, you may want to use the following:

The *CIS* (Congressional Information Service) *Index.* This is published monthly and bound into a volume each year. It covers congressional hearings, reports, and special publications. Each item listed includes an abstract.

The *Congressional Monitor* is the best source of information on congressional hearings, which are listed by subject area for each House and Senate committee.

The *American Statistics Index* covers over five hundred federal government sources of information including numerical data.

The *Guide to U.S. Government Publications,* by John L. Andriot, is an annual guide to the reports and regular publications (magazines, for example) that are produced by more than 2,000 government agencies.

The following are selected United States government publications by topic:

Foreign Policy: *United States Foreign Policy: A Report of the Secretary of State.* This annual report reviews U.S. foreign policy, military and technical assistance, and other international activities country by country.

Federalism: *Catalog of Federal Domestic Assistance.* This publication is compiled by the Office of Management and Budget and lists virtually all federal grant programs to state and local governments. *Intergovernmental Perspective* is published by the Advisory Commission on Intergovernmental Relations four times a year and contains statistical information, analysis, and listings on all aspects of intergovernmental relations.

Voting/Elections: The *Journal of Election Administration* is published by the Federal Election Commission (FEC), which also publishes an array of statistical information on campaigns, voting, and related matters (call toll free, 800-424-9530).

Congress: The *Congressional Record* is published every day Congress is in session and contains the proceedings as well as supplemental documents inserted by members of Congress.

Presidency: The *Weekly Compilation of Presidential Documents* is issued every week and compiled annually as *Public Powers of the President of the United States*. It contains the speeches, messages, statements, and press conferences of the president.

The Supreme Court: The *United States Reports,* published since 1790, is the official publication of Supreme Court decisions. Citation of a case is usually to the *Reports.* For example Miranda v. Arizona, 348 U.S. 436 (1966) means volume 348 of the U.S. Reports, page 436 in the year 1966.

Domestic Policy: One of the best sources of information is the *Budget of the United States* and its appendices or the *United States Budget in Brief,* which contain the specific spending plans and revenue sources of the federal government.

Public Welfare Policy: The book *Characteristics of General Assistance in the United States* provides state-by-state data on federal and state assistance programs for the needy.

Education: data are found in the *Digest of Educational Statistics* published by the Department of Education each year.

The Economy and the Society: Statistic on general aspects of the society and the economy can be found in *Social Indicators: Selected Statistics on Social Conditions and Trends in the U.S.,* published by the Office of Management and Budget.

The U.S. Federal Government: The *United States Government Manual,* describes the agencies of the executive branch, their activities and the names and addresses of key officials. This book can be considered the "official" directory of U.S. government agencies. Government publication can also be obtained from your representative and senators. Find their nearest office in the government section of your local phone book. Ask for the publication by title, date, publication number, and issuing agency. (Have as much of this information as possible.) You can also write or call their office and tell them what general topic you are researching, they will send you material. However, be aware that this will be a random selection from publications they have in their office. You will still need to do further research to make certain you've covered the subject fully.

VI. COMPUTERIZED RESEARCH SOURCES

Computerized searching capabilities are rather recent. The following are useful for students doing research in American government:

The *Social Science Index* is available on CD-ROM floppy disks and also on-line through various library services.

DIALOG Information Service Inc. contains over 350 databases with more than 200 million individual records (units of information generally citations to sources). A typical ten-minute search costs from $5 to $15. It is available twenty-four-hours a day except from 3 A.M. to 1 P.M. EST on Sundays.

One of the most useful files is *U.S. Political Science Documents* #93. This contains 48,970 records starting in 1975 and consisting of detailed abstracts and indexes from roughly 150 of the major American scholarly journals in political science.

Social Science #7 contains over 2.5 million records indexed from the 1,500 most important social science journals throughout the world. It covers every area of the social and behavioral sciences.

PAIS International #49 has 338,817 records with bibliographic information on the public policy literature in a range of disciplines.

Another separate computerized source is the *Monthly Catalog of Government Publications,* which is available on CD-ROM disks under the name MARCIVE, GPO CAT/PAC.

The research librarian at your library is an excellent source for other and computerized sources of information for research projects and papers.

VII. MORE ON RESEARCH

For a more detailed discussion of how to do research in political science, the following are excellent: Carl Kalvelage, Albert P. Melone, and Morley Segal, *Bridges to Knowledge in Political Science: A Handbook for Research,* (Pacific Palisades, CA: Palisades Publishers, 1984), or Robert Weissberg, *Politics: A Handbook for Students* (New York: Harcourt Brace Jovanovich, Publishers, 1985).

Jay M. Shafritz, *The Dorsey Dictionary of American Government and Politics* (Chicago: The Dorsey Press, 1988) is a 661-page treasure of detailed information and reference that you should consider owning. It is richly illustrated and very easy to use.

A

ACTIONABLE   Furnishing grounds for a lawsuit.

ACTION-REACTION SYNDROME   For every action on the part of government, there is a reaction on the part of the affected public. Then the government attempts to counter the reaction with another action, which starts the cycle all over again.

ACTUAL MALICE   Actual desire and intent to see another suffer by one's actions.

ADMINISTRATIVE AGENCIES   Agencies that usually form part of the executive branch, plus independent regulatory agencies and independent agencies; for example, the Federal Trade Commission, the Securities and Exchange Commission, and the Federal Communications Commission.

ADVICE AND CONSENT   The power vested in the U.S. Senate by the Constitution (Article II, Section 2) to give its advice and consent to the president concerning treaties and presidential appointments.

AFFIRM   To declare that a judgment is valid and right and must stand.

AFFIRMATIVE ACTION   Policies issued in job hiring that give special consideration or compensatory treatment to traditionally disadvantaged groups in an effort to overcome present effects of past discrimination.

AGENDA SETTING   The power to determine which public policy questions will be debated or considered by Congress.

AMICUS CURIAE BRIEFS   Latin for "friend of the court"; refers here to persons or groups not parties to a case, but who have an interest in its outcome. These briefs are documents filed with the court that contain legal arguments for a particular desired outcome in a case.

ANARCHY   The state of having no government and no laws. Each member of the society governs him- or herself.

ANTIBALLISTIC MISSILES (ABMs)   A defense system designed to protect targets by destroying the attacking airplanes or missiles before they reach their destination.

ANTI-FEDERALISTS   The Anti-Federalists opposed the adoption of the Constitution because of its centralist tendencies and attacked the failure of the Constitution's framers to include a bill of rights; those individuals who opposed the ratification of the new Constitution in 1787.

APPELLATE COURTS   Those courts that review decisions reached by lower courts.

APPOINTMENT POWER   The authority vested in the president to fill a government office or position. Positions filled by presidential appointment include those in the executive branch, the federal judiciary, commissioned officers in the armed forces, and members of the independent regulatory commissions.

ATTENTIVE PUBLIC   That proportion of the general public that pays attention to foreign policy issues.

AUSTRALIAN BALLOT   A secret ballot prepared, distributed, and tabulated by government officials at public expense. Since 1888, all states have used the secret Australian ballot rather than an open, public ballot.

AUTHORITY   The features of a leader or an institution that compel others to grant it obedience, usually because of ascribed legitimacy. For most societies, government is the ultimate authority in the allocation of values.

B

BAD-TENDENCY RULE   Speech or other First Amendment freedoms may permissibly be curtailed if there is a possibility that such expression might lead to some "evil."

BEAUTY CONTEST   A term used to describe a form of presidential primary in which contending candidates compete for popular votes but the results have little or no impact on the selection of delegates to the national convention.

BENCH TRIAL   Trial before a judge, without a jury.

BICAMERALISM   The division of a legislature into two separate assemblies.

BICAMERAL LEGISLATURE   A legislature made up of two chambers, or parts. The United States Congress, composed of the House of Representatives and the Senate, is a bicameral legislature.

BILL OF RIGHTS   The first ten amendments to the United States Constitution. They contain a listing of the rights a person enjoys and which cannot be infringed upon by the government, such as the freedoms of speech, press, and religion.

BLANKET PRIMARY   A primary in which all candidates' names are printed on the same ballot, regardless of party affiliation. The voter may vote for candidates of more than one party.

BLOCK GRANTS   Federal programs that provide funding to the state and local governments for general functional areas such as criminal justice or mental health programs.

BUREAUCRACY   A large organization that is structured hierarchically to carry out specific functions.

BUSING   The transportation of public school students from areas where they live to schools in other areas to eliminate school segregation based on residential patterns.

C

CABINET   An advisory group selected by the president to aid him in making decisions. The cabinet presently numbers thirteen department secretaries and the attorney general. Depending on the president, the cabinet may be highly influential or relatively insignificant in its advisory role.

CABINET DEPARTMENTS   The fourteen departments of the executive branch (State, Treasury, Defense, Justice, Interior, Agriculture, Commerce, Labor, Health and Human Services, Housing and Urban Development, Education, Energy, Transportation, and Veterans Affairs).

CADRE   The nucleus of political party activists carrying out the major functions of American political parties.

CANVASSING BOARD   An official and normally bipartisan group on a county, city, or state level that receives vote counts from every precinct in the area. The state canvassing board obtains the voting results from all local boards, tabulates the figures, and certifies the winners.

CASEWORK Personal work for constituents by members of Congress.

CATEGORICAL GRANTS Federal grants-in-aid to states or local governments that are for very specific programs or projects.

CAUCUS A closed meeting of party leaders to select party candidates or to decide on policy. Also, a meeting of party members designed to select candidates and propose policies.

CHALLENGE An allegation by a poll watcher that a potential voter is unqualified to vote or that a vote is invalid; designed to prevent fraud in elections.

CHECKS AND BALANCES A major principle of the American governmental system whereby each branch of the government exercises a check upon the actions of the others. Separation of powers, divided power, and checks and balances limit government's power by pitting power against power. For example, the president checks Congress by holding veto power, Congress has the purse strings, and Congress approves presidential appointments.

CHIEF DIPLOMAT The role of the president in recognizing foreign governments, making treaties, and making executive agreements.

CHIEF EXECUTIVE The role of the president as head of the executive branch of the government.

CHIEF LEGISLATOR The role of the president in influencing the making of laws.

CHIEF OF STAFF The person who directs the White House Office and advises the president.

CHIEF OF STATE The role of the president as ceremonial head of the government.

CIVIL LAW The law regulating conduct between private persons over noncriminal matters. Under civil law, the government provides the forum for the settlement of disputes between private parties in such matters as contracts, domestic relations, and business relations.

CIVIL SERVICE A collective term for the body of employees working for the government. Generally, civil service is understood to apply to all those who gain government employment through a merit system.

CIVIL SERVICE COMMISSION The central personnel agency of the national government created in 1883.

CLASS-ACTION SUIT A lawsuit filed by an individual seeking damages for "all persons similarly situated."

CLASS POLITICS Political preferences based on income level and/or social status.

CLEAR AND PRESENT DANGER TEST The test proposed by Justice Holmes for determining when government may restrict free speech. Restrictions are permissible, he argued, only when speech provokes a "clear and present danger" to the public order.

CLIMATE CONTROL Techniques to create favorable public opinion toward an interest group, industry, or corporation.

CLOSED PRIMARY The most widely used primary, in which voters may participate only in the primary of the party with which they are registered.

CLOTURE A method invoked to close off debate and to bring the matter under consideration to a vote in the Senate.

COATTAIL EFFECT The influence of a popular or unpopular candidate on the electoral success or failure of other candidates on the same party ticket. The effect is increased by the party-column ballot, which encourages straight-ticket voting.

COLD WAR The ideological, political, and economic impasse that existed between the United States and the Soviet Union following World War II.

COMMANDER IN CHIEF The role of the president as supreme commander of the military forces of the United States and of the state national guard units when they are called into federal service.

COMMERCE CLAUSE The section of the Constitution in which Congress is given the power to regulate trade among the states and with foreign countries.

COMMERCIAL SPEECH Advertising statements that have increasingly been given First Amendment protection.

COMMON LAW Judge-made law that originated in England from decisions shaped according to prevailing customs. Decisions were applied to similar situations and thus gradually became common to the nation. Common law forms the basis of legal procedures in the United States.

COMMON SENSE Thomas Paine's best-selling pamphlet that argued for a new government in the colonies.

COMPARABLE WORTH The comparable worth idea is that compensation should be based on the worth of the job to an employer and that factors unrelated to the worth of a job, such as the sex of the employee, should not affect compensation; generally used in the argument that women are entitled to comparable wages for doing work that is different from, but of comparable worth and value to, work done by higher-paid men.

COMPLIANCE Accepting and carrying out authoritative decisions.

CONCURRENT MAJORITY A principle advanced by John C. Calhoun whereby democratic decisions could be made only with the concurrence of all segments of society affected by the decision. Without their concurrence, a decision should not be binding on those whose interests it violates.

CONCURRING OPINION An opinion, prepared by a judge who supports the decision of the majority of the court, but wants to make or clarify a particular point or to voice disapproval of the grounds on which the decision was made.

CONFEDERAL SYSTEM A league of independent states, each having essentially sovereign powers, wherein the central government created by such a league has only limited powers over the states.

CONFEDERATION A political system in which states or regional governments retain ultimate authority except for those powers they expressly delegate to a central government. A voluntary association of independent states, in which the member states agree to limited restraints on their freedom of action.

CONFERENCE COMMITTEES Special joint committees appointed to reconcile differences when bills pass the two houses of Congress in different forms.

CONSENSUS General agreement among the citizenry on an issue.

CONSENT OF THE GOVERNED The principle that government is based on the consent or will of the people and can be abolished by them.

CONSENT OF THE PEOPLE The idea that governments and laws derive their legitimacy from the consent of the people living under them.

CONSERVATISM A set of beliefs that includes a limited role for the national government in helping individuals, support for traditional values and life-styles, and a preference for the status quo.

CONSERVATIVE COALITION An alliance of Republicans and southern Democrats that can form in the House or the Senate to oppose liberal legislation and support conservative legislation.

CONSOLIDATION The union of two or more governmental units to form a single unit.

CONSTANT DOLLARS Dollars corrected for inflation; dollars expressed in terms of purchasing power for a given year.

CONSTITUTIONAL INITIATIVE An electoral device whereby citizens can propose a constitutional amendment through petitions signed by the required number of registered voters.

CONSTITUTIONAL POWERS The powers vested in the president by Article II of the Constitution.

CONTAINMENT U.S. diplomatic policy adopted by the Truman administration to "build situations of strength" around the globe to contain communist power within its existing boundaries.

CONTINUING RESOLUTIONS Temporary laws that Congress passes when various appropriations bills have not been decided by the beginning of the new fiscal year on October 1.

COOLEY'S RULE The view that cities should be able to govern themselves, presented in an 1871 decision by Michigan Judge Thomas Cooley.

COOPERATIVE FEDERALISM The theory that the states and the national government should cooperate in solving problems.

CORRUPT PRACTICES ACTS A series of acts passed by Congress in an attempt to limit and regulate the size and sources of contributions and expenditures in political campaigns.

COUNCIL OF ECONOMIC ADVISERS (CEA) A staff agency in the Executive Office that advises the president on measures to maintain stability in the nation's economy. Established in 1946, the council develops economic plans and budget recommendations for maintaining the nation's "employment, production, and purchasing power" and helps the president prepare an annual economic report to Congress.

COUNCILS OF GOVERNMENTS (COGs) Voluntary organizations of counties and municipalities concerned with area-wide problems.

COUNTY The chief government set up by the state to administer state law and business at the local level. Counties are drawn up by area, rather than by rural or urban criteria.

CREDENTIALS COMMITTEE A committee used by political parties at their national convention to determine which delegates may participate. The committee inspects the claim of each prospective delegate to be seated as a legitimate representative of his or her state.

CRIMINAL LAW The law that defines crimes and provides punishment for violations. In criminal cases, the government is the prosecutor since crimes are against the public order.

D

DEFAMATION OF CHARACTER Wrongfully hurting a person's good reputation. The law has imposed a general duty on all persons to refrain from making false, defamatory statements about others.

DEMOCRACY A system of government in which ultimate political authority is vested in the people. Derived from the Greek words *demos* ("the people") and *kratos* ("authority").

DEMOCRATS One of the two major American political parties evolving out of the Democratic Republican (Jeffersonian) group supporting Thomas Jefferson.

DE FACTO SEGREGATION Racial segregation that occurs not as a result of deliberate intentions but because of past social and economic conditions and residential patterns.

DE JURE SEGREGATION Racial segregation that occurs because of laws or administrative decisions by public agencies.

DÉTENTE A French word meaning relaxation of tension. Characterizes U.S.–Soviet policy as it developed under President Nixon and Henry Kissinger. Stresses direct cooperative dealings with cold war rivals but avoids ideological accommodation.

DILLON'S RULE The narrowest possible interpretation of the legal status of local governments, outlined by Judge John F. Dillon, who in 1911 stated that a municipal corporation can exercise only those powers expressly granted by state law.

DIPLOMACY The total process by means of which states carry on political relations with each other; settling conflicts among nations by peaceful means.

DIRECT DEMOCRACY A system of government in which political decisions are made by the people directly, rather than by their elected representatives; probably possible only in small political communities.

DIRECT PRIMARIES An intraparty election in which the voters select the candidates who will run on a party's ticket in the subsequent general election.

DIRECT TECHNIQUES Interest group activities that involve interaction with government officials to further the group's goals.

DISCHARGE PETITION A procedure by which a bill in the House of Representatives may be forced out of a committee (discharged) that has refused to report it for consideration by the House. The discharge motion must be signed by an absolute majority (218) of representatives and is used only on rare occasions.

DISSENTING OPINION A separate opinion in which a judge dissents from the conclusion reached by the majority of the court and expounds his or her own views about the case.

DIVISIVE Public opinion is polarized between two quite different positions.

DUAL CITIZENSHIP The condition of being a citizen of two sovereign political units; being a citizen of both a state and the nation.

DUAL FEDERALISM   A system of government in which the states and the national government each remain supreme within their own spheres. The doctrine looks on nation and state as coequal sovereign powers and holds that acts of states within their reserved powers could be legitimate limitations on the powers of the national government.

E

ECONOMIC AID   Assistance to other nations in the form of grants, loans, or credits to buy American products.

ECONOMIC REGULATION   The regulation of business practices by government agencies.

ELASTIC, or NECESSARY AND PROPER, CLAUSE   The clause in Article I, Section 8, which grants Congress the power to do whatever is necessary to execute its specific powers.

ELECTOR   The partisan slate of electors is selected early in the presidential election year by state laws and applicable political party apparatus, and the electors cast ballots for president and vice president. The number of electors in each state is equal to that state's number of representatives in both houses of Congress.

ELECTORAL COLLEGE   A group of persons called electors who are selected by the voters in each state; this group officially elects the president and the vice president of the United States. The number of electors in each state is equal to the number of each state's representatives in both houses of Congress.

ELECTORAL COLLEGE   The constitutionally required method for the selection of the president and the vice president. To be elected president or vice president, the candidate must have a majority of the electoral votes (currently, 270 out of 538).

ELECTRONIC MEDIA   Broadcasting media (radio and television). The term derives from their method of transmission, in contrast to printed media.

ELITES   The upper socioeconomic classes who control political and economic affairs.

ELITE THEORY   A political perspective holding that society is ruled by the elite.

EMERGENCY POWERS   Inherent powers exercised by the president during a period of national crisis, particularly in foreign affairs.

ENTITLEMENTS   Programs providing benefits to individuals who have an established legal right to them.

ENUMERATED POWERS   The powers specifically granted to the national government by the Constitution. The first seventeen clauses of Article I, Section 8, specify most of the enumerated powers of Congress.

ENVIRONMENTAL IMPACT STATEMENT (EIS)   As a requirement mandated by NEPA, EISs must show the costs and benefits of major federal actions that could significantly affect the quality of the environment.

EQUAL EMPLOYMENT OPPORTUNITY COMMISSION (EEOC)   A commission established by the 1964 Civil Rights Act to (1) end discrimination based on race, color, religion, sex, or national origin in conditions of employment and (2) promote voluntary action programs by employers, unions, and community organizations to foster equal job opportunities.

EQUALITY   A concept that all people are of equal worth.

EQUALIZATION   A method for adjusting the amount of money that a state must put up to receive federal funds that takes into account the wealth of the state or its ability to tax its citizens.

ERA OF DEREGULATION   The early 1980s, characterized by deregulation of several industries including trucking, air transport, and banking.

ERA OF GOOD FEELING   The years from 1817 to 1825 when James Monroe was president and there was, in effect, no political opposition.

ERA OF PERSONAL POLITICS   An era when attention centers on the character of individual candidates rather than on party identification.

ESTABLISHMENT CLAUSE   The part of the First Amendment prohibiting the establishment of a church officially supported by the national government. It is applied to questions of state and local government aid to religious organizations and schools, of the legality of allowing or requiring school prayers, and of the teaching of evolution versus fundamentalist theories of creation.

EUTHANASIA   Killing incurably ill people for reasons of mercy.

EXCISE TAXES   A tax on certain commodities, such as liquor and tobacco, levied on their manufacture or sale within a country.

EXCLUSIONARY RULE   A policy forbidding the admission of illegally seized evidence at trial.

EXECUTIVE AGREEMENT   A binding international obligation made between chiefs of state without legislative sanction.

EXECUTIVE BUDGET   Budget prepared and submitted by the president to Congress.

EXECUTIVE OFFICE OF THE PRESIDENT (EOP)   Established by President Franklin D. Roosevelt by executive order under the Reorganization Act of 1939. It currently consists of nine staff agencies that assist the president in carrying out major duties.

EXECUTIVE ORDER   A rule or regulation issued by the president that has the effect of law. Executive orders can implement and give administrative effect to provisions in the Constitution, to treaties, and to statutes.

EXECUTIVE PRIVILEGE   The right of executive officials to refuse to appear before, or to withhold information from, a legislative committee. Executive privilege is enjoyed by the president and by those executive officials accorded that right by the president.

EXPRESS POWERS   Constitutional and statutory powers of the president, which are expressly written into the Constitution or into congressional law.

EXTRADITE   To surrender an accused criminal to the authorities of the state from which he or she has fled; to return a fugitive criminal to the jurisdiction of the accusing state.

EXTRAORDINARY MAJORITY   A majority that is greater than 50 percent plus one. For example, ratification of amendments to the U.S. Constitution requires the approval of two-thirds of the House and the Senate and three-fourths of the states.

F

FACTION A group or bloc in a legislature or political party acting together in pursuit of some special interest or position.

FAIRNESS DOCTRINE An FCC regulation affecting broadcasting media, which required that "equal time" be made available to legitimate opposing political groups or individuals.

"FAITHLESS" ELECTORS Electors voting for candidates other than those within their parties. They are pledged, but not required by law, to vote for the candidate who has a plurality in the state.

FALL REVIEW Every year, after receiving formal federal agency requests for funding for the next fiscal year, the Office of Management and Budget reviews the requests, makes changes, and submits its recommendations to the president.

FEDERALISTS The first American political party, led by Alexander Hamilton and John Adams. Many of its members had strongly supported the adoption of the new Constitution and the creation of the federal union.

FEDERAL ELECTION CAMPAIGN ACT OF 1972 An act to control the raising and spending of funds for political campaigns.

FEDERAL ELECTION COMMISSION Created by the 1972 Federal Election Campaign Act to enforce compliance with the requirements of the act; the commission consists of six non-partisan administrators.

FEDERAL OPEN MARKET COMMITTEE (FOMC) The most important body within the Federal Reserve System, the FOMC decides how monetary policy should be carried out by the Federal Reserve.

FEDERAL REGISTER A publication of the executive branch that prints executive orders, rules, and regulations.

FEDERAL SYSTEM A system of government in which power is divided by a written constitution between a central government and regional, or subdivisional, governments. Each level must have some domain in which its policies are dominant and some genuine political or constitutional guarantee of its authority.

FIGHTING WORDS Those words that when uttered by a public speaker are so inflammatory that they could provoke the average listener to violence; the words are usually of a racial, religious, or ethnic type.

FILIBUSTER In the Senate, unlimited debate to halt action on a particular bill.

FILIBUSTERING In the Senate, unlimited debate to halt action on a particular bill.

FIRESIDE CHATS Warm, informal talks by Franklin D. Roosevelt to a few million of his intimate friends—via the radio. Roosevelt's fireside chats were so effective that succeeding presidents have been urged by their advisers to emulate him by giving more radio and television reports to the nation.

FIRST BUDGET RESOLUTION A resolution passed by Congress in May setting overall revenue and spending goals and, hence, by definition, the size of the deficit for the following fiscal year.

FIRST CONTINENTAL CONGRESS The first gathering of delegates from the thirteen colonies, held in 1774.

FIRST-STRIKE CAPABILITIES The launching of an initial strategic nuclear attack before the opponent has used any strategic weapons.

FISCAL POLICY Changes in government spending or taxes to alter national economic variables such as the rate of unemployment.

FISCAL YEAR The twelve-month period that is used for bookkeeping, or accounting, purposes. Usually the fiscal year does not coincide with the calendar year. For example, the federal government's fiscal year runs from October 1 through September 30.

FLUIDITY The extent to which public opinion changes over time.

FOREIGN POLICY A nation's external goals and the techniques and strategies used to achieve them.

FOREIGN POLICY PROCESS The steps by which external goals are decided and acted on.

FRANCHISE The legal right to vote, extended to African Americans by the Fifteenth Amendment, to women by the Nineteenth Amendment, and to all citizens age eighteen and over by the Twenty-sixth Amendment.

FRANKING A policy that enables members of Congress to send material through the mail by substituting their facsimile signature (frank) for postage.

FRATERNITY From the Latin *fraternus* ("brother"), the term *fraternity* came to mean, in the political philosophy of the eighteenth century, the condition in which each individual considers the needs of all others; a brotherhood. In the French Revolution of 1789, the popular cry was "liberty, equality, and fraternity."

FREE EXERCISE CLAUSE The provision of the First Amendment guaranteeing the free exercise of religion.

FULL FAITH AND CREDIT CLAUSE A section of the Constitution that requires states to recognize one another's laws and court decisions. It ensures that rights established under deeds, wills, contracts, and other civil matters in one state will be honored by other states.

FUNCTIONAL CONSOLIDATION The cooperation of two or more units of local government in providing services to their inhabitants.

G

"GAG" ORDERS Orders issued by judges restricting publication of news about a trial in progress or a pretrial hearing in order to protect the accused's right to a fair trial.

GENDER GAP Most widely used to describe the difference between the percentage of votes a candidate receives from women voters and the percentage the candidate receives from men. The term was widely used after the 1980 presidential election.

GENERAL LAW CITY A city operating under general state laws that apply to all local government units of a similar type.

GENERAL SALES TAX A tax levied as a proportion of the retail price of a commodity at the point of sale.

GENERATIONAL EFFECTS Events of a particular time period have a long-lasting effect on the political opinions or preferences of those individuals who came of political age at that time.

GERRYMANDERING The drawing of legislative district boundary lines for the purpose of obtaining partisan or factional advantage. A district is said to be gerrymandered when its shape is manipulated by the dominant party in the state legislature to maximize electoral strength at the expense of the minority party.

GOVERNMENT Individuals, institutions, and processes that make society's rules about conflict resolution and the allocation of resources and that possess the power to enforce them.

GOVERNMENT CORPORATION An agency of government that administers a quasibusiness enterprise. Used when an activity is primarily commercial, produces revenue for its continued existence, and requires greater flexibility than permitted for executive departments.

GOVERNMENT IN THE SUNSHINE ACT Requires that all multiheaded federal agencies conduct their business regularly in public session.

GRANDFATHER CLAUSE A device used by southern states to exempt whites from state taxes and literacy laws originally intended to disenfranchise African-American voters. It allowed the voting franchise to anyone who could prove that his grandfather had voted before 1867.

GREAT COMPROMISE The compromise between the New Jersey and the Virginia plans; created one chamber of the Congress based on population and one chamber that represented each state equally. Also called the Connecticut Compromise.

GREENHOUSE EFFECT The trapping of heat within the earth's atmosphere as a result of pollution caused largely by the burning of fossil fuels and emissions of carbon dioxide.

H

HARD, or **COMMAND, POWER** A nation's ability to invade or force others to accept its superiority militarily.

HATCH ACT (POLITICAL ACTIVITIES ACT) This 1939 act prohibits the use of federal authority to influence nominations and elections or the use of rank to pressure federal employees to make political contributions. It also prohibits civil service employees from active involvement in political campaigns.

HECKLERS' VETO Boisterous and generally disruptive behavior by listeners of public speakers that, in effect, vetoes the public speakers' right to speak.

HOME RULE CITY A city with a charter allowing local voters to frame, adopt, and amend their own charter.

HORIZONTAL FEDERALISM Activities, problems, and policies that require state governments to interact with each other.

HOUSE MINORITY LEADER The party leader elected by the minority party in the House.

HYPERPLURALISM An exaggerated form of pluralism in which government is so decentralized and authority so fragmented that it doesn't get anything done.

I

IDEOLOGUE A term applied to an individual whose political opinions are tightly constrained, that is, who has opinions that

are consistent with one another. Ideologues are often described as having a comprehensive world view.

IDEOLOGY A comprehensive and logically ordered set of beliefs about the nature of people and the institutions of government.

IMAGE BUILDING Using public and private opinion polls, the candidate's image is molded to meet the particular needs of the campaign. Image building is done primarily through the media.

IMPEACHMENT As authorized by Article I of the Constitution, impeachment is an action by the House of Representatives and the Senate to remove the president, vice president, or civil officers of the United States from office for crimes of "treason, bribery, or other high crimes and misdemeanors."

INALIENABLE RIGHTS Rights held to be inherent in natural law and not dependent on government; as asserted in the Declaration of Independence, the rights to "life, liberty, and the pursuit of happiness."

INCORPORATION THEORY The view that most of the protections of the Bill of Rights are incorporated into the Fourteenth Amendment's protection against state governments.

INDEPENDENT CANDIDATE A political candidate who is not affiliated with a political party.

INDEPENDENT EXECUTIVE AGENCY A federal agency having a single function that is not part of a cabinet department but reports directly to the president.

INDEPENDENT REGULATORY AGENCY An agency outside the major executive departments charged with making and implementing rules and regulations to protect the public interest.

INDEPENDENT VOTERS Voters who disavow any party affiliation and cast their ballots based on their views of who is the best candidate.

INDIRECT TECHNIQUES Strategies employed by interest groups that use a third party, the general public, or other individuals to influence government officials.

INHERENT POWERS Powers of the president derived from the loosely worded statement in the Constitution that "the executive power shall be vested in a president" and that the president should "take care that the laws be faithfully executed"; defined through practice rather than through constitutional or statutory law.

INITIATIVE A procedure whereby voters can propose a law or a constitutional amendment.

INJUNCTION An order issued by a court in an equity proceeding to compel or restrain the performance of an act by an individual or government official.

INSTITUTIONS Long-standing, identifiable structures or associations that perform functions for society.

INSTRUCTED DELEGATES The concept that legislators are agents of the voters who elected them and that they should vote according to the views of their constituents regardless of their own personal assessments.

INTELLIGENCE COMMUNITY The government agencies involved in gathering information about the capabilities and intentions of foreign governments and engaging in covert activities to further American foreign policy aims.

INTENSITY The strengths of a pro or con position concerning public policy or an issue. Intensity is often critical in generating public action; an intense minority can often win on an issue of public policy over a less intense majority.

INTEREST GROUP An organized group of individuals sharing common objectives who actively attempt to influence government policy makers through direct and indirect methods, including the marshaling of public opinion, lobbying, and electioneering.

INTERPOSITION The act in which a state places itself between its citizens and the national government as a protector, shielding its citizens from any national legislation that may be harmful to them. The doctrine of interposition has been rejected by the federal courts as contrary to the national supremacy clause of Article VI in the Constitution.

INTERSTATE COMPACTS Agreements between two or more states. Agreements on minor matters are made without congressional consent, but any compact that tends to increase the power of the contracting states relative to other states or relative to the national government generally requires the consent of Congress. Such compacts serve as a means by which states can solve regional problems.

INTERSTATE COMPACT An agreement between two or more states to cooperate on a policy or problem such as sharing water resources. It must first be approved by Congress.

INTERVENTIONISM Involvement in foreign affairs; actions directed at changing or preserving the internal political arrangements of other nations.

IRON CURTAIN The term used to describe the division of Europe between the Soviet Union and the West. Popularized by Winston Churchill in a speech portraying Europe as being divided by an iron curtain, with the nations of Eastern Europe behind the curtain and increasingly under Soviet control.

IRON TRIANGLE The three-way alliance among legislators, bureaucrats, and interest groups to make or preserve policies that benefit their respective individual interests.

ISSUE VOTING Voting for a candidate based on how he or she stands on a particular issue.

ITEM VETO The power exercised by the governors of most states to veto particular sections or items of an appropriations bill, while signing the remainder of the bill into law.

J

JOINT COMMITTEE A legislative committee composed of members from both houses of Congress.

JUDICIAL ACTIVISM A doctrine advocating an active role for the Supreme Court in enforcing the Constitution and in using judicial review. An activist Court takes a broad view of the Constitution and involves itself in legislative and executive matters by altering the direction of activities of Congress, state legislatures, and administrative agencies.

JUDICIAL IMPLEMENTATION The way in which court decisions are translated into policy.

JUDICIAL RESTRAINT A doctrine holding that the Court

should rarely use its power of judicial review or otherwise intervene in the political process.

JUDICIAL REVIEW The power of the courts to declare acts of the executive, legislative, and judicial branches unconstitutional. First established in *Marbury v. Madison*.

JURISDICTION The authority of a court to decide certain cases. All courts do not have the authority to decide all cases. Where a case arises and what its subject matter is are two jurisdictional factors.

JUSTICIABLE DISPUTES Disputes that raise questions about the law and are appropriate for resolution before a court of law.

JUSTICIABLE QUESTION A question that may be raised and reviewed in court.

K

KANGAROO COURT A mock hearing in which norms of justice and judicial procedure are ignored.

KEYNESIAN ECONOMICS An economic theory named after English economist John Maynard Keynes, which gained prominence during the Great Depression of the 1930s. Typically associated with the use of fiscal policy to alter national economic variables, for example, increased government spending during times of economic downturns.

KITCHEN CABINET The informal advisers to the president.

L

LABOR MOVEMENT In general, the term refers to the full range of economic and political expression of working-class interests; politically, it describes the organization of working-class interests.

LATENT INTERESTS Interests that are dormant or unexpressed. The group that holds these interests has never organized nor articulated them.

LATENT PUBLIC OPINION Unexpressed political opinions that have the potential to become manifest attitudes or beliefs.

LAWMAKING The process of deciding the legal rules that govern our society. Such laws may regulate minor affairs or establish broad national policies.

LEGISLATIVE VETO Provision in a bill reserving to Congress or to a congressional committee the power to reject an act or regulation of a national agency by majority vote; declared unconstitutional by the Supreme Court in 1983.

LEGISLATURE A government body primarily responsible for the making of laws.

LEGITIMACY A status conferred by the people on the government's officials, acts, and institutions through their belief that the government's actions are an appropriate use of power by a legally constituted governmental authority following correct decision-making policies; regarded as rightful and entitled to compliance and obedience on the part of citizens.

LIBEL Defamation of character in writing.

LIBERALISM A set of beliefs that includes the advocacy of positive government action to improve the welfare of individuals, support for civil rights, and a tolerance for political and social change.

LIBERTY   The greatest freedom of individuals that is consistent with the freedom of other individuals in the society.

LIMITED GOVERNMENT   A form of government based on the principle that the powers of government should be clearly limited either through a written document or through wide public understanding; characterized by institutional checks to ensure that governments serve the public rather than private interests.

LINE ORGANIZATION   Government or corporate units that provide direct services or products for the public.

LITIGATE   To engage in a legal proceeding.

LOBBYING   The attempt by organizations or by individuals to influence the passage, defeat, or contents of legislation and of the administrative decisions of government. The derivation of the term may be traced back over a century ago to the habit of certain private citizens who regularly congregated in the lobby outside the legislative chambers before a session to petition legislators.

LOGROLLING   An arrangement by which two or more members of Congress agree in advance to support each other's bills.

LOOPHOLES   Legal methods by which individuals and businesses are allowed to reduce the tax liabilities owed to the government.

M

MAJORITY   Full age; the age at which a person is entitled by law to the management of his or her own affairs and to the enjoyment of civil rights; also more than 50 percent.

MAJORITY FLOOR LEADER   The chief spokesperson of the major party in the Senate who directs the legislative program and party strategy.

MAJORITY LEADER OF THE HOUSE   A legislative position held by an important party member in the House of Representatives. The majority leader is selected by the majority party in caucus or conference to foster cohesion among party members and to act as spokesperson for the majority party in the House.

MAJORITY OPINION   The views of the majority of the judges.

MAJORITY RULE   A basic principle of democracy asserting that the greatest number of citizens in any political unit should select officials and determine policies.

MANAGED NEWS   Information generated and distributed by the government in such a way as to give government interests priority over candor.

MANDATORY RETIREMENT   Forced retirement when a person reaches a certain age.

MATCHING FUNDS   For many categorical grant programs, the state must "match" the federal funds. Some programs only require the state to raise 10 percent of the funds, whereas others approach an even share.

MEDIA   The technical means of communication with mass audiences. The media have become extremely important in American political life as a means of informing and influencing millions of citizens.

MEDIA ACCESS   The public's right of access to the media. The FCC and the courts have gradually taken the stance that citizens do have an access right to the media.

MERIT SYSTEM   The selection, retention, and promotion of government employees on the basis of competitive examinations.

MILITARY–INDUSTRIAL COMPLEX   The mutually beneficial relationship between the armed forces and defense contractors.

MINORITY FLOOR LEADER   The party officer in the Senate who commands the minority party's opposition to the policies of the majority party and directs the legislative program and strategy of his or her party.

MONETARY POLICY   Changes in the amount of money in circulation to alter credit markets, employment, and the rate of inflation.

MONROE DOCTRINE   The policy statement included in President Monroe's 1823 annual message to Congress, which set out three principles: (1) European nations should not establish new colonies in the Western Hemisphere, (2) European nations should not intervene in the affairs of independent nations of the Western Hemisphere, and (3) the United States would not interfere in the affairs of European nations.

MORAL IDEALISM   A philosophy that sees all nations as willing to cooperate and agree on moral standards for conduct.

MULTIPLE, INDEPENDENTLY TARGETABLE WARHEADS (MIRVs)   Multiple warheads carried by a single missile but directed to different targets.

MUNICIPAL HOME RULE   The power vested in a local unit of government to draft or change its own charter and to manage its own affairs.

MUTUAL ASSURED DESTRUCTION (MAD)   A theory that if the United States and the Soviet Union had extremely large and invulnerable nuclear forces that were somewhat equal, then neither would chance a war with the other.

N

NARROW CASTING   Broadcasting that is targeted to one small sector of the population.

NATIONAL AIR QUALITY STANDARDS (NAQSs)   Standards concerning air quality for sulfur dioxide and other pollutants that are city or region specific and defined by the rules and regulations of the EPA following the passage of the 1963 federal Clean Air Act.

NATIONAL COMMITTEE   A standing committee of a national political party established to direct and coordinate party activities during the four-year period between national party conventions.

NATIONAL CONVENTION   The meeting held every four years by each major party to select presidential and vice presidential candidates, to write a platform, to choose a national committee, and to conduct party business. In theory, the national convention is at the top of a hierarchy of party conventions (the local and state conventions are below it) that considers candidates and issues.

NATIONAL POLITICS   The pursuit of interests that are of concern to the nation as a whole.

NATIONAL SECURITY COUNCIL (NSC) A staff agency in the Executive Office established by the National Security Act of 1947. The NSC advises the president on domestic and foreign matters involving national security.

NATIONAL SECURITY POLICY Foreign and domestic policy designed to protect the independence and political and economic integrity of the United States; policy that is concerned with the safety and defense of the nation.

NATURAL ARISTOCRACY A small ruling clique of the state's "best" citizens, whose membership is based on birth, wealth, and ability. The Jeffersonian era emphasized rule by such a group.

NATURAL RIGHTS Rights held to be inherent in natural law, not dependent on governments. John Locke stated that natural law, being superior to human law, specifies certain rights of "life, liberty, and property." These rights, slightly altered to become "life, liberty, and the pursuit of happiness," are asserted in the Declaration of Independence.

NECESSARIES In contracts, necessaries include whatever is reasonably necessary for suitable subsistence as measured by age, state, condition in life, and so on.

NEGATIVE CONSTITUENTS U.S. citizens who openly oppose government foreign politics.

NEW ENGLAND TOWN Combines the roles of city and county into one governmental unit in the New England states.

NEW FEDERALISM A plan to limit the national government's power to regulate and to restore power to state governments. Essentially, the new federalism was designed to give the states an increased ability to decide for themselves how government revenues should be spent.

NULLIFICATION The act of nullifying or rendering void. John C. Calhoun asserted that a state had the right to declare a national law to be null and void and therefore not binding on its citizens, based on the assumption that ultimate sovereign authority rested with the several states.

O

OFFICE-BLOCK, or MASSACHUSETTS, BALLOT A form of general election ballot in which candidates for elective office are grouped together under the title of each office. It emphasizes voting for the office and the individual rather than for the party.

OFFICE OF MANAGEMENT AND BUDGET (OMB) A division of the Executive Office created by executive order in 1970 to replace the Bureau of the Budget. OMB's main functions are to assist the president in preparing the annual budget, to clear and coordinate all departmental agency budgets, to help set fiscal policy, and to supervise the administration of the federal budget.

OFFSET POLICY A method in which a company wishing to build a plant in a polluted area works out an agreement with another plant in the same area for that other plant to reduce its pollutants.

OMBUDSMAN An individual in the role of hearing and investigating complaints by private individuals against public officials or agencies.

OPEN PRIMARY A direct primary in which voters may cast ballots in the primary of either party without having to declare their party registration. Once voters choose which party primary they will vote in, they must select among only the candidates of that party.

OPINION The statement by a judge or a court of the decision reached in a case tried or argued before them. It expounds the law as applied to the case and details the reasons on which the judgment was based.

OPINION LEADERS Individuals able to influence the opinions of others because of position, expertise, or personality. Such leaders help to shape public opinion either formally or informally.

OPINION POLL A method of systematically questioning a small, selected sample of individuals who are deemed representative of the total population. Widely used by government, business, university scholars, political candidates, and voluntary groups to provide reasonably accurate data on public attitudes, beliefs, expectations, and behavior.

ORAL ARGUMENTS The verbal arguments presented in person by opposing counsel.

ORIGINAL JURISDICTION The authority of a court to hear a case in the first instance.

OVERSIGHT The responsibility Congress has for following up on laws it has enacted to ensure that they are being enforced and administered in the way in which they were intended.

P

PAID-FOR POLITICAL ANNOUNCEMENT A message about a political candidate conveyed through the media, designed to elicit positive public opinion.

PARDON The granting of a release from the punishment or legal consequences of a crime; a pardon can be granted by the president (or a governor) before or after a conviction.

PARTY-COLUMN, or INDIANA, BALLOT A form of general election ballot in which candidates for elective office are arranged in one column under their respective party labels and symbols. It emphasizes voting for the party rather than for the office or individual.

PARTY IDENTIFICATION Linking oneself to a particular political party.

PARTY IDENTIFIERS Those who identify themselves with a political party.

PARTY PLATFORM A document drawn up by the platform committee at each national convention, outlining the policies, positions, and principles of the party; it is then submitted to the entire convention for approval.

PATRONAGE Rewarding faithful party workers and followers with government employment and contracts.

PEER GROUPS Groups consisting of members sharing common relevant social characteristics. They play an important part in the socialization process, helping to shape attitudes and beliefs.

PENDLETON ACT (CIVIL SERVICE REFORM ACT OF 1883) This law, as amended over the years, remains the basic statute regulating federal employment personnel policies. It established the principle of employment on the basis of merit and created the Civil Service Commission to administer the personnel service.

PERIOD OF ISOLATIONISM A period of abstaining from an active role in international affairs or alliances, which characterized most of the nineteenth century.

PERSONAL ATTACK RULE The rule promulgated by the FCC that allows individuals or groups air time to reply to attacks that have previously been aired.

PLURALISM A theory that views politics as conflict among interest groups. Political decision making is characterized by bargaining and compromise.

PLURALITY The winning of an election by a candidate who receives more votes than any other candidate but not necessarily a majority. Most national, state, and local electoral laws provide for winning elections by a plurality vote.

POCKET VETO A special veto power exercised by the chief executive after a legislative body has adjourned. Bills not signed by the chief executive die after a specified period of time. If Congress wishes to reconsider such a bill, it must be reintroduced in the following session of Congress.

POLICE POWER The authority to legislate for the protection of the health, morals, safety, and welfare of the people. In the United States, police power is a reserved power of the states. The federal government is able to legislate for the welfare of its citizens through specific congressional powers such as control over interstate commerce.

POLICY TRADE-OFFS The cost to the nation of undertaking any one policy in terms of all of the other policies that could have been taken; for example, an increase in the expenditures on one federal program means a reduction in expenditures on another program, or an increase in federal taxes.

POLITICAL ACTION COMMITTEES (PACs) Committees set up by and representing corporations, labor unions, or special interest groups; PACs raise and give campaign donations on behalf of the organizations or groups they represent.

POLITICAL CONSULTANT A paid professional hired to devise a campaign strategy and manage a campaign. Image building is the crucial task of the political consultant.

POLITICAL CULTURE The pattern of beliefs and attitudes toward government and the political process held by a community or nation.

POLITICAL PARTY A group of individuals who organize to win elections, to operate the government, and to determine public policy.

POLITICAL QUESTION An issue that the Court believes should be decided by the executive or legislative branches.

POLITICAL REALISM A philosophy that sees each nation acting principally in its own interest.

POLITICAL SOCIALIZATION The process through which individuals learn a set of political attitudes and form opinions about social issues. The family and the educational system are two of the most important forces in the political socialization process.

POLITICAL TOLERANCE The degree to which individuals are able to grant civil liberties to groups that have opinions differing strongly from their own.

POLITICAL TRUST The degree to which individuals express trust in the government and political institutions. This concept is usually measured through a specific series of survey questions.

POLITICO The legislative role that combines the delegate and trustee concepts. The legislator varies the role according to the issue under consideration.

POLITICS According to David Easton, the "authoritative allocation of values" for a society; according to Harold Lasswell, "who gets what, when, and how" in a society.

POLLUTION CREDITS Unused "units" of pollutants that a company has to its credit for a specific plant. In certain instances, these pollution credits can be sold to other companies to allow those other companies to emit more than the standard amount of pollutants.

POLL TAX A special tax that must be paid as a qualification for voting. The Twenty-Fourth Amendment to the Constitution outlawed the poll tax in national elections, and in 1966 the Supreme Court declared it unconstitutional in all elections.

POLL WATCHER An individual appointed by a political party to scrutinize the voting process on election day. Usually, there are two poll watchers at every voting place, representing the Democratic and the Republican parties, both attempting to ensure the honesty of the election.

POPULAR SOVEREIGNTY The natural rights' concept that ultimate political authority rests with the people.

POSITIVE LAW Laws made in and by legislatures to fit a particular circumstance.

POWER The ability to cause others to modify their behavior and to conform to what the power holder wants.

PRECEDENT A court rule bearing on subsequent legal decisions in similar cases. Judges rely on precedents in deciding cases.

PREFERRED-POSITION TEST A court test used in determining the limits of free expression guaranteed by the First Amendment, requiring that limitations only be applied on speech to avoid imminent, serious, and important evils.

PRESIDENTIAL PRIMARY A statewide primary election of delegates to a political party's national convention to help a political party determine its presidential nominee. Such delegates are either pledged to a particular candidate or unpledged.

PRESIDENT PRO TEMPORE The temporary presiding officer of the Senate in the absence of the vice president.

PRESS SECRETARY The individual responsible for representing the White House before the media. The press secretary writes news releases, provides background information, sets up press conferences, and so on.

PRIOR RESTRAINT Restraining an action before the activity has actually occurred. It involves censorship as opposed to subsequent punishment.

PRIVATIZATION, or CONTRACTING OUT The replacement of government paid-for products and services by private firms.

PRIVILEGES AND IMMUNITIES A section of the Constitution requiring states not to discriminate against one another's citizens. A resident of one state cannot be treated as an alien when in another state; he or she may not be denied such privileges and immunities as legal protection, access to courts, travel rights, or property rights.

PROJECT GRANT An assistance grant that can be applied for directly by state and local agencies; established under a national program grant. Project grants allow Congress (and the administration) to bypass state governments and thereby to place the money directly where it is supposedly the most needed.

PROPERTY As conceived by the political philosopher John Locke, a natural right superior to human law (laws made by government).

PROPERTY TAX A tax on the value of real estate; limited to state and local governments and is a particularly important source of revenue for local governments.

PSYCHOACTIVES All substances having a profound or significant effect on mental processes, such as alcohol, nicotine, caffeine, cocaine, the opiates, methamphetamine, and the like.

PUBLIC ADMINISTRATION The science of managing public organizations.

PUBLIC AGENDA Issues that are commonly perceived by members of the political community as meriting public attention and governmental action. The media play an important role in setting the public agenda by focusing attention on certain topics.

PUBLIC DEBT FINANCING Government spending more than it receives in taxes and paying for the difference by issuing U.S. Treasury bonds, thereby adding to the public debt.

PUBLIC INTEREST The best interests of the collective, overall community; the national good, rather than the narrow interests of a self-serving group.

PUBLIC OPINION The aggregate of individual attitudes or beliefs shared by some portion of adults. There is no one public opinion because there are many different "publics."

PUBLIC, or NATIONAL, DEBT The total amount of debt incurred by the federal government since the beginning of the nation.

PUBLIC POLICIES What the government decides to do or not to do.

R

RATIFICATION Formal approval.

RATIONAL IGNORANCE EFFECT When people purposely and rationally decide not to become informed on an issue because they believe that their vote on the issue is not likely to be a deciding one; a lack of incentive to seek the necessary information to cast an intelligent vote.

REAPPORTIONMENT The redrawing of legislative district lines to accord with the existing population distribution.

RECALL A procedure allowing the people to vote to dismiss an elected official from state office before his or her term has expired.

RECOGNITION POWER The president's power, as chief diplomat, to extend diplomatic recognition to foreign governments.

REDISTRICTING Redrawing district lines within the states.

REFERENDUM An electoral device whereby legislative or constitutional measures are referred by the legislature to the voters for approval or disapproval.

REGISTRATION The entry of a person's name onto the list of eligible voters for elections. Registration requires meeting certain legal requirements such as age, citizenship, and residency.

RELEVANCE The extent to which an issue is of concern at a particular time. Issues become relevant when the public views them as pressing or of direct concern to them.

REMAND To send a case back to the court that originally heard it.

REPRESENTATION The function of Congress as elected officials to represent the views of their constituents.

REPRESENTATIVE ASSEMBLY A legislature composed of individuals who represent the population.

REPRESENTATIVE DEMOCRACY A form of government in which representatives elected by the people make laws and policies.

REPRIEVE The president has the power to grant a reprieve to postpone the execution of a sentence imposed by a court of law; usually done for humanitarian reasons or to await new evidence.

REPUBLICAN PARTY One of the two major American political parties, which emerged in the 1850s as an antislavery party. It was created to fill the vacuum caused by the disintegration of the Whig party. The Republican party traces its name—but not its ideology—to Jefferson's Democratic Republican party.

REVENUE-SHARING PROGRAM A program in which the federal government allocated funds to states and cities with virtually no strings attached. Recipient governments could use the funds in any way they saw fit.

REVERSE To annul or make void a judgment on account of some error or irregularity.

REVERSE DISCRIMINATION The charge that affirmative action programs requiring preferential treatment or quotas discriminate against those who have no minority status.

RULES COMMITTEE A standing committee of the House of Representatives that provides special rules under which specific bills can be debated, amended, and considered by the House.

RULE OF FOUR A U.S. Supreme Court procedure requiring four affirmative votes to hear the case before the full Court.

RUN-OFF PRIMARY An election that is held to nominate candidates within the party if no candidate receives a majority of the votes in the first primary election.

S

SAFE SEAT A district that returns the legislator with 55 percent of the vote or more.

SECESSION The act of formally withdrawing from membership in an alliance; withdrawal of a state from the federal union.

SECOND BUDGET RESOLUTION A resolution passed by Congress in September that sets "binding" limits on taxes and spending for the next fiscal year beginning October 1.

SECOND CONTINENTAL CONGRESS The 1775 Congress of the colonies that established the Continental Army.

SECTIONAL POLITICS The pursuit of interests that are of special concern to a region or section of the country.

SELECT COMMITTEE A temporary legislative committee

established for a limited time period for a special purpose.

SELECTPERSONS   The governing group of a town.

SENATORIAL COURTESY   In the case of federal district court judgeship nominations, a Senate tradition allowing a senator of the president's political party to veto a judgeship appointment in his or her state simply by indicating that the appointment is personally "obnoxious." At that point, the Senate may reject the nomination or the president may withdraw consideration of the nominee.

SENIOR EXECUTIVE SERVICE (SES)   A corps of about 8,500 high-level government administrators created in 1978 to provide rewards and incentives for top-ranking civil servants.

SENIORITY SYSTEM   A custom followed in both houses of Congress specifying that members with longer terms of continuous service will be given preference when committee chairpersons and holders of other significant posts are selected.

SEPARATE BUT EQUAL DOCTRINE   The doctrine holding that segregation in schools and public accommodations does not imply the superiority of one race over another; rather, it implies that each race is entitled to separate but equal facilities.

SEPARATION OF POWERS   The principle of dividing governmental powers among the executive, the legislative, and the judicial branches of government.

SERVICE SECTOR   That sector of the economy that provides services—such as food services, insurance, and education—in contrast to that sector of the economy that produces goods.

SEX DISCRIMINATION   Overt behavior in which people are given differential or unfavorable treatment on the basis of sex. Any practice, policy, or procedure that denies equality of treatment to an individual or to a group regardless of sex.

SEXUAL HARASSMENT   Harassment on the basis of sex, in violation of Title VII. This includes unwanted physical or verbal conduct or abuse of a sexual nature that interferes with a recipient's job performance or carries with it an implicit or explicit threat of adverse employment consequences.

SLANDER   The public uttering of a statement that holds a person up for contempt, ridicule, or hatred, when the defamatory statement is made to, or within the hearing of, persons other than the defamed party.

SLIDING-SCALE TEST   Used as a criterion in free-speech cases in which a careful examination of the facts of each individual case must be undertaken.

SNOWBELT   The northern states of the United States characterized by a harsh climate.

SOCIAL CONFLICT   Disagreements arising in society because of differing beliefs, values, and attitudes; conflicts over society's priorities and competition for scarce resources.

SOCIAL CONTRACT   An agreement between individuals to establish a government and to abide by its rules. Early theorists saw the social contract as an agreement between the ruler and the people.

SOCIOECONOMIC STATUS   A category of people within a society who have similar levels of income and similar types of occupations.

SOFT, or COOPTIVE, POWER   The ability to get nations to do what you want them to do without the use of military force.

SOLID SOUTH   A term describing the disposition of the post-Civil War southern states to vote for the Democratic party. (Voting patterns in the South have changed.)

SOVIET BLOC   The Eastern European countries which used to have communist regimes.

SPEAKER OF THE HOUSE   The presiding officer in the House of Representatives. The speaker is always a member of the majority party and is the most powerful and influential member of the House.

SPIN   An interpretation of campaign events or election results that is most favorable to the candidate's campaign strategy.

SPIN-OFF PARTY   A new party formed by a dissident faction within a major political party. Usually, spin-off parties have emerged when a particular personality was at odds with the major party.

SPOILS SYSTEM   The awarding of government jobs to political supporters and friends; generally associated with President Andrew Jackson.

SPRING REVIEW   Every year, the Office of Management and Budget requires federal agencies to review in the spring their programs, activities, and goals, and submit their requests for funding for the next year.

STABILITY   The extent to which public opinion remains constant over a period of time.

STAGFLATION   A period during which the rate of inflation is increasing simultaneously with an increase in the rate of unemployment.

STANDING COMMITTEE   A permanent committee within the House or Senate that considers bills within a subject area.

STARE DECISIS   "To stand on decided cases." The policy of courts to follow precedents established by the decisions of the past.

STATE   A group of people occupying a specific area and organized under one government; either a nation or a subunit of a nation.

STATE CENTRAL COMMITTEE   The principal organized structure of each political party within each state. Responsible for carrying out policy decisions of the party's state convention.

STATE OF THE UNION MESSAGE   An annual message to Congress in which the president proposes a legislative program. The message is not only to Congress but also to the American people and to the world. It offers the opportunity to dramatize policies and objectives and to gain public support.

STATUTORY POWERS   The powers created for the president through laws established by Congress.

STRATEGIC ARMS LIMITATION TREATY (SALT I)   A treaty between the United States and the Soviet Union to stabilize the nuclear arms competition between the two countries. SALT I talks began in 1969 and agreements were signed on May 26, 1972.

SUBPOENA   A legal writ requiring a person's appearance in court to give testimony.

SUBSIDIES   Negative taxes; usually payments to producers given on a per-unit basis according to the amount of production of a particular commodity.

SUFFRAGE   Right to vote; the franchise.

SUNBELT   The southern states of the United States characterized by mild and warm weather.

SUNSET LEGISLATION   A law requiring that an existing program be regularly reviewed for its effectiveness and terminated unless specifically extended as a result of this review.

SUPREMACY CLAUSE   The constitutional provision that makes the Constitution and federal laws superior to all state and local legislation.

SUPREMACY DOCTRINE   A doctrine that asserts the superiority of national law over state or regional laws. This principle is rooted in Article VI of the Constitution, which provides that the Constitution, the laws passed by the national government under its constitutional powers, and all treaties comprise the supreme law of the land.

SYMBOLIC SPEECH   Nonverbal expression of beliefs, which is given substantial protection by the courts.

T

TAX PREFERENCES   Another name for loopholes, or reduced taxes, legally mandated by Congress for particular activities, individuals, or businesses.

TECHNICAL ASSISTANCE   Sending experts with technical skills in agriculture, engineering, or business to aid other nations.

THIRD PARTY   A political party other than the two major political parties (Republican and Democratic). Usually, third parties are composed of dissatisfied groups that have split from the major parties. They act as indicators of political trends and as safety valves for dissident groups.

THIRD-PARTY CANDIDATE   A political candidate running under the banner of a party other than the two major political parties.

TICKET SPLITTING   Voting for candidates of two or more parties for different offices. For example, a voter splits her ticket if she votes for a Republican presidential candidate and for a Democratic congressional candidate.

TOTALITARIAN   A form of government that controls all aspects of the political and social life of a nation. All power resides with the government. The citizens have no power to choose the leadership or policies of the country.

TOWN MANAGER SYSTEM   Form of city government in which voters elect three selectpersons who then appoint a professional town manager, who in turn appoints other officials.

TOWN MEETING   The governing authority of a town. Qualified voters may participate in the election of officers and in the passage of legislation.

TOWNSHIP   Rural units of government based on federal land surveys of the American frontier in the 1780s. They have declined significantly in importance.

TRACKING POLLS   Polls taken for the candidate on a nearly daily basis as election day approaches.

TRIAL COURTS   Those courts in which most cases usually begin, where questions of fact are examined.

TRUMAN DOCTRINE   The policy adopted by President Harry Truman in 1947 to halt communist expansion in southeastern Europe.

TRUSTEES   The idea that a legislator should act according to his or her conscience and the broad interests of the entire society, often associated with the British statesman Edmund Burke.

TWELFTH AMENDMENT   An amendment to the Constitution, adopted in 1804, which specifies the separate election of the president and vice president by the electoral college.

TWENTY-FIFTH AMENDMENT   An amendment to the Constitution adopted in 1967 that establishes procedures for filling vacancies in the two top executive offices and that makes provisions for situations involving presidential disability.

TWO-PARTY COMPETITION   Two strong and solidly established political parties in competition for political control; both parties have a strong chance of winning an election.

U

UNANIMOUS OPINION   Agreement of all judges on the same decision or determination.

UNICAMERAL LEGISLATURES   Legislatures with only one legislative body, as compared with bicameral (two-house) legislatures, such as the United States Congress. Nebraska is the only state in the Union with a unicameral legislature.

UNINCORPORATED AREAS   Areas not located within the boundaries of municipalities.

UNITARY SYSTEM   A centralized governmental system in which local or subdivisional governments exercise only those powers given to them by the central government.

UNIT RULE   All of a state's electoral votes are cast for the presidential candidate receiving a plurality of the popular vote.

UNIVERSAL SUFFRAGE   The right of all adults to vote for their representatives.

U.S. TREASURY BONDS   Evidences of debt issued by the federal government. Similar to corporate bonds, but issued by the U.S. Treasury.

V

VETO MESSAGE   The president's formal explanation of a veto when legislation is returned to the Congress.

VOTER TURNOUT   The percentage of citizens taking part in the election process; the number of eligible voters that actually "turn out" on election day to cast their ballots.

W

WAR POWERS ACT   A law passed in 1973 spelling out the conditions under which the president can commit troops without congressional approval.

WASHINGTON COMMUNITY   Individuals regularly involved with the political circles in Washington, D.C.

WATERGATE BREAK-IN   The 1972 illegal entry into the Democratic campaign offices engineered by the Nixon reelection campaign.

WELFARE   Payments made by the government to specific categories of people whose income is below a certain level.

WHIGS   One of the foremost political organizations in the United States during the first half of the nineteenth century, formally established in 1836. The Whig party was dominated by the same anti-Jackson elements that organized the National Republican faction within the Jeffersonian Republicans and represented a variety of regional interests. It fell apart as a national party in the early 1850s.

WHIPS Assistant floor leaders who aid the majority and minority floor leaders.

WHISTLE BLOWER Someone who brings to public attention gross governmental inefficiency or an illegal action.

WHITE HOUSE OFFICE The personal office of the president which tends presidential political needs and manages the media.

WHITE HOUSE PRESS CORPS A group of reporters assigned full time to cover the presidency.

WHITE PRIMARY State primary election that restrict voting only to whites; outlawed by the Supreme Court in 1944.

WRIT OF CERTIORARI An order issued by a higher court to a lower court to send up the record of a case for review. It is the principal vehicle for U.S. Supreme Court review.

WRIT OF HABEAS CORPUS Literally, "you should have the body." An order that requires jailers to bring a party before a court or judge and explain why the party is being held in prison.

WRIT OF MANDAMUS An order issued by a court to compel performance of an act.

Y

YELLOW JOURNALISM A derogatory term for sensationalistic, irresponsible journalism. Reputedly, the term is short for "Yellow Kid Journalism," an allusion to the cartoon "The Yellow Kid" in the old *New York World,* a paper especially noted for its sensationalism.

Z

ZERO POPULATION GROWTH A stable rate of growth in population, in which the birthrate equals but does not exceed the mortality rate.

PHOTO CREDITS

xxxiv © D. Aubert, Sygma; **xxxiv** (left) © R. Bossu, Sygma; **xxxv** (right) D. Despotovic, Sygma; **xxxv** © Anthony Suau, Black Star; **1** © Eric Meola, The Image Bank; **3** © Jeff Jacobson, Archive Pictures, Inc., **5** Gyorgy Sugar, Gamma-Liaison; **6** Dennis Brack, Black Star; **9** © Peter Miller, Photo Researchers; **11** The Bettmann Archive; **12** © Bill Anderson, Monkmeyer; **13** Baytoff, Black Star; **19** Ira Wyman, Sygma; **25** Dennis Brack, Black Star; **27** The Granger Collection; **28** The Granger Collection; **30** From the Studio of A. Ramsay, © 1767, Courtesy of The National Portrait Gallery, London; **32** Van Bucher, Photo Researchers; **34** The Granger Collection; **36** The Granger Collection; **37** The Granger Collection; **40** Library of Congress; **42** Ted Spiegel, Black Star; **43** (left) Jim Pickerell, Black Star; **43** (middle) Pamela J. Zilly, The Image Bank; **43** (right) The Granger Collection; **44** Library of Congress; **46** Photo by Tom McHugh, Photo Researchers, Courtesy of National Portrait Gallery; **50** Brad Markel, Gamma-Liaison; **57** J. L. Atlan, Sygma; **62** Library of Congress; **63** Rick Friedman, Black Star; **68** Photo by Sygma; **69** Michael Kagan, Monkmeyer; **71** Billy Barnes, Stock Boston; **74** Library of Congress; **76** (left) Collection of William L. Hopkins, Jr., Savannah, Georgia; **76** (right) Courtesy of the New York Historical Society, New York City; **77** The Library of Congress; **79** Library of Congress; **80** Ellis Herwig, Stock Boston; **84** UPI/Bettmann; **88** © P. Durand, Sygma; **89** (top) © Robet White, Sygma; **89** (bottom) © Steve Liss, Gamma-Liaison; **90** Zoja Pictures, Gamma-Liaison; **91** Bob Adelman, Magnum Photos; **93** R. Maiman, Sygma; **98** Rob Nelson, The Picture Group; **99** Bryce Flynn, The Picture Group; **103** UPI/Bettmann; **105** Les Stone, Sygma; **106** (top) Andrew Holbrooke, Black Star; **106** (bottom) Gary Sigman, Black Star; **109** Bart Bartholomew, Black Star; **111** Bob Daemmrich, Stock Boston; **113** (left) Laura Sikes, Sygma; **113** (right) A. Tannenbaum, Sygma; **114** UPI/Bettmann; **118** P. Chauvel, Sygma; **119** Flip Schulke, Black Star; **120** AP/Wide World; **121** Phil Huber, Black Star; **127** Spenser Grant, Stock Boston; **130** Missouri Historical Society; **131** The Granger Collection; **133** From the Dorothy Sterling Collection at the Amistad Research Center; **134** (top) AP/Wide World; **134** (bottom) Burt Glinn, Magnum; **135** Ellis Herwig, Stock Boston; **137** Wide World Photos; **139** UPI/Bettman; **140** (top) Bob East III, The Picture Group; **140** (bottom) Flip Schulke; Black Star, **142** Paul Sakuma, Sygma; **144** Ira Wyman, Sygma; **145** Christina Thomson, Woodfin Camp; **146** P. F. Gero, Sygma; **150** Donald Dietz, Stock Boston; **154** J. P. Laffont, Sygma; **155** The Granger Collection; **156** Rafael Macia, Photo Researchers; **159** Herman Kokojan, Black Star; **163** Terry Ashe, Gamma-Liaison; **166** (top) Paul Conklin, Monkmeyer; **166** (bottom) The Bettmann Archive; **167** The Bettmann Archive; **170** Courtesy of Patricia Ireland; Sygma; **173** Mary Kate Denny, PhotoEdit; **174** Minneapolis Star and Tribune; **179** Paul Conklin, PhotoEdit; **180** Paul Fusco, Magnum Photos; **181** Ron Sachs, Sygma; **182** Burt Bartholomew, Black Star; **183** UPI/Bettmann; **185** Jim Pozarik, Gamma-Liaison; **186** R. Maiman, Sygma; **190** © Dennis Brack, Black Star; **191** (left) Reuters/Bettmann; **191** (right) Rueters/Bettmann Newsphotos; **192** © Bliebtreu, Sygma; **193** Jeff Jacobson, Archive Pictures, Inc.; **195** Billy Barnes, Uniphoto; **198** Arthur Grace, Stock Boston; **200** David Honl, Gamma-Liaison; **205** © Mark McKenna; **209** UPI/Bettmann; **211** Dennis Brack, Black Star; **213** Todd Buchanan, Black Star; **218** Wide World; **221** (top) Randy Taylor, Sygma; **221** (bottom) Arthur Grace, Sygma; **225** Paul Conklin, PhotoEdit; **228** The Bettmann Archive; **230** Mark D. Phillips, Photo Researchers; **231** J. P. Laffont, Sygma; **232** Steve Woit, The Picture Group; **236** Brad Markel, Gamma-Liaison; **237** Dennis Brack, Black Star; **238** Photo courtesy of Earth Island Institute; **243** Lisa Quinones, Black Star; **247** Michael Evans, Sygma; **249** UPI/Bettmann; **251** R. Maiman, Sygma; **254** Wide World; **255** Library of Congress; **257** The Bettmann Archive: **258** (top) The Granger Collection; **258** (bottom) Smithsonian Institutions, Washington, D.C.; **262** R. Maiman, Sygma; **263** Steve Leonard, Black Star; **265** EKM-Nepenthe; **269** J. Traver, Gamma-Liaison; **271** UPI/Bettmann; **273** The Bettmann Archive; **275** Art Resource; **281** Dennis Brack, Black Star; **283** © Bruce S. de Lis Gamma-Liaison; **284** Minnesota Historical Society, St. Paul Pioneer Press; **285** © John Ficara, Woodfin Camp; **287** Paul Conklin, Uniphoto; **289** © Mark McKenna; **291** John Chiasson, Gamma-Liaison; **292** Paul Conklin, Monkmeyer; **296** UPI/Bettmann; **297** (top) UPI/Bettmann Newsphotos; **297** (bottom) Dennis Brack, Black Star; **300** Ira Wyman, Sygma; **304** © Roger P. Watts, Uniphoto Picture Agency; **306** R. Maiman, Sygma; **310** © Bruce Roberts, Photo Researchers; **311** © Susan Meiselas, Magnum Photos, Inc.; **314** Brad Markel, Gamma-Liaison; **315** © Ira Wyman, Sygma; **320** Ira Wyman, Sygma; **325** Dennis Brack, Black Star; **327** Sygma; **328** J. L. Atlan, sygma; **329** UPI/Bettmann Newsphotos; **331** © Andrew Sacks, Art Resource; **332** The Granger Collection; **333** Courtesy of Westinghouse Broadcasting and Cable; **335** Robert Kalfus, Gamma-Liaison; **336** UPI/Bettmann Newsphotos; **337** With the permission of Doyle Dane Bernbach, Inc.; **338** AP/Wide World Photos; **339** National Archives; **341** © Pamela Price,

Uniphoto Picture Agency; **343** © Kenn Bisio, The Picture Group; **344** (top) Franklin D. Roosevelt Library, Photo Researchers; **344** (bottom) Dirck Halstead, Gamma-Liaison; **345** Tom Sobolik, Black Star; **347** © Greg Mathieson, Sygma; **348** Les Stone, Sygma; **352** (left and right) Library of Congress; **353** (top and bottom) Rueters/Bettmann; **355** © Ellis Herwig, Stock Boston; **357** © Consolidated News Pictures; **359** Sygma; **361** © Ashe, Gamma-Liaison, **363** © Paul Conklin, PhotoEdit; **365** Wide World; **366** © Paul Conklin, PhotoEdit; **365** Wide World; **366** From the Dorothy Sterling Collection at the Amistad Research Center; **367** UPI/Bettmann Newsphotos; **368** © Frank Fisher, Gamma-Liaison; **371** UPI/Bettmann; **377** © Terry Ashe, Uniphoto Picture Agency; **379** © Dennis Brack, Black Star; **380** R. Cheney, Gamma-Liaison; **383** © Dennis Brack, Black Star; **384** Shepard Sherbell, The Picture Group; **385** © Ashe, Gamma-Liaison; **386** © Dennis Brack, Black Star; **387** Brad Markel, Gamma-Liaison; **390** Dennis Brack, Black Star; **391** Wide World Photos; **393** © Dennis Brack, Black Star; **395** © Ashe, Gamma-Liaison; **401** © Dennis Brack, Black Star; **403** © Ellis Herwig, Stock Boston; **404** The Bettmann Archive; **405** The Granger Collection; **408** © 1979 Black Star Pool, Black Star; **409** (top) T. Graham, Sygma; **409** (bottom) D. Halstead, Gamma-Liaison; **410** Brad Markel, Gamma-Liaison; **412** Sygma; **413** (top) © Dennis Brack, Black Star; **413** (bottom) © D. Walker, Gamma-Liaison; **414** © D. Walker, Gamma-Liaison; **415** © Brad Markel, Gamma-Liaison; **416** Sygma; **417** © R. Maiman, Sygma; **423** © D. Rodgers, Sygma; **427** © Don Carl Steffan, Photo Researchers; **428** © Fred Ward, Black Star; **429** © Dennis Brack, Black Star; **431** © Dennis Brack, Black Star; **434** © Shelly Katz, Black Star; **435** © G. Mathieson, Sygma; **436** © Sebastiao Salgado, Jr., Magnum; **437** UPI/Bettmann Newsphotos; **441** © David M. Doody, Uniphoto Picture Agency; **445** © Andrew Popper, The Picture Group; **448** © Brad Markel, Gamma-Liaison; **450** (top) © A. Tannenbaum, Sygma; **450** (bottom) UPI/Bettmann; **453** © Brad Markel, Gamma-Liaison; **454** © Susan Leavines, Photo Researchers; **456** © David H. Wells, Black Star; **457** © Bob Daemmrich, Stock Boston; **458** The Bettmann Archive; **459** The Bettmann Archive; **462** © Thomas Iowman, PhotoEdit; **463** UPI/Bettmann; **464** The Associated Press; **469** © Stan Burouh, Uniphoto Picture Agency; **471** © 1985 Stacy Pick, Stock Boston; **474** (left) Library of Congress; **474** (right) Library of Congress; **482** © Dennis Brack, Black Star; **486** © Dennis Brack, Black Star; **488** © Dennis Brack, Black Star; **489** © Shepard Sherbell, The Picture Group; **490** © Terry Ashe, Uniphoto Picture Agency; **491** © Amy E. Powers, Gamma-Liaison; **498** (left) © Cludio Edinger, Gamma-Liaison; **498** (right) F. Hibon, Sygma; **499** (top) © Mark Peters, Sygma; **499** (bottom) © 1989 Vera Lentz, Black Star; **500** Sygma; **501** Sean Haffey, Sygma; **503** © Terry Ashe, Gamma-Liaison; **505** Brian Brainerd, Gamma-Liaison; **511** © 1988 Stacy Pick, Stock Boston; **512** Gamma-Liaison; **514** © Michael Grecco, Stock boston; **515** UPI/Bettmann Newsphotos; **516** © Raoul Hacre, Stock Boston; **517** © Dennis Brack, Black Star; **518** © Paul Conklin, Uniphoto Picture Agency; **525** Rick Friedman, Black Star; **530** © Tannenbaum, Sygma; **531** © Brad Markel, Gamma-Liaison; **532** © Vera Lentz, Black Star; **533** J. L. Atlan, Sygma; **534** © Matt McVay, Black Star; **536** © Ted Spiegel, Black Star; **538** © H. Collart Odinetz, Sygma; **539** © Cynthia Johnson, Gamma-Liaison; **540** © Stephen Ferry, Gamma-Liaison; **541** © Jonathon Wenk, Black Star; **542** Gary Bogdon, Sygma; **546** © Joseph Rodriguez, Black Star; **551** © J. Langevin, Sygma; **553** © Patrick Forestier, Sygma; **555** © Cynthia Johnson, Gamma-Liaison; **555** (bottom) © Pedro Meyer, Black Star; **556** National Archives; **557** © Dennis Brack, Black Star; **558** J. L. Atlan, Sygma; **559** © Ron Dirito, Sygma; **562** © Donald L. Miller, Monkmeyer; **565** Library of Congress; **567** (top) UPI/Bettmann Archive; **567** (bottom) U.S. Air Force; **570** © Julie Houch, Stock Boston; **572** AP/Wide World; **573** UPI/Bettmann; **574** © Ira Wyman, Sygma; **576** © Christopher Morris, Black Star; **578** (top) © Dennis Brack, Black Star; **578** (bottom) © P. Durand, Sygma; **582** (top) © Bisson, Sygma; **582** (bottom) © A. Nogues, Sygma; **583** © J. L. Atlan, Sygma; **590** UPI/Bettmann Newsphotos; **591** (left and right) UPI/Bettmann Newsphotos; **592** Rueters/Bettmann; **593** © Ted Spiegel, Black Star; **595** © Bob Daemmrich, Stock Boston; **597** © J. Campion, Sygma; **602** © Paul Conklin, Monkmeyer; **603** © Bob Daemmrich, Sygma; **609** © Lisa Quinones, Black Star; **614** © Mark McKenna; **616** © Tony Freeman PhotoEdit; **617** (top) Wide World Photos; **617** (bottom) © David Weintraub, Photo Researchers; **618** © Peter Byron, Black Star; **621** © J. P. Laffont, Sygma; **623** © Ron Sachs, Consolidated News Pictures.